2016 release

Adobe Photoshop, Flash & Dreamweaver CC

Web Design Portfolio

Managing Editor: Ellenn Behoriam
Cover & Interior Design: Erika Kendra
Editor: Angelina Kendra
Copy Editor: Liz Bleau

The image on the cover shows the glazed hall at National Gallery of Canada, Ottawa. (©Ckchiu | Dreamstime.com)

10 9 8 7 6 5 4 3 2 1

Print book: 978-1-936201-82-2
Ebook book: 978-1-936201-83-9

4710 28th Street North, Saint Petersburg, FL 33714
800-256-4ATC • www.againsttheclock.com

Acknowledgements

About Against The Clock

Against The Clock, long recognized as one of the nation's leaders in courseware development, has been publishing high-quality educational materials for the graphic and computer arts industries since 1990. The company has developed a solid and widely-respected approach to teaching people how to effectively utilize graphics applications, while maintaining a disciplined approach to real-world problems.

Having developed the *Against The Clock* and the *Essentials for Design* series with Prentice Hall/Pearson Education, ATC drew from years of professional experience and instructor feedback to develop *The Professional Portfolio Series*, focusing on the Adobe Creative Suite. These books feature step-by-step explanations, detailed foundational information, and advice and tips from industry professionals that offer practical solutions to technical issues.

Against The Clock works closely with all major software developers to create learning solutions that fulfill both the requirements of instructors and the needs of students. Thousands of graphic arts professionals — designers, illustrators, imaging specialists, prepress experts, and production managers — began their educations with Against The Clock training books. These professionals studied at Baker College, Nossi College of Art, Virginia Tech, Appalachian State University, Keiser College, University of South Carolina, Gress Graphic Arts Institute, Hagerstown Community College, Kean University, Southern Polytechnic State University, and many other educational institutions.

About the Author

Erika Kendra holds a BA in History and a BA in English Literature from the University of Pittsburgh. She began her career in the graphic communications industry as an editor at Graphic Arts Technical Foundation before moving to Los Angeles in 2000. Erika is the author or co-author of more than thirty books about Adobe graphic design software. She has also written several books about design concepts such as color reproduction and preflighting, and dozens of articles for journals in the graphics industry. Working with Against The Clock for more than fifteen years, Erika was a key partner in developing *The Professional Portfolio Series* of software training books.

Contributing Authors, Artists, and Editors

A big thank you to the people whose artwork, comments, and expertise contributed to the success of these books:

- **Chris Barnes,** Wilson Community College
- **Steve Bird,** Adobe Certified Expert
- **Colleen Bredahl,** United Tribes Technical College
- **Debbie Davidson,** Against The Clock, Inc.
- **Charlie Essers,** photographer, Lancaster, Calif.
- **Matthew Guancale,** Fanboy Photo
- **Pam Harris,** University of North Texas at Dallas
- **Beth Rogers,** Nossi College Of Art
- **Richard Schrand,** International Academy of Design & Technology, Nashville, TN
- **Joseph A. Staudenbaur,** Dakota State University
- **Frank Traina,** Armwood High School
- **Greg Williams,** Keiser University

Finally, thanks to **Angelina Kendra**, editor, and **Liz Bleau**, copy editor, for making sure that we all said what we meant to say.

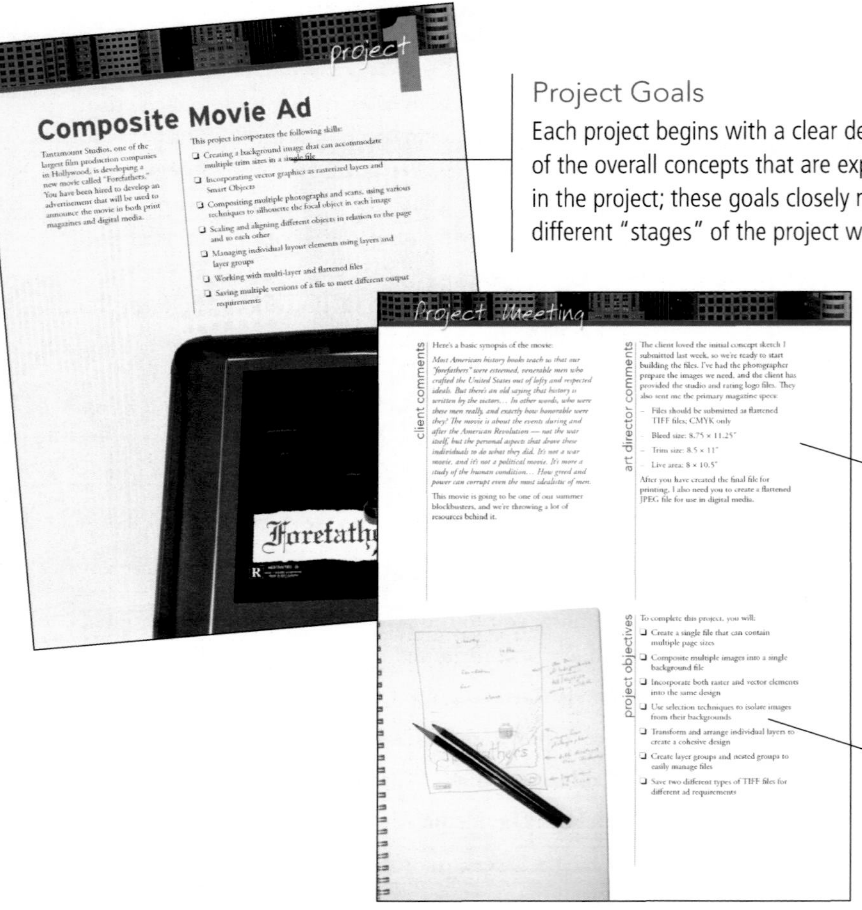

Project Goals

Each project begins with a clear description of the overall concepts that are explained in the project; these goals closely match the different "stages" of the project workflow.

The Project Meeting

Each project includes the client's initial comments, which provide valuable information about the job. The Project Art Director, a vital part of any design workflow, also provides fundamental advice and production requirements.

Project Objectives

Each Project Meeting includes a summary of the specific skills required to complete the project.

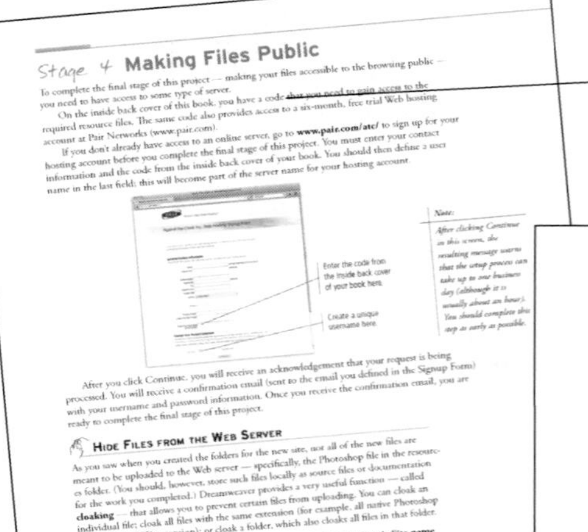

Real-World Workflow

Projects are broken into logical lessons or "stages" of the workflow. Brief introductions at the beginning of each stage provide vital foundational material required to complete the task.

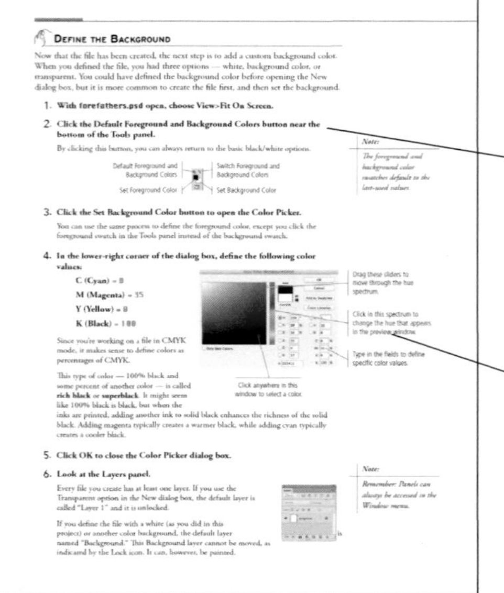

Step-By-Step Exercises

Every stage of the workflow is broken into multiple hands-on, step-by-step exercises.

Visual Explanations

Wherever possible, screen shots are annotated so that you can quickly identify important information.

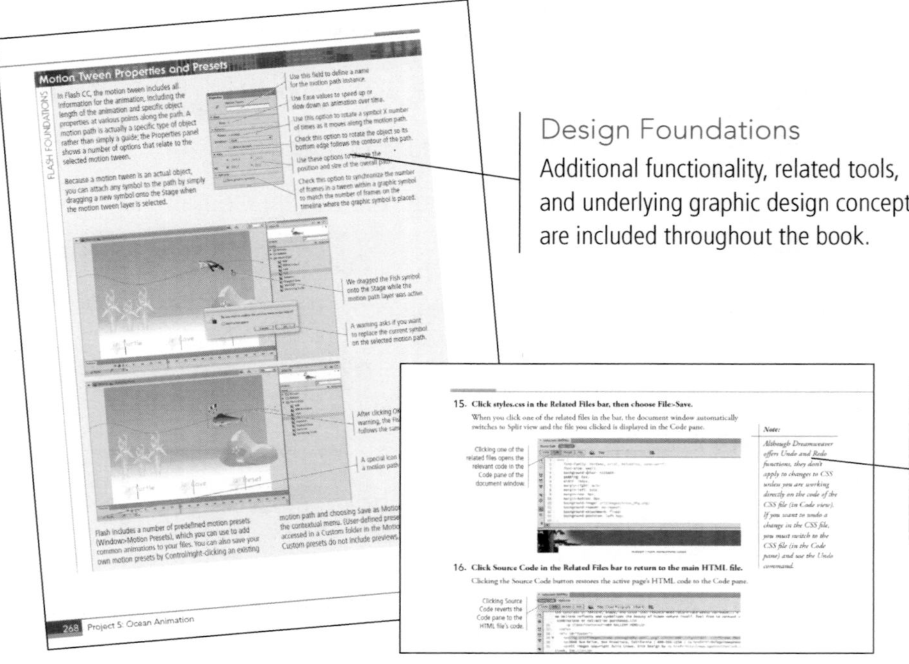

Design Foundations

Additional functionality, related tools, and underlying graphic design concepts are included throughout the book.

Advice and Warnings

Where appropriate, sidebars provide shortcuts, warnings, or tips about the topic at hand.

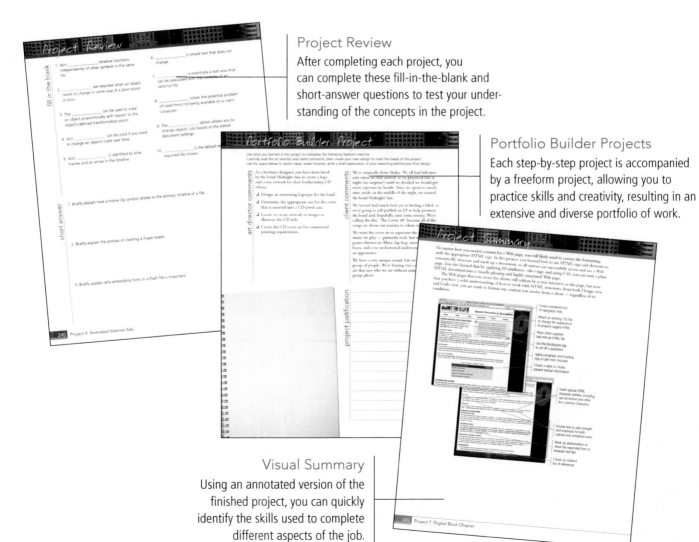

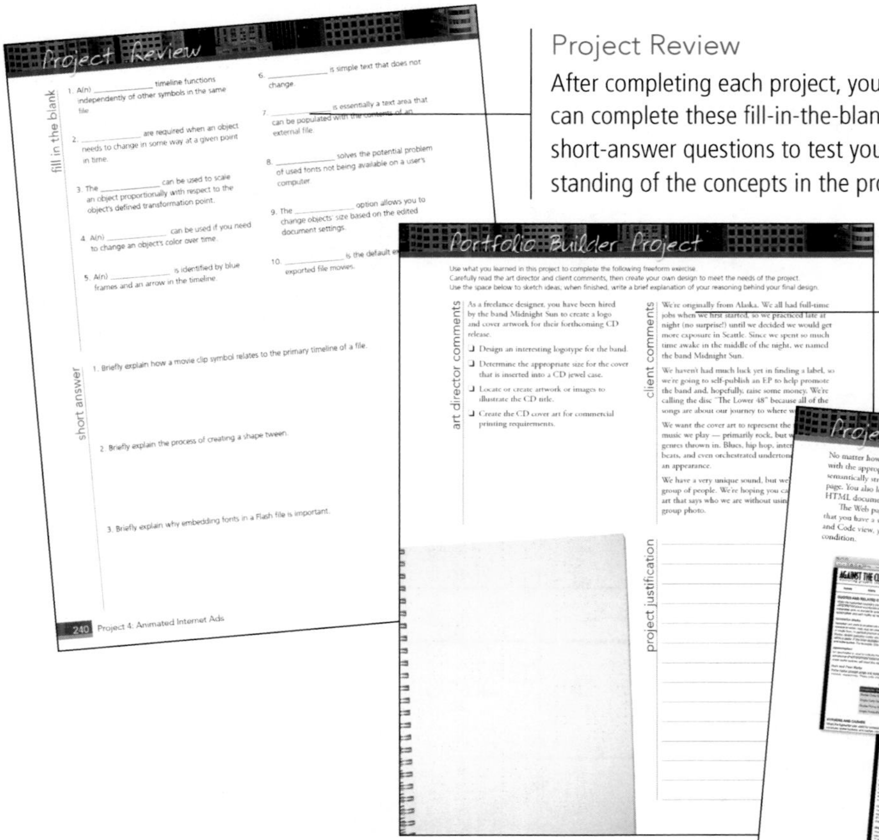

Project Review

After completing each project, you can complete these fill-in-the-blank and short-answer questions to test your understanding of the concepts in the project.

Portfolio Builder Projects

Each step-by-step project is accompanied by a freeform project, allowing you to practice skills and creativity, resulting in an extensive and diverse portfolio of work.

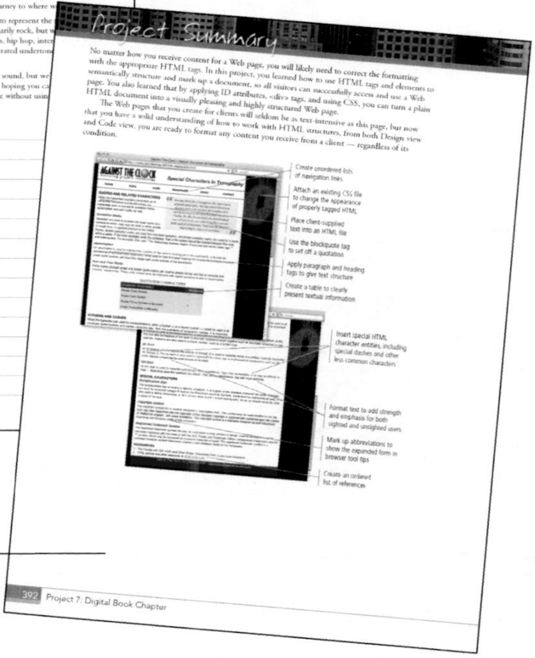

Visual Summary

Using an annotated version of the finished project, you can quickly identify the skills used to complete different aspects of the job.

Projects at a Glance

project 1

Composite Movie Ad

- ❑ Setting Up the Workspace
- ❑ Compositing Images and Artwork
- ❑ Creating Silhouettes
- ❑ Managing Multiple Layers
- ❑ Saving Files for Multiple Media

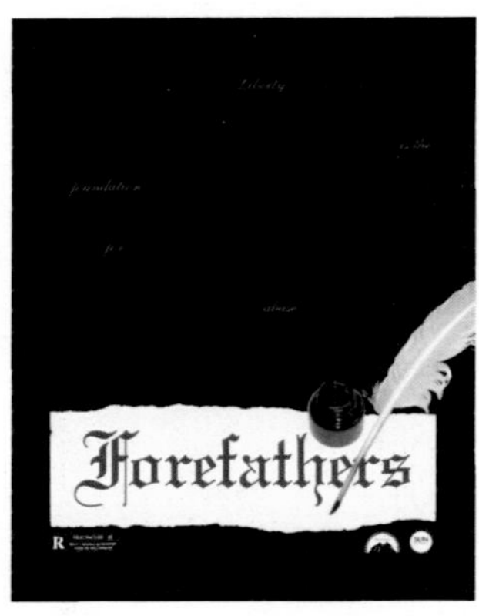

project 2

Web Page Interface

- ❑ Automating Repetitive Tasks
- ❑ Editing Layers for Visual Effect
- ❑ Generating Web-Ready Assets

project 3

Talking Kiosk Interface

- ❑ Working with Symbols
- ❑ Working with Sound
- ❑ Creating Frame Animations

project 4

Animated Internet Ads

- ❑ Animating Symbols
- ❑ Working with Text
- ❑ Repurposing Animate Content

project 5

Ocean Animation

- ❑ Importing Bitmaps and Symbols
- ❑ Animating Symbols
- ❑ Programming Basic Timeline Control

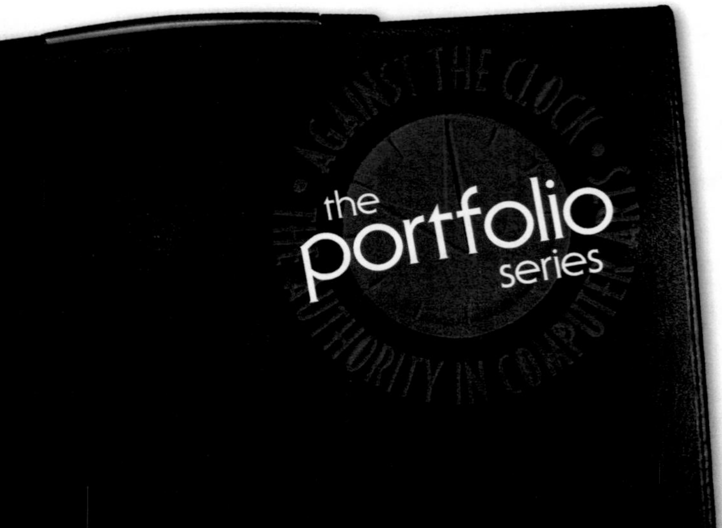

project 6

Bistro Site Organization

- ❏ Exploring Site Structure
- ❏ Organizing the Site Navigation
- ❏ Naming and Titling Documents
- ❏ Making Files Public

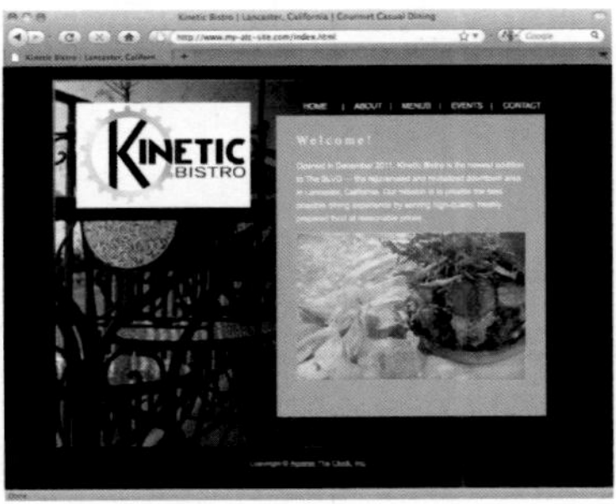

project 9

Museum CSS Layout

- ❏ Creating Layouts with Style Sheets
- ❏ Working with a Template
- ❏ Using CSS to Control Content

project 7

Digital Book Chapter

- ❏ Preparing the Workspace
- ❏ Working with Semantic Markup
- ❏ Working with Special Characters
- ❏ Creating Lists
- ❏ Attaching an External CSS File

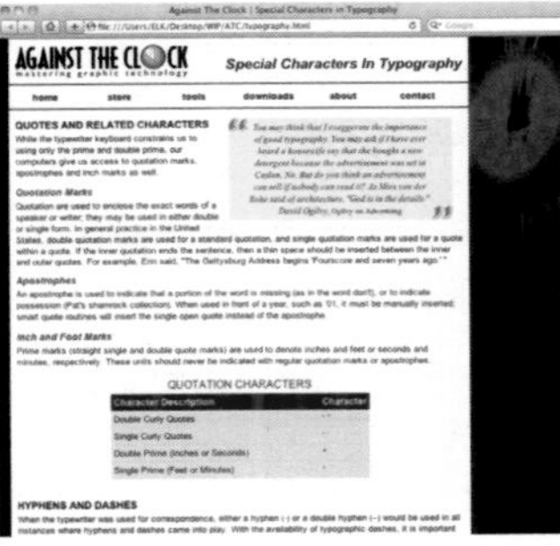

project 8

Photographer's Web Site

- ❏ Placing Static Foreground Images
- ❏ Extracting Photoshop Assets

The Against The Clock *Portfolio Series* teaches graphic design software tools and techniques entirely within the framework of real-world projects; we introduce and explain skills where they would naturally fall into a real project workflow.

The project-based approach in *The Professional Portfolio Series* allows you to get in depth with the software beginning in Project 1 — you don't have to read several chapters of introductory material before you can start creating finished artwork.

Our approach also prevents "topic tedium" — in other words, we don't require you to read pages and pages of information about text (for example); instead, we explain text tools and options as part of a larger project (in this case, as part of a book cover).

Clear, easy-to-read, step-by-step instructions walk you through every phase of each job, from creating a new file to saving the finished piece. Wherever logical, we also offer practical advice and tips about underlying concepts and graphic design practices that will benefit students as they enter the job market.

The projects in this book reflect a range of different types of Web design jobs, from correcting menu images to building a complete Web page with CSS. When you finish the projects in this book (and the accompanying Portfolio Builder exercises), you will have a substantial body of work that should impress any potential employer.

The nine projects are described briefly here; more detail is provided in the full table of contents (beginning on Page viii).

Contents

Project 8
Photographer's Web Site 383

Project 9
Museum CSS Layout 435

Prerequisites

The Professional Portfolio Series is based on the assumption that you have a basic understanding of how to use your computer. You should know how to use your mouse to point and click, as well as how to drag items around the screen. You should be able to resize and arrange windows on your desktop to maximize your available space. You should know how to access drop-down menus, and understand how check boxes and radio buttons work. It also doesn't hurt to have a good understanding of how your operating system organizes files and folders, and how to navigate your way around them. If you're familiar with these fundamental skills, then you know all that's necessary to use the Portfolio Series.

Resource Files

All the files you need to complete the projects in this book — except, of course, the Adobe application files — are on the Student Files Web page at againsttheclock.com. See the inside back cover of this book for access information.

Each archive (ZIP) file is named according to the related project (e.g., **Aquarium_Web16_RF.zip**). At the beginning of each project, you must download the archive file for that project and expand that archive to access the resource files that you need to complete the exercises. Detailed instructions for this process are included in the Interface chapter.

Files required for the related Portfolio Builder exercises at the end of each project are also available on the Student Files Web page; these archives are also named by project (e.g., **Airborne_Web16_PB.zip**).

System Requirements

The Professional Portfolio Series was designed to work on both Macintosh or Windows computers; where differences exist from one platform to another, we include specific instructions relative to each platform. One issue that remains different from Macintosh to Windows is the use of different modifier keys (Control, Shift, etc.) to accomplish the same task. When we present key commands, we always follow the same Macintosh/Windows format — Macintosh keys are listed first, then a slash, followed by the Windows key commands.

ATC Fonts

You must download and install the ATC fonts from the Student Files Web page to ensure that your exercises and projects will work as described in the book. Specific instructions for installing fonts are provided in the documentation that came with your computer. You should replace older (pre-2013) ATC fonts with the ones on the Student Files Web page.

Software Versions

This book was written and tested using the initial versions of the June 2016 release of Adobe Creative Cloud (CC) software:

- Adobe Photoshop 2015.5
- Adobe Animate 2015.2
- Adobe Dreamweaver 2015.2

(You can find the specific version of your applications in the Splash Screen that appears while an application is launching.)

Because Adobe now offers periodic updates rather than new full versions, features and functionality might have changed since publication. Please check the Errata section of the Against The Clock Web site for any issues that might arise from these periodic updates.

Web Hosting

To make Web files accessible to the browsing public, you need to have access to some type of server. On the inside back cover of this book, you have a code that you need to gain access to the required resource files. The same code also provides access to a six-month, free trial Web hosting account at Pair Networks (www.pair.com).

If you don't already have access to an online server, go to **www.pair.com/atc/** to sign up for your hosting account. You must enter your contact information, and the code from the inside back cover of your book. You should then define a user name in the last field; this will become part of the server name for your hosting account.

After clicking Continue in this screen, the resulting message warns that the setup process can take up to one business day (although it is usually about an hour). When the setup process is complete, you will receive an acknowledgement that your request is being processed. You will receive a confirmation email (sent to the email you defined in the Signup Form) with your username and password information. Once you receive the confirmation email, you are ready to complete the final stage of this project.

Adobe Photoshop is the industry-standard application for working with pixels — both manipulating existing ones and creating new ones. Many Photoshop experts specialize in certain types of work. Photo retouching, artistic painting, image compositing, and color correction are only a few types of work you can create with Photoshop. Our goal in this book is to teach you how to use the available tools to succeed with different types of jobs that you might encounter in your professional career.

The simple exercises in this introduction are designed to let you explore the Photoshop user interface. Whether you are new to the application or upgrading from a previous version, we highly recommend following these steps to click around and become familiar with the basic workspace.

Explore the Photoshop Interface

The first time you launch Photoshop, you will see the default user interface (UI) settings as defined by Adobe. When you relaunch after you or another user has quit, the workspace defaults to the last-used settings — including open panels and the position of those panels on your screen. We designed the following exercise so you can explore different ways of controlling panels in the Photoshop user interface.

1. **Create a new empty folder named WIP (Work in Progress) on any writable disk (where you plan to save your work).**

2. **Download the InterfacePS_Web16_RF.zip archive from the Student Files Web page.**

3. **Macintosh users: Place the ZIP archive in your WIP folder, then double-click the file icon to expand it.**

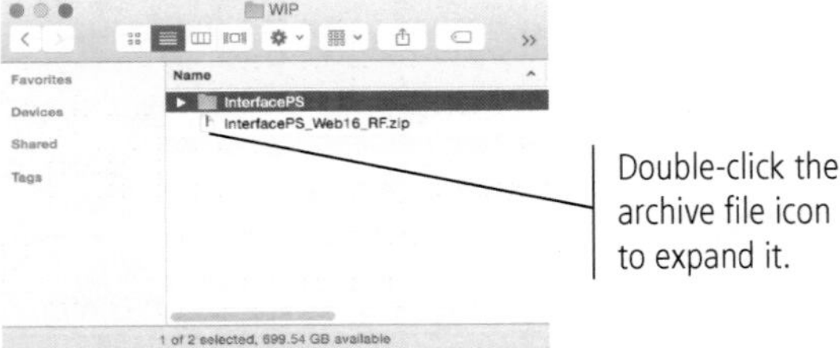

Double-click the archive file icon to expand it.

Windows users: Double-click the ZIP archive file to open it. Click the folder inside the archive and drag it into your primary WIP folder.

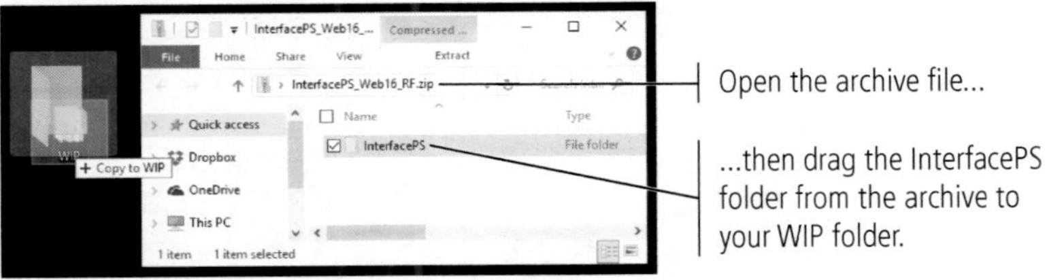

Open the archive file...

...then drag the InterfacePS folder from the archive to your WIP folder.

The resulting **InterfacePS** folder contains all the files you need to complete the exercises in this introduction.

4. **Macintosh users: While pressing Command-Option-Shift, launch Photoshop. Click Yes when asked if you want to delete Settings files.**

   Windows users: Launch Photoshop, and then immediately press Control-Alt-Shift. Click Yes when asked if you want to delete the Settings files.

5. **If you see a message about migrating presets, click No.**

   Presets are saved groups of settings for various tools, swatches, etc., that can be stored for use at a later time. Presets are intended to save time and help avoid the repetitive process of choosing the same settings over and over. To make this process one step easier, Photoshop can import presets created in previous versions — making it unnecessary to redefine presets in the new version of the software.

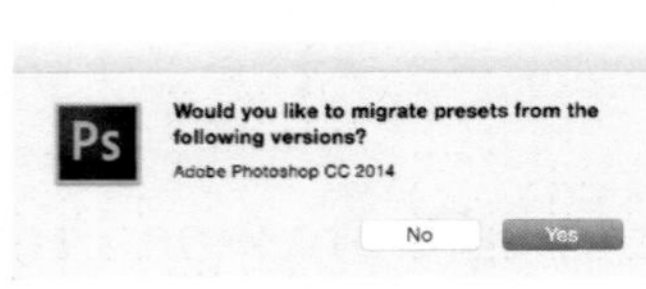

6. **Macintosh users: Open the Window menu and make sure the Application Frame option is toggled on.**

   Many menu commands and options in Photoshop are **toggles**, which means they are either on or off; when an option is already checked, that option is toggled on (visible or active). You can toggle an active option off by choosing the checked menu command, or toggle an inactive option on by choosing the unchecked menu command.

This option should be checked.

Understanding the Application Frame

PHOTOSHOP FOUNDATIONS

On Windows, each running application is contained within its own frame; all elements of the application — including the Menu bar, panels, tools, and open documents — are contained within the Application frame.

Adobe also offers the Application frame to Macintosh users as an option for controlling the workspace. When the Application frame is active, the entire workspace exists in a self-contained area that can be moved around the screen.

All elements of the workspace (excluding the Menu bar) move when you move the Application frame.

The Application frame is active by default, but you can toggle it off by choosing Window>Application Frame. If the menu option is checked, the Application frame is active; if the menu option is not checked, it is inactive. (On Windows, the Application Frame menu command is not available; you can't turn off the Application Frame on the Windows OS.)

When the Application frame is not active, the desktop is visible behind the workspace elements.

When the Application frame is not active, the option is unchecked in the Window menu.

7. Review the options in the Start screen.

The default user interface shows a stored "Start" workspace. No panels are visible in this workspace. Instead, you have one-click access to a list of recently opened files (if any); buttons to create a new file or open an existing one; and links to additional functionality provided by the Adobe Creative Cloud suite.

This workspace appears whenever Photoshop is running but no actual file is open. As soon as you open or create a file, the interface reverts to show the last-used workspace arrangement.

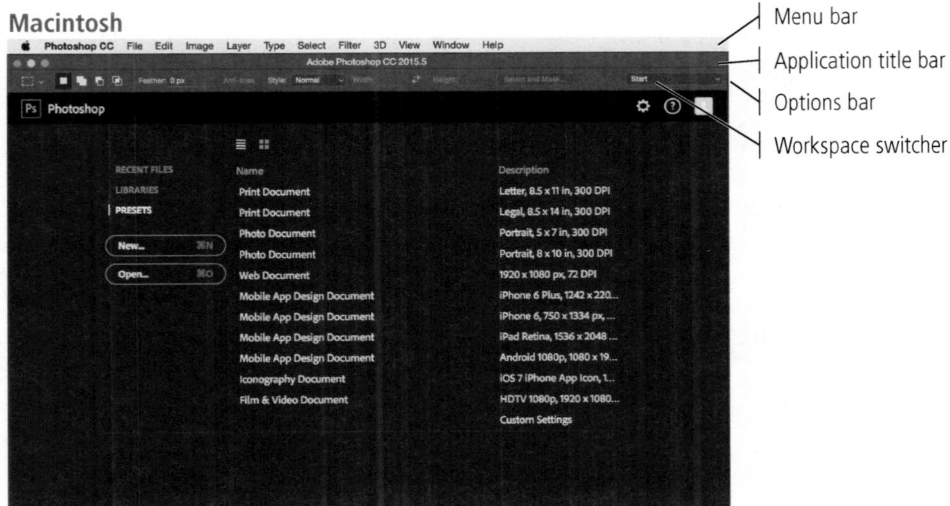

On Windows, the Minimize, Restore, and Close buttons appear on the right end of the Menu bar.

The Macintosh and Windows workspaces are virtually identical, with a few primary exceptions:

- On Macintosh, the application's title bar appears below the Menu bar; the Close, Minimize, and Restore buttons appear on the left side of the title bar, and the Menu bar is not part of the Application frame.
- On Windows, the Close, Minimize, and Restore buttons appear at the right end of the Menu bar, which is part of the overall Application frame.
- Macintosh users have two extra menus (consistent with the Macintosh operating system structure). The Apple menu provides access to system-specific commands. The Photoshop menu follows the Macintosh system-standard format for all applications; this menu controls basic application operations such as About, Hide, Preferences, and Quit.

8. **Open the Workspace switcher in the top-right corner of the workspace and choose Essentials from the menu.**

   Saved **workspaces** provide one-click access to a defined group of panels.

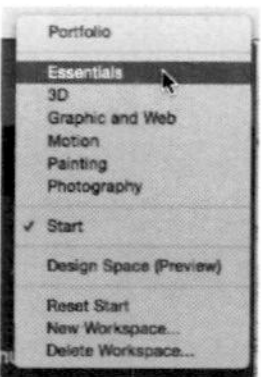

Note:

Saved workspaces can also be accessed in the Window>Workspace menu.

9. **Open the Workspace switcher again choose Reset Essentials.**

   This step might or might not do anything, depending on what was done in Photoshop before you started this project. If you or someone else changed anything and then quit the application, those changes are remembered when Photoshop is relaunched. Because we can't be sure what your default settings show, by completing this step you are resetting the user interface to one of the built-in, default workspaces so your screen shots will match ours.

10. **Review the options available in the overall user interface.**

    The default Essentials workspace includes the Tools panel on the left side of the screen, the Options bar at the top of the screen, and a set of panels attached to the right side of the screen. (The area where the panels are stored is called the **panel dock**.)

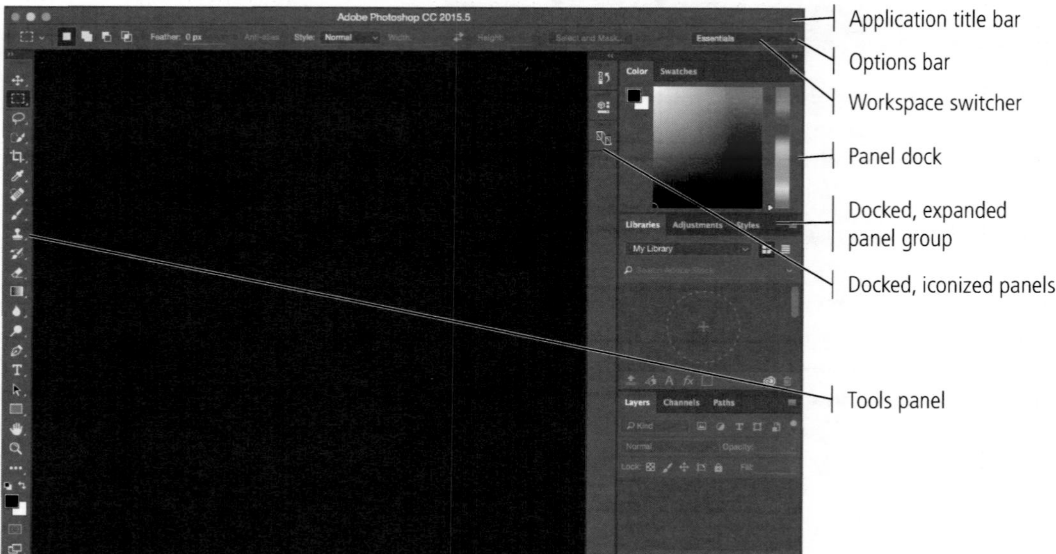

11. Macintosh users: Choose Photoshop>Preferences>Interface.
Windows users: Choose Edit>Preferences>Interface.

Remember that on Macintosh systems, the Preferences dialog box is accessed in the Photoshop menu; Windows users access the Preferences dialog box in the Edit menu.

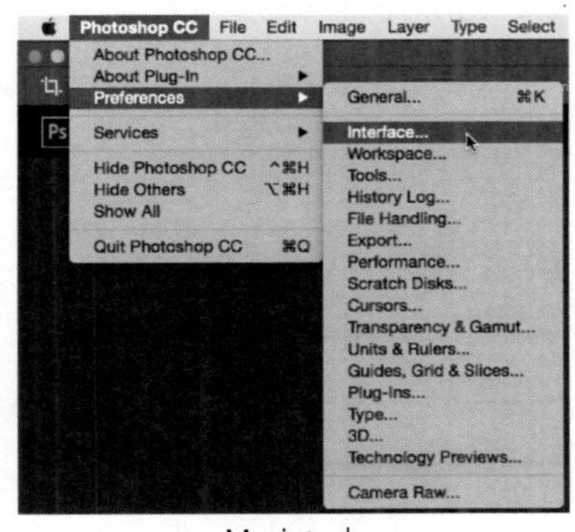

Macintosh

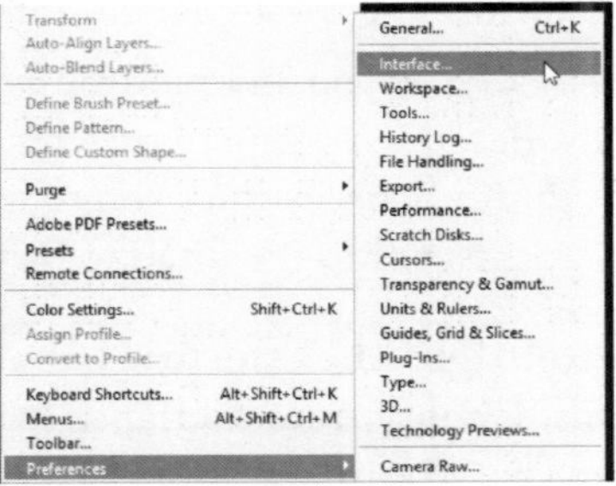

Windows

12. In the Color Theme section, choose any option that you prefer.

Preferences customize the way many of the program's tools and options function. When you open the Preferences dialog box, the active pane is the one you choose in the Preferences submenu. Once open, however, you can access any of the categories by clicking a different option in the left pane.

You might have already noticed the rather dark appearance of the panels and interface background. Photoshop CC uses the medium-dark "theme" as the default. (We used the Light option throughout this book because text in the interface elements is easier to read in printed screen captures.)

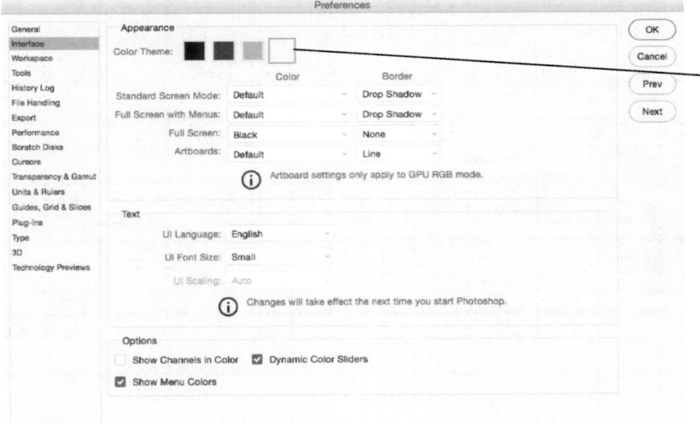

Use these options to lighten or darken the user interface.

> ***Note:***
>
> *As you work your way through this book, you will learn not only what you can do with these different collections of Preferences, but also **why** and **when** you might want to adjust them.*

13. Click OK to close the Preferences dialog box.

14. Continue to the next exercise.

Explore the Arrangement of Photoshop Panels

As you gain familiarity with Photoshop, you will develop personal artistic and working styles. You will also find that different types of jobs often require different but specific sets of tools. Adobe recognizes this wide range of needs and preferences among users; Photoshop includes a number of options for arranging and managing the numerous panels so you can customize and personalize the workspace to suit your specific needs.

We designed the following exercise to give you an opportunity to explore different ways of controlling Photoshop panels. Because workspace preferences are largely a matter of personal taste, the projects in this book instruct you to use certain tools and panels, but where you place those elements within the interface is up to you.

1. **With Photoshop open, Control/right-click the title bar above the left column of docked panel icons. Choose Auto-Collapse Iconic Panels in the contextual menu to toggle on that option.**

   As we explained in the Getting Started section, when commands are different for the Macintosh and Windows operating systems, we include the different commands in the Macintosh/Windows format. In this case, Macintosh users who do not have right-click mouse capability can press the Control key and click to access the contextual menu. You do not have to press Control *and* right-click to access the menus.

   (If you're using a Macintosh and don't have a mouse with right-click capability, we highly recommend that you purchase one.)

   Control/right-clicking a dock title bar opens the dock contextual menu, where you can change the default panel behavior. If you toggle on the Auto-Collapse Iconic Panels option — which is inactive by default — a panel will collapse as soon as you click away from it. (The Auto-Collapse Iconic Panels option is also available in the User Interface pane of the Preferences dialog box, which you can open directly from the dock contextual menu.)

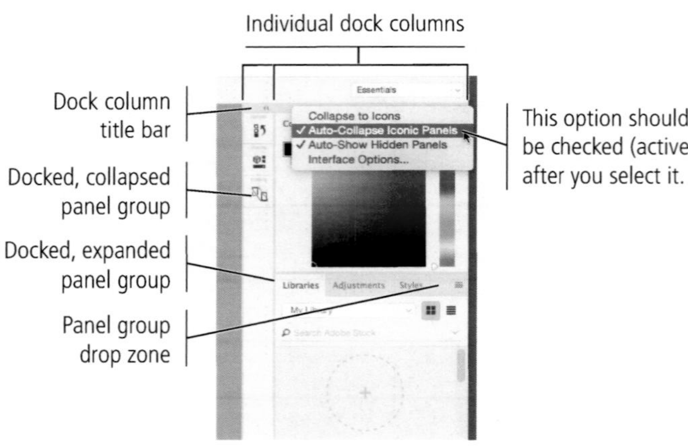

Note:

*Many menu commands and options in Photoshop are **toggles**, which means they are either on or off; when an option is checked, it is toggled on (visible or active). You can toggle an active option off by choosing the checked menu command, or toggle an inactive option on by choosing the unchecked menu command.*

Note:

*Collapsed panels are referred to as **iconized** or **iconic**.*

Note:

When you expand an iconized panel that is part of a group, the entire group expands; the button you clicked is the active panel in the expanded group.

2. **In the left column of the panel dock, hover your mouse cursor over the top button until you see the name of the related panel ("History") in a tool tip.**

3. **Click the History button to expand that panel.**

   The expanded panel is still referred to as a **panel group** even though the History panel is the only panel in the group.

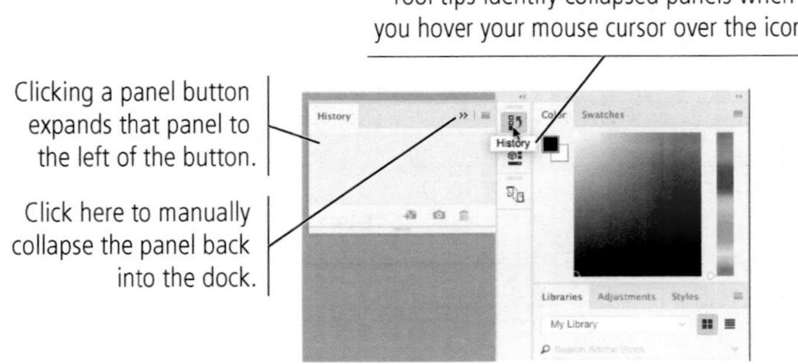

Tool tips identify collapsed panels when you hover your mouse cursor over the icon.
Clicking a panel button expands that panel to the left of the button.
Click here to manually collapse the panel back into the dock.
History
Color
Swatches
Libraries
Adjustments
Styles
My Library

Note:

All panels can be toggled on and off using the Window menu.

If you choose a panel that is open but iconized, the panel expands to the left of its icon.

If you choose a panel that is open in an expanded group, that panel comes to the front of the group.

If you choose a panel that isn't currently open, it opens in the same position as when it was last closed.

4. **Click away from the expanded panel, anywhere in the workspace.**

   Because the Auto-Collapse Iconic Panels option is toggled on (from Step 1), the History panel collapses as soon as you click away from the panel.

5. **Click the History panel button to re-expand the panel. Control/right-click the expanded panel tab and choose Close from the contextual menu.**

   The panel group's contextual menu is the only way to close a docked panel. You can choose Close to close only the active panel, or close an entire panel group by choosing Close Tab Group from the contextual menu.

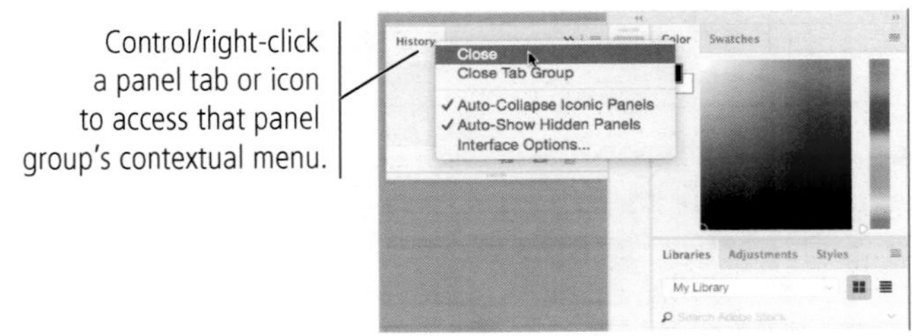

Control/right-click a panel tab or icon to access that panel group's contextual menu.
History
Close
Close Tab Group
✓ Auto-Collapse Iconic Panels
✓ Auto-Show Hidden Panels
Interface Options...
Color
Swatches
Libraries
Adjustments
Styles
My Library

6. **Repeat Step 5 to close the Properties panel and the Device Preview panel.**

   Closing all panels in a column effectively removes that column from the dock.

7. **In the remaining dock column, Control/right-click the drop zone of the Libraries/Adjustments/Styles panel group and choose Close Tab Group from the contextual menu.**

   When you close a docked group, other panel groups in the same column expand to fill the available space.

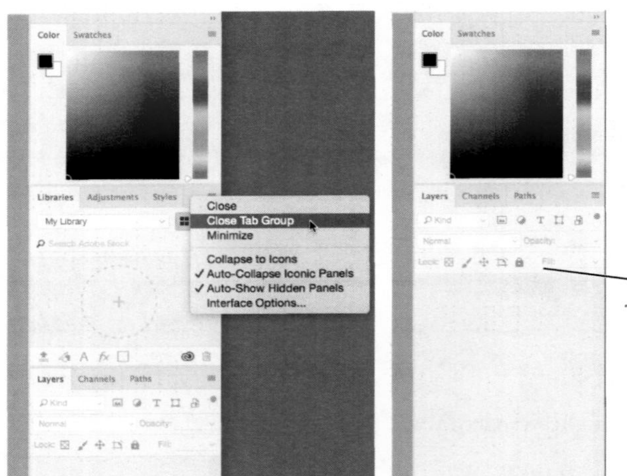

The remaining groups in the dock column expand to fill the available space.

8. **Click the Layers panel tab and drag left, away from the panel dock.**

   A panel that is not docked is called a **floating panel**. You can iconize floating panels (or panel groups) by double-clicking the title bar of the floating panel group.

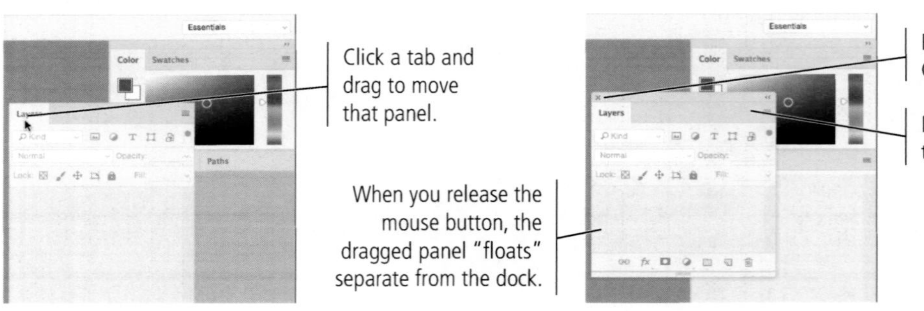

Click a tab and drag to move that panel.

When you release the mouse button, the dragged panel "floats" separate from the dock.

Panel (group) Close button

Floating panel title bar

9. **Click the Layers panel tab (in the floating panel group). Drag between the two existing docked panel groups until a blue line appears, then release the mouse button.**

   To move a single panel to a new location, click the panel tab and drag. To move an entire panel group, click the panel group drop zone and drag. If you are moving panels to another position in the dock, the blue highlight indicates where the panel (group) will be placed when you release the mouse button.

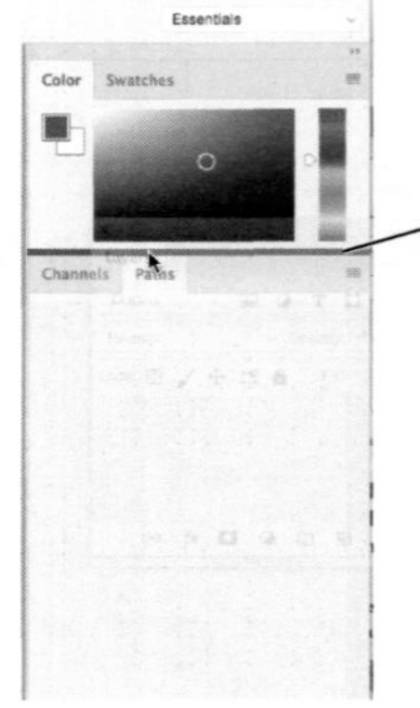

The blue highlight shows where the panel will be placed if you release the mouse button.

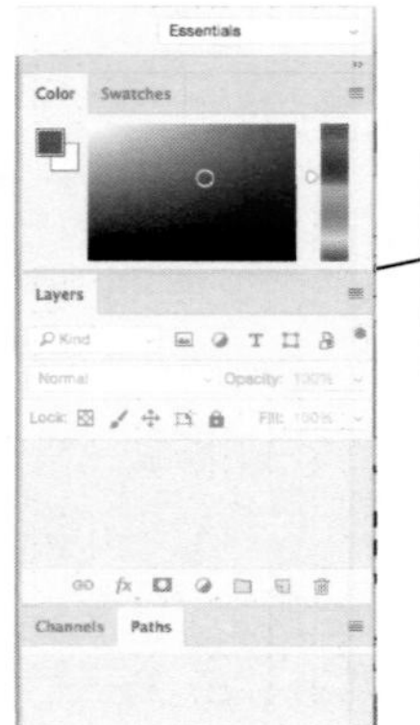

When you release the mouse button, the Layers panel becomes part of a separate panel group.

Note:

Many screen shots in this book show floating panels so we can focus on the most important issue in a particular image. In our production workflow, however, we make heavy use of docked and iconized panels, and we take full advantage of saved custom workspaces.

Note:

To add a panel to an existing group, drag the panel to the target group's drop zone. A blue highlight will surround the group where the moved panel will be added.

Note:

To create a new dock column, drag a panel or panel group until a pop-out "drawer" outlines the edge where the new column will be added.

Each column, technically considered a separate dock, can be expanded or collapsed independently of other columns.

10. Control/right-click the drop zone behind the Colors/Swatches panel group, and choose Minimize from the contextual menu.

When a group is minimized, only the panel tabs are visible. Clicking a tab in a collapsed panel group expands that group and makes the selected panel active.

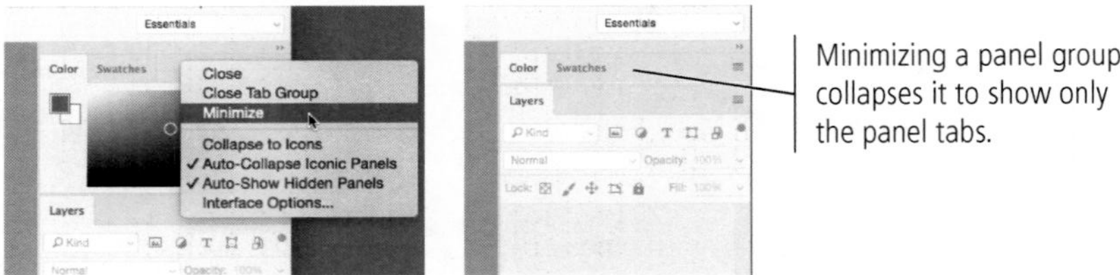

Minimizing a panel group collapses it to show only the panel tabs.

You can also double-click a panel tab to minimize the panel group.

11. Move the cursor over the line between the Layers and Channels/Paths panel groups. When the cursor becomes a double-headed arrow, click and drag down until the Layers panel occupies approximately half of the available dock column space.

You can drag the bottom edge of a docked panel group to vertically expand or shrink the panel; other panels in the same column expand or contract to fit the available space.

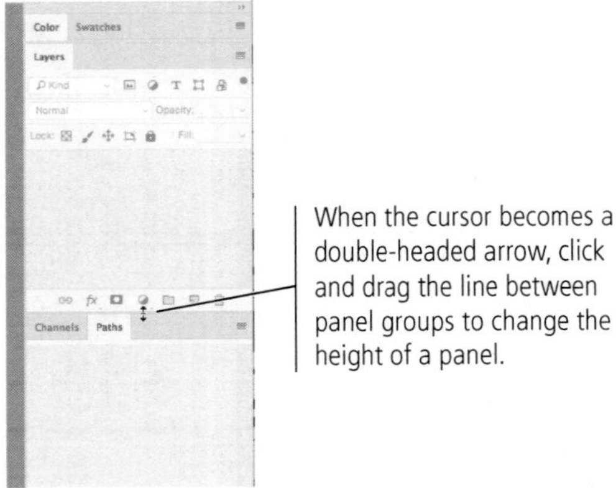

When the cursor becomes a double-headed arrow, click and drag the line between panel groups to change the height of a panel.

12. Double-click the title bar above the column of docked panels to collapse those panels to icons.

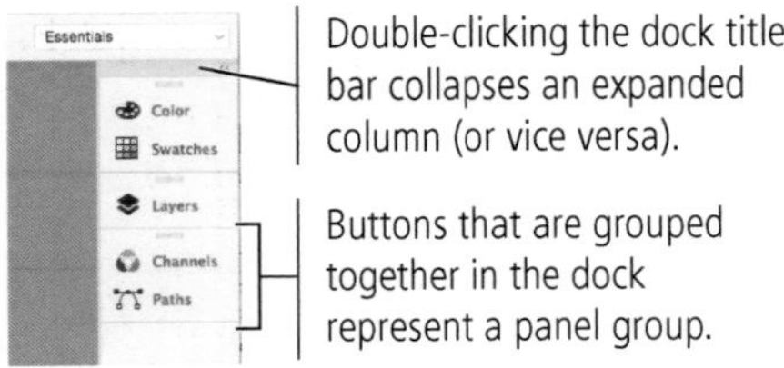

Double-clicking the dock title bar collapses an expanded column (or vice versa).

Buttons that are grouped together in the dock represent a panel group.

13. Move the cursor over the left edge of the dock column. When the cursor becomes a double-headed arrow, click and drag right.

If you only see the icons, you can also drag the dock edge to the left to reveal the panel names. This can be particularly useful until you are more familiar with the application and the icons used to symbolize the different panels.

> ***Note:***
>
> *Dragging the left edge of a dock column changes the width of all panels in that dock column. This works for both iconized and expanded columns.*

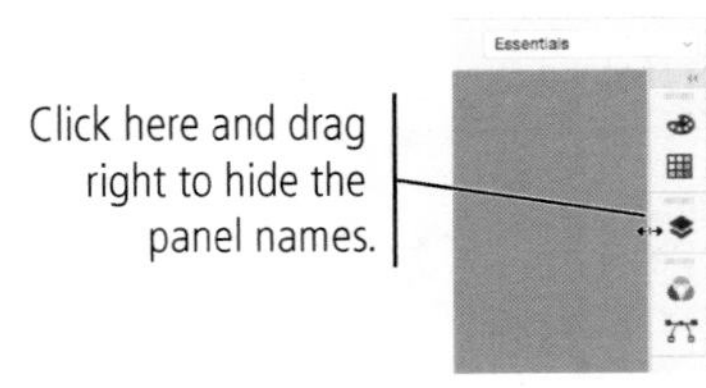

Click here and drag right to hide the panel names.

Accessing Photoshop Tools

In the Tools panel, tools with a small white mark in the lower-right corner have **nested tools**.

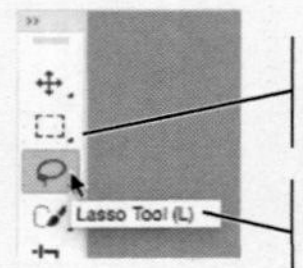

This arrow means the tool has other nested tools.

A tool tip shows the name of the tool.

If you hover your mouse over a tool, a **tool tip** shows the name of the tool, as well as the associated keyboard shortcut for that tool if one exists. (If you don't see tool tips, check the Show Tool Tips option in the General pane of the Preferences dialog box.)

You can access nested tools by clicking the primary tool and holding down the mouse button, or by Control/right-clicking the primary tool to open the menu of nested options.

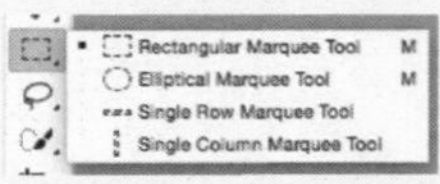

If a tool has a defined shortcut, pressing that key activates the associated tool. Most nested tools have the same shortcut as the default tool. By default, you have to press Shift plus the shortcut key to access the nested variations; for example, press Shift-M to toggle between the Rectangular and Elliptical Marquee tools. You can change this behavior in the General pane of the Preferences dialog box by unchecking the Use Shift Key for Tool Switch option. When this option is off, you can simply press the shortcut key multiple times to cycle through the variations.

Not all nested tools can be accessed with a shortcut. In the marquee tools, for example, the shortcut toggles only between the rectangular and elliptical variations.

Finally, if you press and hold a tool's keyboard shortcut, you can temporarily call the appropriate tool (called **spring-loaded keys**); after releasing the shortcut key, you return to the tool you were using previously. For example, you might use this technique to switch temporarily from the Brush tool to the Eraser tool while painting.

The following chart offers a quick reference of nested tools, as well as the shortcut for each tool (if any). Nested tools are shown indented.

- Move tool (V)
  - Artboard tool (V)
- Rectangular Marquee tool (M)
  - Elliptical Marquee tool (M)
  - Single Row Marquee tool
  - Single Column Marquee tool
- Lasso tool (L)
  - Polygonal Lasso tool (L)
  - Magnetic Lasso tool (L)
- Quick Selection tool (W)
  - Magic Wand tool (W)
- Crop tool (C)
  - Perspective Crop tool (C)
  - Slice tool (C)
  - Slice Select tool (C)
- Eyedropper tool (I)
  - 3D Material Eyedropper tool (I)
  - Color Sampler tool (I)
  - Ruler tool (I)
  - Note tool (I)
  - Count tool (I)
- Spot Healing Brush tool (J)
  - Healing Brush tool (J)
  - Patch tool (J)
  - Content Aware Move tool (J)
  - Red Eye tool (J)
- Brush tool (B)
  - Pencil tool (B)
  - Color Replacement tool (B)
  - Mixer Brush tool (B)
- Clone Stamp tool (S)
  - Pattern Stamp tool (S)
- History Brush tool (Y)
  - Art History Brush tool (Y)
- Eraser tool (E)
  - Background Eraser tool (E)
  - Magic Eraser tool (E)
- Gradient tool (G)
  - Paint Bucket tool (G)
  - 3D Material Drop tool (G)
- Blur tool
  - Sharpen tool
  - Smudge tool
- Dodge tool (O)
  - Burn tool (O)
  - Sponge tool (O)
- Pen tool (P)
  - Freeform Pen tool (P)
  - Add Anchor Point tool
  - Delete Anchor Point tool
  - Convert Point tool
- Horizontal Type tool (T)
  - Vertical Type tool (T)
  - Horizontal Type Mask tool (T)
  - Vertical Type Mask tool (T)
- Path Selection tool (A)
  - Direct Selection tool (A)
- Rectangle tool (U)
  - Rounded Rectangle tool (U)
  - Ellipse tool (U)
  - Polygon tool (U)
  - Line tool (U)
  - Custom Shape tool (U)
- Hand tool (H)
  - Rotate View tool (R)
- Zoom tool (Z)

14. On the left side of the workspace, double-click the Tools panel title bar.

The Tools panel can't be expanded, but it can be displayed as either one or two columns; double-clicking the Tools panel title bar toggles between the two modes.

The one- or two-column format is a purely personal choice. The one-column layout takes up less horizontal space on the screen, which can be useful if you have a small monitor. The two-column format fits in a smaller vertical space, which can be especially useful if you have a widescreen monitor.

The Tools panel can also be floated by clicking its title bar and dragging away from the edge of the screen. To re-dock the floating Tools panel, simply click the title bar and drag back to the left edge of the screen; when the blue line highlights the edge of the workspace, releasing the mouse button puts the Tools panel back into the dock.

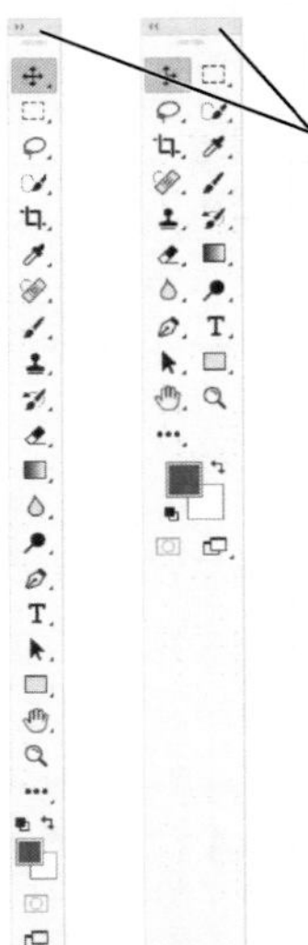

Double-click the Tools panel title bar to toggle between the one-column and two-column layouts.

Note:

Throughout this book, our screen shots show the Tools panel in the one-column format. Feel free to work with the panel in two columns if you prefer.

15. Continue to the next exercise.

Customizing the Photoshop Tools Panel

PHOTOSHOP FOUNDATIONS

Near the bottom of the Tools panel, the Edit Toolbar ··· provides access to a dialog box where you can customize the options that appear in the Tools panel. If you click and hold on this button, you can choose the option to Edit Toolbar in the pop-up menu.

In the Customize Toolbar dialog box, you can select and move individual tools or entire groups of tools into the Extra Tools window. Any tools in that window are moved from their regular position in the default Tools panel to a single position, nested under the Edit Toolbar option.

You can toggle the buttons in the bottom-left corner of the dialog box to show or hide several options in the Tools panel. From left to right:

- Edit Toolbar
- Default Foreground and Background Colors
- Edit in Quick Mask Mode
- Change Screen Mode

If you choose to hide the Edit Toolbar option, any tools in the Extra Tools list are simply hidden; you will not be able to access them unless you customize the Tools panel again. (In this case, you can accomplish this task by choosing Edit>Toolbar).

Clicking the Restore Defaults button in the Customize Toolbar dialog box resets all tools and options in the panel to their original default positions and visibility.

Click and drag tools from the Toolbar list to the Extra Tools list.

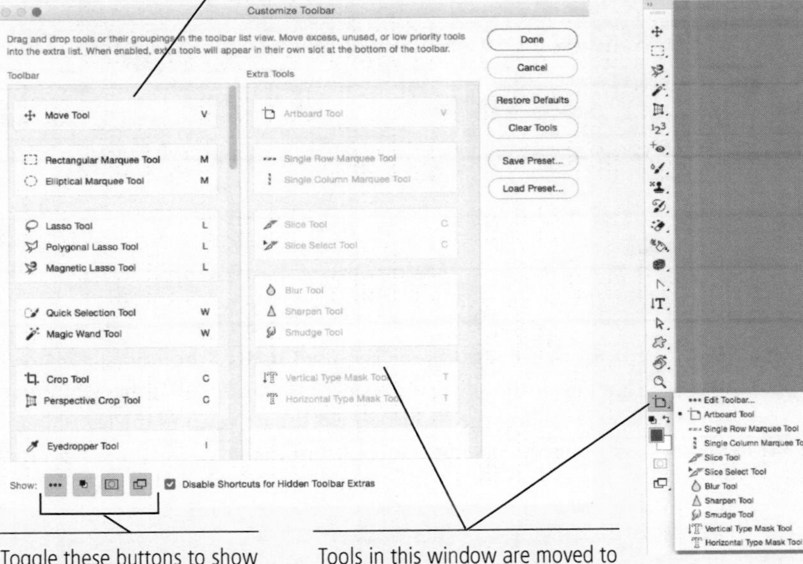

Toggle these buttons to show and hide extra options at the bottom of the Tools panel.

Tools in this window are moved to a single group at the bottom of the Tools panel, nested below the Edit Toolbar option.

Create a Saved Workspace

You have extensive control over the appearance of your Photoshop workspace — you can choose what panels are visible, where they appear, and even the size of individual panels or panel groups. Over time you will develop personal preferences — the Layers panel always appears at the top, for example — based on your work habits and project needs. Rather than re-establishing every workspace element each time you return to Photoshop, you can save your custom workspace settings so they can be recalled with a single click.

> *Note:*
>
> *Because workspace preferences are largely a matter of personal taste, the projects in this book instruct you regarding which panels to use, but not where to place those elements within the interface.*

1. **Choose Window>Workspace>New Workspace.**

   Saved workspaces can be accessed in the Window>Workspace submenu as well as the Workspace switcher on the Options bar.

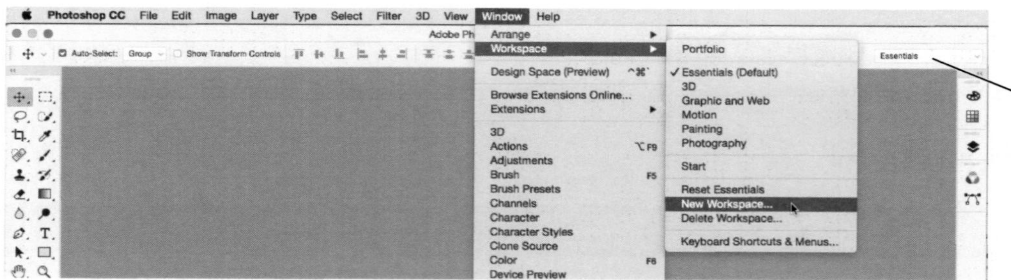

The Workspace switcher is labeled with the last-used saved workspace.

2. **In the New Workspace dialog box, type Portfolio and then click Save.**

   You didn't define custom keyboard shortcuts, menus, or toolbars, so those options are not relevant in this exercise.

> *Note:*
>
> *If a menu option is grayed out, it is not available for the active selection.*

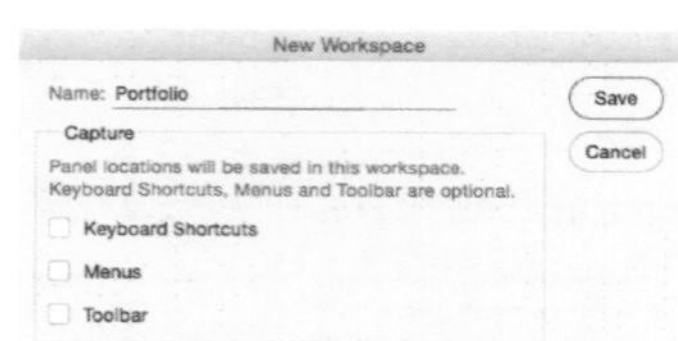

> *Note:*
>
> *The Delete Workspace option opens a dialog box where you can choose a specific user-defined workspace to delete. You can't delete the default workspaces that come with the application.*

3. **Open the Window menu and choose Workspace>Essentials (Default).**

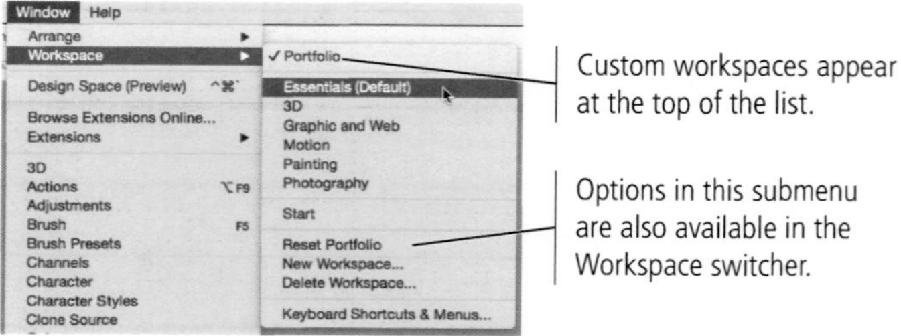

Custom workspaces appear at the top of the list.

Options in this submenu are also available in the Workspace switcher.

   Calling a saved workspace restores the last-used state of the workspace. You made a number of changes since calling the Essentials workspace at the beginning of the previous exercise, so calling the Essentials workspace restores the last state of that workspace — in essence, nothing changes from the saved Portfolio workspace.

The only apparent difference is the active workspace name.

4. **Open the Workspace switcher and choose Reset Essentials (or choose Window>Workspace>Reset Essentials).**

   Remember, saved workspaces remember the last-used state; calling a workspace again restores the panels exactly as they were the last time you used that workspace. For example, if you close a panel that is part of a saved workspace, the closed panel will not be reopened the next time you call the same workspace. To restore the saved state of the workspace, including opening closed panels or repositioning moved ones, you have to use the Reset option.

Note:

If you change anything and quit the application, those changes are remembered even when Photoshop is relaunched.

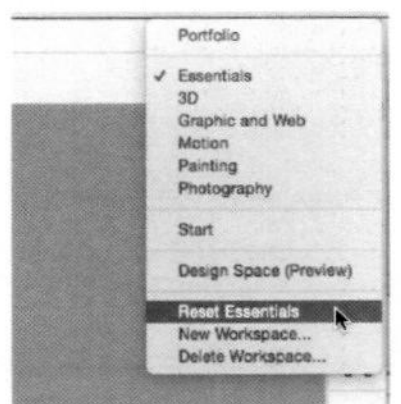

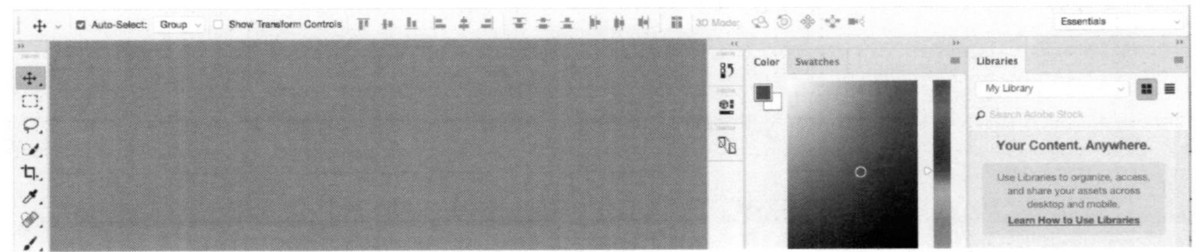

5. **Using the Window>Workspace menu or the Workspace switcher, call the saved Portfolio workspace.**

6. **Continue to the next exercise.**

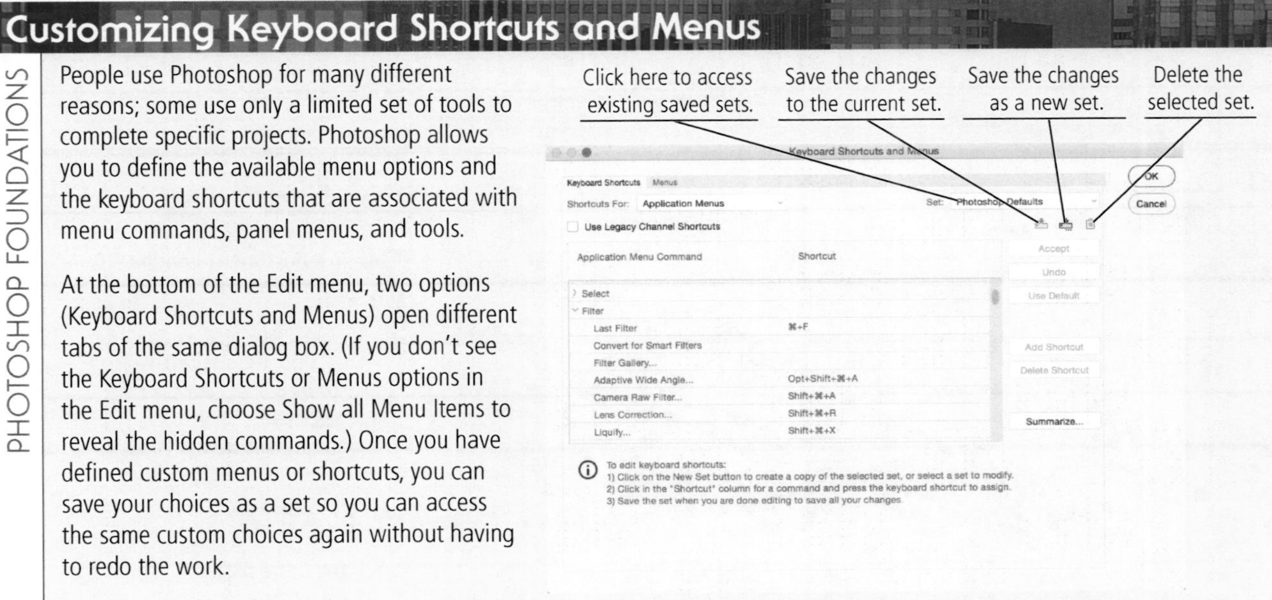

Click here to access existing saved sets.
Save the changes to the current set.
Save the changes as a new set.
Delete the selected set.

Customizing Keyboard Shortcuts and Menus

PHOTOSHOP FOUNDATIONS

People use Photoshop for many different reasons; some use only a limited set of tools to complete specific projects. Photoshop allows you to define the available menu options and the keyboard shortcuts that are associated with menu commands, panel menus, and tools.

At the bottom of the Edit menu, two options (Keyboard Shortcuts and Menus) open different tabs of the same dialog box. (If you don't see the Keyboard Shortcuts or Menus options in the Edit menu, choose Show all Menu Items to reveal the hidden commands.) Once you have defined custom menus or shortcuts, you can save your choices as a set so you can access the same custom choices again without having to redo the work.

Explore the Photoshop Document Views

There is much more to using Photoshop than arranging the workspace. What you do with those panels — and even which panels you need — depends on the type of work you are doing in a particular file. In this exercise, you open a Photoshop file and explore interface elements that will be important as you begin creating digital artwork.

1. **In Photoshop, choose File>Open. If you see a warning message about insufficient vRAM, click OK.**

   The 3D features in Photoshop CC require a graphics card with at least 512 MB of video RAM (vRAM). The first time you try to create a new file or open an existing one, you will see a warning message if your hardware is not sufficient to run those features.

> *Note:*
>
> *If you see this message, you will not be able to complete Project 4: City Promotion Cards.*

2. **Navigate to your WIP>InterfacePS folder and select hubble.jpg in the list of available files. Press Shift, and then click supernova.jpg.**

   The Open dialog box is a system-standard navigation dialog. This is one area of significant difference between Macintosh and Windows users.

   On both operating systems, this step selects all files including and between the two you click. Pressing Shift allows you to select multiple consecutive files in the list. You can also press Command/Control and click to select multiple non-consecutive files.

> *Note:*
>
> *Press Command/Control-O to access the Open dialog box.*

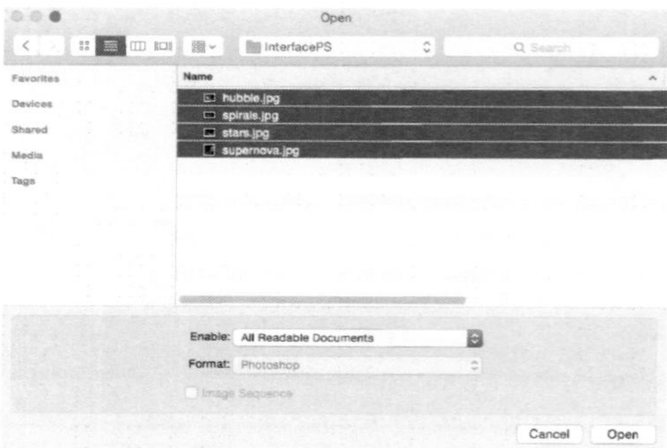

Macintosh

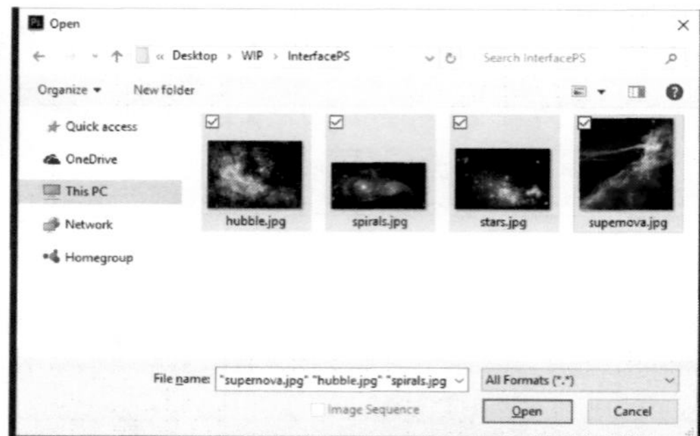

Windows

3. **Click Open.**

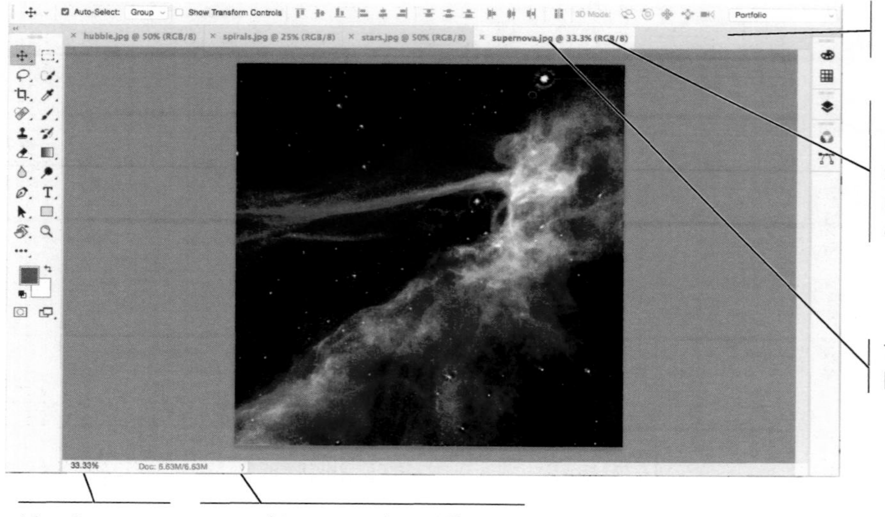

Photoshop files appear in a **document window**.

Each open file is represented by a **document tab**, which shows the file name, view percentage, color space, and current viewing mode.

The active file tab is lighter than other tabs.

View Percentage field

Use this menu to show different document information, such as file size (default), profile, dimensions, etc.

4. **Click the spirals.jpg tab to make that document active.**

5. **Highlight the current value in the View Percentage field (in the bottom-left corner of the document window). Type 45, then press Return/Enter.**

   Different people prefer larger or smaller view percentages, depending on a number of factors (eyesight, monitor size, and so on). As you complete the projects in this book, you will see our screen shots zoom in or out as necessary to show you the most relevant part of a particular file. In most cases we do not tell you what specific view percentage to use for a particular exercise, unless it is specifically required for the work being done.

Note:

Macintosh users: If you turn off the Application frame, opening multiple files creates a document window that has a separate title bar showing the name of the active file.

Click the tab to activate a specific file in the document window.

Changing the view percentage of the file does not affect the size of the document window.

6. **Choose View>100%.**

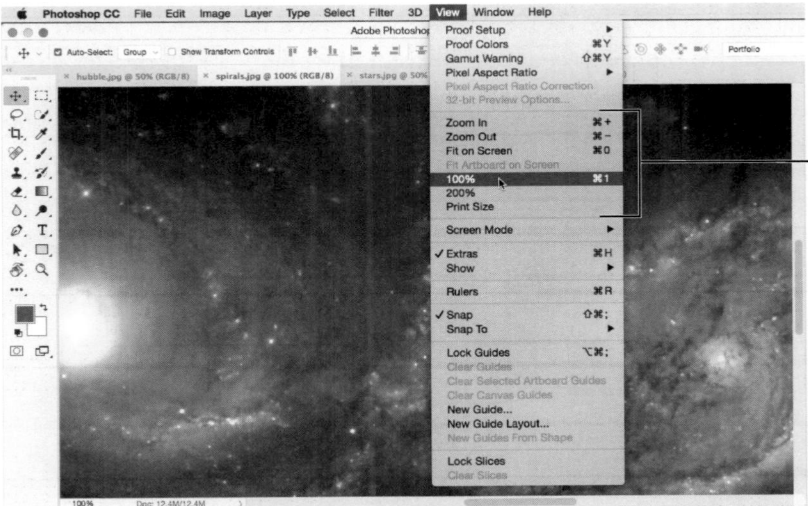

These options affect the file's view percentage.

7. **Click the Hand tool (near the bottom of the Tools panel). Click in the document window, hold down the mouse button, and drag around.**

The Hand tool is a very easy and convenient option for changing the area of an image that is currently visible in the document window.

(If the Scroll All Windows option is checked in the Options bar, dragging in one window affects the visible area of all open files.)

> ***Note:***
>
> *You can press the Spacebar to access the Hand tool when another tool (other than the Type tool) is active.*

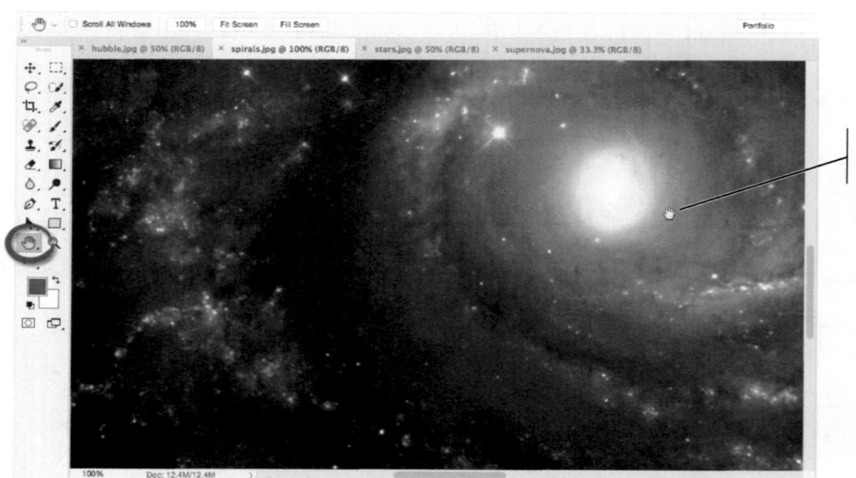

Hand tool cursor

8. **Click the Zoom tool in the Tools panel. Press Option/Alt, and then click anywhere in the document window.**

One final reminder: we list differing commands in the Macintosh/Windows format. On Macintosh, you need to press the Option key; on Windows, press the Alt key. (We will not repeat this explanation every time different commands are required for the different operating systems.)

Clicking with the Zoom tool enlarges the view percentage in specific, predefined percentage steps. Pressing Option/Alt while clicking with the Zoom tool reduces the view percentage in the reverse sequence of the same percentages.

> ***Note:***
>
> *You can zoom a document between approximately 0.098% and 3200%. We say approximately because the actual smallest size is dependent on the original image size; you can zoom out far enough to "show" the image as a single tiny square, regardless of what percentage of the image that represents.*

When the Zoom tool is active, pressing Option/Alt changes the cursor to the Zoom Out icon.

> ***Note:***
>
> *Dragging with the Zoom tool enlarges the selected area to fill the document window.*

9. **In the Options bar, click the Fit Screen button.**

The Options bar appears by default at the top of the workspace below the Menu bar. It is context sensitive, which means it provides different options depending on which tool is active. When the Zoom tool is active:

- If Resize Windows to Fit is checked, zooming in a floating window affects the size of the actual document window.
- If Zoom All Windows is checked, zooming in one window affects the view percentage of all open files.
- Scrubby Zoom enables dynamic image zooming depending on the direction you drag in the document window.
- The 100% button changes the view percentage to 100%.
- The Fit Screen option changes the image view to whatever percentage is necessary to show the entire image in the document window. (This has the same effect as choosing Window>Fit on Screen.)
- The Fill Screen button changes the image view to whatever percentage is necessary to fill the available space in the document window.

The Fit Screen command automatically calculates view percentage based on the size of the document window.

Note:

You can toggle the Options bar on or off by choosing Window>Options.

Note:

If you check the Enable Narrow Options Bar option in the Workspace pane of the Preferences dialog box, many options in the Options bar will appear as small icons that you can click to toggle on and off. This saves horizontal space on narrow monitors.

10. **In the Tools panel, choose the Rotate View tool (nested under the Hand tool). Click in the document window and drag right to turn the document clockwise.**

The Rotate View tool turns an image without permanently altering the orientation of the file; the actual image data remains unchanged. This tool allows you to more easily work on objects or elements that are not oriented horizontally (for example, working with text that appears on an angle in the final image).

In the Options bar, you can type a specific angle in the Rotation Angle field or click the rotation proxy icon to dynamically rotate the view. At any time, you can click the Reset View button to restore the original rotation (0°) of the image. If Rotate All Windows is checked, dragging in one window affects the view angle of all open files.

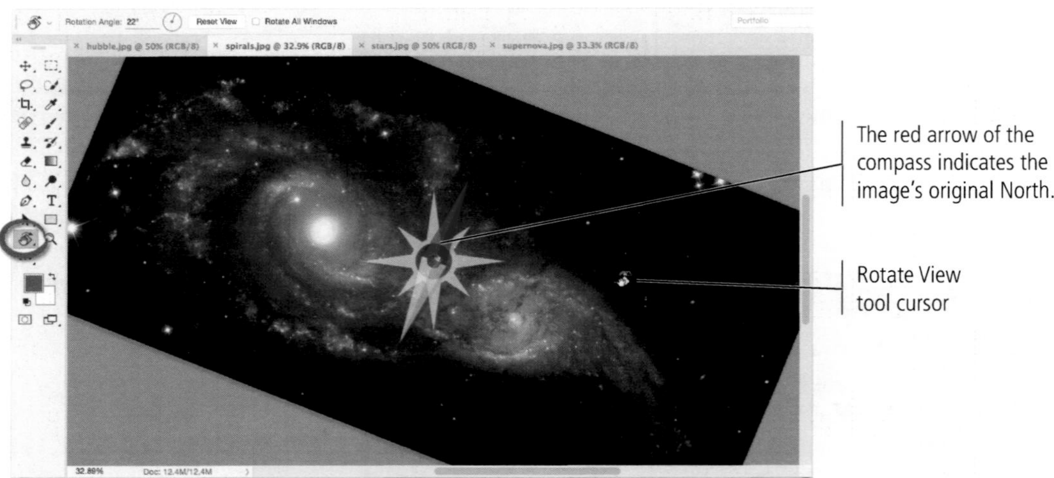

The red arrow of the compass indicates the image's original North.
Rotate View tool cursor

If you are unable to rotate the image view, your graphics processor does not support OpenGL — a hardware/software combination that makes it possible to work with complex graphics operations. If your computer does not support OpenGL, you will not be able to use a number of Photoshop features (including the Rotate View tool).

11. **In the Options bar, click the Reset View button.**

As we said, the Rotate View tool is **non-destructive** (i.e., it does not permanently affect the pixels in the image). You can easily use the tool's options to define a specific view angle or to restore an image to its original orientation.

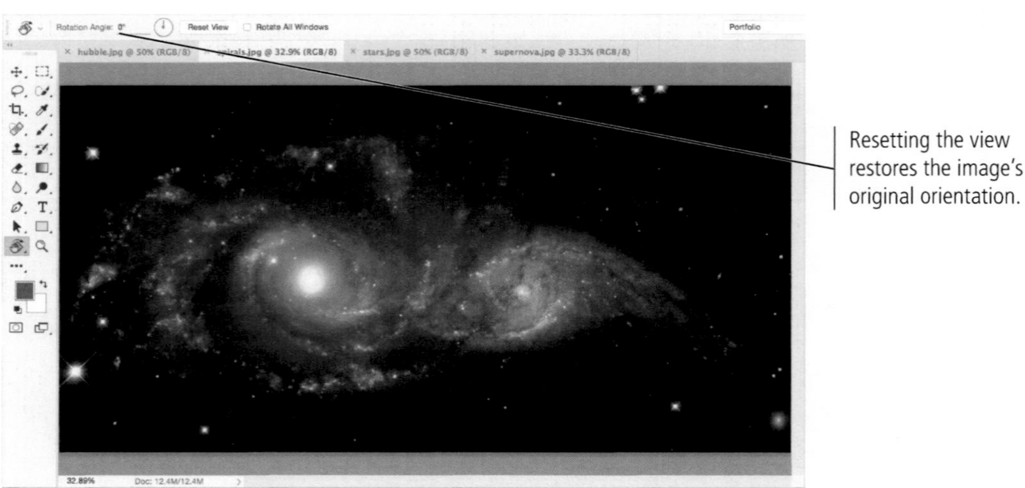

Resetting the view restores the image's original orientation.

12. **Continue to the next exercise.**

Summing Up the Photoshop View Options

Most Photoshop projects require some amount of zooming in and out to various view percentages, as well as navigating around the document within its window. As we show you how to complete different stages of the workflow, we usually won't tell you when to change your view percentage because that's largely a matter of personal preference. However, you should understand the different options for navigating around a Photoshop file so you can easily and efficiently get to what you want, when you want to get there.

View Percentage Field

You can type a specific percentage in the View Percentage field in the bottom-left corner of the document window.

View Menu

The View menu also provides options for changing the view percentage, including the associated keyboard shortcuts. (The Zoom In and Zoom Out options step through the same predefined view percentages that the Zoom tool uses.)

Zoom In	Command/Control-plus (+)
Zoom Out	Command/Control-minus (-)
Fit On Screen	Command/Control-0 (zero)
Actual Pixels (100%)	Command/Control-1

Zoom Tool

You can click with the **Zoom tool** to increase the view percentage in specific, predefined intervals. Pressing Option/Alt with the Zoom tool allows you to zoom out in the same predefined percentages. If you drag a marquee with the Zoom tool, you can zoom into a specific location; the area surrounded by the marquee fills the available space in the document window.

When the Zoom tool is active, you can also activate the Scrubby Zoom option in the Options bar. This allows you to click and drag left to reduce the view percentage, or drag right to increase the view percentage; in this case, the tool does not follow predefined stepped percentages.

Hand Tool

Whatever your view percentage, you can use the **Hand tool** to drag the file around in the document window. The Hand tool changes only what is visible in the window; it has no effect on the actual pixels in the image.

Mouse Scroll Wheel

If your mouse has a scroll wheel, rolling the scroll wheel up or down moves the image up or down within the document window. If you press Command/Control and scroll the wheel, you can move the image left (scroll up) or right (scroll down) within the document window. You can also press Option/Alt and scroll the wheel up to zoom in or scroll the wheel down to zoom out.

(In the General pane of the Preferences dialog box, the Zoom with Scroll Wheel option is unchecked by default. If you check this option, scrolling up or down with no modifier key zooms in or out and does not move the image within the document window.)

Navigator Panel

The **Navigator panel** is another method of adjusting how close your viewpoint is and what part of the page you're currently viewing (if you're zoomed in close enough so you can see only a portion of the page). The Navigator panel shows a thumbnail of the active file; a red rectangle represents exactly how much of the document shows in the document window.

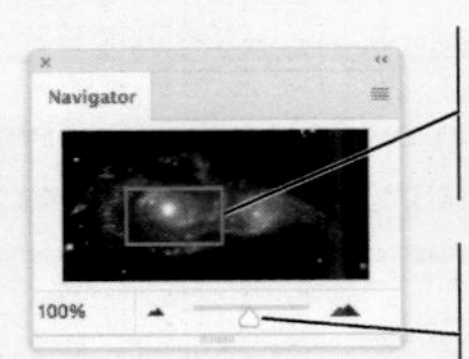

Drag the red rectangle to change the visible portion of the file.

Use the slider and field at the bottom of the panel to change the view percentage.

Explore the Arrangement of Multiple Documents

You will often need to work with more than one Photoshop file at once. Photoshop incorporates a number of options for arranging multiple documents. We designed the following simple exercise so you can explore these options.

1. **With all four files from the WIP>InterfacePS folder open, click the hubble.jpg document tab to make that the active file.**

2. **Choose Window>Arrange>Float in Window.**

   You can also separate all open files by choosing Window>Arrange>Float All In Windows.

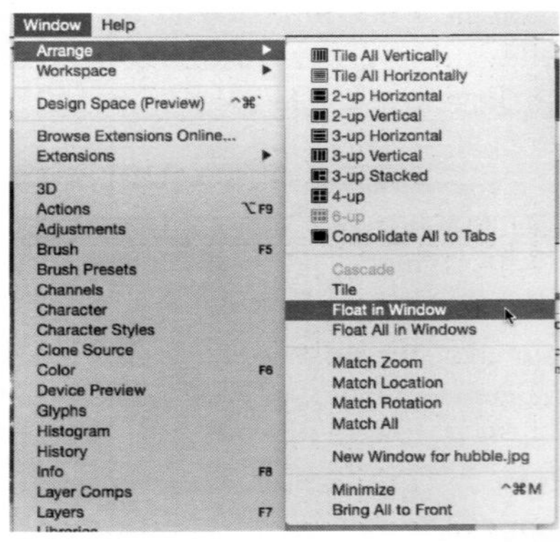

Floating a document separates the file into its own document window.

The title bar of the separate document window shows the same information that was in the document tab.

3. **Choose Window>Arrange>4-up.**

   The defined arrangements provide a number of options for tiling multiple open files within the available workspace. These arrangements manage all open files, including those in floating windows.

   The options' icons suggest the result of each command. The active file remains active; this is indicated by the brighter text in the active document's tab.

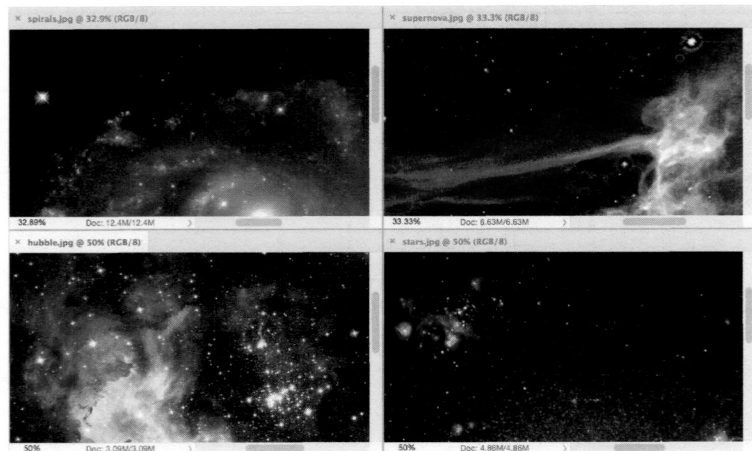

> ***Note:***
>
> *All open files are listed at the bottom of the Window menu.*
>
> ✓ hubble.jpg
> spirals.jpg
> stars.jpg
> supernova.jpg

> ***Note:***
>
> *If more files are open than what a specific arrangement indicates, the extra files will be consolidated as tabs into the window with the active file.*

4. **Choose Window>Arrange>Consolidate All to Tabs.**

   This command restores all documents — floating or not— into a single tabbed document window.

5. **At the bottom of the Tools panel, click the Change Screen Mode button.**

   Photoshop has three different **screen modes**, which change the way the document window displays on the screen. The default mode, which you saw when you opened these three files, is called Standard Screen mode.

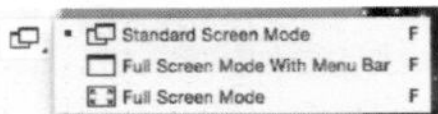

6. **Choose Full Screen Mode with Menu Bar from the Change Screen Mode menu.**

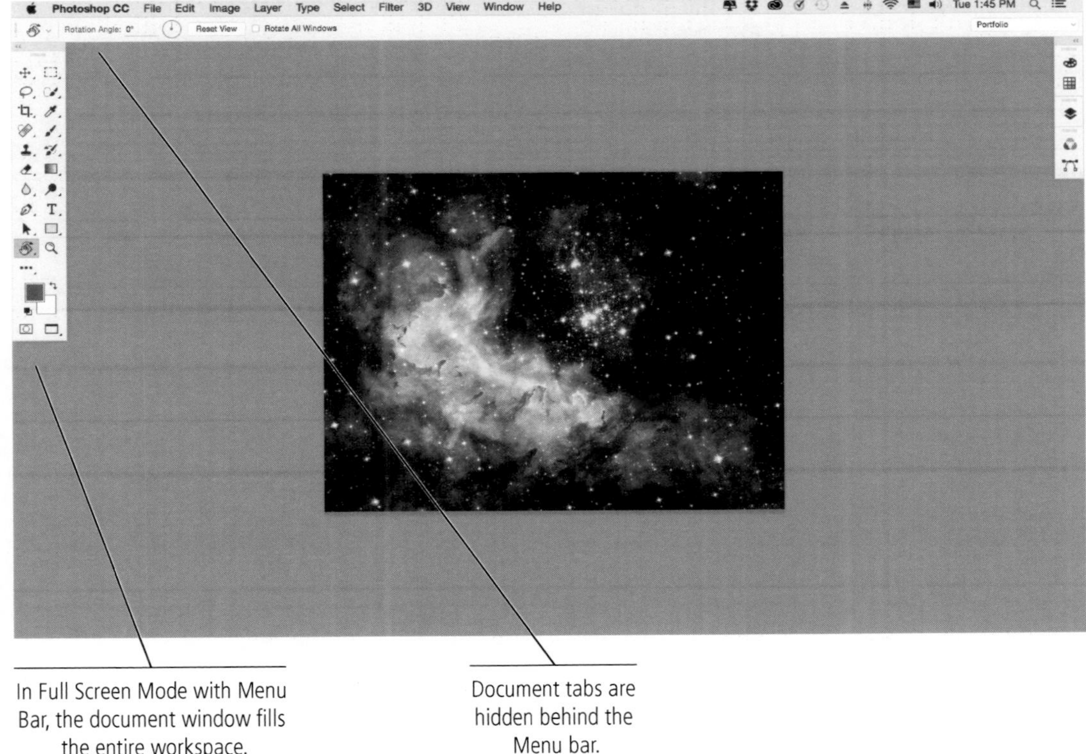

7. **Click the Change Screen Mode button in the Tools panel and choose Full Screen Mode. Read the resulting warning dialog box, and then click Full Screen.**

In Full Screen Mode, the Menu bar, title bar, and all panels are hidden.

Adobe Photoshop

In Full Screen Mode, panels are hidden. They can be accessed on the sides of the screen, or revealed by pressing Tab.

While in Full Screen Mode, you can return to Standard Screen Mode by pressing 'F' or Esc.

Don't show again

Cancel Full Screen

Move your mouse cursor to the left edge of the screen to temporarily show the Tools panel.

Move your mouse cursor to the right edge of the screen to temporarily show docked panels.

8. **Press the Escape key to return to Standard Screen mode.**

9. **Click the Close button on the hubble.jpg tab.**

10. **Macintosh: Click the Close button in the top-left corner of the Application frame.**

    Closing the Macintosh Application frame closes all open files, but does *not* quit the application.

    Windows: Click the Close button on each document tab to close the files.

    Clicking the Close button on the Windows Menu bar closes all open files *and* quits the application. To close open files *without* quitting, you have to manually close each file.

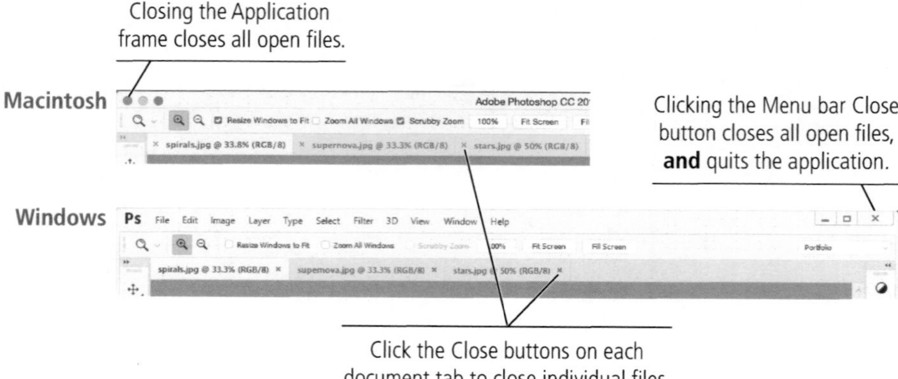

Closing the Application frame closes all open files.
Macintosh
Windows
Clicking the Menu bar Close button closes all open files, **and** quits the application.
Click the Close buttons on each document tab to close individual files.

Composite Movie Ad

Tantamount Studios, one of the largest film production companies in Hollywood, is developing a new movie called "Forefathers." You have been hired to develop an advertisement that will be used to announce the movie in both print magazines and digital media.

This project incorporates the following skills:

- ❑ Creating a background image that can accommodate multiple trim sizes in a single file
- ❑ Incorporating vector graphics as rasterized layers and Smart Objects
- ❑ Compositing multiple photographs and scans, using various techniques to silhouette the focal object in each image
- ❑ Scaling and aligning different objects in relation to the page and to each other
- ❑ Managing individual layout elements using layers and layer groups
- ❑ Working with multi-layer and flattened files
- ❑ Saving multiple versions of a file to meet different output requirements

Project Meeting

client comments

Here's a basic synopsis of the movie:

Most American history books teach us that our "forefathers" were esteemed, venerable men who crafted the United States out of lofty and respected ideals. But there's an old saying that history is written by the victors… In other words, who were these men really, and exactly how honorable were they? The movie is about the events during and after the American Revolution — not the war itself, but the personal aspects that drove these individuals to do what they did. It's not a war movie, and it's not a political movie. It's more a study of the human condition… How greed and power can corrupt even the most idealistic of men.

This movie is going to be one of our summer blockbusters, and we're throwing a lot of resources behind it.

art director comments

The client loved the initial concept sketch I submitted last week, so we're ready to start building the files. I've had the photographer prepare the images we need, and the client has provided the studio and rating logo files. They also sent me the primary magazine specs:

- Files should be submitted as flattened TIFF files; CMYK only
- Bleed size: 8.75 × 11.25″
- Trim size: 8.5 × 11″
- Live area: 8 × 10.5″

After you have created the final file for printing, I also need you to create a flattened JPEG file for use in digital media.

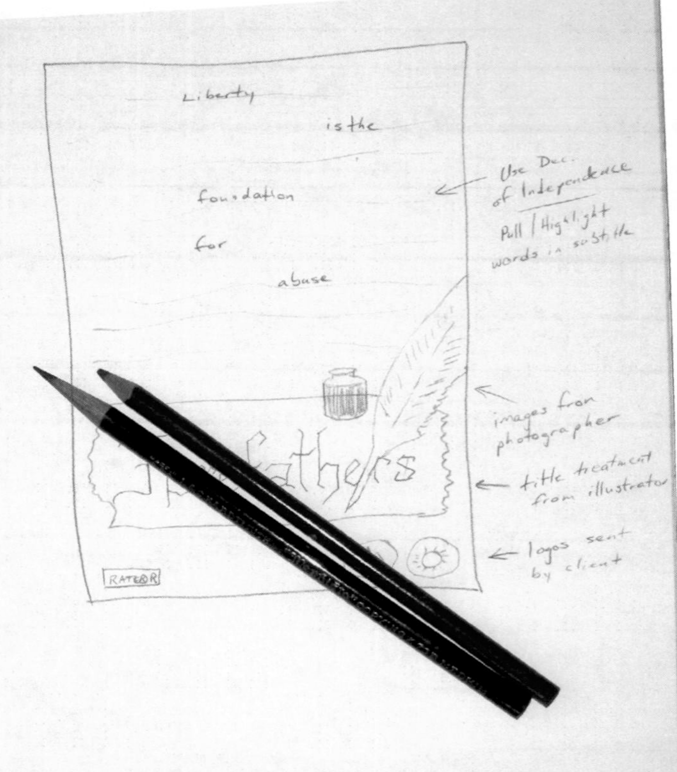

project objectives

To complete this project, you will:

- ❑ Create a single file that can contain multiple page sizes
- ❑ Composite multiple images into a single background file
- ❑ Incorporate both raster and vector elements into the same design
- ❑ Use selection techniques to isolate images from their backgrounds
- ❑ Transform and arrange individual layers to create a cohesive design
- ❑ Create layer groups and nested groups to easily manage files
- ❑ Save two different types of TIFF files for different ad requirements

Stage 1 Setting Up the Workspace

There are two primary types of artwork: vector graphics and raster images.

- **Vector graphics** are composed of mathematical descriptions of a series of lines and geometric shapes. These files are commonly created in illustration ("drawing") applications like Adobe Illustrator. Vector graphics are **resolution independent**; they can be freely scaled and are automatically output at the resolution of the output device.
- **Raster images** are made up of a grid of individual pixels (rasters or bits) in rows and columns (called a **bitmap**). Raster files are **resolution dependent** — their resolution is determined when you scan, photograph, or create the file. (**Line art**, sometimes categorized as a third type of image, is actually a type of raster image that includes only black and white pixels.)

Note:

Why is this information important? The ad you're building in this project will be placed in print magazines, so you have to build the new file with the appropriate settings for commercial printing. When the composition is finished, you will convert it to a resolution and file format that is more appropriate for digital media display.

Photoshop is what some people call a "paint" program — it is primarily used to create and manipulate pixel-based or raster images. Raster-image quality depends directly on the resolution; when you create files in Photoshop, you need to understand the resolution requirements from the very beginning of the process.

Pixels per inch (ppi) is the number of pixels in one horizontal or vertical inch of a digital raster file. As a general rule, commercial print jobs require 240–300 pixels per inch at the final output size to achieve good image quality in the printed piece. Some digital media such as desktop Web browsers typically require much lower resolution, commonly 72 ppi, although monitors and mobile devices with HD display capabilities support higher-resolution images.

It is important to realize that you cannot significantly increase image resolution once a raster image has been created or captured. When you create files that will be used for both print and digital media — as in the case of this project — you should start with the higher resolution and then reduce the resolution after the composition is complete.

The same raster image is reproduced here at 300 ppi (left) and 72 ppi (right). Notice the obvious degradation in quality when the resolution is set to 72 ppi.

Create the New File

When you create a file in Photoshop, you can define a number of important parameters in the New Document dialog box. In this exercise you will define the size, resolution, and color mode of the file that will serve as the background for the composition you create throughout this project.

1. **Download Liberty_Web16_RF.zip from the Student Files Web page.**
2. **Expand the ZIP archive in your WIP folder (Macintosh) or copy the archive contents into your WIP folder (Windows).**

   This results in a folder named **Liberty**, which contains all the files you need to complete this project. You should also use this folder to save all files that you create in this project. (If necessary, refer to Page 1 of the Photoshop Interface chapter for specific instructions on expanding or accessing the required resource files.)

3. In Photoshop, choose File>New.

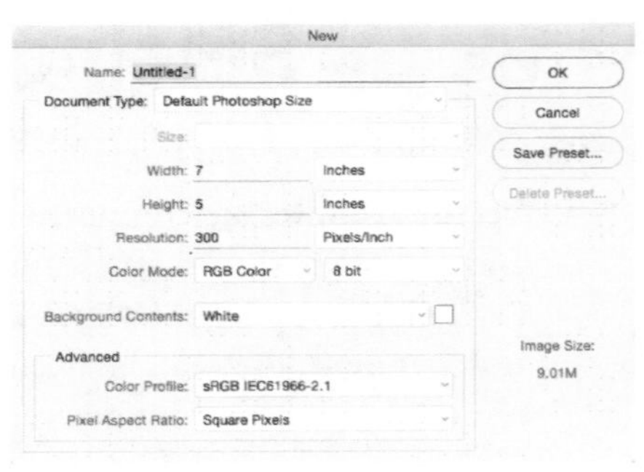

The New dialog box defaults to the Clipboard preset (if you have anything copied) or to the last-used settings.

If Clipboard is showing in the Preset menu, the new file settings will match the current contents of the system clipboard (whatever you last copied in any application).

You can create new files based on a number of included presets, including standard paper sizes (U.S. Paper, International Paper, and Photo) and standard sizes for different devices (Web, Mobile & Devices, and Film & Video). If you choose one of these presets, the Size menu shows secondary options for the selected preset (such as Letter, Legal, or Tabloid for U.S. Paper). Choosing any of these presets automatically changes the values in the other fields.

4. Highlight the Name field and type `forefathers`.

When you save the file, the file name defaults to the name you define when you create the file (in this case, "forefathers"). The name you assign here also appears in the Window menu and on the document tab at the top of the document window.

5. Press Tab until the Width field is highlighted.

Like most applications, you can press Tab to move through the fields of a dialog box. Pressing Shift-Tab moves to the previous field in the dialog box.

Note:

On Windows, you have to press the Tab key two times to move from the Name field to the Width field.

6. Click the menu to the right of the Width field and choose Inches.

When you change one unit of measurement (width), the other (height) changes too. (Don't worry about the default values. You're going to define exactly what you need in the following steps.)

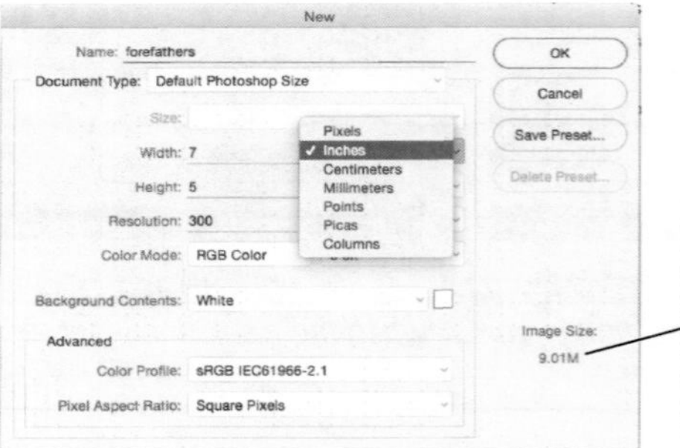

The Image Size area shows the base file size of the file you're defining. This number changes dynamically whenever you change an option in this dialog box.

Note:

You can change the default unit of measurement in the Preferences>Units & Rulers dialog box.

7. Highlight the Width field, then type `8.75` as the new value.

As soon as you change any field, the Preset menu switches to "Custom" — you are defining a "custom" file size.

Note:

Depending on the default options, some of the settings in this exercise might already be selected in your New dialog box.

8. Highlight the Height field, then type `11.25` as the new value.

9. Change the Resolution field to `300`; make sure the menu shows Pixels/Inch.

Pixels/cm is primarily used in countries that use the metric system of measurement. But if you inadvertently set the field to 300 pixels/cm, you'll create a file that is 762 pixels/inch, which is far more than you need for this project.

You are creating this file to meet print-resolution requirements; when you have finished the ad, you will save a second file with a reduced resolution that is more appropriate for digital media. You are starting with the higher resolution because you can't significantly increase resolution once a file has been created without degrading image quality.

10. **Click the Color Mode menu and choose CMYK.**

11. **Choose White in the Background Contents menu.**

    You can set the default background of any new file to White, the current Background Color, or Transparent.

12. **In the Advanced options, click the Color Profile menu and choose Don't Color Manage this Document from the top of the menu.**

    Color management is basically a process for controlling color shift from one color space to another. (This advanced topic is not covered in this book.)

Note:

A detailed explanation of color management is provided in the Against The Clock book ***Adobe Photoshop CC: The Professional Portfolio****.*

13. **Leave the Pixel Aspect Ratio menu set to Square Pixels.**

    The options in this menu are primarily used for editing video. Since this is a print project, you don't want to alter the pixel ratio.

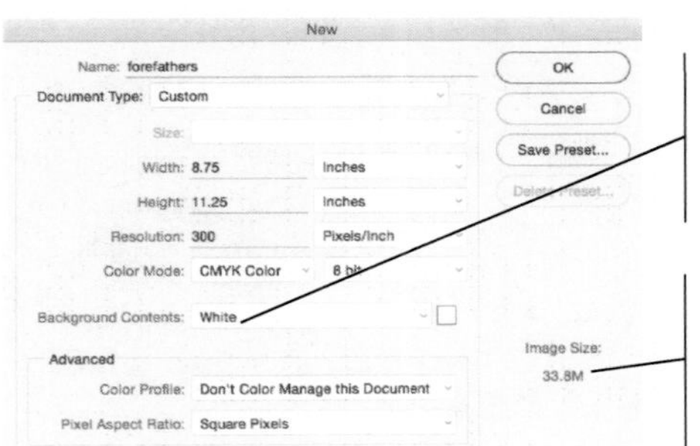

Use this menu to determine the default background color of the file (if any).

When you changed color modes, the Image Size changed to reflect the impact on the file's size.

14. **Click OK to create the new file.**

Understanding Color Modes

PHOTOSHOP FOUNDATIONS

The **color mode** (or color space) defines the structure of the colors in your file.

Bitmap color reproduces all pixels in the image as either black or white; there are no shades of gray.

Grayscale color reproduces all tones in the file as shades of gray. This type of image has only one channel (you learn about color channels later in this book).

RGB creates color by combining different intensities of red, green, and blue light (collectively referred to as the "additive primaries"). Computer monitors and mobile devices display color in RGB, which has a **gamut** or range of more than 16.7 million different colors. An RGB file has three color channels, one for each of the additive primaries.

CMYK ("process") color is based on the absorption and reflection of light. Four process inks — cyan, magenta, yellow, and black (collectively referred to as the "subtractive primaries") — are used in varying combinations and percentages to produce the range of printable colors in most commercial printing. A CMYK file has four color channels, one for each of the four subtractive primaries.

Theoretically, a mixture of equal parts of cyan, magenta, and yellow would produce black. Pigments, however, are not pure, so the result of mixing these colors is a muddy brown (called **hue error**). To obtain vibrant colors (and so elements such as type can be printed cleanly), black ink is added to the three primaries. Black is represented by the letter "K" for "key color."

LAB color is device independent; the colors it describes don't depend upon the characteristics of a particular printer, monitor, or scanner. In theory, LAB bridges the gap between the various color models; it is used in the background when converting images from one color space to another.

The problem with using RGB for print jobs is that the RGB colors eventually need to be converted to CMYK separations for a commercial printing press, and many colors in the RGB model do not exist in the CMYK model. Since you're creating this file for both print and digital media, it's a better idea to create it in the smaller color model to avoid unwanted color shift later in the process.

15. If you don't see rulers on the top and left edges of the document window, choose View>Rulers to toggle rulers on.

As we explained in the Interface chapter, the panels you see depend on what was done the last time you (or someone else) used the Photoshop application. Because workspace arrangement is such a personal preference, we tell you what panels you need to use but we don't tell you where to put them.

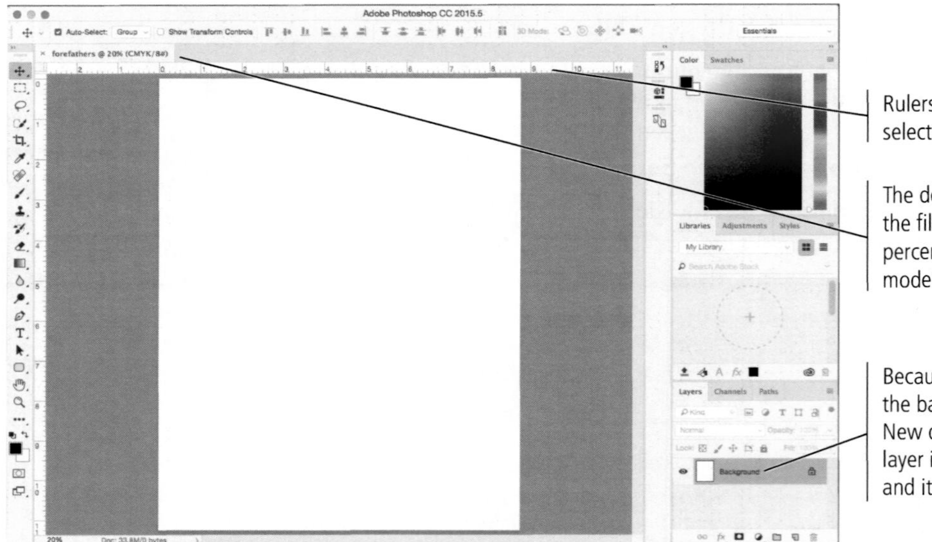

Rulers display the selected unit values.

The document tab shows the file name, view percentage, and color model of the active file.

Because you chose White as the background color in the New dialog box, the default layer is named "Background" and it is locked.

16. Choose File>Save As. Navigate to your WIP>Liberty folder as the location for saving this file.

Because you named the file when you created it (in the New dialog box), the Save As field is automatically set to the file name you already assigned. The extension is automatically added on both Macintosh and Windows computers.

17. Choose Photoshop in the Format menu.

You can save a Photoshop file in a number of different formats, all of which have specific capabilities, limitations, and purposes. While you are still working on a file, it's best to keep it as a native Photoshop (PSD) file.

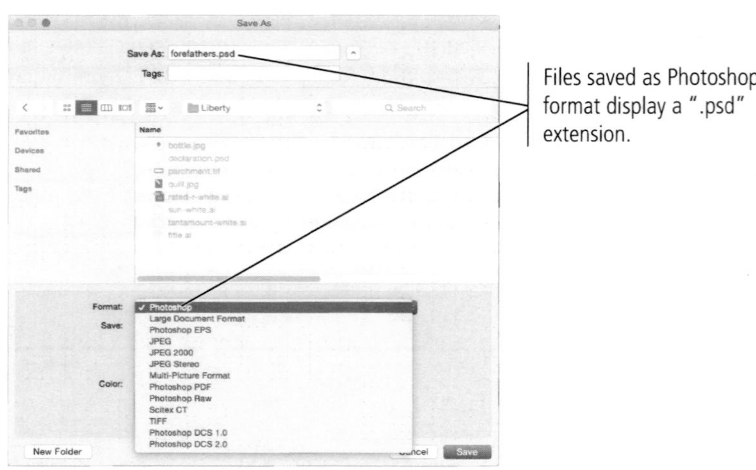

Files saved as Photoshop format display a ".psd" extension.

> ***Note:***
>
> *Since this is the first time you're seeing this series of dialog boxes (New and Save As), we explained a fairly large number of options. In the following projects, the basic file set-up instructions will be considerably shorter. Whenever you create a new file, refer to this section if you need help.*

18. Leave any remaining options unchecked and click Save.

Since this is a very basic file with only a white background, most of the other options in the Save As dialog box are not available at this time.

19. Continue to the next exercise.

Define the Background

Now that the file has been created, the next step is to add a custom background color. When you defined the file, you had three options — white, background color, or transparent. You could have defined the background color before opening the New dialog box, but it is more common to create the file first, and then set the background.

1. **With `forefathers.psd` open, choose View>Fit On Screen.**

2. **Click the Default Foreground and Background Colors button near the bottom of the Tools panel.**

   By clicking this button, you can always return to the basic black/white options.

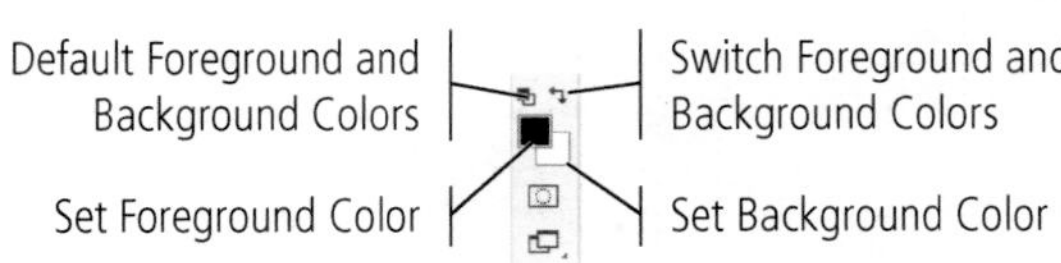

Note:

The foreground and background color swatches default to the last-used values.

3. **Click the Set Background Color button to open the Color Picker.**

   You can use the same process to define the foreground color, except you click the foreground swatch in the Tools panel instead of the background swatch.

4. **In the lower-right corner of the dialog box, define the following color values:**

   C (Cyan) = `0`

   M (Magenta) = `35`

   Y (Yellow) = `0`

   K (Black) = `100`

   Since you're working on a file in CMYK mode, it makes sense to define colors as percentages of CMYK.

Drag these sliders to move through the hue spectrum.

Click in this spectrum to change the hue that appears in the preview window.

Type in the fields to define specific color values.

Click anywhere in this window to select a color.

   This type of color — 100% black and some percent of another color — is called **rich black** or **superblack**. It might seem like 100% black is black, but when the inks are printed, adding another ink to solid black enhances the richness of the solid black. Adding magenta typically creates a warmer black, while adding cyan typically creates a cooler black.

5. **Click OK to close the Color Picker dialog box.**

6. **Look at the Layers panel.**

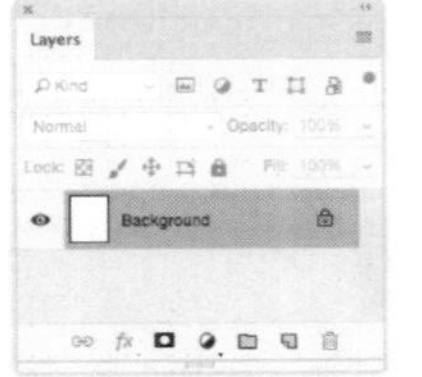

   As we explained in the Interface chapter, the panels you see depend on what was done the last time you (or someone else) used the Photoshop application. Because workspace arrangement is such a personal preference, we tell you what panels you need to use, but we don't tell you where to put them.

   Every file you create has at least one layer. If you use the Transparent option in the New dialog box, the default layer is called "Layer 1" and it is unlocked.

   If you define the file with a white (as you did in this project) or another color background, the default layer is named "Background." This Background layer cannot be moved, as indicated by the Lock icon. It can, however, be painted.

Note:

Remember: Panels can always be accessed in the Window menu.

Note:

We typically show floating panels so that we can focus on the current topic of discussion. Feel free to dock the panels, grouped or ungrouped, iconized or expanded, however you prefer.

7. **With nothing selected in the file, choose Edit>Fill.**

8. **Choose Background Color in the Contents menu and click OK.**

   The file has only one layer, so that layer is selected by default. Because no area of the file is currently selected, the Fill process fills the entire selected layer. (Depending on the accuracy of your monitor, you'll see the "rich" magenta color underneath the black — hence the name "rich black").

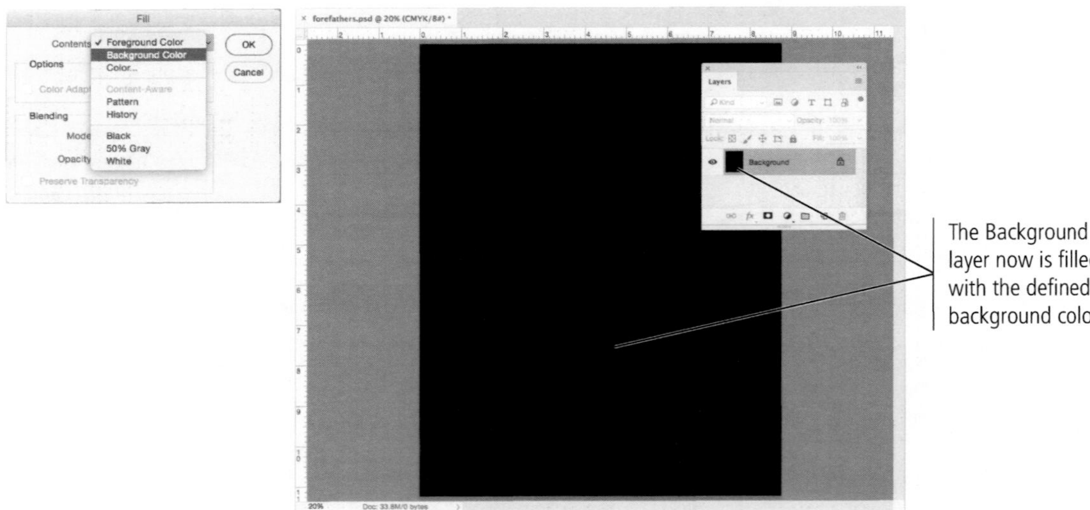

The Background layer now is filled with the defined background color.

9. **Save the file and continue to the next exercise.**

Place Page Guides

The final step in preparing the workspace is defining the live area of the page; all of the important elements of the design need to fit inside the live area.

According to your client, the magazine trim size is 8.5″ × 11″. (**Trim size** is the actual size of a page once it has been cut out of the press sheet.)

You might have noticed that you created the file 0.25″ larger than the larger file size. That's because a file for printing has to incorporate **bleeds** that will print right up to the edge of the paper; to create this effect, you have to extend the page elements and background beyond the page trim size (called **bleed allowance**). Most print applications require at least 1/8″ bleed allowance on any bleed edge.

> *Note:*
>
> *You should familiarize yourself with the most common fraction-to-decimal equivalents:*
>
> *1/8 = 0.125*
>
> *1/4 = 0.25*
>
> *3/8 = 0.375*
>
> *1/2 = 0.5*
>
> *5/8 = 0.625*
>
> *3/4 = 0.75*
>
> *7/8 = 0.875*

1. **With `forefathers.psd` open, choose View>New Guide Layout.**

   This dialog box makes it very easy to define a page grid using non-printing guides. The dialog box defaults to add 8 columns with a 20-pixel (0.067 in) gutter. In the document window, you can see the guides (blue lines) that will be created based on the active settings in the New Guide Layout dialog box.

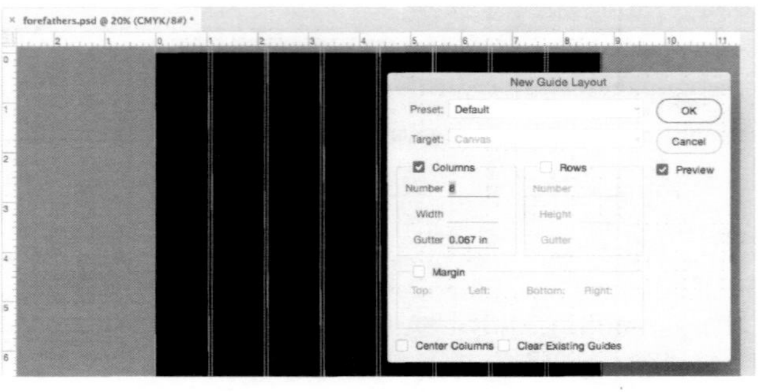

2. **Uncheck the Columns option and check the Margin option. Type 0.125 in each of the available margin fields.**

   You can use the Margin fields to place guides at specific distances from each edge of the canvas. You don't need to type the unit of measurement because the default unit for this file is already inches. Photoshop automatically assumes the value you type is in the default unit of measurement.

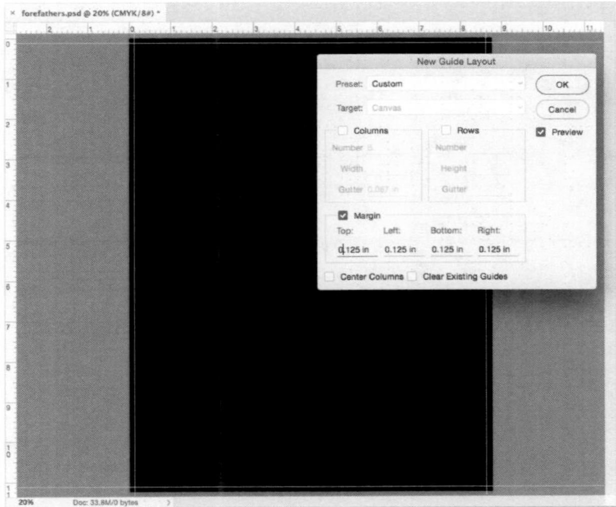

Note:

It is not necessary to type the unit of measurement in the dialog box as long as you are using the default units for the active file.

3. **Click OK to return to the document and add the required margin guides.**

   At this point you should have four guides – two vertical and two horizontal, each 1/8″ from the file edges. These mark the trim size of your final 8.5 × 11″ file.

4. **Choose View>100%.**

   It helps to zoom in to a higher view percentage if you want to precisely place guides. To complete the following steps accurately, we found it necessary to use at least 100% view.

5. **In the top-left corner of the document window, click the zero-point crosshairs and drag to the top-left intersection of the guides.**

   You can reposition the zero point to the top-left corner of the bleed allowance by double-clicking the zero-point crosshairs.

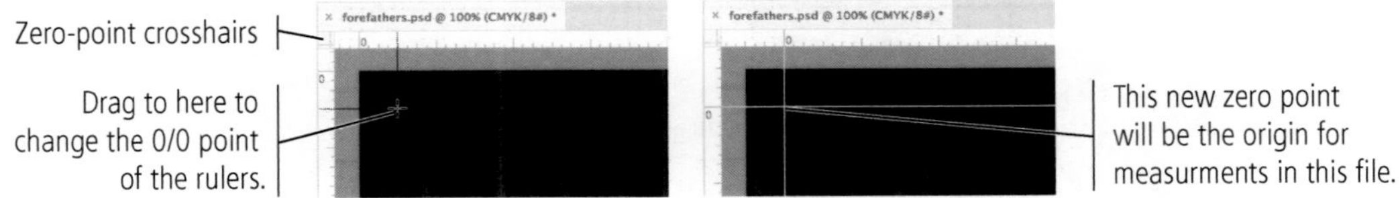

Zero-point crosshairs
Drag to here to change the 0/0 point of the rulers.
This new zero point will be the origin for measurments in this file.

6. **Choose the Move tool in the Tools panel.**

   For this file, the live area (the area in which important objects should be placed) should be 0.25″ inset from the trim edge. This is how we determined that number:

   [Width] 8.5″ – 8.0″ = 0.5 ÷ 2 = 0.25″

   [Height] 11″ – 10.5″ = 0.5″ ÷ 2 = 0.25″

   In the next few steps you will add guides that identify the live area.

7. **Click the horizontal page ruler at the top of the page and drag down to create a guide positioned at the 1/4″ (0.25″) mark.**

   If you watch the vertical ruler, a marker indicates the position of the cursor. The live cursor feedback shows the precise numeric position of the guide you are dragging.

   You might need zoom in further to place precise guides; we found it necessary to zoom in to 200% to accurately place them.

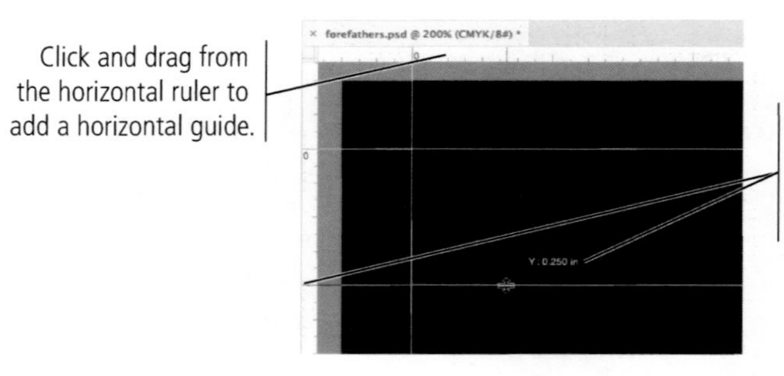

Note:

Press Option/Alt and click a guide to change it from vertical to horizontal (or vice versa). The guide rotates around the point where you click, which can be useful if you need to find a corner based on the position of an existing guide.

8. **Click the vertical ruler at the left and drag right to place a guide at the 0.25″ mark.**

   Watch the marker on the horizontal ruler to judge the guide's position.

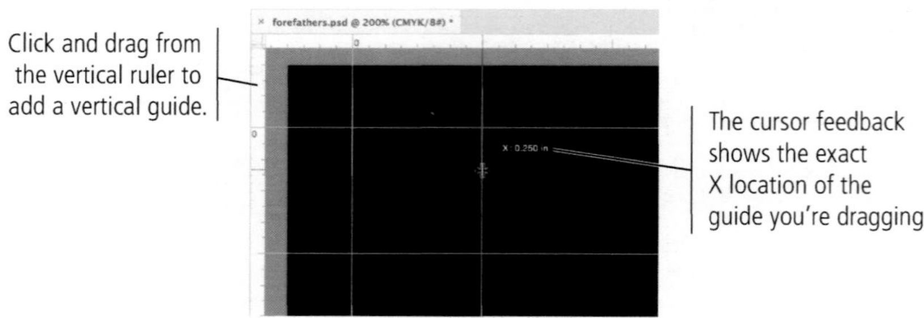

Click and drag from the vertical ruler to add a vertical guide.
The cursor feedback shows the exact X location of the guide you're dragging.

9. **Double-click the intersection of the two rulers.**

   This resets the file's zero point to the original position (the top-left corner of the canvas).

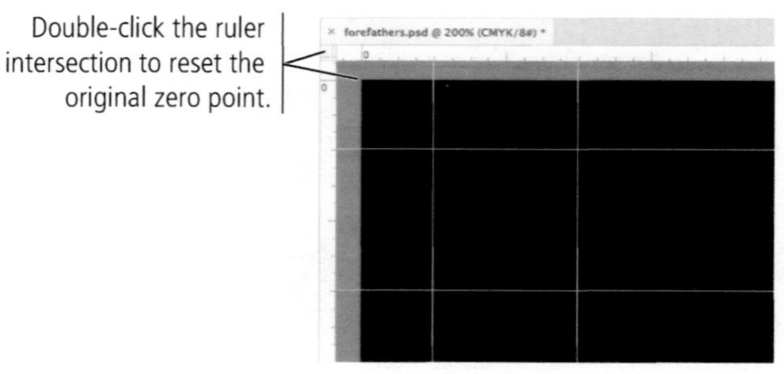

Double-click the ruler intersection to reset the original zero point.

Note:

Use the Move tool to reposition placed guides. Remove individual guides by dragging them back onto the ruler.

If you try to reposition a guide and can't, choose View>Lock Guides. If this option is checked, guides are locked; you can't move them until you toggle this option off.

10. **Zoom out so you can see the entire canvas in the document window (View>Fit On Screen).**

11. **Choose View>New Guide. In the resulting dialog box, choose the Horizontal option and type `10.875` in the field and click OK.**

This dialog box makes it easy to precisely position guides without dragging, which means you won't have to continually adjust the view percentage to find an exact position.

This dialog box always measures the position of guides from the canvas's top-left corner, regardless of the zero point as reflected in the rulers.

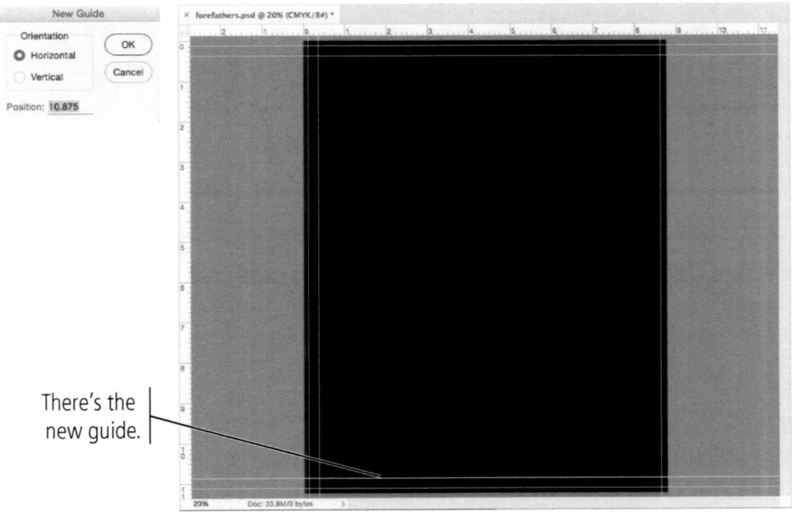

12. **Choose View>New Guide again. Choose the Vertical option and type `8.375` in the field. Click OK.**

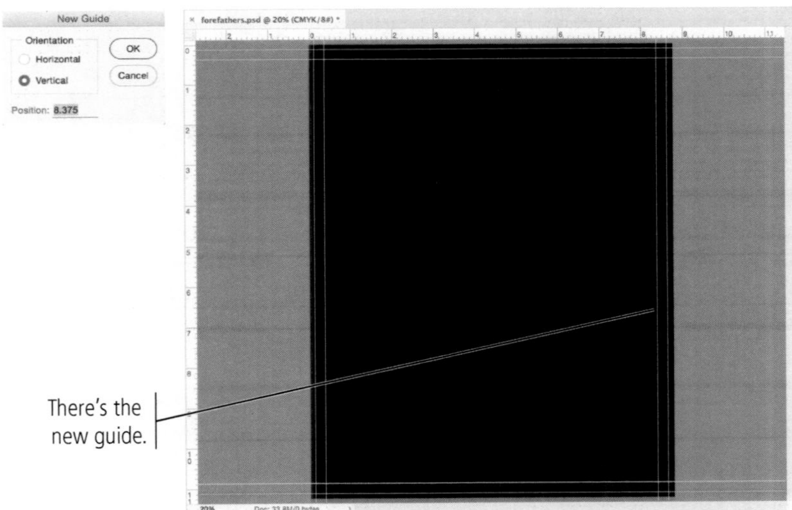

13. **Click the View menu and make sure a checkmark appears to the left of Lock Guides. If no checkmark is there, choose Lock Guides to toggle on that option.**

    After you carefully position specific guides, it's a good idea to lock them so you don't accidentally move or delete them later. If you need to move a guide at any point, simply choose View>Lock Guides to toggle off the option temporarily.

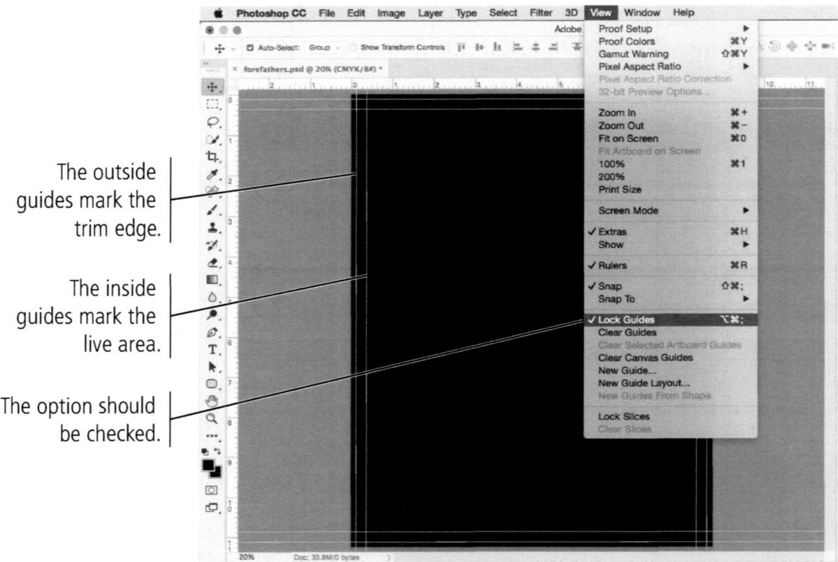

14. **Save the file and continue to the next stage of the project.**

    Because you have already saved this working file with a new name, you can simply choose File>Save, or press Command/Control-S to save without opening a dialog box. If you want to change the file name, you can always choose File>Save As.

Stage 2 Compositing Images and Artwork

Many of the projects you complete in Photoshop involve compositing two or more images into the same file. Technically speaking, **compositing** is the process of combining any two or more objects (images, text, illustrations, etc.) into an overall design. Image compositing might be as simple as placing two images into different areas of a background file, and then adding blurred edges; or it could be as complex as placing a person into a group photo, carefully clipping out the individual's background, and adjusting the shadows to match the lighting in the group.

The movie ad you're building in this project requires compositing three individual images — one that has been scanned and two digital photographs. You'll also incorporate title treatment and logo files that were created in Adobe Illustrator by other members of your creative team. The various elements that make up the ad are fairly representative of the type of work you can (and probably will) create in Photoshop as your career progresses.

Copy and Paste Layers

Compositing multiple images in Photoshop is a fairly simple process — or at least, it starts out that way. But there are a number of technical and aesthetic issues you must resolve whenever you combine multiple images into a single design.

In this and the next several exercises, you will use several methods to composite multiple images into a single Photoshop file. In the next stage of the project, you will learn various techniques for combining the different pieces into a unified design.

Note:

Digital photographs and scans are pixel-based, which is why you use Photoshop to edit and manipulate those types of files.

1. **With forefathers.psd open, choose File>Open.**

2. **Navigate to your WIP>Liberty folder. Select bottle.jpg, parchment.tif, and quill.jpg, then click Open.**

   Remember, you can press Command/Control to select multiple non-consecutive files in the Open dialog box. If you press Shift, you select multiple consecutive files.

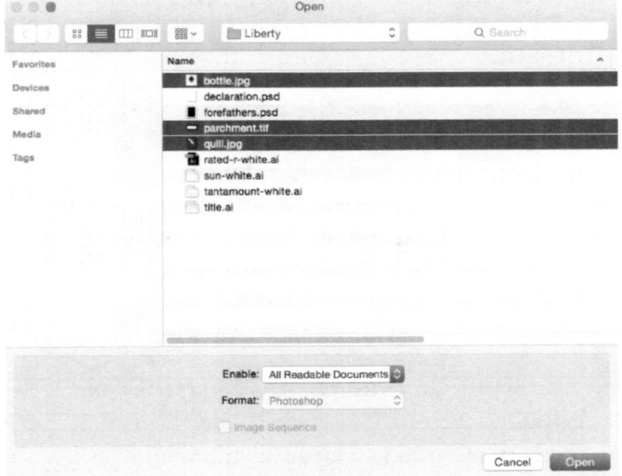

   You should now have four images open in Photoshop — the background file you created earlier, the parchment scan, and the bottle and quill photographs. The document tabs show the color model of each file.

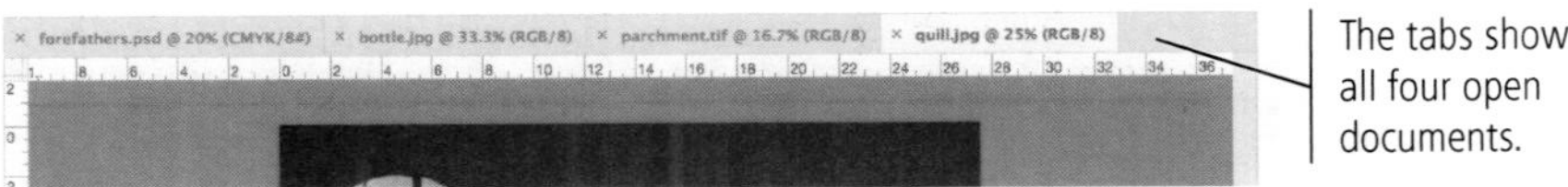

The tabs show all four open documents.

3. **Choose Window>Arrange>4-Up to show all four images in the document window at one time.**

   As you saw in the Interface chapter, these options are useful for arranging and viewing multiple open files within your workspace.

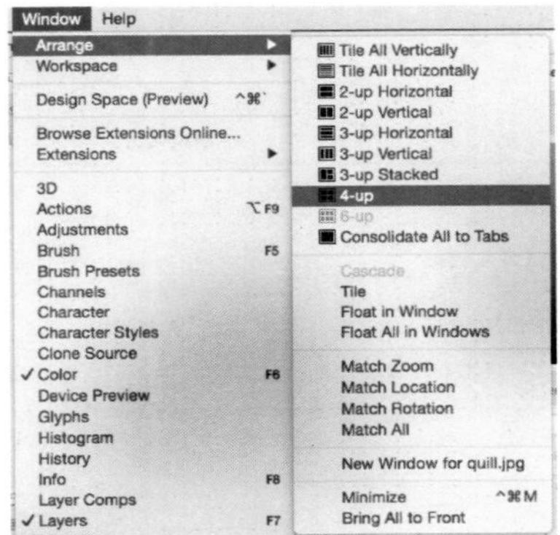

4. **Click the parchment window to activate that file.**

   Like the file you created, this file has only one layer — Background. Every scan and digital photograph has this characteristic.

5. **With nothing selected, choose the Move tool at the top of the Tools panel.**

6. **Click in the parchment file window and drag to the forefathers.psd file window.**

   Since you didn't select anything specific in the parchment file, you can drag the entire active layer into another file.

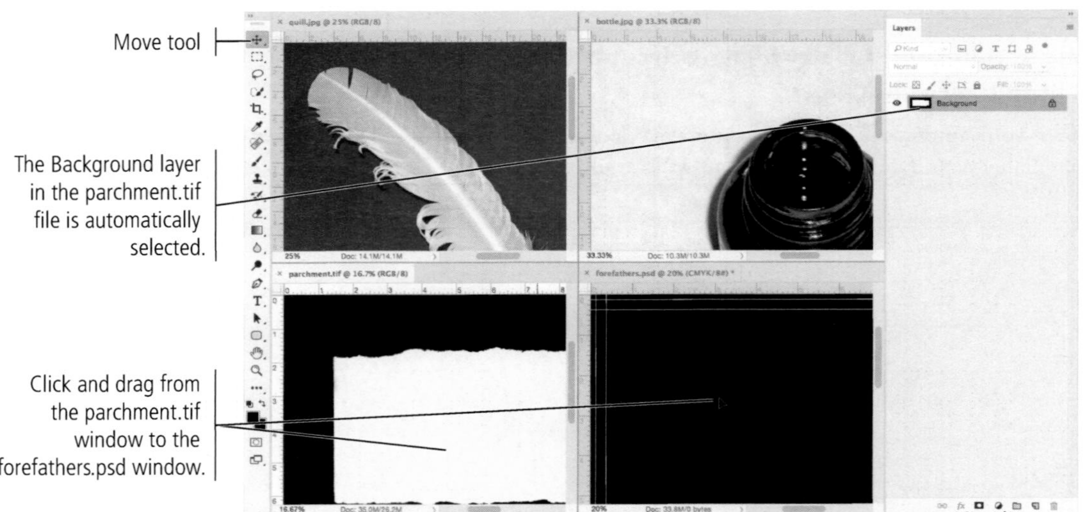

   When you release the mouse button, the forefathers.psd file — where you dragged to — is active and it now has two layers: Background (the one you created) and Layer 1 (the parchment image you just copied). When you copy or drag a layer from one file into another, it is automatically placed on a new layer with the default name "Layer *n*", where "n" is a sequential number.

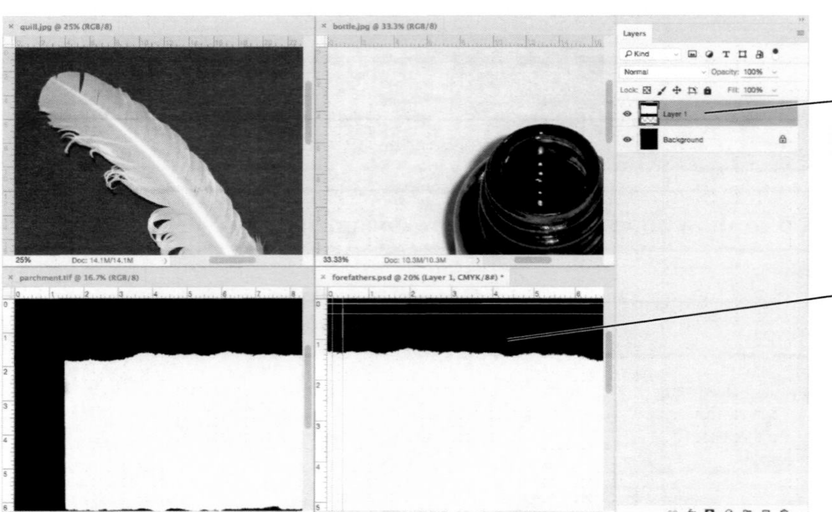

Dragging the parchment file onto the forefathers file generates a new layer (Layer 1) for the dragged image layer.
When you release the mouse button, the forefather.psd file becomes the active file.

   The parchment image was scanned in RGB color mode, as you can see in the document's tab. Photoshop cannot maintain multiple color modes in a single file. The RGB parchment image layer is automatically converted to the CMYK color mode you're using in the background file.

7. **Close the parchment.tif file.**

8. **Click the bottle.jpg window to activate that file. If you can't see the entire bottle, zoom out until you can.**

9. **Choose the Rectangular Marquee tool in the Tools panel.**

   In addition to dragging entire layers into other files, you can also select specific areas of a file to copy using one of the selection tools.

10. **Using the Rectangular Marquee tool, click in the bottle.jpg window and drag around the entire shape of the bottle.**

    By default, dragging with the selection tool creates a new selection. You can use the buttons on the left end of the Options bar to add to the current selection, subtract from the current selection, or intersect with the current selection.

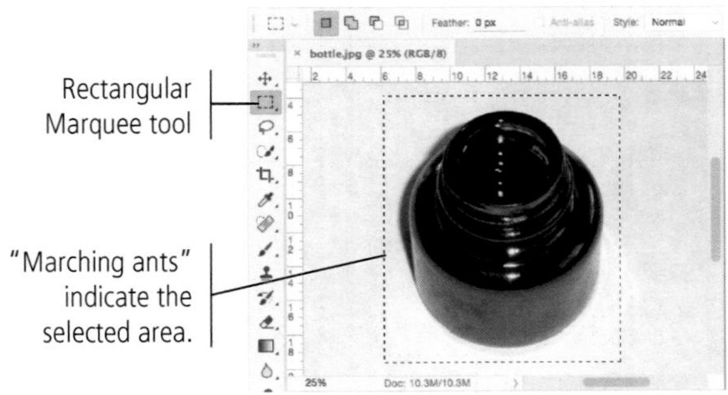

11. **Click the Subtract From Selection button on the Options bar.**

    When one of the marquee tools is selected, the Options bar gives you better control over what you are selecting.

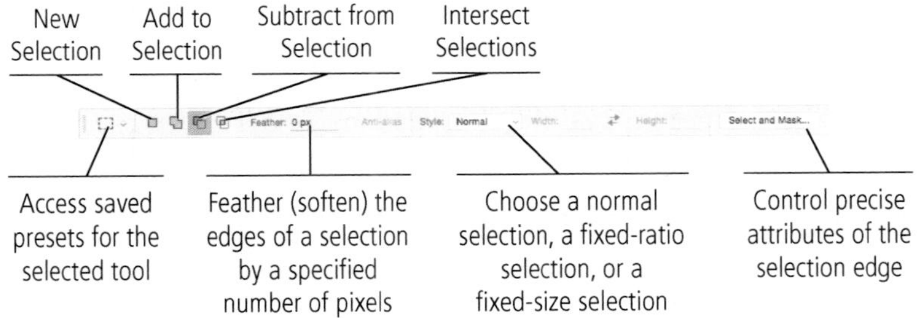

12. **Drag a new marquee that overlaps the upper corner of the first selection but doesn't include any part of the bottle.**

    When you release the mouse button, the selection is the area of the first marquee, minus the area of the second marquee. (This isn't particularly necessary in this case, but you should know how to add to and subtract from selections.)

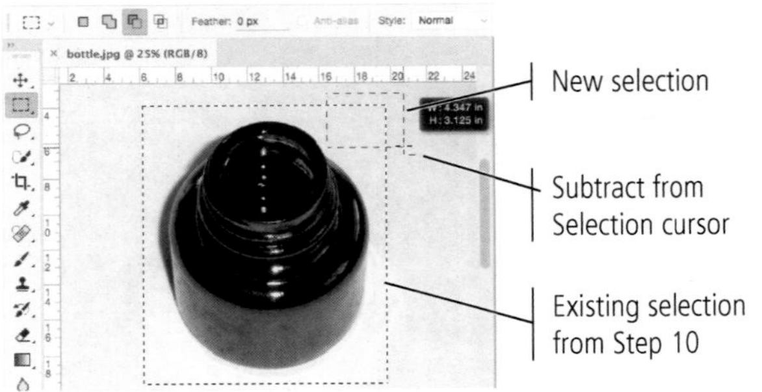

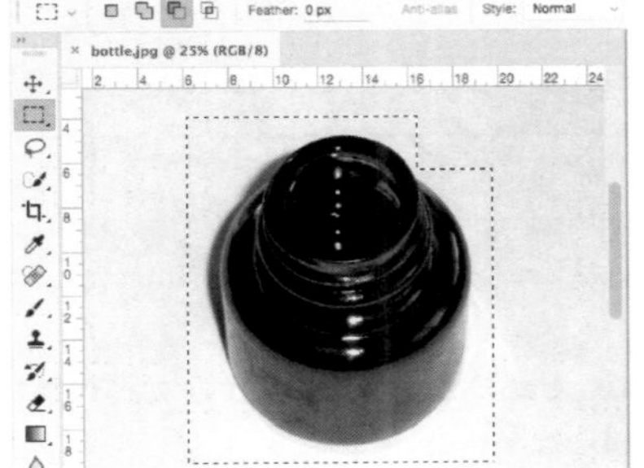

13. **Choose Edit>Copy.**

Note:

Use the marquee tools to create simple-shape selections such as rectangular, elliptical, single row of pixels, or a single column of pixels.

Note:

***Marching ants** is an industry term for the animated edge of an active selection marquee.*

Note:

Press Shift while dragging a new marquee to constrain the selection to a square (using the Rectangular Marquee tool) or circle (using the Elliptical Marquee tool).

Note:

When using one of the selection tools, press Shift before dragging to add to the current selection, or press Option/Alt to subtract from the current selection.

14. Click the forefathers.psd file window to activate that file, then choose Edit>Paste.

The standard Cut and Paste options are available in Photoshop, just as they are in most applications. Whatever you have selected will be copied to the Clipboard, and whatever is in the Clipboard will be pasted.

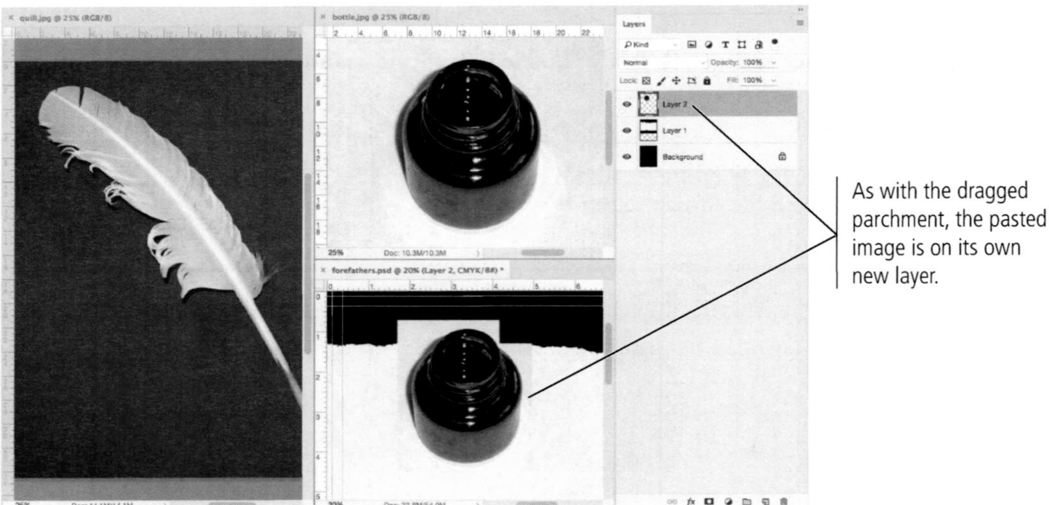

As with the dragged parchment, the pasted image is on its own new layer.

15. Close the bottle.jpg file.

16. Click the quill.jpg window to activate that file, and zoom out so you can see the entire image.

17. Select the Lasso tool in the Tools panel.

The lasso tools allow you to make irregular selections — in other words, selections that aren't just rectangular or elliptical.

18. Drag a shape around the entire quill.

When you release the mouse button, the end point automatically connects to the beginning point of the selection.

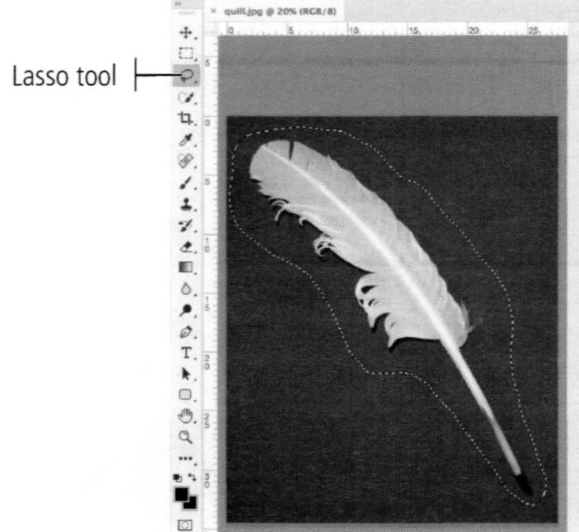

19. Copy the selection and paste it into the forefathers.psd file window, just as you did for the bottle selection.

20. Close the quill.jpg file.

21. **Choose View>Fit On Screen to fit the image into the document window.**

You now have a file with four layers, but the composited images are simply stacked one on top of another. You'll fix this problem as you complete the rest of the project.

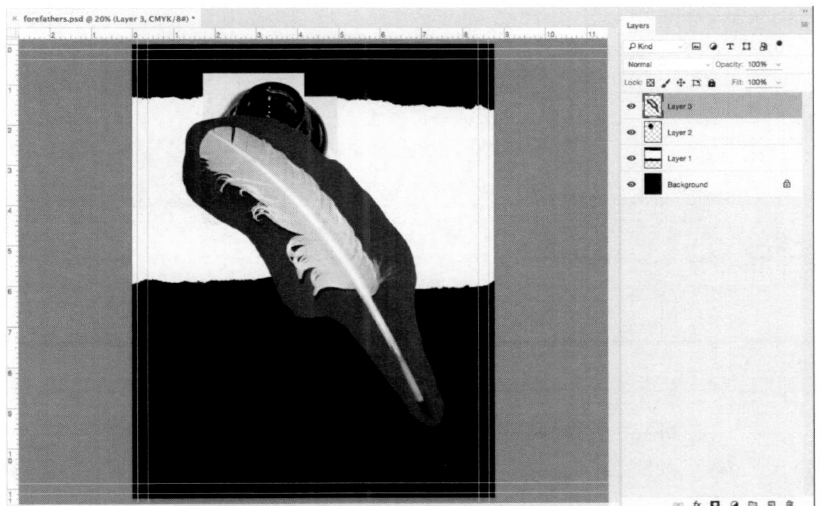

> *Note:*
>
> *You might notice that the parchment image doesn't fit into the background. You'll fix this problem later.*

22. **Choose File>Save.**

Because this is the first time you've saved the file after adding new layers, you should see the Photoshop Format Options dialog box, with the Maximize Compatibility check box already activated. It's a good idea to leave this check box selected so your files will be compatible with other CC applications and other versions of Photoshop.

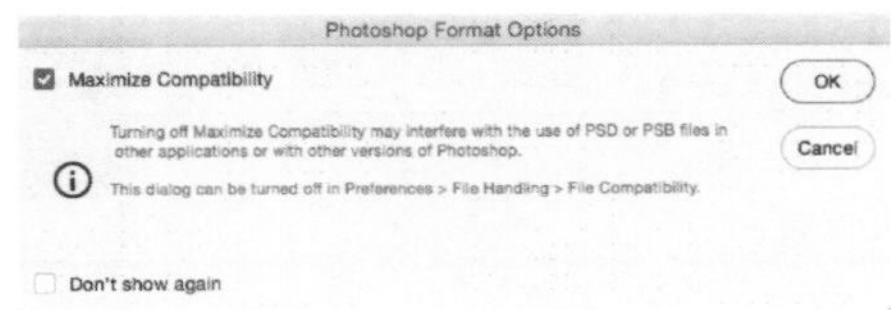

> *Note:*
>
> *If you don't see this dialog box, check the File Handling pane of the Preferences dialog box. You can set the Maximize PSD and PSB File Compatibility menu to Always, Never, or Ask.*

23. **Make sure the Maximize Compatibility check box is selected and click OK. Continue to the next exercise.**

PHOTOSHOP FOUNDATIONS

Understanding Effective Resolution

You might have noticed that the bottle and quill images were physically very large — both over 26 inches wide — but they are only 72 dpi. When you copied these images into the forefathers.psd file, however, they were nowhere near 26 inches wide. This is because copied images adopt the resolution of the file you paste them into. On the surface this seems simple; but you should understand what is actually happening behind the scenes, so you don't accidentally lose image quality.

If you open the Image Size dialog box (Image>Image Size) for the bottle.jpg file, you can see that the file's physical dimensions, in pixels, are 1887 × 1917 at 72 dpi. In other words, the bottle image has 1887 pixels in a horizontal row. If you divide 1887 pixels by 72 pixels/inch, you end up with the size in inches: the image is approximately 26.21 inches wide.

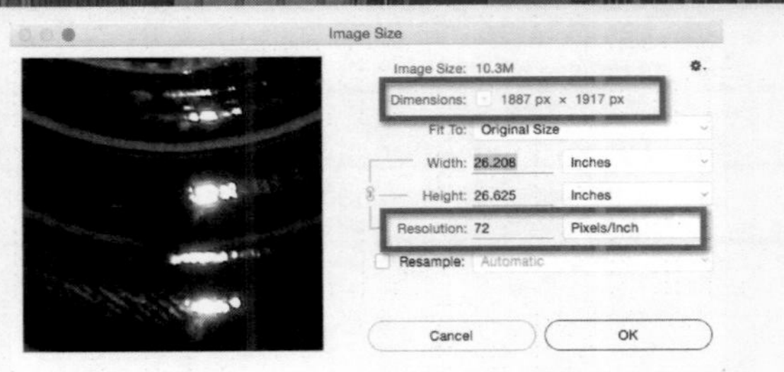

When the image is copied into a 300 dpi file, the bottle has the same 1887 pixels across. But when those 1887 pixels are divided by 300 dpi, the pasted image is about 6.3 inches wide. This is why the bottle you pasted into the forefathers.psd file was so much smaller than it appeared in its own file window — the same number of pixels takes up a much smaller space when more pixels fit into an inch. This is the principle of **effective resolution**.

Working with CC Libraries

If you have an individual-user subscription to the Adobe Creative Cloud, you have access to CC Library functionality, which allows you to easily share assets across various Adobe CC applications. This technology makes it very easy to maintain consistency across a design campaign — for example, using the same color swatches for all pieces, whether created in Illustrator, InDesign, or Photoshop.

In Photoshop, you can create new libraries from scratch (using the menu at the top of the Libraries panel), or use the "Auto-Vacuum" feature to create a library based on an existing file's contents.

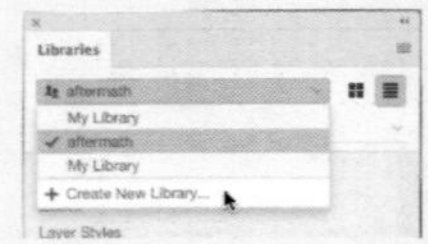

Once you create a library, it is stored in your Creative Cloud account so you can access the same assets in other Adobe applications. You can add new assets to the active library using the buttons at the bottom of the Libraries panel.

A Library list
B Show Items as Icons
C Show Items in a List
D Library from Document
E Add Graphic
F Add Character Style
G Add Layer Style
H Add Foreground Color
I Libraries Sync Status
J Delete

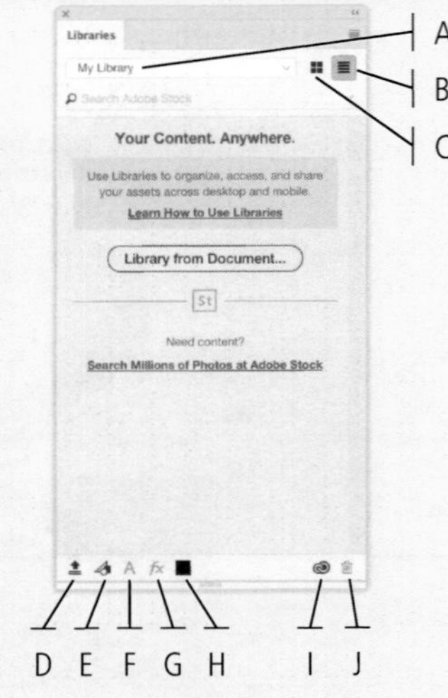

Creating Library Items

You can use the buttons at the bottom of the Libraries panel to create new items in the active library.

Add Graphic adds the content on the active layer as an object ("graphic") in the library.

- If you add a Smart Object layer, the layer becomes linked to the new library item instead of to the original file that created the Smart Object layer.
- If you add a regular layer, it is not dynamically linked to the new library item.

Add Character Style creates a type style in the library based on the active type layer. If more than one set of character formatting options is applied within the type layer, only the formatting options in the first character of the layer are stored in the library item.

Add Layer Style creates an item in the library that includes all layer styles applied to the active layer when you click.

Add Foreground Color stores the active foreground color as a color swatch in the library.

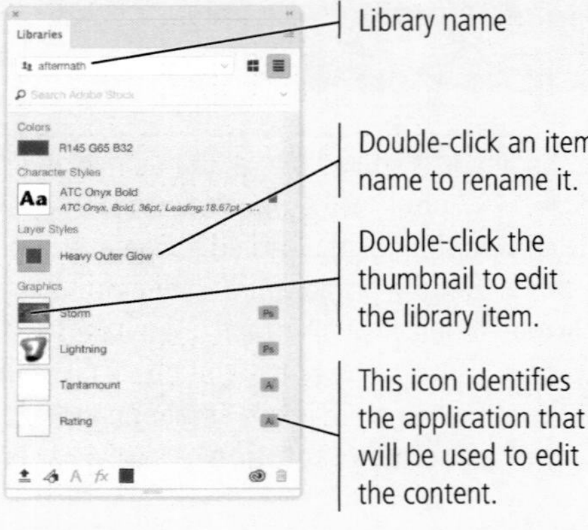

Library name
Double-click an item name to rename it.
Double-click the thumbnail to edit the library item.
This icon identifies the application that will be used to edit the content.

Understanding Auto-Vacuum

When you open a file with more than a flat background layer, you will see a dialog box asking if you want to create a new library from the document you are opening. If you click Cancel, no library is created. However, you can always initiate the Auto-Vacuum function using the Library from Document button at the bottom of the Libraries panel, or the Create New Library from Document item in the panel's Options menu.

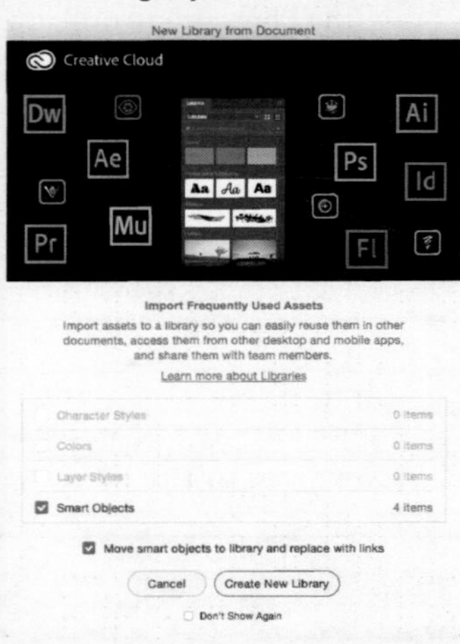

If you use the Auto-Vacuum feature, the new library automatically adopts the name of the file from which the library is created. Any character styles, defined color swatches, applied layer styles, and smart object layers are added to the new library by default.

Working with CC Libraries (continued)

Working with Library Items

Clicking a color swatch in the library changes the active foreground color in Photoshop.

Clicking a layer style in the library applies the stored layer styles to the active layer (in the Layers panel).

Clicking a character style applies the defined formatting options to all text on the active type layer. (You cannot apply a library character style to only certain characters on a type layer.)

To place a graphic from a library, simply drag it from the Libraries panel onto the Photoshop canvas. This creates a linked Smart Object layer, in this case linked to the Library item instead of to an external file on your desktop.

Linked Smart Object layers in Photoshop are identified by a special icon in the Layers panel.

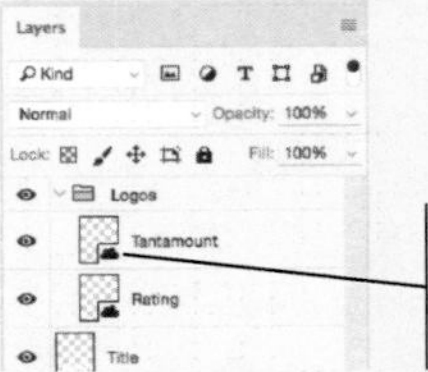

This icon identifies a Smart Object layer that is linked to a library item.

By default, objects placed from a library are linked to the library file. Any changes you make to the library item will reflect in all placed instances.

Say you change the color of text in a logo. Any instance of that logo that has been placed from the library — in any Adobe CC application — will automatically reflect the new type color as long as the library link is active.

If you press Option/Alt when you drag an object from the panel, you create a non-linked regular layer with the content from the object you dragged onto the canvas. In this case, there is no dynamic link to the library.

Sharing and Collaboration

Libraries also offer a powerful opportunity to communicate assets with other users.

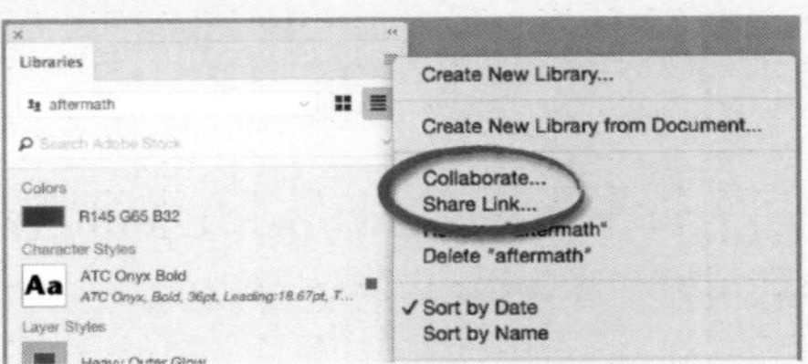

- If you invite others to collaborate, authorized users can edit assets in the library.
- If you share a link to a library, invited users can view a library's contents but not edit those assets.

The options in the Libraries panel submenu navigate to your online Adobe CC account page, and automatically ask you to invite specific users (for collaborating) or create a public link (for sharing).

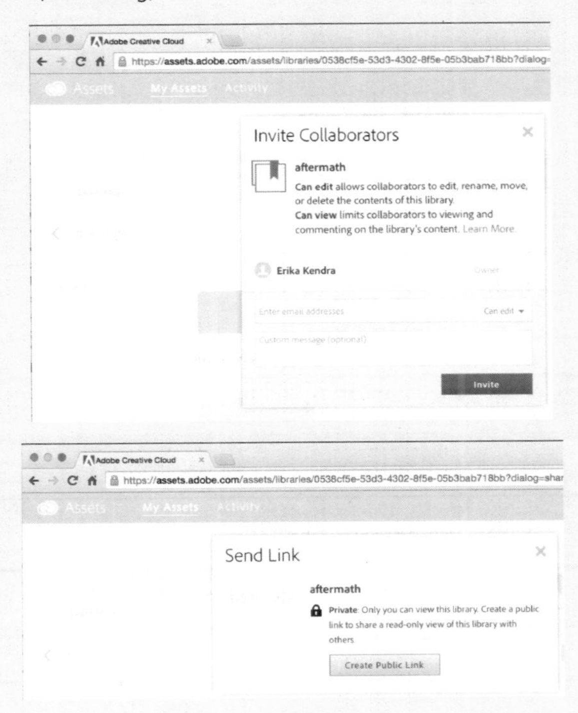

Rasterize a Vector File

As you already know, vector graphics are based on a series of mathematical descriptions that tell the computer processor where to draw lines. Logos and title treatments — such as the ones you use in this project — are commonly created as vector graphics. Although Photoshop is typically a "paint" (pixel-based) application, you can also open and work with vector graphics created in illustration programs like Adobe Illustrator.

1. **With forefathers.psd open, choose File>Open and navigate to the WIP>Liberty folder.**

2. **Select title.ai in the list of files, then click Open.**

   This is an Adobe Illustrator file of the movie title text treatment. The Format menu defaults to Photoshop PDF because Illustrator uses PDF as its underlying file structure.

   When you open a vector file (Illustrator, EPS, or PDF) in Photoshop, it is rasterized (converted to a raster graphic). The Import PDF dialog box allows you to determine exactly what and how to rasterize the file. The default values in this box are defined by the contents of the file you're opening.

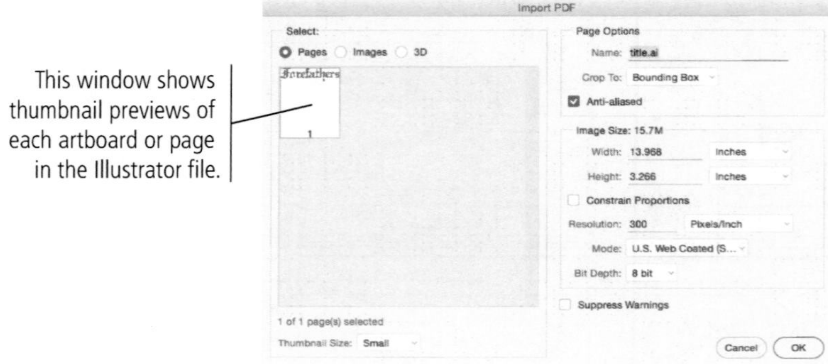

   The Crop To options determine the size of the file you import. Depending on the type of file you're importing and how it was created, some of these values might be the same as others:

   - **Bounding Box** is the outermost edges of the artwork in the file.
   - **Media Box** is the size of the paper as defined in the file.
   - **Crop Box** is the size of the page including printer's marks.
   - **Bleed Box** is the trim size plus any defined bleed allowance.
   - **Trim Box** is the trim size as defined in the file.
   - **Art Box** is the area of the page as defined in the file.

   The Image Size fields default to the settings of the bounding box you select. You can change the size, resolution, color mode, and bit depth by entering new values.

3. **Choose Inches in the Width menu, make sure the Constrain Proportions option is checked, and then change the Width field value to 8.**

   You know the page size of the smaller ad you're building is 8″ wide, so you can import this file at a size small enough to fit into that space.

   Because the Constrain Proportions option is checked, the height changes proportionally to match the new width.

4. **Make sure the Resolution field is set to `300` pixels/inch, and then choose CMYK Color from the Mode menu.**

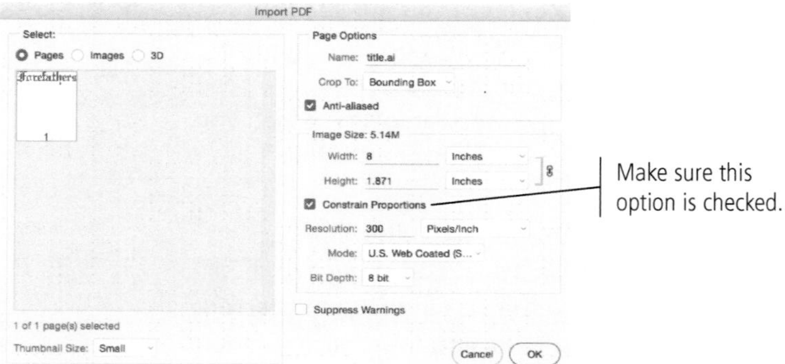

Make sure this option is checked.

5. **Click OK.**

   The title treatment file opens in Photoshop. The checked area behind the text indicates that the background is transparent. If you look at the Layers panel, you'll see that Layer 1 isn't locked; because it's transparent, it is not considered a background layer.

6. **Choose the Move tool in the Tools panel, then choose Select>All.**

   This command creates a selection marquee around the entire canvas in the active file.

7. **Choose Edit>Copy to copy the selected area.**

8. **Close the title file. If asked, don't save it.**

9. **With the forefathers.psd file active, choose Edit>Paste.**

   Again, the pasted contents are added on a new layer. (If you still have the entire canvas visible in the document window, you might also notice that the pasted content is placed in the center of the document window.)

   Because the title artwork has a transparent background, the other layers are visible behind the text in the composite file.

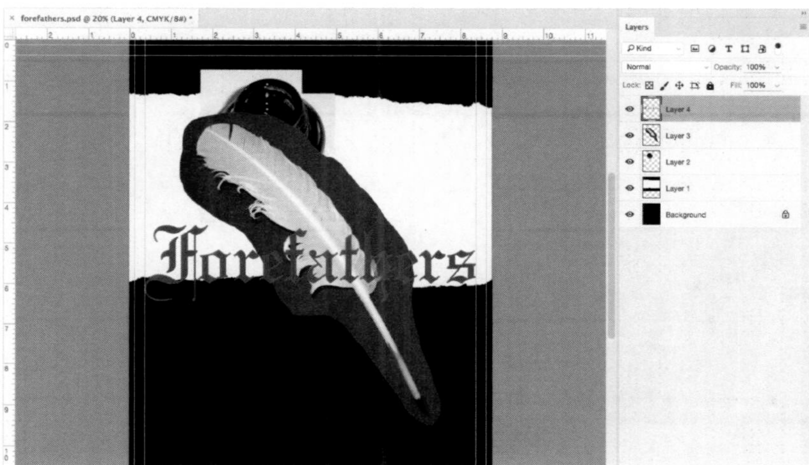

10. **Save forefathers.psd, then continue to the next exercise.**

Place Vector Graphics as Smart Object Layers

As you have seen in the last few exercises, copying layer content from one file to another results in new regular layers for the pasted content. Photoshop also supports Smart Object layers, in which you place one file into another instead of pasting layer content. Smart Objects provide a number of advantages over regular layers, which you will explore later in this project. In this exercise, you will create the Smart Object layers for the remaining image elements.

Vector graphics offer several advantages over raster images, including sharper edges and free scaling without deteriorating image quality. To take advantage of these benefits, you might want to maintain vector files as vector objects instead of rasterizing them. Photoshop gives you the option to do exactly that — maintaining vector information and raster information in the same file.

1. **With `forefathers.psd` open, choose File>Place Embedded.**

   Two options in the File menu — Place Embedded and Place Linked — give you the option to embed the placed file data into active file, or to place smart objects as links to the original placed file. (See Page 46 For more about placing linked files.)

   The Place Embedded dialog box is virtually the same as the Open dialog box. You can use this function any time you want to place one entire file directly into another without dragging or copying and pasting (as you did in the previous exercises).

2. **Navigate to and select `rated-r-white.ai` and click Place.**

3. **In the resulting Place PDF dialog box, choose Art Box in the Crop To menu and then click OK.**

   The Crop To options in this dialog box are the same as those that are available when you rasterize a native Illustrator file.

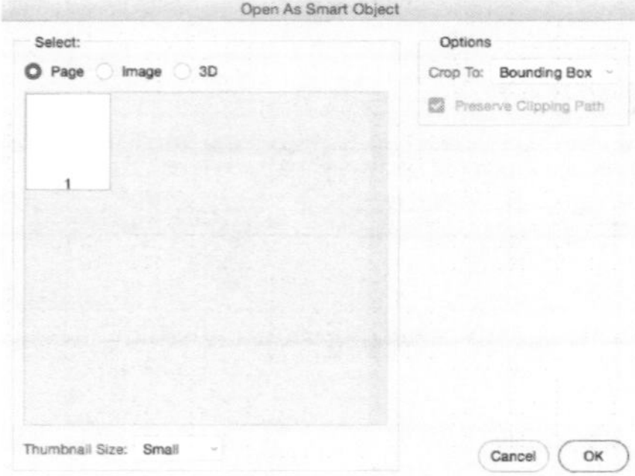

   When the Place PDF dialog box disappears, the placed file appears centered in the document window. Crossed diagonal lines indicate that the placement has not yet been finalized. (You can press the ESC key to cancel the placement.)

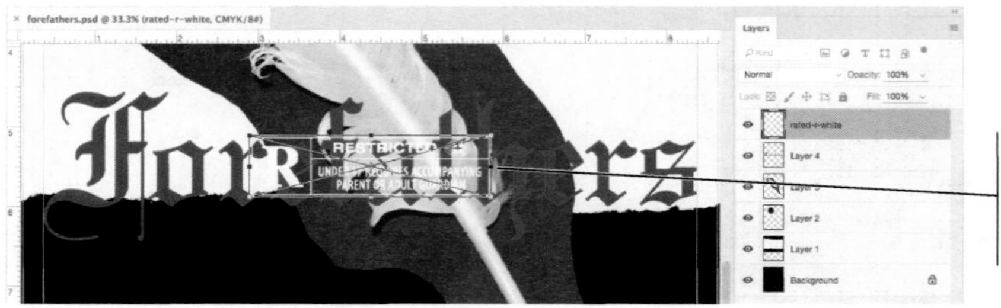

Crossed diagonal lines indicate that the placement is not yet final.

> ***Note:***
>
> *You can place either raster or vector files as Smart Objects. If you place a raster file as a Smart Object, double-clicking the thumbnail opens the placed raster file in another Photoshop window.*

4. **Press Return/Enter to commit (finalize) the placement.**

   After you finalize the placement, the bounding box handles and crossed diagonal lines disappear. In the Layers panel, the placed file has its own layer (just as the copied layers do). This layer, however, is automatically named, based on the name of the placed file.

   The layer's thumbnail indicates that this layer is a **Smart Object** — it is linked to the file that you placed. Because you are essentially placing a link to the vector file, it isn't rasterized into the Photoshop file; the vector information is maintained.

Smart Object thumbnail
When you place a file into a Photoshop file, the placed file name is used as the layer name.

5. **Repeat Steps 1–4 to place the two remaining logo files (sun-white.ai and tantamount-white.ai) as Smart Objects into the composite file.**

   When you place Smart Objects, they are automatically placed into the center of the document window. So right now, you have a fairly incomprehensible mess of four raster images and three vector objects all piled on top of one another. You'll start to make sense of these files in the next stage.

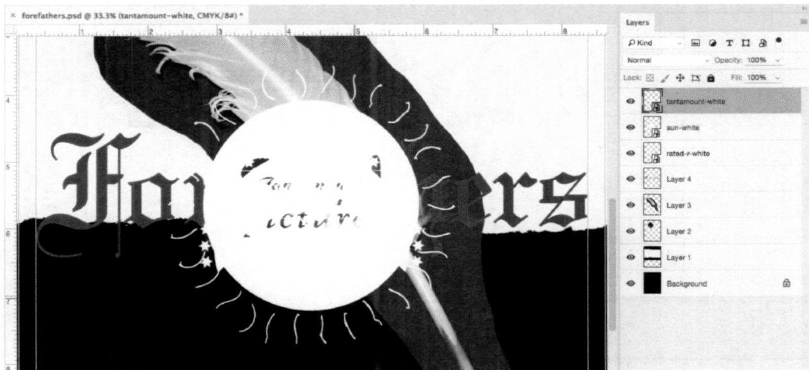

6. **Save the file and continue to the next stage of the project.**

Note:

Smart Objects provide extremely tight integration between Adobe Photoshop and Adobe Illustrator. You can take advantage of the sophisticated vector-editing features in Adobe Illustrator, and then place those files into Photoshop without losing the ability to edit the vector information.

Note:

Unfortunately you can only place one file at a time using the Place Embedded command.

Working with Embedded and Linked Smart Objects

In the previous exercise you used the Place Embedded option to create Smart Object layers that contain the placed file data. Using that method the embedded file data becomes a part of the parent file.

If you double-click the thumbnail icon of an embedded Smart Object, the embedded file opens in an application that can edit the stored data — AI files open in Illustrator; PSD, TIFF, and JPEG files open in Photoshop.

When you first open a Smart Object file, the application provides advice for working with Smart Objects:

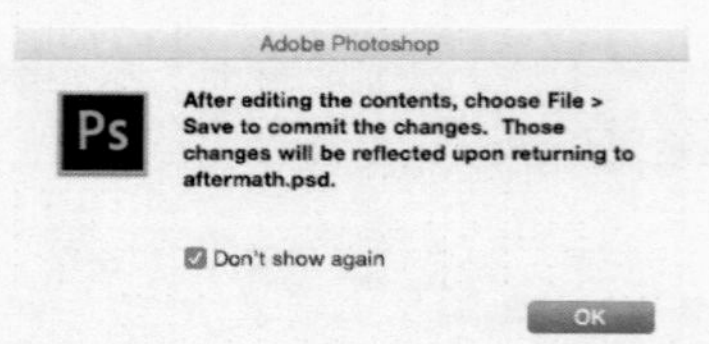

After you make necessary changes, you can save the file and close it, then return to Photoshop (if necessary). Your changes in the Smart Object file will automatically reflect in the parent file where the Smart Object layer is placed.

Important note: Do not use the Save As option when editing Smart Object layers. The changes will not reflect in the parent file if you save changes with a different file name.

If you choose the Place Linked option in the File menu, Smart Object layer stores a link to the original file data rather than embedding that data inside the parent file.

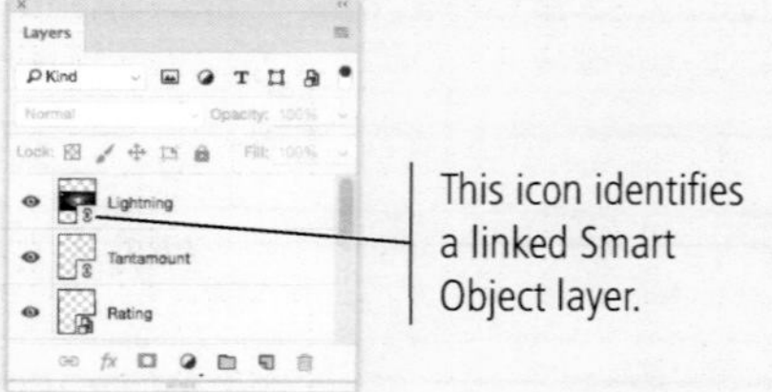

This icon identifies a linked Smart Object layer.

This provides an opportunity for maintaining consistency because you only need to change one instance of a file to reflect those changes anywhere the file is placed.

Say you place a logo created in Illustrator into a Photoshop file. The same logo is also placed as a link in a number of InDesign documents. If you open the logo in Illustrator and change the main color (for example), then save the changes in the original logo file, the new color automatically reflects in any file — whether InDesign or Photoshop — that is linked to the edited logo.

If you use the Place Embedded option in Photoshop, the Smart Object layer is not linked to the original, edited logo file; you would have to open the embedded Smart Object and make the same color change a second time.

Linked files also have potential disadvantages. As we mentioned previously, double-clicking a Smart Object layer thumbnail opens the linked or embedded file in an application that can edit the relevant data. If you are working with *linked* Smart Object layers, any changes you make affect the original file data. This means your changes appear not only in the parent Photoshop file where it is linked, but also any other file that links to the same data.

For a file to output properly, linked Smart Object layers must be present and up to date at the time of output.

If the linked file has been modified while the parent file is open, the changes automatically reflect in the parent file when you return to that document. If the parent file is not open in Photoshop when the linked file is edited, you will see a Modified icon for the linked Smart Object layer.

If the linked file is deleted or moved to another location after it has been placed, the parent file will show a Missing icon for the linked Smart Object layer.

If a linked Smart Object has been moved while the parent file is not open, you will see a warning dialog box when you open the parent Photoshop file. You can use that dialog box to locate the missing link, or close it and use the options in the Layers panel to correct the problem.

Control/right-clicking a linked Smart Object layer name opens a contextual menu with options to update modified content and resolve broken links.

This icon identifies a linked, modified Smart Object layer.

This icon identifies a linked, missing Smart Object layer.

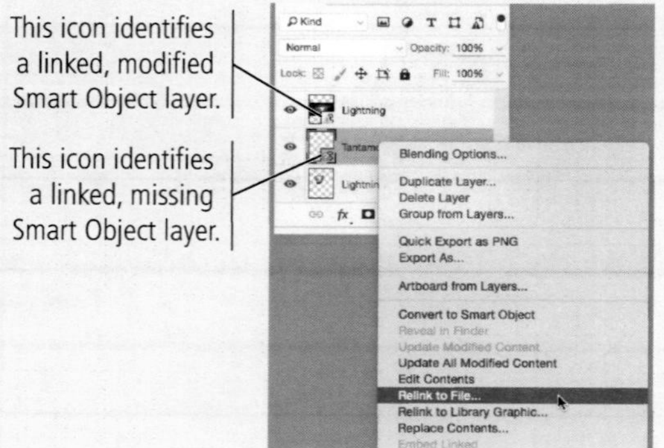

To avoid potential problems with missing linked files, you can use the File>Package command to create a job folder. The parent file is copied to a new folder, along with a Links subfolder containing any files that are placed as linked Smart Object layers.

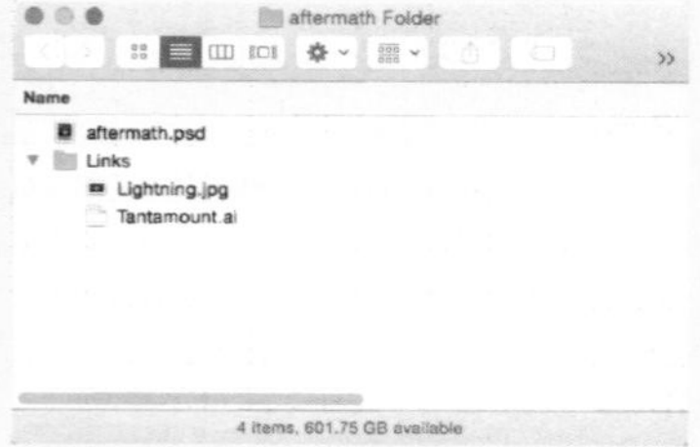

Stage 3 Creating Silhouettes

At this stage of the project, you have a single file that contains all of the necessary graphic elements, but you still have a few issues to resolve: the images are stacked on top of one another, some images don't fit into the page area, and some images have border edges that don't fit into the overall design (the blue background around the quill, for example). In this stage, you start fixing these problems.

Virtually any Photoshop project involves making some kind of selection. Making selections is so important, in fact, that there are no fewer than nine tools dedicated specifically to making selections, as well as a whole Select menu and a few other options for making and refining selections.

In an earlier lesson you learned how to use the marquee and lasso tools to draw selections. In the next series of exercises, you use several other selection methods to isolate the graphics from their backgrounds (called **silhouetting**).

Transform a Layer

Before you start silhouetting the different elements of the ad, it's a good idea to make them fit into the page area. Photoshop makes scaling, rotating, and other transformations fairly easy to implement.

1. **With forefathers.psd open, choose View>Fit on Screen.**

2. **Option/Alt-click the eye icon for Layer 1 to hide all other layers.**

   Toggling layer visibility is an easy way to see only what you want to see at any given stage in a project.

   Clicking the eye icon for a specific layer hides that layer; clicking the empty space where the eye icon should be shows the hidden layer. To show or hide a series of consecutive layers, click the visibility icon (or empty space) for the first layer you want to affect, hold down the mouse button, and drag down to the last layer you want to show or hide.

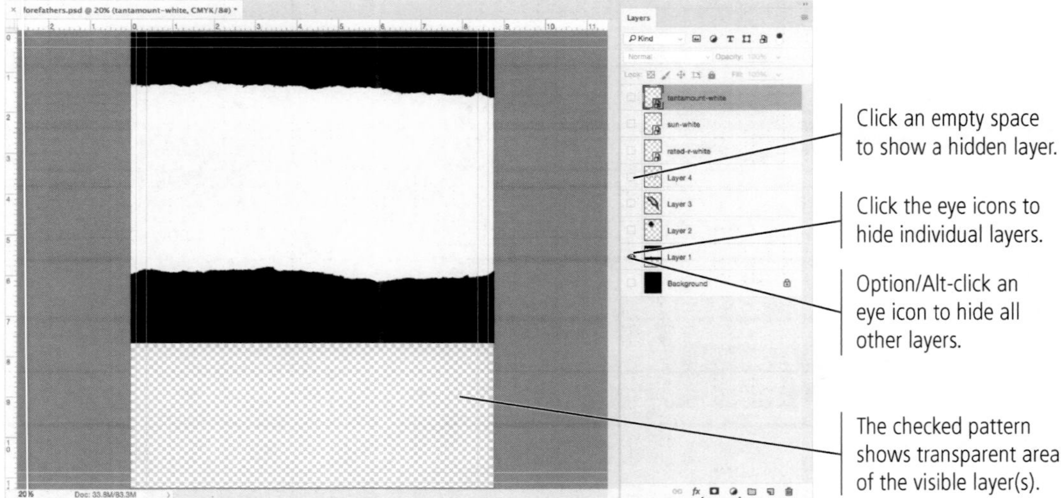

Click an empty space to show a hidden layer.
Click the eye icons to hide individual layers.
Option/Alt-click an eye icon to hide all other layers.
The checked pattern shows transparent areas of the visible layer(s).

3. **Double-click the Layer 1 layer name and type Parchment.**

You can rename any layer by simply double-clicking the name and typing. It's always a good idea to name your layers because it makes managing the file much easier — especially when you work with files that include dozens of layers. Even with only four unnamed layers in this file, it would be tedious to have to toggle each layer on to find the one you want.

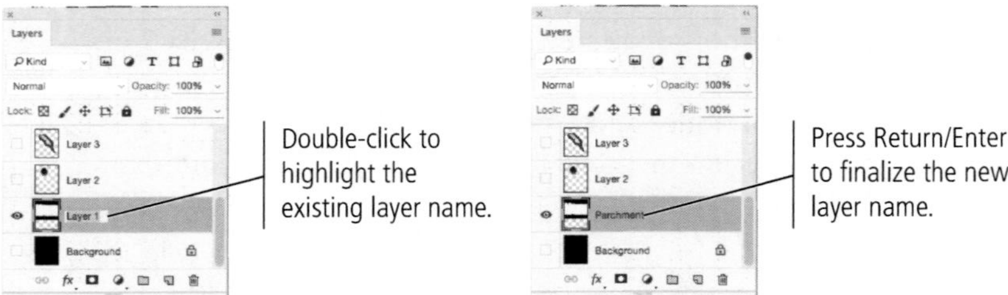

Double-click to highlight the existing layer name.
Press Return/Enter to finalize the new layer name.

4. **With the parchment layer selected, choose Edit>Transform>Scale.**

You can use this menu to apply any specific transformation to a layer or selection.

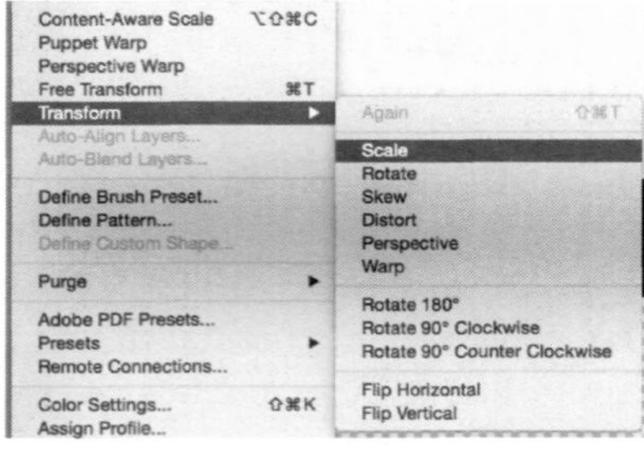

When you use the transform options, bounding box handles surround the selection; although the parchment doesn't fit inside the area of your file, you can still see the edges outside the page area. Since the parchment file is so much wider than the background file you created, some of the handles might not be visible.

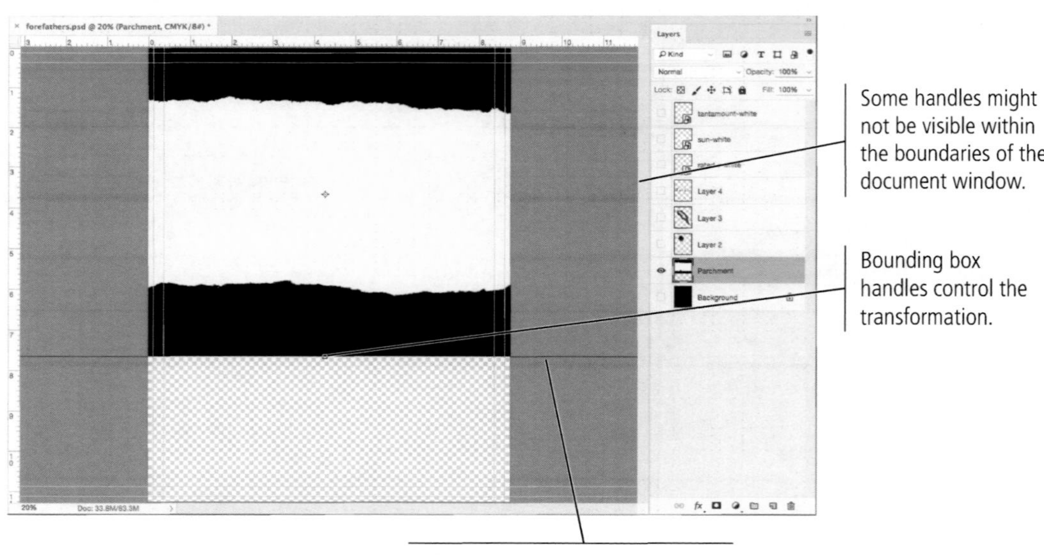

The edge of the bounding box shows that some parts of the layer do not fit within the current file dimensions.

5. **Choose View>Zoom Out until you can see all eight bounding box handles.**

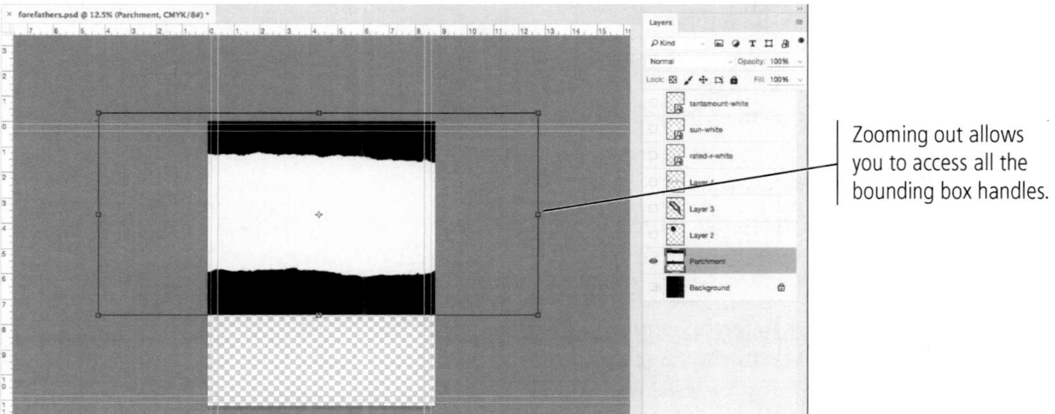

Zooming out allows you to access all the bounding box handles.

6. **Place the cursor within the bounding box. Drag until the left edge of the bounding box snaps to the left edge of the image.**

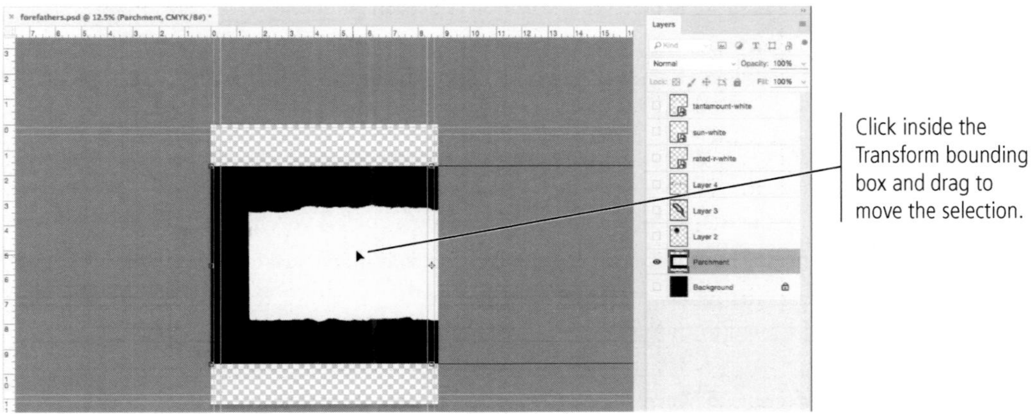

Click inside the Transform bounding box and drag to move the selection.

7. **If necessary, zoom out again (or adjust your user interface) until you can see all eight bounding box handles.**

8. **Press Shift, click the bottom-right bounding box handle, and then drag up and left until the right edge of the bounding box is just past the right edge of the canvas.**

   The image dynamically changes as you scale the layer. Pressing Shift while you drag a handle constrains the image proportions as you resize it. When you release the mouse button, the handles remain in place until you finalize ("commit") the transformation.

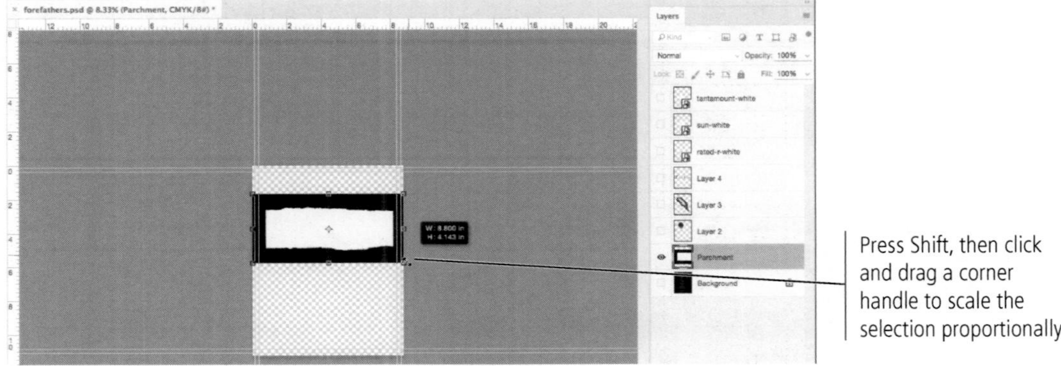

Press Shift, then click and drag a corner handle to scale the selection proportionally.

9. **Look at the Options bar.**

When you use the transform options, bounding box handles surround the selection in the document window. The Options bar gives you a number of options for controlling the transformations numerically:

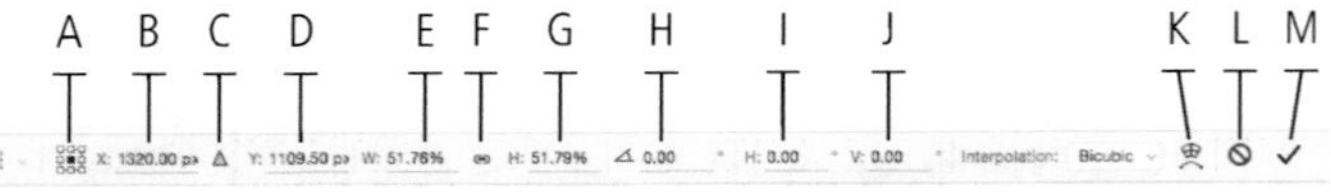

A. **Reference Point Location.** This point determines the point around which transformations are made. It always defaults to the center point.

B. **Set Horizontal Position of Reference Point.** This is the X position of the reference point for the content being transformed. If the center reference point is selected, for example, this is the X position of the center point of the content.

C. **Use Relative Positioning for Reference Point.** If this option is active, the Set Horizontal Position and Set Vertical Position fields default to 0; changing these values moves the reference point by the value you type. For example, typing "–25" in the Set Horizontal Position field moves the active content 25 pixels to the left.

D. **Set Vertical Position of Reference Point.** This is the Y position of the reference point for the content being transformed.

E. **Set Horizontal Scale.** Use this field to change the horizontal scale percentage of the transformed content.

F. **Maintain Aspect Ratio.** When active, the horizontal scale and vertical scale fields are locked to have the same value.

G. **Set Vertical Scale.** Use this field to change the vertical scale percentage of the transformed content.

H. **Rotate.** Use this field to rotate the transformed content by a specific angle.

I. **Set Horizontal Skew.** This field is used to transform an object so that it appears to lean to the left or right.

J. **Set Vertical Skew.** This field is used to transform an object so that it appears to lean to the up or down.

K. **Switch Between Free Transform and Warp Modes.** If available, click this button to apply a built-in warp to the active selection.

L. **Cancel Transform.** Click this button (or press the Esc key) to exit Free Transform mode without applying any transformation.

M. **Commit Transform.** Click this button (or press Return/Enter) to finalize the transformation that you applied while in Free Transform mode.

Note:

*The Options bar includes a "hidden" feature called the **scrubby slider**. If you place your cursor over a field name, it turns into a pointing hand with left- and right-facing arrows. While you see this cursor, you can drag across the Options bar to increase (drag right) or decrease (drag left) the value in the selected field.*

10. **In the Options bar, type 51 in Width field and then click the Maintain Aspect Ratio button.**

Type in these fields to define a specific transformation.

Click this icon to constrain the height and width.

11. **Click the Commit Transform button on the Options bar or press Return/ Enter to apply the transformation.**

12. **Choose Edit>Transform>Scale again and look at the Options bar.**

    Once you commit the transformation, it is final. Looking at the Options bar now, you can see that it shows the layer at 100% instead of the 51% from Step 10.

After committing the original transformation, the new size becomes the layer content's actual size.

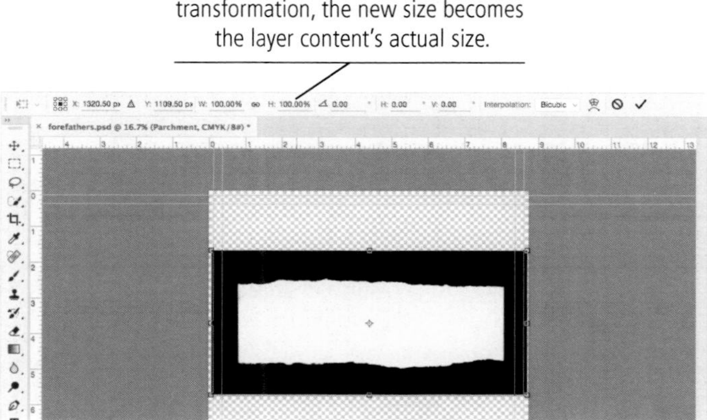

Note:

When you resize a Smart Object, the scale percentage is maintained even after you finalize the change (unlike scaling a regular layer, where the layer reverts to 100% once you finalize the scaling).

13. **Click the Cancel button in the Options bar or press the ESC key.**

14. **Choose the Move tool, then click and drag the selected layer until the pink guides show the selection is centered on the canvas.**

    While the Move tool is active, pressing the Arrow keys nudges the selected layer by a few pixels at a time. This method is useful for slight movements.

    The pink lines that appear as you drag are smart guides, which help you to reposition objects (including selection marquees) relative to other objects or to the canvas.

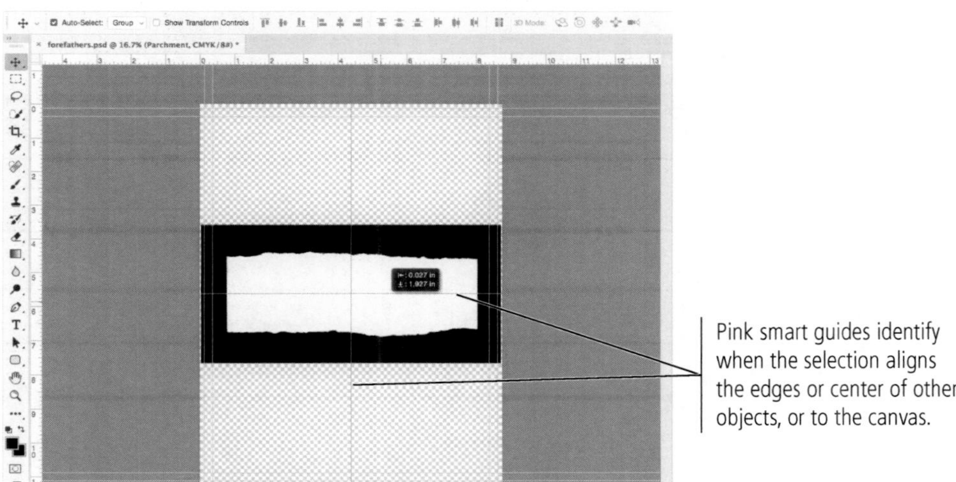

Pink smart guides identify when the selection aligns the edges or center of other objects, or to the canvas.

15. **Save the file and continue to the next exercise.**

Understanding Smart Guides

PHOTOSHOP FOUNDATIONS

As you dragged the selection marquee in the previous exercise, you might have noticed a series of pink lies appearing in different locations. These lines are a function of Smart Guides, which make it easier to align layer content to other layers or to the overall canvas.

Smart Guides are active by default, but you can toggle them on and off in the View>Show submenu.

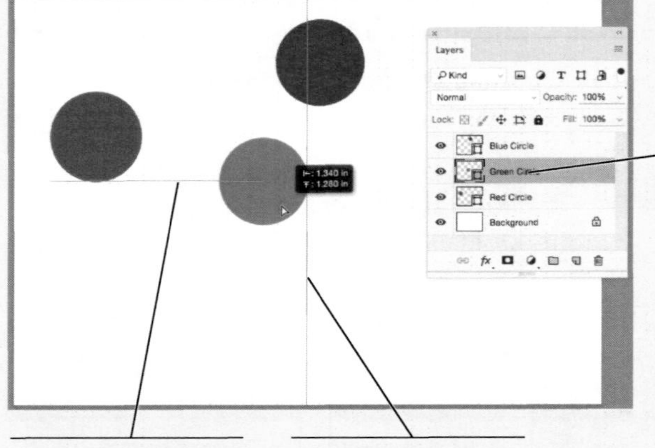

We dragged the Green Circle layer with the Move tool.

Smart Guides identify the center and edges of content on other layers.

Smart Guides identify the center and edges of the overall canvas.

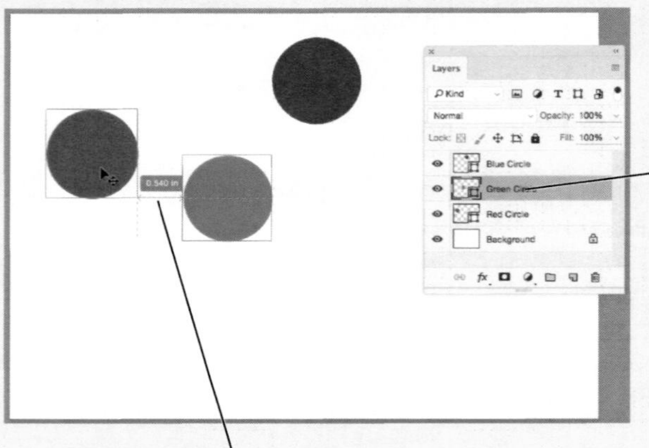

The Green Circle layer is selected.

Press Command/Control and hover over an object to find the distance between it and the selected layer.

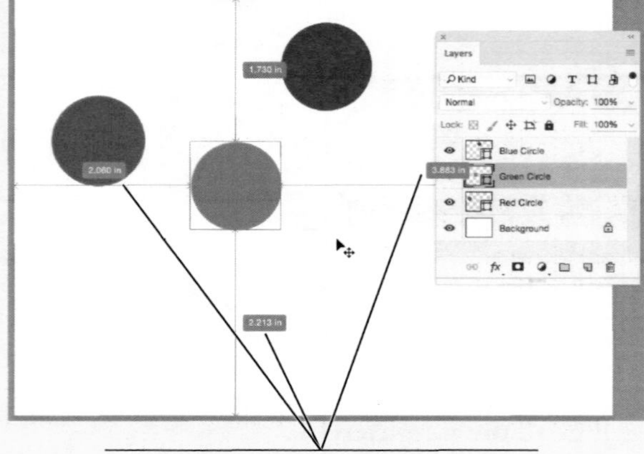

Press Command/Control and hover over the canvas find the distance between the selected layer content and the canvas edges.

Make and Refine a Quick Selection

Rather than drawing a selection area, you can make selections based on the color in an image. This technique is especially useful when you want to select large areas of solid color, or in photos with significant contrast between the foreground and background.

1. **With forefathers.psd open, zoom in so you can clearly see the Parchment layer content.**

2. **Choose the Quick Selection tool (nested with the Magic Wand tool) in the Tools panel. In the Options bar, make sure the New Selection option is active.**

   As with the other selection tools, the Quick Selection tool can create a new selection, add to the existing selection, or subtract from the existing selection (using the three buttons on the left side of the Options bar).

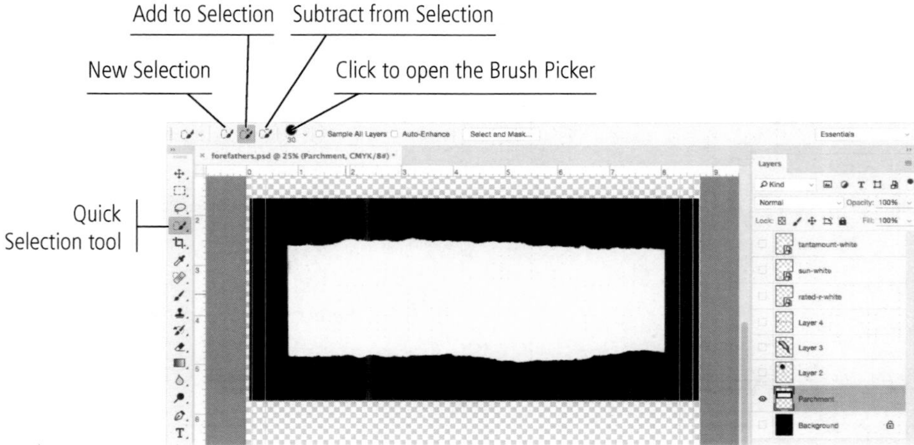

3. **Click at the left edge of the parchment and drag to the right.**

   The Quick Selection tool essentially allows you to "paint" a selection. As you drag, the selection expands and automatically finds the edges in the image. Because the varying shades in the parchment aren't significantly different, the resulting selection should closely — but not exactly — match the parchment edges.

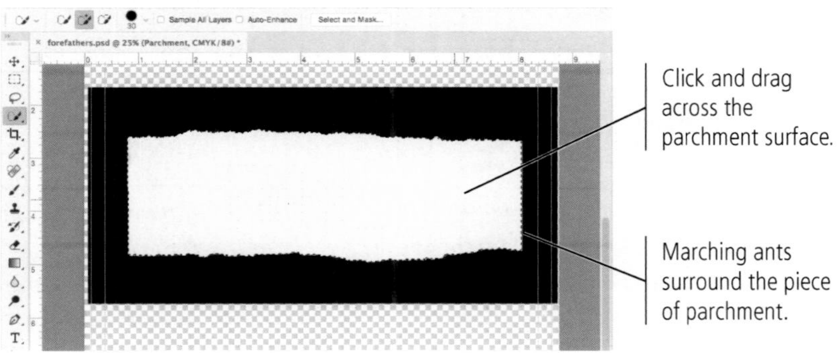

Click and drag across the parchment surface.
Marching ants surround the piece of parchment.

> ***Note:***
>
> *If you stop dragging and then click in a nearby area, the selection grows to include the new area.*

5. **Click the Select and Mask button in the Options bar.**

The Select and Mask workspace is a specialized workspace that contains only the tools you need to refine a complex selection.

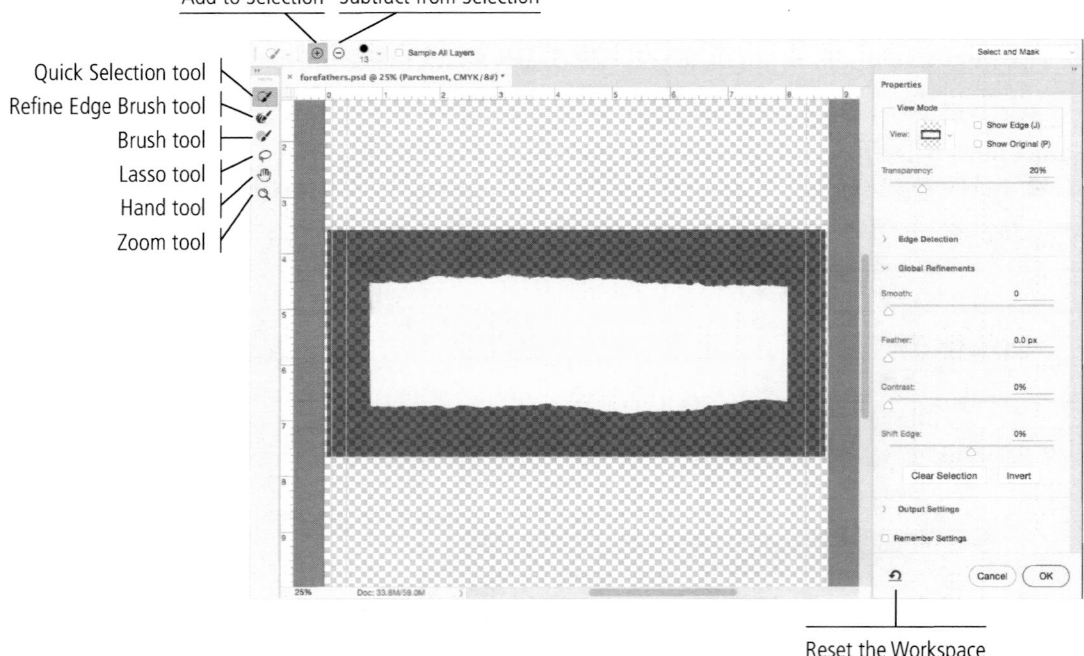

6. **In the Properties panel, open the View menu and click the On White option.**

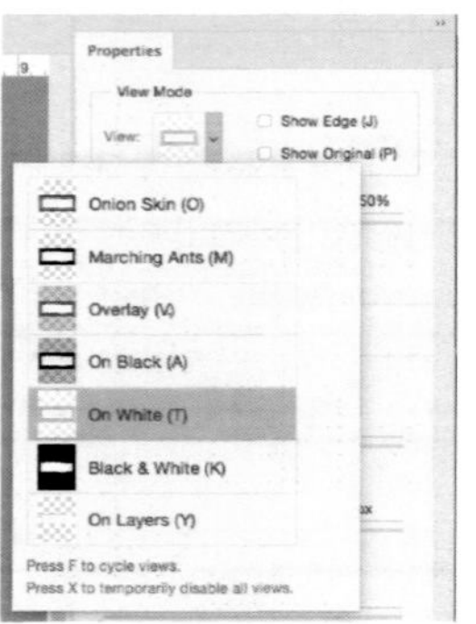

The different types of preview change the way your image appears while you refine the edges within the workspace.

- **Onion Skin**, the default, shows unselected (masked) areas as semi-transparent, based on the value in the Transparency slider. You can make the masked areas more or less transparent by increasing or decreasing (respectively) the Transparency value.
- **Marching Ants** shows the basic standard selection.
- **Overlay** shows the unselected areas with a Quick Mask overlay.
- **On Black** shows the selection in color against a black background.
- **On White** shows the selection in color against a white background.
- **Black & White** shows the selected area in white and the unselected area in black.
- **On Layers** shows only the selected area; unselected areas are hidden so that underlying layers are visible in masked areas in the preview.

> ***Note:***
>
> *If the Show Edge option is checked, only the edge of the selection area will be visible in the preview.*

7. **Change the Opacity slider to 100%.**

Using the default setting, the masked areas appear at 50% opacity in the Select and Mask workspace. By changing this setting to 100%, masked pixels are entirely hidden by the white area.

8. **Experiment with the adjustments in the Properties panel until you're satisfied with the selection edge.**

   You want to include a small amount of darkness around the edge so that when you invert the selection to remove the hole in the wall, there is no light halo effect left by the selection edge. We used the Shift Edge slider to slightly expand the selection edge.

   - **Radius** (accessed by expanding the Edge Detection section) is the number of pixels around the edge that are affected. Higher radius values (up to 250 pixels) improve the edge in areas of fine detail.
   - **Smooth** reduces the number of points that make up your selection and, as the name suggests, makes a smoother edge. You can set smoothness from 0 (very detailed selection) to 100 (very smooth selection).
   - **Feather** softens the selection edge, resulting in a transition that does not have a hard edge (in other words, blends into the background). You can feather the selection up to 250 pixels.
   - **Contrast** is the degree of variation allowed in the selection edge. Higher Contrast values (up to 100%) mean sharper selection edges.
   - **Shift Edge** shrinks or grows the selection edge by the defined percentage (from –100% to 100%).
   - **Decontaminate Colors** (accessed by expanding the Advanced Output Settings section) can be checked to remove a certain percentage of color from the edge of a selection.

> ***Note:***
>
> *It might help to work with a closer view while you refine edges. You can use the Zoom and Hand tools in the Refine Edge dialog box to change the image view behind the open dialog box.*

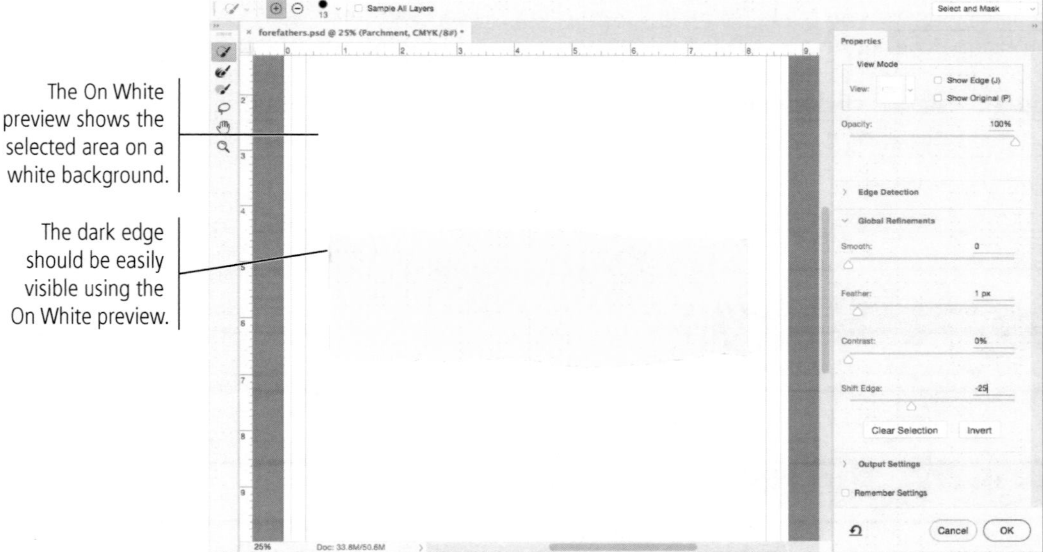

9. **At the bottom of the Properties panel, expand the Output Settings section.**

10. **Choose the Layer Mask option in the Output To menu.**

    This menu can be used to create a new layer or file (with or without a mask) from the selection. You want to mask the existing layer, so you are using the Layer Mask option.

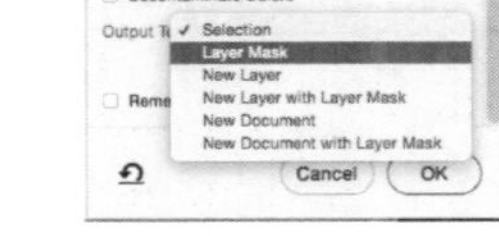

    Rather than simply deleting the unwanted background area, another option for isolating an object with a path is to create a **layer mask** that hides the unwanted pixels. Areas outside the mask are hidden but not deleted, so you can later edit the mask to change the visible part of the image.

11. **Click OK to accept your refined selection.**

A **layer mask** is a map of areas that will be visible in the masked layer. The mask you just created is a raster-based pixel mask, based on the active selection when you created the mask. This is a non-destructive way to hide certain elements of a layer without permanently deleting pixels; you can edit or disable the layer mask at any time.

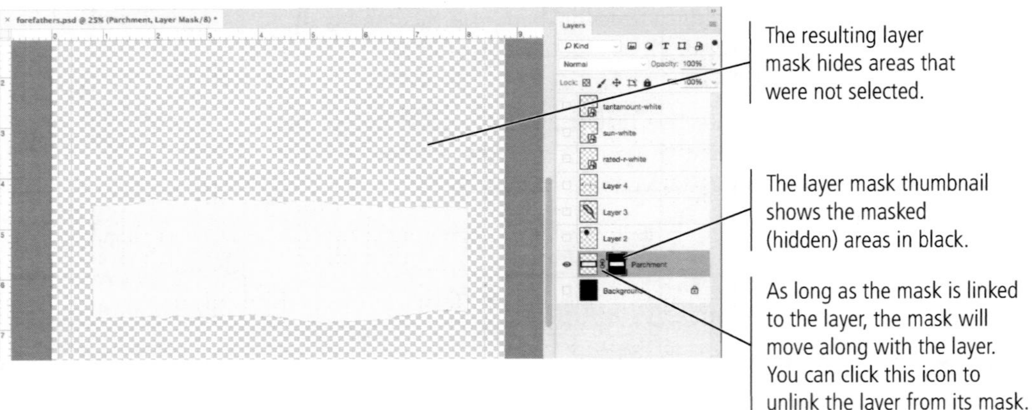

The resulting layer mask hides areas that were not selected.
The layer mask thumbnail shows the masked (hidden) areas in black.
As long as the mask is linked to the layer, the mask will move along with the layer. You can click this icon to unlink the layer from its mask.

12. **Click the mask thumbnail in the Layers panel to select only the mask, and then open the Properties panel (Window>Properties).**

Like the Options bar, the Properties panel is contextual. Different options are available in the panel depending on what is selected in the Layers panel. When a layer mask is selected, you can manipulate a variety of properties related to the selected mask.

13. **In the Properties panel, click the Invert button.**

This button reverses the mask, so now only the background pixels are visible.

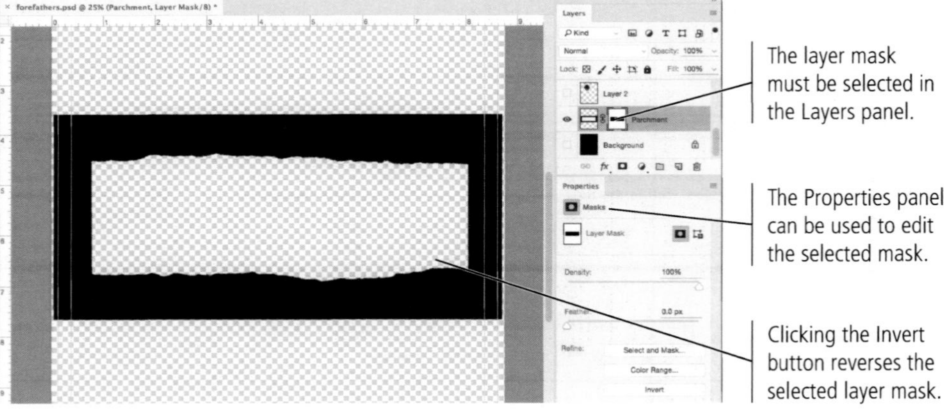

The layer mask must be selected in the Layers panel.
The Properties panel can be used to edit the selected mask.
Clicking the Invert button reverses the selected layer mask.

14. **Click the Invert button again to restore the parchment area of the layer.**

Remember, layer masks are non-destructive. You can edit the mask to show or hide different areas of a layer; the actual layer pixels are not affected.

15. In the Layers panel, Control/right-click the mask thumbnail and choose Disable Layer Mask from the contextual menu.

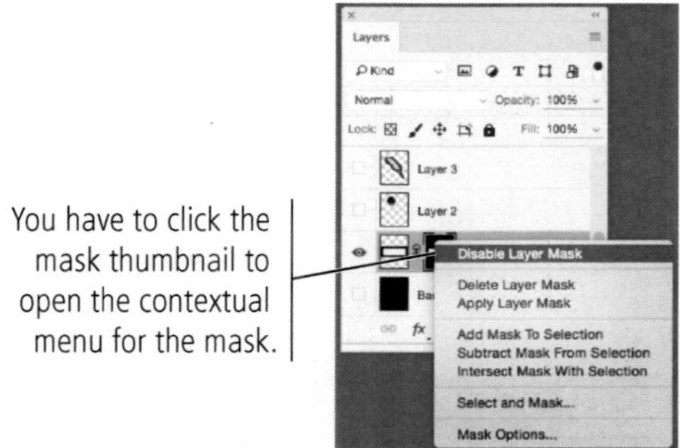

When you disable the mask, the background pixels are again visible. Again, this is one of the advantages of using masks — the background pixels are not permanently removed, they are simply hidden.

> *Note:*
>
> *If you choose Apply Layer Mask from the contextual menu, the mask is no longer attached to the layer and the previously masked pixels are permanently removed from the layer.*

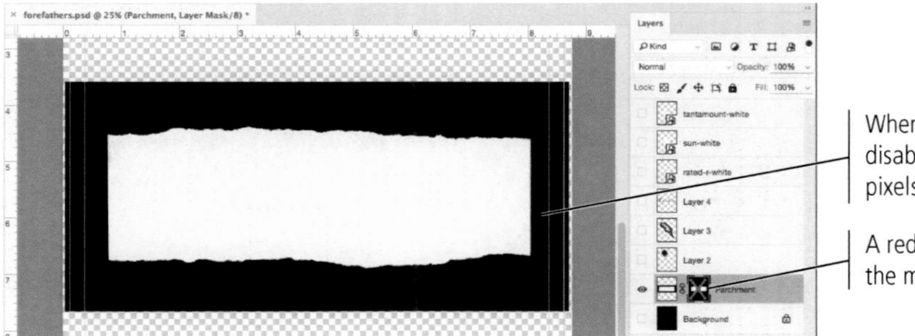

When the mask is disabled, the masked pixels are visible.
A red X indicates that the mask is disabled.

16. Control/right-click the mask thumbnail and choose Enable Layer Mask from the contextual menu.

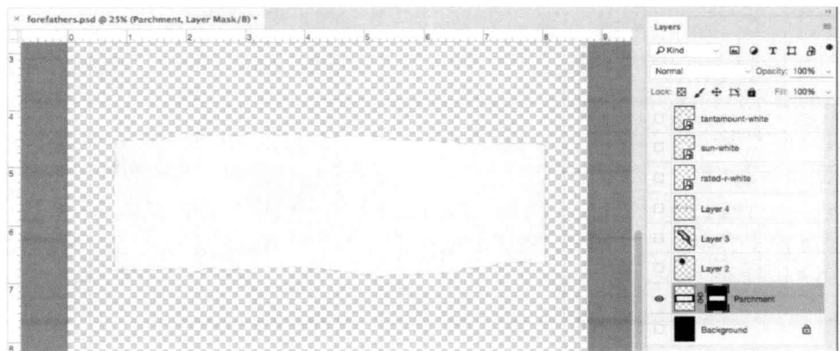

> *Note:*
>
> *Creating selections and then deleting the pixels surrounding an object is a common method for creating silhouettes — but not necessarily the best method. Masks protect the original pixels while providing exactly the same result.*

17. Save the file and continue to the next exercise.

Draw a Vector Path

In some cases, the image content makes it difficult (or at least tedious) to select by color. The bottle image in this ad, for example, has only black colors — the bottle is black, the shadow is a medium black, and the background is a mottled light gray. Selecting by color range will almost certainly result in some of the selection intruding into the bottle shape, and some of the background/shadow area being omitted from the selection. The good news is that Photoshop has other ways for making selections, including several that are specifically designed for selecting areas with hard edges.

Understanding Anchor Points and Handles

PHOTOSHOP FOUNDATIONS

An **anchor point** marks the end of a line **segment**, and the point **handles** determine the shape of that segment. That's the basic definition of a vector, but there is a bit more to it than that. (The Photoshop Help files refer to handles as direction lines, and distinguishes different types of points. Our aim here is to explain the overall concept of vector paths, so we use the generic industry-standard terms. For more information on Adobe's terminology, refer to the Photoshop Help files.)

Each segment in a path has two anchor points, and can have two associated handles.

You can create corner points by simply clicking with the Pen tool instead of clicking and dragging. Corner points do not have their own handles; the connected segments are controlled by the handles of the other associated points.

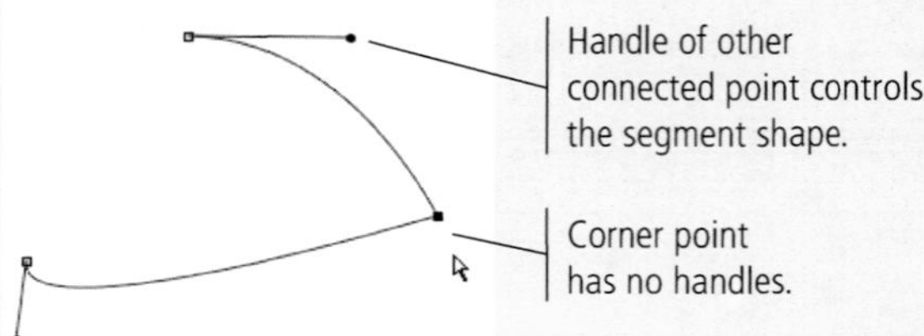

Handle of other connected point controls the segment shape.

Corner point has no handles.

In the following image, we first clicked to create Point A and dragged (without releasing the mouse button) to create Handle A1. We then clicked and dragged to create Point B and Handle B1; Handle B2 was automatically created as a reflection of B1 (Point B is a **symmetrical point**).

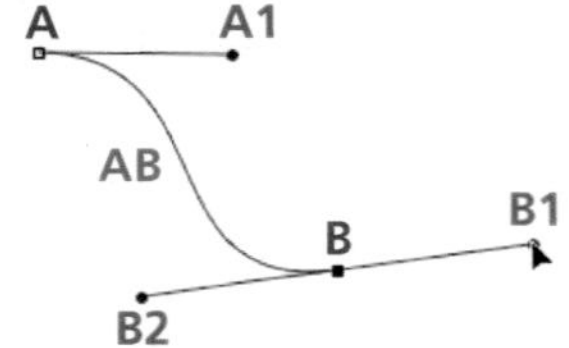

This image shows the result of dragging Handle B1 to the left instead of to the right when we created the initial curve. Notice the difference in the curve here, compared to the curve above. When you drag a handle, the connecting segment arcs away from the direction you drag.

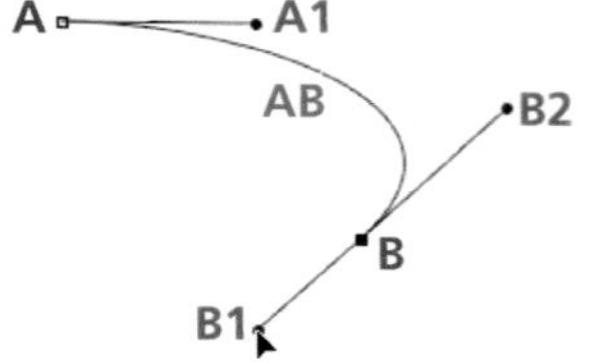

It's important to understand that every line segment is connected to two handles. In this example, Handle A1 and Handle B2 determine the shape of Segment AB. Dragging either handle affects the shape of the connected segment.

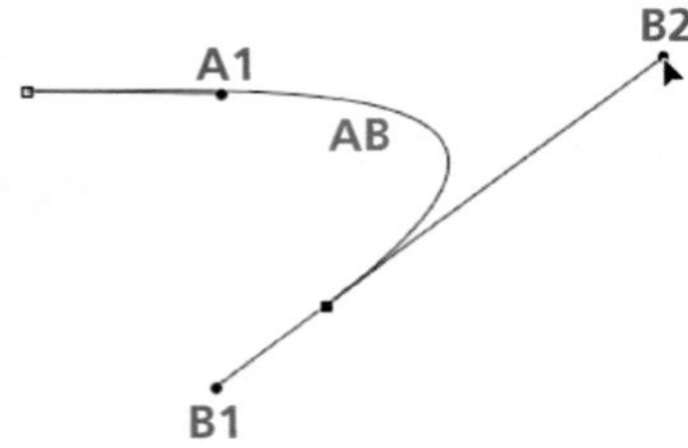

When you use the Pen tool, clicking and dragging a point creates a symmetrical (smooth) point; both handles start out at equal length, directly opposite one another. Changing the angle of one handle of a symmetrical point also changes the opposing handle of that point. In the example here, repositioning Handle B1 also moves Handle B2, which affects the shape of Segment AB. (You can, however, change the length of one handle without affecting the length of the other handle.)

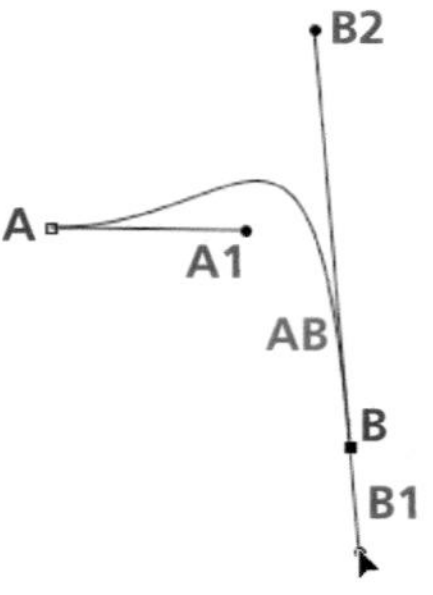

1. **With forefathers.psd open, hide the Parchment layer and show Layer 2.**

2. **Choose Select>Deselect to make sure any selection marquees from previous exercises are turned off.**

   Pressing Command/Control-D deselects selections more quickly and easily than choosing Select>Deselect from the Menu bar. You should learn — and use — keyboard shortcuts wherever you can. They result in measurable time savings.

3. **In the Layers panel, double-click the Layer 2 name and rename it Bottle.**

4. **Zoom in so you can more clearly see the bottle edges.**

   When drawing paths, it helps to work with high view percentages so that you can see the edges more clearly. We're using 50% in our screen shots; you should use whatever works best for you. It isn't necessary to keep the entire image in the project window if you're more comfortable working at higher percentages; you can scroll around the project window while you create paths.

5. **Choose the Pen tool in the Tools panel.**

   The Pen tool can be used to create shape layers or paths. Shape layers are vector-based, which means they have mathematically defined edges and can be filled with colors or pixel-based images. Paths are also vector-based, but they do not create their own layers and cannot be directly filled; instead, paths (or clipping paths, to use their full name) are most commonly used to isolate certain portions of an image.

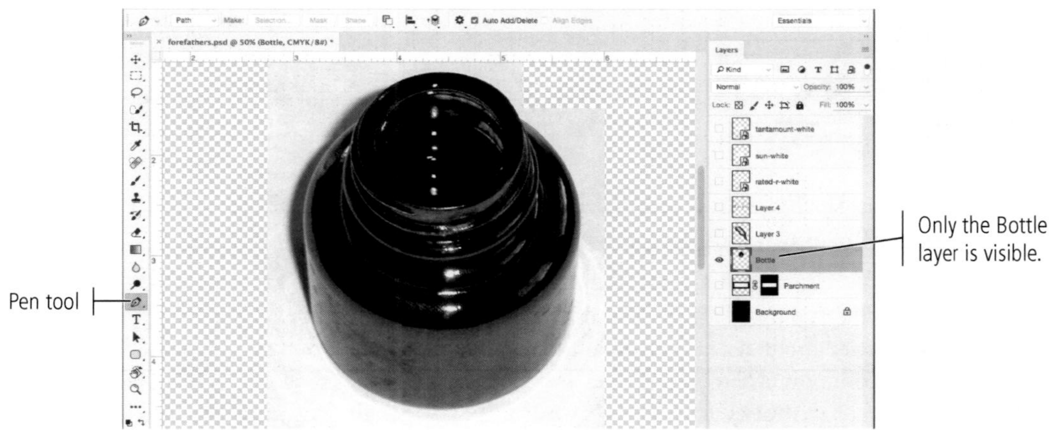

Pen tool
Only the Bottle layer is visible.

6. **In the Options bar, make sure Path is selected in the left menu.**

   You can use this menu to create a path or a vector shape layer. When you use the Path option, the result will be a vector path that is stored in the Paths panel; nothing is added to the active layer.

   If you choose the Shape option, you can define fill color, stroke weight and color, and a number of other shape attributes in the Options bar. The resulting vector path is stored on a special layer called a shape layer.

7. **Open the Path Operations menu and choose the Combine Shapes option.**

These options define how a new path will interact with any existing paths.

- **New Layer**, available when Layer is selected in the Tool Mode menu, creates a new shape layer every time you draw a new path.
- **Combine Shapes** adds new paths to an already selected path or shape layer. Each path's shape is maintained as a separate vector path.
- **Subtract Front Shape** removes the area of secondary shapes from existing shapes.
- **Intersect Shape Areas** results in a shape that is only the area where a new shape overlaps an existing shape.
- **Exclude Overlapping Shapes** is similar to Subtract; overlapping areas are removed from the existing shape, but non-overlapping areas of the new shape are filled with the shape color.
- The **Merge Shape Components** option, available when a single path contains more than one shape, results in a single (possibly compound) shape. Any overlapping paths are combined into one shape/path.

Note:

If the Subtract Front Shape option is selected, the vector mask you create later will essentially be reversed, hiding the areas within the shape you draw.

8. **Click in the image where the bottle opening meets the side of the bottle.**

Click here with the Pen tool to add a single anchor point.

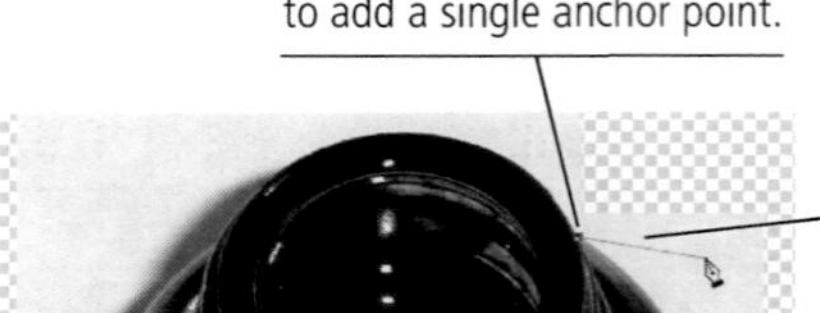

A line connects from the placed point to the tool cursor, previewing the appearance of the connecting segment if you click again.

Note:

If you don't see the ne connecting the anchor point and the tool cursor, open the Geometry Options menu in the Options bar and check the Rubber Band option.

9. **Move your cursor down and to the right along the curved edge of the bottle. Click to add an anchor point and drag down and to the right before releasing the mouse button.**

When you click and drag with the Pen tool, you are defining the handles for the anchor point. Without getting too heavily into detailed explanations of geometry, you should simply understand that the anchor points determine the ends of line segments, and the handles determine the curve shape of the segments that are connected to that point.

Click here and hold down the mouse button ...

... then drag down and to the right; the curve takes shape as you drag.

Note:

The Auto Add/Delete option in the Options bar, which is active by default, allows you to add or remove points on an active path without manually switching to the Add Anchor Point or Delete Anchor Point tool (nested under the Pen tool).

10. **Move the cursor down and to the right, then click and drag down to create another anchor point and handles.**

The shape of this line segment is defined by the handles of the two connecting anchor points.

Click here...

...then drag to here.

11. Move the cursor down and click to add another anchor point. For this point, don't drag a handle.

When you click without dragging, no handles are created for that point. This creates a corner point.

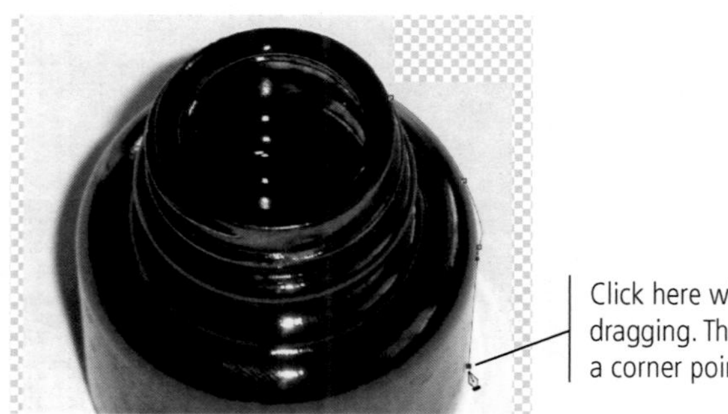

Click here without dragging. The result is a corner point.

12. Move down and to the left, and then click and drag to the left to create another smooth anchor point.

13. Continue clicking and dragging points until you have outlined the entire bottle. Use a corner point where the left side of the bottle opening meets the left side of the bottle.

14. When you reach the first point you created, place your cursor over the point and click to close the path.

This small hollow circle in the cursor icon indicates that clicking will close the path.

Don't worry if your path isn't perfect. You can edit a path at any point, which you will do next.

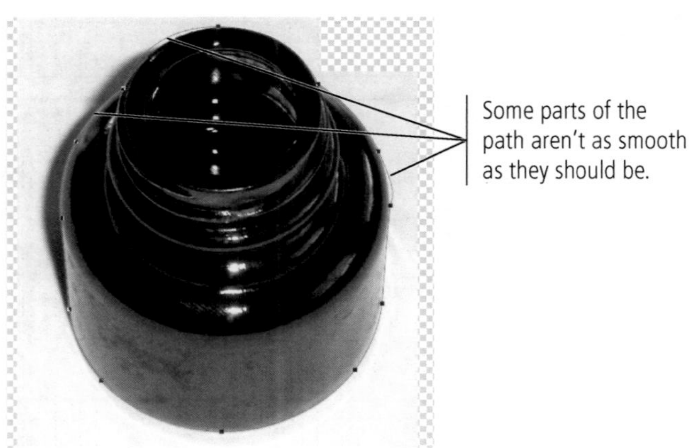

Some parts of the path aren't as smooth as they should be.

15. Save the file and continue to the next exercise.

Note:

A smooth point allows the path to flow continuously from one segment to another. A corner point creates a sharp angle, allowing you to change directions of the path.

Click a smooth point with the Convert Point tool to change it to a corner point. Click and drag a corner point with the Convert Point tool to change a corner point to a smooth point.

Edit a Vector Path

In most cases, the first path you draw won't be perfect; you'll probably need to edit at least one or two points or segments, move existing points, or even add or delete points before your path exactly matches the shape you're outlining. As you complete this exercise, we show you how to correct the path in our screen shots. You should follow the general directions to correct the path that you drew in the previous exercise.

1. **With `forefathers.psd` open, open the Paths panel.**

   When you use the Pen tool to draw a path, it automatically appears in the Paths panel as the Work Path (in italics).

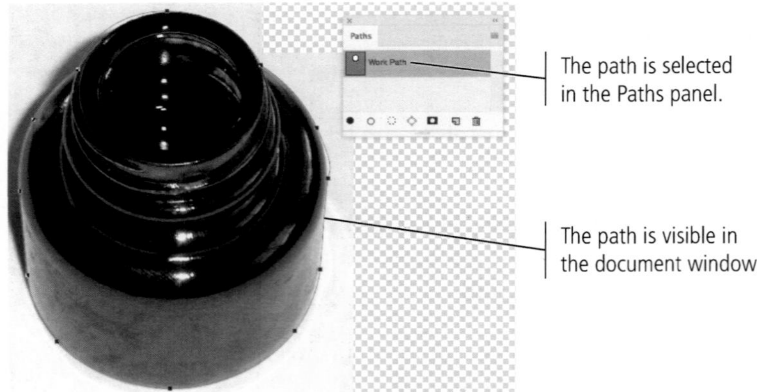
Paths
Work Path
The path is selected in the Paths panel.
The path is visible in the document window.

2. **Click the empty area in the Paths panel (below the work path).**

   This effectively "turns off" the path; it is still in the Paths panel, but the points and handles are no longer visible in the file window.

Paths
Work Path

Note:

If you deselect the work path and then draw a new path, your first work path will be lost. You have to manually save the work path if you want to access it again later.

3. **Click Work Path in the Paths panel to show the current work path in the document window.**

4. **Choose the Path Selection tool in the Tools panel and click the path in the document window.**

   The Path Selection tool selects the entire path.

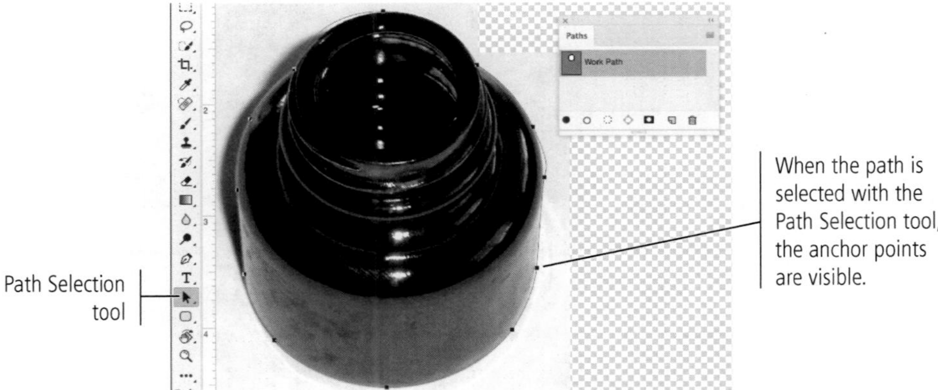

Paths
Work Path
Path Selection tool
When the path is selected with the Path Selection tool, the anchor points are visible.

5. **Click away from the path to deselect it, then choose the Direct Selection tool (nested under the Path Selection tool).**

   The Direct Selection tool selects individual points and segments of a path.

6. **Zoom in if necessary, and then click one of the segments of your path that needs to be edited.**

   When you select a segment with the Direct Selection tool, you can see the handles that are associated with that segment.

7. **Drag the handle and/or point to correct the bad segment.**

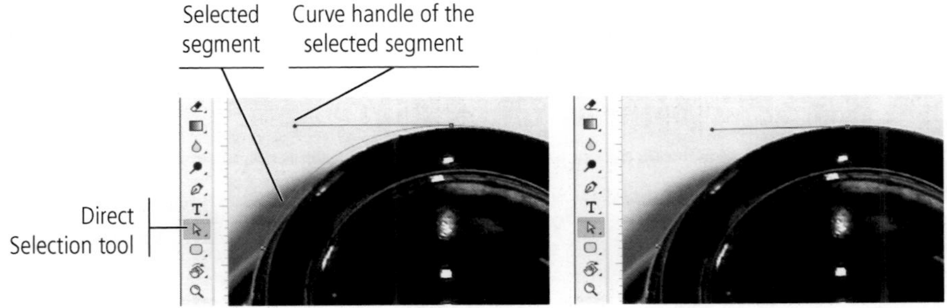

> *Note:*
>
> *If you click a point with the Direct Selection tool, the point appears solid. Unselected points appear hollow.*

8. **Continue editing the path until you are satisfied with the result. If you need to add or remove points from the path, use the related tools nested under the Pen tool.**

   This is one place where we can't give you specific instructions because everyone's path will be a bit different. Keep the following points in mind as you refine your shape:

   - Use the Direct Selection tool to select and edit specific segments or points on the path. You can move points to a new position by dragging (or using the Arrow keys), or move their handles to change segment shapes.
   - Use the Add Anchor Point tool to add a point to the path.
   - Use the Delete Anchor Point tool to remove a point from the path.
   - Use the Convert Point tool to change a corner point to a smooth point, and vice versa.

   As you work more with paths, anchor points, and handles, you'll become more comfortable with how changing a handle affects the associated line segments. In this case, the best teacher is practice.

9. **When you're satisfied with your path, open the Paths panel Options menu and choose Save Path.**

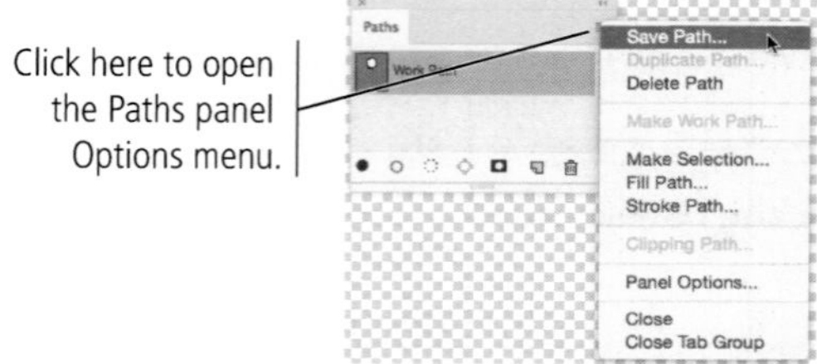

10. **In the Save Path dialog box, name the path** `Bottle Outline` **and click OK.**

    Trust us — when you get into very complicated files with multiple paths, you'll thank yourself for using names that indicate the purpose of a layer, path, or other element.

    After you save a path, it stays in the Paths panel; if you draw a new path now, you create a new work path.

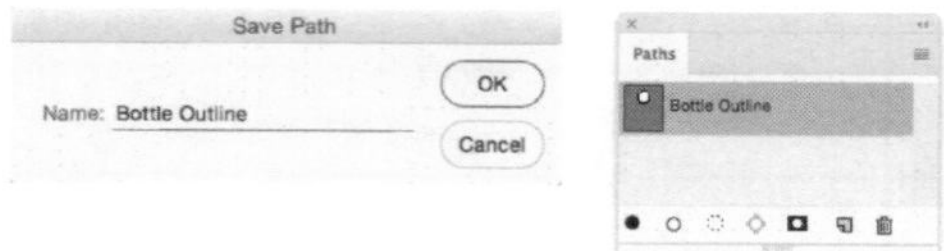

11. **Save the file and continue to the next exercise.**

Create a Vector Mask

You now have a path that outlines the bottle shape, but the bottle background is still in the image. Since you've already selected the shape (with the path), you can easily remove the background using the path you created in the previous exercises.

One option for completing this task is to make a selection based on the path (choose Make Selection in the Paths panel Options menu) and simply delete the pixels outside the selection. This is a pixel-based option, even though the path is a vector. When you make the selection, it will be a rendered version of the original vector path.

The second option for isolating an object with a path is to create a vector-based mask. This option maintains the vector data as the outside edge of the image; areas of the image outside the vector path are hidden but not deleted, so you can later edit the path to change whatever part of the image is visible if necessary.

1. **With forefathers.psd open, make sure the Bottle Outline path is selected in the Paths panel.**

2. **Display the Layers panel and make sure the Bottle layer is selected.**

3. **Choose Layer>Vector Mask>Current Path.**

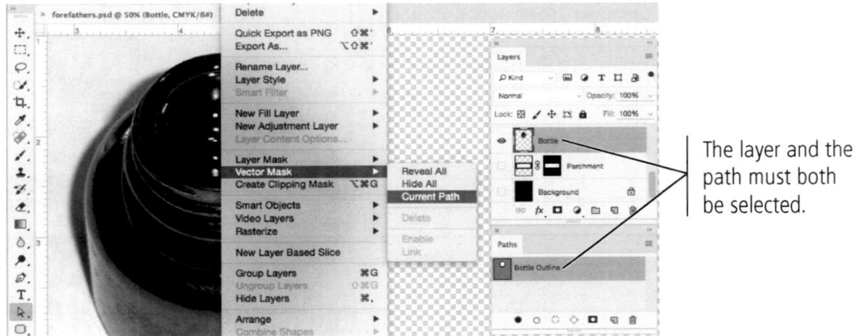

The layer and the path must both be selected.

After applying the mask, a second path appears in the Paths panel. The name identifies the path as a specific layer's vector mask (in this case, "Bottle Vector Mask"). The name is in italics because it is temporary; it only appears in the panel when the masked layer is selected in the Layers panel.

There is no link between the original path (Bottle Outline) and the vector-mask path. If you want to edit the vector mask, you have to first select the masked layer and then use the vector-editing tools to edit the layer's vector-mask path.

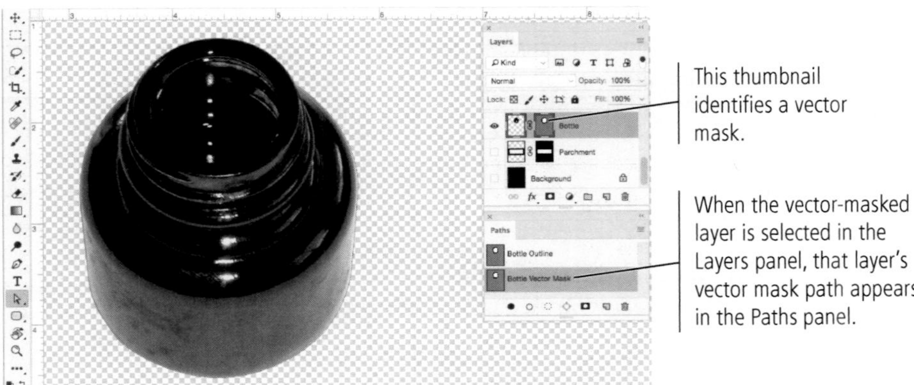

This thumbnail identifies a vector mask.

4. **Save the file and continue to the next exercise.**

Select a Color Range

As we said earlier, there is a host of selection options in Photoshop, each with its own advantages and disadvantages. You've already used the marquee tools and lasso tools to select general areas of images; you've used the Quick Selection tool to easily select an entire background, and then refined the edges of that selection; and you've used the Pen tool to select an object with a well-defined edge.

Some images aren't quite as clear-cut as the ones you've silhouetted so far. In fact, many images have both hard and soft edges, and/or very fine detail that needs to be isolated from its background (think of a model's blowing hair overlapping the title on the cover of a magazine). In this type of image, other tools can be used to create a very detailed selection based on the color in the image.

1. **With forefathers.psd open, hide the Bottle layer and show Layer 3.**

2. **Rename Layer 3 as Quill and zoom out so you can see the entire feather.**

3. **Choose the Magic Wand tool (under the Quick Selection tool). In the Options bar, make sure the New Selection button is active and set the Tolerance field to 32.**

   The Magic Wand tool is an easy way to select large areas of solid color.

   The first four options in the Options bar are the same as those for the Marquee tools (New Selection, Add to Selection, Subtract from Selection, and Intersect with Selection).

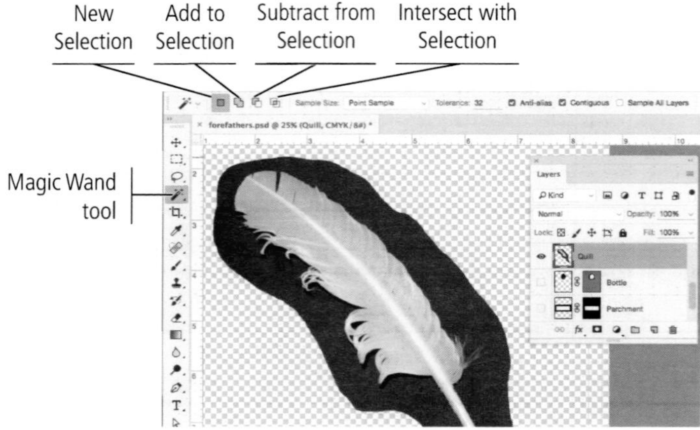

   Tolerance is the degree of variation between the color you click and the colors Photoshop will select; higher tolerance values select a larger range based on the color you click. If you're trying to select a very mottled background (for example), you should increase the tolerance; be careful, however, because increasing the tolerance might select too large a range of colors if the parts of the foreground object falls within the tolerance range.

   The **Anti-alias** check box, selected by default, allows edges to blend more smoothly into the background, preventing a jagged, stair-stepped appearance.

   When **Contiguous** is selected, the Magic Wand tool only selects adjacent areas of the color; unchecking this option allows you to select all pixels within the color tolerance, even if some pixels are non-contiguous (for example, inside the shape of the letter Q).

   By default, selections relate to the active layer only. You can check Sample All Layers to make a selection of all layers in the file.

   The **Refine Edge** button opens the same dialog box you used when you isolated the parchment image with the Quick Selection tool.

Note:

The 'W' key automatically picks and toggles between the Magic Wand and the Quick Selection tools (both in the same place on the Tools panel).

Note:

Using any of the selection tools, press Shift and select again to add to the current selection. Press Option/Alt and select again to subtract from the current selection. If you use these modifier keys, you'll see a plus sign (Add To) or minus sign (Subtract From) in the tool cursor.

Note:

Anti-aliasing is the process of blending shades of pixels to create the illusion of sharp lines in a raster image.

4. **Click anywhere in the blue area of the image.**

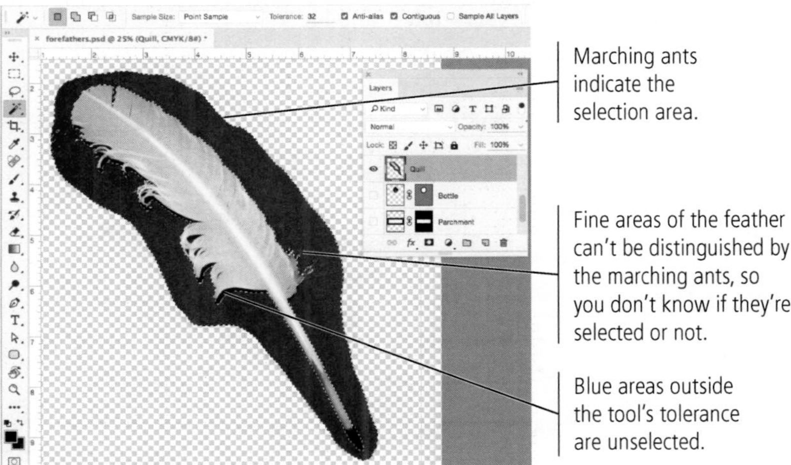

Marching ants indicate the selection area.
Fine areas of the feather can't be distinguished by the marching ants, so you don't know if they're selected or not.
Blue areas outside the tool's tolerance are unselected.

5. **Choose Select>Deselect to turn off the current selection.**

   Although you could keep adding to the selection with the Magic Wand tool, the marching ants can't really show the fine detail, and they don't show shades of gray. There's a better way to isolate the feather from its blue background.

Note:

Press Command/ Control-D to turn off the current selection.

6. **Choose Select>Color Range.**

7. **Make sure the Localized Color Clusters option is unchecked.**

   This option can be used to select specific areas of a selected color. When this option is checked, the Range slider defines how far away (in physical distance) a color from the point you click can be located and still be included in the selection.

8. **At the bottom of the dialog box, choose None in the Selection Preview menu.**

   The options here are the same as those in the Refine Edge dialog box.

9. **Set the Fuzziness value to 24 and click anywhere in the blue area around the feather image (in the document window).**

   Fuzziness is similar to the Tolerance setting for the Magic Wand tool. Higher Fuzziness values allow you to select more variation from the color you click.

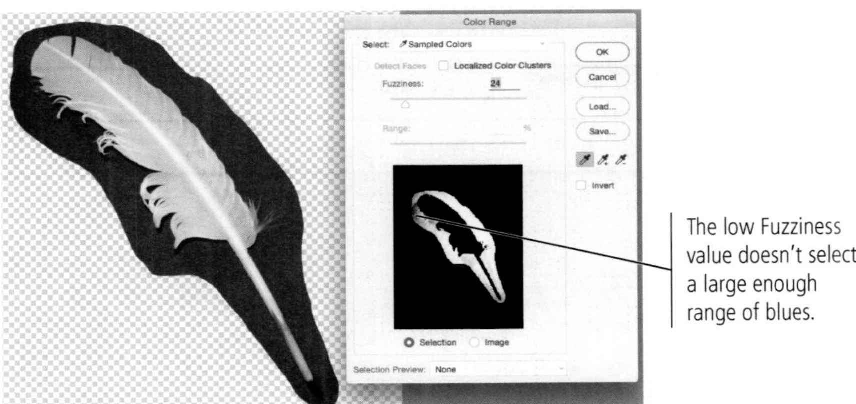

9. **Change the Fuzziness value to `60` and watch the effect on the dialog box preview.**

   Changing the Fuzziness value expands (higher numbers) or contracts (lower numbers) your selection. Be careful, however, since higher fuzziness values also eliminate very fine lines and details.

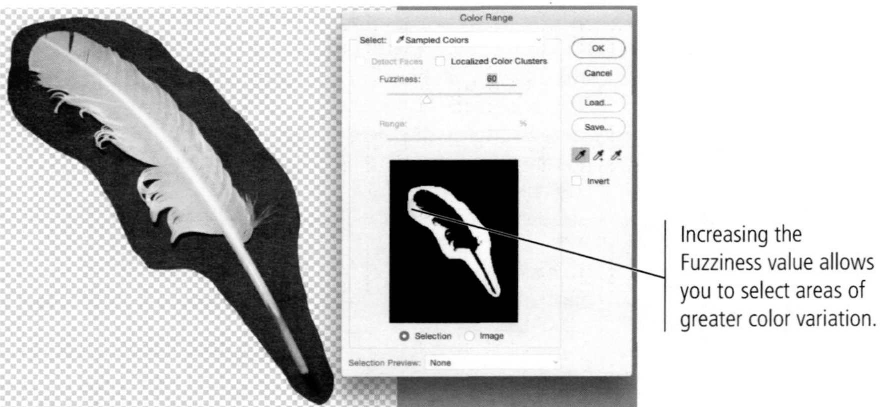

Increasing the Fuzziness value allows you to select areas of greater color variation.

10. **Choose White Matte in the Selection Preview menu.**

    By changing the Selection Preview mode, you can more easily determine exactly what is selected. Using the White Matte preview, anything visible is selected.

    You can preview color range selections in the image window as grayscale (areas outside the selection are shown in shades of gray), against a black matte (unselected areas are shown in black), against a white matte (unselected areas are shown in white), or using the default Quick Mask settings. If you choose None in the Selection Preview menu, the document window displays the normal image.

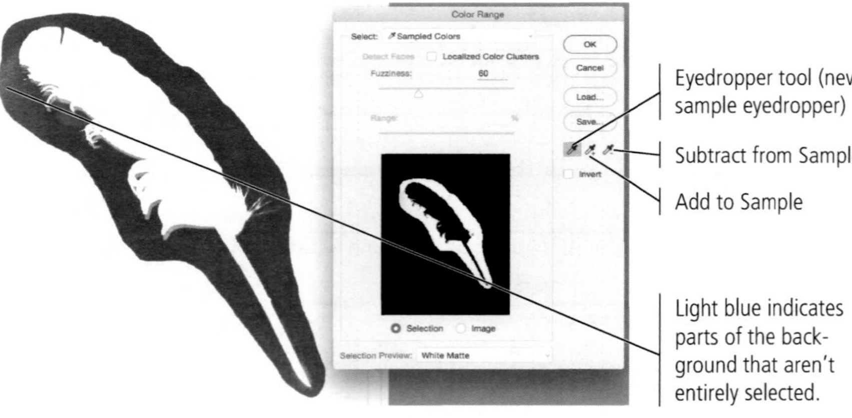

Eyedropper tool (new sample eyedropper)

Subtract from Sample

Add to Sample

Light blue indicates parts of the background that aren't entirely selected.

Note:

Because the dialog box preview is so small, we prefer to rely on the preview in the document window, which is controlled in the Selection Preview menu at the bottom of the dialog box.

Depending on where you clicked, your selection might not exactly match what you see in our screen shot. For now, the important point is to know that the visible areas indicate the current selection.

11. **Click the Add to Sample eyedropper and click in the image where parts of the blue background are not shown in full strength (light blue).**

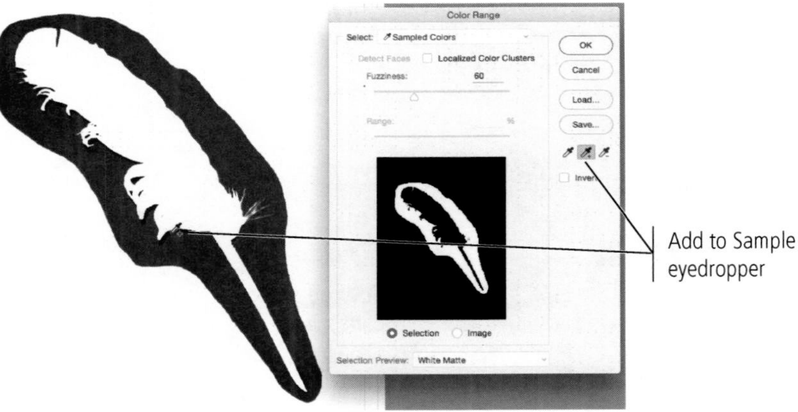

12. **Check the Invert box in the Color Range dialog box.**

Because your goal is to isolate the feather and not the background, it helps to look at what you want to keep instead of what you want to remove.

13. **Continue adding to (or subtracting from, if necessary) your selection until you are satisfied that all the blue background is gone.**

14. **Click OK when you're satisfied with your selection.**

When you return to the image window, the marching ants indicate the current selection. In the Color Range dialog box, you selected the blue and inverted the selection — in other words, your selection is everything that isn't blue.

If you zoom out to see the entire file, you'll see the marching ants surround the file as well as the blue background. Since the transparent area is not blue, it is included in the selection.

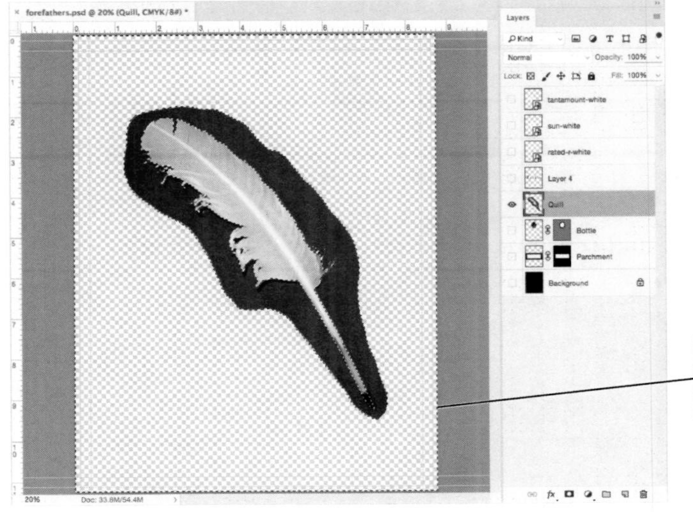

Marching ants surround the image edge.

15. **Choose the Magic Wand tool in the Tools panel and choose the Subtract from Selection option on the Options bar.**

16. **Click anywhere in the transparent area (the gray-and-white checkerboard) to remove that area from the selection.**

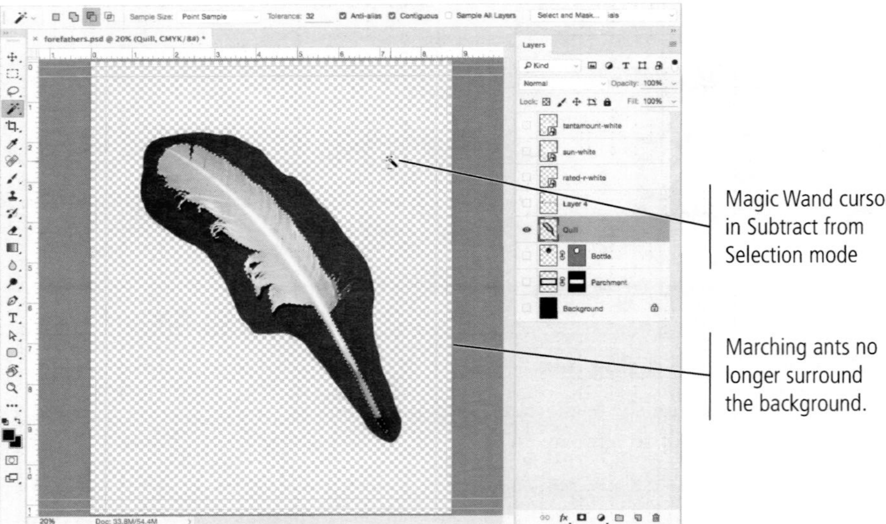

17. **In the Layers panel, click the Add Layer Mask button.**

    Similar to the vector mask you created in the previous exercise, this layer mask shows a new icon linked to the layer icon. A layer mask works on the same principle as the vector mask, except that the layer mask is raster-based instead of vector-based. You can disable the layer mask in the same way you disabled the vector mask in the previous exercise.

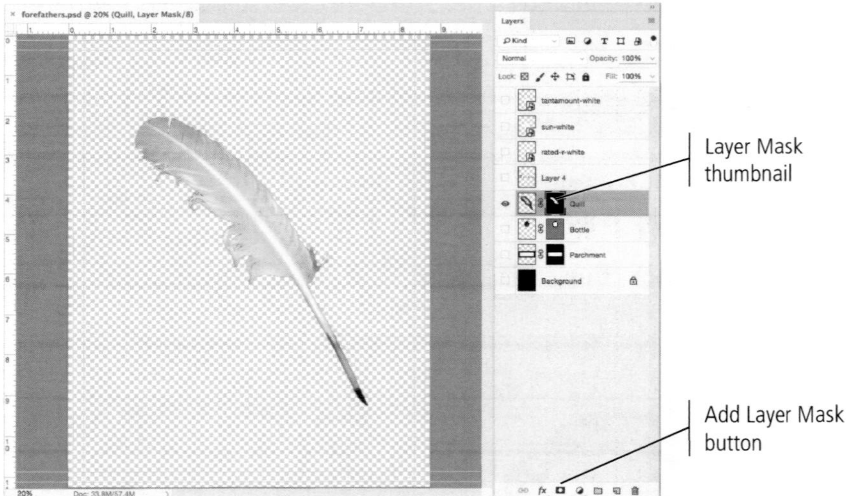

18. **Save the file and continue to the next stage of the project.**

Stage 4 Managing Multiple Layers

Your ad file has most of the necessary pieces. If you show all of the layers, however, you'll still see a bunch of stacked images. It's not yet an actual design, just a pile of images. When you composite images into a cohesive design, you almost certainly need to manipulate and transform some of the layers to make all the pieces work together.

Photoshop includes a number of tools for managing layers, from resizing the layer (as you did for the parchment) to rotating and flipping layers, to aligning different layers to each other, to grouping individual layers so you can work on multiple images at once.

Manipulate and Arrange Layers

1. **With `forefathers.psd` open, hide the Quill layer and show the Background, Parchment, and Layer 4 layers.**

2. **Rename Layer 4 as `Title`.**

   Right now the title is too large to fit into the parchment layer, so you need to resize it.

3. **With the Title layer selected in the Layers panel, choose Edit>Transform>Scale.**

Note:

Press Command/Control-T to display the transform handles.

4. **Click one of the corner handles, press Shift, and drag until the Options bar shows the layer at approximately 85%.**

   Because you pressed Shift, the layer automatically rescales proportionally.

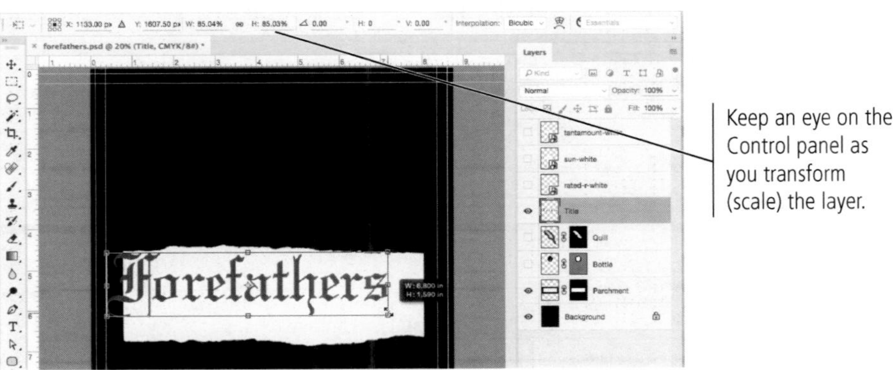

Keep an eye on the Control panel as you transform (scale) the layer.

   Once you've resized the title to fit into the parchment, you need to reposition the title in the center of the parchment. You could do this manually, but Photoshop includes tools that make this task much easier.

5. **Press Return/Enter to commit (finalize) the rescaling.**

6. **Using the Move tool, click and drag the Title layer content until smart guides show it aligned horizontally and vertically to the canvas.**

   Remember, you earlier aligned the Parchment layer content to be centered on the canvas, so this step aligns the Title layer content to the Parchment layer as well as to the canvas.

> *Note:*
>
> *Command/Control-clicking a layer thumbnail results in a selection around the contents of that layer.*

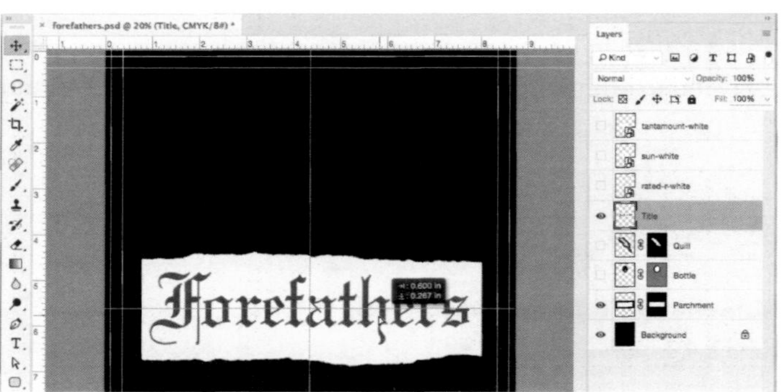

7. **In the Layers panel, press Command/Control and click the Parchment layer name to add that layer to the active selection.**

   Since the Title layer was already selected, the Parchment layer should now be a second selected (highlighted) layer.

   You can select noncontiguous layers by pressing Command/Control. You can select contiguous layers by pressing Shift while you click.

8. **With the two layers selected, click the Create a New Group button at the bottom of the panel.**

   This button creates a group that automatically contains the selected layers. The new group is automatically named "Group N" (N is simply a sequential number); of course, you can rename a layer group just as easily as you can rename a layer.

Click here to open the panel Options menu.
Two layers are selected.
Create a New Group button
The new group automatically contains the selected layers.

> *Note:*
>
> *You can also choose New Group from Layers in the panel Options menu.*

   To create a new empty layer group, make sure nothing is selected in the Layers panel before clicking the Create a New Group button. Alternatively, choose New Group in the panel Options menu; this option results in an empty layer group even if layers are currently selected.

9. **Double-click the Group 1 name in the Layers panel to highlight it, then type** Parchment Title**. Press Return/Enter to finalize the new layer group name.**

   As with any other layer, you should name groups based on what they contain so you can easily identify them later.

10. Click the arrow to the left of the Parchment Title group name to expand the layer group.

You have to expand the layer group to be able to access and edit individual layers in the group. If you select the entire layer group, you can move all layers within the group at the same time. Layers in the group maintain their position relative to one another.

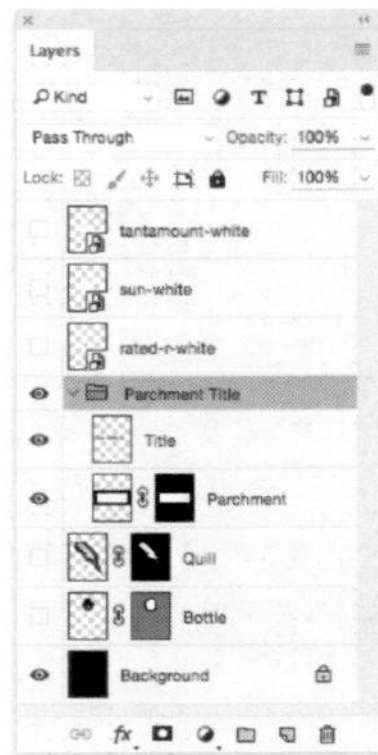

Note:

You can click the eye icon for a layer folder to hide the entire layer group (and all layers inside the folder).

11. Collapse the group by clicking the arrow left of the group name.

12. With the Parchment Title group selected in the Layers panel, use the Move tool to position the Parchment Title group in the bottom third of the document window.

Because the current selection is the layer group, both layers contained within that group are moved in the document window.

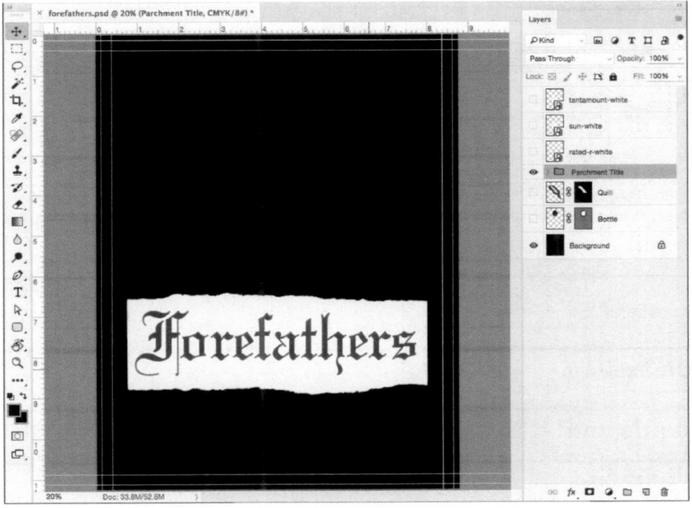

13. Save the file and continue to the next exercise.

Create a Nested Group

1. **With forefathers.psd open, show and select the Bottle layer.**

2. **In the Layers panel, click the Bottle layer and drag up until a heavy bar appears above the Parchment Title layer group.**

   You can move a layer to any position in the **stacking order** (the top-to-bottom position of a layer) by simply dragging it to a new position in the Layers panel.

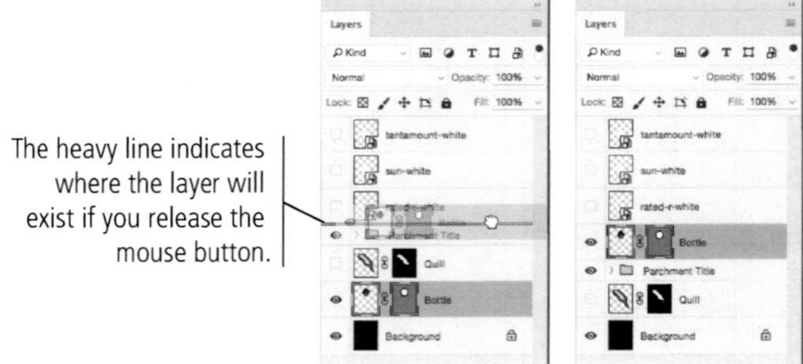

The heavy line indicates where the layer will exist if you release the mouse button.

3. **With the Bottle layer selected, press Command/Control-T to enter into Free Transform mode. Use the Options bar to scale the layer to 40% proportionally.**

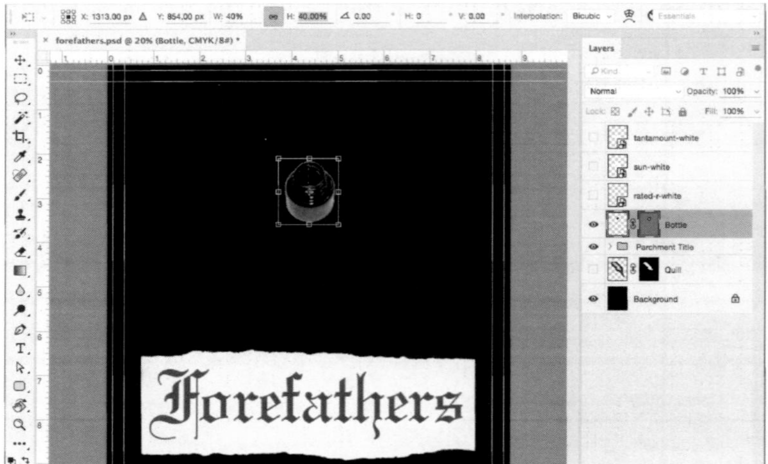

4. **Press Return/Enter to finalize the scaling.**

5. **Using the Move tool, drag the bottle until it is directly above the "he" in the title.**

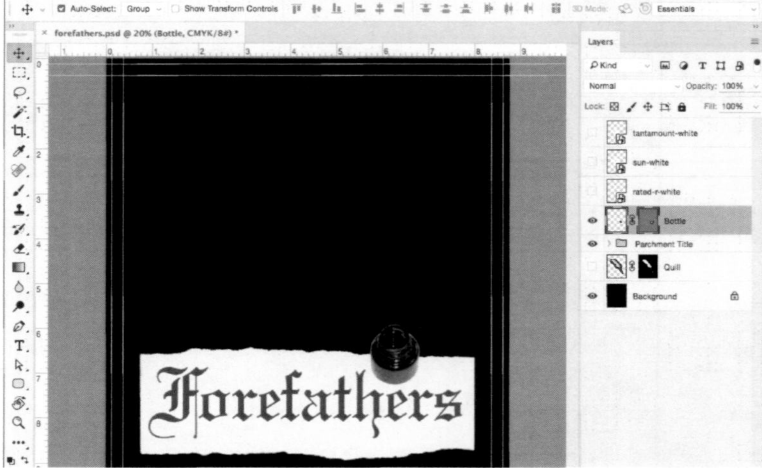

6. **Show and select the Quill layer. In the Layers panel, move it above the Bottle layer.**

7. **With the Quill layer selected, enter into Free Transform mode and resize it to 65% proportionally.**

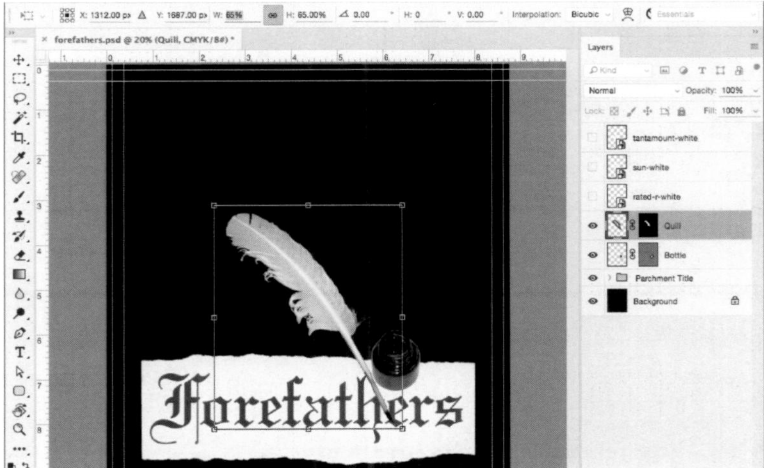

8. **Press Return/Enter to finalize the scaling.**

9. **With the quill layer still selected, choose Edit>Transform>Flip Horizontal.**

10. **Using the Move tool, drag the selected layer so that the quill image overlaps the "er" in the title, and the tip is within the edges of the parchment. (Use the following image as a placement guide.)**

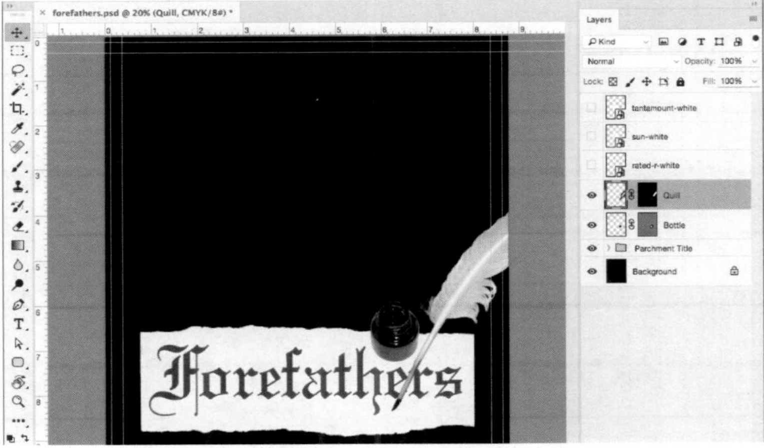

11. **In the Layers panel, select the Bottle and Quill layers and group them together in a group named `Bottle and Quill`.**

12. **Click the new layer group and drag down. When a heavy border appears around the Parchment Title group, release the mouse button.**

    This places the Bottle and Quill group inside the Parchment Title group (called nesting).

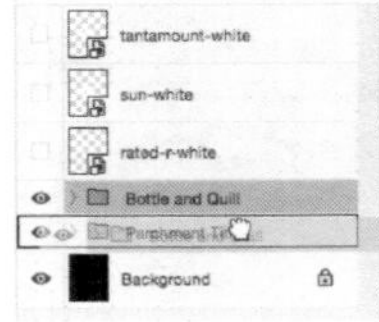

12. **Expand the Parchment Title layer group.**

    The nested group is automatically placed at the bottom of the group's stacking order, so the bottle and quill are behind the parchment.

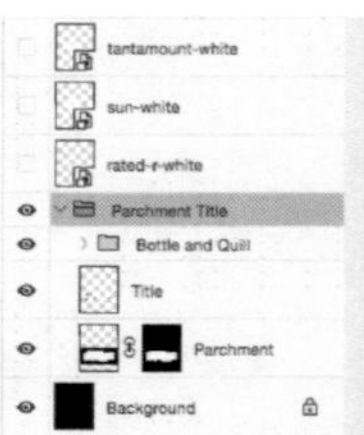

13. **Collapse the Parchment Title layer group.**

14. **Save the file, then continue to the next exercise.**

Finish the Ad

1. **With forefathers.psd open, show the three remaining layers (the logo Smart Object layers).**

2. **Resize the Sun logo to 13% and drag it to the bottom-right corner (inside the live area guides of the smaller ad).**

3. **Resize the Tantamount logo to 20% and drag it to the bottom live area guide, about 1/4" to the left of the Sun logo.**

4. **Resize the rating logo to 45%. Drag it to the bottom-left corner of the live area.**

5. **Using smart guides, align the vertical centers of all three logo layers.**

6. **Combine the three logo layers in a layer group named Logos.**

7. **Choose File>Place Embedded to place the file declaration.psd (from the WIP>Liberty folder) as a Smart Object.**

8. **Make sure the placed file is scaled at 100% and reaches all edges of the image.**

    Placed files are sometimes automatically scaled below 100% when you place them. To check, choose Edit>Transform>Scale and look at the W or H field in the Options bar.

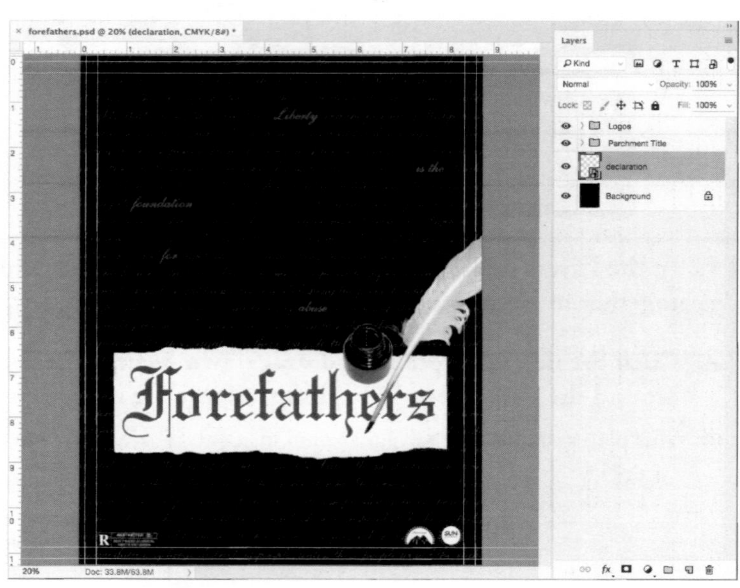

9. **In the Layers panel, drag the declaration layer below the Parchment Title layer group.**

    Be careful that you don't drop the declaration layer onto the Parchment Title group folder, which would place it inside that group instead of behind it.

10. **Save the file and continue to the final stage of the project.**

Stage 5 Saving Files for Multiple Media

At the beginning of the project, you saved this file in Photoshop's native format (PSD). However, many Photoshop projects require saving the completed file in at least one other format. Many artists prefer to leave all files in the PSD format since there is only one file to track. Others prefer to send only flattened TIFF files of their artwork because the individual elements can't be changed.

Ultimately, the format (or formats, if the file is being used in multiple places) you use will depend on where and how the file is being placed. For this project, you have been asked to create a flattened, high-resolution, CMYK TIFF file and a low-resolution JPEG file for use on a Web site.

Save a Flat TIFF File

The printed magazine suggests that ads created in Photoshop be submitted as flat TIFF files. Since you designed the ad to incorporate bleeds for pages up to 8.5 × 11″, all you have to do for this version is save the file in the appropriate format.

1. **With forefathers.psd open, choose File>Save As.**

2. **If necessary, navigate to your WIP>Liberty folder as the target location for saving the final files.**

   The Save As dialog box defaults to the last-used location. If you continued the entire way through this project without stopping, you won't have to navigate.

3. **Open the Format/Save as Type menu and choose TIFF.**

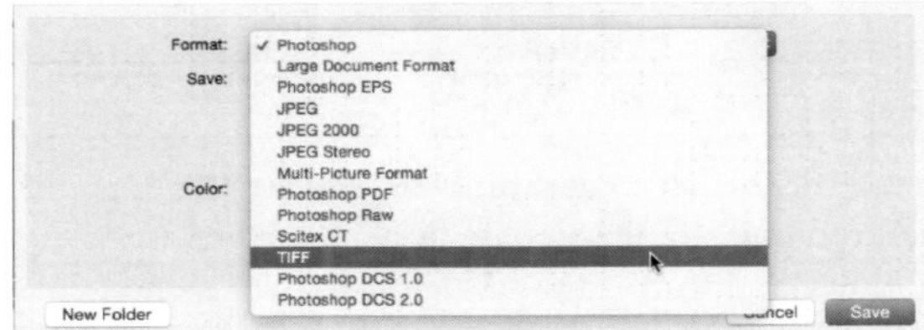

4. **In the lower half of the dialog box, uncheck the Layers option.**

   Because this file contains layers, this option is probably checked by default. If your file contained alpha channels, annotations, or spot colors, those check boxes would also be available. When you uncheck the Layers option, the As a Copy check box is automatically activated.

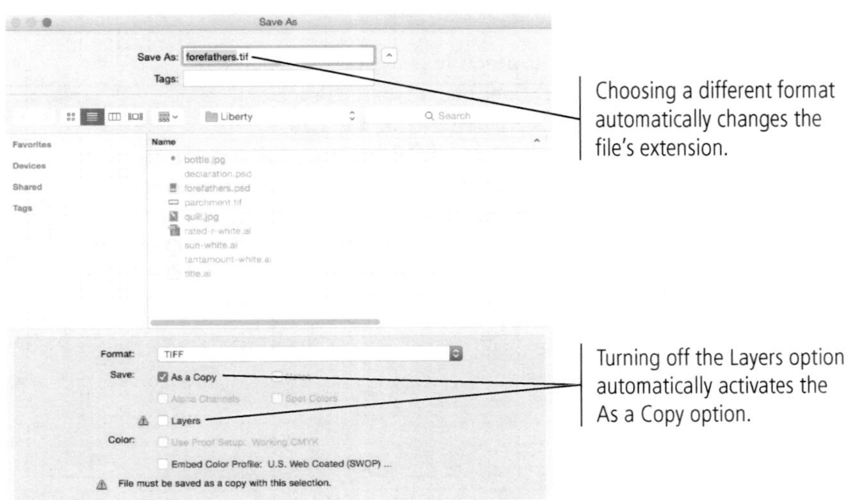

Choosing a different format automatically changes the file's extension.

Turning off the Layers option automatically activates the As a Copy option.

> ***Note:***
>
> *You can manually flatten a file by choosing Layer>Flatten Image.*

5. **Click Save.**

   Most file formats include additional options, which you should understand before you simply click OK.

6. **In the TIFF Options dialog box, make sure the (Image Compression) None radio button is selected.**

   TIFF files can be compressed (made smaller) using one of three schemes:

   - **None** (as the name implies) applies no compression to the file. This option is safe if file size is not an issue, but digital file transmission often requires files to be smaller than a full-page, multi-layered Photoshop file.
   - **LZW** (Lempel-Ziv-Welch) compression is lossless, which means all file data is maintained in the compressed file.
   - **ZIP** compression is also lossless, but is not supported by all desktop publishing software (especially older versions).
   - **JPEG** is a **lossy** compression scheme, which means some data will be thrown away to reduce the file size. If you choose JPEG compression, the Quality options determine how much data can be discarded. Maximum quality means less data is thrown out and the file is larger. Minimum quality discards the most data and results in the smaller file size.

7. **Leave the Pixel Order and Byte Order options at their default values.**

   Pixel Order determines how channel data is encoded. The Interleaved (RGBRGB) option is the default; Per Channel (RRGGBB) is called "planar" order.

   Byte Order determines which platform can use the file, although this is somewhat deceptive. Even in older versions of most desktop publishing software, Macintosh systems can read the PC byte order but Windows couldn't read the Macintosh byte order. If you don't know which platform will ultimately be used, choose IBM PC.

   Save Image Pyramid creates a tiered file with multiple resolution versions; this isn't widely used or supported by other applications, so you can typically leave it unchecked.

   If your file contains transparency, the Save Transparency check box will be available. If you don't choose this option, transparent areas will be white in the saved file.

8. **Click OK to save the file.**

   When you return to the document, the original native Photoshop file is still active. The TIFF file that you just created is saved in the target location, but it is not the active file because the As a Copy option was checked in the Save As dialog box. If you had included layers and not intentionally check the As a Copy option, the active file would be the TIFF file that you saved instead of the original native Photoshop file.

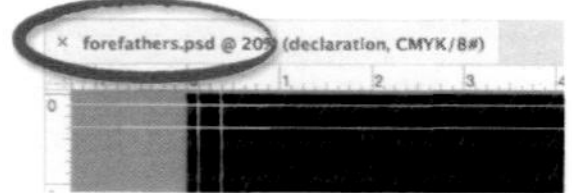

9. **Continue to the next exercise.**

Save a JPEG File for Digital Media

Your client has also requested a low-resolution JPEG file using the RGB color model. Several extra steps are required to create this file with the required settings.

1. **With `forefathers.psd` open in Photoshop, choose File>Save As.**

   To protect your work, you are saving this file with a different file name *before* making significant destructive changes.

2. **Choose JPEG in the Format/Save as Type menu. Change the file name to `forefathers-web.jpg`, then click Save.**

   JPEG files do not support multiple layers; when you choose the JPEG format, the Layers option is automatically unchecked and the As a Copy option is automatically activated.

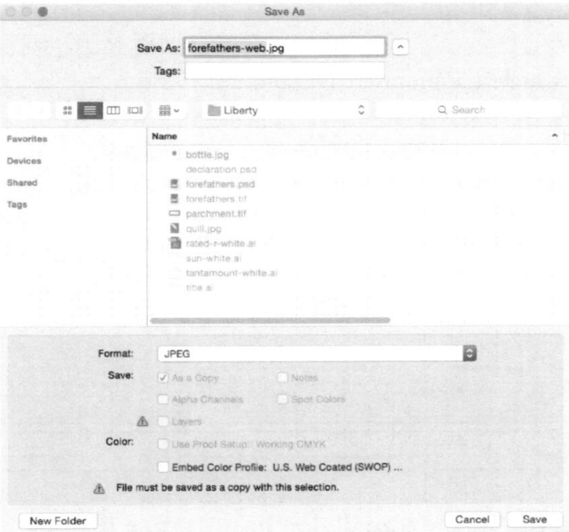

3. **In the JPEG Options dialog box, choose High in the Quality menu and then click OK.**

   You can use these options to reduce the weight of the resulting JPEG file. Keep in mind that JPEG is a lossy compression scheme; the application throws away what it perceives as redundant data to reduce the file weight. Lower quality settings mean more compression and smaller file weight (and thus, shorter download time), but you might notice significant deterioration in image quality.

   The right side of the dialog box shows the estimated file size — in this case, just over 1 megabyte.

4. **Close the forefathers.psd file.**

   Remember, when the As a Copy option is checked, the file you had open before the save remains active in the document window. You need to manually open the JPEG file so you can make the necessary changes for Web distribution.

5. **Open `forefathers-web.jpg` from your WIP>Liberty folder.**

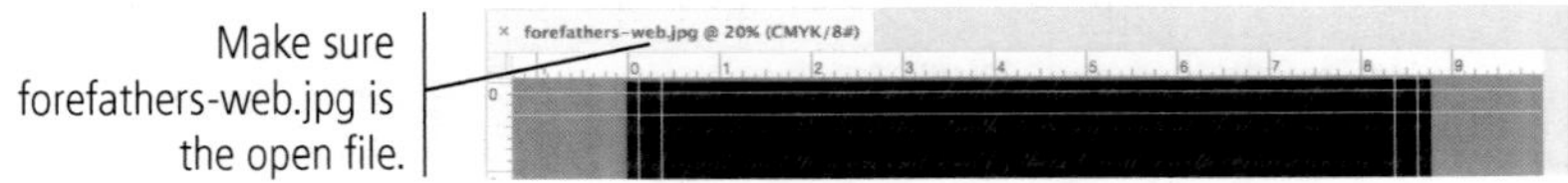

Make sure forefathers-web.jpg is the open file.

6. **With `forefathers-web.jpg` open, choose Image>Mode>RGB Color.**

   Remember, you created this file using the CMYK color model, which requires four color channels — one for each primary color (cyan, magenta, yellow, and black). Converting the image from CMYK to RGB means the file now requires only three channels (red, green, and blue). This significantly reduces the file weight, which will help to reduce the download time.

Note:

Converting colors from one model to another can result in color shift if you are converting from a larger model to one with a smaller gamut (for example, from RGB to CMYK). Converting from CMYK to RGB is usually safe, and does not typically result in noticeable color shift.

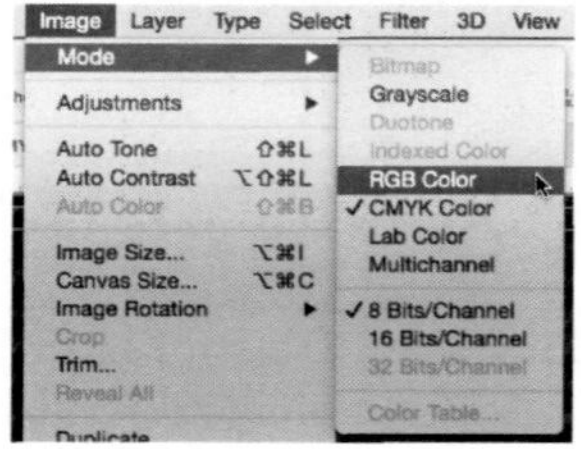

7. **Choose Image>Image Size.**

   You created this file at 300 pixels per inch, which is appropriate for commercial print requirements. For Web distribution, however, 300 ppi is far more than you need. To further reduce the file weight and resulting download time, you should downsample the file to 72 ppi — an appropriate resolution for most Web display requirements.

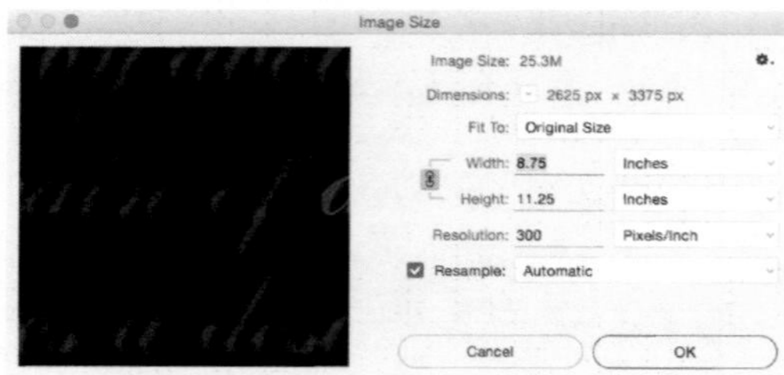

8. **With the Resample option checked in the Image Size dialog box, change the Resolution field to `72`.**

   When the Resample option is checked, changing the resolution does not affect the file's physical size; the actual number of pixels is reduced. In this case, at 72 ppi, only 630 × 810 pixels are required for a file that is 8.75 × 11.25″.

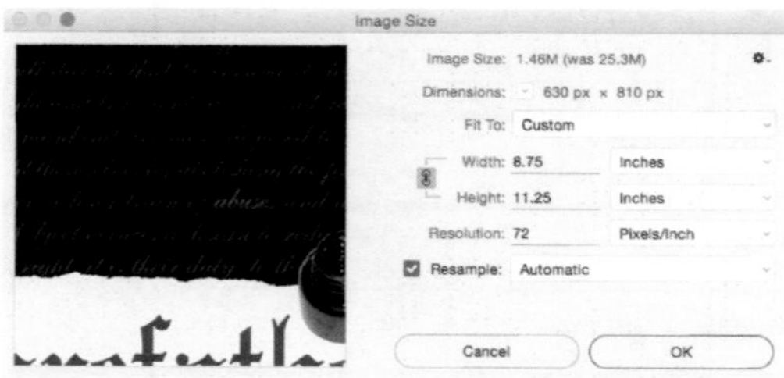

9. **Click OK to finalize the change.**

10. **Choose File>Save As. Leave the options at their default values and click Save.**

    You are using the Save As process so that you can review the compression settings that will be applied in the resulting JPEG file.

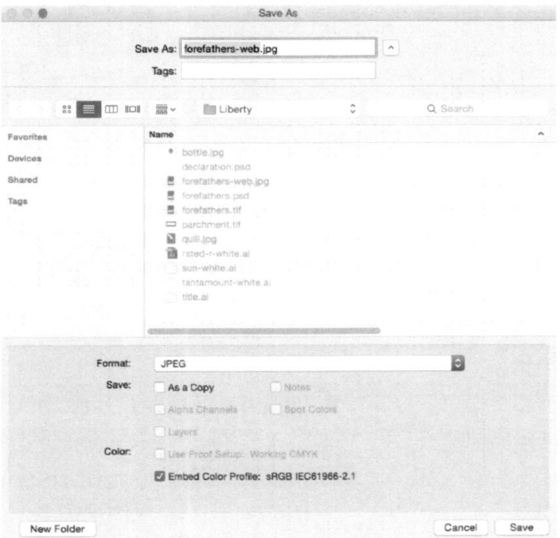

11. **In the resulting warning message, click Replace/OK.**

    Because you did not change the file name, you are asked to confirm whether you want to overwrite the existing JPEG file.

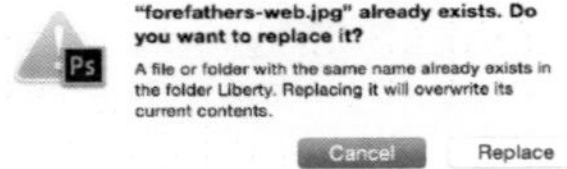

12. **In the JPEG Options dialog box, make sure High is selected in the Quality menu and click OK.**

    When you first saved the file at the beginning of this exercise, the resulting JPEG file was just over 1 megabyte. By converting the color mode and reducing the resolution, the file is now approximately 152 kilobytes.

13. **Close the active file.**

fill in the blank

1. The _______________ is the range of visible and available color in a particular color model.
2. Commercial print applications typically require _______________ pixels per inch.
3. A _______________ is a linked file that you placed into a Photoshop document.
4. The _______________ is context sensitive, providing access to different functions depending on what tool is active.
5. The _______________ is the final size of a printed page.
6. The _______________ tool is used to draw irregular-shaped selection marquees.
7. The _______________ tool is used to create precise shapes based on anchor points and connecting line segments.
8. The _______________ tool can be used to drag layer contents to another position within the image, or into another open document.
9. When selecting color ranges, the _______________ value determines how much of the current color range falls into the selection.
10. _______________ is a lossy compression method that is best used when large file size might be a problem.

short answer

1. Briefly describe the difference between raster images and vector graphics.

2. Briefly explain three separate methods for isolating an image from its background.

3. Briefly describe the relationship between anchor points and handles (direction lines) on a vector path.

Portfolio Builder Project

Use what you learned in this project to complete the following freeform exercise.
Carefully read the art director and client comments, then create your design to meet the needs of the project.
Use the space below to sketch ideas; when finished, write a brief explanation of the reasoning behind your design.

art director comments

Tantamount Studios is pleased with your work on the Forefathers ad, and they would like to hire you again to create the ad concept and final files for another movie that they're releasing early next year.

To complete this project, you should:

- ❏ Find appropriate background and foreground images for the movie theme (see the client's comments at right).
- ❏ Incorporate the title artwork, logos, and rating placeholder that the client provided. (These files are included in the **Airborne_Web16_PB.zip** archive on the Student Files Web page.)
- ❏ Composite the different elements into a single completed file; save both a layered version and a flattened version.

client comments

The movie is titled *Above and Beyond*. Although the story is fictionalized, it will focus on the men who led the first U.S. Airborne unit (the 501st), which suffered more than 2,000 casualties in the European theater of World War II.

We already have the title artwork, which we sent to your art director.

We don't have any other images in mind, but the final ad should reflect the time period (the 1940s) of the movie. The 501st Airborne was trained to parachute into battle, so you should probably incorporate some kind of parachute image.

This movie is another joint venture between Sun and Tantamount, so both logos need to be included in the new ad. It isn't rated yet, so please use the "This Movie Is Not Yet Rated" artwork as a placeholder.

Create this ad big enough to fit on an 8.5 × 11″ page, but keep the live area an inch inside the trim, so the ad can be used in different sized magazines.

project justification

Project Summary

Making selections is arguably the most important skill you will learn to do in Photoshop. Selections are so important that Photoshop dedicates an entire menu to the process.

As you created the ad in this project, you used a number of skills and techniques that you will apply in many (if not all) projects you build in Photoshop. You learned a number of ways to make both simple and complex selections — and you'll learn additional methods in later projects. You also learned that after you make a selection, you can create composite images, move pixels to silhouette an object against its background, and much more.

Finally, you learned how to save files for Web distribution by changing color mode and reducing file resolution.

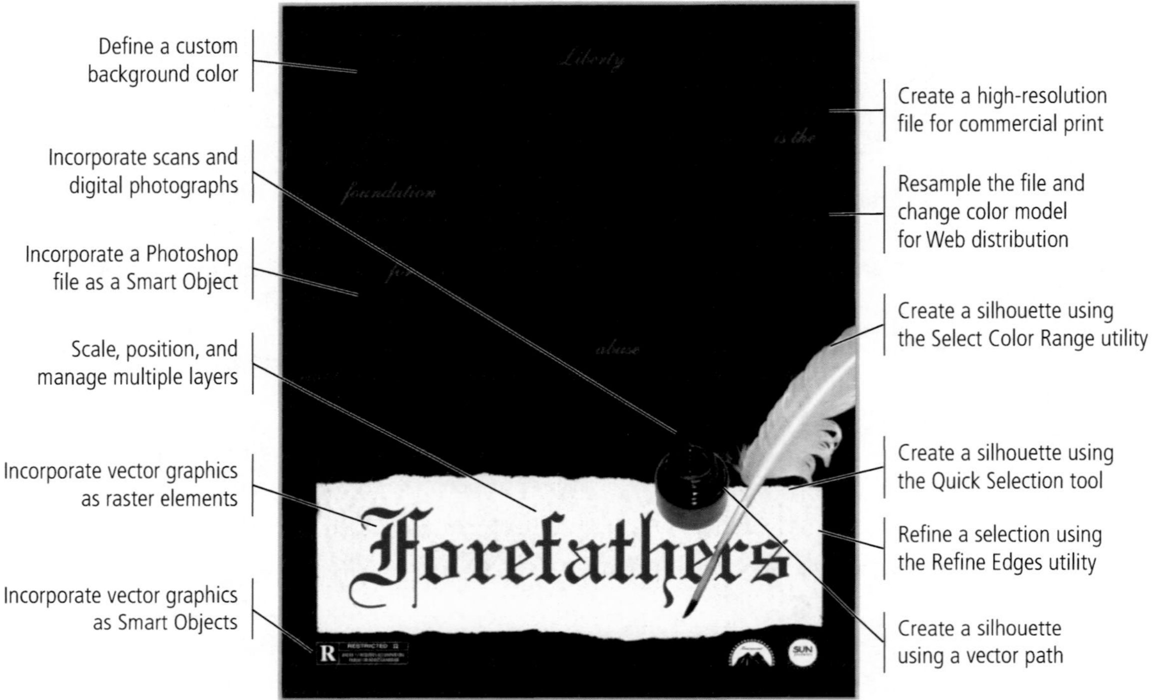
Define a custom background color
Incorporate scans and digital photographs
Incorporate a Photoshop file as a Smart Object
Scale, position, and manage multiple layers
Incorporate vector graphics as raster elements
Incorporate vector graphics as Smart Objects
Create a high-resolution file for commercial print
Resample the file and change color model for Web distribution
Create a silhouette using the Select Color Range utility
Create a silhouette using the Quick Selection tool
Refine a selection using the Refine Edges utility
Create a silhouette using a vector path
Forefathers

Web Page Interface

Your client is a photographer in the San Francisco Bay area who has hired your agency to create a new Web site interface. Your job is to take the first draft and add a number of finishing touches to add visual appeal to the overall site. You must then generate the required pieces that will be used by a Web developer to create the functioning HTML file.

This project incorporates the following skills:

- ❑ Using actions and batches to automate repetitive processes and improve productivity
- ❑ Adding depth and visual interest with 3D extrusion and puppet warping
- ❑ Generating image assets from Photoshop layers and layer groups, as required by the HTML developer
- ❑ Communicate design intent using cascading style sheets

Project Meeting

client comments

I really like the general idea that you created. I sorted through some photos and selected six that I want to include as the thumbnails at the bottom of the page. I think they're a good representation of the type of photography I enjoy most.

My only real complaint is that the top part is rather bland. Right now everything is just too horizontal. I don't have a real logo at this point, but is there anything you can do with the word "Metro" to make it a bit more visually interesting? And maybe something to make the longer filmstrip less horizontal too.

art director comments

All of the client's points are reasonable, and you can use Photoshop's built-in tools to meet each of her specific goals.

First, you need to scale down her images to make them fit as thumbnails into the space at the bottom of the layout. I also think it would be a nice touch to convert them to grayscale so the variety of color isn't too distracting in the main interface. Keep in mind, though, that you need to keep the original color images because the Web developer will need them for the actual slideshow widget.

For the top, I want you to bend the filmstrip a bit. That will break the horizontal syndrome, and create a sort of frame around her studio name. You can also use the 3D functionality to add some depth to the studio name itself.

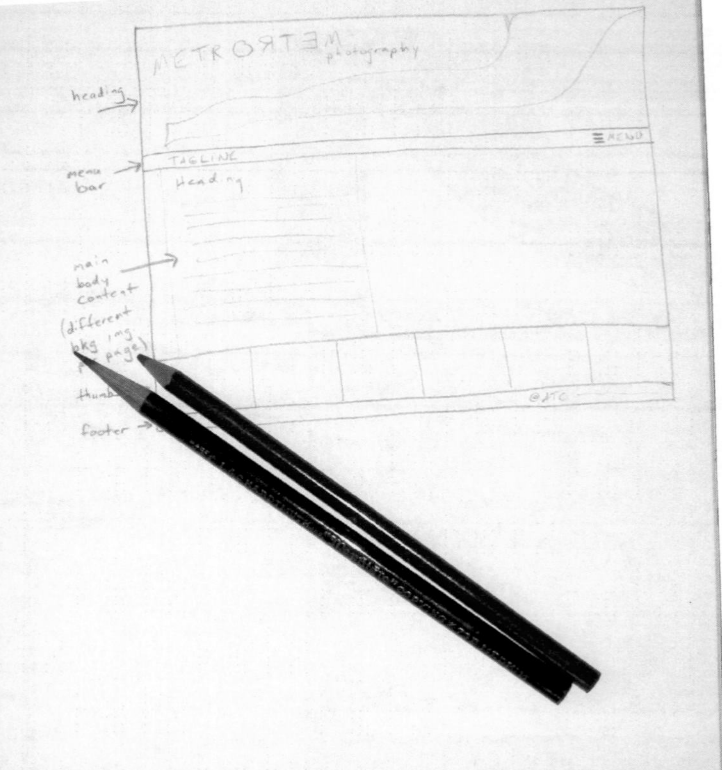

project objectives

To complete this project, you will:

- ❑ Review the initial site design
- ❑ Save an action set
- ❑ Create a new action
- ❑ Batch-process files
- ❑ Place and align thumbnails on the page
- ❑ Extrude a text layer to 3D
- ❑ Use Puppet Warp to transform a layer
- ❑ Generate image assets from layers
- ❑ Copy CSS for text and shape layers

Stage 1 Automating Repetitive Tasks

Actions are some of the most powerful (yet underused) productivity tools in Photoshop. In the simplest terms, actions are miniature programs that run a sequence of commands on a particular image or selected area. An action can initiate most of the commands available in Photoshop — alone or in sequence — to automate repetitive and potentially time-consuming tasks.

Running an action is a fairly simple process: highlight the appropriate action in the Actions panel and click the Play button at the bottom of the panel. Some actions work on an entire image, while others require some initial selection. If you use the actions that shipped with the Photoshop application, the action name tells you (in parentheses) what type of element the action was designed to affect; in most cases, however, you can run an action on other elements without a problem.

The Actions Panel in Depth

PHOTOSHOP FOUNDATIONS

The default Actions panel (Window>Actions) shows the Default Actions set, which contains several pre-built actions. A folder icon indicates an **action set**, which is used to create logical groupings of actions. You can expand an action set to show the actions contained within that set, and you can expand a specific action to show the steps that are saved in that action; any step in an action marked with an arrow can be further expanded to see the details of that step.

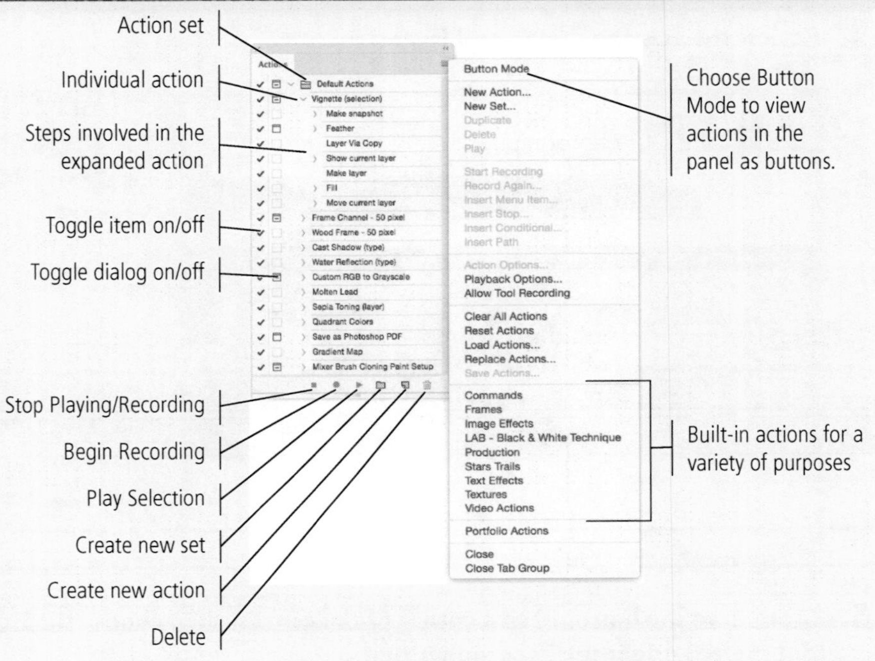

The left column of the Actions panel shows a checkmark next to each action set, individual action, and step within an expanded action. All elements of pre-recorded actions are active by default, which means that playing an action initiates each step within the action. You can deactivate specific steps of an action by clicking the related checkmark. (If the checkmark next to an action is black, all elements of that action are active. If the checkmark is red, one or more steps of that action are inactive.)

Modal Controls

The second column in the Actions panel controls the degree of user interaction required when running an action. If an icon appears in this column, the Photoshop dialog box relevant to that step opens when the action runs. These are called **modal controls**; the action pauses until you take some required action. You can deactivate modal controls for:

- An entire action set by clicking the dialog box icon next to a set name
- An individual action by clicking the icon next to the action name
- A single step by clicking the icon next to the step

If the modal controls are turned off, Photoshop applies the values that were used when the action was recorded. This increases the automatic functionality of the action, but also offers less control over the action's behavior.

Some actions require a certain degree of user interaction, in which case the modal controls can't be entirely deactivated. In this case, the dialog box icon appears grayed out in the panel, even when the remaining modal controls are turned off. (If an action shows a black dialog box icon, all modal controls within the action are active. If an action shows a red dialog box icon, one or more modal controls within the action have been turned off.)

Button Mode

Choosing Button Mode in the panel Options menu makes running an action one step easier. Each action is represented as a colored button, which you can simply click to run the action.

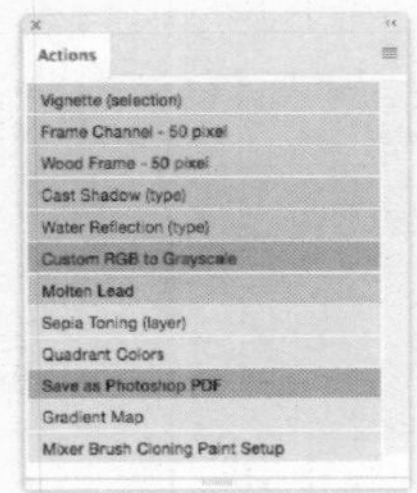

Review the Initial Site Design

Because this project starts from a partially completed file, your first task is to evaluate the existing file and determine what needs to be accomplished.

> *Note:*
>
> *You must install the ATC fonts from the Student Files Web site to complete the rest of this project.*

1. **Download Metro_Web16_RF.zip from the Student Files Web page.**
2. **Expand the ZIP archive in your WIP folder (Macintosh) or copy the archive contents into your WIP folder (Windows).**

   This results in a folder named **Metro**, which contains the files you need for this project.
3. **Open the metro-site.psd file from the WIP>Metro folder. If you get a warning about missing or mismatched color profiles, choose the option to use the embedded profile.**
4. **Review the existing design and layer structure.**

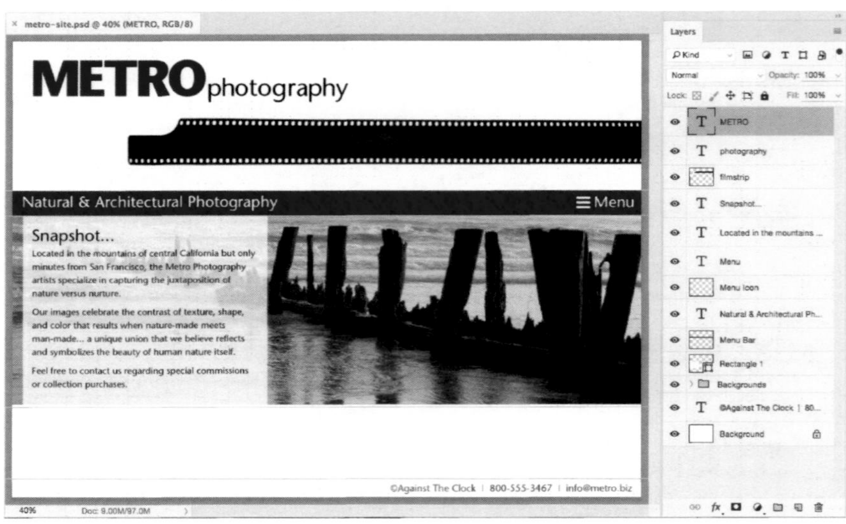

5. **Zoom in to the bottom-right corner of the canvas, then choose the Ruler tool (nested under the Eyedropper tool).**
6. **If you don't see the blue guides, choose View>Show>Guides.**
7. **Click the third horizontal ruler guide from the top of the canvas. Hold down the mouse button and drag down until the tool cursor snaps to the fourth ruler guide.**

   In the Options bar, you can see that the space between guides is 245 pixels high. This is the measurement you need when resizing the gallery images in the next exercise.

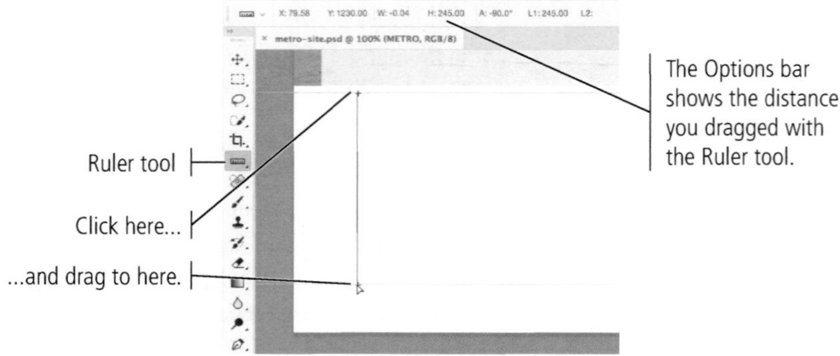

Ruler tool
Click here...
...and drag to here.
The Options bar shows the distance you dragged with the Ruler tool.

8. **Close the file, and then continue to the next exercise.**

Save an Action Set

Whenever you need to perform the same task more than two times, it's a good idea to automate as much of the process as possible. This project requires you to create thumbnails from nine images. Creating a single "negative" thumbnail for this project requires at least five steps:

1. Open the file (any number of clicks, depending on the default location in the Open dialog box).
2. Resize the image to a specific height to fit into the designated space in the site layout (at least two clicks, possibly three if the Resample check box is active, as well as typing the new dimensions).
3. Convert the reduced image to black-and-white.
4. Save the file in a new folder with a revised file name (any number of clicks, depending on the default location in the Save dialog box), as well as typing the new file name.
5. Close the file.

> ***Note:***
>
> *It's important to remember when creating actions that, "just because you can, doesn't mean you should." There are many powerful tools in Photoshop that require human judgment and intervention if they are to be effective. Color correction, for example, is different for every image, and should never be left entirely to a computer to implement.*

This process can be streamlined by using an action, which you have to record only once.

1. **In Photoshop with no file open, open the Actions panel (Window>Actions).**
2. **Choose Clear All Actions from the Actions panel Options menu.**

   Rather than editing an existing action set, you are going to create your own action set to store the action you define. If you did not clear the existing actions, the set you define would include all of the default actions as well as the one you create.

> ***Note:***
>
> *You can add actions to the Actions panel by choosing a defined set or by choosing **Load Actions** in the panel Options menu.*
>
> ***Reset Actions** restores the default set to the Actions panel. You have the option to replace the existing actions or append the default set to the current sets.*
>
> ***Replace Actions** replaces the current action sets with whatever set you load in the resulting dialog box.*

3. **Click OK in the warning message dialog box.**

   Clear All Actions removes everything from the Actions panel. You can also remove a specific action or set from the panel by highlighting the item in the panel and clicking the Delete button, or by choosing Delete from the Actions panel Options menu. These commands remove the actions or sets from the panel, but they do not permanently delete saved actions or sets. If you delete an action from one of the built-in sets, you can reload the set to restore all items that originally existed in the set.

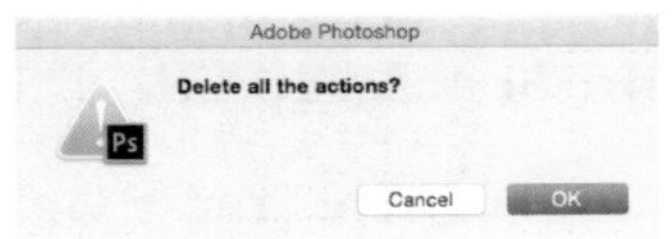

4. **Click the Create New Set button at the bottom of the Actions panel.**

5. **In the New Set dialog box, name the new set Portfolio Actions, and then click OK.**

   You can name the set whatever you prefer, but the action set name should indicate what the set contains, whether it's a set of actions for a specific type of project, for a specific client, or any other logical group.

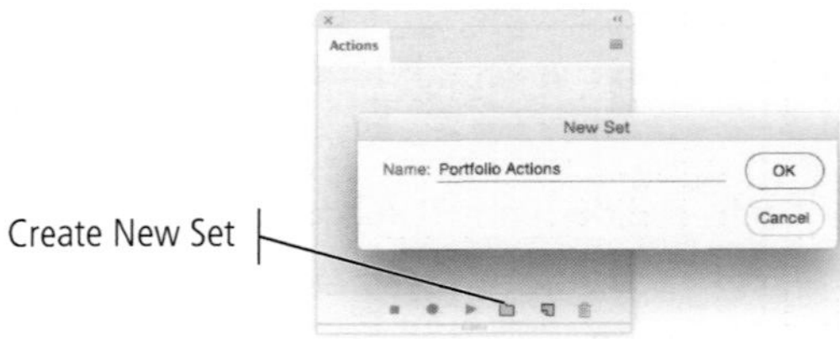

6. **Continue to the next exercise.**

Create a New Action

Recording an action is a fairly simple process: open a file, click the Record button in the Actions panel, and perform the steps you want to save in the action. Click the Stop button to stop recording, either permanently when you're done or temporarily if you need to do something else in the middle of creating the action. (If you stop recording, you can later select the last step in the existing action and start recording again by clicking the Record button.)

1. **In Photoshop, open windmill.jpg from your WIP>Metro>images folder. If you get a profile mismatch warning, use the embedded profile.**

   When you apply this action in the next exercise, you can determine how color profile problems are managed by the automated batch processing.

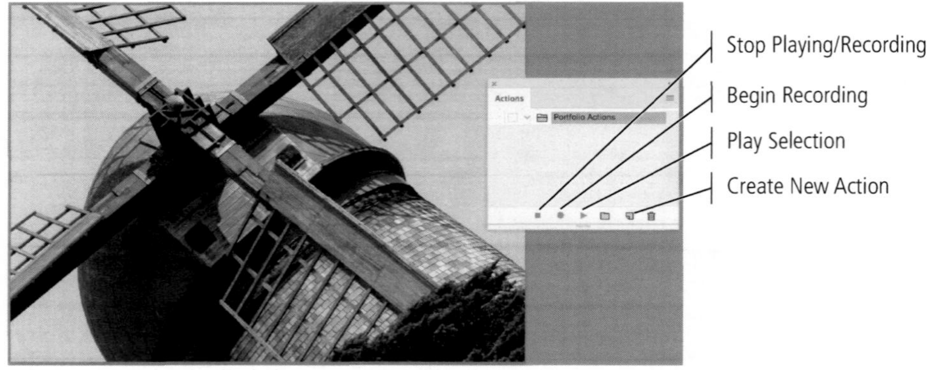

> *Note:*
>
> *You can change the name, keyboard shortcut, and/or button color of any action by selecting it in the Actions panel and choosing Action Options from the panel Options menu.*

2. **Open the Actions panel if necessary, then click the Create New Action button at the bottom of the Actions panel.**

3. **In the New Action dialog box, type Create Web Thumbnail in the Name field.**

   By default, new actions are added to the currently selected set. You can add the action to any open set by choosing from the Set menu. The Function Key menu allows you to assign a keyboard shortcut to the action, so an "F" key (with or without modifiers) can initiate that action. The Color menu defines the color of the button when the Actions panel is viewed in Button mode.

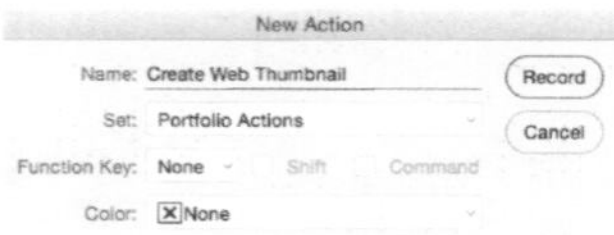

> *Note:*
>
> *As with any user-defined element, you should use descriptive names for your actions.*

4. **Click Record to close the dialog box.**

   In the Actions panel, the Record button automatically becomes red, indicating that you are now recording; anything you do from this point forward is recorded as a step in the action until you intentionally stop the recording by clicking the Stop button at the bottom of the Actions panel.

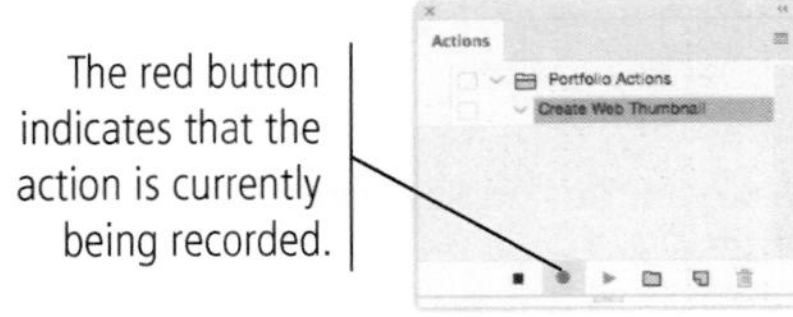

The red button indicates that the action is currently being recorded.

5. **With windmill.jpg open, choose Image>Image Size.**

6. **Make sure the Resample option is checked.**

   You want the thumbnails to be proportionally sized, and you want them to remain at 72 ppi.

7. **With the Constrain Aspect Ratio option active, choose Pixels in the Height Units menu and then change the Pixel Dimensions height to `245 pixels`.**

   Because the Resample option is active, reducing the number of pixels results in a proportionally smaller document size.

The image's physical dimensions are reduced proprtionally.

Change this value to 245 pixels.

Make sure the Resample option is checked.

8. **Click OK to close the Image Size dialog box and apply the change.**

9. **Choose Image>Mode>Grayscale. Read the resulting warning, then click Discard.**

   You are converting to the small thumbnails to grayscale simply for aesthetic purposes, so you don't need to control the precise conversion.

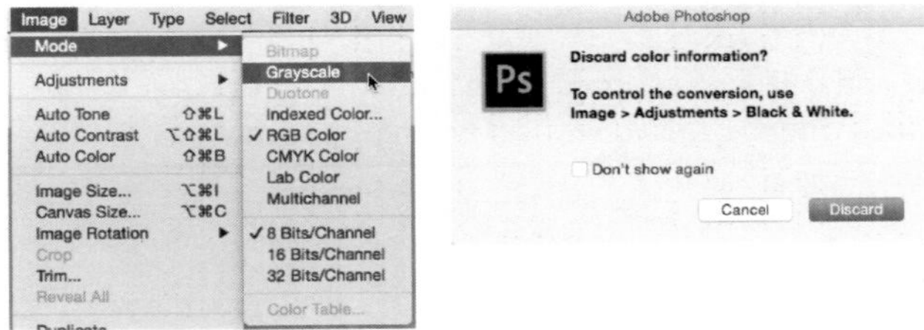

10. **In the Actions panel, click the Stop Playing/Recording button.**

11. **Expand the Image Size item in the Create Web Thumbnail action.**

12. **Click Portfolio Actions in the Actions panel to select the set, then choose Save Actions in the panel Options menu.**

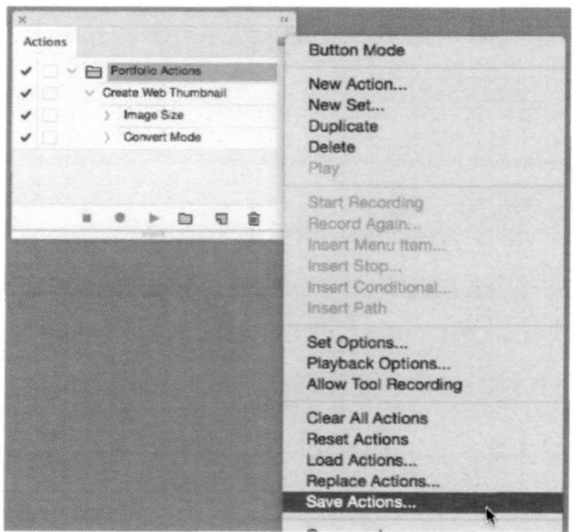

13. **In the Save dialog box, review the options and then click Save.**

Action sets are saved by default in the Photoshop>Presets>Actions folder with the extension ".atn" (which is automatically added for you). If you are using a shared computer, you might not be able to save files in the application's default location. If this is the case, navigate to your WIP>Metro folder to save the Portfolio Actions.atn file.

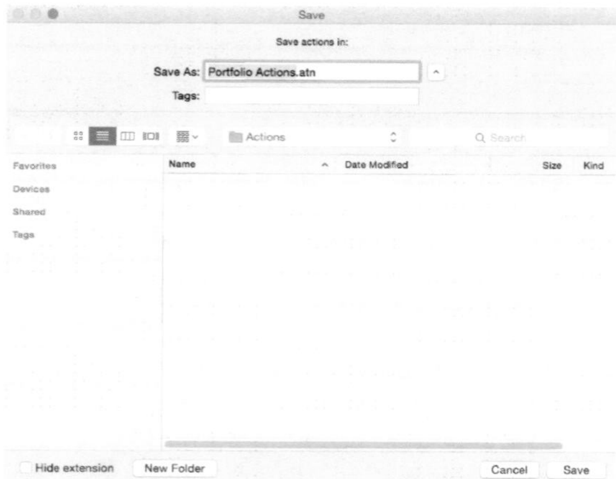

If you make changes to a set — whether you delete an existing action from the set or add your own custom actions — without saving the altered set, you will have to repeat your work the next time you launch Photoshop.

> ***Note:***
>
> *The default file name is the same as the set name that you defined when you created the set.*

> ***Note:***
>
> *Action sets are stored by default in the Presets>Actions folder in the Photoshop Application folder on your computer. You can also load an action from another location, such as when someone sends you an action that was created on another computer.*

14. **Close the windmill.jpg file without saving.**

You don't need to save the changes since this file will be processed when you run the action on the entire images folder.

15. **Continue to the next exercise.**

Inserting Action Stops and Menu Options

Action Stops

When you record actions, you can insert an intentional pause by choosing **Insert Stop** from the Actions panel Options menu. When you insert a stop, the Record Stop dialog box allows you to type a message — for example, specific instructions or reminders to the user — that displays when the action runs.

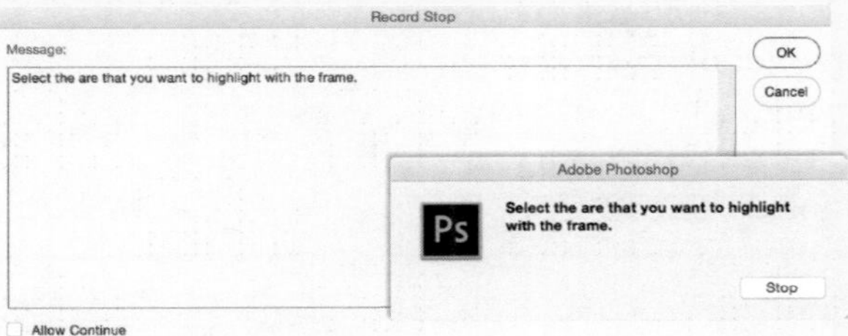

When a user runs the action and the action reaches a stop, the message you entered into the Record Stop dialog box appears. The user must click Stop, perform the required step, and then click the Play button in the Actions panel to complete the rest of the action. (If you check the Allow Continue option when you define the Stop, the resulting message includes a Continue button; if the user clicks Continue, the action resumes.)

Menu Items

You can cause an action to open a specific dialog box or execute a menu command by choosing **Insert Menu Item** from the Actions panel Options menu. When the Insert Menu Item dialog box appears, you can make a selection from the application menus, and then click OK. When a user runs the action, the specified dialog box opens or the menu command executes.

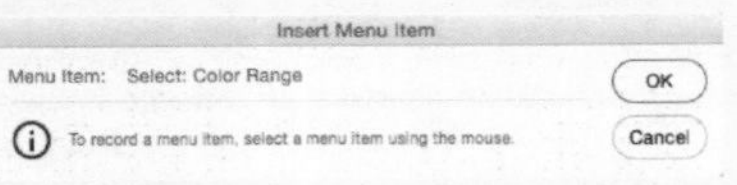

When you insert a menu item that opens a dialog box (such as Select>Color Range), you are adding a modal command that can't be turned off. When a user runs the action, even with modal commands turned off, the dialog box opens and requires user interaction. Although an action can automate many steps in a repetitive process, there are still some things that can't be entirely automatic.

Conditional Actions

You can also define steps in an action that occur if a specific condition is met by choosing **Insert Conditional** from the Actions panel Options menu. In the Conditional Actions dialog box:

- If Current defines the condition that will be evaluated. You can choose from the available list conditions.
- Then Play Action menu defines what will occur if the condition is true. You can choose any action that exists in the same set as the action you are recording.
- Else Play Action defines what happens if the condition is *not* true. You can choose any action that exists in the same set as the action you are recording.

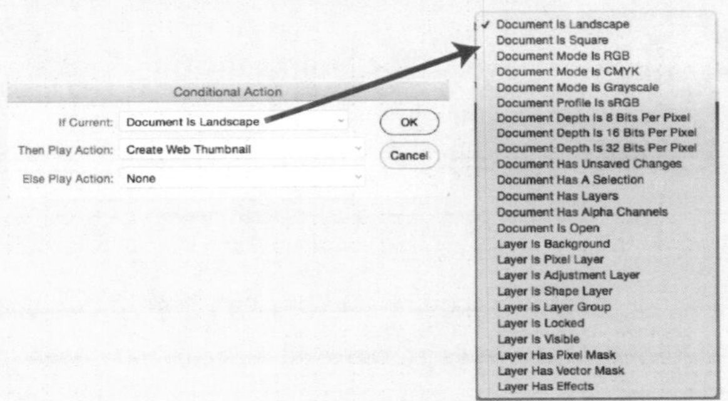

Batch-Process Files

The ability to batch-process files further enhances and automates productivity. If you have a large group of files that all require the same adjustments, you can build an action, set up a batch, and go to lunch (or, depending on your computer processor and number of files, go home for the night).

For example, when we write the Portfolio books, we take screen shots in RGB mode at 100%. Before the books are laid out for print production, the screen shots are converted to the U.S. Web Coated (SWOP) v2 CMYK profile and resized (not resampled) to 40%. As you have probably noticed, there are a lot of screen shots in these books. Rather than sitting for several days and modifying each file (or even sitting for one full day and running an action on each file), we set up a batch that converts all screen shots for an entire book in about 25 minutes.

1. **In Photoshop, choose File>Automate>Batch.**

   At the top of the Batch dialog box, the Set and Action menus default to the active selection in the Actions panel. In this case, there is only one available choice, so the Create Web Thumbnail action is already selected. You can choose to run a batch for any action in any open set.

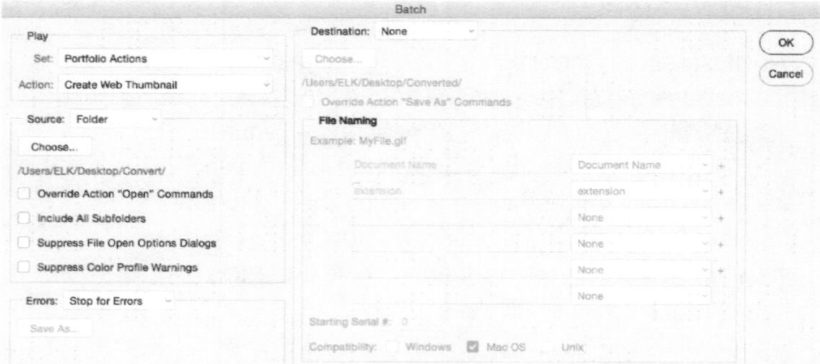

2. **Choose Folder in the Source menu.**

   The Source menu allows you to choose which files are batched:

   - **Folder** processes a complete group of images arranged within a single folder on your computer.
   - **Import** acquires and processes a group of images from a scanner or digital camera.
   - **Open Files** processes all files currently open in the application.
   - **File Browser** processes files selected in the File Browser.

   When Folder is selected, you can also choose to override "Open" commands that are recorded in the selected action, include subfolders within the selected folder, and suppress color profile warnings for the files being processed.

3. **Click the Choose button and navigate to the WIP>Metro>images folder and click Choose/OK to return to the Batch dialog box.**

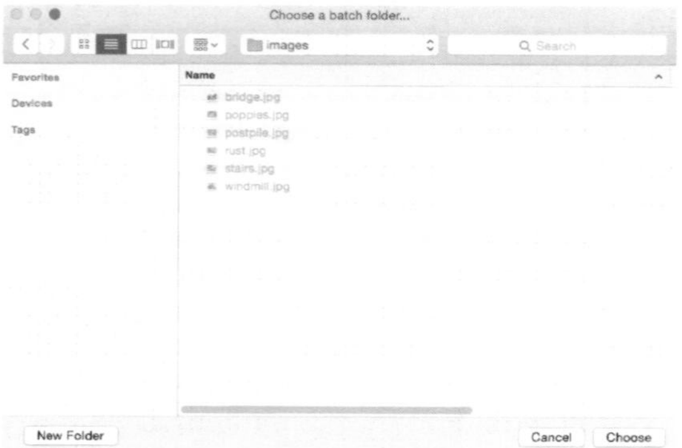

4. **Make sure the Suppress Color Profile Warnings option is checked to prevent the batch from stopping if color management policies are violated.**

   This is a matter of some debate, but when processing images for the Web, color management is not considered as critical as it is for print.

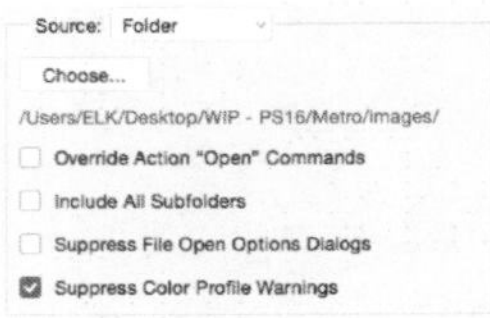

5. **Choose Folder in the Destination menu.**

   The Destination menu in the Batch dialog box presents three options:

   - **None** simply means that the action will be run. If the action saves and closes the files, those commands will be completed. If the action does not save and close the files, you might end up with a large number of open files and eventually crash your computer.
   - **Save and Close** saves the modified file in the same location with the same name, overwriting the original file.
   - **Folder** allows you to specify a target folder for the files after they have been processed. This option is particularly useful because it saves the processed files as copies of the originals in the defined folder; the original files remain intact.

6. **Click the Choose button (in the Destination area), navigate to the WIP>Metro>thumbnails folder, and click Choose/OK.**

Note:

*You can create a **droplet** from an action, which allows you to run the action using a basic drag-and-drop technique (as long as Photoshop is running). The Create Droplet dialog box (File>Automate>Create Droplet) presents most of the same options as the Batch dialog box, with a few exceptions. Clicking Choose at the top of the dialog box allows you to define the name of the droplet and the location to save it. The dialog box does not include Source options because the source is defined when you drag files onto the droplet.*

7. **In the File Naming area, open the menu for the first field and choose document name (lowercase) from the menu.**

   The File Naming fields allow you to redefine file names for the modified files. You can choose a variable from the pop-up menu, type specific text in a field, or use a combination of both. The example in the File Naming area shows the result of your choices in these menus.

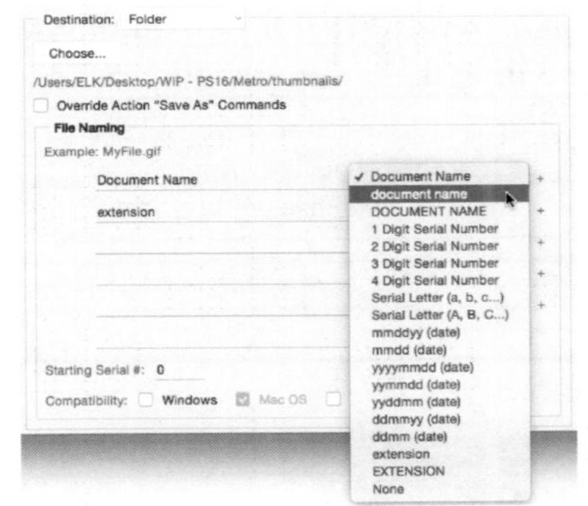

Note:

These options are only available when Folder is selected in the Destination menu.

8. **In the second field, type -thumb.**

   This identifies the images as thumbnails, differentiating them from the full-size images with the same names.

9. **Choose extension (lowercase) from the menu for the third field.**

Note:

*The Errors section of the Batch dialog box determines what happens if an error occurs during a batch. **Stop for Errors** (the default setting) interrupts the batch and displays a warning dialog box. **Log Errors to File** batch-processes every file and saves a record of all problems.*

10. **Click OK to run the batch.**

    When the process is complete, you will have six thumbnail images in your WIP>Metro>thumbnails folder.

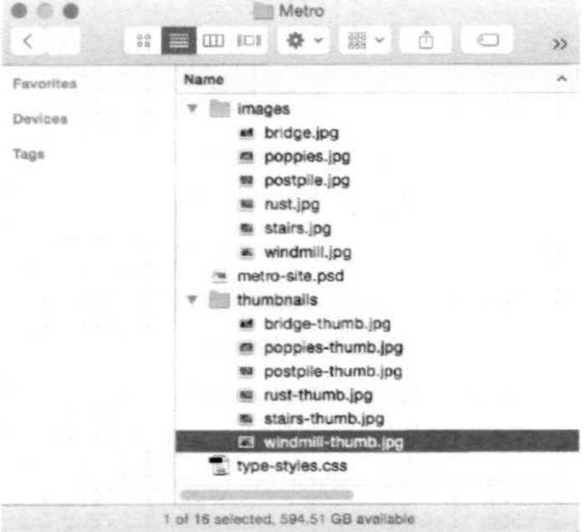

11. **Continue to the next exercise.**

Place and Align Thumbnails on the Page

Now that the thumbnail images have been created, you can arrange them in the gallery file so it can be animated, sliced, and saved for the Web.

1. **Open the file metro-site.psd from the WIP>Metro folder. If you receive a missing profile warning, choose the option to use the embedded profile.**

2. **In the Layers panel, select the Background layer to make it active.**

   New layers are automatically added above the previously selected layer. In this case, the new layers will be added directly above the Background layer.

3. **On your desktop, navigate to the WIP>Metro>thumbnails folder. Select all six files in the folder and drag them onto the Photoshop document window.**

Drag multiple files from the desktop to the Photoshop document window to place more than one at a time.

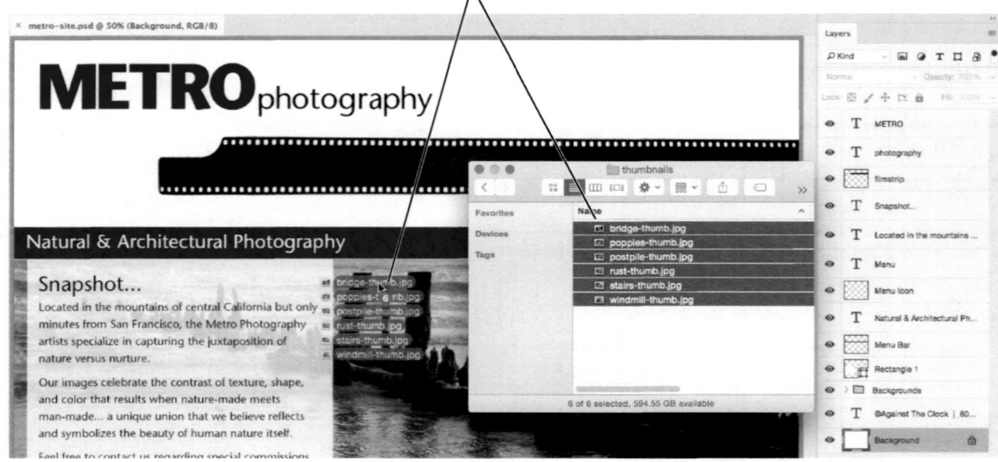

4. **Make the Photoshop application active again.**

The first dragged file shows the crossed diagonal lines, indicating that you need to finalize the placement.

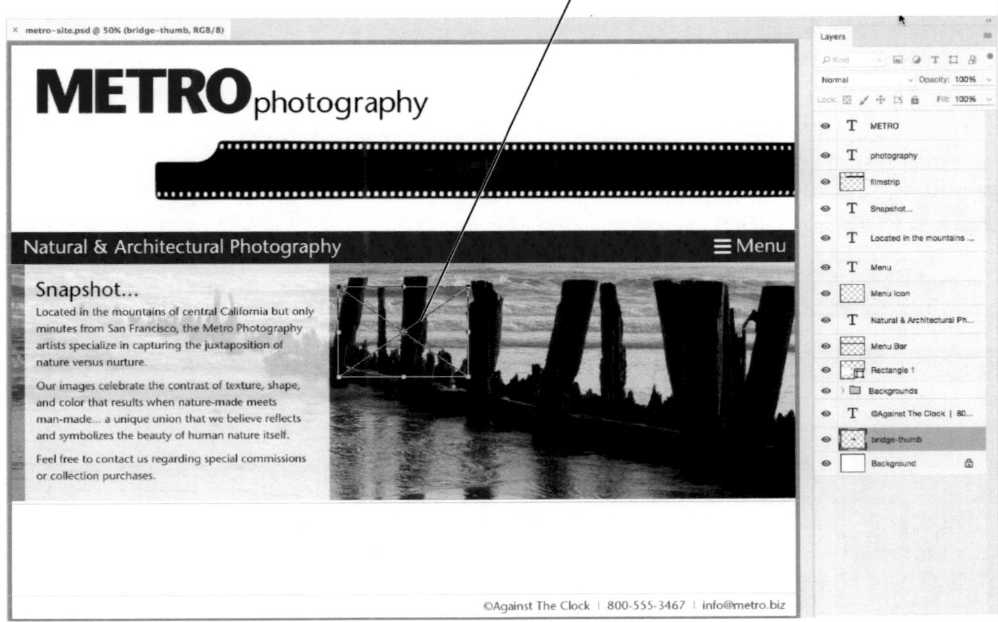

5. **Press Return/Enter six times to finalize the placement of each image.**

   This method make this process of placing multiple files far easier than using the File>Place Embedded command, which only allows placement of a single image at once.

6. **Choose the Move tool. In the Options bar, make sure the Auto-Select option is not checked.**

   By turning off Auto-Select, you can click anywhere in the document window to move the contents of the selected layer. Turning this option off prevents you from accidentally moving the content of a different layer.

7. **In the Layers panel, select the windmill-thumb layer.**

   When Auto-Select is not active, the Move tool moves the content of whatever layer is active in the Layers panel.

8. **Make sure the Snap option is toggled on in the View menu.**

9. **Open the View>Snap To submenu and make sure Document Bounds is active.**

   When the Snap options are turned on, arranging layers relative to one another is fairly easy (as you will see in the next few steps).

Make sure Snap is toggled on.

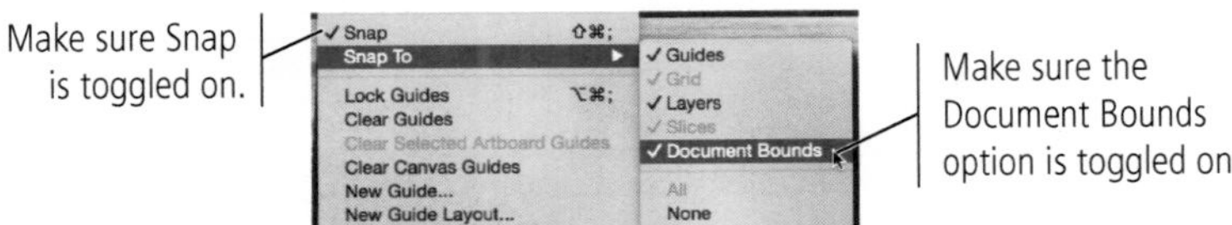

Make sure the Document Bounds option is toggled on.

10. **Click inside the document window and drag down and right until the windmill-thumb layer content snaps to the right canvas edge and the third and fourth horizontal ruler guides.**

    If guides are not visible, choose View>Show>Guides.

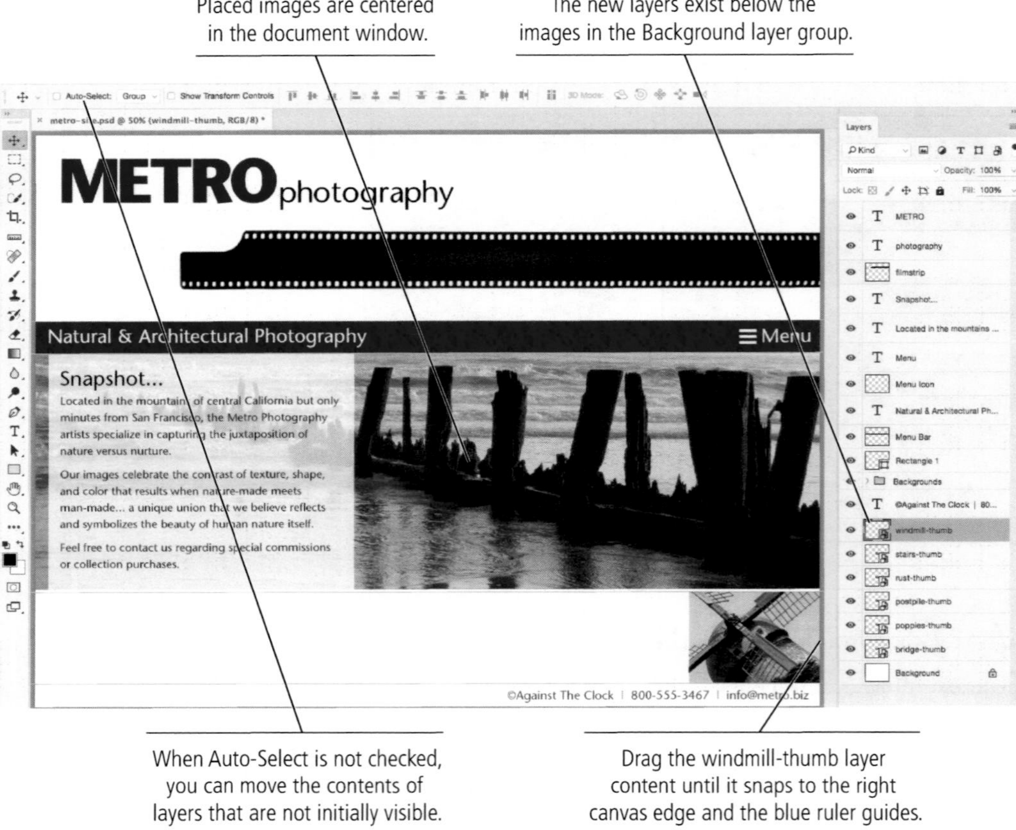
Placed images are centered in the document window.
The new layers exist below the images in the Background layer group.
When Auto-Select is not checked, you can move the contents of layers that are not initially visible.
Drag the windmill-thumb layer content until it snaps to the right canvas edge and the blue ruler guides.
METRO photography
Natural & Architectural Photography
Menu
Snapshot...

11. **Select the bridge-thumb layer in the layers panel, then drag it to the left side of the canvas between the third and fourth ruler guides.**

12. **In the Layers panel, Shift-click to select all six thumbnail image layers.**

    When multiple layers are selected in the Layers panel, a number of alignment options become available in the Options bar. These are very useful for aligning or distributing the content of multiple layers relative to one another.

13. **In the Options bar, click the Align Bottom Edges button, then click the Distribute Horizontal Centers button.**

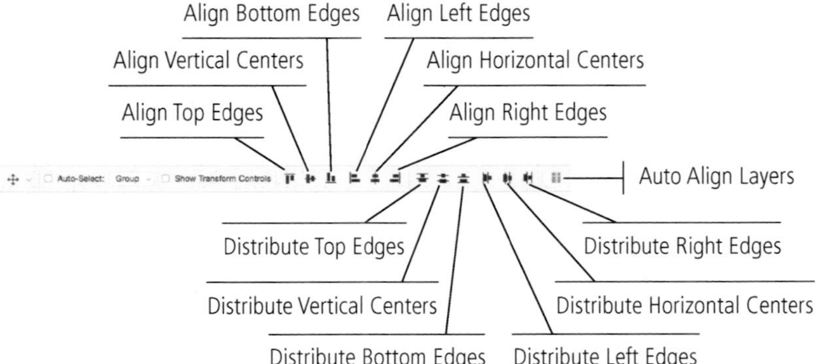

Aligning the bottom edges moves the four previously hidden layers to match the bottom-most edge of all selected layers — in this case, the bottom edge of the windmill and bridge images.

The Distribute Horizontal Centers option places an equal amount of space between the horizontal center point of each selected layer. The centers of the six thumbnail images are now exactly spaced in relation to one another.

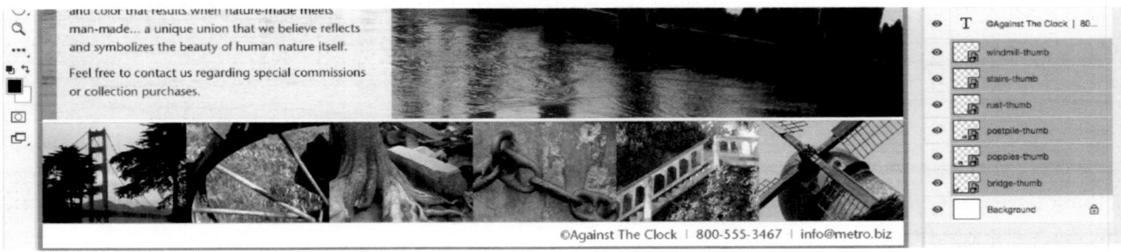

14. **Save the file and continue to the next stage of the project.**

Working with Type in Photoshop

When you click with the Horizontal or Vertical Type tool, you create a new type layer. The insertion point flashes at the location where you click to create the layer. Typing adds text to the type layer; after clicking the Commit button in the Options bar (or choosing a different tool in the Tools panel), the type layer adopts text on the layer as the layer name

Point Type

Simply clicking with the Horizontal Type tool creates a point-type layer, which starts at a single point and extends along or follows a single path.

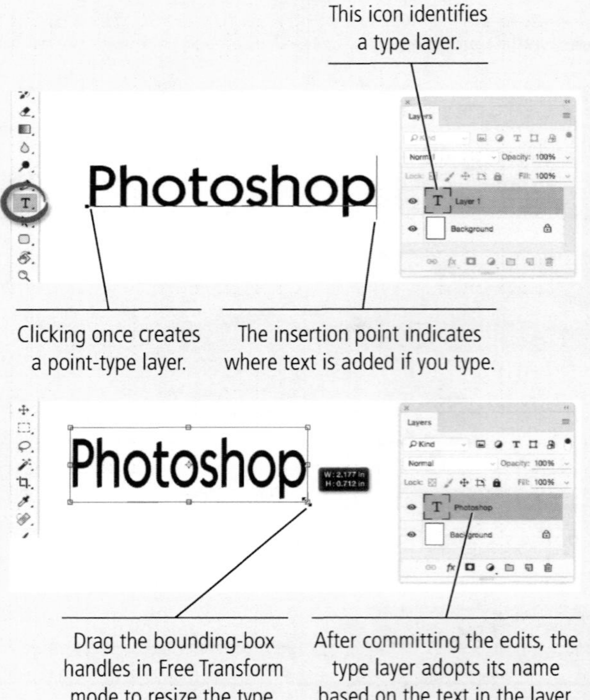

You can access the bounding-box handles of a point-type layer by entering Free Transform mode (Edit>Transform>Free Transform). In this case, dragging the bounding-box handles resizes the type on the layer.

When you change the paragraph alignment of point type, the point remains in the same position; text on the layer moves relative to the fixed point.

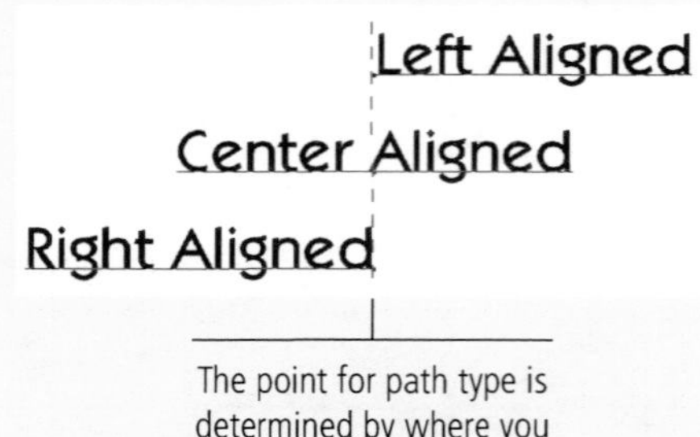

Left Aligned
Center Aligned
Right Aligned
The point for path type is determined by where you click to place the object.

Area Type

Clicking and dragging with the Horizontal Type tool creates an area-type layer, in which text flows inside a defined area; you can resize the area to change the way text wraps.

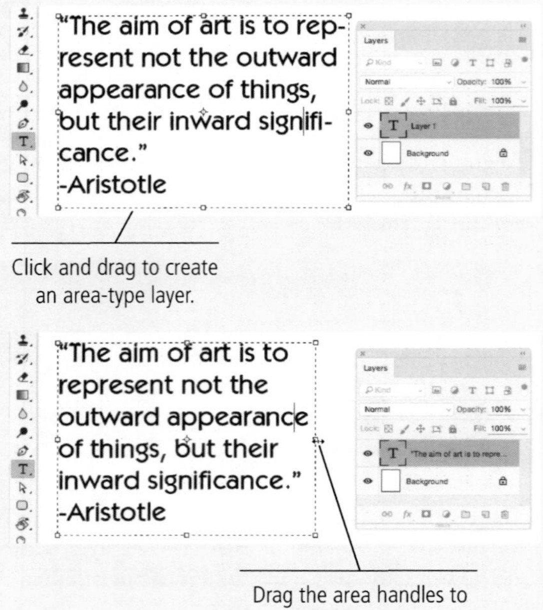

Drag the area handles to adjust the area dimensions.

When the Horizontal Type tool is active, you can drag a type area's bounding-box handles to change the size of the type area. Text in the area reflows to fit into the adjusted space; the size of the text is not affected.

Working with Type in Photoshop (continued)

When you work with type in Photoshop, a number of formatting options are available in the Options bar.

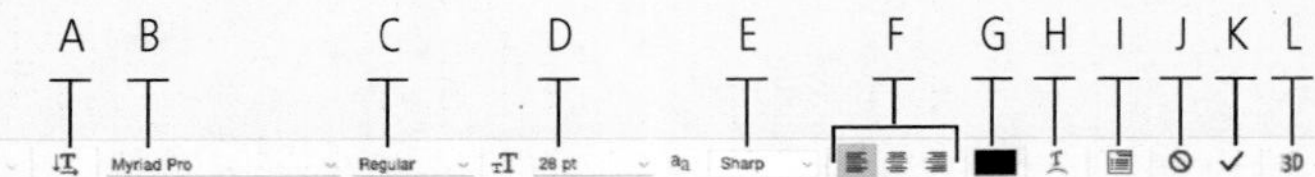

- A Toggle Text Orientation
- B Font Family
- C Font Style
- D Font Size
- E Anti-Aliasing Method
- F Paragraph Alignment Options
- G Text Color
- H Create Warped Text
- I Toggle the Character and Paragraph Panels
- J Cancel Current Edits
- K Commit Current Edits
- L Create 3D from Text

Character Panel Options

All of the options that are available in the Options bar are also available in the Character panel. However, the Character panel includes a number of other options that control the appearance of type in your document.

Keep in mind that changes to character formatting affect only selected characters. If you make changes before typing, the changes apply to all characters you type from the insertion point.

- A **Font Family** is the general font that is applied, such as Minion or Warnock Pro.
- B **Font Style** is the specific variation of the applied font, such as Italic, Bold, or Light.
- C **Font Size** is the size of the type in points.
- D **Leading** is the distance from one baseline to the next. If you change the leading for only certain characters in a line, keep in mind that the adjusted leading will apply to the entire line where the adjusted characters exist; for example:

  > In this sentence, we changed the leading for only the underlined word; all text in the same line moves to accommodate the adjusted leading of the characters in that word.

- E **Kerning** increases or decreases the space between pairs of letters. Kerning is used in cases where particular letters in specific fonts need to be manually spread apart or brought together to eliminate a too-tight or too-spread-out appearance.
- F **Tracking** refers to the overall tightness or looseness across a range of characters. Tracking and kerning are applied in thousandths of an **em** (or the amount of space occupied by an uppercase "M," which is usually the widest character in a typeface).
- G, H **Vertical Scale** and **Horizontal Scale** artificially stretch or contract the selected characters. This scaling is a quick way of achieving condensed or expanded type if those variations of a font don't exist.
- I **Baseline Shift** moves the selected type above or below the baseline by a specific number of points.
- J **Text Color** changes the color of selected characters.
- K **Type Styles** apply artificial styling such as Faux Bold, Faux Italic, All Caps, Small Caps, Superscript, Subscript, Underline, and Strikethrough.
- L **Opentype Attributes** replace characters with alternative glyphs if those are available in the applied font.
- M **Language Dictionary** defines the language that is used to check spelling in the story.
- N **Anti-Aliasing** can be used to help smooth the apparent edges of type when it is rasterized.

Paragraph Panel Options

Paragraph formatting options, available in the Paragraph panel, apply to all type in the selected paragraph — wherever characters are highlighted or the insertion point is placed.

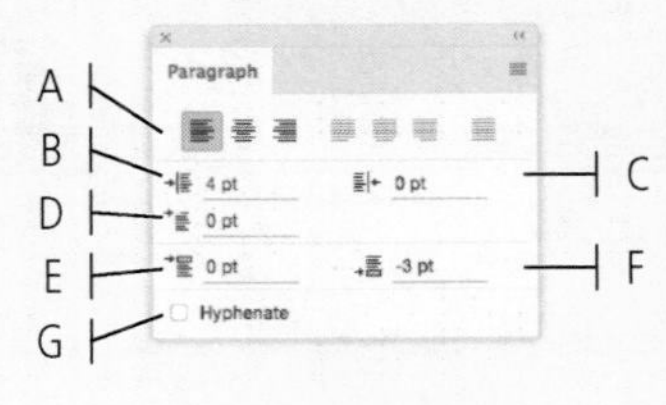

- A Alignment options
  - Left Align Text
  - Center Text
  - Right Align Text
  - Justify Last Left
  - Justify Last Centered
  - Justify Last Right
  - Justify All
- B Indent Left Margin
- C Indent Right Margin
- D Indent First Line
- E Add Space Before Paragraph
- F Add Space After Paragraph
- G Allow Automatic Hyphenation

Keep in mind that justification options are only available when you work with area type, and some options are not relevant for point type that only occupies a single line.

Working with Type in Photoshop (continued)

If you type in the Font Family menu of the Options bar or Character panel, the software presents a list of fonts that match the characters you type.

If you click the arrow to the right of the Font Family menu, you see a menu of all fonts that are available to Photoshop on your computer.

The top section of the menu lists the ten most **recent fonts**. By default, these appear in the order they were used (the most recently used appears at the top of the menu). In the Type pane of the Preferences dialog box, you can change the number of displayed fonts.

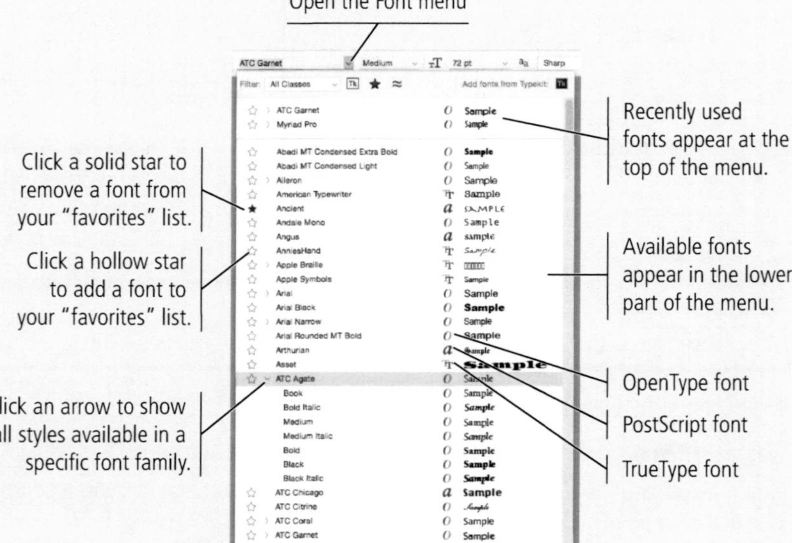

Open the Font menu
Click a solid star to remove a font from your "favorites" list.
Click a hollow star to add a font to your "favorites" list.
Click an arrow to show all styles available in a specific font family.
Recently used fonts appear at the top of the menu.
Available fonts appear in the lower part of the menu.
OpenType font
PostScript font
TrueType font

Each font listed in the Font menu includes a number of elements:

- You can use the star icons on the left side of the font menu to define "favorite" fonts. You can then use the button at the top of the menu to show only those fonts that you have marked as favorites.
- The font family names in each section appear in alphabetical order.

  An arrow to the left of a font name indicates that a specific font family includes more than one style. You can click the arrow to show all possible styles.

  If you apply a font that includes more than one style, the style you choose appears in the Font Style menu below the Font Family field. You can open the Font Style menu to change the style without changing the font family.

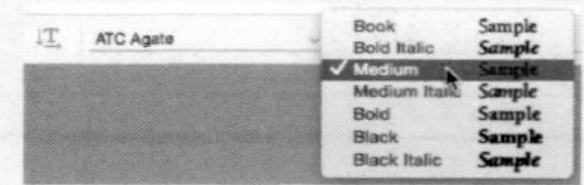

- An icon identifies the type of each font.

  PostScript (Type 1) fonts have two file components (outline and printer) that are required for output.

  TrueType fonts have a single file, but (until recently) were primarily used on the Windows platform.

  OpenType fonts are contained in a single file that can include more than 60,000 glyphs (characters) in a single font. OpenType fonts are cross-platform; the same font can be used on both Macintosh and Windows systems.
- A sample of each font appears at the right side of the menu. You can change the size of the sample in the Type>Font Preview Size menu.

The top of the Font menu includes options for filtering fonts. (If you have an individual-user subscription to Adobe Creative Cloud, you can also show only fonts that are installed through the Adobe Typekit Web site; see Project 5: Calendar Cover.)

Show only certain categories of fonts.

Show only fonts that are marked as favorites.

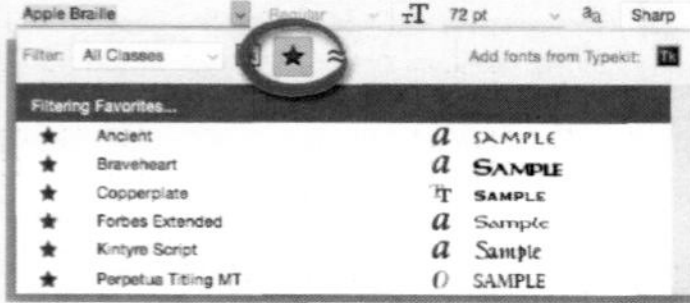

Show only fonts that are similar to the currently active font.

Stage 2 Editing Layers for Visual Effect

At the meeting, your client asked for some way to break up the horizontal uniformity in the top half of the interface design. Photoshop offers a number of tools for distorting layers, from simple scaling to the Free Transform mode to the Liquify filter. If you completed the other projects in this book, you have already used all of these techniques to fulfill specific project goals. In this stage of this project, you will learn two more methods for transforming layer content — 3D extrusion and puppet warping — to achieve effects that can't easily be created with other methods.

Extrude a Text Layer to 3D

Photoshop CC includes a very sophisticated set of tools for working with 3D graphics. In this exercise, you will use some of the basic options to create three-dimensional shapes from a type layer.

Important Note: If you see a message about insufficient vRAM when you first launch the application, you will not be able to complete this exercise. You must have at least 512 MB vRAM to work with Photoshop's 3D features.

1. **With metro-site.psd open, hide the filmstrip and photography layers.**
2. **Select the METRO layer in the layers panel and then select the Horizontal Type tool.**

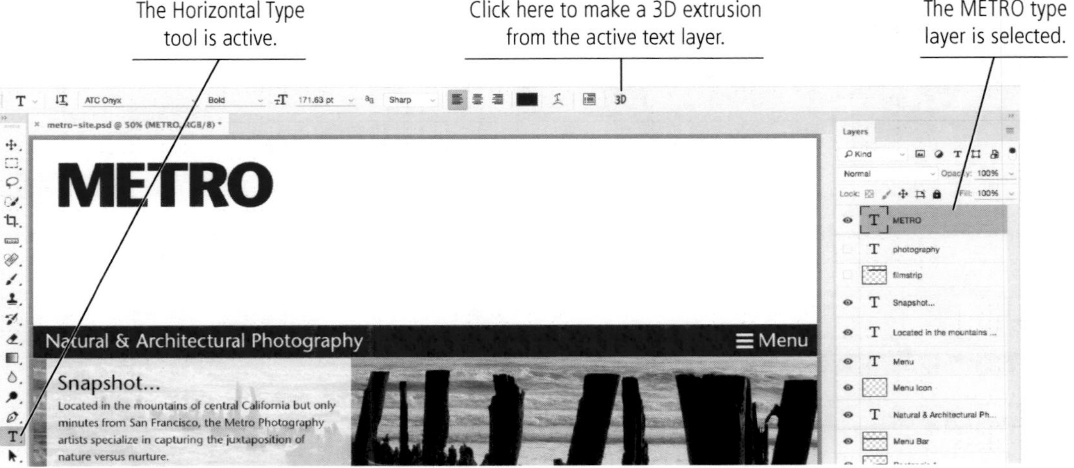

3. **Click the 3D button in the Options bar.**

   You don't need to place the insertion point to apply 3D effects to a type layer. Simply select the layer you want to affect in the Layers panel and make sure the Horizontal Type tool is active.

4. **Read the resulting message and then click Yes.**

   To work effectively with 3D objects, you need (at least) the Layers panel, the 3D panel, and the Properties panel. The built-in 3D workspace automatically shows those panels.

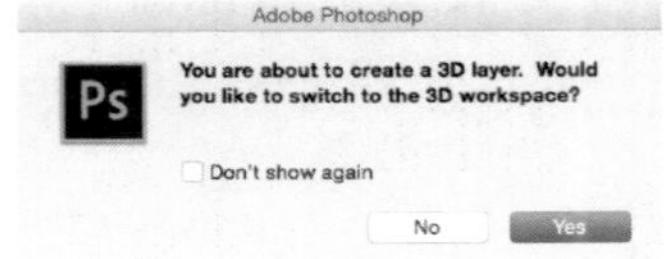

   When you create a 3D layer from the existing Type layer, Photoshop automatically asks if you want to switch to that workspace.

Note:

We are only touching the surface of what you can do when you work in three dimensions; our goal is to show you some of the options that will be useful for creating 3D effects in a 2D medium such as print or Web design.

5. **Click the word "Metro" in the top-left corner of the canvas to select it.**

6. **Open the View>Show submenu. Turn off the 3D Secondary View and 3D Ground Plane options; turn on the 3D Lights and 3D Selection options.**

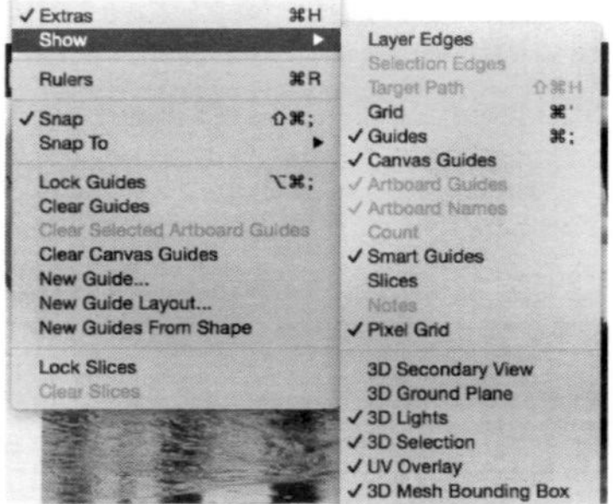

You're only manipulating a single word of type, so the secondary view and ground plane aren't particularly helpful in this instance. The lights and selection options, however, can be very helpful for manipulating the 3D shape on screen.

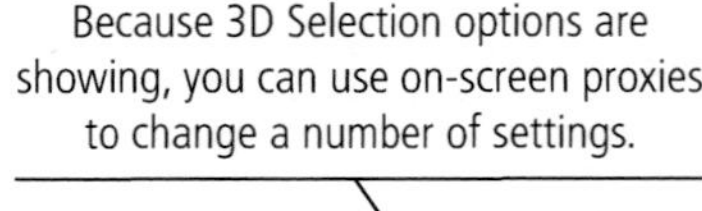

Because 3D Selection options are showing, you can use on-screen proxies to change a number of settings.

Move the mouse over various parts of the on-screen mesh to change different properties.

Options related to the new 3D layer are available in the 3D and Properties panels.

The Type layer now shows the 3D layer icon.

As you complete this exercise, keep in mind that the 3D panel lists all of the elements that make up a 3D object:

- The Environment is everything around the 3D object.
- The Scene is basically everything that makes up the 3D effect.
  - Current View defines properties of the camera, or the perspective from which the scene is being viewed.
  - Light defines the specific light sources that shine on the 3D model.
  - [Object Name] defines properties related to the actual 3D model, including:
    - Materials, which are the appearances of the surfaces
    - Constraints, which are the shapes that make up the 3D mesh

7. **Select the Metro object in the 3D panel, then review the options in the Properties panel.**

When the 3D type object is selected, the Properties panel has four modes:

- Mesh options relate to the overall 3D shape. You can change how the mesh casts and catches shadows, and choose a shape preset to distort the 3D mesh.

  At the bottom of the Properties panel, you can use the Text swatch and Character Panel buttons to make changes to the type formatting. Clicking the Edit Source button opens a separate file with the live type layer — which means you can edit the text (and its formatting) even after converting it to a 3D layer.

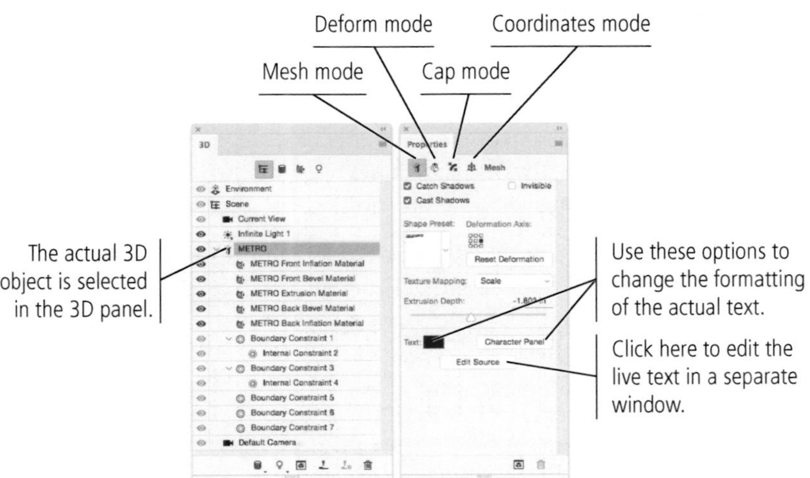

Deform mode
Coordinates mode
Mesh mode
Cap mode
The actual 3D object is selected in the 3D panel.
Use these options to change the formatting of the actual text.
Click here to edit the live text in a separate window.

- Deform options control the depth, twist, taper, bend, and shear of the 3D extrusion.
- Cap options control the beveling and inflation effects that are applied to the front and/or back surfaces of a 3D shape.
- Coordinates options are the same as for the Scene, but apply only to the selected object.

8. **Click the Deform button at the top of the Properties panel, then place the mouse cursor over the Bend control of the on-screen Deform proxy.**

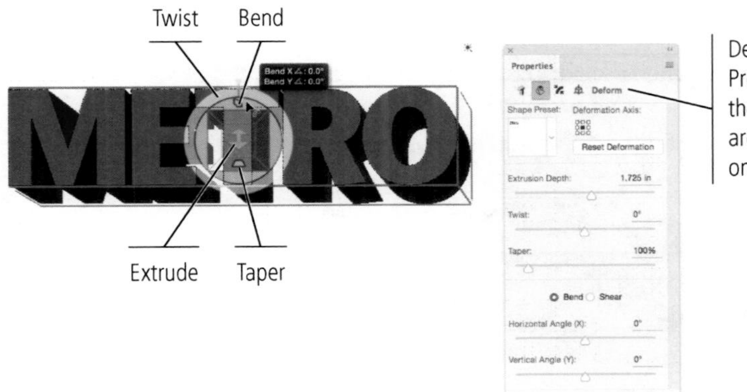

Note:

Press V to toggle through various modes of the Properties panel.

9. **Click and drag right until the cursor feedback shows (approximately) Bend X: 180°.**

   Dragging right or left changes the horizontal bend (Bend X). Dragging up or down changes the vertical bend (Bend Y).

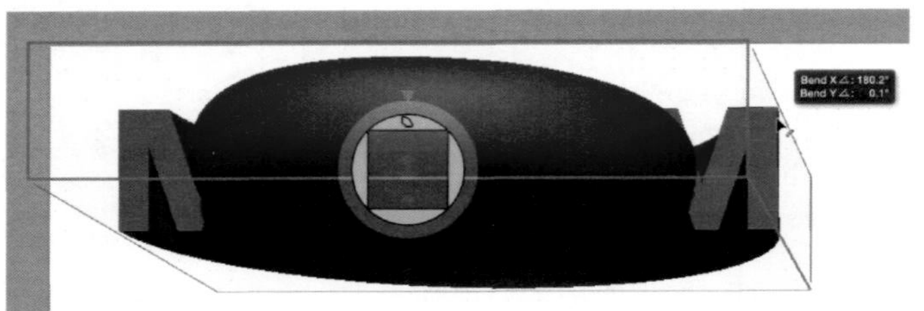

Note:

In either the Mesh or Deform properties, you can apply a predefined group of shape options using the Shape Preset menu. Different presets change the Extrude options, which define the shape that is created.

10. **In the Properties panel, click the right-center point in the Deformation Axis proxy.**

    You might have to reselect the Deform button at the top of the panel after changing the bend value. This appears to be a minor bug in the software that requires selecting the Deform button again after making any change to the object's properties.

    The registration point defines the origin of the bend or shear. As you can see in this example, the bend is now applied around the right-center point of the original object.

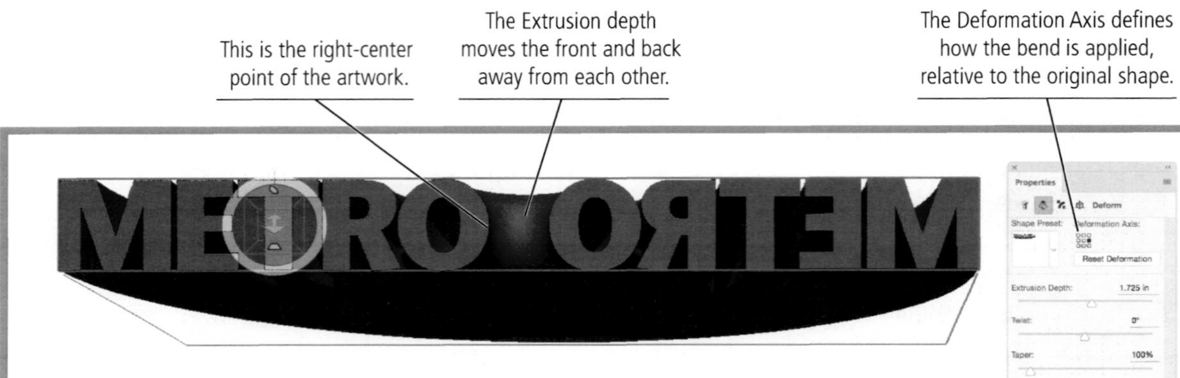
This is the right-center point of the artwork.
The Extrusion depth moves the front and back away from each other.
The Deformation Axis defines how the bend is applied, relative to the original shape.

11. **Place the cursor over the Extrude control of the on-screen Deform proxy. Click and drag down until the two "o" shapes overlap, as shown in the following image.**

    Changing the Extrusion Depth moves the front and back sides closer together or farther apart.

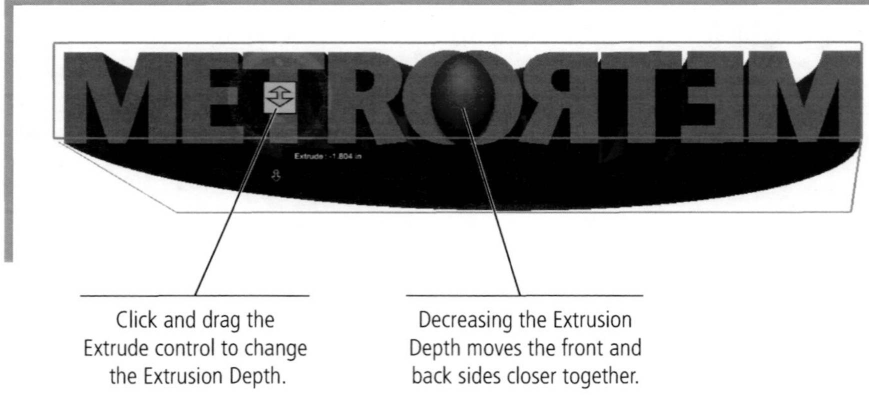
Click and drag the Extrude control to change the Extrusion Depth.
Decreasing the Extrusion Depth moves the front and back sides closer together.

12. **With the Metro object still selected in the 3D panel, click the Cap button at the top of the Properties panel.**

Cap properties control the same options that are available in the on-screen proxy.

13. **Place the mouse cursor over the Bevel Width control in the on-screen Cap proxy. Click and drag right to apply a 15% bevel.**

Bevel options change the contour map for the front and/or back of the shape. The Inflate options can be used to create a bubble effect.

14. **In the Properties panel, choose Front and Back in the Sides menu.**

Note:

Sometimes the 3D panel changes automatically to select the scene instead of the object; this appears to be a bug in the software. You should make sure the correct element is selected in the 3D panel.

Cap settings can be changed for the front, the back, or both.

Cap mode is active.

Front Bevel Angle

Front Bevel Width

Front Inflation Strength

Front Inflation Angle

15. **In the 3D panel, click METRO Extrusion Material to select only that mesh.**

When a specific material is selected, you can change the color and texture that apply to the selected material.

16. **In the Properties panel, open the Material Picker. Scroll down to find the No Texture option, then click it to remove the texture from the extrusion mesh.**

Click these swatches to change the color of the various lights that affect the material.

Click here to change the texture for the selected material.

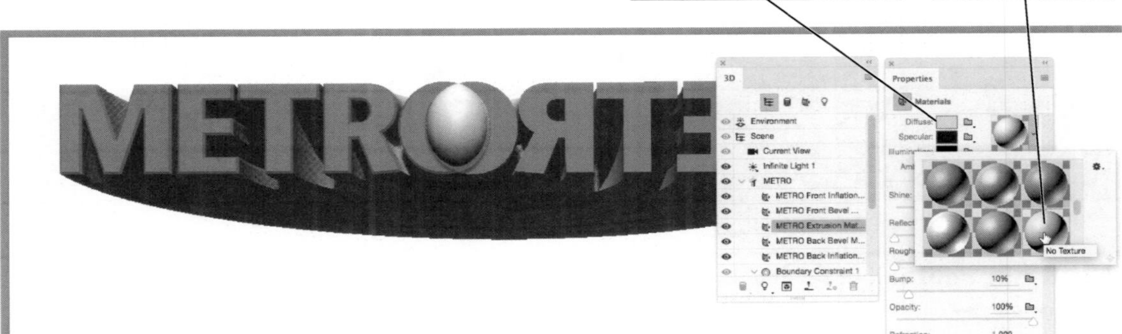

In the Properties panel, the color of various lights changes the appearance of the selected material:

- Diffuse is the color of the surface material, or the file that makes up the reflective surface of the object.
- Specular defines the color of specular highlights (i.e., areas where the light is 100% reflected).
- Illumination is the color of surface areas where the material is transparent; this setting results in the effect of interior lighting, such as a painting on a light bulb.
- Ambient defines the color of ambient light that's visible on reflective surfaces.

17. **In the 3D panel, click the METRO object to select it.**

18. **Make the Move tool active in the Tools panel. Move the cursor near the front-top edge of the 3D object cage until the cursor feedback shows "Rotate Around X Axis"**

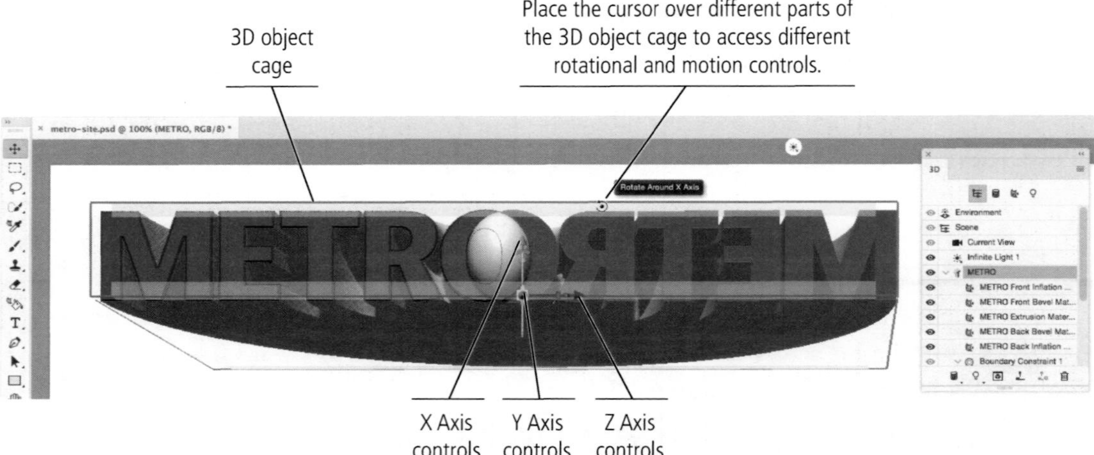

3D object cage
Place the cursor over different parts of the 3D object cage to access different rotational and motion controls.
Rotate Around X Axis
X Axis controls
Y Axis controls
Z Axis controls

19. **Click and drag down until cursor feedback shows (approximately) Rotate X: 20°.**

20. **Move the cursor near the right-top edge of the object cage until the cursor feedback shows Rotate Around Z Axis.**

21. **Click and drag until cursor feedback shows (approximately) Rotate Z: 2.0°.**

22. **Move the Metro type layer closer to the top and left edges of the canvas.**

23. **In the Layers panel, make the "photography" type layer visible.**

    You hid these layers earlier to better focus on the 3D object. Now you need to scale the 3D object to fit into the available space, so you have to make those layers visible again.

24. **Using the Move tool, drag the "photography" type layer until the "h" ascender sits between the T and E on the reversed "METRO" (as shown here).**

25. **Save the file and continue to the next exercise.**

Use Puppet Warp to Transform a Layer

Puppet Warp provides a way to transform and distort specific areas of a layer without affecting other areas of the same layer. It is called "puppet" warp because it's based on the concept of pinning certain areas in place and then bending other areas around those pin locations — mimicking the way a puppet's joints pivot. In this exercise, you use puppet warping to bend and distort the top filmstrip image layer.

Note:

Puppet warping can be applied to image, shape, and text layers, as well as layer and vector masks.

1. **With metro-site.psd open, make the filmstrip layer visible.**

2. **Control/right-click the filmstrip layer in the Layers panel. Choose Convert to Smart Object from the contextual menu.**

   By first converting this layer to a Smart Object, you can apply the puppet warp non-destructively.

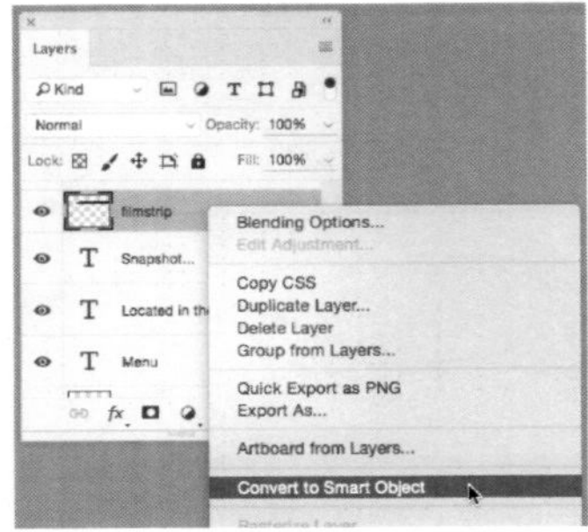

3. **With the filmstrip Smart Object layer selected in the Layers panel, choose Edit>Puppet Warp.**

   When you enter Puppet Warp mode, a mesh overlays the active layer content. This mesh represents the joints in the shape that can bend when you warp the layer content.

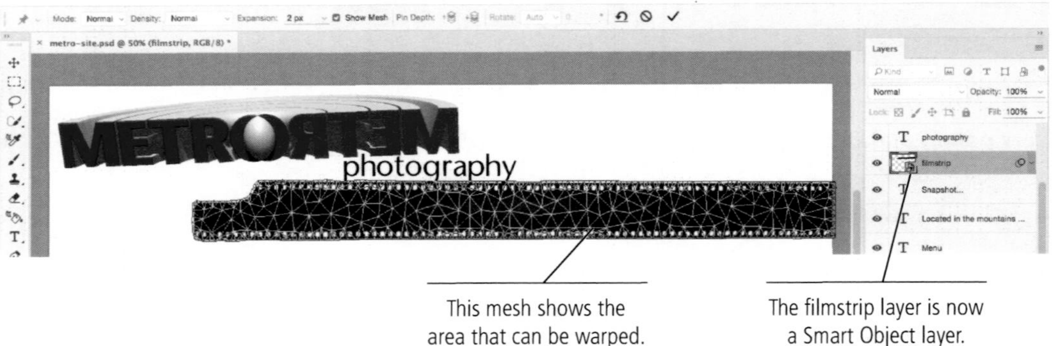

This mesh shows the area that can be warped.
The filmstrip layer is now a Smart Object layer.

4. **In the Options bar, choose Fewer Points in the Density menu.**

   In the Options bar, you can change the mesh density from the default Normal to show Fewer Points or More Points.

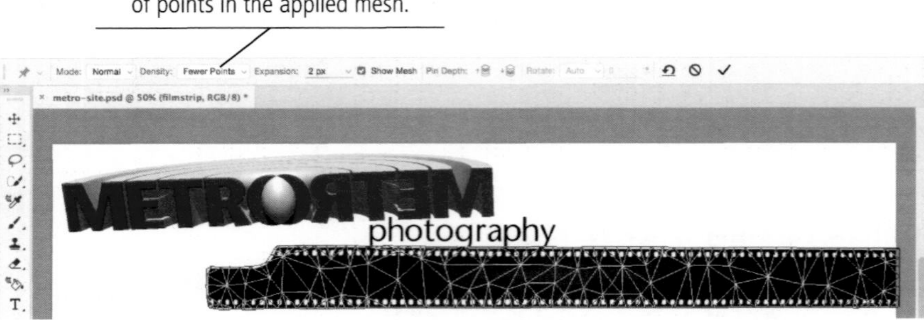

Use this menu to change the number of points in the applied mesh.

5. **Click the mesh near the center of the filmstrip art to place an anchoring pin.**

   Clicking the mesh places a pin, which anchors the layer at that location.

6. **Click the top-right corner of the mesh and, without releasing the mouse button, drag up above the top edge of the image.**

   Clicking and dragging places a new pin and rotates the image around the location of the existing pin. Because you have placed one other pin on the layer, the entire shape rotates around the first pin location.

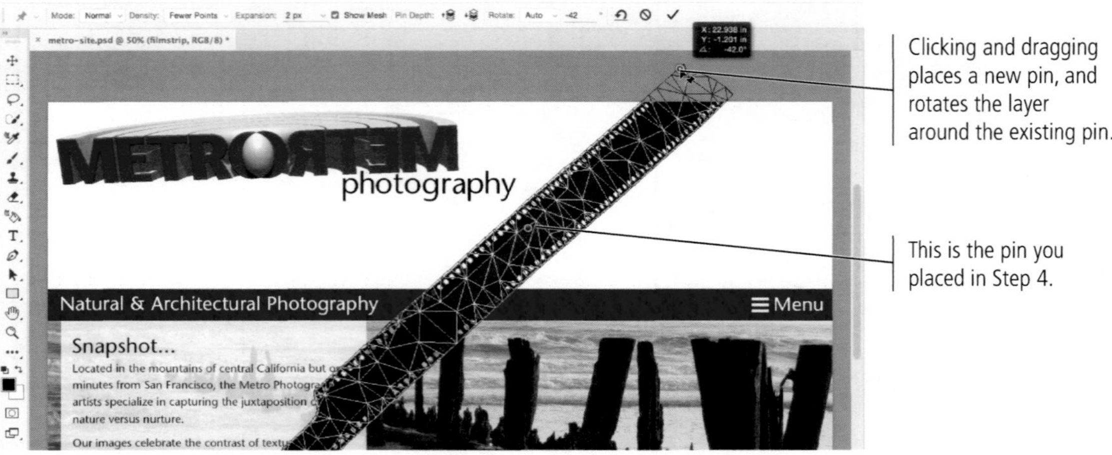

This is the pin you placed in Step 4.

7. **Click the left-center edge of the layer and drag up to move the filmstrip end back into the heading area.**

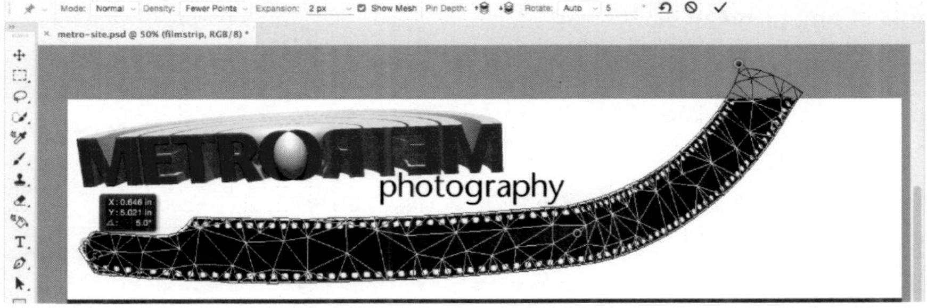

8. **Add another pin to the bottom-right corner of the filmstrip. Drag the new point until the filmstrip edge is past the canvas edge (as shown here).**

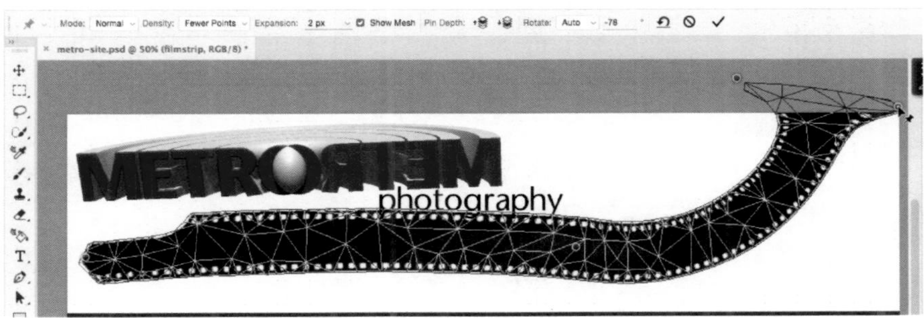

9. **In the Options bar, choose the Distort option in the Mode menu.**

   As you can see, Distort mode warps the object based on the position and angle of existing pins.

In Distort mode, the layer content distorts based on the position and angle of pins.

10. **Click the center pin and drag left to change the distorted shape.**

    This changes the distortion between the center pin and the pins on the either end of the filmstrip. The bend on the right end of the filmstrip is reduced.

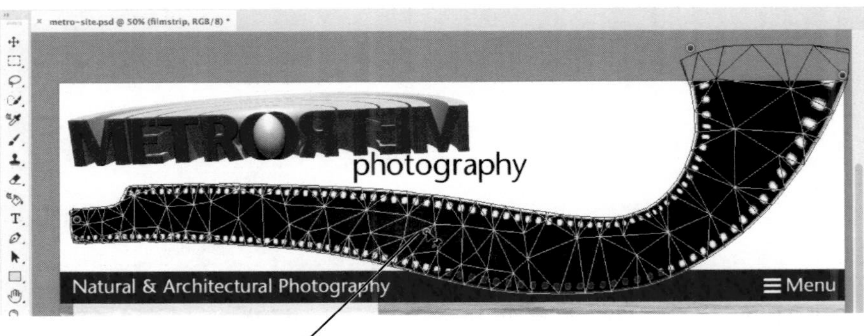

Moving a pin changes the overall shape distortion.

Note:

Pressing Command/Control-Z while working in Puppet Warp mode undoes the last action you performed inside the puppet warp mesh. You can only undo one action; after you finalize the warp, the Undo command undoes the entire warp — everything you did since you entered Puppet Warp mode.

11. **Continue manipulating the filmstrip warp until you are satisfied with the result. Keep the following points in mind:**

    - **Click to add new pins at any point in the process.**
    - **Option/Alt click an existing, selected pin to remove it from the mesh.**
    - **Press Option/Alt to change the selected pin from an Auto rotation angle to a Fixed rotation angle.**
    - **With a specific pin selected, press Option/Alt, then click the rotation proxy and drag to change the angle of that pin.**
    - **Uncheck the Show Mesh option to get a better preview of your warp.**

    Our solution is shown here.

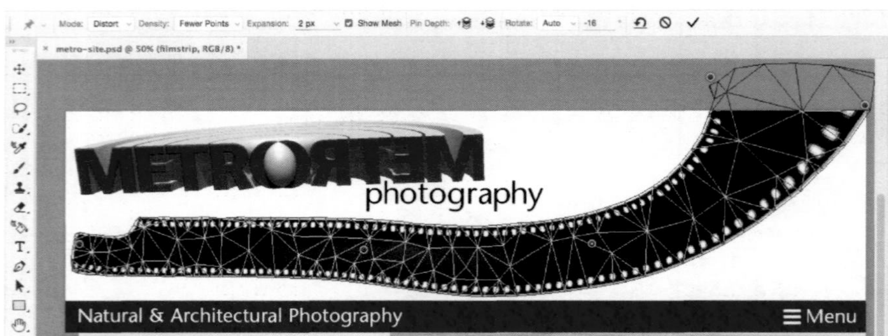

Note:

The Expansion option in the Options bar determines how far the mesh extends beyond the edge of the layer content.

Note:

If you warp a layer so that the mesh overlaps, you can use the Pin Depth buttons in the Options bar to show pins on underlying layers.

12. **Press Return/Enter to finalize the warp.**

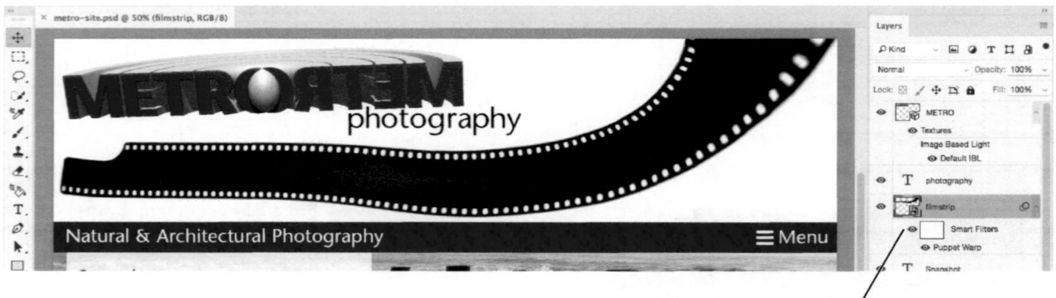

Because you converted the layer to a Smart Object, you can double-click the Puppet Warp effect to change the warp settings.

13. **Save the file, then continue to the next stage of the project.**

Stage 3 Generating Web-Ready Assets

It is common practice to create the look and feel of a Web site in Photoshop, and then hand off the pieces for a programmer to assemble in a Web-design application such as Adobe Dreamweaver. In the second half of this project, you complete a number of tasks to create the necessary pieces for the final Web site, including the different styles that will be used to properly format various elements in the resulting HTML page.

This site is a very simple example, using only a few elements to illustrate the process of properly mapping Photoshop objects to create the pieces that are necessary in an HTML page; we kept the site design basic to minimize the amount of repetition required to complete the project. The skills and concepts you complete in this project would apply equally to more complex sites.

Define a New Artboard

Responsive design is a term used to describe how page layouts change based on the size of display being used to show a specific Web page. This technique typically requires different settings for various elements (type size, alignment, etc.), and even different content that will — or will not — appear in different-size displays (for example, removing thumbnail images from extra-small or phone display sizes).

Although this is not a book about Web design, you should understand that responsive design technology generally recognizes four different display sizes:

Display size	Designation	Display Width
Extra-small for phones	xs	< 768 pixels
Small for tablets	sm	768–991 pixels
Medium for desktops	md	992–1199 pixels
Large for large desktops	lg	1200+ pixels

Photoshop artboards are a special type of layer group that make it easier to manage content for multiple display sizes within a single Photoshop file.

In this exercise, you are going to define an artboard to contain the existing project layout, which was designed for large display sizes. In a later exercise, you will duplicate and modify the existing layout elements to create the required files for extra-small displays.

1. **With metro-site.psd open, choose the Artboard tool (nested under the Move tool).**

   If you don't see the Move tool, call the Essentials workspace in the Workspace switcher. The Artboard tool ios not available in the built-in 3D workspace.

2. **Select the Background layer in the Layers panel. Open the Layers panel Options menu and choose Artboard from Layers.**

   This command creates a new artboard with the boundaries at the outer edges of the selected layer(s). Using the Background layer, your new artboard will be the same size as the canvas for this site layout — which means it will also encompass all the other layers in the file.

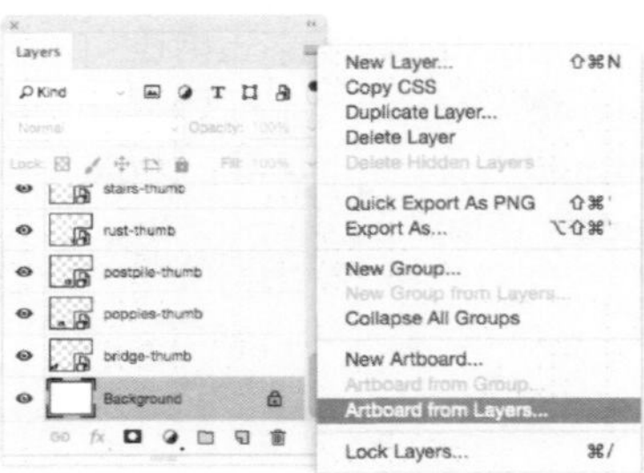

3. **In the resulting dialog box, type `LG Display` in the Name field and choose iPad Retina (1536, 2048) in the Set Artboard to Preset menu.**

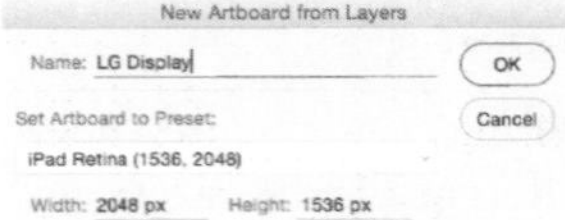

4. **Review the Layers panel.**

   Artboards contain all the layers with content that appears at least partially within the artboard bounds. When you define a new artboard, the locked Background layer is automatically converted to a solid-color fill layer named "Layer 0."

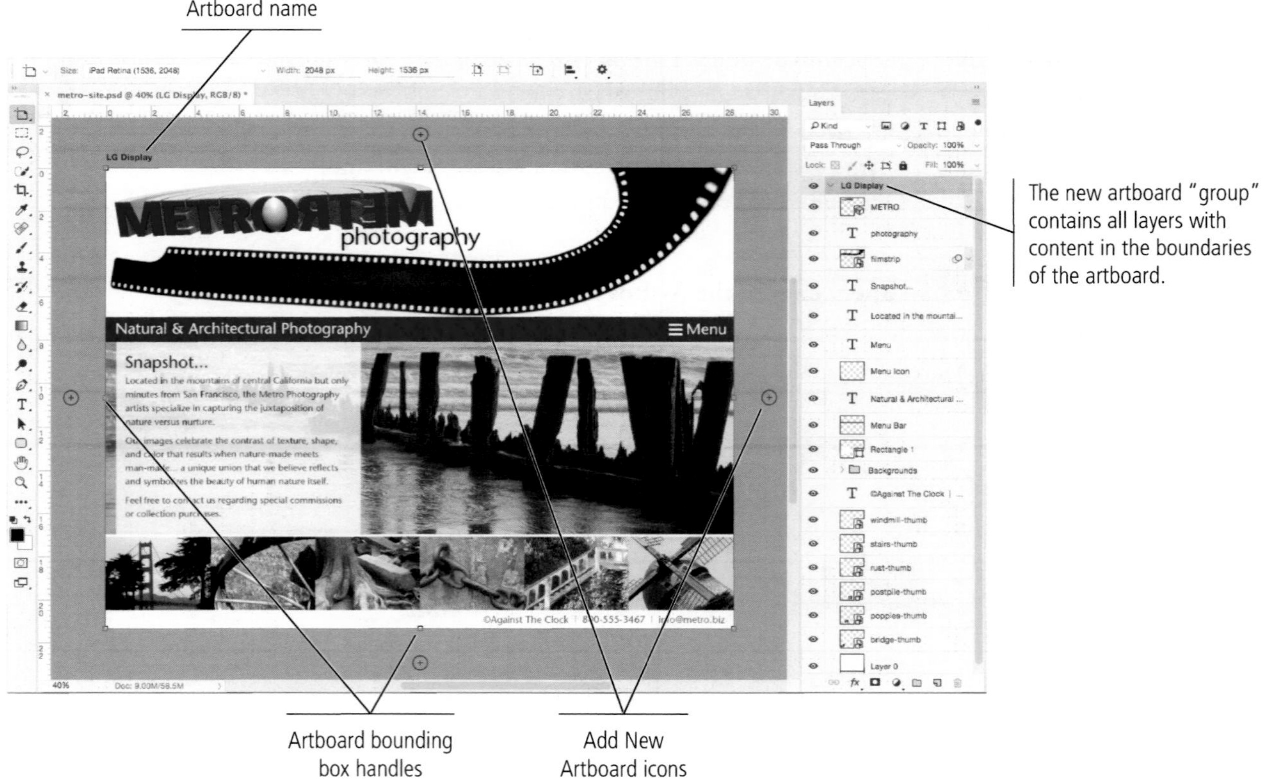

5. **Save the file, then continue to the next exercise.**

Generate Image Assets from Layers

Adobe Generator is a Photoshop plug-in that makes it very easy to create the required web-ready assets from layers in any Photoshop file. Any transformations applied to layer content are processed and become a permanent part of the generated asset.

Three image formats are primarily used for digital delivery:

- **JPEG** (Joint Photographic Experts Group), which supports 24-bit color, is used primarily for continuous-tone images with subtle changes in color, such as photographs or other images that are created in Adobe Photoshop. The JPEG format incorporates **lossy compression**, which means that pixels are thrown away in order to reduce file size; when areas of flat color are highly compressed, speckles of other colors (called artifacts) often appear, which negatively impacts the quality of the design.
- **GIF** (Graphics Interchange Format), which supports only 8-bit color and basic on-or-off transparency, is best used for graphics with areas of solid color, such as logos or other basic illustrations. The GIF format uses **lossless compression** to reduce file size while ensuring that no information is lost during the compression.
- **PNG** (Portable Network Graphics), which supports 8- and 24-bit color, as well as a special 32-bit format allowing support for various degrees of transparency, can be used for both illustrations and continuous-tone images. The PNG format uses lossless compression to create smaller file size without losing image data.

Note:

***Bit depth** refers to how many bits define the color value of a particular pixel. A **bit** is a unit of information that is either on or off (represented as 1 and 0, respectively). One bit has two states or colors, eight bits have 256 possible colors (2×2×2×2×2×2×2×2=256), and 24 bits have 16,777,216 (2^{24}) possible colors.*

In an RGB photograph, three color channels define how much of each primary color (red, green, and blue) makes up each pixel. Each channel requires 8 bits, resulting in a total of 24 bits for each pixel ("true color").

1. **With `metro-site.psd` open, open the Plug-Ins pane of the Preferences dialog box.**
2. **Make sure the Enable Generator option is checked (active), then click OK.**

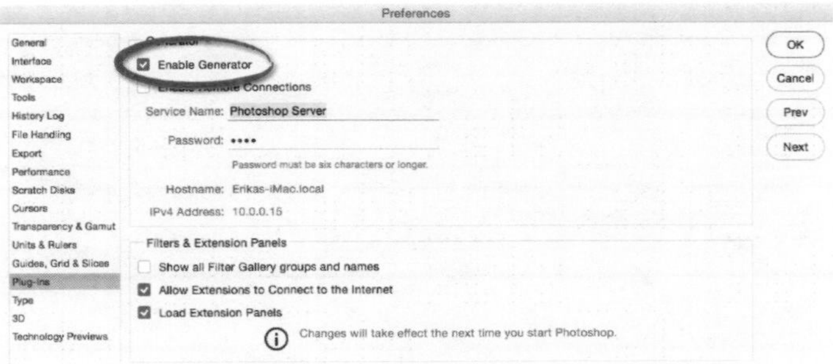

3. **Open the Generate submenu in the File menu and make sure the Image Assets option is checked (active).**

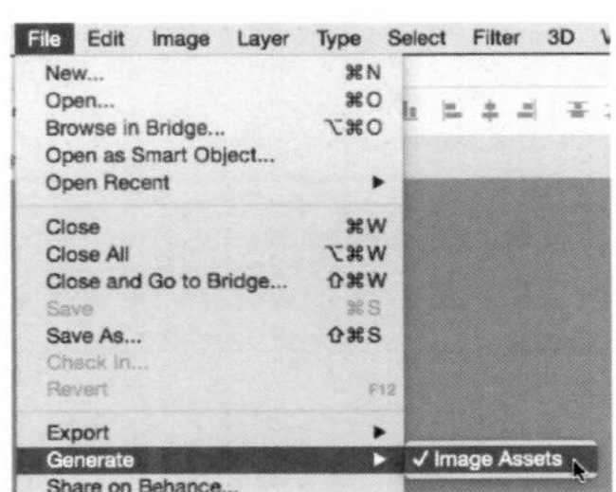

Note:

To disable image asset generation for the active file, deselect File>Generate>Image Assets.

To disable image asset generation for all Photoshop files, uncheck the Enable Generator option in the Plug-Ins pane of the Preferences dialog box.

4. **In the Layers panel, select both the METRO and photography layers. Click the Create a New Group button at the bottom of the Layers panel.**

   You want the two layers to function together as a single logo in the Web page, so you are grouping them together.

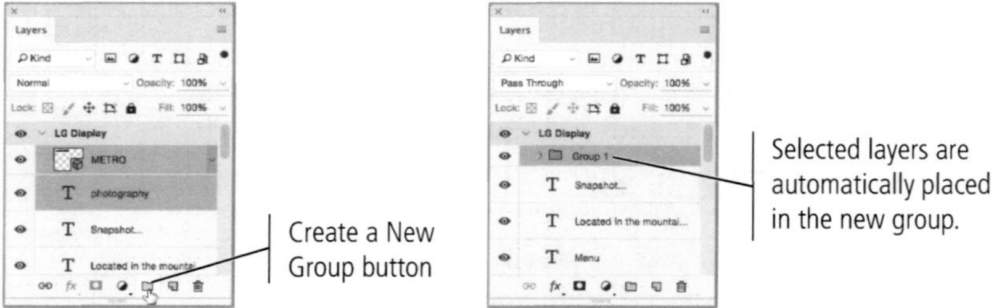

5. **Double-click the new layer group name to select it. Type** `logotype-lg.png` **as the new name, then press Return/Enter.**

   Renaming a layer group is the same process as renaming a layer.

   You are using the "lg" designation to differentiate this file from the one you will create for extra-small displays in a later exercise.

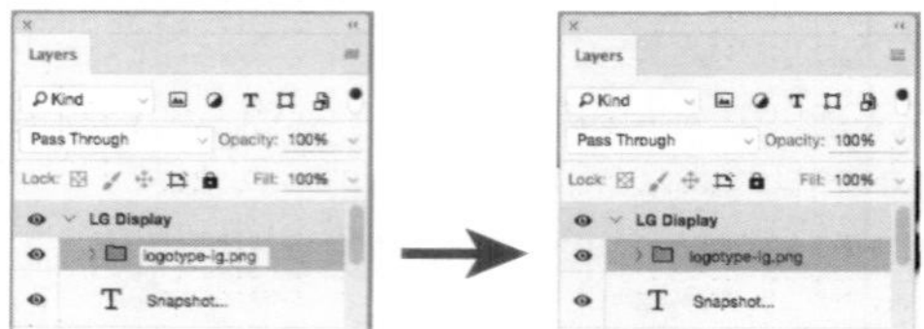

6. **On your desktop, open the WIP>Metro folder.**

   Adobe Generator creates new web assets as soon as you define a layer name that includes an appropriate extension (.jpg, .gif, or .png). A new folder — metro-site-assets — has been added. The logotype-lg.png file, which was generated as soon as you defined the layer group name, exists inside that folder.

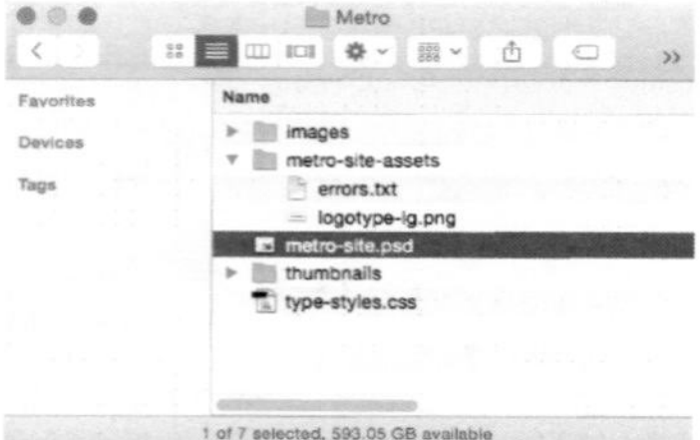

7. **In Photoshop, double-click the filmstrip layer name to highlight it. Type** `filmstrip-lg.png` **as the new layer name, then press Return/Enter.**

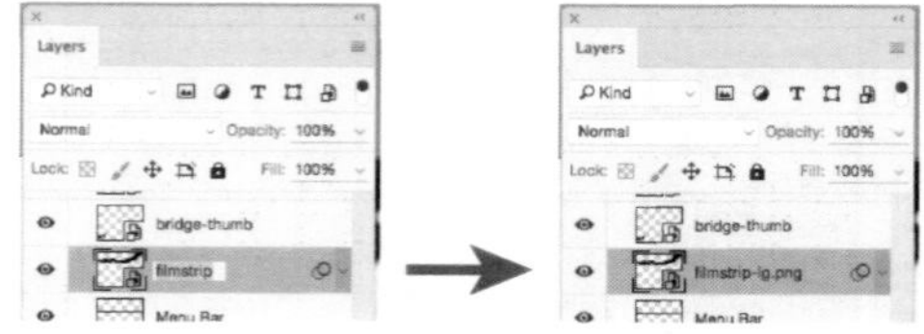

Note:

At the time of this writing, original layer order is not maintained when you create a new artboard. Because of this bug in the software, your filmstrip layer might be at a different location in the layer order.

8. **Repeat Step 7 for the following layers:**

Layer	Rename as:
Menu Icon	menu-icon-lg.gif
Menu Bar	menu-bar-lg.jpg
Backgrounds>pilings	pilings-bkg-lg.jpg
Backgrounds>waves	waves-bkg-lg.jpg
Backgrounds>fountain	fountain-bkg-lg.jpg
Backgrounds>arches	arches-bkg-lg.jpg
windmill-thumb	windmill-thumb.jpg
stairs-thumb	stairs-thumb.jpg
rust-thumb	rust-thumb.jpg
postpile-thumb	postpile-thumb.jpg
poppies-thumb	poppies-thumb.jpg
bridge-thumb	bridge-thumb.jpg

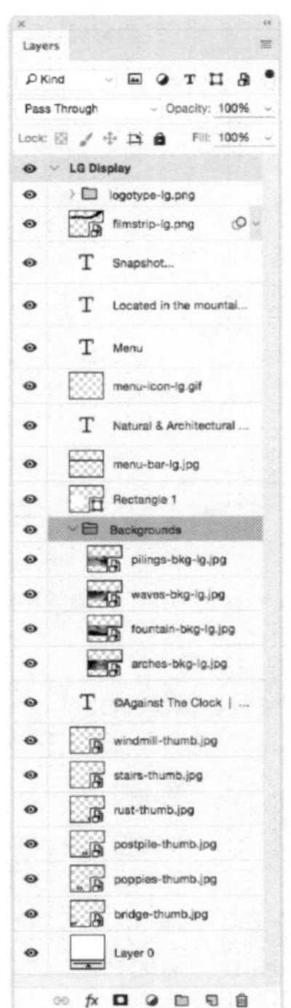

More about Using Adobe Generator

As you saw in this exercise, Generator creates Web assets as soon as you define an appropriate file extension for a specific layer (or layer group).

You can also generate multiple files from a single layer by separating asset names with a comma in the Layers panel. For example, the layer name:

menu-bar.jpg, menu-bar.png

creates two separate files in the metro-site-assets folder.

Creating Asset Subfolders

If you want to create subfolders inside the main assets folder, simply include the subfolder name and a forward slash in the modified layer name. For example:

thumbnails/bridge_small.jpg

Changing Asset Quality Settings

You can use complex layer/layer group names to define different compression, quality, and size options in the generated assets. By default:

- JPG assets are generated at 90% quality by default.
- PNG assets are generated as 32-bit images by default.
- GIF assets are generated with basic alpha transparency.

While renaming layers or layer groups in preparation for asset generation, you can customize quality and size.

For JPEG files, you can define a different quality setting by appending a number to the end of the layer name, such as filename.jpg(1-10) or filename.jpg(1-100%). For example:

menu-bar.jpg50%

creates a JPEG file with medium image quality.

For PNG files, you can change the output quality by appending the number 8, 24, or 32 to the layer name. For example:

filmstrip.png24

creates a 24-bit PNG file instead of the default 32-bit file.

Changing Asset Size Settings

You can also use layer names to define a specific size for the generated assets. Simply add the desired output size — relative or specific — as a prefix to the asset name. (Remember to add a space character between the prefix and the asset name.) For example:

200% menu-bar.jpg

10in x 2in logotype.png

50 x 25 menu-icon.gif

If you specify the size in pixels, you can omit the unit; other units must be included in the layer name prefix.

9. **On your desktop, review the contents of the metro-site-assets folder.**

10. **In Photoshop, save metro-site.psd and then continue to the next exercise.**

 Copy CSS for Text and Shape Layers

You do not need to be a Web programmer to design a site in Photoshop. However, to take best advantage of some of the tools that are available for moving your work into a functional HTML page, you should understand at least the basics of HTML:

- An HTML page contains code that defines the **elements** that make up a page.
- Individual page elements are defined with **tags**. For example, a <div> tag identifies a division or area of the page, and a <p> tag identifies a paragraph of text. Available tags are defined by the version of HTML being used; you can't simply make up tags.
- Specific elements can be identified with user-defined classes, which helps to differentiate them from other same-type elements. For example:

```
<div class="feature-image">
<div class="text-area">
```

- Cascading Style Sheets (CSS) are used to define the properties of HTML elements. CSS files define **selectors**, which contain **property:value pairs** to control the appearance of specific elements in an HTML page. For example:

```
header {
    width: 780px;
    height: 75px;
}
```

- Two types of CSS selectors are relevant to site design in Photoshop:
  - **Tag selectors** define the appearance of HTML tags. These selectors simply use the tag name as the selector name; for example, the **div** selector defines the appearance of all **<div>** tags.
  - **Class selectors** define the appearance of any tag that is identified with the defined class. These selector names always begin with a period; for example, the **.text-area** selector would apply to any element that has the **class="text-area"** attribute.

In this exercise, you will use Photoshop to create CSS classes, which the Web designer can apply to various page elements so that your design choices are maintained in the final HTML page.

1. **With metro-site.psd open in Photoshop, change the Snapshot type layer name to h1-lg.**

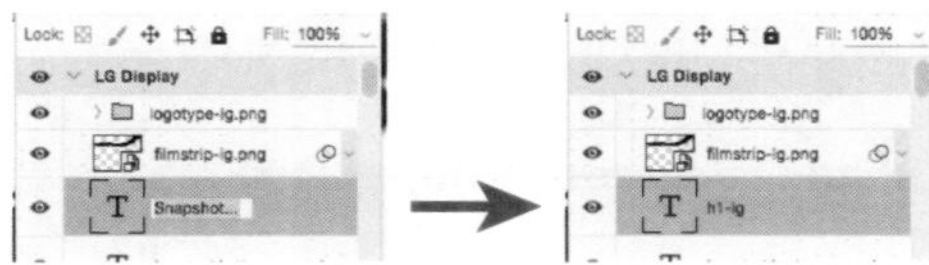

2. **Control/right-click the h1-lg type layer and choose Copy CSS from the contextual menu.**

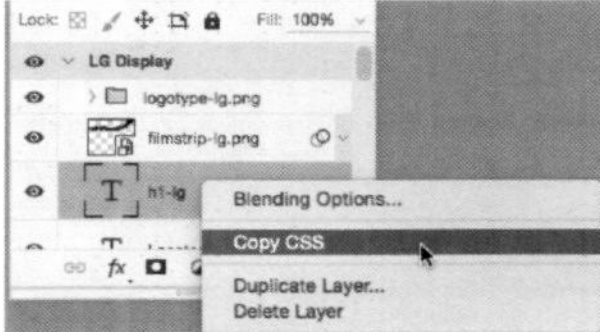

3. **Using any text-editing application, open the file type-styles.css from the WIP>Metro folder.**

   We use TextEdit on a Macintosh in our screen shots, but you can use any text editor to complete the following steps.

4. **Place the insertion point on the first empty line at the end of the file, then press Command/Control-V to paste the CSS that was copied in Step 2.**

   All CSS copied from Photoshop is created as a class. The selector name, beginning with a period, is taken from the relevant Photoshop layer.

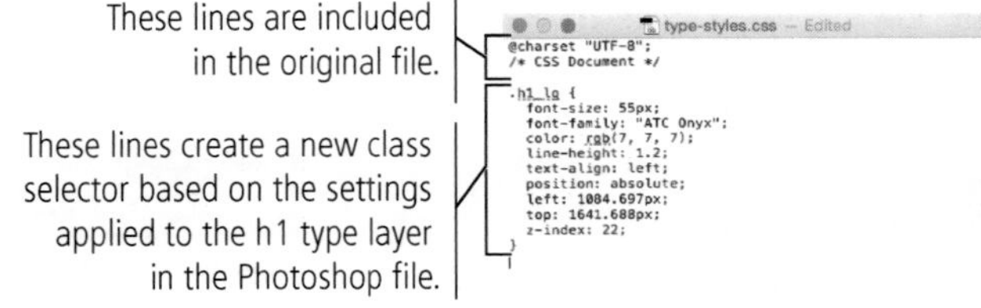

5. **Repeat Steps 1–4 to rename the remaining type layers in the Photoshop file and create the required CSS for each.**

Layer	Rename as:
Located in ...	body-copy-lg
Menu	menu-lg
Natural & ...	subhead-lg
©Against the ...	footer-lg

6. **In the Layers panel, rename the Rectangle 1 shape layer as** main-content-lg**.**

   Although this is not a type layer, you want to communicate the area's transparency to the Web designer. Photoshop can generate CSS for any layer that is not a smart object.

7. **Control/right-click the main-content-lg shape layer and choose Copy CSS from the contextual menu.**

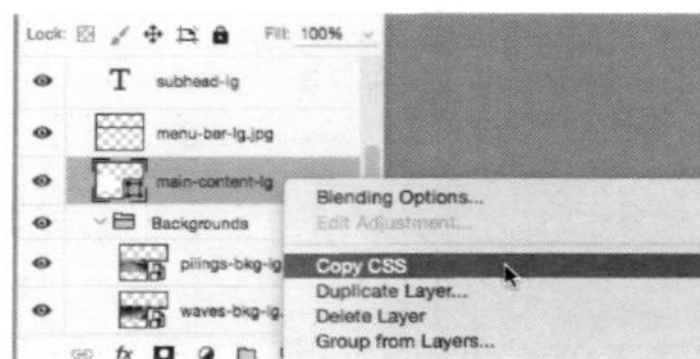

8. **Paste the copied CSS into the type-styles.css file.**

9. **In the .main-content-lg selector, select and delete all but the background-color and opacity lines.**

10. **Save type-styles.css, then close it.**

11. **In Photoshop, collapse the LG Display artboard.**

12. **Save the file, then continue to the next exercise.**

Creating Image Slices

PHOTOSHOP FOUNDATIONS

Although the Slice tool was intended to cut apart pieces of a Web page comp for reassembly in a Web design application, it can be used for any situation in which you need to cut up a single image into multiple bits.

In addition to creating image assets from layers and layer groups, you can also create image slices; all visible layers in the slice area are included in the resulting images.

Photoshop offers a number of options for creating slices in your artwork:

- Manual draw a slice area with the Slice tool.
- When the Slice tool is active, click Slices from Guides in the Options bar to automatically slice the file based on existing ruler guides.
- When the Slice Select tool is active and a specific slice is selected in the file, click Divide in the Options bar to divide the slice horizontally or vertically into a specific number of equal-size slices.
- Create a new slice based on specific layer content by selecting one or more layer sin the Layers panel, then choosing Layer>New Layer Based Slice

Once slices are created, you can double-click select a specific slice with the Slice Selection tool to edit its settings. In the resulting dialog box:

- Name is the file name of the image that is created from the slice.
- URL is the file that opens if a user clicks the slice.
- Target is the location where the URL opens when a user clicks the slice.
- Message Text appears in the browser's status bar.
- Alt Tag appears if image display is disabled.

(URL, Target, and Message are better handled in a Web design application such as Adobe Dreamweaver.)

Dimensions fields are automatically filled with the size of the selected slice. You can also change the slice background type and color if the slice contains areas of transparency.

Copy and Edit Artboard Sizes

As we explained earlier, a Photoshop artboard is basically a way of organizing and managing layers so you can create more than one layout in the same Photoshop file. In this exercise, you are going to create a second artboard to create the files you need for extra-small (<768 pixels wide) displays such as smart phones.

1. **With `metro-site.psd` open, make sure the LG Display artboard is selected in the Layers panel and then activate the Artboard tool in the Tools panel.**

2. **Option/Alt-click the Add New Artboard icon to the right of the existing artboard.**

   When the Artboard tool is active, the Add New Artboard icons appear on all four sides of the active artboard. Clicking one of these icons adds a new blank artboard adjacent to the existing one (the new artboard appears on the same side as the icon you click).

   If you Option/Alt-click one of the icons, the new artboard is a duplicate of the existing one, including all the layers that existed on the previous artboard.

3. **In the Layers panel, expand the LG Display copy artboard.**

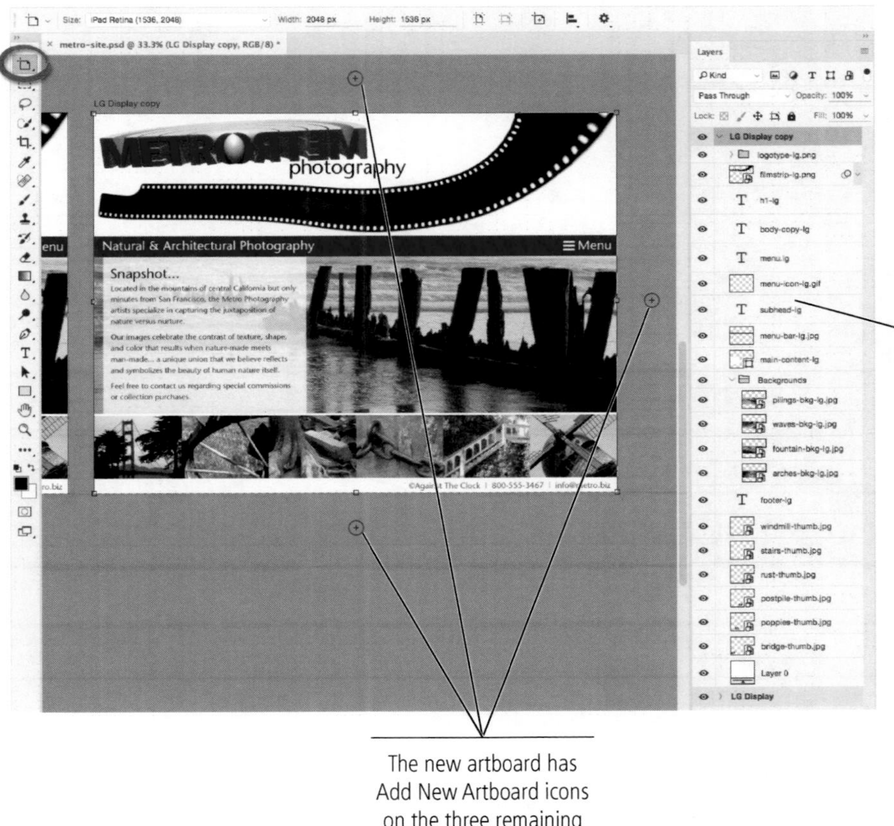

Layers on the original artboard are duplicated in the new artboard.

The new artboard has Add New Artboard icons on the three remaining available sides.

4. **In the Layers panel, change the name of the LG Display copy artboard to `XS Display`.**

   Renaming artboards uses the same process as renaming layers and layer groups — double-click the existing name in the Layers panel, then type the new name.

5. **With the XS Display artboard active, choose iPhone 6 (750, 1334) in the Options bar Size menu, then click the Make Portrait button.**

   When you change the size of an artboard, any layers that no longer have content within the bounds of the artboard are automatically moved outside the artboard group in the Layers panel.

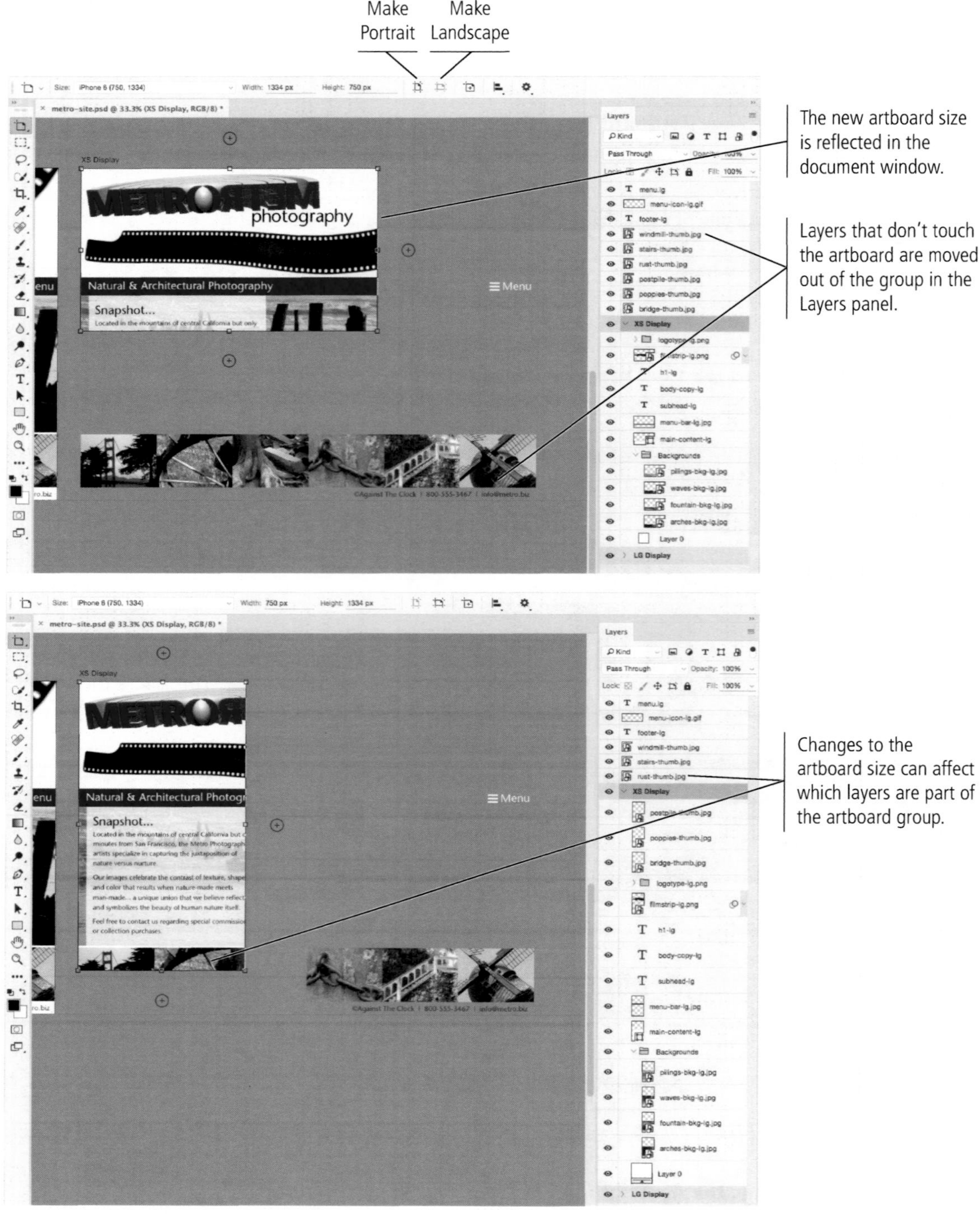

Make Portrait
Make Landscape
The new artboard size is reflected in the document window.
Layers that don't touch the artboard are moved out of the group in the Layers panel.
Changes to the artboard size can affect which layers are part of the artboard group.

6. **In the Layers panel, press Command/Control, then click the following layer names:**

menu-lg	**windmill-thumb.jpg**
stairs-thumb.jpg	**rust-thumb.jpg**
postpile-thumb.jpg	**poppies-thumb.jpg**
bridge-thumb.jpg	**filmstrip-lg.png**

7. **With all eight layers selected, click the panel's Delete button; click Yes to confirm the deletion.**

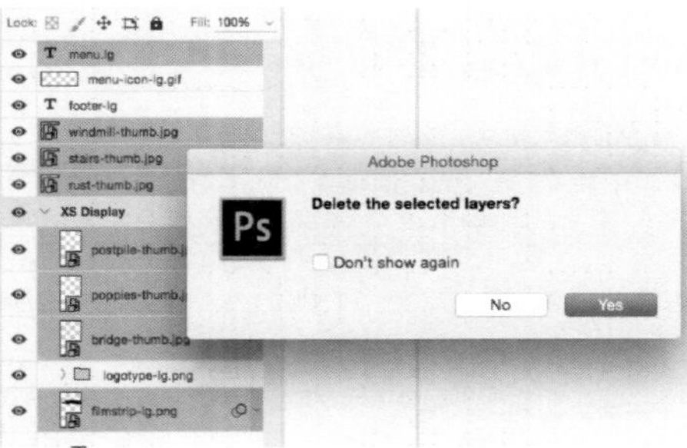

On an extra-small display size, most sites would not include the type of thumbnail images that you see in the large display layout. Because space is at a premium on extra-small displays, you are also deleting the purely decorative filmstrip and the word identifier word "Menu."

8. **Save the file and continue to the next exercise.**

Adjust Image Content for Alternate Display Sizes

1. **With metro-site.psd open, activate the Move tool in the Tools panel. Turn off the Auto Select option in the Options bar.**

2. **Select the logotype-lg.png layer group in the Layers panel, then press Command/Control-T to enter Free Transform mode for the layer group.**

3. **Shift-click and drag the bottom-right bounding box handle until the entire logotype fits in the artboard bounds.**

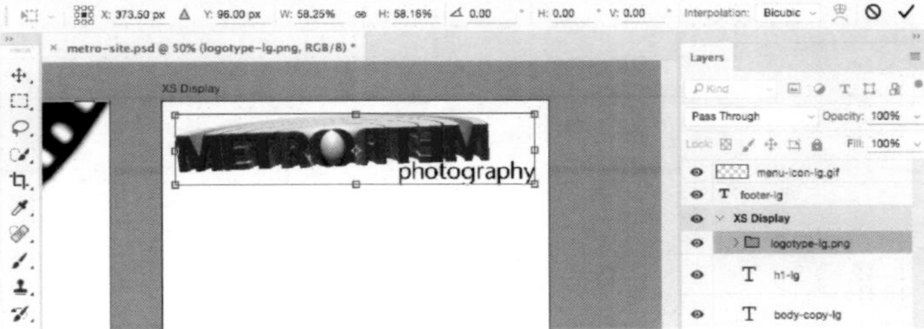

4. **Press Return/Enter to finalize the transformation.**

5. **In the Layers panel, change the name of the resized layer group to `logotype-xs.png`.**

   If you don't define a separate name for the resized group, Photoshop does not generate a new version of the logotype image. The original logotype-lg,png file is maintained, and it is not overwritten with the resized version.

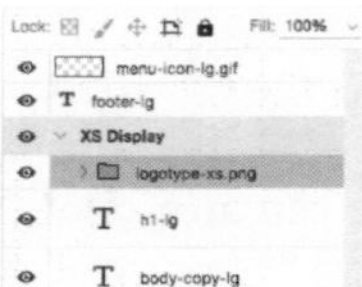

6. **Choose the menu-bar-lg.jpg layer, then move it up until only a small amount of white space appears below the logotype.**

   Because you did not transform this layer, you do not need to generate a separate file for this image in an extra-small display.

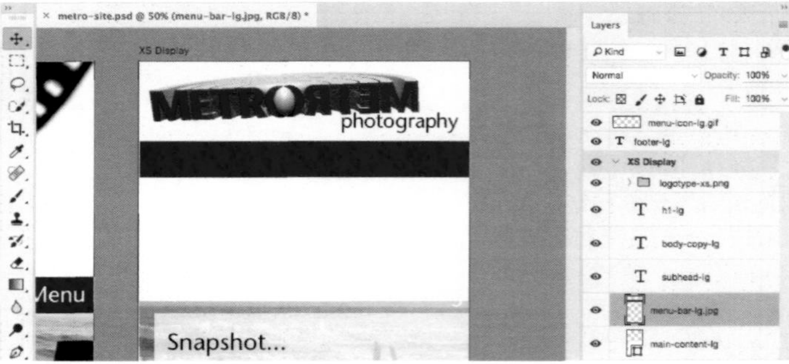

7. **Select the menu-icon-lg.gif layer, then click and drag until the icon artwork appears in the right side of the menu bar area.**

   Because the Auto Select option is not active, you do not have to carefully click the narrow bars of the icon to move this layer's content.

   As soon as you move the layer content within the artboard bounds, the menu-icon-lg.gif layer is moved into the XS Display artboard in the Layers panel.

   Again, you do not need a separate file for this icon so you do not need to change the layer name.

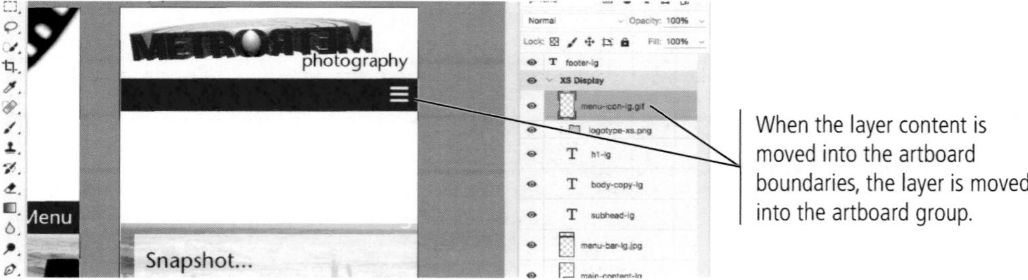

When the layer content is moved into the artboard boundaries, the layer is moved into the artboard group.

8. **In the Layers panel, select the Backgrounds layer group. Press Command/Control-T to enter Free Transform mode for the entire group.**

   By transforming the entire group, you are transforming all layers in the group at one time.

9. **Enlarge the group, anchoring the bottom-left corner, until the images fill the white space below the menu bar.**

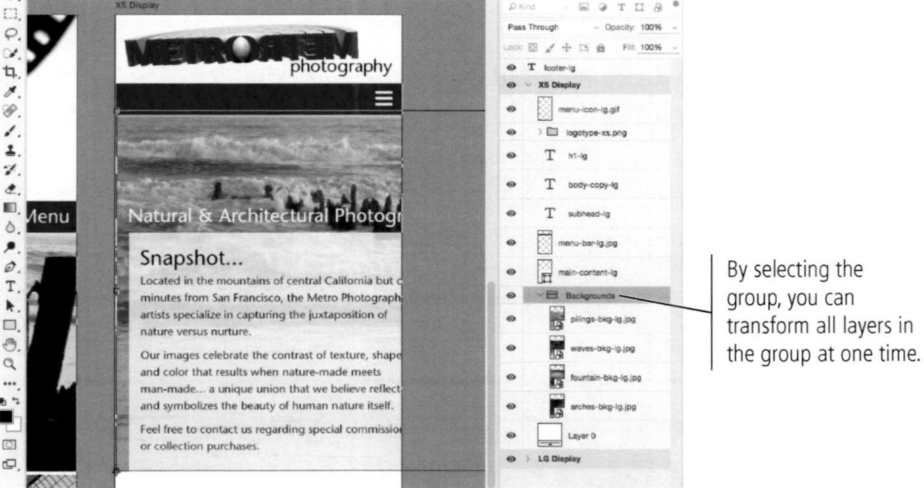

By selecting the group, you can transform all layers in the group at one time.

10. **Press Return/Enter to finalize the transformation.**

11. **In the Layers panel, change the "lg" in each background layer name to `xs`.**

    When Photoshop generates an image based on layer content, the resulting image is cropped at the artboard edges. The background images generated in this step will have significantly different dimensions than the large-size background images generated in the earlier exercise.

12. **Save the file and continue to the next exercise.**

 Generate Type CSS for Alternate Display Sizes

1. **With `metro-site.psd` open, select the subhead-lg layer in the XS Display artboard group.**

2. **Using the Move tool, click and drag until the layer text appears in the menu bar area (as shown after Step 3).**

    As you can see, the type size for the large display does not fit within the available space in the extra-small display. You need to change the type size, then generate additional CSS for the smaller display size.

3. **Activate the Horizontal Type tool, then click to place the insertion point in the layer.**

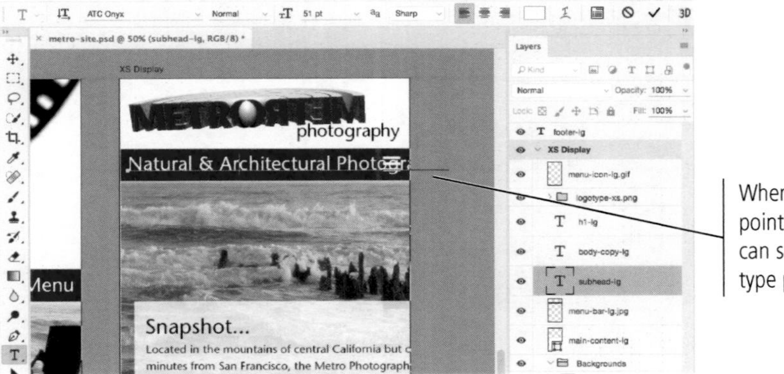

When the insertion point is placed, you can see the entire type path.

4. **Triple-click the active type layer to select all text on that line.**

   When the insertion point is placed in a type layer, you can also press Command/Control-A to select all type on that layer.

5. **Press Command/Control-Shift-< repeatedly to reduce the type size, until the entire heading fits inside the artboard boundaries.**

   This keyboard shortcut reduces the type size by one point. You can press Command/Control-Shift-> to increase the type size by one point.

   If you use the Transform controls to reduce type size on a type layer, the CSS generated by Photoshop does not recognize the transformed type size. For the type size to change in the CSS, you have to manually reduce the type size when the actual type is highlighted.

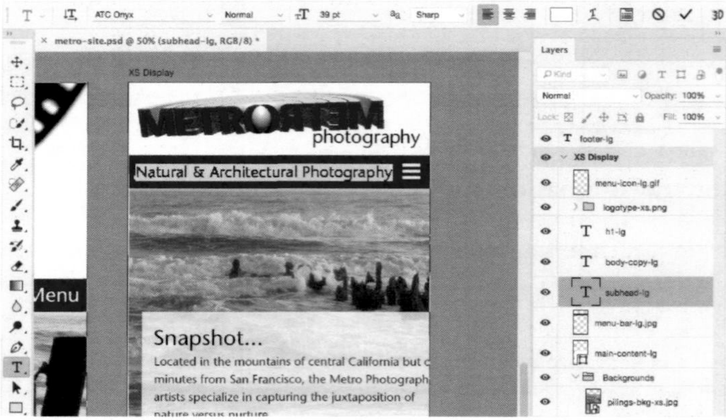

6. **In the Layers panel, change the subhead-lg layer name to `subhead-xs`.**

7. **Command/Control-click the subhead-xs layer and choose Copy CSS in the contextual menu.**

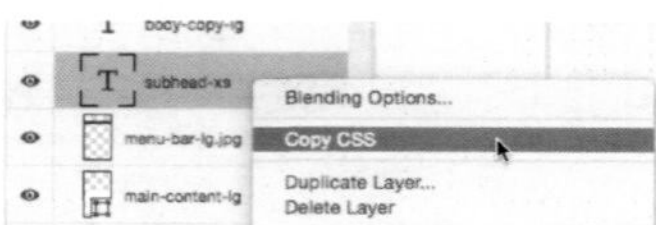

8. **Open `type-styles.css` (from your WIP>Metro folder) in a text-editing application.**

9. **Place the insertion point at the end of the existing copy and press Command/Control-V to paste the CSS from Step 7.**

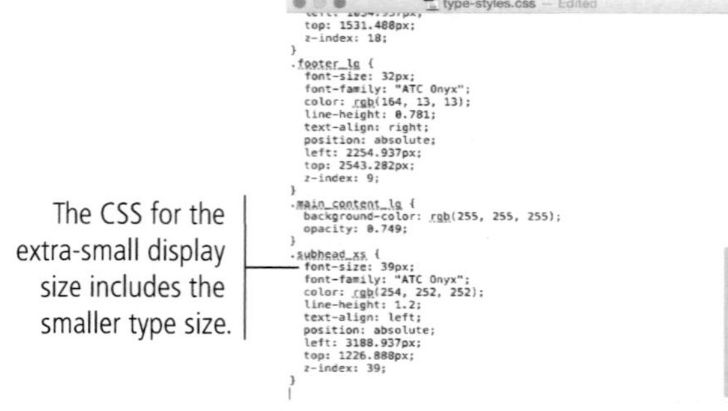

10. **Return to Photoshop. In the Layers panel, Command/Control-click to select the h1-lg, body-copy-lg, and main-content-lg layers.**

11. **Using the Move tool, drag the selected layer content left until it snaps to the artboard edge.**

    Because you selected all three layers, their positions relative to one another remains the same when you move the three layers at one time.

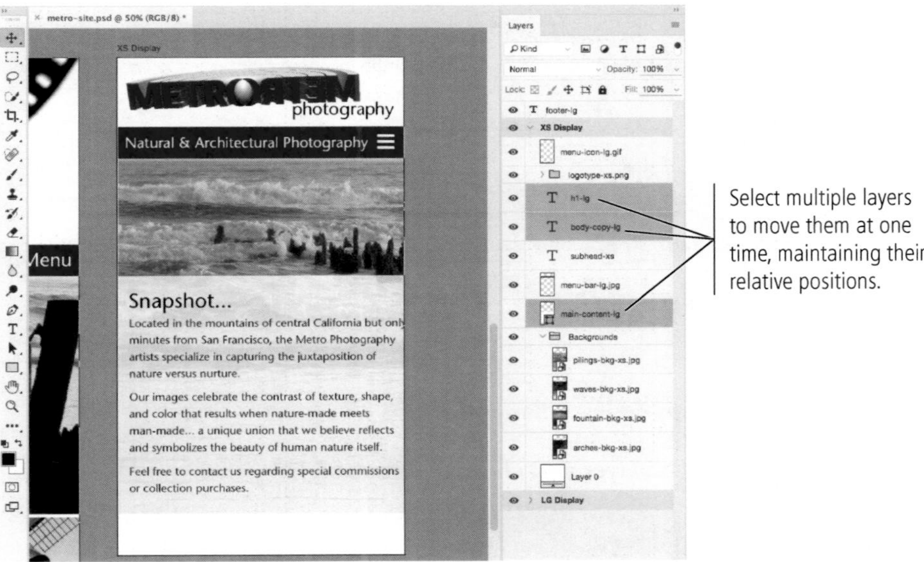

Select multiple layers to move them at one time, maintaining their relative positions.

12. **Using the Horizontal Type tool, click to place the insertion point in the body copy text ("Located in the...").**

    Because this is an area-type object, you have to place the insertion point to access the area handles.

13. **Drag the right-center handle until the right edge of the area is approximately 1/8″ inside the artboard edge.**

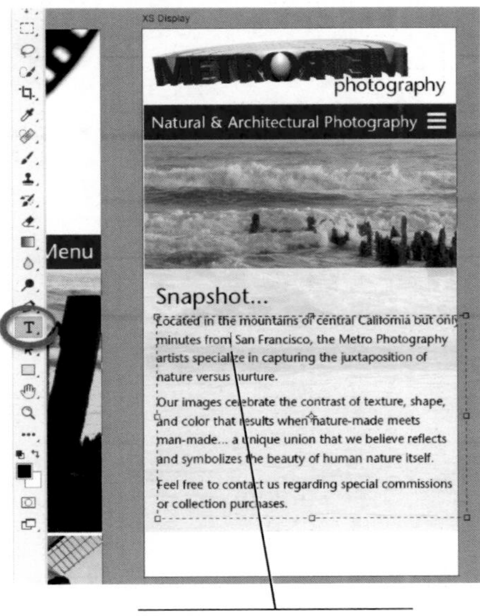

Place the insertion point to access the type area handles.

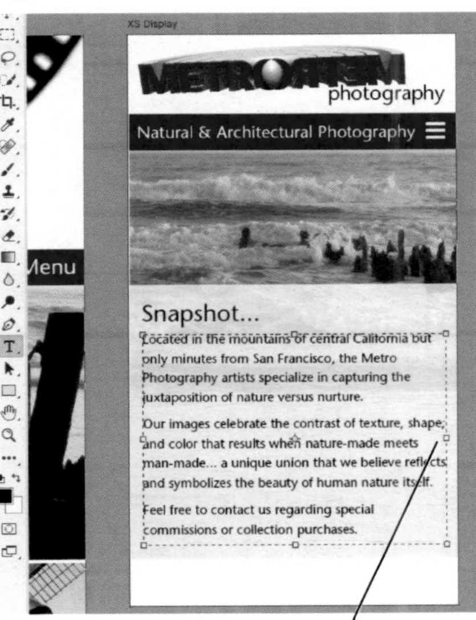

Drag the handles to change the size of the type area.

14. **Click the body-copy-lg layer name to select the layer.**

    This step also deactivates the type area handles.

15. **Using the Character panel, define a `24 pt` font size with `36 pt` leading.**

    When the layer is selected and the insertion point is not placed, changing type settings affects all text on the selected layer.

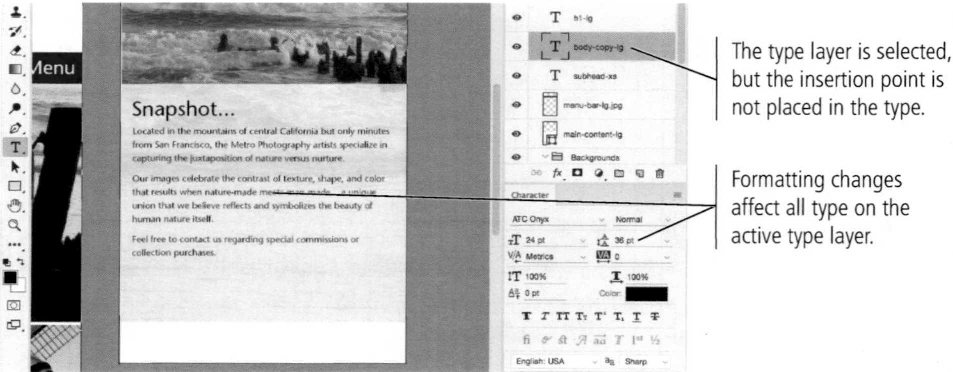

The type layer is selected, but the insertion point is not placed in the type.
Formatting changes affect all type on the active type layer.

16. **In the Layers panel, change the body-copy-lg layer name to `body-copy-xs`.**

17. **Command/Control-click the body-copy-xs layer and choose Copy CSS in the contextual menu.**

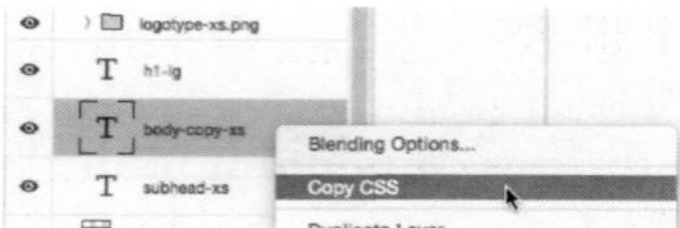

18. **If necessary, open `type-styles.css` (from your WIP>Metro folder) in a text-editing application.**

19. **Place the insertion point at the end of the existing copy and press Command/Control-V to paste the CSS from Step 12.**

type-styles.css — Edited

```
}
.main_content_lg {
  background-color: rgb(255, 255, 255);
  opacity: 0.749;
}
.subhead_xs {
  font-size: 39px;
  font-family: "ATC Onyx";
  color: rgb(254, 252, 252);
  line-height: 1.2;
  text-align: left;
  position: absolute;
  left: 3188.937px;
  top: 1226.888px;
  z-index: 39;
}
.body_copy_xs {
  font-size: 24px;
  font-family: "ATC Onyx";
  color: rgb(0, 0, 0);
  line-height: 1.5;
  text-align: left;
  position: absolute;
  left: 3198.834px;
  top: 1757.538px;
  width: 673px;
  height: 348px;
  z-index: 40;
}
```

20. Repeat Steps 14–19 to change the type on the h1-lg layer to 44 pt with Auto leading. Change the layer name to h1-xs, then copy and paste the layer's CSS into the type-styles.css file.

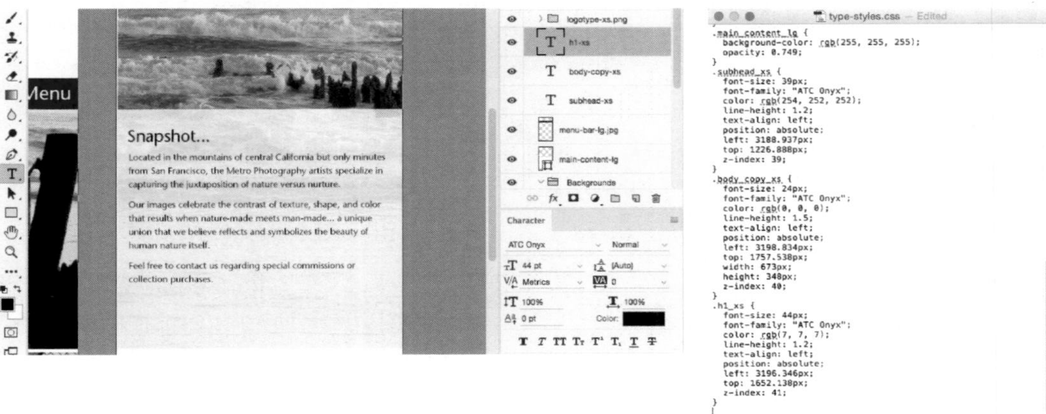

21. Using the basic process you learned in this exercise, make the following changes for the footer text:

- Change the text on the footer-lg type layer to 22 pt with centered paragraph alignment.
- Position the layer so the text is centered in the white space at the bottom of the artboard.
- Change the layer name to footer-xs, copy the CSS for that layer, and paste it into the text-styles.css file.

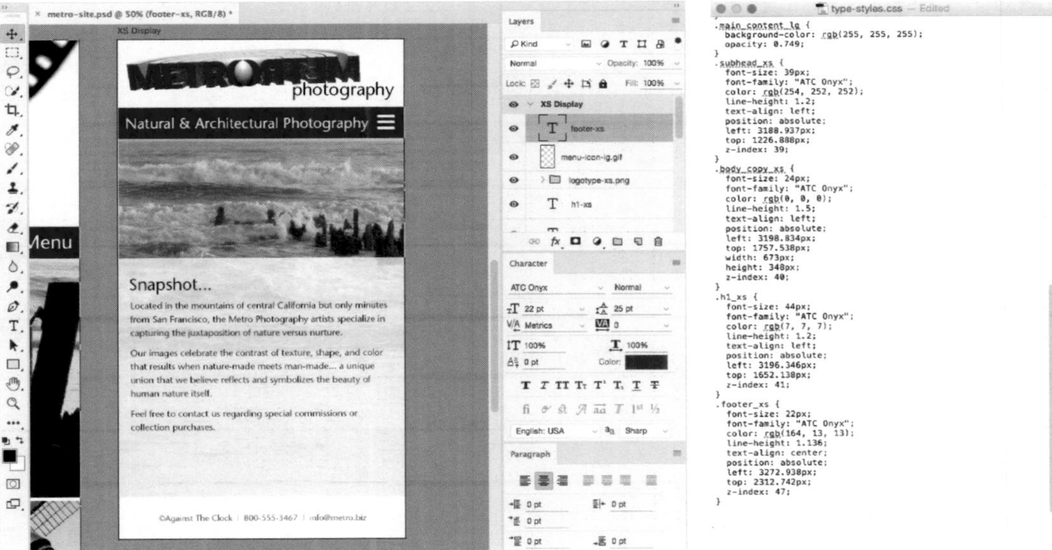

22. Save and close text-styles.css.

23. Save and close metro-site.psd.

Project Review

fill in the blank

1. The _______________ command can be used to run an action on all files in a specific folder without user intervention.

2. Align options are available in the _______________ when multiple layers are selected in the Layers panel.

3. True or False: You can edit the text in a type layer that has been converted to 3D. _______________

4. The _______________ tool is used to manually cut apart a page into smaller pieces for Web delivery.

5. The _______________ image format allows lossy compression and does not support transparency; it is best used for photos.

6. The _______________ format supports only 8-bit color; it is best used for artwork or graphics with large areas of solid color.

7. The _______________ format supports both continuous-tone color and degrees of transparency.

8. _______________ are used to define the properties of HTML elements.

9. CSS files define _______________, which contain property:value pairs to control the appearance of specific elements in an HTML page.

10. All CSS copied from Photoshop is created as a _______________. The selector name, beginning with a period, is taken from the relevant Photoshop layer.

short answer

1. Briefly explain how actions can be used to improve workflow.

2. Briefly explain three file formats that are used for images on the Web.

3. Briefly explain the concept of CSS in relation to Web design.

Portfolio Builder Project

Use what you learned in this project to complete the following freeform exercise.
Carefully read the art director and client comments, then create your own design to meet the needs of the project.
Use the space below to sketch ideas; when finished, write a brief explanation of your reasoning behind your final design.

art director comments

As a freelance designer, you have been hired by the band Midnight Sun to create a logo and cover artwork for their forthcoming CD release.

- ❑ Design an interesting logotype for the band.
- ❑ Determine the appropriate size for the cover that is inserted into a CD jewel case.
- ❑ Locate or create artwork or images to illustrate the CD title.
- ❑ Create the CD cover art for commercial printing requirements.
- ❑ Save a file with appropriate settings for digital display on a Web site.

client comments

We're originally from Alaska. We all had full-time jobs when we first started, so we practiced late at night (no surprise!) until we decided we would get more exposure in Seattle. Since we spent so much time awake in the middle of the night, we named the band Midnight Sun.

We haven't had much luck yet in finding a label, so we're going to self-publish an EP to help promote the band and, hopefully, raise some money. We're calling the disc "The Lower 48" because all of the songs are about our journey to where we are now.

We want the cover art to represent the type of music we play — primarily rock, but with other genres thrown in. Blues, hip hop, international beats, and even orchestrated undertones all make an appearance.

We have a very unique sound, but we're an eclectic group of people. We're hoping you can create cover art that says who we are without using a boring group photo.

project justification

Project Summary

The graphic design workflow typically revolves around extremely short turnaround times, which means that any possible automation will only be a benefit. Photoshop actions can be useful whenever you need to apply the same sets of options to more than one or two images. Every click you save will allow you to do other work, meet tight deadlines, and satisfy your clients. In the case of running a batch on multiple images, you are completely freed to work on other projects, be in other places, or even (technically) "work" while you're gone for the evening.

Although many developers use dedicated Web-design software like Adobe Dreamweaver to build sophisticated Web sites, the images for those sites have to come from somewhere. It is very common for a designer to build the "look and feel" of a site in Photoshop, then generate the pieces so the developer can more easily reassemble them in the Web-design application. As you saw by completing this project, Photoshop can even be used to create cascading style sheets to communicate the type and object formatting that you define in Photoshop.

Create a 3D extrusion from a type layer
Use puppet warping to distort a layer
Use artboards to create multiple versions in one file
Define an action to resize images
Run a batch to resize and rename multiple images
Generate Web assets based on layers and layer groups
Create CSS from type and shape layers
photography
Natural & Architectural Photography
Menu
Snapshot...

Adobe Animate (formerly Flash Professional) is an industry-standard application for building animations and other interactive content. Mastering the tools and techniques of the application can significantly improve your potential career options.

Typical Animate work ranges from simply moving things around within a space to building fully interactive games and Web sites, complete with sound and video files. Animate is somewhat unique in the communications industry because these different types of work often require different sets of skills — specifically, a combination of both visual creativity and logical programming. Depending on the type of application you're building, you should have a basic understanding of both graphic design and code.

Our goal in this section is to teach you how to use the available tools to create various types of work that you might encounter in your professional career. As you complete the projects, you explore the basic drawing techniques, and then move on to more advanced techniques such as adding animation and interactivity.

The simple exercises in this introduction are designed to let you explore the Animate user interface. Whether you are new to the application or upgrading from a previous version, we highly recommend that you follow these steps to click around and become familiar with the basic workspace.

Explore the Animate Interface

Much of the Animate interface functions in the same way as the Photoshop user interface. Panels can be opened, moved, and grouped in the same manner, and you can save custom workspaces to call specific sets of panels. The first time you launch the application, you'll see the default workspace settings defined by Adobe. When you relaunch after you or another user has quit, the workspace defaults to the last-used settings — including specific open panels and the position of those panels on your screen. Because Flash has a different basic purpose than Photoshop, there are some inherent differences that you should recognize.

1. **Download the InterfaceAN_Web16_RF.zip archive from the Student Files Web page.**

2. **Expand the ZIP archive in your WIP folder (Macintosh) or copy the archive contents into your WIP folder (Windows).**

   This results in a folder named **InterfaceAN**, which contains all of the files you need for this project.

3. **In Animate, open the Window menu and choose Workspaces>Essentials.**

   Remember: Saved workspaces, accessed in the Window>Workspaces menu or in the Workspace switcher on the Application bar, provide one-click access to a defined group of tools.

4. **Choose Window>Workspace>Reset 'Essentials'. If asked if you're sure about resetting the workspace, click Yes.**

   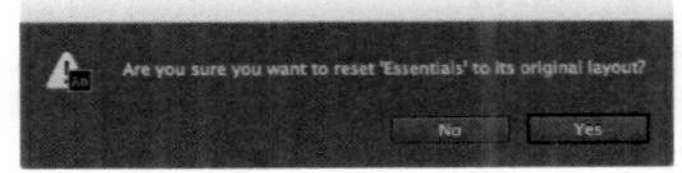

   As in Photoshop, saved workspaces in Flash remember the last-used state; to restore the saved state of the workspace, you have to use the Reset option.

   The Welcome Screen appears by default when no file is open, unless you (or someone else) checked the Don't Show Again option. The Welcome Screen provides quick access to recently opened files, and links for creating a variety of new documents. If you don't see the Welcome Screen when no files are open, you can turn this feature back on by choosing Welcome Screen in the On Launch menu of the General pane of the Preferences dialog box. After you quit and relaunch the application, the Welcome Screen reappears.

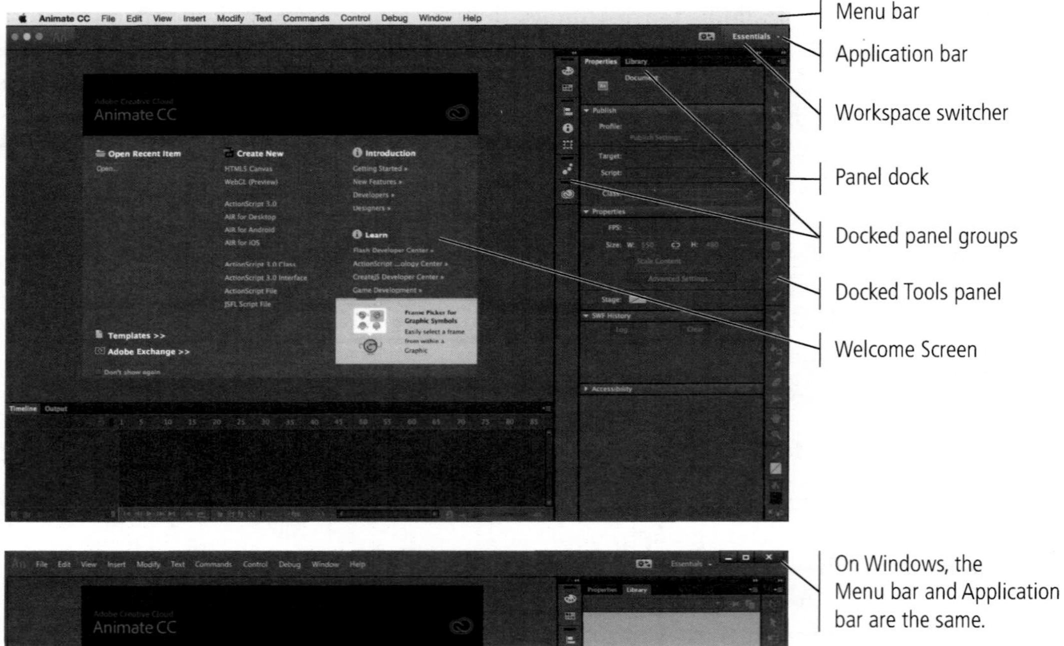

Menu bar
Application bar
Workspace switcher
Panel dock
Docked panel groups
Docked Tools panel
Welcome Screen
On Windows, the Menu bar and Application bar are the same.

The Welcome Screen appears by default when no file is open, unless someone checked the Don't Show Again option. If you don't see the Welcome Screen when no files are open, you can turn this feature back on by choosing Welcome Screen in the On Launch menu of the General pane of the Preferences dialog box. After you quit and relaunch the application, the Welcome Screen reappears.

Customizing Animate Keyboard Shortcuts

ANIMATE FOUNDATIONS

Different people use Animate for various reasons, sometimes using a specific, limited set of tools to complete only one type of project. In addition to customizing the workspace and the Tools panel, you can also customize the various keyboard shortcuts used to access different commands (Animate>Keyboard Shortcuts on Macintosh or Edit>Keyboard Shortcuts on Windows). Once you have defined custom menus or shortcuts, you can save your choices as a set so you can access the same custom choices again without having to redo the work.

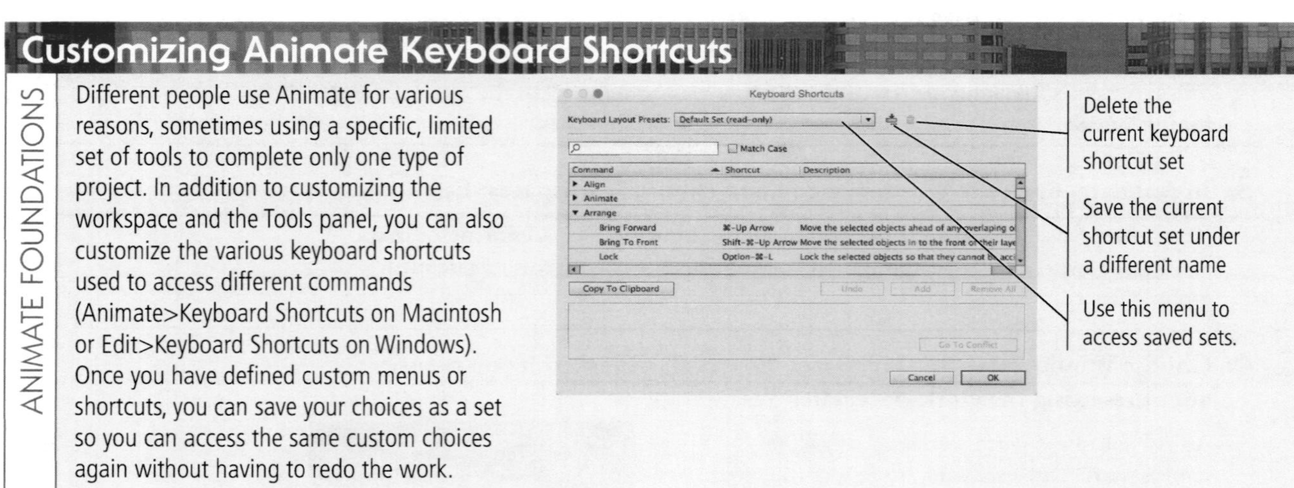

Delete the current keyboard shortcut set
Save the current shortcut set under a different name
Use this menu to access saved sets.

5. **Macintosh users: Choose Animate CC>Preferences.**
   Windows users: Choose Edit>Preferences.

   Remember that on Macintosh systems, the Preferences dialog box is accessed in the Animate CC menu; Windows users access the Preferences dialog box in the Edit menu.

   Preferences customize the way many of the program's tools and options function. Once open, you can access any of the Preference categories by clicking a different option in the left pane; the right side of the dialog box displays options related to the active category.

Macintosh **Windows**

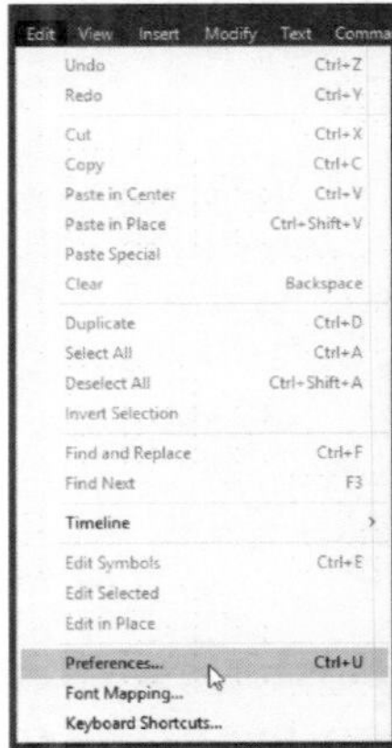

6. **With General selected in the list on the left side of the Preferences dialog box, choose any option that you prefer in the User Interface menu.**

   You might have already noticed the rather dark appearance of the panels and interface background. The application uses the dark "theme" as the default. (We used the Light option throughout this book because text in the interface elements is easier to read in printed screen captures.)

7. **Check the option to Auto-Collapse Iconic Panels, then click OK to close the Preferences dialog box.**

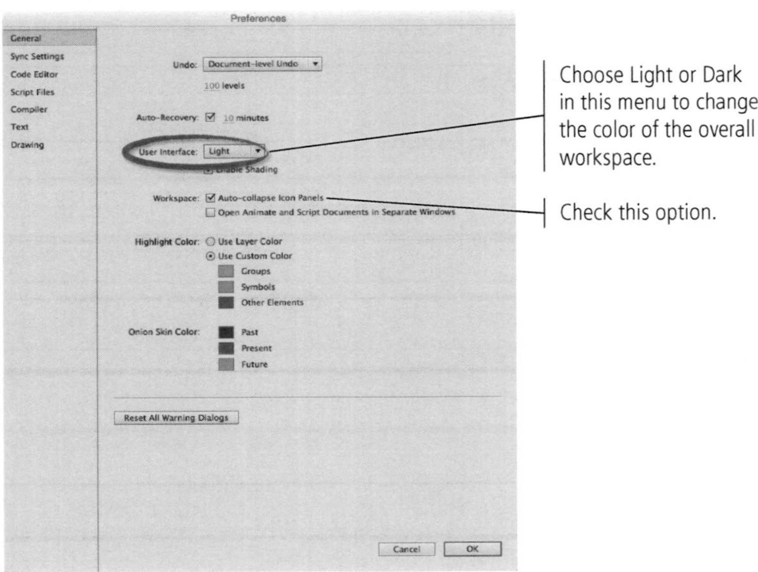

Choose Light or Dark in this menu to change the color of the overall workspace.

Check this option.

8. **On the right side of the workspace, click the Tools panel title bar and drag away from the dock into the middle of the workspace.**

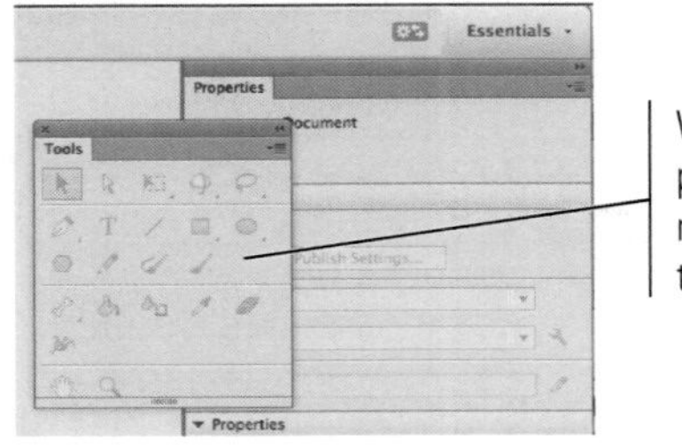

When floating, the Tools panel defaults to a standard rectangular panel with the tools in several rows.

9. **Click the Tools panel title bar and drag left until a blue line appears on the left edge of the workspace.**

   This step docks the Tools panel on the left edge of the workspace.

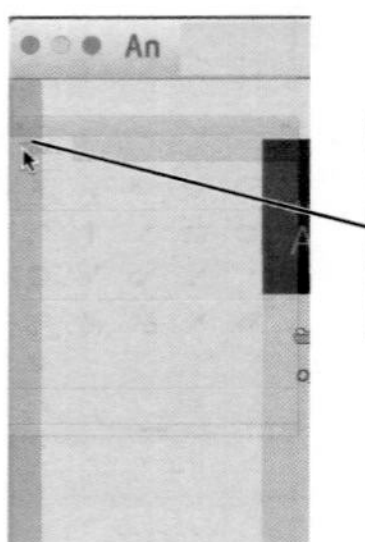

This pop-up "drawer" indicates that you are adding a column to the panel dock (in this case, on the left edge of the workspace).

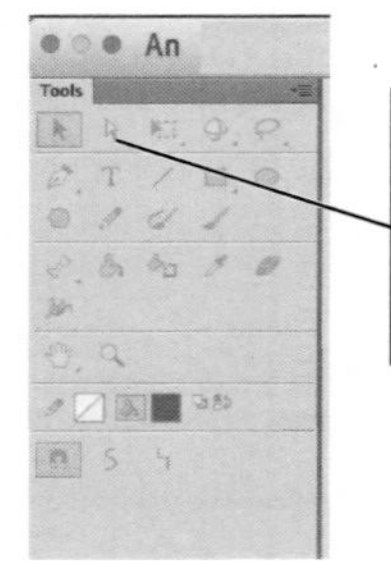

After docking the Tools panel, the panel might still appear in the same configuration as the floating panel (with multiple rows of tools).

10. **Click the right edge of the Tools panel and drag left until all the tools appear in a only one or two columns.**

    If you are working with a small monitor such as a laptop, you might not be able to fit all of the Tools panel options in a single column. If this is the case, drag until all options appear in two columns.

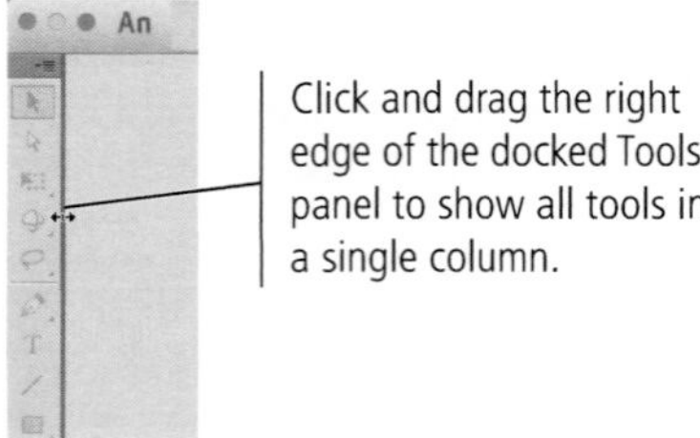

Click and drag the right edge of the docked Tools panel to show all tools in a single column.

11. **Click the button on the right side of the Tools panel title bar and choose Lock in the panel Options menu.**

    If the menu shows "Unlock," the panel is already locked. Simply move the mouse away from the menu and click to dismiss the menu.

    When a panel is locked, it can't be removed from the dock (although it can be resized, collapsed, or expanded).

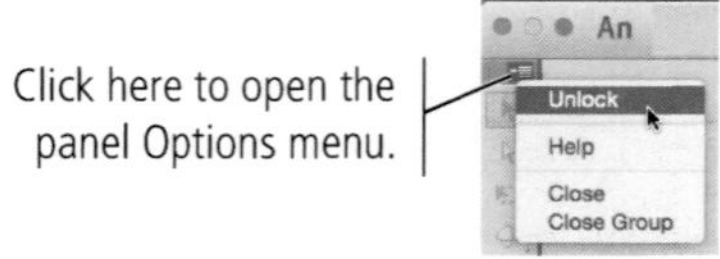

Click here to open the panel Options menu.

12. **Continue to the next exercise.**

ANIMATE FOUNDATIONS

Identifying and Accessing Tools in Animate

In addition to a wide variety of panels, Animate includes 31 tools — a large number that indicates the power of the application. You can change the docked Tools panel to more than one column by dragging the right edge of the panel. When the Tools panel is floating, it defaults to show the various tools in rows.

You learn how to use these tools as you complete the projects in this book. For now, you should simply take the opportunity to identify the tools and their location on the Tools panel. The image to the right shows the icon, tool name, and keyboard shortcut (if any) that accesses each tool. Nested tools are shown indented.

Keyboard Shortcuts & Nested Tools

When you hover your mouse over a tool, the pop-up tooltip shows the name of the tool and a letter in parentheses. Pressing that letter activates the associated tool (unless you're working with type, in which case pressing a key adds that letter to your text). If you don't see tooltips, check the General pane of the Preferences dialog box; the Show Tooltips check box should be active. (Note: You must have a file open to see the tooltips and access the nested tools.)

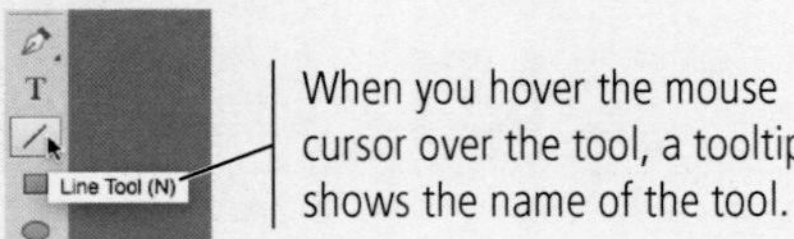
Line Tool (N)
When you hover the mouse cursor over the tool, a tooltip shows the name of the tool.

Any tool with an arrow in the bottom-right corner includes related tools nested below it. When you click a tool and hold down the mouse button, the nested tools appear in a pop-up menu. If you choose one of the nested tools, that variation becomes the default choice in the Tools panel.

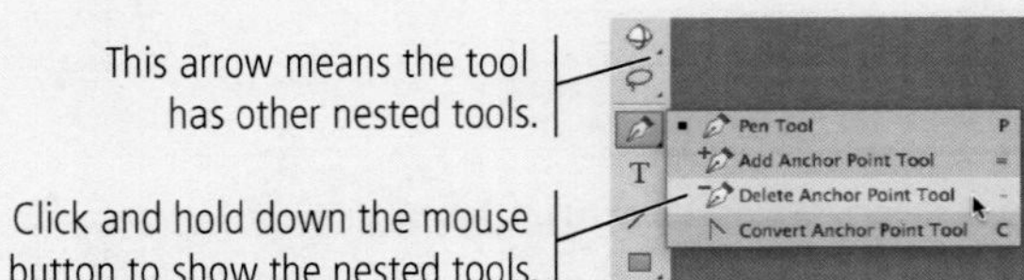
This arrow means the tool has other nested tools.
Click and hold down the mouse button to show the nested tools.
Pen Tool P
Add Anchor Point Tool =
Delete Anchor Point Tool -
Convert Anchor Point Tool C

Tool Options

In addition to the basic tool set, the bottom of the Tools panel includes options that control the fill and stroke colors, as well as options that change depending on the selected tool.

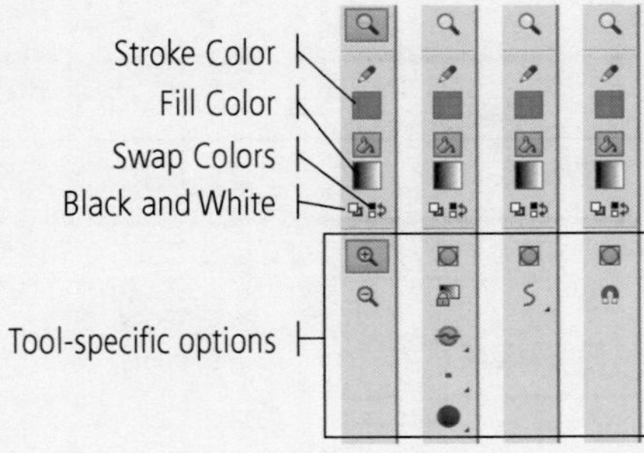
Stroke Color
Fill Color
Swap Colors
Black and White
Tool-specific options

- Selection tool (V)
- Subselection tool (A)
- Free Transform tool (Q)
  - Gradient Transform tool (F)
- 3D Rotation tool (W)
  - 3D Translation tool (G)
- Lasso tool (L)
  - Polygon tool (L)
  - Magic Wand (L)
- Pen tool (P)
  - Add Anchor Point tool (=)
  - Delete Anchor Point tool (-)
  - Convert Anchor Point tool (C)
- Text tool (T)
- Line tool (\)
- Rectangle tool (R)
  - Rectangle Primitive tool (R)
- Oval tool (R)
  - Oval Primitive tool (O)
- Polystar tool (R)
- Pencil tool (Shift-Y)
- Paint Brush tool (Y)
- Brush tool (B)
- Bone tool (M)
  - Bind tool (M)
- Paint Bucket tool (K)
- Ink Bottle tool (S)
- Eyedropper tool (I)
- Eraser tool (E)
- Width tool (U)
- Hand tool (H)
- Zoom tool (Z)

Explore the Animate Document Window

There is far more to using Animate than arranging panels around the workspace. What you do with those panels — and even which panels you need — depends on the type of work you are doing in a particular file. In this exercise, you open an Animate file and explore the interface elements that you will use to create digital animations.

1. **In Animate, choose File>Open.**

2. **Navigate to your WIP>InterfaceAN folder and select `capcarl.fla` in the list of available files.**

   The Open dialog box is a system-standard navigation dialog. Press Shift to select and open multiple contiguous (consecutive) files in the list. Press Command/Control to select and open multiple non-contiguous files.

> *Note:*
>
> *Press Command/Control-O to access the Open dialog box.*

Macintosh

Windows

3. **Click Open.**

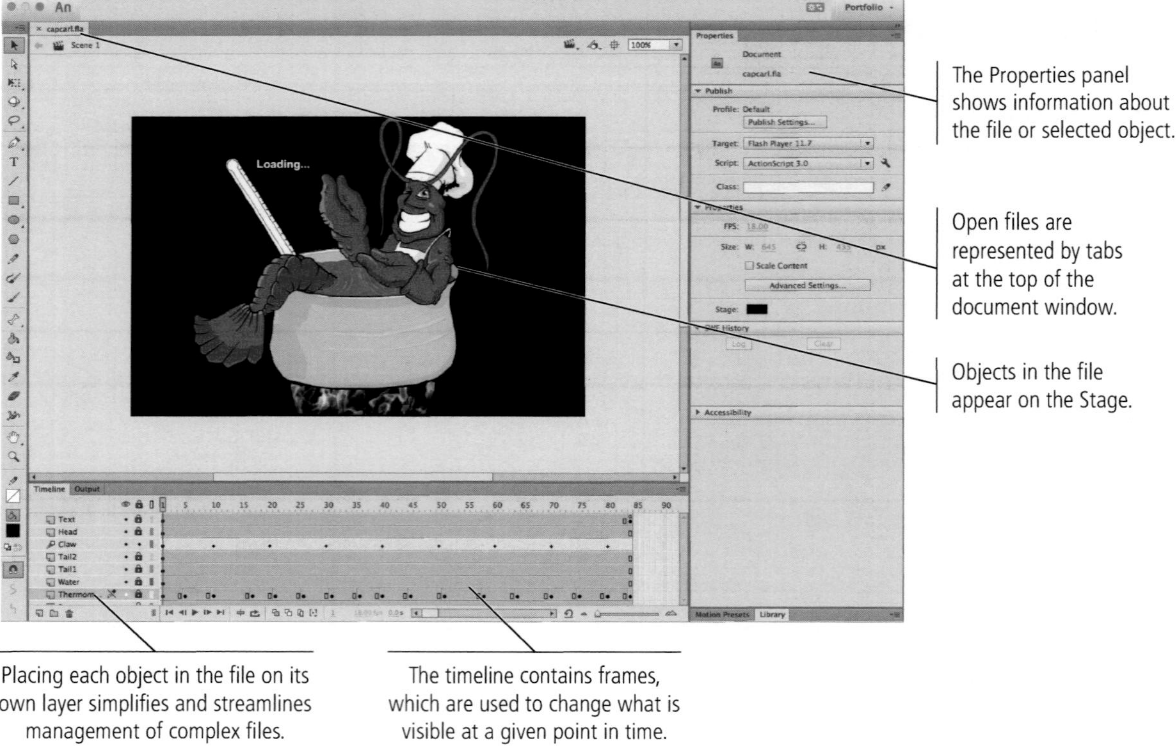

The Properties panel shows information about the file or selected object.

Open files are represented by tabs at the top of the document window.

Objects in the file appear on the Stage.

Placing each object in the file on its own layer simplifies and streamlines management of complex files.

The timeline contains frames, which are used to change what is visible at a given point in time.

4. **Above the top-right corner of the Stage, open the View Percentage menu and choose Fit in Window.**

5. **Click the bar that separates the Stage area from the Timeline panel. Drag up to enlarge the panel and show all the layers in the file.**

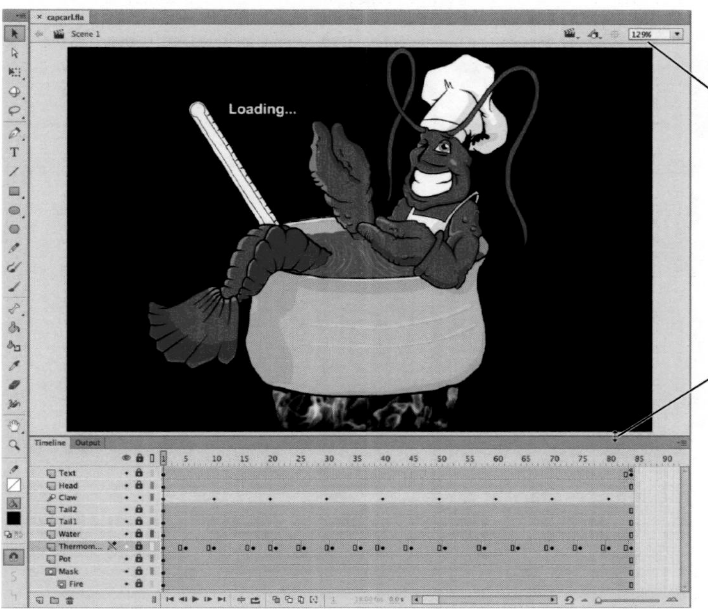

6. **Review the Timeline panel.**

The Timeline panel is perhaps the most important panel in Animate. It represents the passage of time within your animation, and it enables you to control what happens to objects in your file, as well as when and where changes occur.

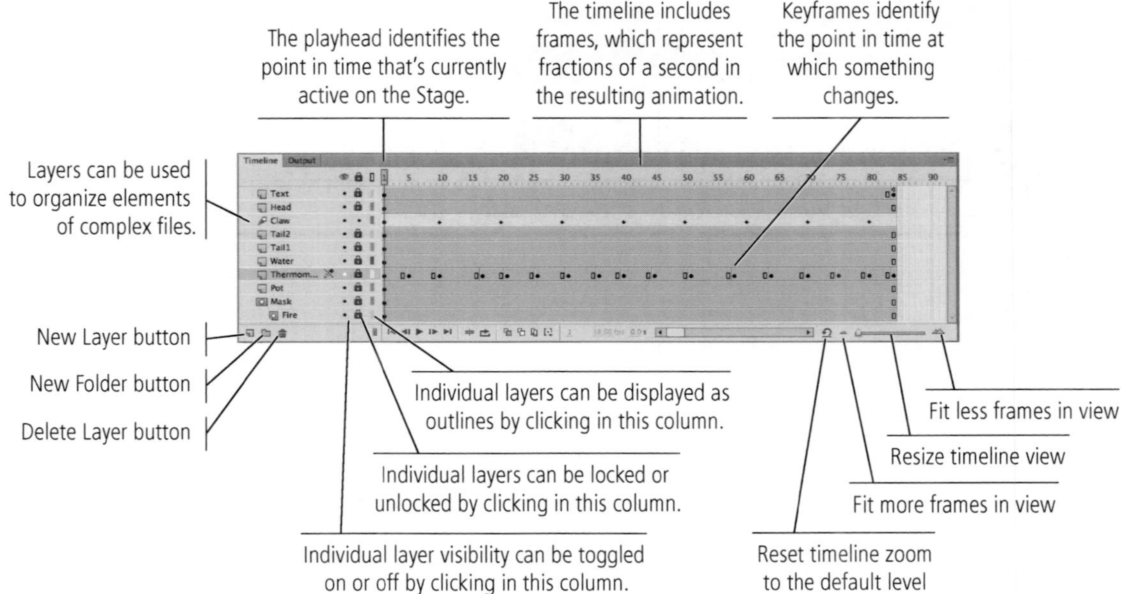

The playhead identifies the point in time that's currently active on the Stage.
The timeline includes frames, which represent fractions of a second in the resulting animation.
Keyframes identify the point in time at which something changes.
Layers can be used to organize elements of complex files.
New Layer button
New Folder button
Delete Layer button
Individual layers can be displayed as outlines by clicking in this column.
Individual layers can be locked or unlocked by clicking in this column.
Individual layer visibility can be toggled on or off by clicking in this column.
Fit less frames in view
Resize timeline view
Fit more frames in view
Reset timeline zoom to the default level

7. **Choose the Selection tool from the Tools panel and click the lobster's right claw on the Stage.**

Although we will not discuss all 20+ Animate panels here, the Properties panel deserves mention. This important panel is **context sensitive**, which means it provides various options depending on what is selected on the Stage.

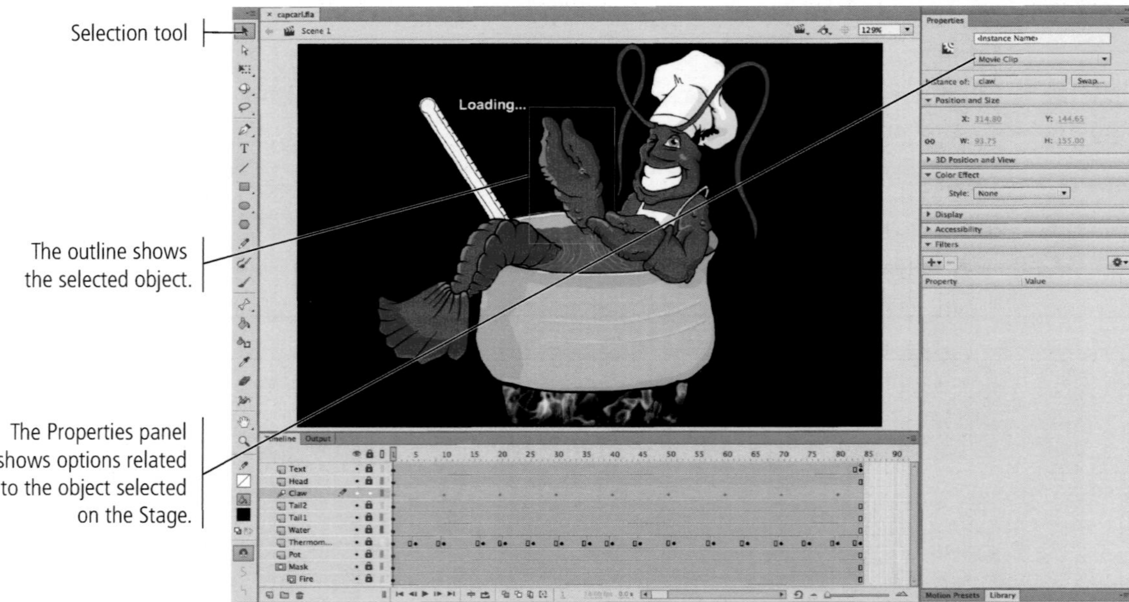

Selection tool
The outline shows the selected object.
The Properties panel shows options related to the object selected on the Stage.
As you drag right, the claw moves back and forth in a waving motion (based on objects on the Claw layer).
The mercury in the thermometer rises (based on objects on the Thermometer layer).
Loading...

8. **Click the playhead above the timeline frames and drag right.**

This technique of dragging the playhead above the timeline is called **scrubbing**.

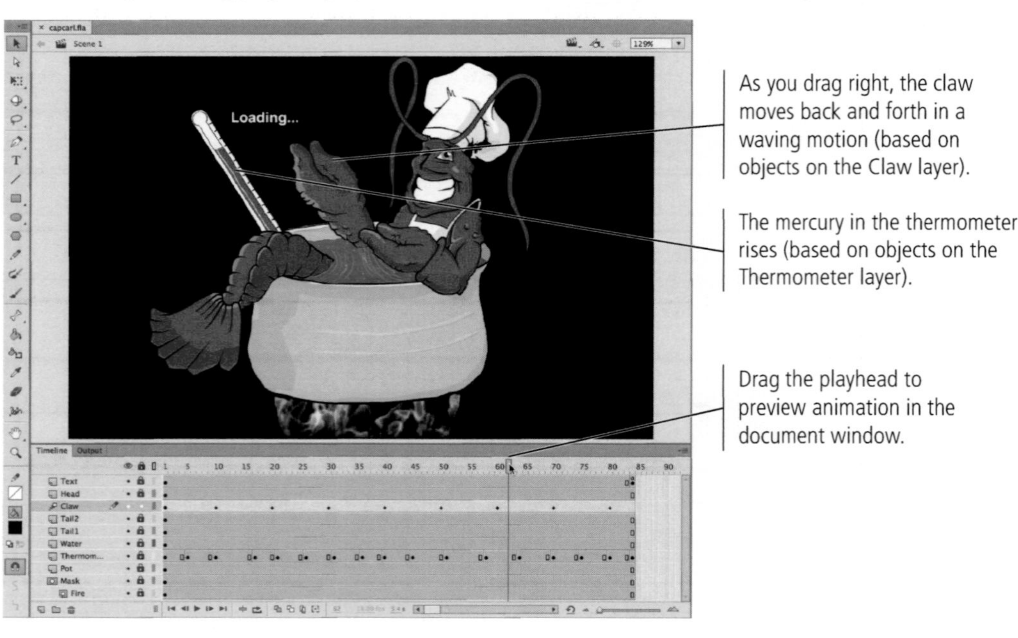

9. **Click the gray area outside of the Stage to deselect everything, then press Return/Enter.**

   One final reminder: throughout this book, we list differing commands in the Macintosh/Windows format. On Macintosh, you need to press the Return key; on Windows, press the Enter key. (We will not repeat this explanation every time different commands are required for the different operating systems.)

   This keyboard shortcut plays the movie on the Stage from the current location of the playhead. If the playhead is already at the end of the frames, it moves back to Frame 1 and plays the entire movie.

> *Note:*
>
> *When a movie is playing on the Stage, press the Escape key to stop the playback.*

10. **Press Command-Return/Control-Enter.**

    Instead of simply playing the movie on the Stage, you can preview the file to see what it will look like when exported. This keyboard shortcut, which is the same as choosing Test Movie in the Control menu, exports a SWF file from the existing FLA file so you can see what the final file will look like.

    In the separate Player window, you see some animated elements that did not appear when you played the movie on the Stage. This is a perfect example of why you should test actual animation files rather than relying only on what you see on the Stage. (This is especially true if you did not create the file, as in this case.)

The exported SWF file appears in a Player window and begins playing.

Some animation does not play on the Stage, but does play in the Player window.

> *Note:*
>
> *As you complete the projects in this book, you'll see our screen shots zoom in or out as necessary to show you the most relevant part of a particular file. In most cases we do not tell you what specific view percentage to use for a particular exercise, unless it's specifically required for the work being done.*

11. **Close the Player window and return to Animate.**

12. **Click the Close button on the capcarl document tab. If asked, click Don't Save/No to close the file without saving.**

    Clicking the Close button on the Application frame closes all open files and quits the application.

Macintosh

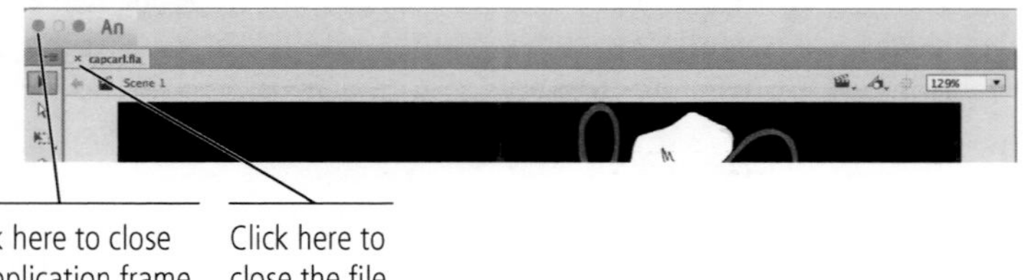

Click here to close the application frame.

Click here to close the file.

> *Note:*
>
> *Press Command/Control-W to close the active file.*

Windows

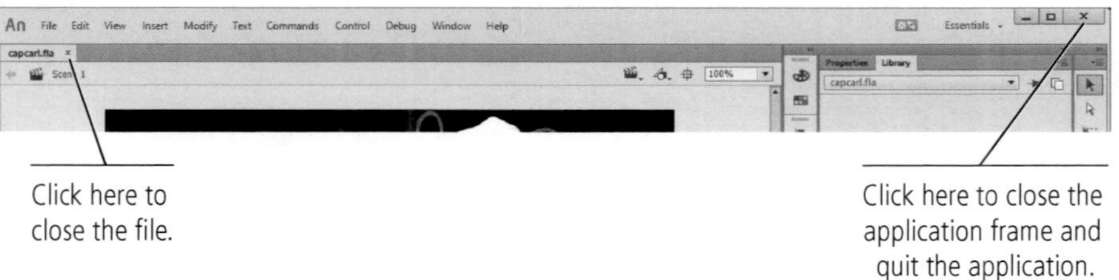

Click here to close the file.

Click here to close the the application frame and quit the application.

Understanding the Animate View Options

Most Animate projects require some amount of zooming in and out, as well as navigating around the document within its window. As we show you how to complete different stages of the workflow, we usually won't tell you when to change your view percentage because that's largely a matter of personal preference. You should understand the different options for navigating around an Animate file, however, so you can more easily get to what you want, when you want to get there.

Zoom Tool

You can click with the Zoom tool to increase the view percentage in specific, predefined intervals (the same intervals you see in the View Percentage menu in the top-right corner of the document window). Pressing Option/Alt with the Zoom tool allows you to zoom out in the same predefined percentages. If you drag a marquee with the Zoom tool, you can zoom into a specific location; the area surrounded by the marquee fills the available space in the document window.

Click with the Zoom tool to zoom in.

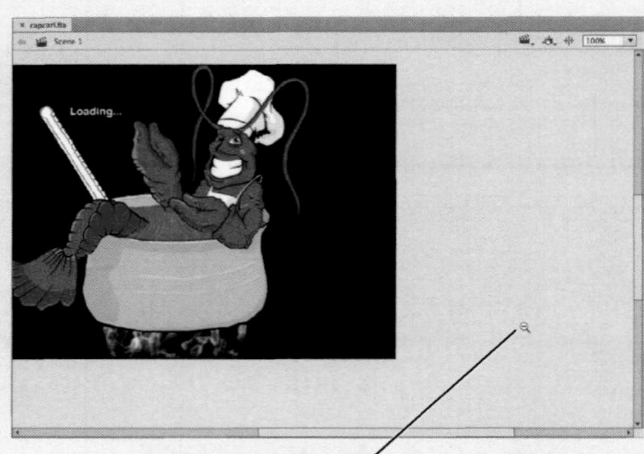

Option/Alt-click with the Zoom tool to zoom out.

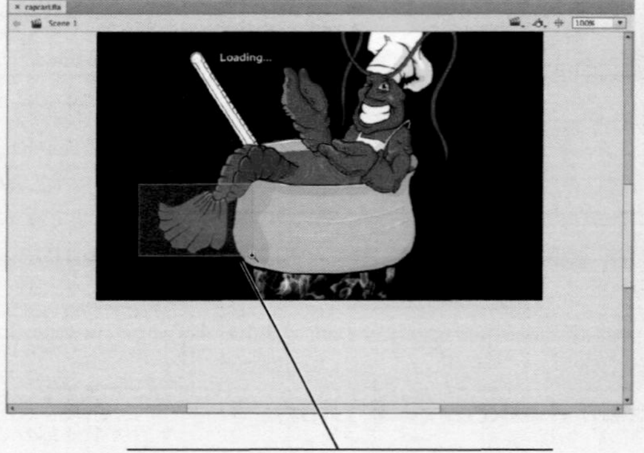

Draw a marquee with the Zoom tool...

...to fill the document window with the selected area.

View Menu

The View>Magnification menu also provides options for changing the view percentage, including their associated keyboard shortcuts. (The Zoom In and Zoom Out options step through the same predefined view percentages you see by clicking with the Zoom tool.)

Zoom In	Command/Control-equals (=)
Zoom Out	Command/Control-minus (–)
100%	Command/Control-1
Show Frame	Command/Control-2
Show All	Command/Control-3
400%	Command/Control-4
800%	Command/Control-8

View Percentage Field

In addition to the predefined view percentages in the menu, you can also type a specific percentage in the View Percentage field in the top-right corner of the document window.

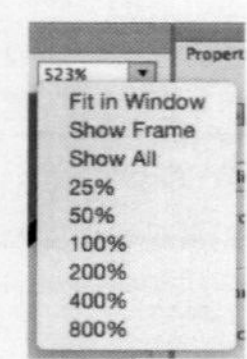

Hand Tool

If scroll bars appear in the document window, you can use the Hand tool to drag the file around within the document window. The Hand tool changes the visible area in the document window; it has no effect on the actual content of the image.

When using a different tool other than the Text tool, you can press the Spacebar to temporarily access the Hand tool.

Double-clicking the Hand tool in the Tools panel fits the Stage to the document window.

Talking Kiosk Interface

You were hired to create an animated introduction for a shopping mall information kiosk. The Animate-based animation must feature a character who offers shoppers assistance in finding various facilities. Each button should also offer audio instructions that explain the link's purpose. As part of the Animate development team, your job is to prepare the interface artwork that will be handed off to the programmer, who will script the interactivity.

This project incorporates the following skills:

- ❑ Importing and managing artwork from Adobe Illustrator
- ❑ Using the Library panel to manage a complex file
- ❑ Building a frame-by-frame animation
- ❑ Editing various button states
- ❑ Importing sound files into Animate
- ❑ Adding event and stream sounds to the Animate timeline
- ❑ Controlling volume and duration of sound
- ❑ Applying built-in sound effects
- ❑ Synchronizing sound to animation
- ❑ Defining sound compression settings

Project Meeting

client comments

Throughout the facility grounds, we are replacing all of the static "You Are Here" maps with interactive kiosks that will help users more quickly find the shops they are looking for.

I'd like the interface to be personal — a person actually talking to the user. We thought about the video route, but I'm convinced an animated character would be better (plus we won't have to pay an actor to use her image).

The interface should provide a link to four different categories of shops: Shoes & Apparel, Home Furnishings, Music & Electronics, and Casual & Fine Dining. We might break it down into more specific categories later, but the important point for now is to get the first version of this thing into use quickly.

art director comments

I already had all of the kiosk components created. I need you to assemble everything in Animate and prepare the various elements for the programmer, who will create all of the necessary code and links.

The artwork was created in Adobe Illustrator. Our illustrator is fairly knowledgeable about Animate requirements, so you should be able to import the artwork without too many problems. He even created the basic appearance of the navigation buttons, so you'll just need to modify those rather than create them from scratch.

When I reviewed the sound files, it seemed like the background music was very loud compared to the spoken intro. You should fix the music so that the talking is audible above the background.

The lip-syncing part of the interface requires some careful attention to detail, but overall, it isn't a difficult job. Just take your time and try to make the mouths follow the words.

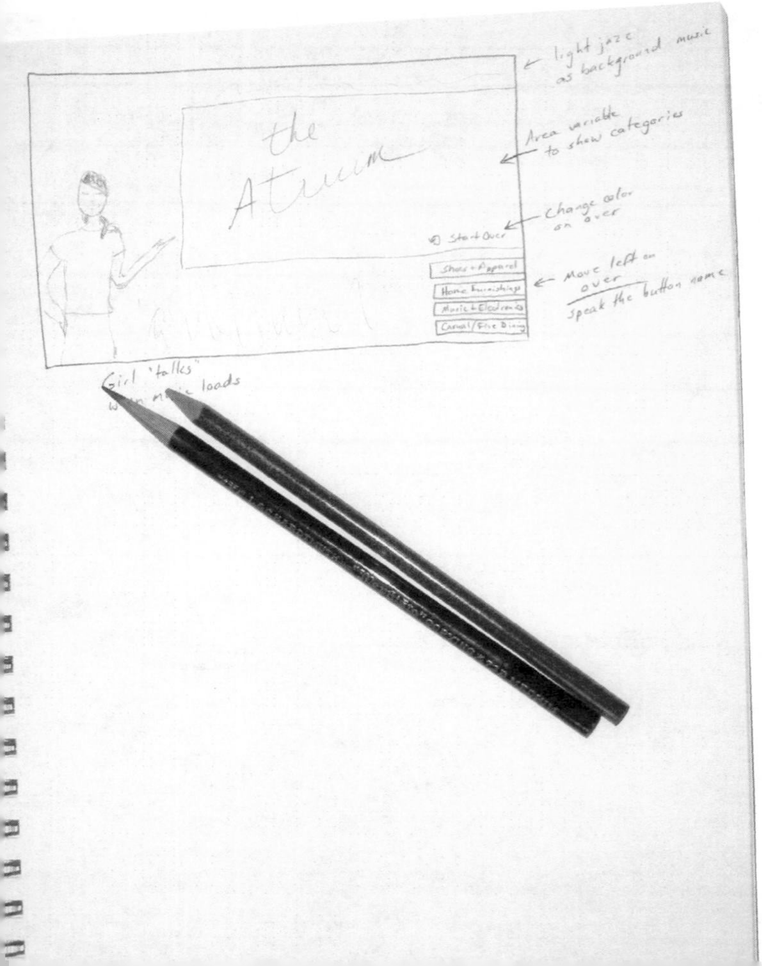

project objectives

To complete this project, you will:

- ❑ Create symbols from imported Illustrator files
- ❑ Place and manage instances of symbols on the Stage
- ❑ Control timing using keyframes
- ❑ Add visual interactivity to button symbols
- ❑ Import sound files into Animate
- ❑ Add event and stream sounds to a movie
- ❑ Use the start and stop sync methods for button sounds
- ❑ Edit a sound envelope to control volume and duration
- ❑ Swap graphics at precise moments in time
- ❑ Define sound compression settings

Stage 1 Working with Symbols

Although Animate can be used to create extraordinary interactive content, the program can also create extremely large files that take a very long time to download. (The size of a file is often referred to as a file's **weight**.) Users will not wait for more than a few seconds to download a file, so you should always try to keep file weight to a minimum — and that's where symbols come into play.

Symbols are objects that can be used repeatedly without increasing file size. The original symbol resides in the Library panel; **symbol instances** are copies of the symbol that you place onto the Stage. Although a regular graphic object adds to the overall file weight every time you use it on the Stage, a symbol counts only once no matter how many times you use it — which can mean dramatically smaller file sizes.

As another benefit, changes made to the content of an original symbol reflect in every placed instance of that symbol. For example, if you have placed 40 instances of a bird symbol, you can simultaneously change all 40 birds from blue jays to cardinals by changing the primary symbol in the Library panel.

A third benefit of symbols is that you can name placed instances, which means those instances can be targeted and affected by programming — one of the keys to animation and interactive development.

Note:

There are three primary types of symbols — graphic, movie clip, and button — and a number of other types of assets, such as audio and video files. In Animate, all of these assets are automatically stored in the Library panel.

The Library Panel in Depth

ANIMATE FOUNDATIONS

Assets in Animate are stored in the Library panel. Additional information about each asset is listed on the right side of the panel, including the name by which an asset can be called using a script (Linkage), the number of instances in the current file (Use Count), the date the asset was last modified (Date Modified), and the type of asset (Type). To show the additional information, you can either make the panel wider or use the scroll bar at the bottom of the panel. In addition to storing and organizing assets, the Library panel has a number of other uses:

- Each type of asset is identified by a unique icon. Double-clicking a symbol icon enters into Symbol-Editing mode, where you can modify the symbol on its own Stage. Double-clicking a non-symbol icon (sounds, bitmaps, etc.) opens the Properties dialog box for that file.
- You can use the Library menu to switch between the libraries of currently open files.
- The Preview pane shows the selected asset. If the asset includes animation, video, or sound, you can use the Play and Stop buttons to preview the file in the panel. (The Stage background color appears in the Preview pane; if you can't see the Play button, move your mouse over the area of the button to reveal it.)
- If a file has a large number of assets (which is common), you can use the Search field to find assets by name.
- Clicking the Pin button to the right of the Library menu attaches the current library to the open Animate file.
- Clicking the New Library Panel button opens a new version of the Library panel, which allows you to view multiple libraries at one time.
- Clicking the New Symbol button opens the Create New Symbol dialog box, where you can define the name and type of the new symbol you want to create.
- Clicking the New Folder button adds a new folder in the current file's library.
- Clicking the Properties button opens a dialog box that shows information about the selected library asset.
- Clicking Delete removes an asset from the library. Placed instances of that symbol are deleted from the file.

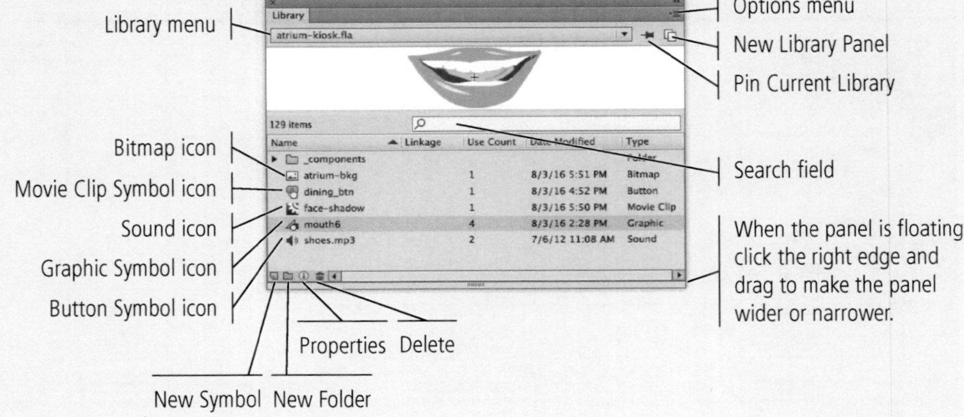

Create a New Animate File

When you begin a new Animate project, the first step (obviously) is to create a new file. You can use the options in Welcome Screen to create new files using the default settings, or choose File>New to define a new file using the New Document dialog box.

1. **Download Atrium_Web16_RF.zip from the Student Files Web page.**
2. **Expand the ZIP archive in your WIP folder (Macintosh) or copy the archive contents into your WIP folder (Windows).**

   This results in a folder named **Atrium**, which contains the files you need for this project. You should also use this folder to save the files you create in this project.

3. **In Animate, choose File>New. Choose the AIR for Desktop option in the Type list.**

   The Type pane lists the types of documents you can create in Animate. You are creating this file to be a standalone app on a self-contained computer system.

   You can use the options on the right side of the dialog box to define the Stage size, units of measurement, frame rate, and background color of the Stage.

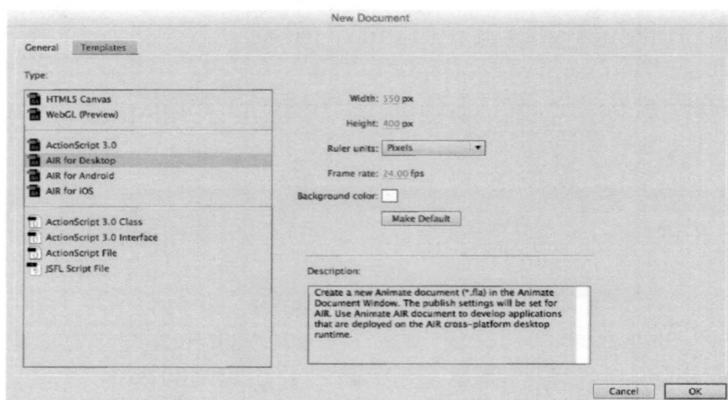

4. **Click OK to create the new file.**

   When you create a new file, the new Stage appears in the document window. The Stage color is determined by the Background color defined in the New Document dialog box (white by default). Every file includes one default layer, named "Layer 1," in the timeline.

   When nothing is selected on the Stage, the Properties panel shows a number of file-specific options, including the target device, type of script being used, and frame rate.

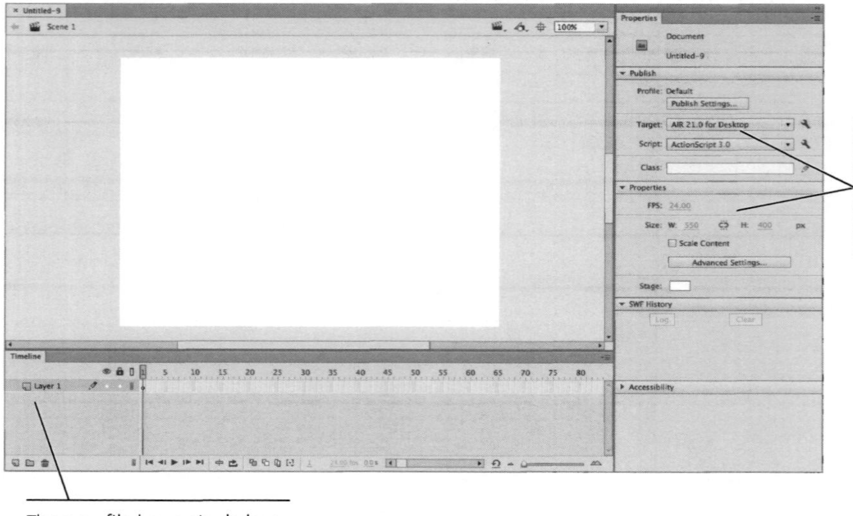

File-specific options are avaiable in the Properties panel when nothing is selected on the Stage.

The new file has a single layer, named Layer 1 by default.

5. **Choose File>Save. Navigate to your WIP>Atrium folder as the target location, then change the Save As field to `atrium-kiosk.fla`. Click Save to save the file.**

   The File Format menu defaults to Animate Document (*.fla). This option creates a native Animate file, which you can open and edit in Animate as necessary. When you have finished your work, you can export the Animate file to another format that will present the animation on digital media.

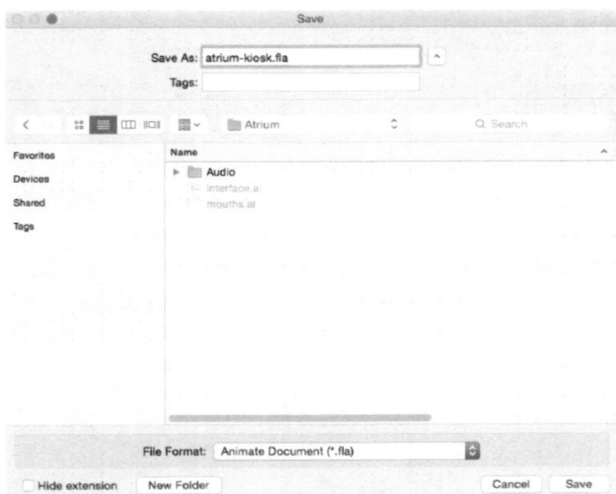

> ***Note:***
>
> *In this project, you will use the Tools, Properties, Library, Align, and Timeline panels. You should arrange your workspace to best suit your personal preferences.*

6. **Continue to the next exercise.**

Import Adobe Illustrator Artwork

You can use the built-in Animate tools to draw complex custom artwork. In many cases, however, your work in Animate will incorporate files that were created in other applications. For example, illustrations and other vector graphics for animation are typically created in Adobe Illustrator. This project incorporates a number of external files, which you need to import into your Animate file.

> ***Note:***
>
> *Learn more about Adobe Illustrator in the companion book of this series,* ***Adobe Illustrator CC: The Professional Portfolio****.*

1. **With `atrium-kiosk.fla` open, choose File>Import>Import to Stage.**

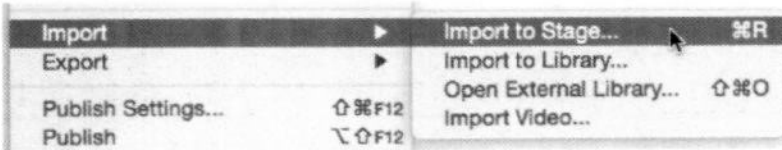

2. **At the bottom of the dialog box, choose All Openable Formats in the Enable menu. Navigate to `interface.ai` in the WIP>Atrium folder, and click Open.**

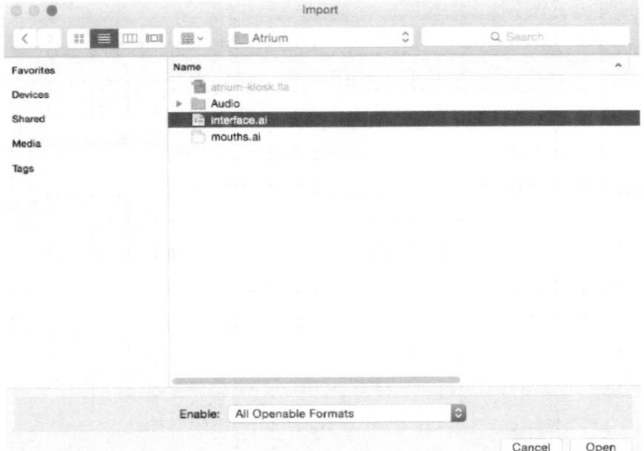

3. **If the button at the bottom of the resulting dialog box shows "Hide Advanced Options," click that button to show only the basic import options.**

When advanced options are visible, you can review the individual layers (and their contents) that will be imported in the Illustrator file. You are importing the entire file in this project, so you don't need to examine each layer and sublayer.

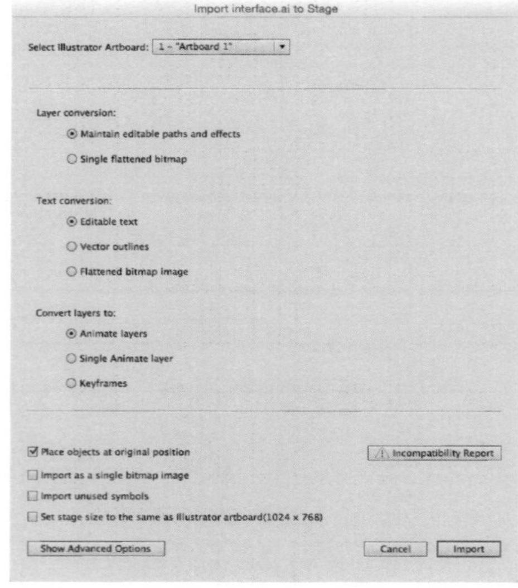

The **Artboard** menu lists all artboards that exist in the Illustrator file you are importing. (An Illustrator artboard is the equivalent of the Animate Stage; it defines the visible area in the final artwork.)

The **Layer Conversion** options determine whether Illustrator objects will be editable after being imported into Animate.

- Maintain Editable Paths and Effects option means you can use the Animate Subselection tool to manipulate the anchor points and handles on the imported paths.
- If you select the Single Flattened Bitmap option, you will not be able to edit the vector paths within Animate.

The **Text Conversion** options determine whether text objects in Illustrator will be editable with the Animate Text tool.

- Editable Text, selected by default, imports text objects that you can edit using the Animate Text tool.
- If you choose Vector Outlines, text objects import as a group of vector shapes; you can't edit the text in these objects (other than manipulating the vector paths).
- If you choose Flattened Bitmap Image, text objects import as raster objects that cannot be edited with either the Text tool or the Subselection tool.

Note:

The Incompatibility Report button tends to disappear and reappear when you make changes in other areas of the dialog box. This is a minor bug in the software.

The **Convert Layers To** options determine how layers in the Illustrator file are managed in the Animate timeline.

- The Animate Layers option maintains the existing layers from the original artwork; each Illustrator layer becomes a layer in the Animate file. This is useful if you aren't sure about what you're importing; you can always change or delete imported layers if you don't need them.
- If you choose Single Animate Layer, all layers in the original artwork are flattened into one layer (named with the imported file name) on the Animate timeline.
- If you choose Keyframes, each layer in the artwork is added as a keyframe on the default Layer 1. (You will learn about keyframes in Stage 2 of this project.)

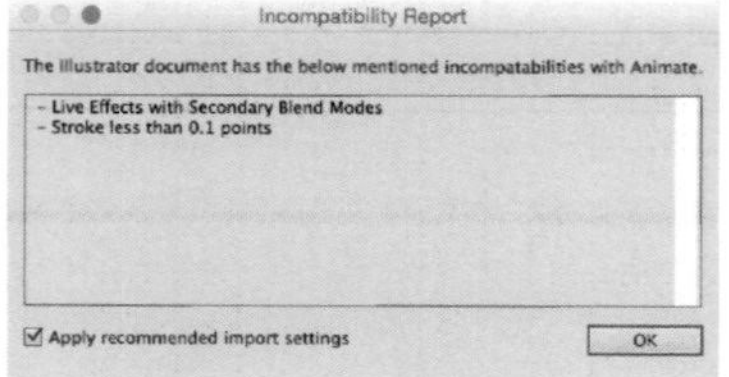

Many objects created in Illustrator are fully compatible with Animate drawing capabilities, so they are imported as regular drawing objects. Any objects that don't fit the Animate drawing model (primarily, ones with some type of applied transparency) are imported in a way that allows Animate to maintain the overall artwork integrity. If an **Incompatibility Report** button appears in the Import to Stage dialog box, you can click it to see what effects are causing the problem.

When **Place Objects at Original Position** is checked, the objects imported onto the Animate Stage have the same position relative to one another as they did in the original Illustrator file.

If you check **Import as a Single Bitmap Image**, the entire file is flattened into a raster image; you are not able to access the individual elements that made up the original artwork in Illustrator.

The Illustrator artboard is the area that defines the physical dimensions of the file, just as the Stage defines the physical size of an Animate file. The **Set Stage Size...** option shows the dimensions of the imported file's artboard; if you know the Illustrator file was created to the correct dimensions, you can use this option to automatically change the Stage size to match the imported artwork.

Illustrator can be used to create graphic and movie clip symbols (but not buttons), which are stored in a file's Symbols panel. This can include symbols that are not placed in the file, but which might be necessary for the overall project. If you don't know what a file contains, you can check the **Import Unused Symbols** option to be sure all of the necessary bits are imported; you can always delete unwanted symbols once they have been imported. For this project, we are telling you that all required symbols in the imported artwork are placed on the artboard.

4. **Make the following changes to the default import settings:**
   - **Choose the Vector Outline option in the Text Conversion section.**
   - **Check the Set Stage Size option.**

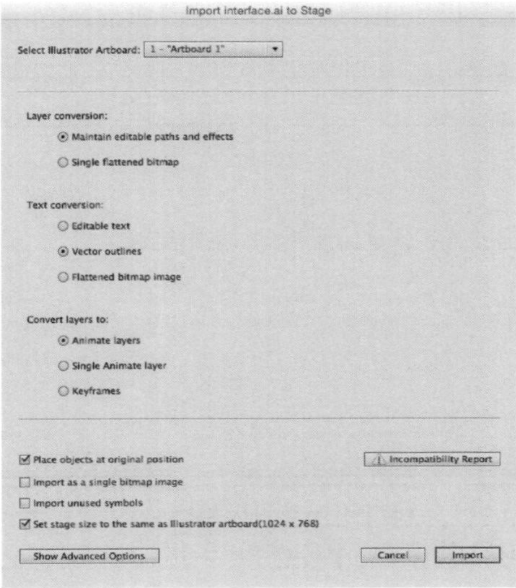

5. **Click OK to import the Illustrator artwork.**
6. **Fit the Stage in the document window, then click away from all objects on the Stage to deselect them.**

All objects are automatically selected after being imported to the Stage. Deselecting them allows you to review the Animate file's properties.

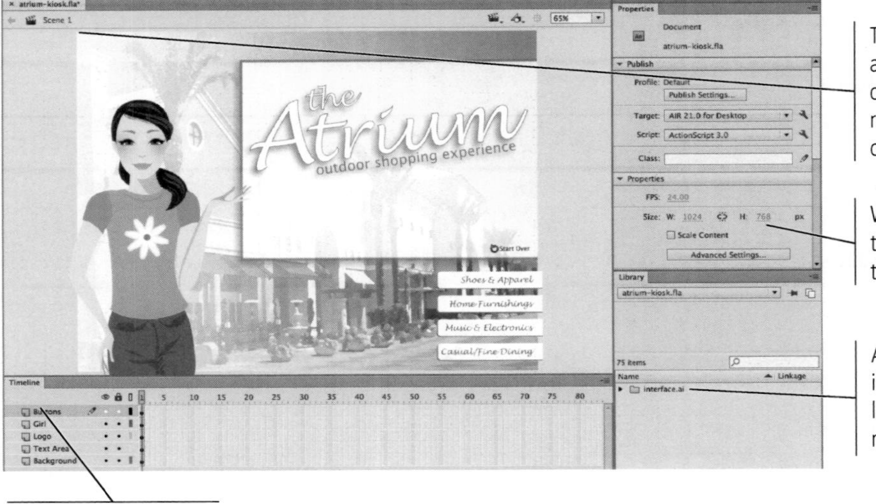

The imported artwork is aligned to the top-left corner of the Stage, matching its relative position on the original Illustrator artboard.

With nothing selected, the Properties panel shows the adjusted Stage size.

A folder (named the same as the imported file) is added to the library, containing all the pieces necessary for the imported artwork.

Five layers are added to the Timeline panel.

7. **In the Library panel, click the arrow to the left of the interface.ai folder to expand it, and then click the arrows to expand all but the Girl folder.**

   Imported assets are sorted by layer; folder names match the imported layer names to help you understand where different pieces are required. A separate folder for Illustrator Symbols is included.

> *Note:*
>
> *The Girl folder includes a long list of paths and groups that were imported as movie clips to preserve transparency effects that were applied in the Illustrator file. We did not include that folder in this instruction simply because the list is so long.*

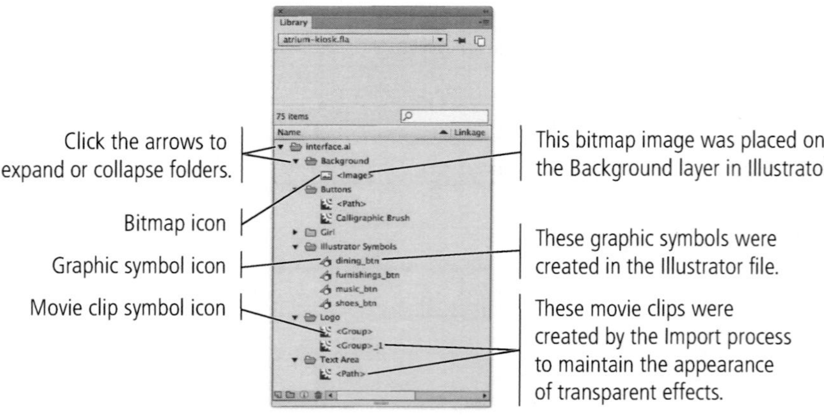
Click the arrows to expand or collapse folders.
Bitmap icon
Graphic symbol icon
Movie clip symbol icon
This bitmap image was placed on the Background layer in Illustrator.
These graphic symbols were created in the Illustrator file.
These movie clips were created by the Import process to maintain the appearance of transparent effects.

8. **In the Library panel, collapse the subfolders in the interface.ai folder.**

9. **Save the file and continue to the next exercise.**

Import Files to the Library

In addition to importing files to the Animate Stage, you can also import external files directly into the Animate file's Library panel. This option is particularly useful when certain objects aren't going to be placed on the main Stage, or if you don't yet know how you will use a particular object.

1. **With atrium-kiosk.fla open, choose File>Import>Import to Library. Navigate to the file mouths.ai in the WIP>Atrium folder and click Open.**

   When you import an Illustrator file directly to the Library panel, most of the options are the same as for importing to the Stage. The Set Stage Size... option is not available because it does not apply to files that only exist (for now) in the file's library.

> *Note:*
>
> *Animate defaults to the last-used folder, so you might not have to navigate to the folder you used in the previous exercise.*

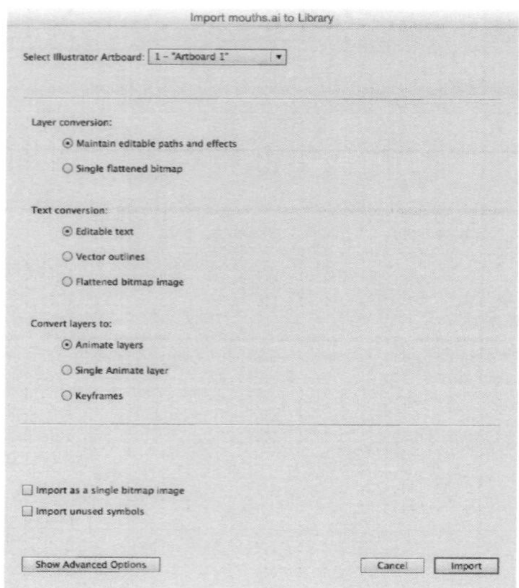

2. **Click OK to import the artwork to the library.**

   The Library panel shows that the resulting object was imported as a graphic symbol. Nothing is added to the Stage or the timeline.

3. **In the Library panel, click the mouths.ai item to select it.**

   The top portion of the panel shows a preview of the selected item.

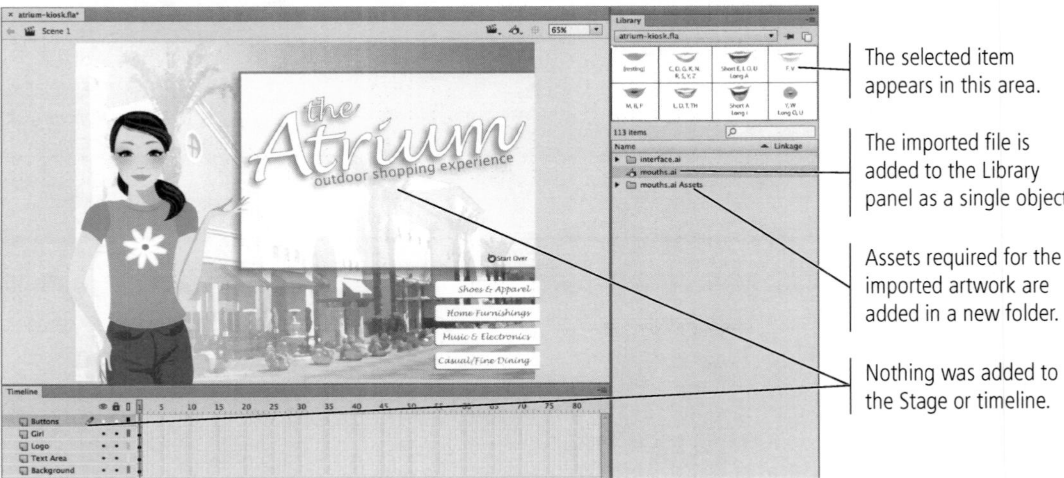

The selected item appears in this area.
The imported file is added to the Library panel as a single object.
Assets required for the imported artwork are added in a new folder.
Nothing was added to the Stage or timeline.

4. **Save the file and continue to the next exercise.**

Convert Objects to Symbols

You now have a number of assets in your file's Library panel. The mouths.ai graphic contains eight groups of graphics — the different mouth shapes that you will use later in this project to synchronize the character to a sound file. For the process to work, you need to separate each mouth shape into a distinct symbol so the correct artwork can be placed at the appropriate point in the file.

1. **With `atrium-kiosk.fla` open, choose the Selection tool. Double-click the mouths.ai symbol icon to enter into the symbol.**

2. **Zoom as necessary so you can clearly see all the objects on the symbol Stage.**

   Every symbol technically has its own Stage, which is theoretically infinite and separate from the main Stage of the base file. When you double-click the symbol icon in the Library panel, you enter **Symbol-Editing mode** for that symbol; other elements of the base file are not visible on the Stage.

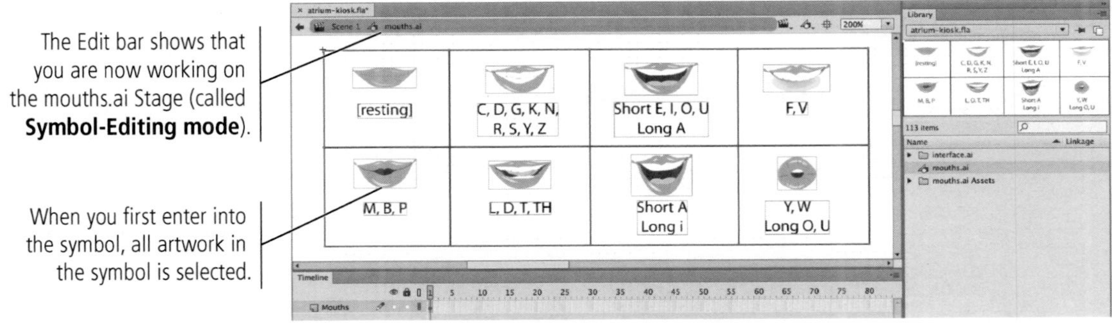

3. **Click away from the artwork to deselect everything, then click the top-left mouth shape to select that group (but not the word "resting").**

   Grouping in the original artwork is maintained in the imported artwork.

4. **Control/right-click the selected artwork and choose Convert to Symbol from the contextual menu.**

Note:

You can also drag an object onto the Library panel to open the Convert to Symbol dialog box for that object.

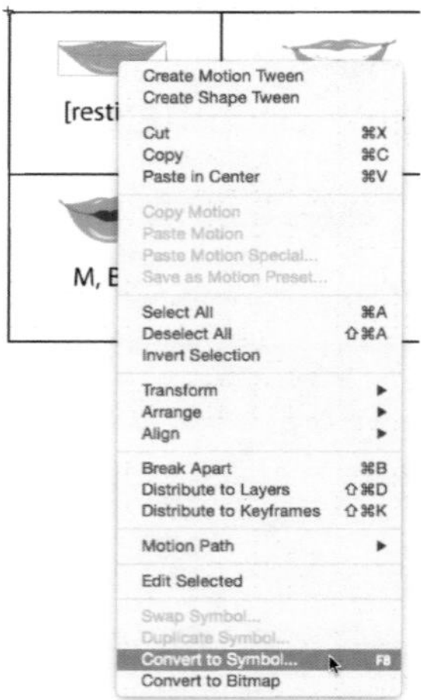

5. **In the resulting dialog box, type `mouth1` in the Name field and choose Graphic in the Type menu.**

   A graphic symbol is the most basic type of symbol. It is typically used for objects that will simply be placed on the Stage. (A graphic symbol can include animation; you will explore these options in Project 5: Ocean Animation.) The type of animation you create in the third stage of this project — simply swapping one symbol with another at various points in time — is ideally suited to graphic symbols.

6. **Select the center point in the registration proxy icon.**

   The registration grid affects the placement of the symbol's registration point, which is the 0,0 point for the symbol. (This will make more sense shortly when you begin editing symbols on their own Stages.)

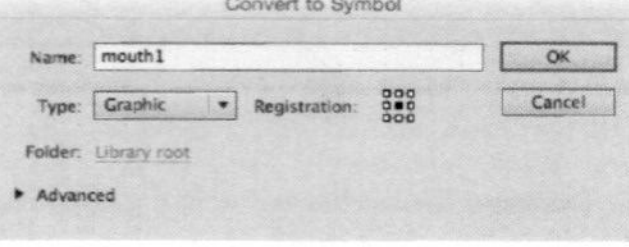

7. **Click OK to create the new symbol.**

   The Properties panel now shows that the selected object is an instance of the mouth1 symbol, which has been added to the Library panel.

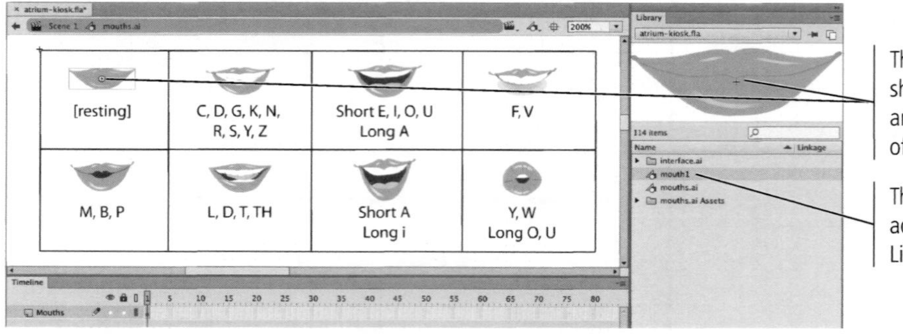

8. **Click the second mouth shape (to the right) to select it, then press the F8 key.**

   If you are using a laptop or an abbreviated keyboard, you have to press the FN key while you also press the F8 key.

   If you don't have access to function keys, simply Control/right-click the group and choose Convert to Symbol.

9. **Type `mouth2` in the Name field and click OK.**

   The Convert to Symbol dialog box remembers the last-used settings. The Type menu is already set to Graphic, and the center registration point is already selected.

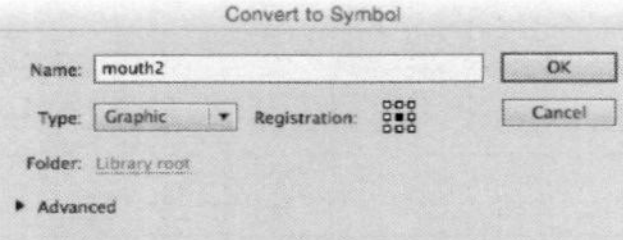

10. **Repeat Steps 8–9 to convert the rest of the mouth shapes into symbols, working from left to right across the top row and then left to right across the bottom row.**

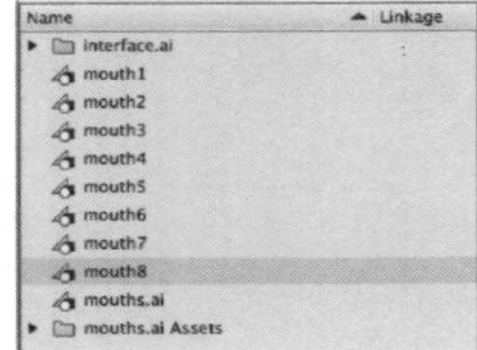

11. **Click Scene 1 in the Edit bar to return to the main Stage.**

12. **Using the Selection tool, click the mouth shape on the Stage to select it.**

    When you select the mouth shape, the layer containing the object (Girl) automatically becomes the active layer.

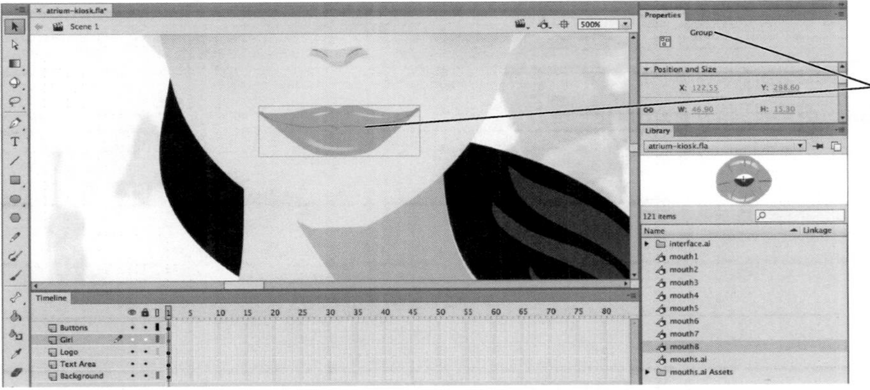

13. **In the Timeline panel, click the New Layer button to add a new layer.**

    When you click the New Layer button, the new layer is automatically added above the previously selected layer. The new layer is also automatically selected as the active layer.

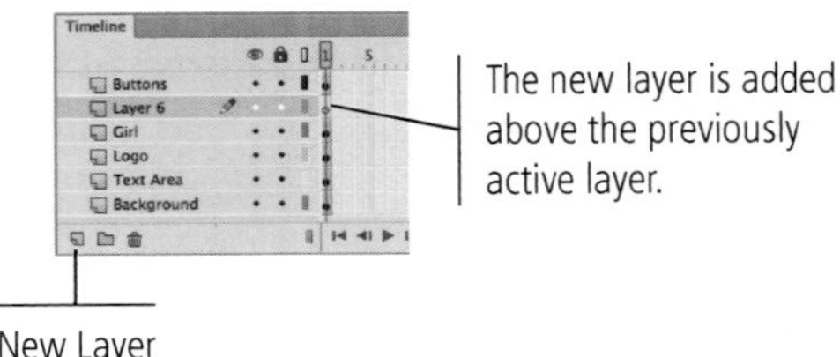

14. **Double-click the new layer name to highlight it. Type Mouths, then press Return/Enter to finalize the new layer name.**

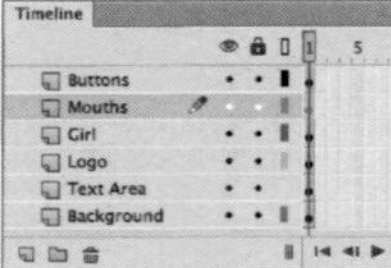

15. **Click mouth1 in the Library panel and drag an instance onto the Stage.**

16. **Use the Selection tool to drag the placed instance to the same position as the mouth group on the underlying Girl layer.**

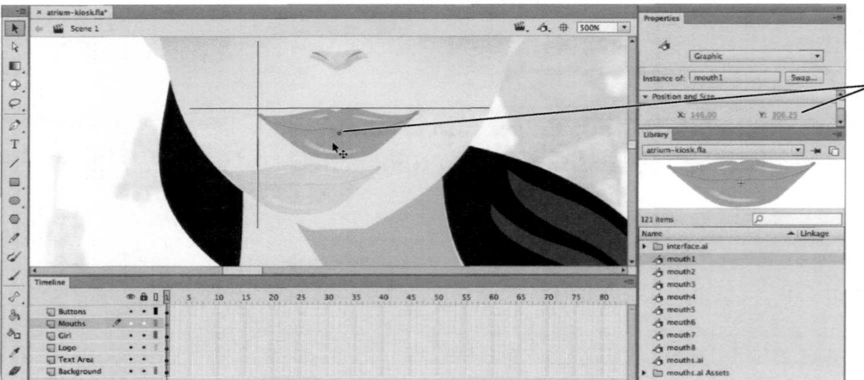

The X and Y fields show the position of the instance's registration point.

> ***Note:***
>
> *Don't confuse the symbol registration point (the crosshairs) with the transformation point (the hollow circle).*

17. **In the Timeline panel, click in the Eye column to the right of the Mouths layer name to hide that layer.**

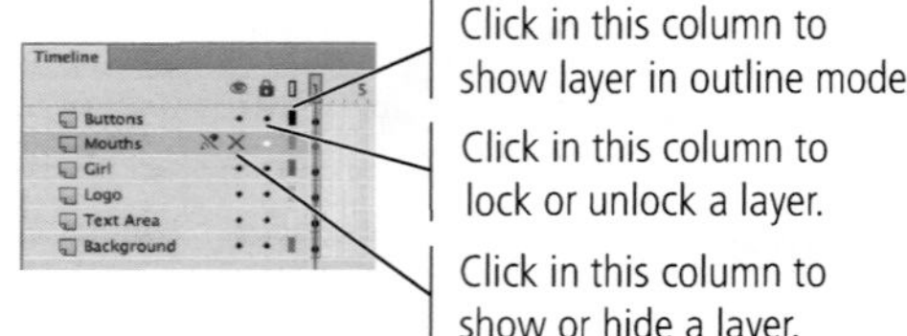

Click in this column to show layer in outline mode.
Click in this column to lock or unlock a layer.
Click in this column to show or hide a layer.

18. **Select the mouth group on the Girl layer and delete it.**

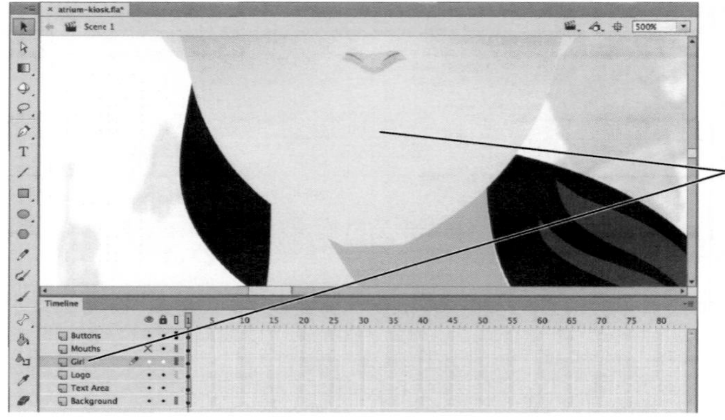

Because the Mouths layer is hidden, you can select and delete the underlying group from the Girl layer.

19. **Show the Mouths layer again, then save the file and continue to the next exercise.**

Create a Button Symbol

Buttons, one of the three main symbol types in Animate, are interactive assets that change when a user interacts with them. A button symbol has four "states":

- A button's **Up state** (also referred to as the idle or default state) is the basic appearance of a button when a user first loads a file.
- The **Over state** occurs when a mouse pointer rolls over a button. (When a user places a mouse cursor over a rollover area, the cursor often turns into a pointing finger or some other custom shape.)
- The **Down state** occurs when a user clicks a button.
- The **Hit state** defines the size of a rollover area (**hot spot**) of a button.

Note:

Buttons can be both animated and idle at the same time; idle simply means that no one has passed over or clicked the button with the mouse pointer.

This file includes five buttons. Four were created as symbols in the Illustrator artwork, and one was imported onto the Stage as a group.

1. **With atrium-kiosk.fla open, use the Selection tool to select the group containing the words "Start Over".**
2. **Press F8, or Control/right-click the selected group and choose Convert to Symbol in the contextual menu.**
3. **In the resulting dialog box, type start_over in the name field. Choose Button in the Type menu and choose the center registration point (if it is not already selected).**

Choose Button in this menu.

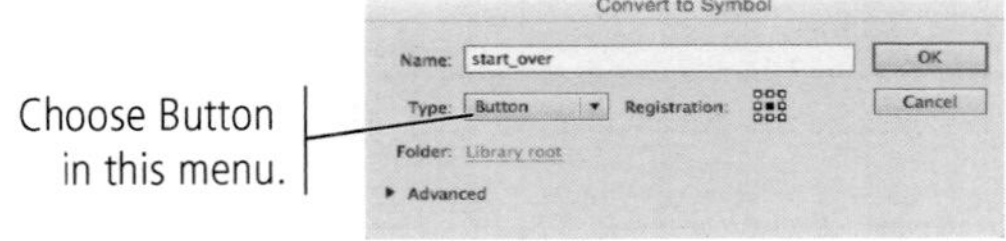

4. **Click OK to create the new symbol.**

   Because you created the symbol from objects on the Stage, the Properties panel shows that the selection is automatically an instance of the new symbol.

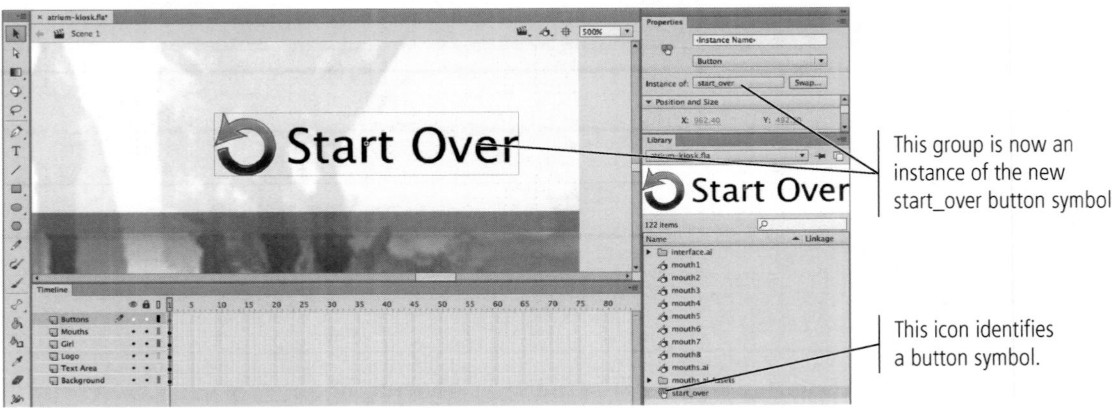

This group is now an instance of the new start_over button symbol.

This icon identifies a button symbol.

5. **Double-click the Start Over button on the Stage to enter into the symbol.**

This method of editing a symbol is called **editing in place**. Other objects on the Stage are still visible, but they are screened back and cannot be accessed.

As we explained earlier, a button is a special type of symbol with four distinct states. Each possible state is represented as a frame in the special Button symbol timeline.

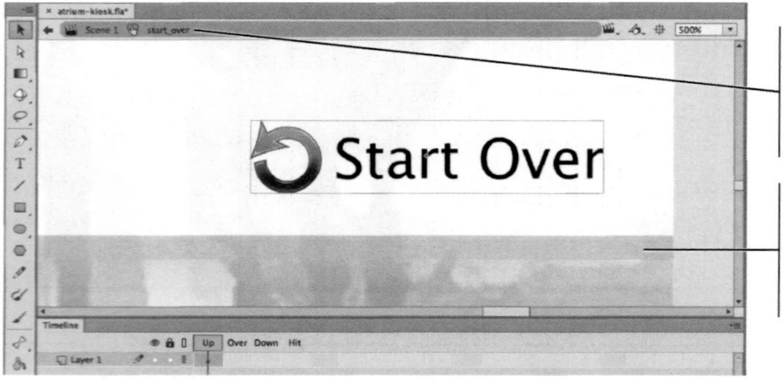
Start Over
The Edit bar shows that you are editing on the start_over button symbol Stage.
Editing a symbol in place means you can see — but not access — the other objects on the Stage.

6. **In the Timeline panel, Control/right-click the Over frame of Layer 1 and choose Insert Keyframe from the contextual menu.**

A **keyframe** defines a point where something changes. If you want to make something appear different from one frame to the next — whether inside a symbol or on the main Stage — you need to place a keyframe at the point where the change should occur.

Note:

You can also insert a keyframe by choosing Insert>Timeline> Keyframe, or pressing F6.

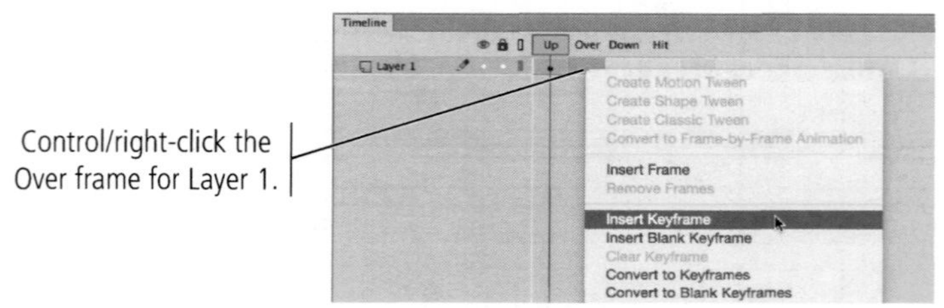
Control/right-click the Over frame for Layer 1.
Insert Frame
Insert Keyframe
Insert Blank Keyframe
Convert to Keyframes
Convert to Blank Keyframes

7. **Make sure the Over frame is selected in the Timeline panel, then double-click the words "Start Over" in the graphic to enter into that group.**

The contents of the Over frame will appear when the user's mouse moves over the button area. You are going to change the color of the letters in this button.

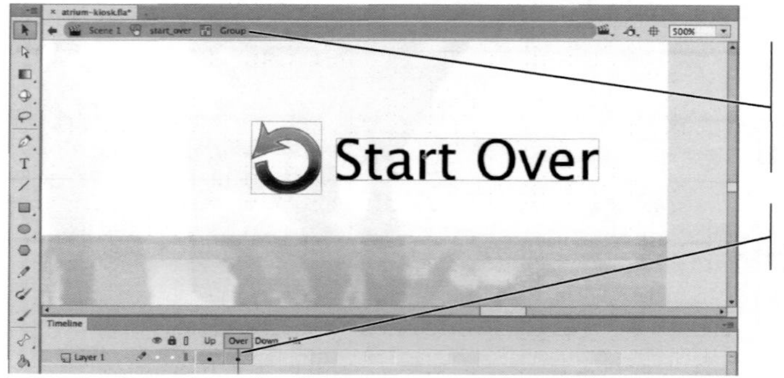
Start Over
Double-clicking "enters into" the group of objects, so you can access individual members of the group.
You are editing only the Over frame.

8. **Double-click any letter in the group to access the individual letters that make up the group.**

Remember, Animate remembers the groupings from the original Illustrator file. Depending on how a file was created, you might have to enter into a number of nested groups before you get to the level you need.

9. **With the individual letter shapes selected, click the Fill Color swatch in the Properties panel. Click a medium blue swatch in the color palette to change the fill color of the selected objects.**

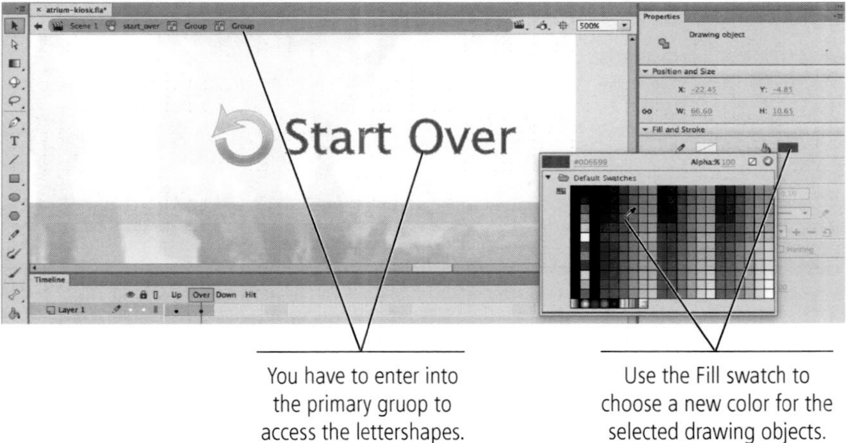
Start Over
You have to enter into the primary gruop to access the lettershapes.
Use the Fill swatch to choose a new color for the selected drawing objects.

10. **Click Scene 1 in the Edit bar to return to the main Stage.**

    Even if you have drilled into multiple levels of Symbol-Editing mode, you can return to the main Stage with a single click on the Edit bar. You can also return to any particular nesting level by clicking a specific item (called "breadcrumbs") in the Edit bar.

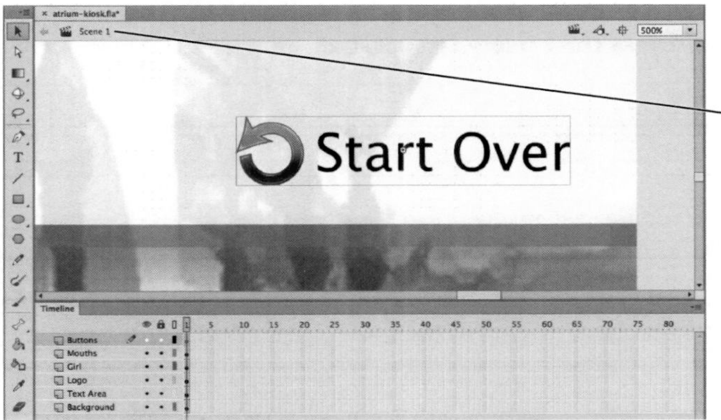
Start Over

Click Scene 1 in the Edit bar to return to the main Stage.

Note:

You will test the button's functionality in the next exercise.

11. **Save the file and continue to the next exercise.**

Define a Hit Frame

A button symbol mimics a four-frame Animate animation; it is the basic concept behind all Animate buttons. You add keyframes and modify the content of each frame; the movie displays the appropriate frame when a user hovers over or clicks the object.

In the previous exercise, you changed the color of button text in the Over frame. However, there is still a problem — the button currently works only if the mouse pointer touches the icon or one of the letter shapes. If the pointer lies between two letters, for example, the button fails to activate. All spaces within the button should be active. Moving the pointer close to or on top of the button should trigger the desired action. To resolve the problem, you need to define the Hit frame, which determines where a user can click to activate the button.

1. **With atrium-kiosk.fla open, choose Control>Enable Simple Buttons to toggle that option on.**

   This command allows you to test button states directly on the Animate Stage.

2. **Check the current condition of the Start Over button by positioning the pointer between the two words in the button.**

   There are "dead" areas within the button that don't cause the color change to occur. (You might need to zoom in to verify this problem.)

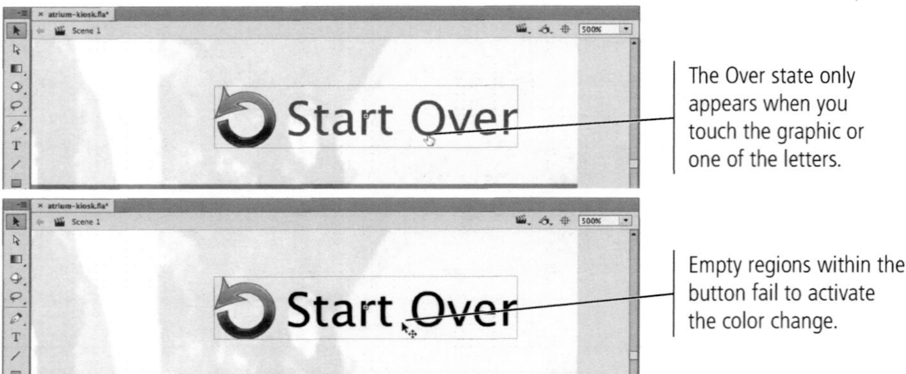
Start Over
The Over state only appears when you touch the graphic or one of the letters.
Start Over
Empty regions within the button fail to activate the color change.

3. **Choose Control>Enable Simple Buttons to toggle that option off.**

   When this option is active, you can't select a button instance on the Stage — which means you can't double-click the button to edit the symbol in place.

4. **Double-click the Start Over button on the Stage to edit the symbol in place.**

5. **Select the Hit frame in the Timeline and then Press the F6 key to insert a new keyframe on the selected frame.**

   If you can't use the function keys, Control/right-click the Hit frame and choose Insert Keyframe from the contextual menu.

   The **Hit frame** defines the live area of the button, or the area where a user can click to activate the button. Objects on this state do not appear in the movie; you only need to define the general shapes.

Note:

You can use the Insert Blank Keyframe command to add a blank keyframe to the timeline that (as the name suggests) has no content.

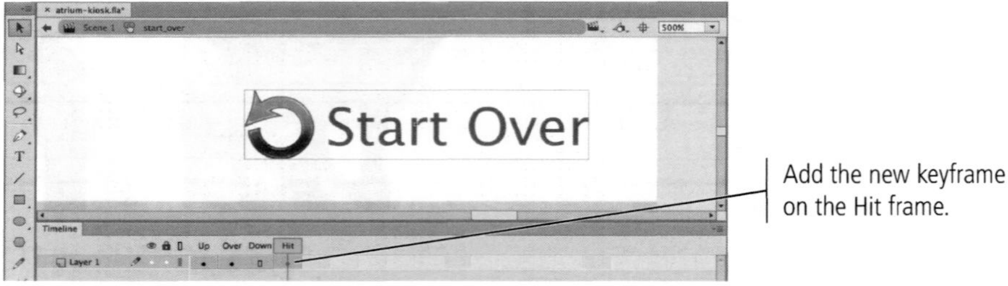
Start Over
Add the new keyframe on the Hit frame.

6. **Choose the Rectangle tool from the Tools panel.**

7. **In the Properties panel, turn off the Object Drawing toggle.**

   When this option is turned off (not highlighted), new drawing shapes drop to the back of the stacking order on the active layer.

   Because merge-drawing shapes drop to the back of the stacking order, this method allows you to still see the button artwork in front of the "hit" shape.

8. **Set the Stroke color to None, and choose a contrasting color as the Fill color.**

9. **Draw a rectangle that covers the entire contents of the button.**

   We used a green color that contrasted with the blue text, but any color will work because the Hit frame content doesn't appear on the Stage when you play the movie.

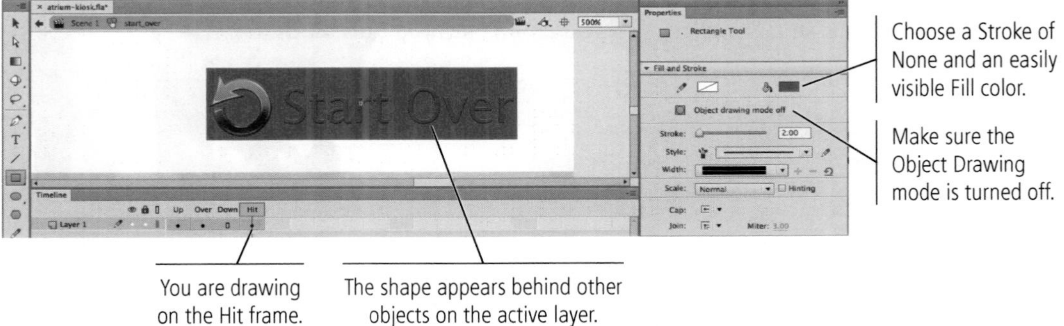

Choose a Stroke of None and an easily visible Fill color.
Make sure the Object Drawing mode is turned off.
You are drawing on the Hit frame.
The shape appears behind other objects on the active layer.

10. **Click Scene 1 in the Edit bar to return to the main Stage.**

11. **Choose Control>Enable Simple Buttons to toggle the option back on, then move the mouse cursor between the words in the button.**

    The button now works even if you hover over the white areas or between the letters. The Hit frame rectangle determines the live (hit) area of the button.

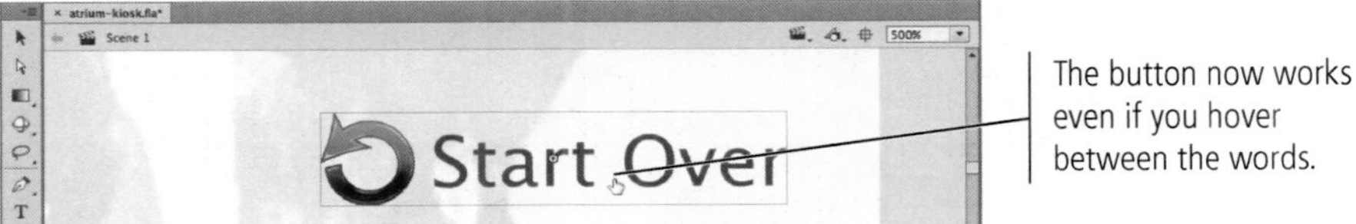

12. **Choose Control>Enable Simple Buttons to toggle off that option.**

13. **Save the file and continue to the next exercise.**

Edit Symbol Properties

The control buttons, which you imported as graphic symbols, are the final pieces of artwork for this movie. Illustrator, does not create button symbols; you need to convert the imported graphic symbols into the necessary button symbols.

1. **With atrium-kiosk.fla open, expand the interface.ai>Illustrator Symbols folder in the Library panel (if necessary).**

   Remember, you can't select a button on the Stage if this control is toggled on.

2. **Control/right-click the shoes_btn symbol icon in the Library panel and choose Properties from the contextual menu.**

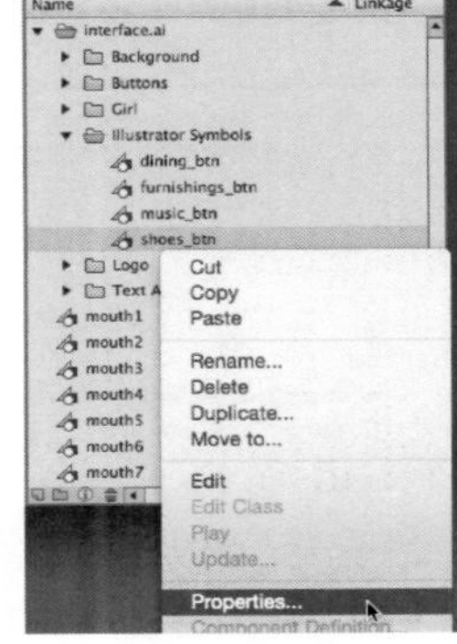

3. **In the Symbol Properties dialog box, choose Button in the Type menu, and then click OK.**

   The Symbol Properties dialog box is nearly the same as the Create New Symbol dialog box; it does not have registration options because that has already been defined for the symbol. To move the symbol artwork relative to the registration point, you can edit the symbol on its Stage.

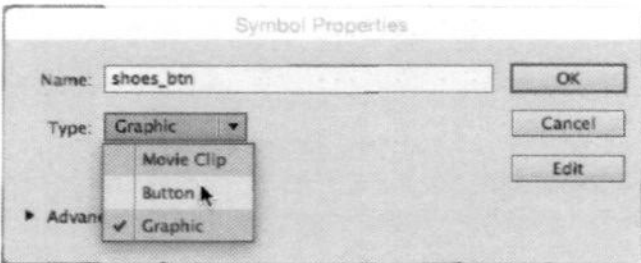

4. **Using the Selection tool, select the Shoes & Apparel button on the Stage.**

5. **In the Properties panel, open the top menu and choose Button.**

   Unlike changing the content of a symbol, changes to the symbol type do not reflect in placed instances. When you change the type of a symbol that has already been placed on the Stage, you also have to change the instance type in the Properties panel.

Choose Button in this menu to change the behavior of the placed instance.

The symbol now shows the button icon instead of the original graphic icon.

6. **Repeat Steps 2–5 to convert the remaining three graphic symbols to buttons.**

7. **Save the file and continue to the next exercise.**

Explore the Symbol Registration Point

Now that the buttons are symbols rather than graphics, you can define the various states of the buttons. You are going to edit the artwork so that the buttons seem to move when the mouse cursor rolls over the hit area.

1. **With atrium-kiosk.fla open, open the Align panel (Window>Align).**

2. **Double-click the Shoes & Apparel button instance to edit the symbol in place.**

   The crosshairs in the middle of the symbol artwork identify the **symbol registration point**; all measurements for placed instances begin at this location.

Symbol registration point

When editing the symbol, the X and Y fields show the position of the top-left corner relative to the symbol's registration point.

3. **In the Align panel, make sure the Align To Stage option is active and then click the Align Right Edge button.**

   The right edge of the symbol artwork is now aligned to the symbol registration point. Because you are editing the symbol in place, you can see the effect of the new alignment relative to the overall file artwork. This illustrates that the registration point is fixed, and the artwork is the thing that moves — not the other way around.

Note:

Use the Align panel with the Align To Stage option active to align the placed object to the symbol's registration point.

4. **Click Scene 1 in the Edit bar to return to the main Stage.**

5. **With the Shoes & Apparel button selected, click the current X value in the Properties panel to access the field.**

On the main Stage, the X and Y fields define the position of the registration point for the instance.

Click the existing value to access the field.

6. **Type `1034` in the highlighted X field and press Return/Enter to apply the change.**

   As we explained earlier, the symbol registration point is the origin of measurements for placed instances. When you change the X position, you are defining the horizontal location of the symbol registration point for the selected instance.

   The Stage for this file is 1024 pixels wide (as defined by the imported Illustrator artboard); you are placing the right edge of the button 10 pixels past the Stage edge.

   In the next few steps, you will use this position as the basis for changing the object's position when a user moves the cursor over the button (i.e., triggers the Over frame).

7. **Double-click the Shoes & Apparel button again to enter back into the symbol Stage.**

8. **Insert a new keyframe on the button's Over frame. With the Over keyframe selected, click the button artwork to select it.**

   The object must be selected to change its properties. Selecting the frame in the timeline also selects the object on that frame.

9. **In the Properties panel, click the current X value in the Properties panel to access the field.**

10. **Place the insertion point after the existing value and type `-10` after the existing value. Press Enter to move the selected object.**

    Using mathematical operators makes it easy to move an object a specific distance without manually calculating the change:

    - Subtract from the X position to move an object left.
    - Add to the X position to move an object right.
    - Subtract from the Y position to move an object up.
    - Add to the Y position to move an object down.

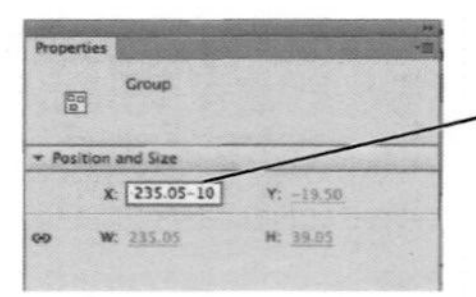

Type **–10** after the current value.

The new X value moves the artwork 10 pixels to the left.

You are editing the Over frame.

11. **Click Scene 1 in the Edit bar to return to the main Stage.**

12. **Repeat Steps 2–11 for the three remaining buttons.**

13. **Choose Control>Enable Simple Buttons to toggle the option back on. Move your mouse cursor over the buttons to test the Over state functionality.**

The buttons should move 10 pixels to the left when the mouse cursor enters the button area.

14. **Save the file and continue to the next exercise.**

> ***Note:***
>
> *Because this button artwork includes a solid-filled white rectangle, you don't need to define a separate hit frame. The artwork itself is sufficient to trigger the button.*

Organize Your Library with Folders

Library folders work the same as layer folders; they help you organize and structure complex files. Movies often contain dozens or even hundreds of assets — and the more complex a movie becomes, the more useful it is to clearly organize those assets. Although this step isn't strictly necessary, it is always a good idea to organize your work so that you can more easily organize your thoughts and processes going forward.

1. **With atrium-kiosk.fla open, expand the interface.ai folder in the Library panel.**

2. **Click the Illustrator Symbols folder (inside the interface.ai folder) and drag down to the empty area at the bottom of the panel.**

   This moves the Illustrator Symbols folder to the first level of the library. The symbols, which are placed on the Stage, are not affected by the move.

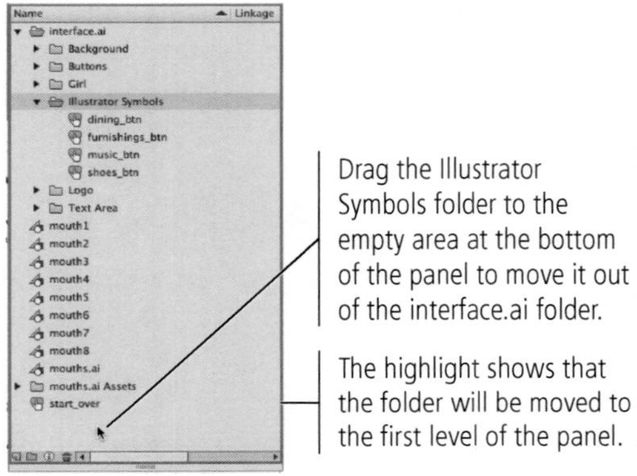

Drag the Illustrator Symbols folder to the empty area at the bottom of the panel to move it out of the interface.ai folder.

The highlight shows that the folder will be moved to the first level of the panel.

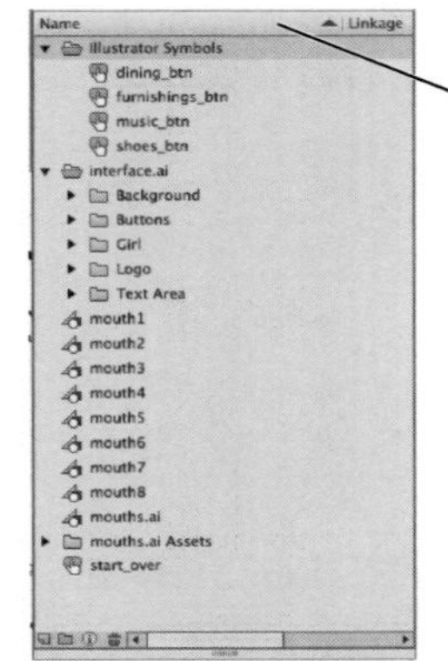

Click a column heading to sort library items by that category.

3. **Double-click the Illustrator Symbols folder name to highlight the name. Type `Buttons` to change the folder name.**

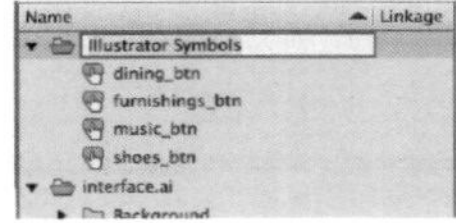

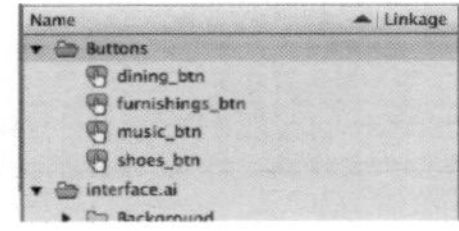

Note:

If your Library panel is too short to show an empty area below the current assets, Control/right-click any of the existing first-level assets and choose Paste. The pasted symbols are pasted at the same level as the asset where you Control/right-click.

4. **Click the start_over button symbol icon and drag it into the Buttons folder.**

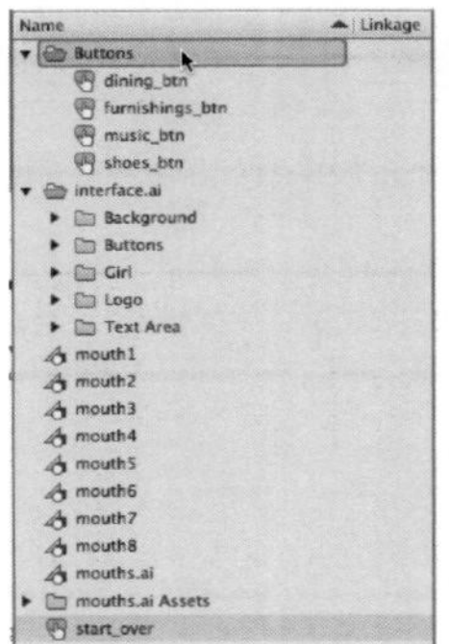

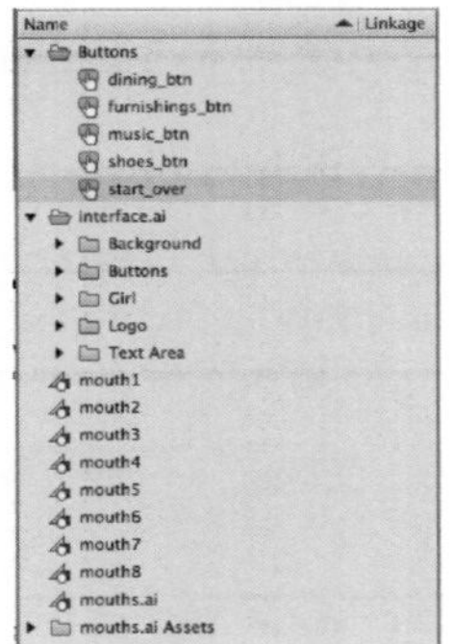

5. **Double-click the interface.ai folder name to highlight the name. Type `Component Artwork` to change the folder name.**

6. **Click the mouths.ai Assets folder and drag it into the Component Artwork folder.**

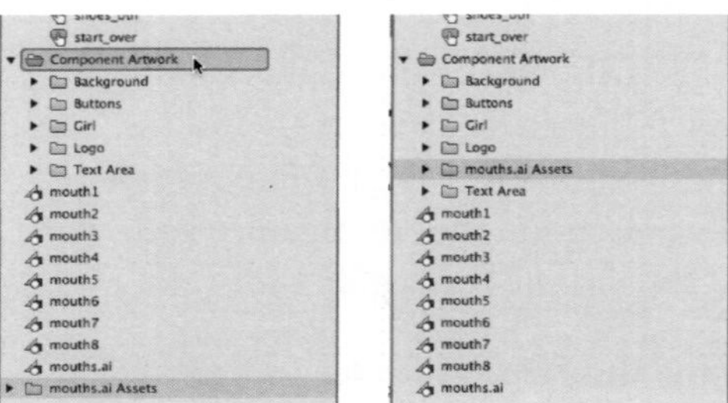

7. **Click the empty area at the bottom of the panel to deselect all assets and folders.**

8. **Click the New Folder button at the bottom of the Library panel. Type Mouth Graphics as the new folder name.**

   The new folder is added at the main level of the library, alphabetized with other items at the same level. If you didn't deselect in Step 7, the new folder would have been created at the same nesting level as the selected item.

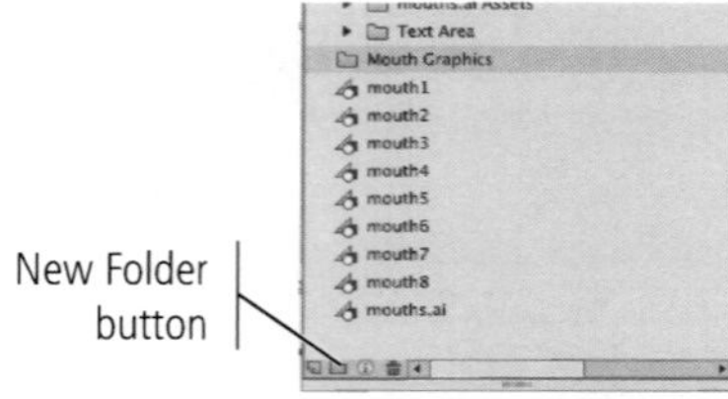
New Folder
button

9. **Click the mouth1 symbol to select it, then Shift-click the mouth8 symbol to select it and all files in between.**

   Press Shift to select multiple contiguous items in the panel, or press Command/Control to select multiple, non-contiguous items.

10. **Click the icon of any selected file and drag into the Mouth Graphics folder.**

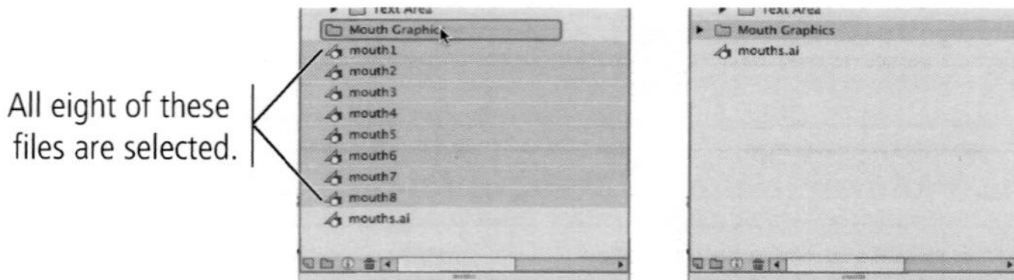
All eight of these
files are selected.

11. **Click the mouths.ai graphic symbol and click the panel's Delete button.**

    Although you used this artwork to create the individual mouth symbols, this symbol is not used in the file, so it can be safely deleted from the library. If you delete a symbol that is used in the file, the placed instances will also be deleted from the file.

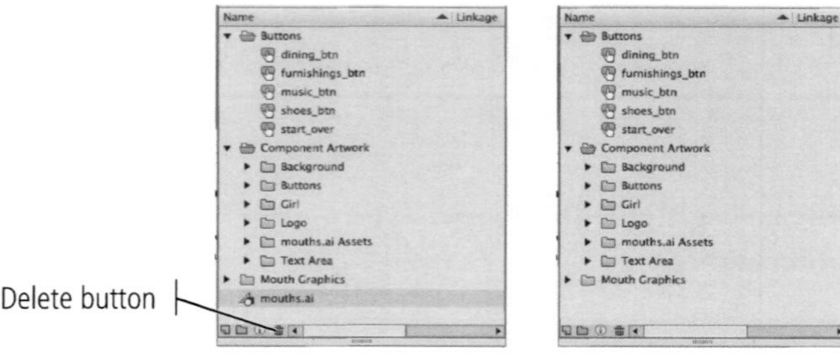
Delete button

12. **Collapse all library folders, then save the file and continue to the next stage of the project.**

Stage 2 Working with Sound

Sound files can be categorized into three basic types: uncompressed, compressed (lossless), and compressed (lossy). **Uncompressed sound files** encode all sounds with the same number of bits per unit of time. In an uncompressed format, two sound files of the same duration — whether a symphony or a simple beep — have the same size (which is typically very large). Such files are commonly used for archiving or other situations where file size is not an issue.

Lossless compression sound files lose no data during compression; these files are smaller than uncompressed files, but not as small as lossy compression file formats. **Lossy compression sound files** lose some data but retain good sound quality; a large number of these files can be stored in relatively small amounts of space.

Animate handles most major audio formats, including the ones most commonly used today:

- The **MP3** format is the most commonly used audio format. This format compresses a music file in the most efficient manner, so file size is reduced without compromising quality. MP3 playback does require more processing power than other formats because the data has to be decoded every time the file plays.
- The **WAV** format is an uncompressed format with very high quality. This file type can be used in Animate animations for desktop applications, but should be avoided for Web-based movies because the files are huge and take a long time to download.
- The **AIFF** format (Audio Interchange File Format) is common on Macintosh computers. This format is generally uncompressed, so file sizes are large compared to the MP3 format. AIFF files are suitable for applications specifically targeted for Macintosh computers.
- The **Audio** (AU) file format, developed by Sun Microsystems, transmits sound files over the Internet and can be played in Java programs. These files are smaller than AIFF and WAV formats, but the quality of sound is not as good as regular WAV files.
- The **QuickTime** (MOV) format is technically a video format, but it can also include audio.

Import Sound Files

In general, there are three methods for incorporating sound into an Animate movie. Sounds in a file's library can be placed directly on the timeline, or you can use code to call a library sound based on a particular event. You can also use code to load and play external sound files (those that don't exist in the Animate library).

In this project, you will use the timeline method to add the various sounds that are needed for the kiosk to function properly. The first step is to import the necessary sound files into the Animate library.

1. **With atrium-kiosk.fla open, choose File>Import>Import to Library. In the resulting dialog box, select all files in the WIP>Atrium>Audio folder, then click Open.**

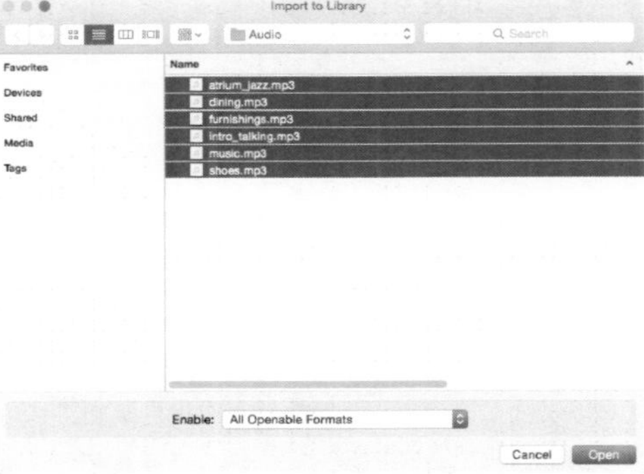

2. **Open the Library panel and review the contents.**

   The sound files are automatically imported into the file's Library panel.

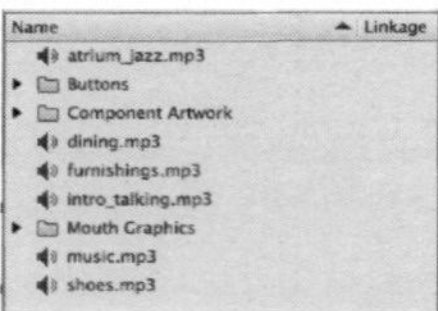

3. **Click the New Folder button at the bottom of the Library panel. Rename the new folder `Audio`.**

4. **Command/Control-click all six imported audio files and drag them into the Audio folder.**

5. **Expand the Audio folder so you can see the available files.**

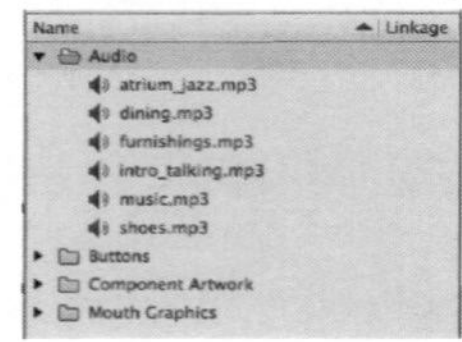

6. **Save the file and continue to the next exercise.**

Note:

It's always a good idea to keep your library well organized while developing a file with numerous assets.

Add Event Sound

Event sounds are "timeline independent" — they play independently of the movie timeline. They are downloaded completely and stored in the user computer's memory; this means they can be played repeatedly (including continuously looping) without having to redownload the file.

1. **With the file `atrium-kiosk.fla` open, click to select the atrium_jazz.mp3 file in the Library panel.**

   This file will be the background music for the entire file. It will play in an infinite loop as long as the kiosk file is open.

2. **Click the Play button in the top-right corner of the Preview area.**

   You can use the Library panel to hear imported sounds before they are used on the Stage.

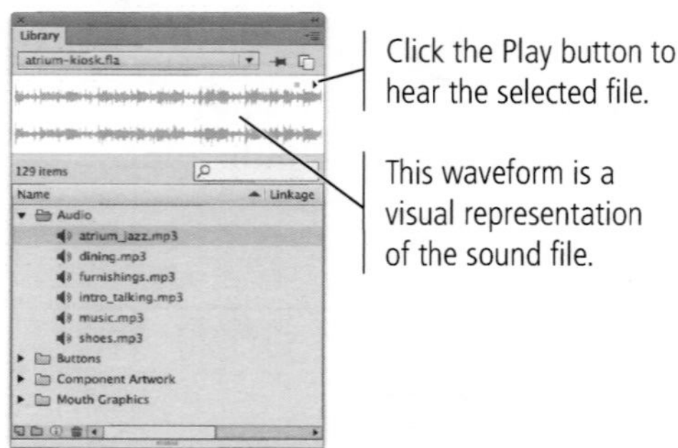

3. **Select the Frame 1 keyframe on the Background layer.**

Note:

Because event sounds must be downloaded completely before they can play, they can cause buffering delays in playback.

4. **In the Sound section of the Properties panel, choose atrium_jazz.mp3 in the Name menu.**

5. **In the Sync menu, choose Event.**

Event sounds default to the Repeat 1 method, which means the sound plays one time. You can change the number in the Repeat field to play the sound a specific number of times.

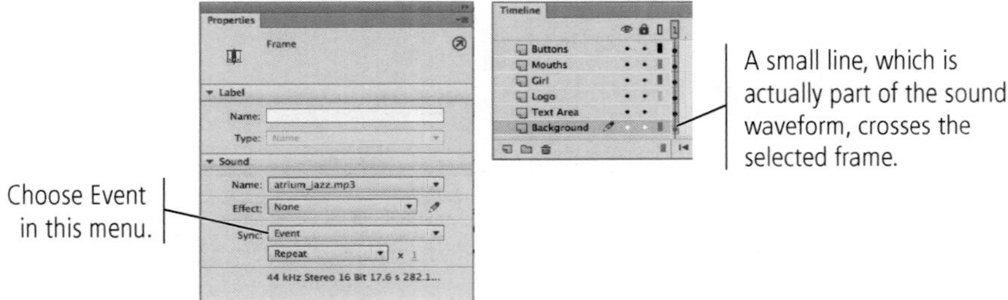

Choose Event in this menu.
A small line, which is actually part of the sound waveform, crosses the selected frame.

6. **Choose Control>Test.**

Because you created this file targeting AIR for Desktop, this command opens the file in a separate AIR Debug Launcher window. This shows you what the exported file will look and sound like. Although the sound waveform only appears on Frame 1 of the Background layer, the entire sound plays from start to finish when you test the file.

> ***Note:***
>
> *Press Command-Return/Control-Enter to test the movie in an Animate Player window.*

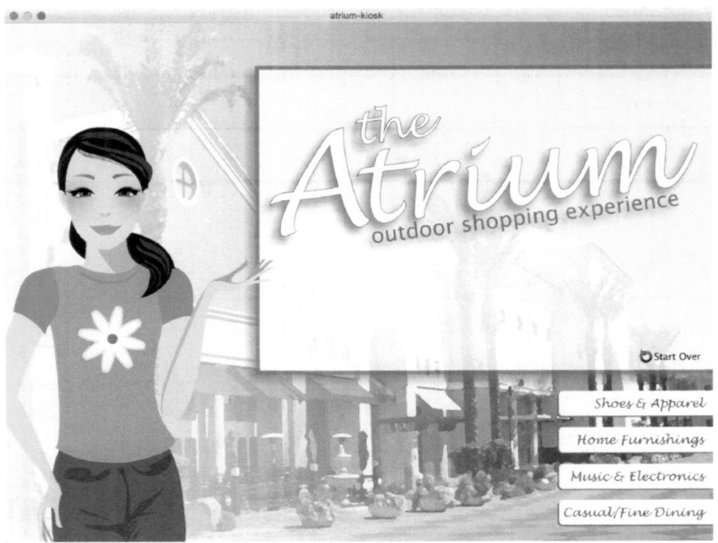

7. **Close the Player window and return to Animate.**

8. **With Frame 1 of the Background layer selected, choose Loop in the menu under the Sync menu (in the Sound area of the Properties panel).**

   Using the Loop method, the event sound plays continuously as long as the movie remains open.

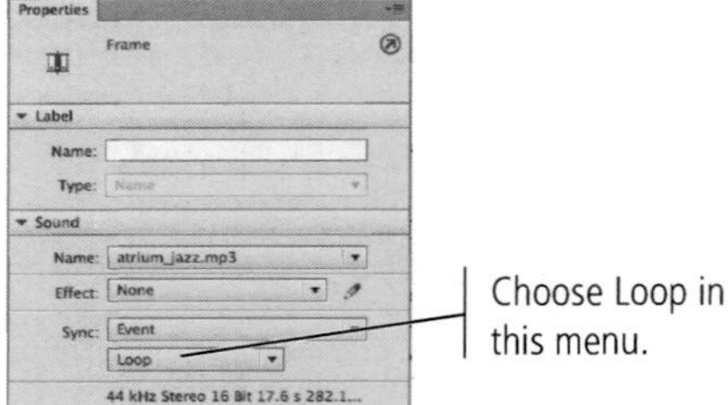

Choose Loop in this menu.

9. **Press Command-Return/Control-Enter to test the movie again.**

   The background sound now plays from start to finish, and then repeats to create a continuous background sound track.

10. **Close the Player window and return to Animate.**

11. **Save the file and continue to the next exercise.**

Edit a Sound Envelope to Control Volume

Although Animate is not intended to be a sound-editing application, you can apply a limited number of effects to control the volume and length of sounds on the Animate timeline. These options are available in the Effect menu of the Properties panel when a sound is attached to a keyframe.

1. **With atrium-kiosk.fla open, click Frame 1 of the Background layer to select the frame where you attached the sound in the previous exercise.**

2. **In the Properties panel, open the Effect menu and choose Custom to open the Edit Envelope dialog box.**

   The Edit Envelope dialog box shows the waveforms for each channel in a sound file. (In many cases, both channels have the same waveform.) You can view the sound waves by seconds or frames, and you can zoom in or out to show various portions of the sound. The left and right channels refer to sound output systems that have more than one speaker — one on the left and one on the right.

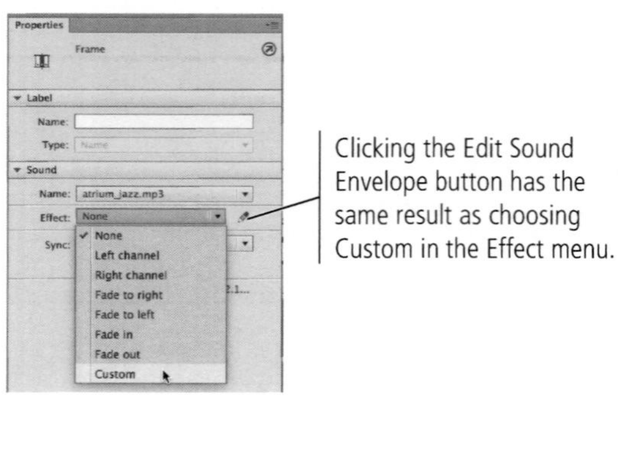

Clicking the Edit Sound Envelope button has the same result as choosing Custom in the Effect menu.

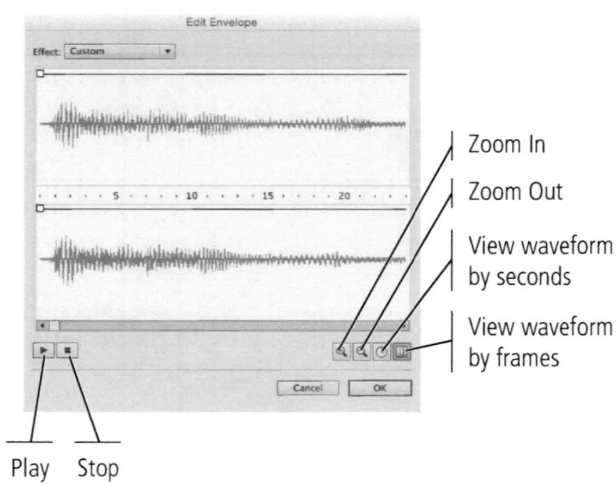

Zoom In
Zoom Out
View waveform by seconds
View waveform by frames
Play
Stop

3. **Click the Frames button to show the sound based on frames (if this isn't already active).**

4. **In the left channel area (the top waveform), click the handle on the left end of the waveform, and drag down to below the existing waveform.**

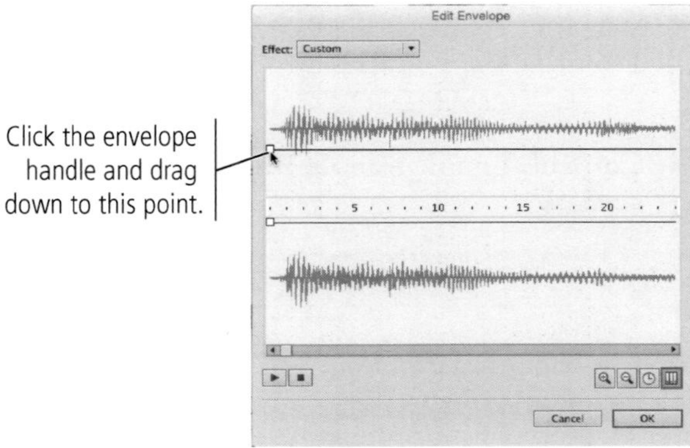

> *Note:*
>
> *Click the envelope line to add a new handle to the envelope. Click an existing handle and drag it away from the window to remove a point from the envelope.*

5. **Repeat Step 4 for the right channel (the bottom waveform).**

   By lowering the envelope handles, you reduced the volume of the sound file.

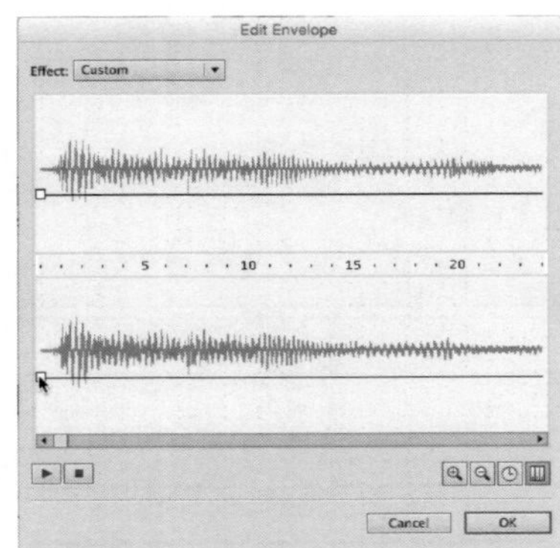

6. **Click OK to close the Edit Envelope dialog box and apply the change.**

7. **Save the file and continue to the next exercise.**

More about Editing Sound Files

ANIMATE FOUNDATIONS

The Effect menu in the Properties panel lists a number of common sound envelope effects built into Animate. These sound effects do not alter the sound in the files; they simply control how the sound data plays.

- **Left Channel** plays only the left channel of the sound.
- **Right Channel** plays only the right channel of the sound.
- **Fade to Right** gradually lowers the sound level of the left channel, and then gradually raises the sound level of the right channel.
- **Fade to Left** gradually lowers the sound level of the right channel, and then gradually raises the sound level of the left channel.
- **Fade In** gradually raises the sound level at the beginning of the sound file.
- **Fade Out** gradually lowers the sound level at the end of the sound file.
- **Custom** opens the Edit Envelope dialog box, where you can define your own sound effects.

Use the Start and Stop Sync Methods for Buttons

The four category buttons will link to different screens in the kiosk. Each button needs to trigger a sound that plays when the user's mouse rolls over the button. To achieve this result, you can attach the relevant sound to each button using the same technique you applied in the previous exercise. Because of the four-frame nature of button symbols, however, a few extra steps are required to make the sounds play only when you want them to play.

1. **With atrium-kiosk.fla open, choose Control>Enable Simple Buttons to make sure that option is toggled on.**

2. **In the Library panel, double-click the shoes_btn symbol icon to enter Symbol-Editing mode for that symbol.**

   Remember, you can edit a symbol by double-clicking the symbol icon. This is especially useful when the Enable Simple Buttons feature is toggled on because you can't select buttons on the Stage in that mode.

   In Symbol-Editing mode, a discrete Stage appears when you double-click a symbol icon in the Library panel; the name of the symbol appears to the right of the Scene name in the Edit bar, indicating that you're working on the symbol instead of the main scene. You can also access this option by Control/right-clicking a placed instance on the Stage and choosing Edit.

3. **Select the Over frame of Layer 1. In the Properties panel, choose shoes.mp3 in the Sound menu and set the Sync menu to Event.**

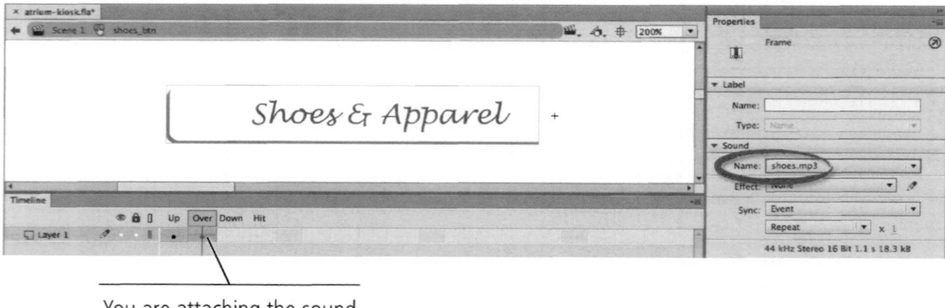

You are attaching the sound to the button's Over frame.

4. **Click Scene 1 in the Edit bar to return to the main Stage.**

5. **Move your mouse cursor over the Shoes & Apparel button to hear the attached sound.**

Moving the mouse over the button triggers the Over state, including the attached sound file.

6. **Move your mouse cursor away, and then move back over the Shoes & Apparel button to trigger the sound again.**

   When the mouse re-enters the button area — triggering the Over frame — the message plays again. (Because the sound is very short, this might not be apparent unless you move the mouse back into the button area very quickly.)

7. **Double-click the shoes_btn symbol icon in the Library panel to enter back into the button Stage. Select the Over frame, then change the Sound Sync menu to Start.**

   The Start sync option is similar to the Event method. The difference is that the Start method allows only one instance of the same sound to play at a time; this prevents the overlap problem caused by the Event method.

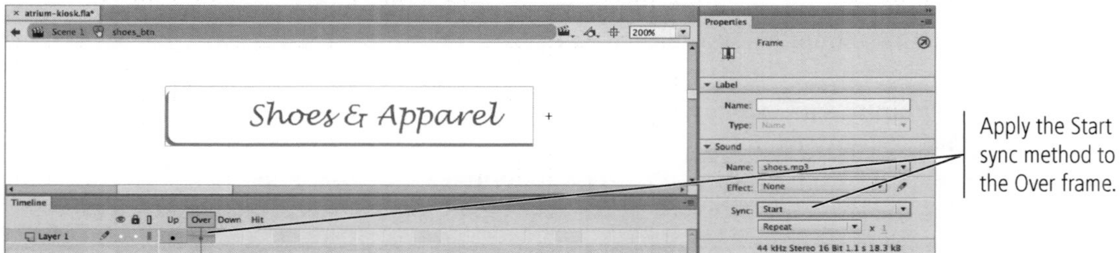

Apply the Start sync method to the Over frame.

8. **Select the Down frame and press F6 to insert a new keyframe, or Control/right-click the Down frame and choose Insert Keyframe from the contextual menu.**

9. **In the Properties panel, choose shoes.mp3 in the Sound menu and choose Stop in the Sync menu.**

   The Stop option stops all instances of the selected sound from playing. When a user clicks the Shoes & Apparel button, the sound triggered on the Over frame will stop playing.

Apply the Stop sync method to a keyframe on the Down frame.

10. **Click Scene 1 to return to the main Stage.**

11. **Repeat the same basic process to add the appropriate event sounds to the other three navigation buttons:**
    - Double-click the button symbol icon to enter the symbol's Stage.
    - Select the Over frame and attach the appropriate sound file using the Start sync option.
      - For the Home Furnishings button, use the furnishings.mp3 sound file.
      - For the Music & Electronics button, use the music.mp3 sound file.
      - For the Casual/Fine Dining button, use the dining.mp3 sound file.
    - Add a keyframe to the Down frame.
    - Attach the same sound you used for the Over frame, and apply the Stop sync option.

12. **If you haven't done so already, click Scene 1 in the Edit bar to return to the main Stage.**

13. **Roll your mouse cursor over the four buttons to test all four sounds. Click each to make sure the sounds stop when they're supposed to.**

14. **Save the file and continue to the next stage of the project.**

Stage 3 Creating Frame Animations

The basic underlying premise of animation is that objects change over time — from complex transitions in color, shape, and opacity to moving a character to a new position. The most basic type of animation is to simply replace one object with another at specific points in time; you will create this type of animation in this stage of the kiosk project to make it seem like the girl is talking.

Repositioning or replacing objects on successive frames results in the appearance of movement when you watch an animation; in reality, your brain is being fooled — you're simply seeing a series of images Animate before your eyes (hence the application's name). Your brain thinks it's seeing movement, when in fact it's simply processing a series of still images displayed in rapid succession.

To make an animation appear to run continuously, you can **loop** it so it starts over at Frame 1 after reaching the last frame. (In fact, as you will see, looping is the default state of an animation; you have to use code to prevent the timeline from automatically looping in the exported file.)

To create animation, you need to understand several terms and concepts:

- The Animate Timeline panel shows a visual depiction of the passage of time. Each fraction of a second is represented by a frame (the rectangles to the right of the layer names). The **playhead** indicates the current point in time, or the frame that is visible on the Stage.
- The number of frames in one second (called **frames per second**, **FPS**, or **frame rate**) determines the length and quality of the overall animation. New Animate files default to 24 fps, which is the standard frame rate of most film movies in the United States (although HD formats range as high as 120 fps). Animations only for the Web are commonly developed at 15 fps.
- A **keyframe** indicates the point in time at which something changes. If you want to change something, you need to insert a keyframe at the appropriate moment on the timeline.
- Regular frames between keyframes have the same content as the preceding keyframe.

Note:

*The term **playhead** is a throwback to the days when animation and video were shown on physical tape-reading machines. The playhead is the component under which the tape moves, and the tape is read by the player. By sliding the tape back and forth underneath the playhead, an animator could make a movie run forward and backward.*

Add Streaming Sound

Unlike the event sounds that you used in the previous exercises, **stream sounds** play as soon as enough data is downloaded (called **progressive downloading**) to the user's computer. Stream sounds cannot be saved on a user's computer; the sound file must be redownloaded every time it is played. Stream sounds are linked to the timeline, which means they stop playing if the timeline stops (i.e., they are "timeline dependent").

1. **With atrium-kiosk.fla open, add a new layer named Talking immediately above the Mouths layer.**

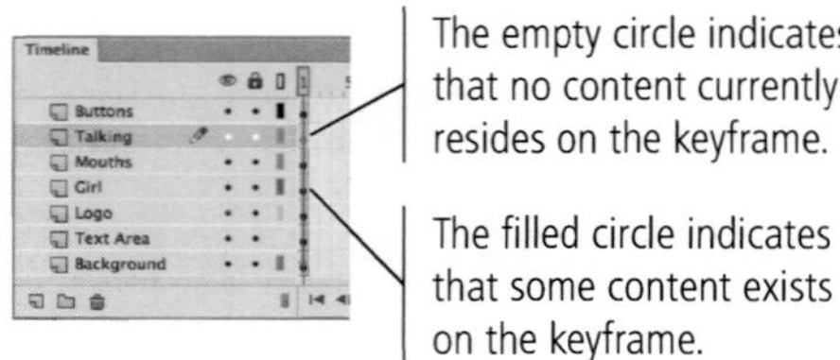

The empty circle indicates that no content currently resides on the keyframe.

The filled circle indicates that some content exists on the keyframe.

2. **Select the Frame 1 keyframe of the Talking layer.**

   By default, the first frame of every layer is a keyframe.

3. **In the Properties panel, choose intro_talking.mp3 from the Sound menu and choose Stream in the Sync menu.**

> *Note:*
>
> *Because stream sounds are typically larger files (longer sounds equal more data and larger file size), the quality of these sounds might be poor for users who have slow Internet connections.*

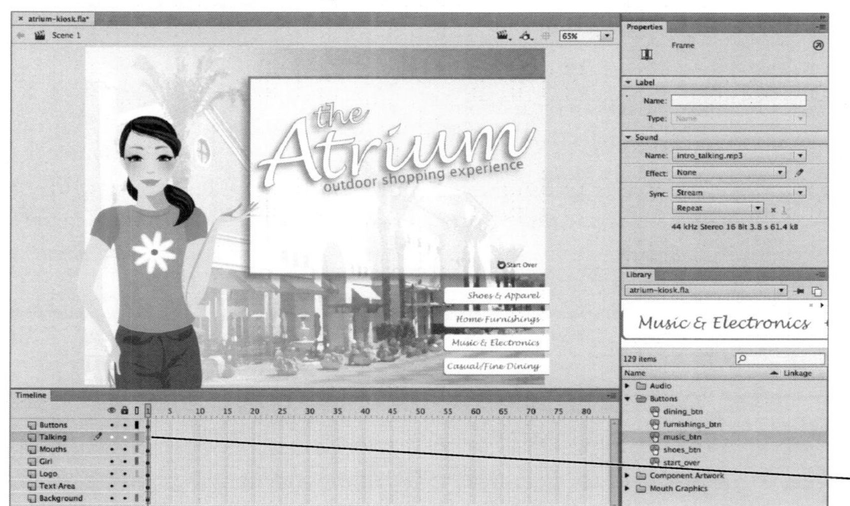

Frame 1 of the Talking layer is selected.

4. **Choose Control>Test to test the movie.**

   The background sound plays as expected, but the intro_talking sound does not. Remember, stream sounds are related to the position of the playhead on the timeline (they are timeline dependent). Because this file currently has only one frame, the playhead has nowhere to move, so the sound file does not play in the Player window.

5. **Close the external window and return to Animate.**

6. **In the timeline, Control/right-click Frame 95 of the Talking layer and choose Insert Frame from the contextual menu.**

Frame numbers appear in the frame ruler at the top of the timeline.

Control/right-click Frame 95 of the Talking layer to open the contextual menu.

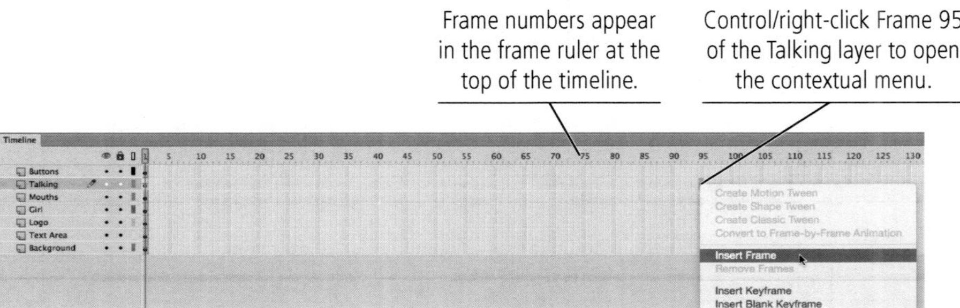

When you add a new frame, you extend the layer's timeline to the point where you place the new frame. The red playhead above the timeline shows the currently active frame.

You can now see the entire waveform of the sound that is attached to Frame 1 of the Talking layer. As you can see, however, none of the graphics are visible on the Stage because you have not added frames to the other layers. In other words, objects on those layers don't yet exist at Frame 95.

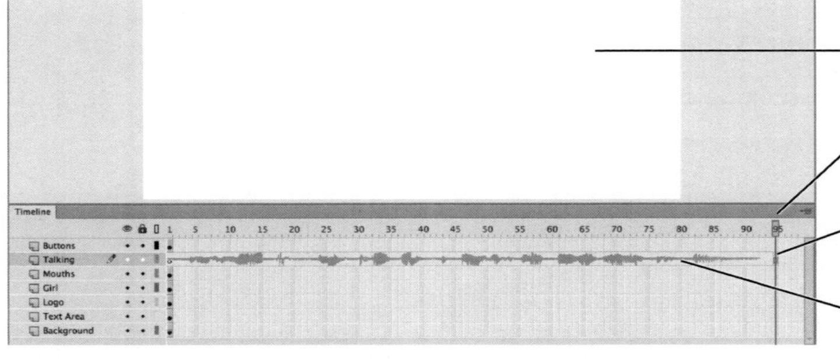

Other layers are not yet extended to Frame 95, so the graphics on those layers are not visible.

The playhead shows the currently active frame.

Adding a frame extends the layer's timeline.

The waveform on the Talking layer is now entirely visible.

7. **Click Frame 95 of the Buttons layer to select it, then press F5.**

   This keyboard shortcut inserts a new frame at the selected location on the timeline; it is the same as choosing Insert Frame from the contextual menu.

   If you are using a laptop or keyboard that has system-specific functions assigned to the Function keys, you can either press FN plus the required function key, or use the Insert>Timeline menu commands to insert frames and keyframes.

   After adding the new frame to the Buttons layer, objects on that layer are now visible at Frame 95. The other graphics are still not visible because those layers do not yet have frames at Frame 95.

> ***Note:***
>
> *You can also insert a frame, keyframe, or blank keyframe by Control/right-clicking a specific frame in the Timeline panel and choosing from the contextual menu.*

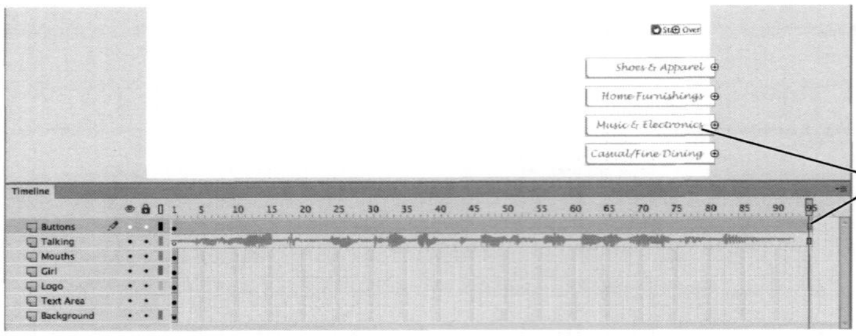

Objects on the Buttons layer are visible once that layer has been extended to Frame 95.

8. **Click Frame 95 of the Mouths layer, then Shift-click Frame 95 of the Background layer.**

9. **Press F5 to add new frames to all five selected layers.**

   Because all of the layers now "exist" on Frame 95, all of the kiosk graphics are now visible on the Stage.

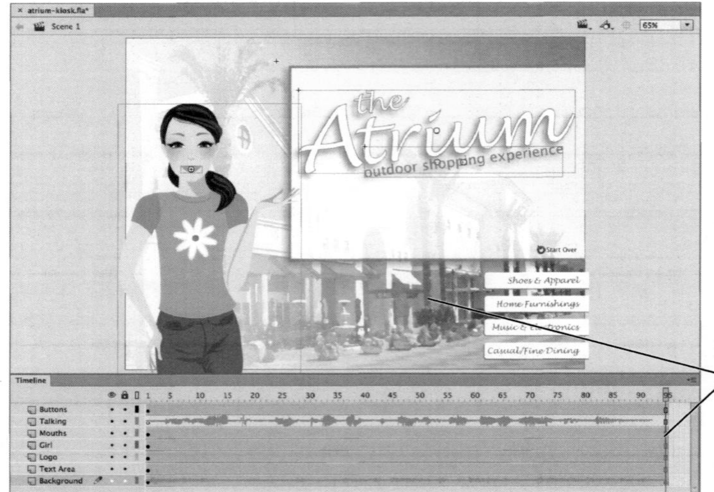

Because all layers now extend to Frame 95, all graphics in the interface are visible on the Stage.

10. **Click Frame 1 of any layer to move the playhead to the beginning of the timeline.**

    The playhead identifies the current point in time on the Animate timeline. If you don't move the playhead back to Frame 1, the background sound will not play.

11. **Press Return/Enter to test the movie on the Animate Stage.**

    You should now hear two sounds: the character talking and the background music.

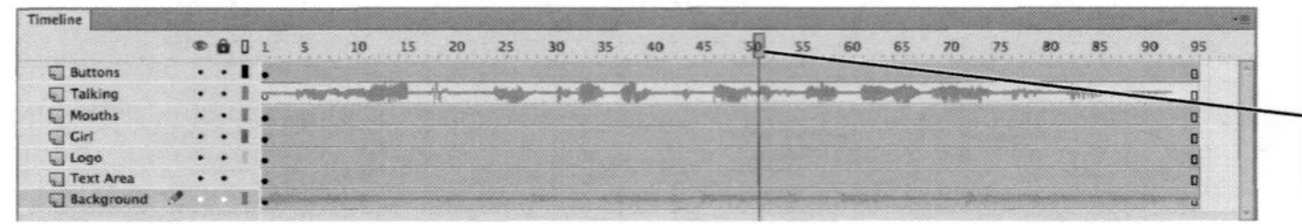

Pressing Return/Enter causes the playhead to move, playing the movie directly on the Stage.

12. **Choose Control>Test to test the movie in the external debugger window.**

The movie plays entirely through and then starts over again (**loops**) — this is what would happen in the actual exported file.

To make the timeline play only once, you have to use code to intentionally stop the playhead from looping. This code will be implemented by your developer partner after you are finished creating the lip-syncing animation.

Note:

You can choose Control>Loop Playback to allow the playhead to loop on the Animate Stage.

13. **Close the external window and return to Animate.**

14. **Save the file and continue to the next exercise.**

Prepare for Lip Syncing

If you have ever watched cartoons, you have probably seen the results of the time-consuming and painstaking work involved in synchronizing a character's movements to sounds. Realistic lip syncing is an extremely complex art that requires precise attention to detail, as well as in-depth study of behavioral movement. Other projects, such as this one, do not call for the precision and detail required for lifelike animation; rather, they use representative movements to create the effect of a character talking.

1. **Sit or stand in front of a mirror. Say the following sentence slowly, paying careful attention to the shape of your mouth for each syllable:**

   Need help? Use the buttons to find exactly what you're looking for.

Note:

To better understand how to sync lip movements to sounds, you should study the different facial movements that are involved in spoken sound (called phonology).

2. **With `atrium-kiosk.fla` open in Animate, expand the mouth graphics folder in the Library panel.**

3. **Click each mouth symbol in the Library panel and review the shapes.**

   The illustrator for this project created eight different mouth shapes to represent the various "talking" sounds. Note that each symbol was created with the registration point at the center.

Symbol	Use for:	Symbol	Use for:	Symbol	Use for:	Symbol	Use for:
mouth1	Silent, M, B, P	mouth2	C, D, G, J, K, N, R, S, Y, Z	mouth3	Short E, I, O, U Long A	mouth4	F, V
mouth5	M, B, P	mouth6	L, D, T, Th	mouth7	Short A, E Long I	mouth8	Ch, Sh, Qu, W Long O, U

4. **In the timeline layers area, double-click the icon to the left of the Talking layer name to open the Layer Properties dialog box.**

5. **Choose 300% in the Layer Height menu and click OK.**

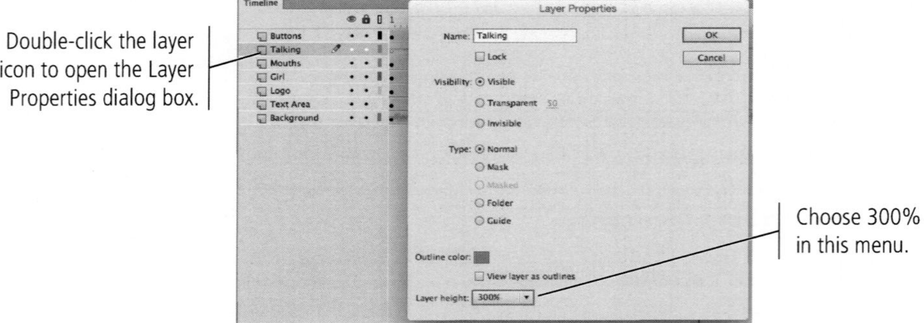

It's easier to sync movement to sound when you can see the variations in the sound file. By enlarging the layer height, you can see the peaks and valleys of the waveform directly on the timeline.

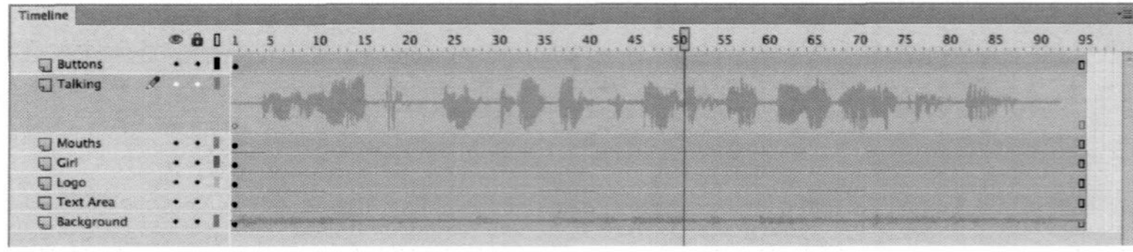

6. **Continue to the next exercise.**

 Create Lip Sync Animation

While lip syncing might seem complicated, it's actually quite simple — you show the graphic that supports the sound heard at a particular frame on the timeline. Because the different mouth shapes for this project have already been created, the most difficult part of the process is determining which shape to place at which point on the timeline.

1. **Click Frame 1 above the timeline to reset the playhead to the beginning of the movie.**

2. **Click the playhead and drag quickly to the right.**

   Dragging the playhead, a technique called **scrubbing the timeline**, allows you to manually preview portions of an animation. Because the sound on the Talking layer is a stream sound, you hear the sound as you drag the playhead. The background music — an event sound — is not related to the playhead, so scrubbing the playhead does not play the background music.

   As you drag the playhead from Frame 1, you hear the first sound in the spoken message beginning at Frame 4 (also indicated by the rise in the waveform).

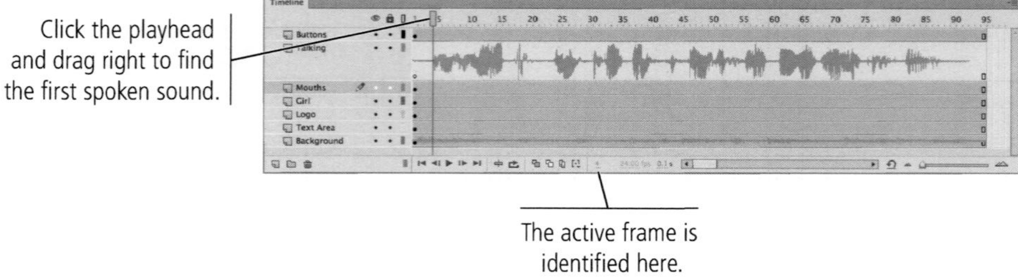

Click the playhead and drag right to find the first spoken sound.
The active frame is identified here.

3. **Select Frame 3 of the Mouths layer, then press F6 to insert a new keyframe.**

   Remember, a keyframe is the point at which something changes. In this case, you are going to change the mouth shape, so you need to add a keyframe at the appropriate point in time (when the mouth begins to move to make the spoken sound).

   Content on the preceding frame is automatically duplicated on the new keyframe.

   Although the sound begins at Frame 4, people's mouths usually start moving before actual words are spoken. You are adding a keyframe one frame earlier than the sound to accommodate for this behavior.

4. **Click the mouth symbol on the Stage to show its properties in the Properties panel.**

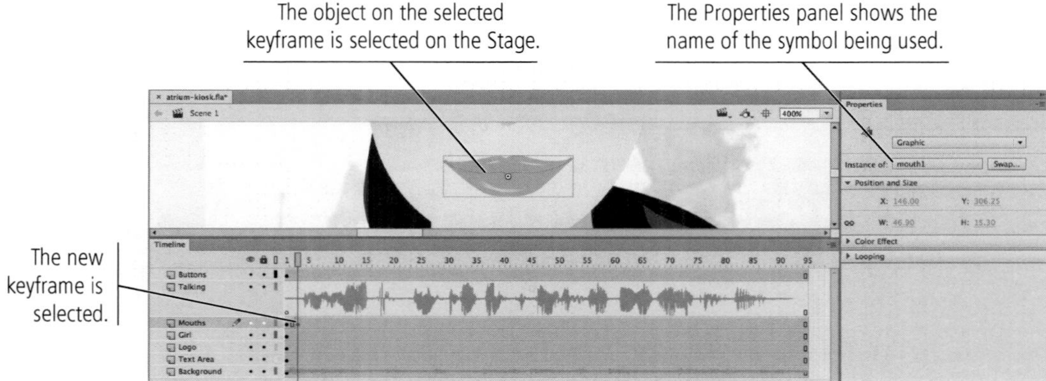

The object on the selected keyframe is selected on the Stage.
The Properties panel shows the name of the symbol being used.
The new keyframe is selected.

5. **With the mouth shape on the Frame 3 keyframe selected, click the Swap button in the Properties panel.**

   Lip syncing requires one primary task: swapping symbols to show the graphics that correlate to the sound at that particular moment.

6. **In the Swap Symbol dialog box, choose the mouth2 graphic symbol.**

   This is the mouth that correlates to the "N" sound at the beginning of the word "Need".

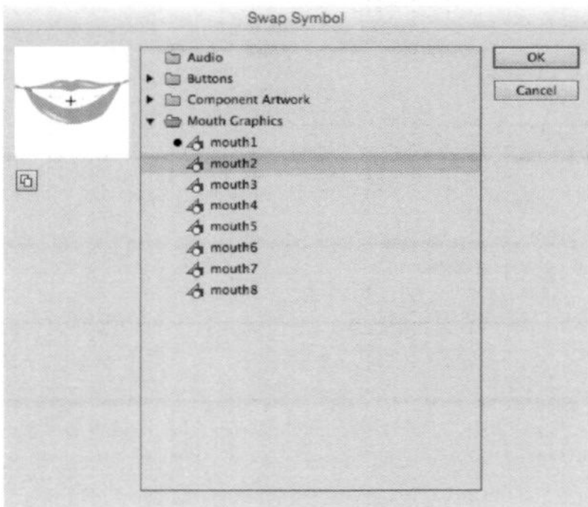

7. **Click OK to close the Swap Symbol dialog box.**

   The new mouth now appears on Frame 3. The mouth symbol (mouth1) on the previous keyframe will remain visible until the playhead reaches Frame 3.

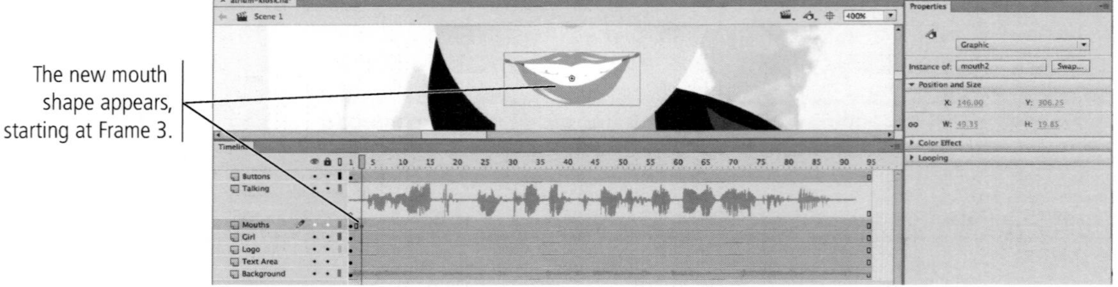
The new mouth
shape appears,
starting at Frame 3.

8. **Drag the playhead right to find the next significant change in sound.**

   The brief pause between the words "need" and "help" suggests a change in the speaker's mouth position at Frame 8.

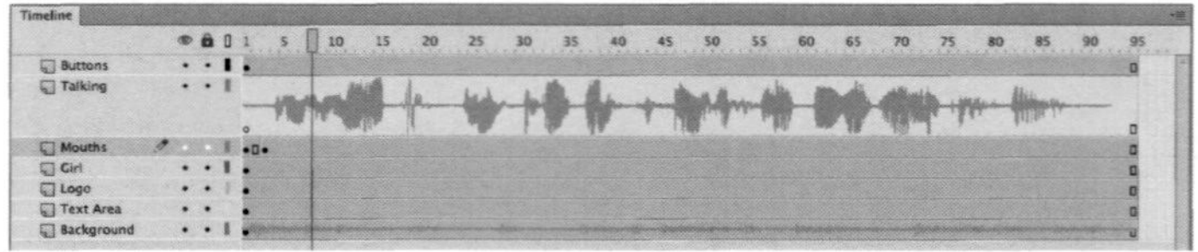

9. **Select Frame 8 on the Mouths layer, then add a new keyframe to the selected frame.**

10. **With the mouth on the Frame 8 keyframe selected, click to select the mouth shape on the Stage, then click the Swap button in the Properties panel. In the Swap Symbol dialog box, choose the mouth5 symbol and click OK.**

    This mouth shape is nearly closed, so it works well for the brief pause between words. It correlates to the short "I" sound, but it also works well as a good transition shape between a wide-open mouth and a closed mouth.

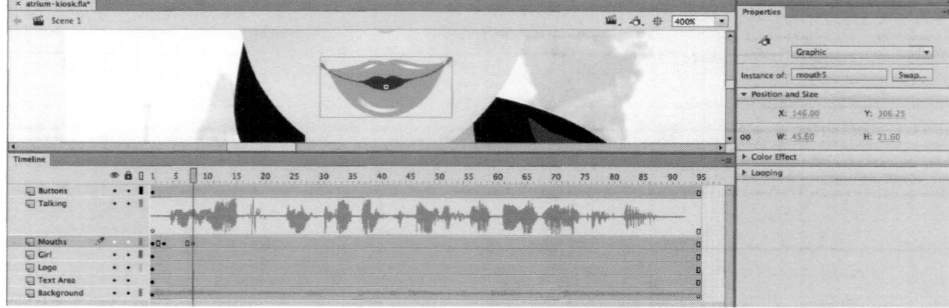

11. **Insert a new keyframe at Frame 10 of the Mouths layer. Select the mouth shape on the Stage, open the Swap Symbol dialog box, and replace the mouth shape with the mouth3 symbol.**

    This shape correlates to the "short e" sound in "help". (The "h" sound typically blends into the vowel sound.)

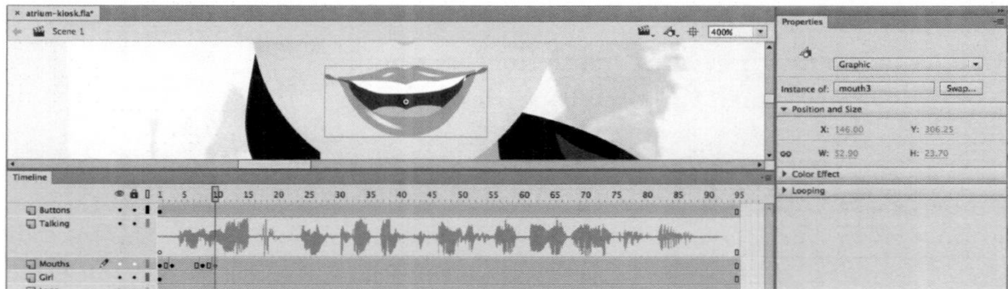

12. **Return the playhead to Frame 1 and press Return/Enter to play the movie on the Stage.**

    So far you have only three changes in the character's mouth, but you should begin to see how the different symbols appear at the appropriate points in the playback. In general, lip syncing in Animate is a relatively simple process. The hardest parts are determining when to change the graphics in relation to the sound, and deciding which shape best suits the animation at any given point.

13. **Applying the same process you used to create the first three mouth changes, continue scrubbing the playhead to identify points of change. Insert keyframes and swap symbols on the Mouths layer at the appropriate locations. In our example, we used the following locations and symbols:**

Frame	Symbol	Frame	Symbol	Frame	Symbol
15	mouth1	43	mouth4	64	mouth3
23	mouth8	46	mouth3	66	mouth2
27	mouth2	48	mouth2	68	mouth8
30	mouth6	50	mouth3	70	mouth2
31	mouth1	52	mouth2	72	mouth6
33	mouth3	55	mouth7	74	mouth2
36	mouth6	57	mouth2	79	mouth4
39	mouth2	60	mouth6	82	mouth8
41	mouth8	62	mouth2	84	mouth2

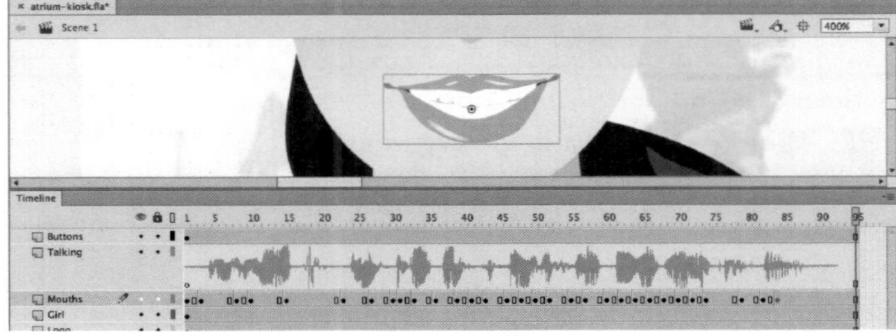

14. **Return the playhead to Frame 1, then press Return/Enter test the animation.**

    By swapping the mouth symbol at various points on the timeline in relation to the sounds on the Talking layer, you now have a character who appears to be talking.

15. **Save the file and continue to the next exercise.**

Define Sound Compression Settings

Before you export the final movie file, you should optimize the sounds to produce the smallest possible files while still maintaining the best possible quality. You can define default export settings for all stream sounds and all event sounds, but you can also experiment with different compression settings for individual sound files in the library.

1. **With atrium-kiosk.fla open, Control/right-click the atrium_jazz.mp3 file in the Audio folder of the Library panel. Choose Properties from the contextual menu.**

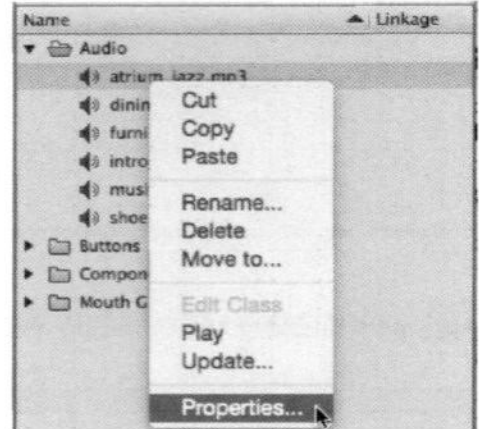

2. **In the resulting Sound Properties dialog box, make sure the Options tab is active at the top of the dialog box.**

3. **Choose MP3 in the Compression menu. If available, uncheck the Use Imported MP3 Quality option.**

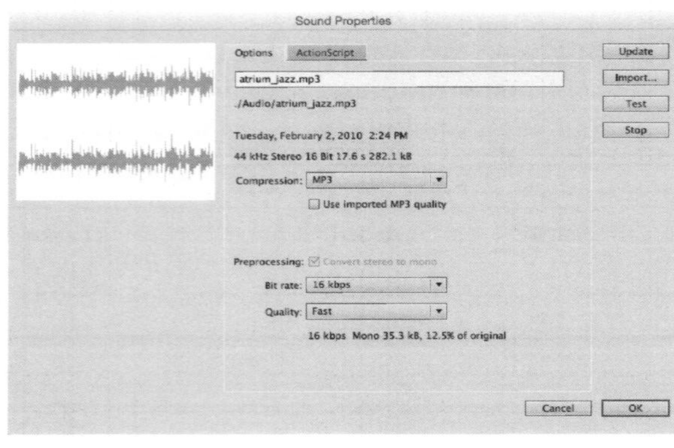

Animate supports five sound compression options:

- **Default.** This option uses the global compression settings (mp3, 16kbps, mono) defined in the Publish Settings dialog box when you export your SWF file. If you select Default, no additional export settings are available.
- **ADPCM.** This option converts sounds into binary data. ADPCM encoding is not as efficient as MP3 compression, but it is useful if you need to export a file to be compatible with older versions of Animate.
- **MP3.** Over the past few years, this format has become a *de facto* standard for audio on the Web. MP3 compression produces small files with very good quality, but it can cause problems for older computers with limited processing power.
- **Raw.** This option does not compress the audio data, which results in very large file sizes. This option should only be used for files that will be delivered on the desktop instead of over the Internet.

  ADPCM and Raw use less processing power on each playback than MP3. They are recommended for very short (small) sounds that are played back rapidly. A shooting game in which guns fire many times a second, for example, might benefit from encoding the gun sound in ADPCM or Raw; the cost in file size would probably be less than 1k, and processor performance would be significantly enhanced.
- **Speech.** This option uses a compression algorithm designed specifically for compressing spoken sounds. Sounds compressed with this option are converted to mono sounds (instead of stereo). Speech-compressed sounds require Animate Player 6 or higher.

Note:

The Preprocessing check box, enabled by default, converts stereo sounds to mono sounds.

4. **Choose 48 kbps in the Bit Rate menu.**

   Depending on the selected compression option, you can also change the bit rate or the sample rate to affect the quality of the exported sound.

   - The **Sample Rate** menu is available for ADPCM, Raw, and Speech compression; lower sample rates decrease file size, but can also decrease sound quality. The 22 kHz setting is recommended for reasonably good quality of most sounds.
   - The **Bit Rate** menu is available for MP3 compression. This option determines the bits per second in the exported sound. Higher bit rates result in better sound quality. Most experts recommend at least 20 kbps for speech, and 48 kbps for reasonably good quality of complex sounds such as music.

Note:

Animate cannot increase the sample rate or bit rate of an imported sound above its original settings.

5. **Choose Best in the Quality menu.**

   Three quality options — in order of file size (from small to large) and quality (from low to high) — are available for MP3 sounds: Fast, Medium, and Best.

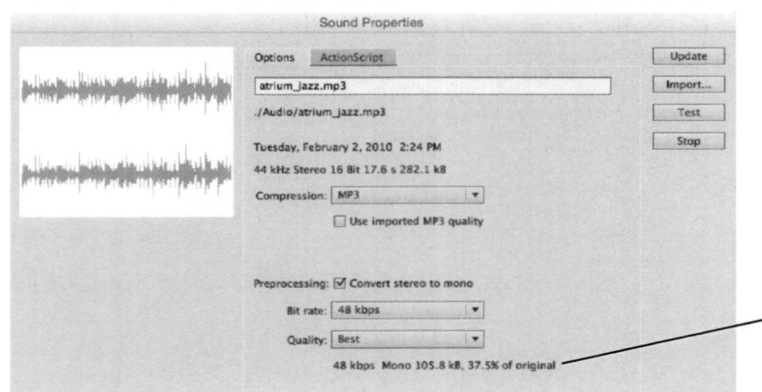

The dialog box provides feedback regarding the size of the file using the selected settings.

6. **Click OK to change the export settings for the selected sound file.**
7. **Open the Sound Properties dialog box for the intro_talking sound file.**
8. **Choose Speech in the Compression menu.**
9. **Choose 11 kHz in the Sample Rate menu, and then click the Test button.**

   When the sound plays, you might notice some popping or hissing noises behind the spoken message.

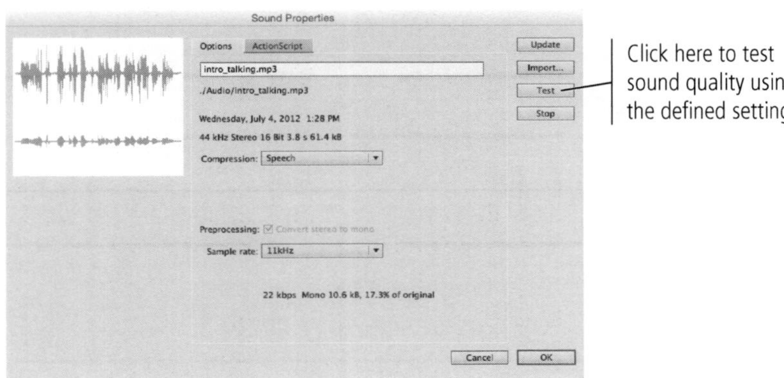

Click here to test sound quality using the defined settings.

Note:

You can change the default sound export settings in the Publish Settings dialog box.

10. **Choose 44 kHz in the Sample Rate menu, and then click the Test button.**

    This sample rate results in much better quality. Because this kiosk will not be downloaded over the Internet, the larger file size is not a problem.

11. **Click OK to apply the new compression settings for this sound file.**
12. **Save the Animate file and close it.**

fill in the blank

1. In a Button symbol, the _______________ defines the area where a user can click to trigger the button.

2. _______________ to edit a symbol in place on the Stage.

3. The _______________ marks the location of the defined X and Y values of a placed instance.

4. A(n) _______________ defines the point in time when a change occurs.

5. _______________ is the number of animation frames that occur in a second.

6. _______________ sounds are timeline independent; they must download completely before they play.

7. _______________ sounds are timeline dependent; they play as soon as enough of the data has downloaded to the user's computer.

8. The _______________ sync method prevents more than one instance of the same sound from playing at the same time.

9. You can use the _______________ dialog box to change the length of a specific sound file.

10. Use the _______________ option to replace one symbol with another at a specific frame.

short answer

1. Briefly describe at least three uses of the Library panel.

2. Briefly explain the difference between event sounds and stream sounds.

3. Briefly explain the concept of lip syncing, as it relates to symbols and the Animate timeline.

Portfolio Builder Project

Use what you learned in this project to complete the following freeform exercise.
Carefully read the art director and client comments, then create your own design to meet the needs of the project.
Use the space below to sketch ideas; when finished, write a brief explanation of your reasoning behind your final design.

art director comments

Your client is a company that provides technical support for children's online video games. The owner wants an introduction page for that site similar to the kiosk interface with a talking character that identifies the options.

To complete this project, you should:

- ❑ Download the client's supplied files in the **Robot_Web16_PB.zip** archive on the Student Files Web page.
- ❑ Review the client-supplied sound and artwork files.
- ❑ Develop a site intro page with a talking robot and two different buttons.
- ❑ If you use the client's artwork, import the file into Animate and create movie clips as necessary from the different elements.
- ❑ If you don't use the supplied file, create or find artwork as appropriate.

client comments

We want to build a new introduction page to our video game site. We're using a robot avatar throughout the video game site, and want that character to be featured on the intro page — I even recorded the intro message with a "mechanical" sounding voice. (Feel free to re-record the audio if you want to, as long as the message stays the same.)

I found a robot illustration that I like, but I'm not an artist; I'd be happy to review other artwork if you have a better idea. I also want you to develop some kind of background artwork that makes the piece look like a cohesive user interface.

You need to include two buttons: one that links to online technical support and one that links to a telephone support page.

In the final file, I want the robot to look like it's talking, but I also want the robot to point to the related buttons when the appropriate part of the intro sound plays.

project justification

Project Summary

This project introduced many of the basic concepts and techniques of animating objects in Animate. You learned about frames and keyframes, as well as two different types of symbols that will be used in many Animate projects, both throughout this book and in your professional career. You also learned how to import artwork that was created in Adobe Illustrator — a very common workflow in the graphic design/animation market.

You should understand how frames on the Animate timeline relate to the passage of actual time, and how keyframes are used to make changes at specific points in an animation. You should also understand the basic concept of symbols and instances, including the different ways to edit the conent of a specific symbol. You will build on these skills as you complete the rest of the projects in this book.

This project also showed you how to add audio content to a movie — placing a looped sound in the background of a file, triggering specific sounds with a button's Over state, and even synchronizing graphics to a spoken message.

Import artwork from Adobe Illustrator files
Add a streaming sound as the interface introduction
Create symbols from imported artwork
Synchronize graphics to sound to create a "talking" effect
Add an event sound that loops continuously in the background
Edit a sound envelope to control the sound volume
Attach and control button sounds
Edit button symbols to change different button states
the Atrium
outdoor shopping experience
Start Over
Shoes & Apparel
Home Furnishings
Music & Electronics
Casual/Fine Dining

project 4

Animated Internet Ads

Your client wants to create a series of ads to place on Web sites that are used by existing and potential customers. They have asked you to create a short animation rather than just a static image in hopes of attracting more attention when the ad appears in a browser with other content.

This project incorporates the following skills:

- ❑ Creating shape tweens to animate changes in shape and color
- ❑ Creating classic tweens to animate changes in position and opacity
- ❑ Adding text to an Animate movie
- ❑ Adapting file content to match different file dimensions
- ❑ Publishing a file to SWF for distribution

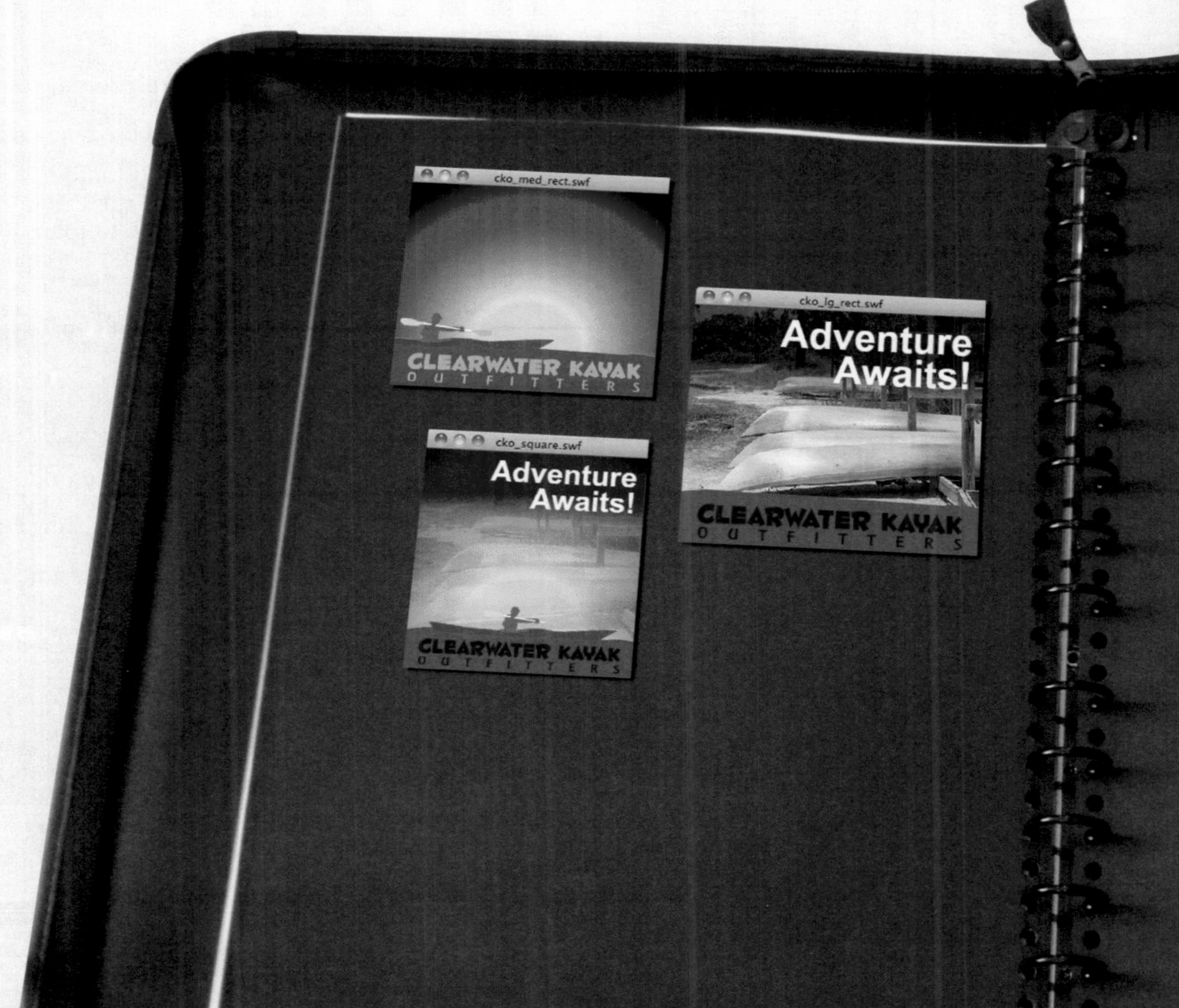

Project Meeting

client comments

We've provided you with our logo and an image that we want to use in the ads. Since these are going to be placed into a variety of Web sites, we want some kind of animation that might help catch a user's eye.

Most of the sites where we're planning on advertising use standard ad sizes. I'm not sure exactly which sizes we're going to purchase, but we do like the rectangle and square shapes better than the narrow banners.

We might decide on some of the other options later, but we'd like to get started with three common sizes:

- 300 × 250 pixels
- 336 × 280 pixels
- 250 × 250 pixels

art director comments

Animate includes predefined templates for most of the common ad sizes, so that's the easiest way to start the first file.

I want you to animate different aspects of the client's logo over the course of the animation. The kayaker is ideally suited to move across the stage. He should paddle across the stage while the sun rises. Halfway through, he should pause and wait until the tagline appears, then move the rest of the way across while the image gradually appears in place of the sunrise.

After you create the initial ad, you can use several built-in techniques to repurpose the content for other sizes.

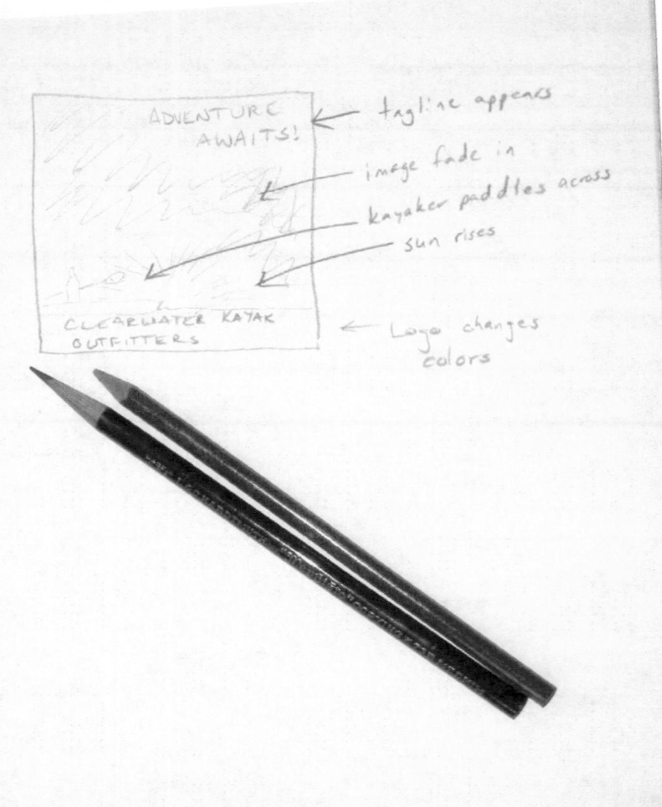

project objectives

To complete this project, you will:

- ❑ Create a file based on a template
- ❑ Create a shape tween
- ❑ Tween an object's color
- ❑ Create a classic tween
- ❑ Tween an object's opacity
- ❑ Stop the animation timeline
- ❑ Create and control a text object
- ❑ Define font embedding
- ❑ Control object stacking order
- ❑ Scale content to document properties
- ❑ Publish files to SWF

Stage 1 Animating Symbols

Animation — the true heart of Animate — can be created in a number of different ways. To create the animated ads for this project, you will use **shape tweening** and **classic tweening**.

In this project, you work with movie clip symbols. Both graphic symbols and movie clip symbols can include animation, but movie clips offer a number of advantages over graphic symbols.

Movie clips are **timeline independent**; the animation contained in a movie clip requires only a single frame on the timeline where it is placed (called the **parent timeline**). A movie clip timeline might include 500 frames, but the entire animation will play on a single frame of the parent timeline.

An animated graphic symbol, on the other hand, is **timeline dependent**; it requires the same number of frames on the parent timeline that are present inside the symbol's timeline. In other words, a 500-frame animation inside the graphic symbol requires 500 corresponding frames on the timeline where the symbol is placed.

Because movie clip timelines function independently of the parent timeline, you can more easily incorporate animations of different duration onto the same parent timeline.

Note:

Another advantage of movie clips is that placed instances can be named, which means they can be addressed — and controlled — using code. You will learn more about this option in Project 5: Ocean Animation.

Planning a movie

When you start any new project, you should begin by analyzing what you need to accomplish. A bit of advance planning can help you avoid unnecessary rework and frustration — in the project planning phase, you can determine, for example, that an independent movie clip is a better option than animating an object directly on the main timeline.

The ad that you are going to create in this project has the following plan or **storyboard**:

- The entire animation should last four seconds.
- The logotype will change from white to dark blue throughout the entire four-second animation.
- The kayaker will move across the Stage throughout the entire four-second duration, pausing halfway until the client's tagline appears.
- The sun is going to rise while the kayaker moves across the Stage. The sunrise animation should be finished when the kayaker gets halfway across the Stage.
- An image will gradually appear to replace the sunrise.

This information tells you a number of things about what you need to do:

- The finished ad requires four separate animations — the logo changing colors, the moving kayaker, the sunrise, and the image fading in.
- Each animation requires different timing. The sunrise and the image fade-in each occupy only half the time of the moving kayaker.
- The animations also require different starting points. The sunrise and the moving kayaker need to start as soon as the file opens. The image fade-in doesn't start until the sunrise animation is complete.

As you complete this project, you are going to use movie clip symbols and timeline frames to achieve the stated goals.

Create an Ad File

The final goal of this project is three separate ads that can be placed on Web sites where your client has decided to advertise. Because Internet ads typically use standard sizes, Animate includes those sizes as templates in the New Document dialog box.

In the first stage of this project, you are going to create the initial ad using one of the defined templates. Later you will use Animate's built-in tools to repurpose the existing content into the other required ad sizes.

1. **Download Kayaks_Web16_RF.zip from the Student Files Web page.**

2. **Expand the ZIP archive in your WIP folder (Macintosh) or copy the archive contents into your WIP folder (Windows).**

   This results in a folder named **Kayaks**, which contains the files you need for this project. You should also use this folder to save the files you create in this project.

3. **Choose File>New. In the General tab of the New Document dialog box, choose ActionScript 3.0 in the Type list.**

4. **Click the Templates tab to display those options. Select Advertising in the left pane, then select 300 × 250 Medium Rectangle in the right pane.**

   Animate includes templates for a number of standard file sizes, including the most common ads that are placed on the Internet.

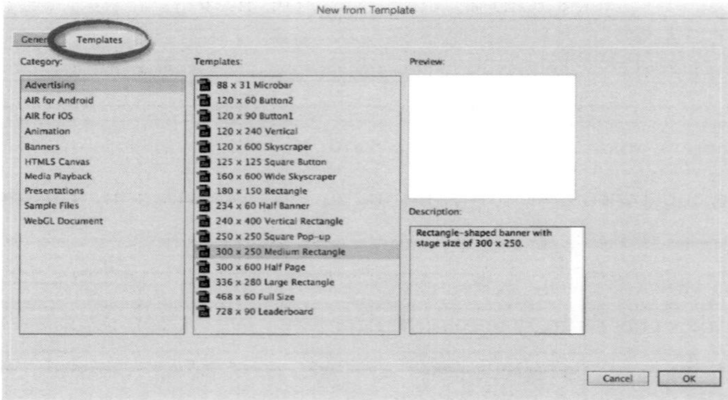

5. **Click OK to create the new file.**

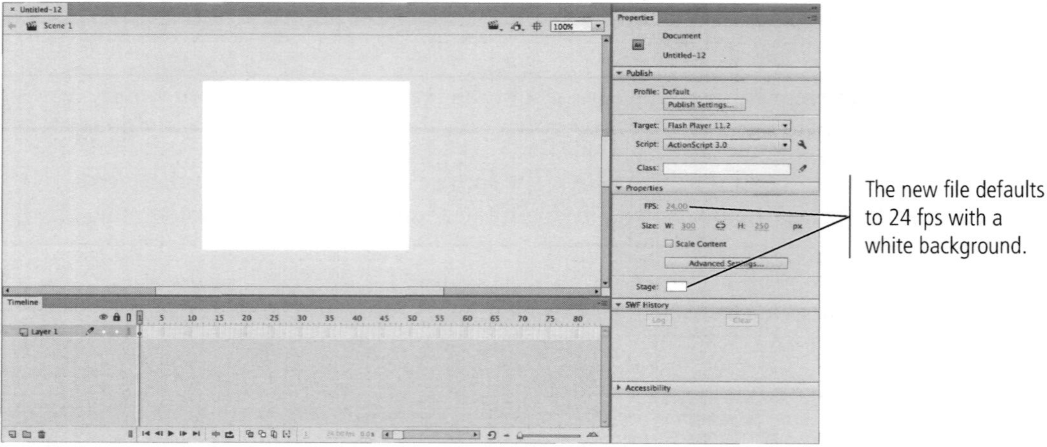

The new file defaults to 24 fps with a white background.

6. **Choose File>Import>Import to Stage. Select `cko_logo.ai` (in the WIP>Kayaks folder) and click Open.**

7. **In the Import to Stage dialog box, choose the following options:**

Layer Conversion	**Maintain Editable Paths and Effects**
Convert Layers To	**Animate Layers**
Import as a Single Bitmap Image	**Unchecked**
Import Unused Symbols	**Unchecked**
Set Stage Size...	**Unchecked**

You created this Animate file at a specific file size to meet specific needs, so you are not converting the Stage to match the imported artwork.

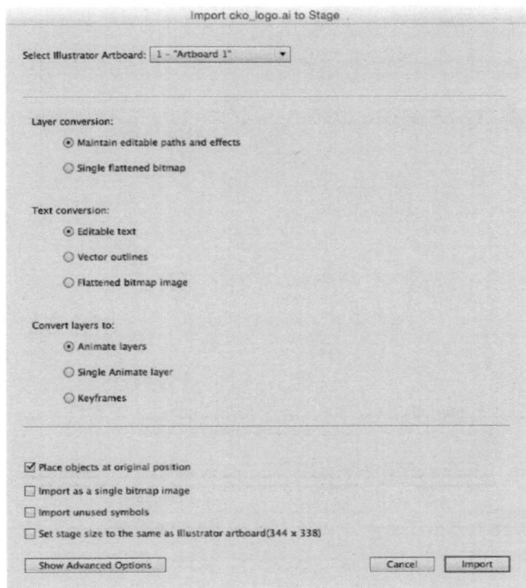

> ***Note:***
>
> *Refer to Project 3: Talking Internet Kiosk for an explanation of these options.*

8. **Click OK to import the artwork to the Stage.**

The imported Illustrator file was created with four layers, each containing a different element of the logo. The Animate file now includes four layers, matching the layers in the original Illustrator file. All the imported artwork is automatically selected. As you complete this project, you will use several techniques to animate different parts of the logo artwork.

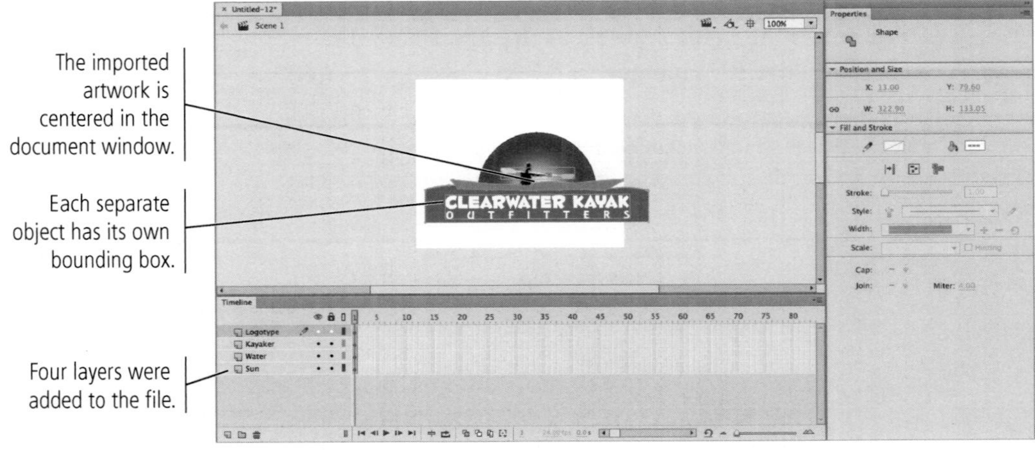

9. **Using the Selection tool, drag the selected artwork until the bottom edge snaps to the bottom edge of the Stage, and the artwork appears to be centered horizontally.**

   Each logo component, identified by the various bounding boxes, is an individual object (or group). If you tried to use the Align panel to align the artwork to the bottom and center of the Stage, each individual component would be aligned to the bottom of the Stage; the objects' positions relative to one another would not be maintained.

Note:

Because these objects all reside on different layers, you can't use the Group command to treat them as a single object for positioning purposes.

Use the Selection tool to move all selected objects at one time without changing their positions relative to one another.

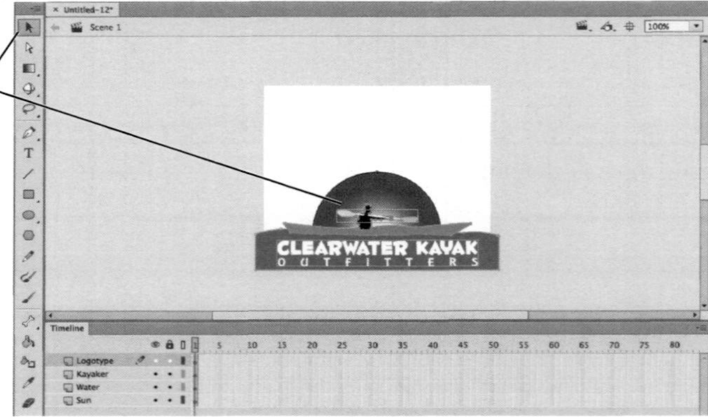

10. **Click away from everything on the Stage to deselect everything.**

11. **In the Properties panel, click the Stage swatch and choose Black from the pop-up color panel.**

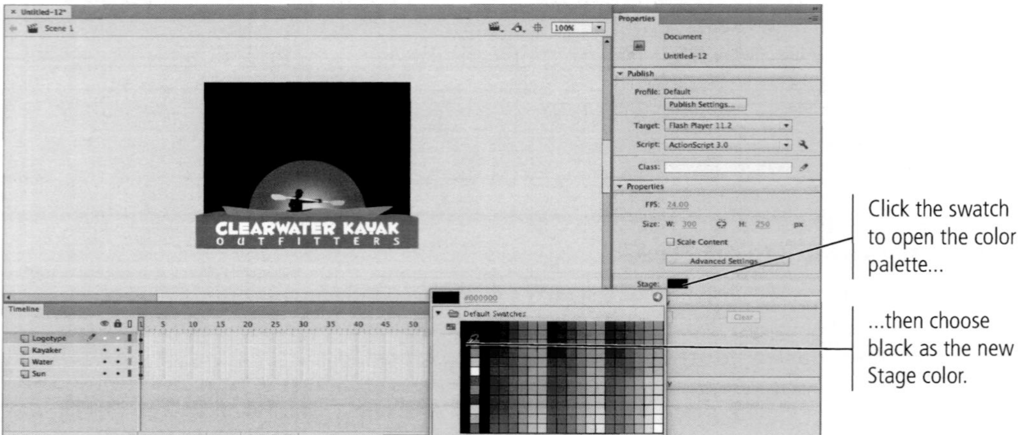

Click the swatch to open the color palette...

...then choose black as the new Stage color.

12. **Click the FPS hot text to access the field. Type 15 as the new FPS value, then press Return/Enter to finalize the change.**

    The ads you are creating are only going to be distributed over the Internet; 15 fps is high enough for good-quality display. (Higher frame rate would result in larger file sizes that are unnecessary for this type of file and could be problematic for users with slower download speeds.)

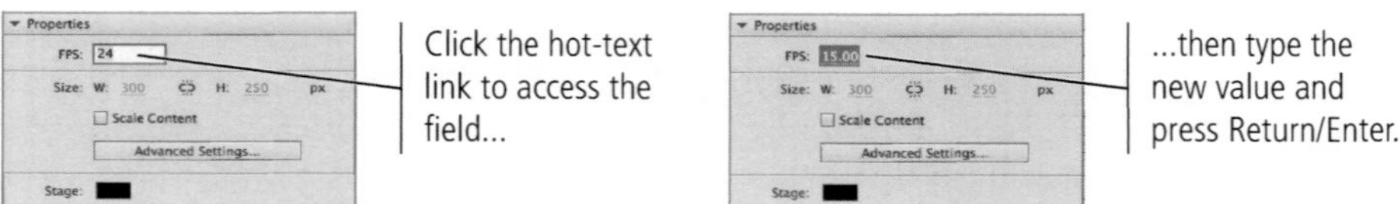

Click the hot-text link to access the field...

...then type the new value and press Return/Enter.

13. **Save the file as cko-med-rect.fla in your WIP>Kayaks folder, then continue to the next exercise.**

Create a Shape Tween

A **shape tween** allows you to convert one shape into another over time. You define the starting and ending shape, then Animate creates the in-between frames (hence the name "tween") that create the appearance of continuous movement when the finished animation plays.

You will use this type of tween to create the sunrise animation, as well as change the colors of the logotype.

1. **With `cko-med-rect.fla` open, use the Selection tool to select the sun object on the Stage.**

2. **Open the Color panel.**

   This object was created with a gradient fill. You are going to edit the gradient so the edge of the shape blends smoothly into the Stage background color.

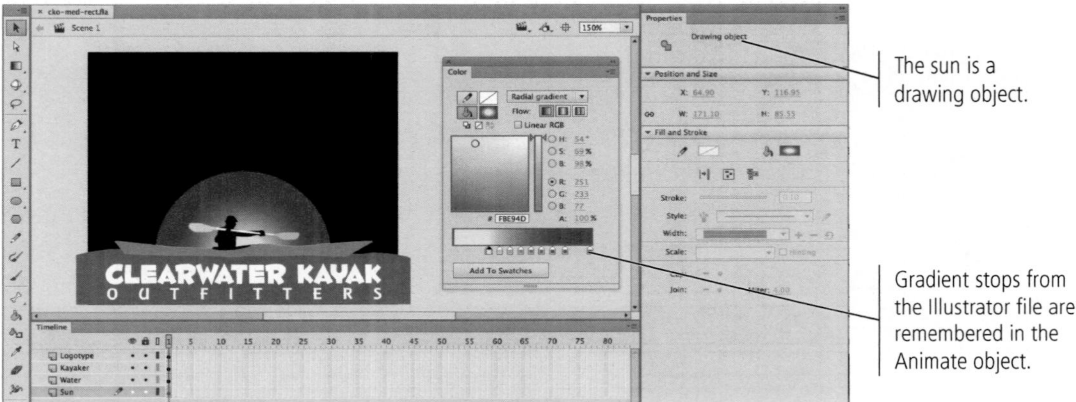

CLEARWATER KAYAK
OUTFITTERS
The sun is a drawing object.
Gradient stops from the Illustrator file are remembered in the Animate object.

3. **Click the right gradient stop to select it, then change the Alpha value of the selected stop to `0`.**

   Alpha refers to transparency; a value of 0 means something is entirely transparent.

   This step makes the last gradient stop entirely transparent. Colors between the next-to-last and last stop will now transition from entirely opaque (100% Alpha) to entirely transparent (0% Alpha), which allows the object to blend into the background without a harsh edge.

CLEARWATER KAYAK
OUTFITTERS
Change the Alpha value of the last stop on the gradient.

4. **With the sun object selected, press F8 to convert the object to a symbol, or Control/right-click the selected object and choose Convert to Symbol.**

5. **Define the following settings in the Convert to Symbol dialog box:**

Name:	**sun_mc**
Type:	**Movie Clip**
Registration:	**Bottom center**

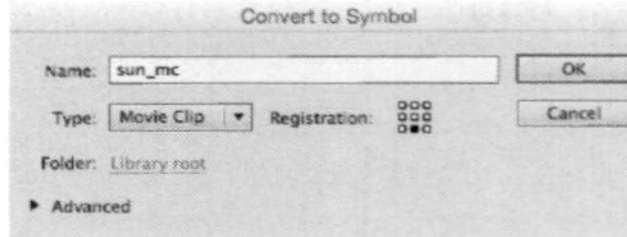

   You are using the bottom-center registration point because you want the sun object to grow out from that point.

6. **Click OK to create the new symbol.**

   When you create a symbol from existing artwork, the original object is automatically converted to an instance of that symbol.

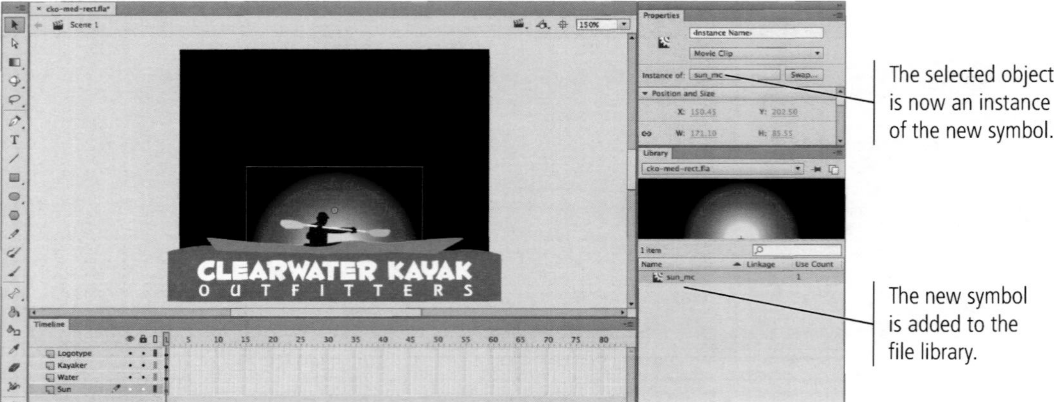

The selected object is now an instance of the new symbol.
The new symbol is added to the file library.
CLEARWATER KAYAK
OUTFITTERS

7. **Double-click the instance on the Stage to enter into Symbol-Editing mode.**

   You are editing this symbol in place because you need to be able to see the shape's size relative to the Stage on which it is placed.

8. **Select Frame 30 in the timeline, then press F6 to add a new keyframe.**

   The completed ad needs to last four seconds. At 15 fps, the entire ad will require 60 frames; the sunrise should take half that time to complete, so this movie clip needs 30 frames.

   When you add a keyframe to a layer, the contents of the previous keyframe are automatically copied to the new keyframe. You can edit the contents on each keyframe independently without affecting the same contents on other keyframes.

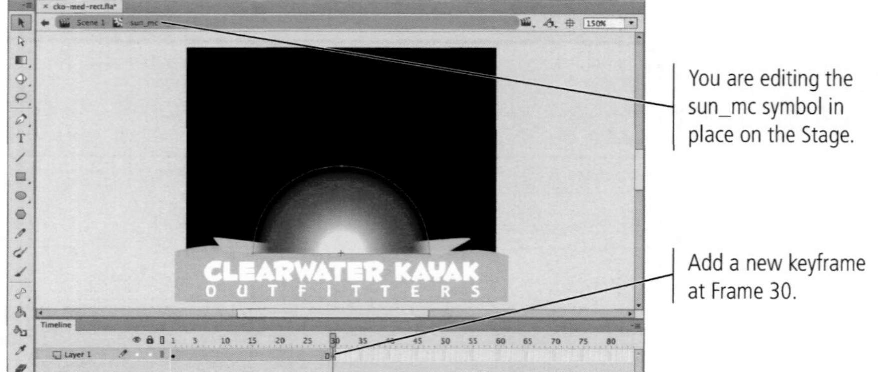

Note:

If you can't use, or don't have, Function keys, you can use the Insert>Timeline submenu, or the frame's contextual menu, to insert a frame, keyframe, or blank keyframe.

Note:

Remember, keyframes are required when an object needs to change in some way at a given point in time.

9. **Choose the Free Transform tool.**

   When the Free Transform tool is active, a solid white circle on the selected object identifies the transformation point, or the point around which transformations will be made. Think of the transformation point as a pin that keeps that spot in place when you apply specific transformations.

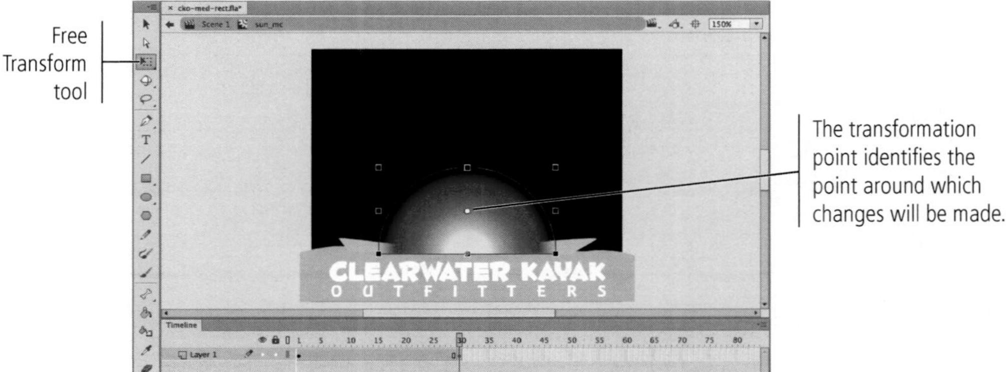

Free Transform tool
The transformation point identifies the point around which changes will be made.
CLEARWATER KAYAK
OUTFITTERS

10. **With Frame 30 selected in the timeline and the sun object selected on the Stage, move the transformation point to the object's bottom-center bounding-box handle.**

    When you create the animation, you want the sun to appear as if it is growing out from the horizon. To accomplish this, you are going to make the sun shape larger, using the bottom-center point as the anchor.

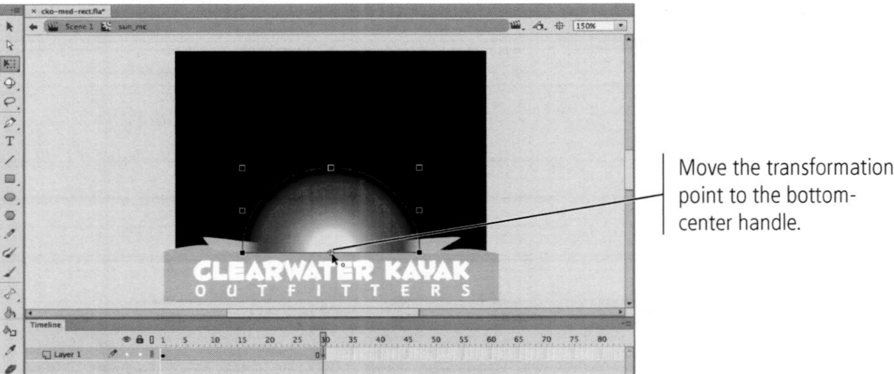

Move the transformation point to the bottom-center handle.
CLEARWATER KAYAK
OUTFITTERS

11. **Zoom out so you can see the area around the Stage on all four sides.**

    Feel free to zoom in and out as necessary while you complete the projects in this book.

12. **Open the Transform panel. At the top of the panel, make sure the Constrain icon is active.**

    The Transform panel can be used to make precise numerical changes or simply to monitor the changes you make with the Free Transform tool.

    When the Constrain icon appears as two connected chain links, the object's width and height are linked to maintain object's original aspect ratio. If this icon is a broken chain, you can change one value without affecting the other.

13. **Place the cursor over the existing Width value. When you see the scrubby-slider cursor, click and drag right to enlarge the object until none of the black background color is visible.**

Although you can use the Properties panel to change an object's height and/or width, those changes apply from the top-left corner of the selection instead of the defined transformation point that you set in Step 10. Changes made through the Transform panel respect the defined transformation point, so this is a better option for making this type of change.

Note:

This technique of dragging to change a property value is called ***scrubbing****.*

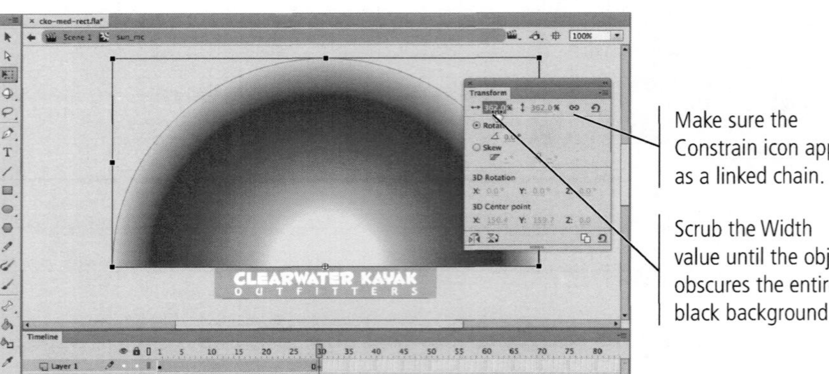

Make sure the Constrain icon appears as a linked chain.
Scrub the Width value until the object obscures the entire black background.

14. **Control/right-click any frame between Frame 1 and Frame 30, and choose Create Shape Tween from the contextual menu.**

In the timeline, Animate identifies the shape tween with green frames and an arrow between keyframes.

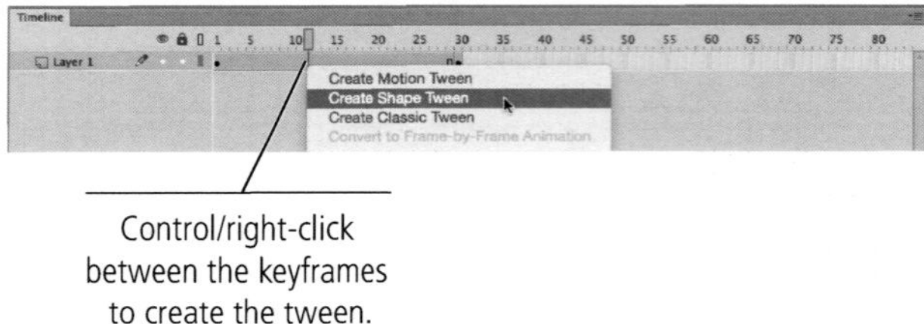

Note:

You can't create a shape tween for a group.

15. **Click Frame 1 in the timeline to move the playhead back to the beginning of the animation.**

16. **Press Return/Enter to play the animation on the Stage.**

Flash defines the object's size at each frame in the tween.
A shape tween is identified by green frames and an arrow.

Understanding Transformation Options

The Transform Panel

At times, you might need to apply very specific numeric transformations, such as scaling an object by a specific percentage. Rather than manually calculating new dimensions and defining the new dimensions in the Properties panel, you can use the Transform panel to make this type of change.

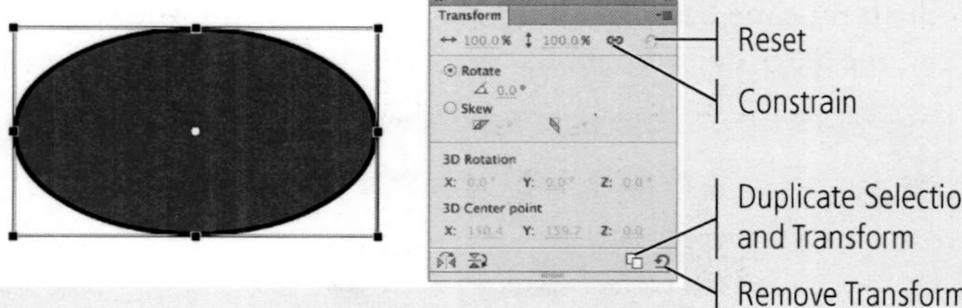

When you change a value in the Transform panel, press Return/Enter to apply the change, or click the Duplicate Selection and Transform button to make a copy of the object and apply the change to the copy.

Keep in mind that all transformations made in the Transform panel apply around the defined transformation point.

The Modify>Transform Submenu

The Modify>Transform submenu has a number of valuable options for transforming objects.

Free Transform displays a set of eight bounding box handles, which you can drag horizontally or vertically to scale, stretch, skew, and rotate an object. During a free transform, an object's overall shape is maintained (an oval remains an oval, a square remains a square, and so on).

Distort displays a set of eight bounding box handles. If you drag one of the corner handles, you can "stretch" the object out of its original shape. For example, you can drag one corner of a rectangle to create a polygon with odd angles.

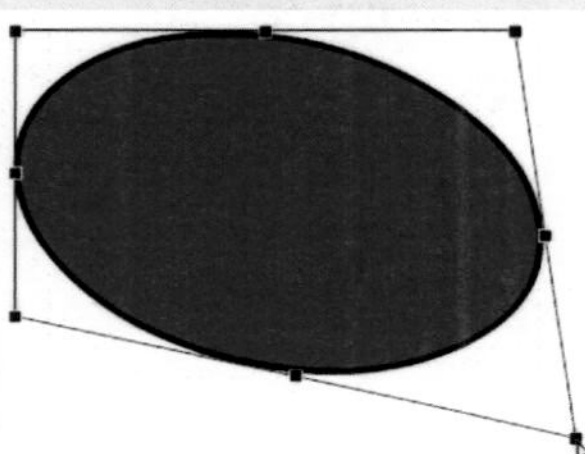

Scale and Rotate opens a dialog box where you can define specific scale percentages or rotation angles. You can also use the **Rotate 90°** (Clockwise and Counterclockwise) options for a selected object.

Envelope adds control handles to the object's anchor points, which you can use to warp the shape. You can drag the handles to reshape the connecting curves, and/or drag the anchor points to new positions to create an entirely different shape than the original.

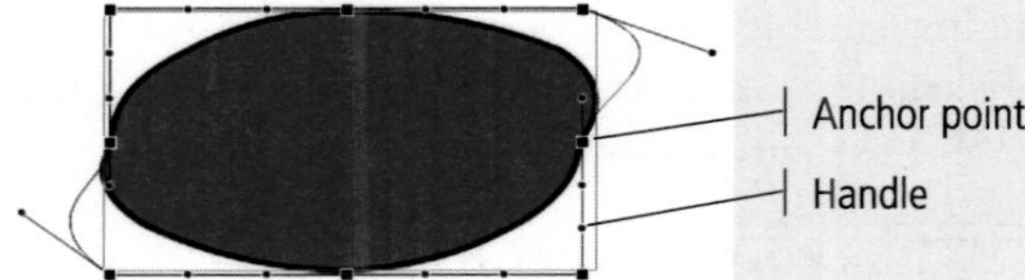

Scale is a subset of Free Transform. You can see the eight bounding box handles, but you can only scale or stretch the object; you can't rotate or skew it.

Rotate and Skew are also subsets of Free Transform. You can see the eight bounding box handles, but you can only skew or rotate the object; you can't scale or stretch it.

Flip Horizontal or **Flip Vertical** options allow you to flip objects on either axis.

Even though you can transform objects, Animate remembers the object's original size and shape. You can remove any transformation — except envelope distortion — from drawing objects and symbol instances using the **Remove Transform** option. (You can't remove a transformation from a merge-drawing object after you have deselected the object.)

To remove an envelope distortion, you have to choose Modify>Combine Objects>Delete Envelope.

17. **Click Scene 1 in the Edit bar to return to the main Stage.**

    Remember, pressing Return/Enter plays the *current* timeline on the Stage. Because the main timeline has only one frame, this command would have no effect. Testing a movie on the Stage does not initiate the timeline of movie clips that are placed on the Stage.

    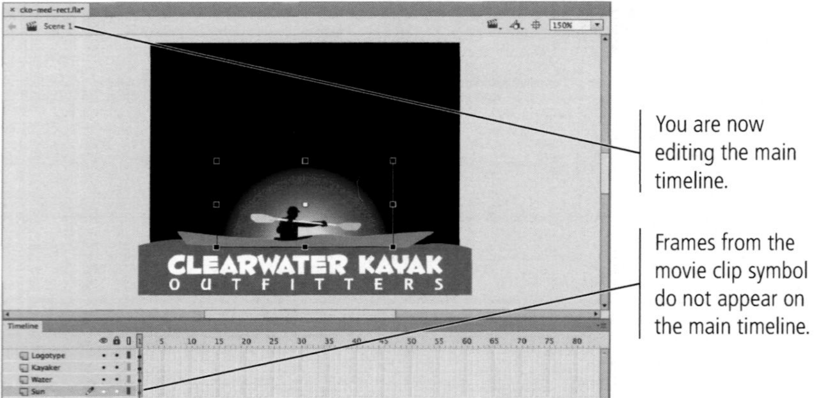

18. **Save the file and continue to the next exercise.**

Tween an Object's Color

Changing an object from one color to another is a common animation task. This is simply accomplished using a shape tween, using the same method you used to change the size of the sun symbol.

1. **With cko-med-rect.fla open, use the Selection tool to select the logotype on the Stage.**

    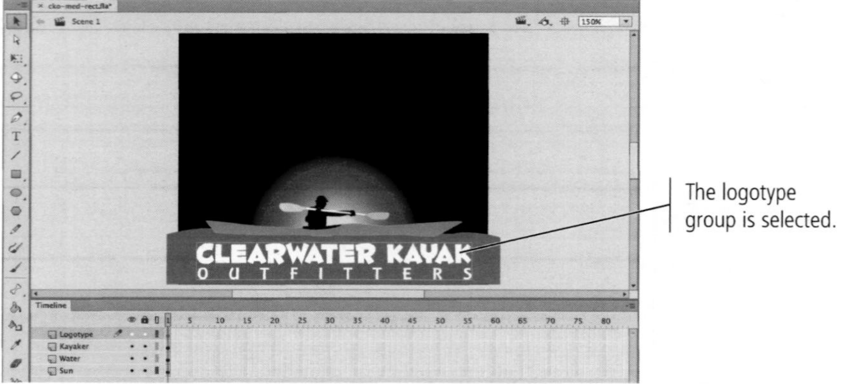

2. **With the logotype object selected, press F8 to convert the object to a symbol, or Control/right-click the selected object and choose Convert to Symbol.**

    As we continue through this project, remember your options for converting an object to a symbol. We will no longer repeat the entire instruction for accomplishing this task.

3. **Define the following settings in the Convert to Symbol dialog box:**

    Name: logo_mc
    Type: Movie Clip
    Registration: Leave at default

    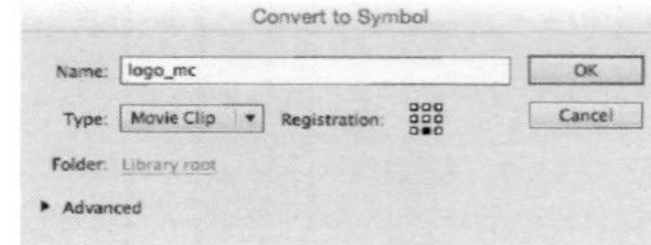

    You will only change the color of the logotype, so the registration point is not important for this symbol.

4. **Click OK to create the new symbol.**

   In this animation, you are simply going to change the color of the text. Because nothing is moving, the symbol registration point does not matter; you can leave it at the default location.

5. **Double-click the symbol instance on the Stage to enter into it.**

6. **With the logotype selected on the Stage, choose Modify>Ungroup.**

   You can't create a shape tween with a group, so you first have to ungroup the letters. After ungrouping, you can see that each letter is a separate drawing object.

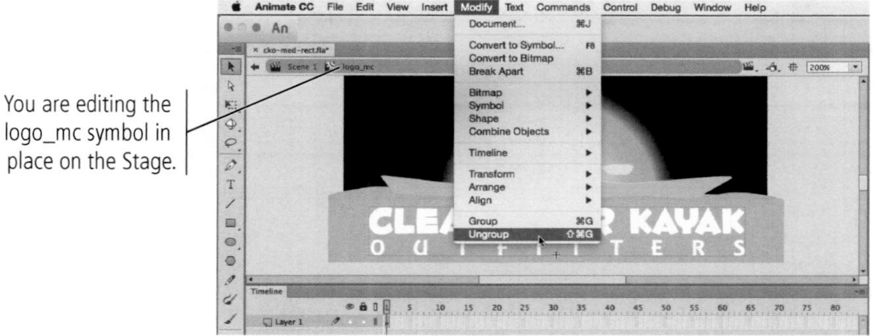

7. **Click Frame 60 in the timeline to select it, then press F6 to add a new keyframe.**

   When you add or select a frame on the timeline, the frame becomes the active selection.

   This is deceptive because the objects' bounding boxes are still visible, suggesting that they are selected — even though they are not.

8. **Click the filled area of any of the drawing objects on the Stage to make them the active selection.**

   To edit an object's properties, you first have to remember to intentionally reselect the object(s) on the Stage. If you aren't sure what is actually selected, look at the top of the Properties panel.

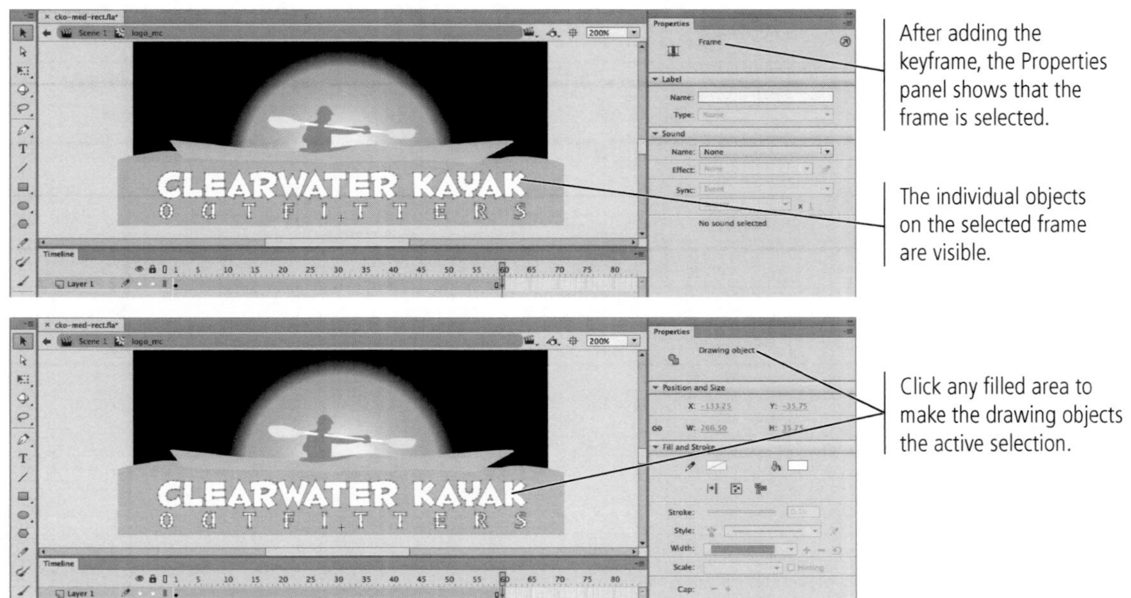

After adding the keyframe, the Properties panel shows that the frame is selected.
The individual objects on the selected frame are visible.
Click any filled area to make the drawing objects the active selection.
CLEARWATER KAYAK
OUTFITTERS
Frame
Drawing object

> ***Note:***
>
> *You could also choose Modify>Break Apart (or press Command/Control-B) to accomplish the same general effect.*

Creating and Controlling Shape Tweens

In addition to changing object properties in a shape tween, you can also create a **shape tween** to change one shape into another over time (as the name suggests). A shape tween requires two existing keyframes — one with the starting shape and one with the ending shape.

If you Control/right-click between two keyframes, choosing Create Shape Tween generates the shape tween; the tween frames automatically change the shape of the object as necessary to convert Shape A into Shape B. The following illustrations show a simple shape tween that changes a blue square into a green circle.

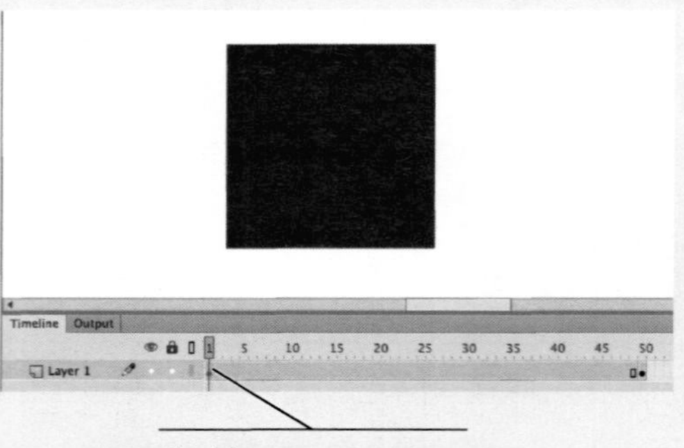

The blue square exists on the Frame 1 keyframe.

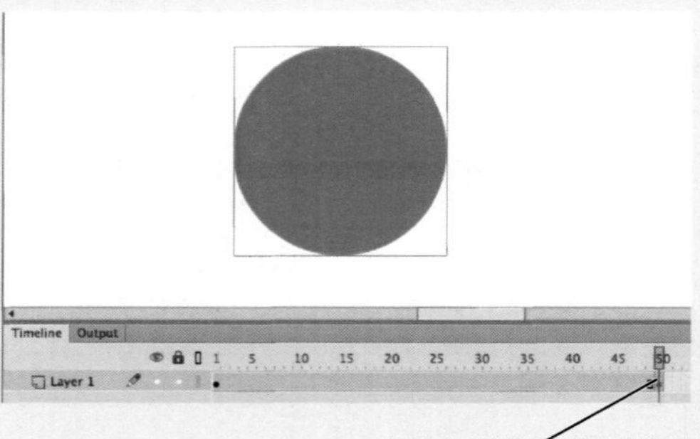

The green circle exists on the Frame 50 keyframe.

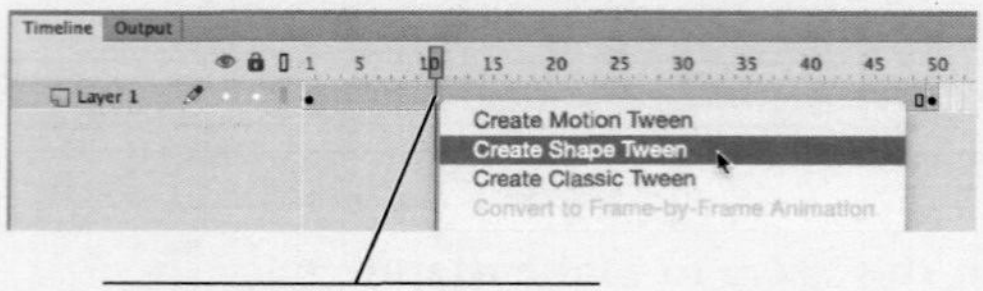

Control/right-click between the two keyframes and choose Create Shape Tween.

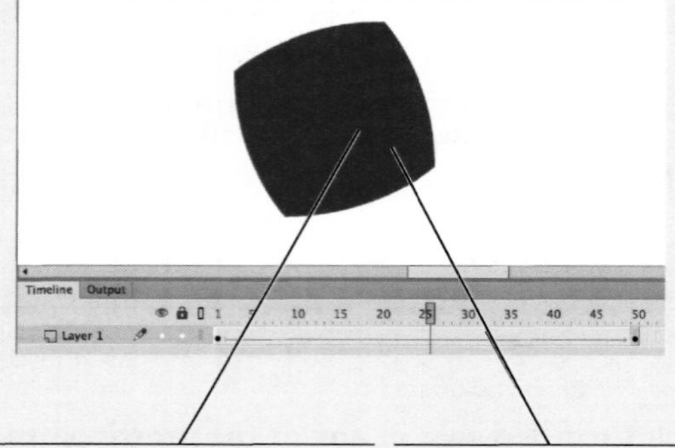

Because the two keyframe objects are different colors, the tween also calculates the required change in color for each frame.

Playing the animation shows the object twisting from a square to a circle.

9. **Using the Fill swatch in the Properties panel, change the objects' fill color to #000033.**

After ungrouping, click any of the active objects to select them.

Use the Properties panel to change the fill color to #000033 with 100% Alpha.

10. **Control/right-click any frame between Frame 1 and Frame 60, and choose Create Shape Tween from the contextual menu.**

    Although you did not change the objects' shapes, a shape tween is still an appropriate method for changing an object's color over time.

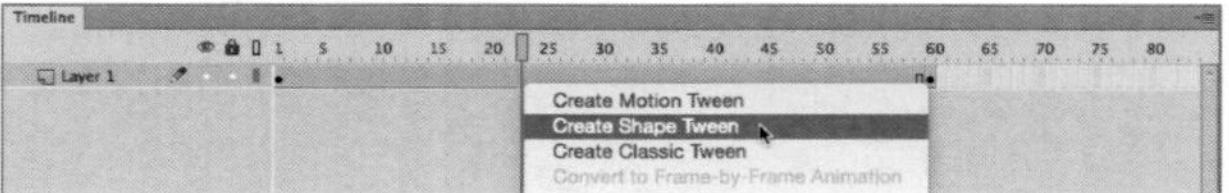

11. **Move the playhead to Frame 1, then press Return/Enter to test the animation on the Stage.**

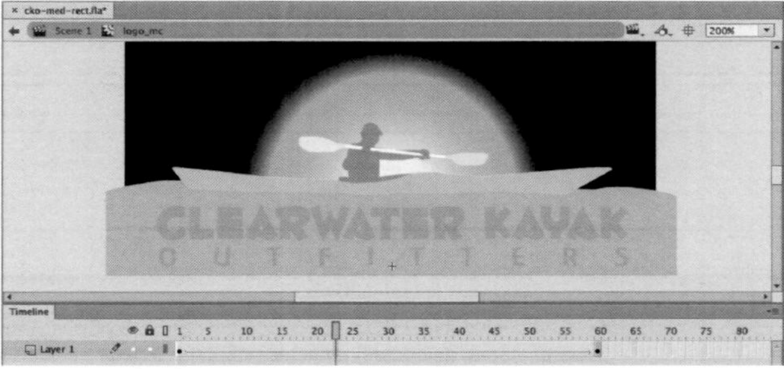

12. **Click Scene 1 in the Edit bar to return to the main Stage.**

    Again, there is only one frame on the main timeline, so there is nothing to play. Remember, a movie clip symbol operates independently of the main timeline; you can't view the movie clip's animation directly on the Animate stage.

13. **Save the file and continue to the next exercise.**

More about Working in the Timeline Panel

Reducing and Enlarging the Timeline View

At the bottom-right corner of the Timeline panel, you have several options for adjusting the size of frames that are visible in the panel.

Two buttons can be used to show more or less frames in the panel, effectively reducing or enlarging (respectively) the size of the visible frames. You can also use the slider between the two buttons to manually resize the visible frames.

You can click the Reset button ( ) to restore the frames to their default size in the panel.

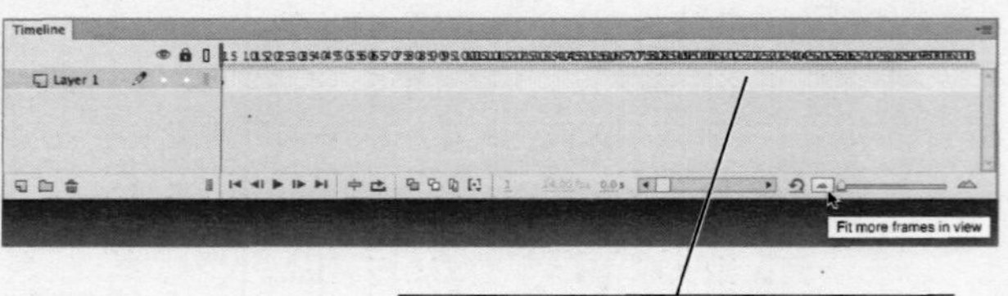

Fitting more frames in the view reduces the size of frames in the panel.

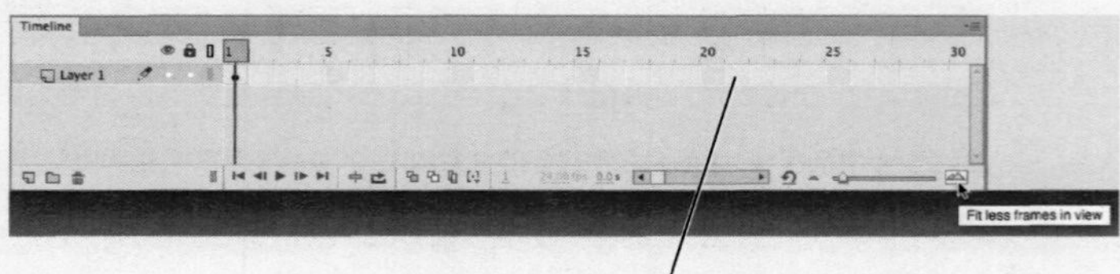

Fitting less frames in the view enlarges the size of frames in the panel.

Adding Frames to the Timeline

If you create animations with very long timelines, you might need to extend the timeline beyond what is available by default. To accomplish this, scroll the timeline all the way to the right and then add a regular frame to the layer near the end of the visible timeline.

When you add a frame after the last visible frame, the timeline scroll bar moves to the middle of the panel, indicating that more frames are now available in the timeline. You can then scroll again to the new end of the timeline and add another frame, which again extends the length of the available timeline. Continue this process until you have the number of frames you need.

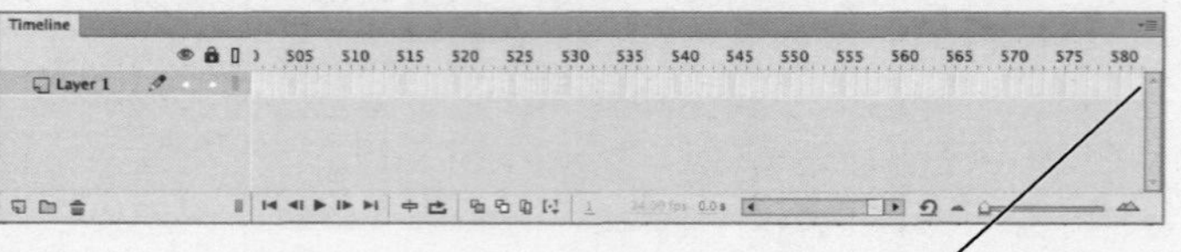

The default timeline only goes up to a certain frame number.

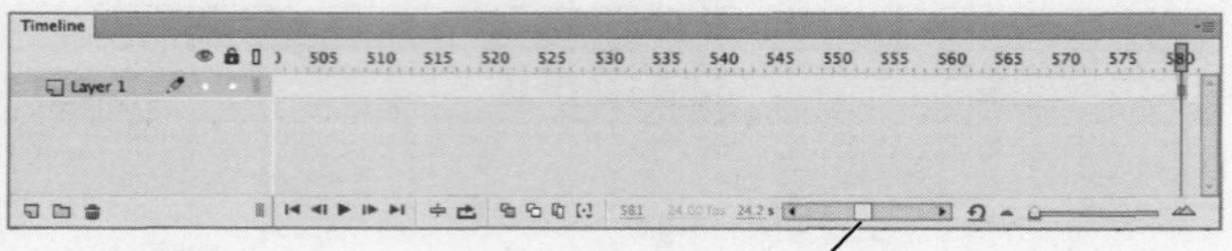

After adding a regular frame near the end of the default timeline, the scroll bar indicates that more frames are available.

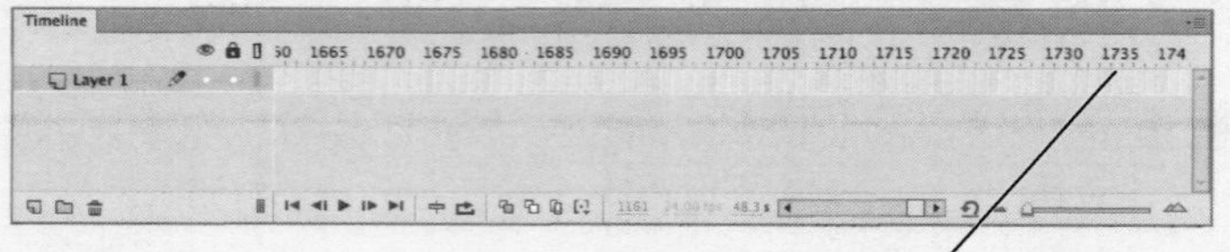

Continue adding regular frames and scrolling the timeline until you have the number of frames you need.

Create a Classic Tween

As you can probably guess, there is much more to animation than changing an object's shape or color. In this exercise, you will create very simple classic tweens that move the kayaker across the Stage, using keyframes to control the movement's timing.

1. **With `cko-med-rect.fla` open, click the Kayaker layer in the timeline to select all objects on the layer.**

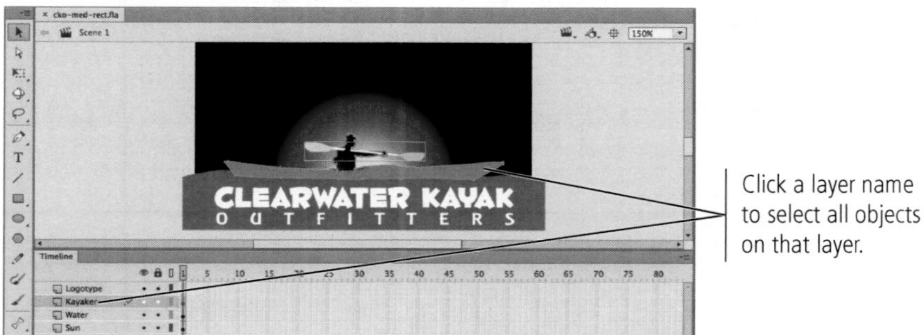

2. **Convert the selected object to a symbol. Define the following settings in the Convert to Symbol dialog box:**

Name:	`kayaker_mc`
Type:	**Movie Clip**
Registration:	**Right center**

3. **Click OK to create the new symbol.**
4. **With the new symbol instance selected on the Stage, change the X value in the Properties panel to `0`.**

   Remember, the X and Y properties define the position of a symbol's registration point. Because you chose the right-center registration point, changing the X value to 0 moves the kayaker entirely off the Stage.

You are editing the symbol instance on the main timeline.

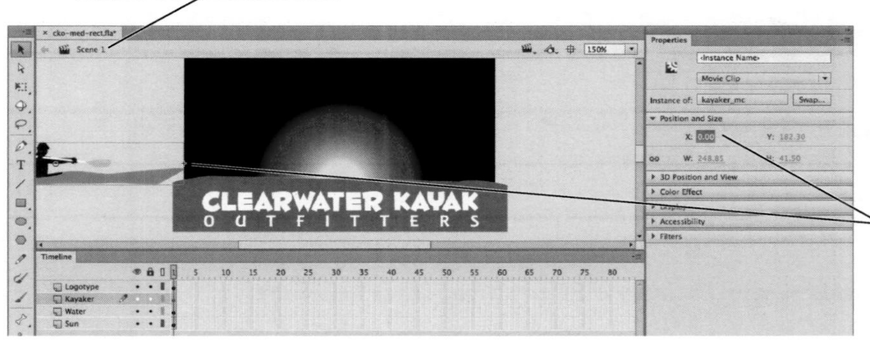

The X property defines the position of the symbol's registration point.

5. Click Frame 30 of the Kayaker layer and press F6 to add a new keyframe.

6. Click the kayaker symbol instance to select it, then scrub the X property in the Property panel until the instance is approximately centered on the Stage (as shown here).

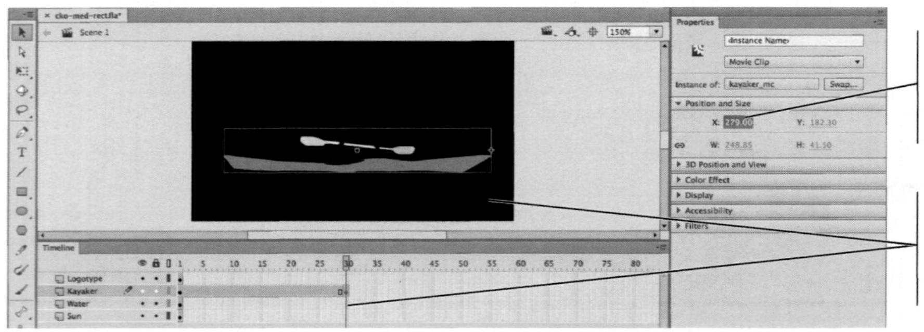

Scrub the X value to move the selected instance horizontally across the stage.

Other objects are not visible because those layers don't yet exist on Frame 30.

7. Control/right-click any frame between Frame 1 and 30 of the Kayaker layer and choose Create Classic Tween from the contextual menu.

A classic tween is one method for creating motion in an Animate animation. Like the shape tweens you created already, you have to define the starting and ending keyframes, then create the tween; Animate automatically determines the instance's position on the in-between frames.

In Project 5: Ocean Animation, you will learn about Motion Tweens, which provide far more control over numerous aspects of a tween. You should understand what a classic tween is, though, so you can recognize one if you find one in a file — especially files created in older versions of the software.

> ***Note:***
>
> *This is called a "classic" tween because this technique was available in previous versions of the application.*

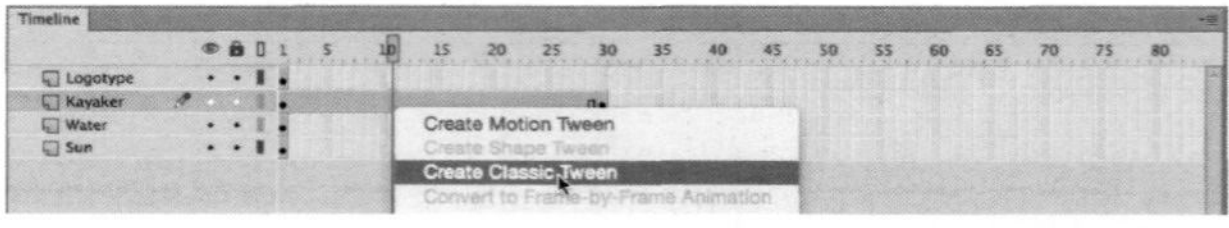

In the timeline, Animate identifies the classic tween with blue frames and an arrow between keyframes.

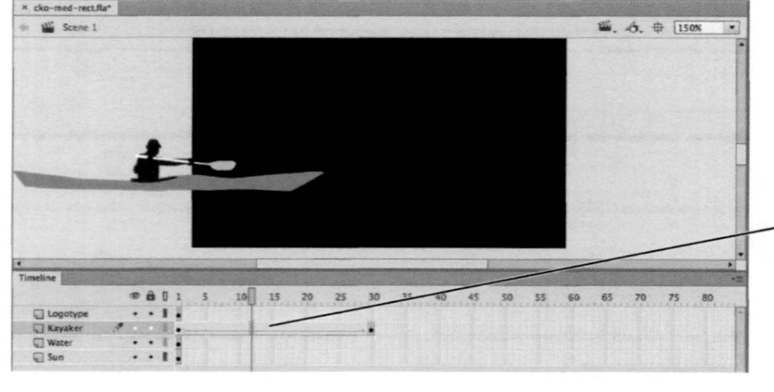

A classic tween is identified by blue frames and an arrow between keyframes.

8. Select Frame 38 on the Kayaker layer, then press F6 to add another keyframe.

Remember: when you add a new keyframe, Animate duplicates the content on the previous keyframe. By adding this keyframe at Frame 38, you are holding the symbol instance in place for approximately half a second.

(We say "approximately half a second" because the frame rate in this file is 15 fps, which is not equally divisible by 2. Because you can't have half a frame, you are using slightly more than half a second for the pause in animation.)

9. Select Frame 60 of the Kayaker layer and add a new keyframe.

10. **Select the symbol instance on the Stage, then change the X property in the Properties panel until the instance is entirely past the right edge of the Stage.**

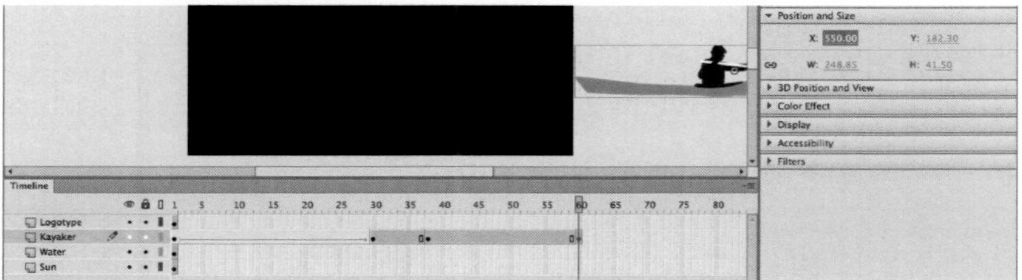

11. **Control/right-click any frame between Frame 38 and 60 of the Kayaker layer and choose Create Classic Tween from the contextual menu.**

    The new tween occupies the entire range of frames between the keyframes that you defined on Frames 38 and 60.

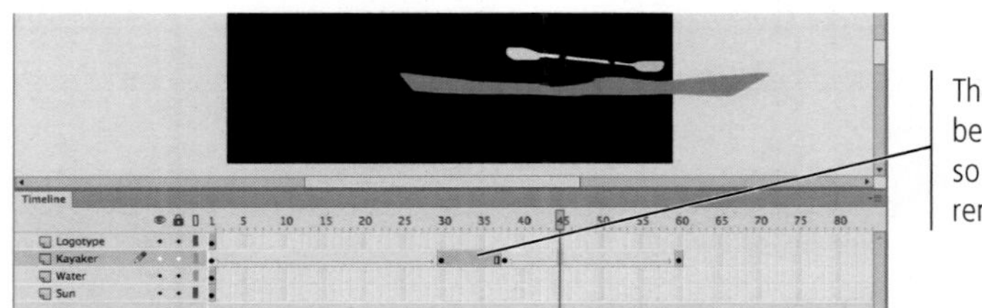

There is no tween between these keyframes, so the instance will remain in place.

12. **Select Frame 60 of the Logotype layer. Press Command/Control, then click Frame 60 of the Water and Sun layers to add them to the active selection.**

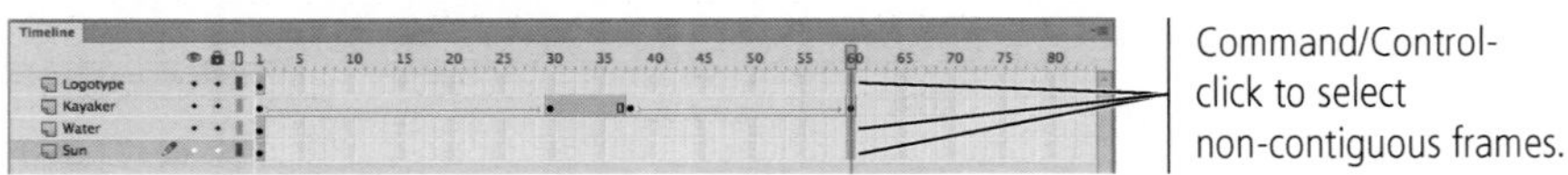

Command/Control-click to select non-contiguous frames.

> *Note:*
>
> *You can press Shift to select contiguous frames, or press Command/Control to select non-contiguous layers.*

Although two of these layers contain animated movie clips, those movie clips' timelines do not transfer to the main movie timeline. They will not exist in the main movie beyond Frame 1 unless you extend those layers' timelines on the main Stage.

13. **Press F5 to add regular frames to the three selected layers.**

    This extends all three layers to Frame 60, so their content will be visible throughout the entire animation.

14. **Click Frame 1 to select it, then press Return/Enter to test the animation on the timeline.**

    Remember, you can't see the sunrise and logotype animations because those are created inside the individual symbols. To see all three animations together, you have to test the movie in the Player window. (You will do this after you create the final required animation in the next exercise.)

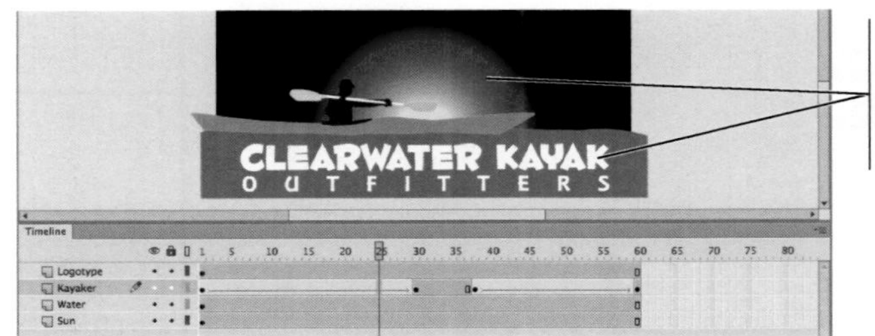

The sunrise and logotype animations do not play on the main Stage.

15. **Save the file and continue to the next exercise.**

Tween an Object's Opacity

The last required animation for this movie is an image that fades in after the sun finishes rising. In this exercise you will create a new layer on the timeline and use a blank keyframe to prevent the image from appearing too early.

1. **With `cko-med-rect.fla` open, create a new layer named `Photo` directly above the Sun layer.**

2. **Control/right-click Frame 30 on the new layer and choose Insert Blank Keyframe.**

   You are inserting a blank keyframe before placing the image onto the Stage at Frame 30, so the preceding frames (1–29) will remain blank — preventing the image from appearing until halfway through the movie.

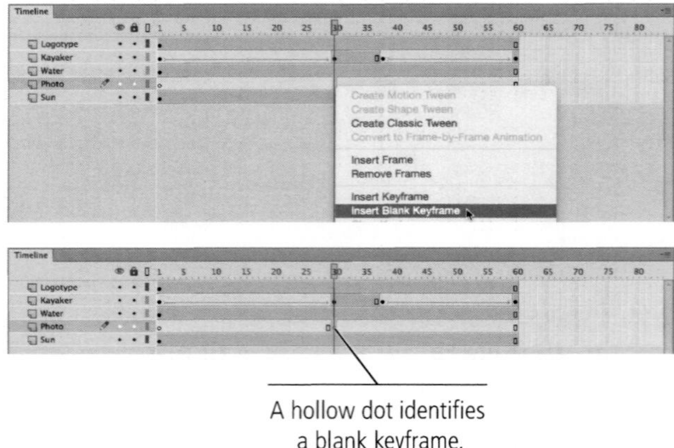

A hollow dot identifies a blank keyframe.

3. **With the blank keyframe on Frame 30 selected, choose File>Import>Import to Stage.**

4. **Choose the file `kayaks.jpg` in your WIP>Kayaks folder, then click Open.**

5. **Align the image to the top of the Stage, centered horizontally.**

   Unlike the imported Illustrator artwork, you can use the Align panel to move the image into the correct position.

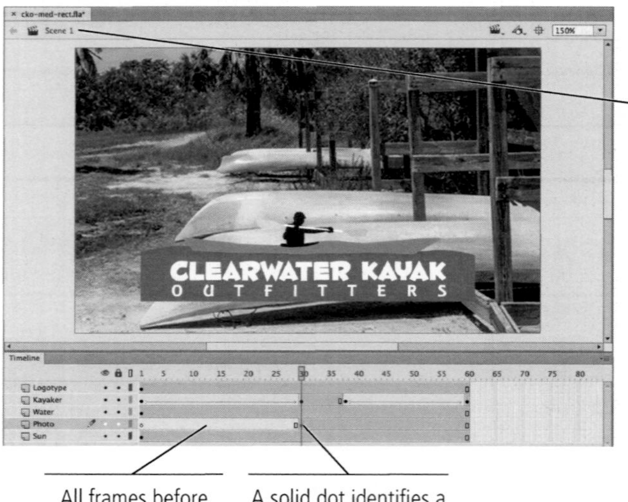

You are working on the main Stage.

All frames before Frame 30 are empty.

A solid dot identifies a keyframe with content.

6. **Choose the Free Transform tool, then move the image's transformation point to the top-center bounding-box handle.**

7. **Using the Transform panel, reduce the image scale (proportionally) until the bottom edge is just hidden by the blue shape that makes up the water.**

   You can't animate a bitmap object; to cause this image to appear gradually over time, you first need to convert it to a symbol.

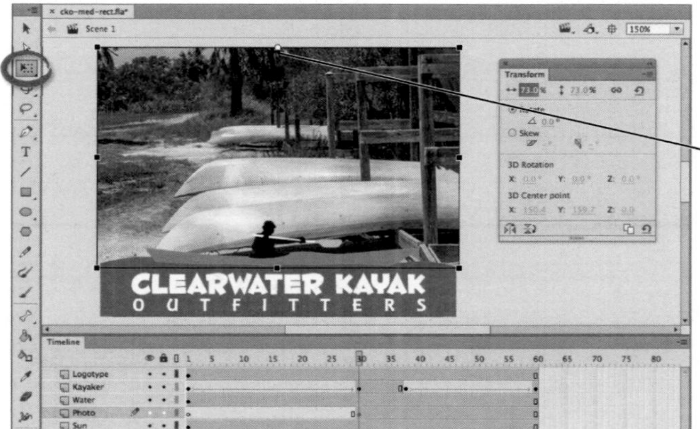

Because you moved the transformation point, the top-center point of the image remains in place when you scale it.

8. **Convert the selected object to a symbol. Define the following settings in the Convert to Symbol dialog box:**

   Name: `photo_mc`

   Type: **Movie Clip**

   Registration: **Top center**

9. **Click OK to create the new symbol.**

   Symbols have a number of properties that are not available for bitmap or drawing objects. In this case you are going to edit and animate the Color Effect property to change the alpha (transparency) value of the symbol over time.

10. **In the Properties panel, expand the Color Effect options, then choose Alpha in the Style menu. In the secondary Alpha field that appears, change the Alpha value to `0`.**

    Remember, the Alpha value controls an object's opacity; a value of 0 means the object is not visible.

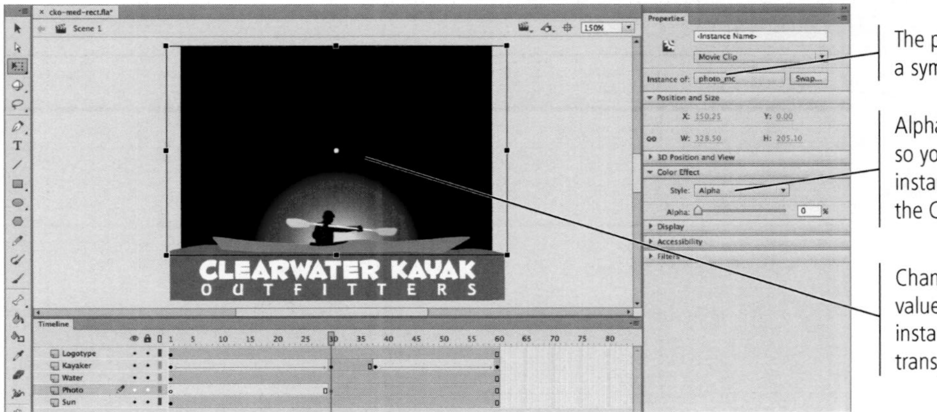

The placed image is a symbol instance.

Alpha is related to color, so you can change an instance's Alpha value in the Color Effect properties.

Changing the Alpha value to 0 makes the instance entirely transparent on the Stage.

11. **Add a new keyframe to Frame 60 of the Photo layer.**

12. **Using the Selection tool, click inside the area of the photo to select the instance on the Stage.**

    The symbol instance is not visible because its Alpha value is currently 0; you can still click inside the image area to select it.

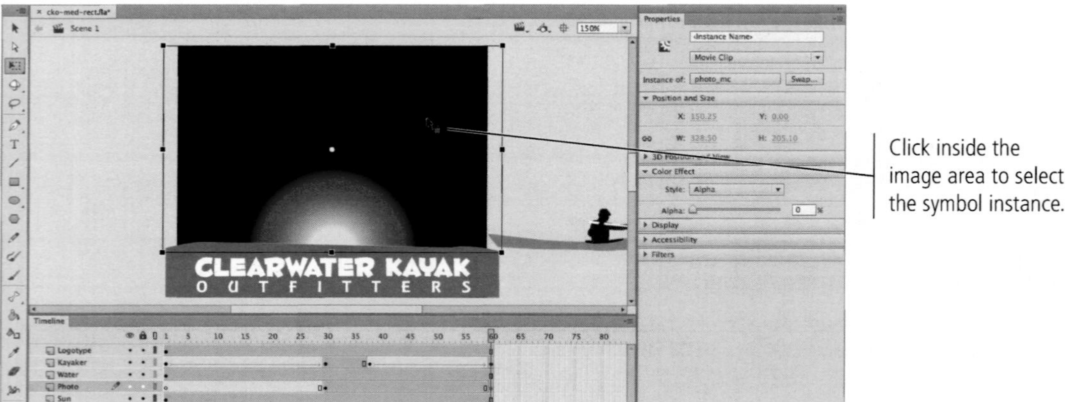
CLEARWATER KAYAK
OUTFITTERS
Click inside the image area to select the symbol instance.

13. **In the Properties panel, change the Alpha value to 100%.**

CLEARWATER KAYAK
OUTFITTERS
Change the Alpha value to 100%.
The Frame 60 keyframe is active.

14. **Control/right-click anywhere between Frames 30 and 60 in the Photo layer and choose Create Classic Tween.**

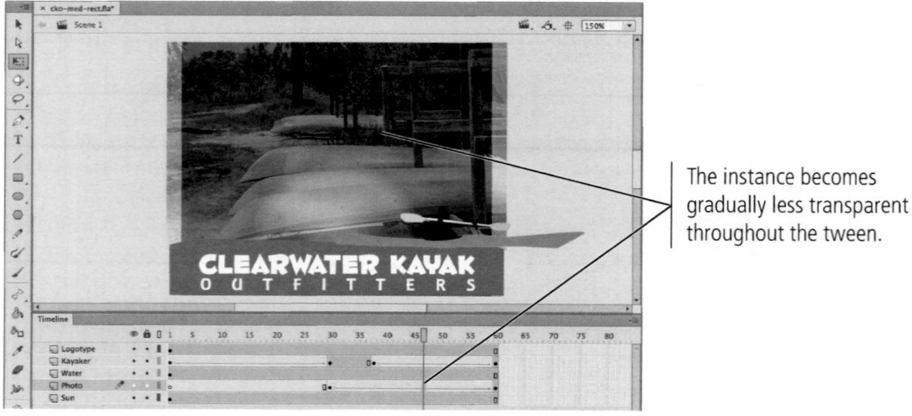
CLEARWATER KAYAK
OUTFITTERS
The instance becomes gradually less transparent throughout the tween.

15. **Save the file and continue to the next exercise.**

Stop the Animation Timeline

Remember, movie clips each have their own timelines, which are independent of other movie clips and of the main movie timeline. As soon as the playhead reaches the end of the timeline in each symbol, it automatically returns to the beginning and plays again (called **looping**). To prevent this, you have to add the Stop command to the timeline.

1. **With `cko-med-rect.fla` open, press Command-Return/Control-Enter to test the movie in the Player window.**

   As you can see, the four animations in your movie play repeatedly. You should also notice that the sun rises twice in the time it takes the logotype to change colors and the kayaker to move out of the movie area.

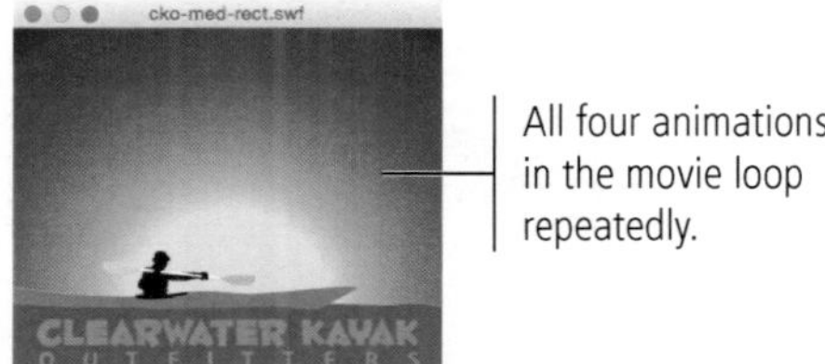

All four animations in the movie loop repeatedly.

2. **Close the Player window and return to Animate.**

3. **In the timeline, select Frame 60 of the Kayaker layer.**

   It really doesn't matter what layer you selected because the Stop command applies to the entire timeline. Any animation on this timeline — the main movie timeline — will be stopped when the playhead reaches Frame 60.

4. **Open the Code Snippets panel. Expand the ActionScript folder, then expand the Timeline Navigation subfolder.**

   The Code Snippets panel is intended to make it easier for non-programmers to add a certain level of interactivity to an Animate movie. Different types of common commands are available, grouped into logical sets or folders. Each snippet includes a plain-English name; if you move your mouse over a snippet, more information about that item appears in a tool tip.

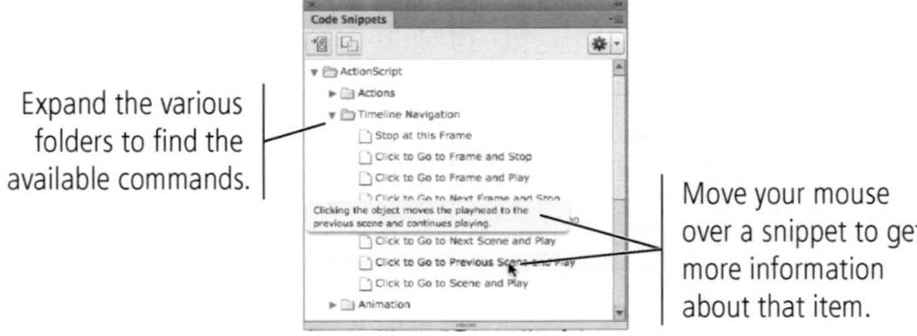

Expand the various folders to find the available commands.

Move your mouse over a snippet to get more information about that item.

5. **Double-click Stop at this Frame in the Code Snippets panel.**

   The Actions panel opens and shows the code that is required to stop the timeline from playing more than once.

   A new Actions layer is added at the top of the layer stack on the main timeline. A small "a" in the selected keyframe (Frame 60) indicates that code exists on that frame.

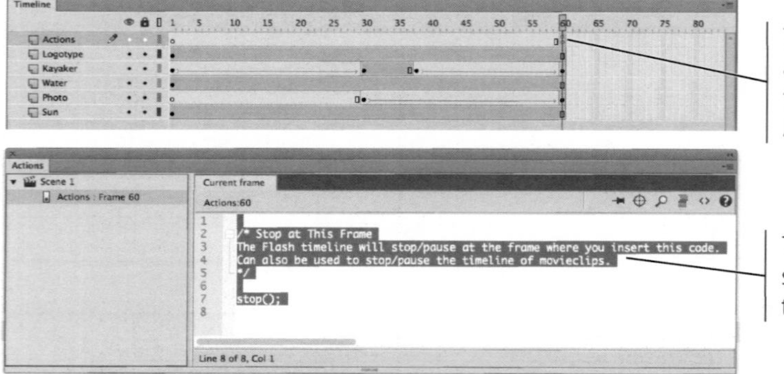

The code was added to the active frame on a new Actions layer.

The Actions panel shows the code that was added.

> ***Note:***
>
> *Although we are not going to go into any depth about code until Project 5: Ocean Animation, this is a fundamental requirement for many Animate animations. The Code Snippets panel makes it easy to add the necessary code without any programming knowledge.*

6. **Press Command-Return/Control-Enter to test the animation in the Player window.**

   The kayaker and photo animations play once and stop; however, the two movie clip animations continue to loop. It is important to note that the stop command does not stop movie clip animations that are placed on the current timeline.

The two animations on the main timeline stop after playing once.

The sunrise and logotype movie clip animations still loop.

   Remember, movie clip timelines are independent of other movie clips and of the main timeline; you have to add the stop command to each symbol timeline to prevent them from looping.

7. **Close the Player window and return to Animate.**

8. **In the Library panel, double-click the sun_mc icon to enter into the symbol.**

9. **Select Frame 30 in the timeline, then double-click Stop at this Frame in the Code Snippets panel.**

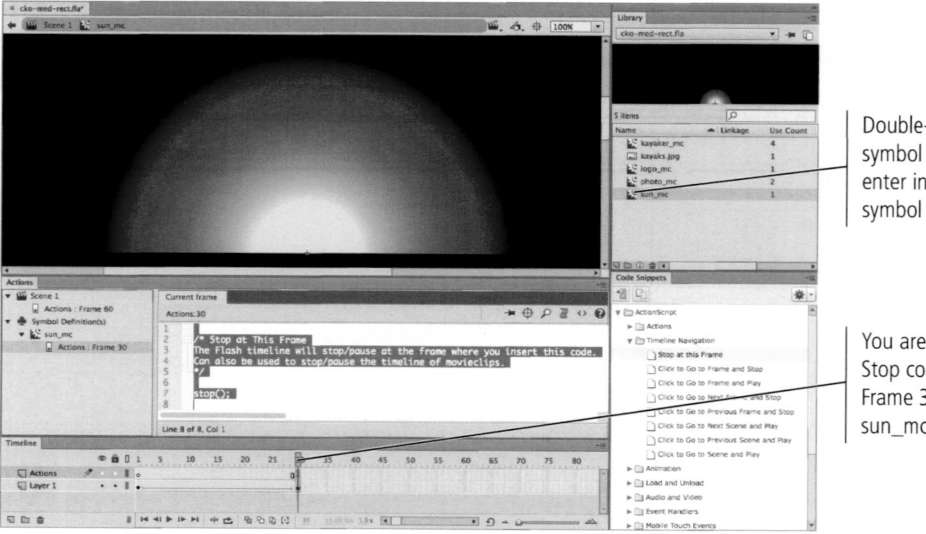

Double-click the symbol icon to enter into the symbol Stage.

You are adding the Stop command to Frame 30 of the sun_mc symbol.

10. **In the Library panel, double-click the logo_mc symbol icon to enter into that symbol.**

When you use the Library panel to enter into a symbol, you don't need to return to the main movie Stage before entering into a different symbol. You can simply double-click the symbol icons to navigate from one symbol to another.

11. **Select Frame 60 in the timeline, then double-click Stop at this Frame in the Code Snippets panel.**

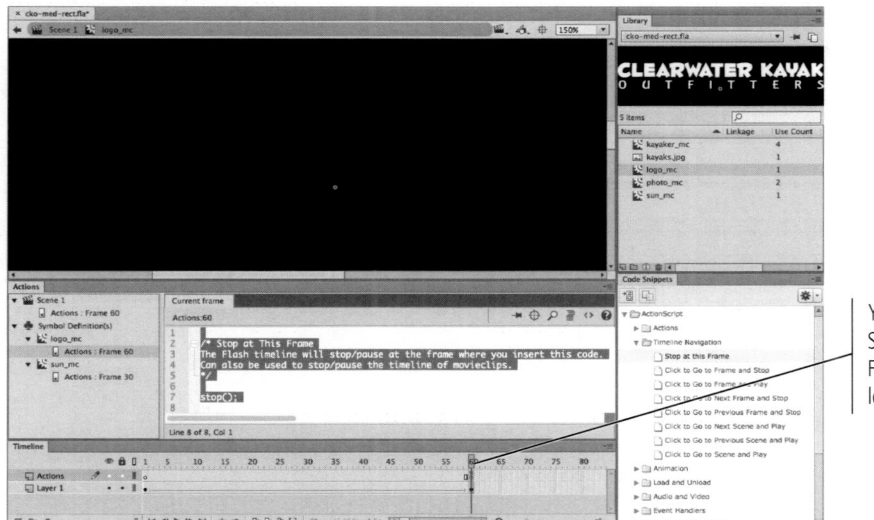

You are adding the Stop command to Frame 60 of the logo_mc symbol.

12. **Click Scene 1 in the Edit bar to return to the main Stage.**

13. **Press Command-Return/Control-Enter to test the movie in the Player window.**

All four animations now play once and stop.

14. **Close the Player window and return to Animate.**

15. **Save the file and continue to the next stage of the project.**

Stage 2 Working with Text

One of the more frustrating aspects of Web design is working with text elements; this is because the appearance of type is dependent on the available fonts on a user's computer. Animate movies are not subject to this limitation because used fonts are embedded in the exported SWF file, which means you can use any font you like in an Animate file, and it will appear exactly as expected in the movie.

The Text tool is used to add text elements to movies; the tool includes options that tie text fields to variables using ActionScript. This added functionality means text fields can automatically update from formulas and databases, or they can take user input from online forms.

Animate allows you to create three types of text:

- **Static text** is placed, kerned, aligned, and manually edited with the Text tool. To create static text, simply select the Text tool, click the Stage, and type.
- **Dynamic text** is basically an area into which a separate file (such as text-only or XML) can be read.
- **Input text** is a field in which users can type to submit information (as you would find in an online form).

> ***Note:***
>
> *The words "static" and "dynamic" do not, in this context, indicate movement. In the case of text in an Animate file, these terms refer instead to whether the text is manually placed with the Text tool (static text) or is data-driven with variables (dynamic text).*

Create a New Text Object

Your client wants a very simple text message added to the top of the ad. The message shouldn't appear until halfway through the animation, so you will again use blank keyframes to prevent the message from appearing until it should.

1. **With `cko-med-rect.fla` open, choose View>Magnification>Fit in Window.**

   You are going to create a heading across the top of the entire movie, so it will help to see the entire Stage.

2. **Add a new layer at the top of the layer stack named Text.**

3. **Create a new keyframe at Frame 37 of the Text layer, then select that frame as the active one.**

4. **Choose the Text tool in the Tools panel. At the top of the Properties panel, choose Static Text in the Text Type menu.**

5. **In the Character section of the Properties panel, change the Family menu to a sans-serif font such as Arial or Helvetica. Choose a Black, Heavy, or Bold variation of the selected font in the Style menu.**

   Any formatting you define before clicking with the Text tool will be applied in the new text area.

> ***Note:***
>
> *You might need to choose a different tool and then rechoose the Text tool to show the appropriate options in the Properties panel.*

6. **Click the current Size link to access the field. Type 24 in the field and press Return/Enter.**

7. **Click the Color swatch to open the Color palette, and choose white (#FFFFFF) as the text color.**

8. **In the Paragraph section of the Properties panel, click the Align Right format option.**

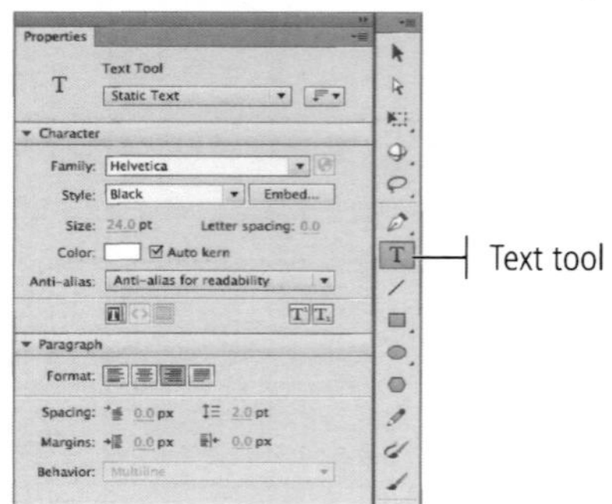

Controlling Text Properties

A number of options for controlling text appear in the Properties panel when the Text tool or an existing text element is selected.

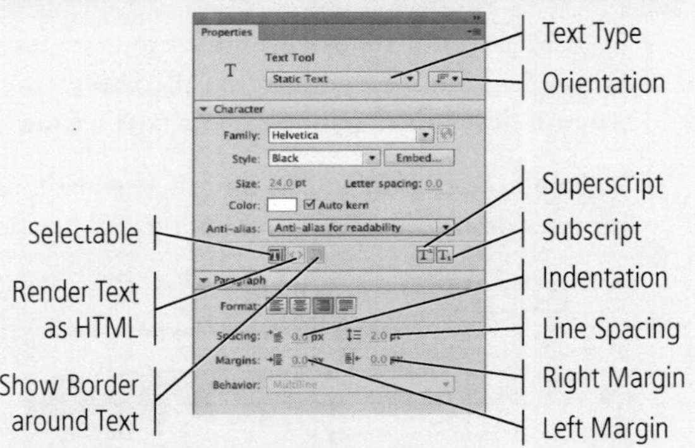

- **Text Type menu.** This menu defines a text field as static, dynamic, or input text.
- **Orientation menu.** When creating a static text object, you can use this menu to orient text horizontally, vertically, or vertically left-to-right within the text object.

Character Options

- **Family and Style menus.** As with any computer application, the font defines the appearance of the text. The entire list of fonts installed on your machine appears in the Family menu. The Style menu lists available variants of the selected font (Bold, Italic, etc.).
- **Embed button.** This button allows you to embed selected fonts or specific characters to ensure that text will appear on users' computers in the font you define.
- **Size.** The size of the text (in points) can be changed in the Font Size field or selected from the menu.
- **Letter Spacing (Tracking) field.** This option is used to increase or decrease the spacing between a selected range of characters.
- **Color.** This swatch changes the fill color of selected characters.
- **Auto Kern check box.** You can uncheck this option to prevent Animate from applying a font's default kerning values in static text.
- **Anti-aliasing menu.** This menu determines the level of anti-aliasing applied (if any).
- **Selectable button.** When you create static or dynamic text, you can activate this option to allow users to select the text within the Player window. (If you are adding text to a button, you should make sure this option is turned off so the text does not interfere with the click properties of the button.)
- **Render Text as HTML button.** When you create dynamic or input text fields, you can activate this option to show text in the field using default HTML settings instead of your specific fonts. This is usually a good choice, but when you choose it, you won't have ultimate control over the appearance of text in these areas.
- **Show Border Around Text button.** For dynamic or input text areas, you can use this option to add a visible black line around the text area, so users can more easily identify the area. This option is particularly useful for input text fields when the background is not sufficient to differentiate the field area.
- **Type Style buttons.** These buttons change the style of text to (from left) superscript (such as the TH in 4th) or subscript (the 2 in H_20).

Paragraph Options

- **Paragraph Format buttons.** Text can be aligned to the left, center, or right of its containing area, or it can be justified so that all lines fill the available horizontal space.
- **Spacing: Indentation.** This option defines how far the first line of the paragraph is indented from the left edge of the remaining text in the same paragraph.
- **Spacing: Line Spacing.** This option defines the distance between the bottoms of lines in the same type area (basically, this is the type leading).
- **Margins.** These options define how far text is moved from the left and right edges of the containing area.
- **Behavior.** This menu is only available when you are creating dynamic or input text areas. A text area can be a single line, multiple lines, or multiple lines with no wrap. If you are creating an input text field, you can also define the field as a password field.

9. **Click near the top-left corner of the Stage and drag to create a rectangular text area about the width of the movie.**

To include text in a movie, you have to first create an area to hold the text characters. As you drag, notice that dragging affects only the width of the rectangle. The area's height is determined by the current type settings defined in the Properties panel.

When you release the mouse button, the text area appears as a white box. When the insertion point is flashing, you can type in the box to add text.

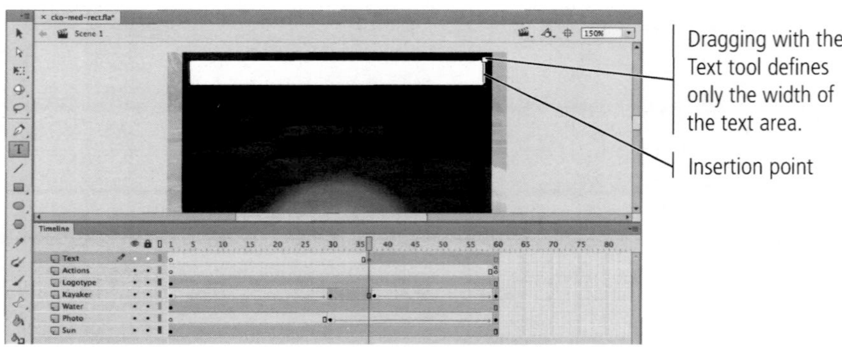
Dragging with the Text tool defines only the width of the text area.
Insertion point

> **Note:**
>
> *You can't define the height of a static text area; it automatically changes to accommodate the text in the area.*

10. **Type Adventure Awaits!.**

The text appears in the text area you just created, using the character and paragraph formatting options that you already defined. (Because you chose white as the text color, the text appears gray in the area so you can see it as you type.)

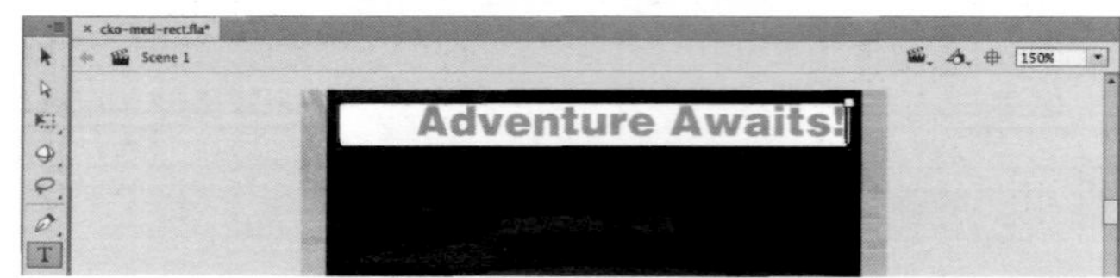
Adventure Awaits!

> **Note:**
>
> *The insertion point appears on the right side of the area because you chose the Align Right paragraph formatting option in Step 8.*

11. **Choose the Selection tool, and then expand the Position and Size options in the Properties panel. Change the properties of the selected text area to:**

    X: 0 **Y: 10**
    W: 280

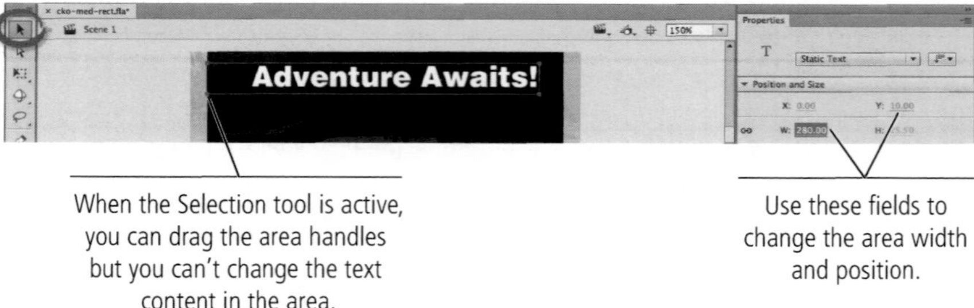
Adventure Awaits!
When the Selection tool is active, you can drag the area handles but you can't change the text content in the area.
Use these fields to change the area width and position.

Using the Position and Size properties, you can define specific numeric parameters for the area. You can also reposition a text area by clicking inside the area with the Selection tool and dragging to a new location, or resize the area by dragging any of the handles that appear on the outside edges of the object.

> **Note:**
>
> *When the insertion point is flashing in a text area, you can't use the one-key shortcuts to choose other tools.*

> **Note:**
>
> *Depending on how wide you create a text area, the height of a text area might enlarge if the text you type requires a second line.*

> **Note:**
>
> *Using the Free Transform tool on a text area stretches or condenses type inside the area.*

12. **With the text area still selected, change the Size value (in the Character section of the Properties panel) to 40.**

When a text area is selected, changes to character and paragraph formatting apply to all text inside the area. You can change the formatting of only certain characters by highlighting the target characters with the Text tool before making changes in the Properties panel.

The text area automatically expands to accommodate the new text formatting; in this case, it is high enough to show two lines of text.

When the entire text object is selected, formatting changes affect all text in the area.

The text object height expands to accommodate the new formatting.

13. **Click away from the text area to deselect it.**

14. **Save the file and continue to the next exercise.**

Define Font Embedding

When you use text in a movie, the fonts you use must be available to other users who open your file. If not, the users' systems will substitute some font that is available — which can significantly change the appearance of your movie. To solve this potential problem, you can embed fonts into your movies so the required fonts are always available.

1. **With cko-med-rect.fla open, select the Text tool.**

2. **Click inside the heading text area to place the insertion point and reveal the formatting for that area.**

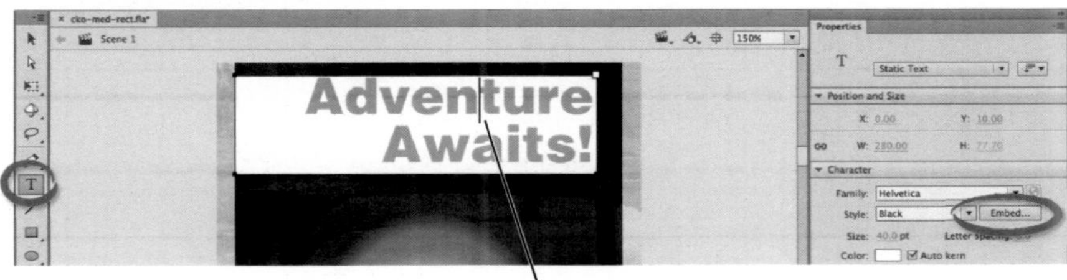

The insertion point is placed in the text.

3. **In the Character section of the Properties panel, click the Embed button.**

   This button opens the Font Embedding dialog box. The currently applied font is automatically selected in the Family and Style menus.

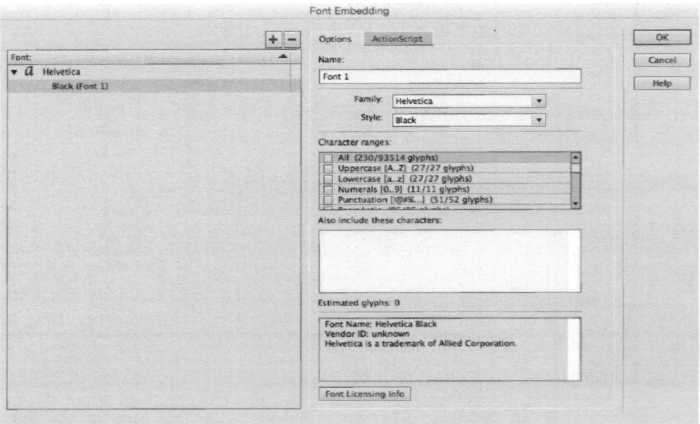

4. **Change the Name field to `Heading Font`.**

5. **In the Character Ranges list, check the Uppercase, Lowercase, and Punctuation options.**

   Remember, embedding characters from fonts increases the resulting file size. You know only letters and punctuation were used in this document, so you can limit the embedded characters to only these ranges rather than embedding every possible character of the font.

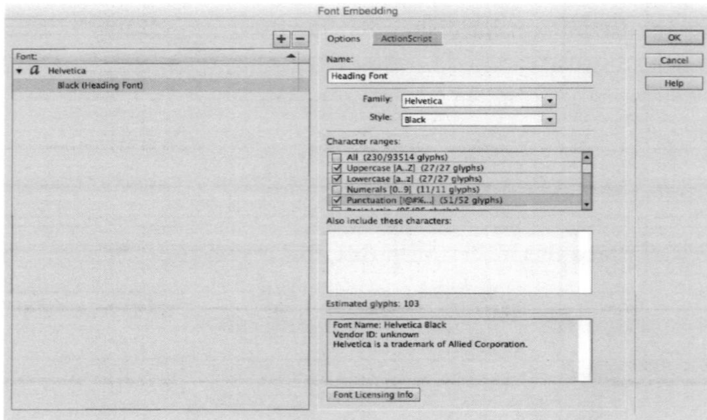

6. **Click OK to close the dialog box.**

7. **Review the Library panel.**

   When you embed a font into the file, it is added to the file's library.

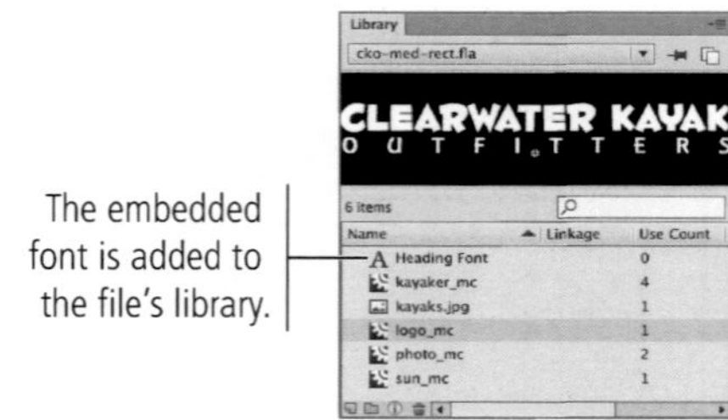

Note:

Keep in mind that embedding fonts adds to the resulting file size and increases download time. The font outline (embedded character) is stored as part of the SWF file, so repeatedly using the same character of the same font in the movie does not increase the file size (the same theory as using instances of symbols). Keeping the number of fonts in a movie to a minimum ensures a faster-loading movie.

Note:

The item on the left side of the dialog box won't reflect the new name until you click away from the Name field.

8. **Press Command-Return/Control-Enter to test the file in the Player window.**

   When the movie ends, you might notice a problem — the white text is difficult to read when the image is entirely opaque. You will solve this problem in the next exercise.

cko-med-rect.swf
Adventure
Awaits!
CLEARWATER KAYAK
O U T F I T T E R S

9. **Close the Player window and return to Animate.**

10. **Save the file and continue to the next exercise.**

Control Object Stacking Order

It is not uncommon for designers to use individual layers for each object in the file — which makes things much easier to find as long as you use descriptive layer names.

You should also understand, however, that stacking order applies to multiple objects that are created on the same layer. Drawing objects and symbols exist from bottom to top in the order they were created *on a single layer*. It is easy to create something in the wrong order, but fortunately, Animate makes it relatively easy to rearrange the stack.

1. **With `cko-med-rect.fla` open, select Frame 37 of the Text layer.**

2. **Using the Selection tool, click an empty area around the Stage to deselect the text object.**

3. **Choose the Rectangle tool, and make sure Object-Drawing mode is active.**

4. **In the Color panel, change the Stroke color to None.**

5. **Click the Fill button to make it the active attribute, then open the Color Type menu and chose Linear Gradient.**

6. **Open the Fill color palette and choose the white-to-black linear gradient swatch.**

7. **Click the left gradient stop to select it, then change the Alpha value to `0%`.**

8. **Click the right gradient stop to select it, and drag it to the 50% point along the gradient. Change the stop color to `#000033`, and change the Alpha value to `50%`.**

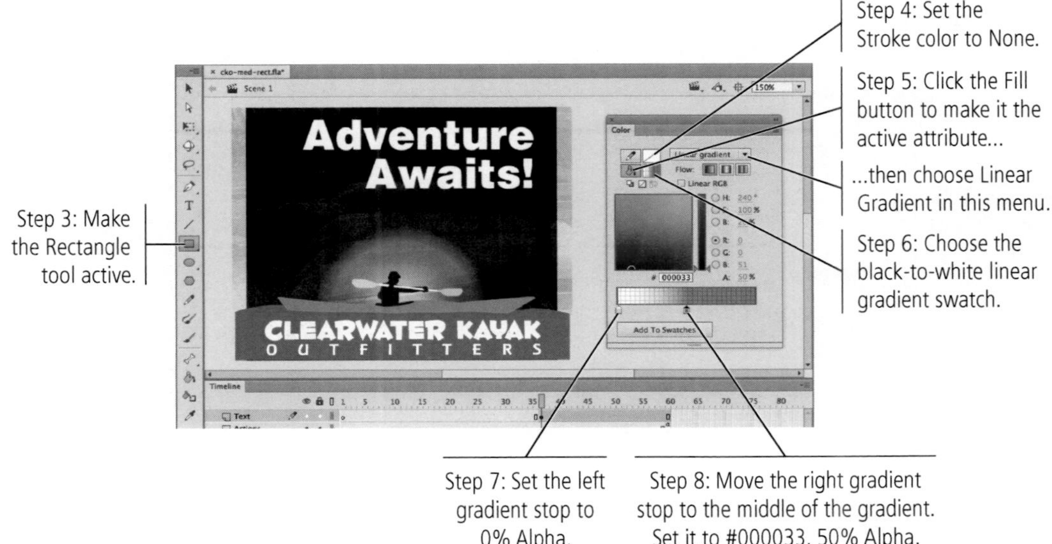

Step 3: Make the Rectangle tool active.
Step 4: Set the Stroke color to None.
Step 5: Click the Fill button to make it the active attribute...
...then choose Linear Gradient in this menu.
Step 6: Choose the black-to-white linear gradient swatch.
Step 7: Set the left gradient stop to 0% Alpha.
Step 8: Move the right gradient stop to the middle of the gradient. Set it to #000033, 50% Alpha.
Adventure
Awaits!
CLEARWATER KAYAK
O U T F I T T E R S
Add To Swatches

9. **With Frame 37 of the Text layer selected, click and drag to create an object that fills the top half of the Stage.**

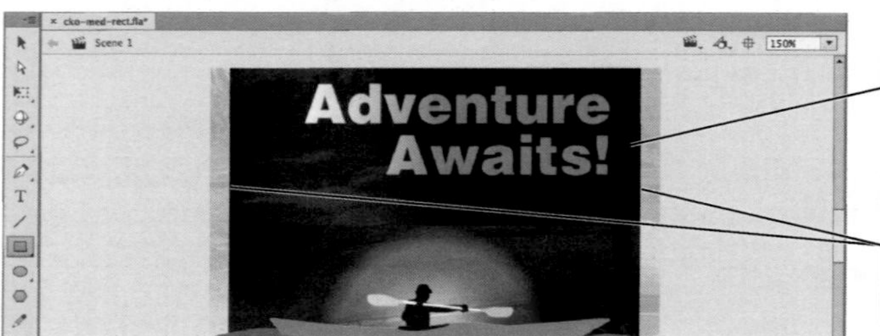

The gradient defaults to fill the object from left to right.

The gradient goes from entirely transparent to 50% transparent (the Alpha value of each stop on the gradient).

10. **Choose the Gradient Transform tool in the Tools panel. If necessary, click the gradient-filled rectangle to reveal the gradient-editing handles.**

11. **Rotate the gradient 90° counterclockwise, then use the gradient width handle to make the gradient the same size as the object's height.**

Drag this handle to rotate the gradient.

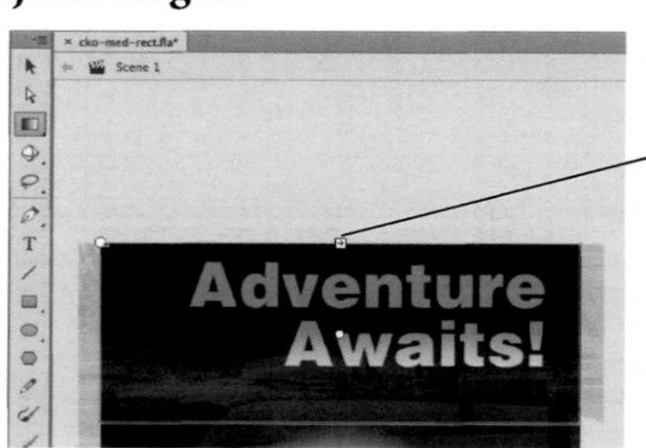

Drag this handle to change the gradient width.

12. **Using the Selection tool, select the gradient-filled rectangle.**

The gradient-filled shape is currently on top of the text object. You want the text to appear on top of the gradient, so you need to rearrange the object stacking order.

13. **Choose Modify>Arrange>Send to Back.**

Options in the Modify>Arrange submenu control the stacking order of objects on the active layer. These options have no effect on the relative stacking of objects on different layers.

> *Note:*
>
> *Merge-drawing shapes, which result when the object-drawing mode is not toggled on, are always created at the back of the stacking order, behind any other objects on the layer (symbol instances, object-drawing shapes, type areas, etc.).*

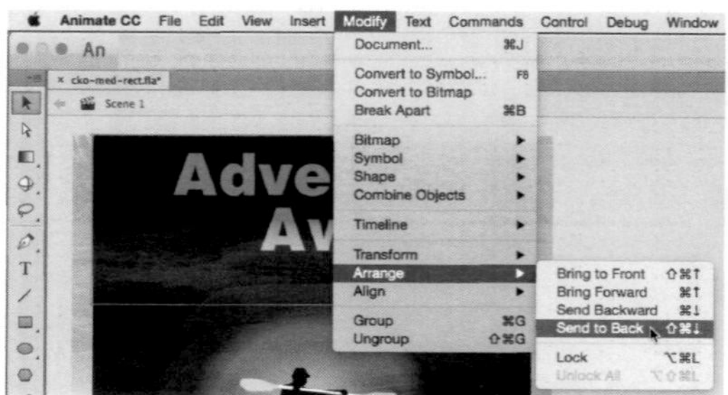

By placing the gradient-filled rectangle behind the text object but in front of the underlying layers, the white text will be more easily visible when the background photo is entirely visible at the end of the animation.

14. **Save the file and continue to the next stage of the project.**

Stage 3 Repurposing Animate Content

The first ad required for this project is now complete. However, the entire job calls for three versions of the same ad, using different standard ad sizes but the same content in each ad. Rather than simply creating a new file and then copying the existing content into it, you will use two different techniques to scale the existing content to suit the alternate file sizes.

 Scale Content to Document Properties

To complete the entire assignment, you need two more versions of the ad: one is a slightly larger rectangle size (336 × 280 px), and one is a 250 × 250-pixel square.

You could use the New Document dialog box to create the file using the built-in templates, then copy and paste all of the necessary content from one file to another. However, that process is time-consuming and introduces the potential for error since you need to copy the entire timeline as well as the objects on the Stage.

1. **With `cko-med-rect.fla` open, make sure nothing is selected on the Stage and the Selection tool is active.**

2. **In the Properties panel, click the Advanced Settings button.**

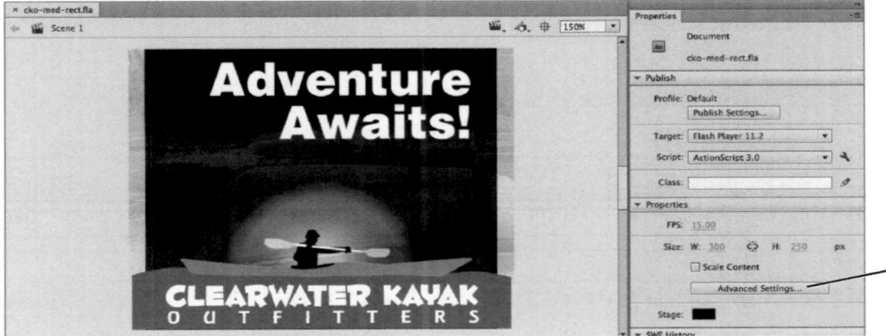

With nothing selected on the Stage, click here to open the Document Settings dialog box.

3. **In the resulting dialog box, change the Width dimension to `336` px and change the Height dimension to `280` px.**

4. **Check the Scale Content option, then click OK to apply the change.**

   Because the new file dimensions have the same width-to-height aspect ratio (6:5), the objects in the new file are easily scaled up and require no further manipulation to function properly. By using the existing file as the basis of the new one, the Scale Content option made the entire process possible in only a few clicks.

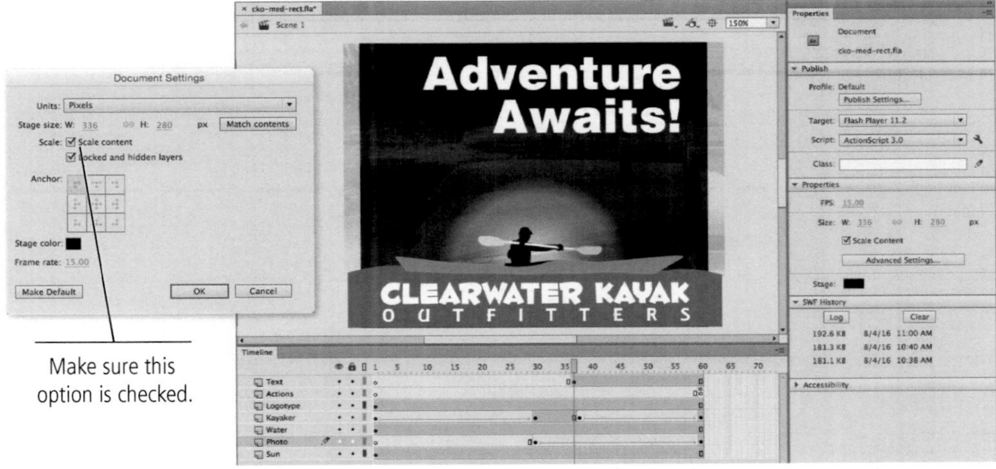

Make sure this option is checked.

5. **Choose File>Save As. Make sure your WIP>Kayaks folder is the target destination, change the Save As/File Name field to `cko-lg-rect.fla`, then click Save.**

6. **Close the active Animate file, then continue to the next exercise.**

Manually Adjust Content to Document Properties

Because the new file size in the previous exercise had the same aspect ratio as the original, you did not need to make any further changes other than saving the file with a new name. In many cases, the new file size will not have the same aspect ratio as the original; you will have to make some manual adjustments to keep the content in the same general position as in the original.

1. **Choose File>Open. Select `cko_med.rect.fla` in your WIP>Kayaks folder and click Open.**

2. **Deselect everything on the Stage, then click the Advanced Settings button in the Properties panel.**

3. **In the resulting dialog box, change the Width and Height dimensions to `250` px. Choose the top-center anchor, then check the Scale Content with Stage option.**

   For some reason, the anchor options are unavailable when Scale Content with Stage is active. You have to select the appropriate anchor first.

4. **Click OK to finalize the change.**

   In this case, the new file does not use the same aspect ratio as the original. As you can see, Animate is not able to interpret the necessary positions of all elements in the file. Although this is a good start, you still need to make some adjustments manually.

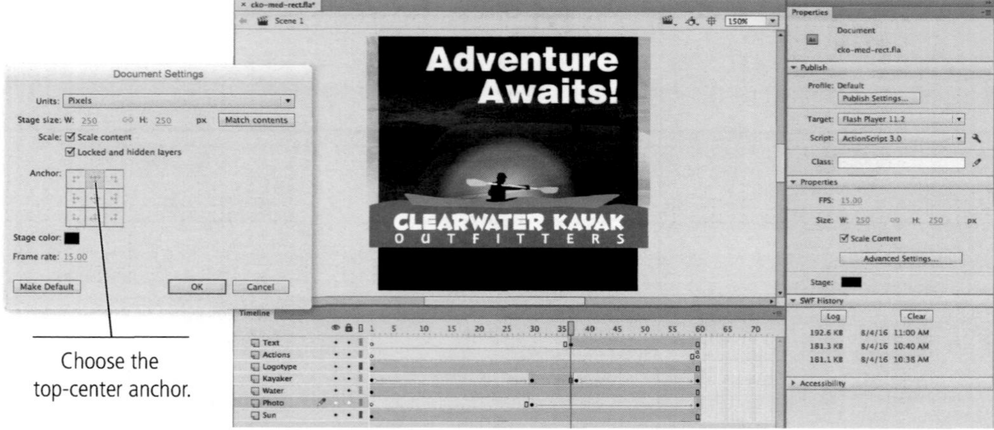

Choose the top-center anchor.

4. **Save the file as `cko-square.fla` in your WIP>Kayaks folder.**

   By immediately saving the new file with a different name, you avoid accidentally changing something in the wrong file.

5. **Click Frame 1 in the timeline to move the playhead to the beginning of the movie.**

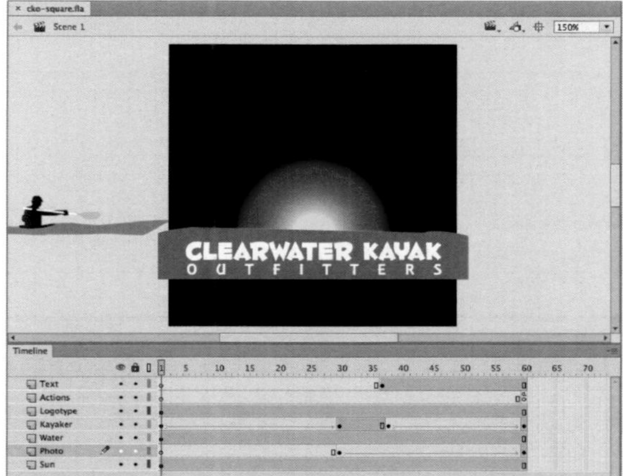

CLEARWATER KAYAK
OUTFITTERS

6. **In the Timeline panel, Command/Control-click to select the Logotype, Kayaker, Water, and Sun layers.**

   You need to move the content on all four of these layers down to the bottom of the adjusted Stage. You don't want to move the Photo layer content because you want it to remain attached to the top of the Stage.

7. **Using the Selection tool, click any of the selected objects on the Stage, press Shift, and drag down until the water aligns with the bottom of the Stage.**

   By moving the content on all four layers at once, you maintain the same relative positions between the selected objects.

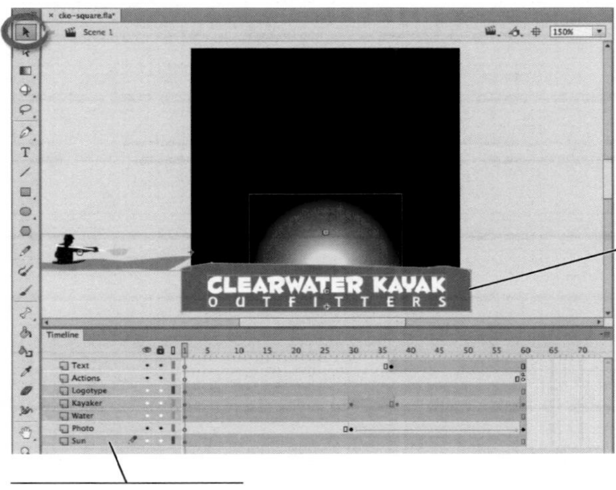

CLEARWATER KAYAK
OUTFITTERS
Shift-drag the selected objects until they align to the bottom of the Stage.
Command/Control-click each layer to select the content on all four layers.

8. **Press Return/Enter to play the movie on the Stage.**

   You should notice the kayaker symbol instance moves up and away from the water as the playhead progresses. If you review the timeline, remember that this layer has four separate keyframes, each of which define a specific position in a classic tween. To keep the kayaker paddling straight across the Stage, you have to change the instance's position on each keyframe in the layer.

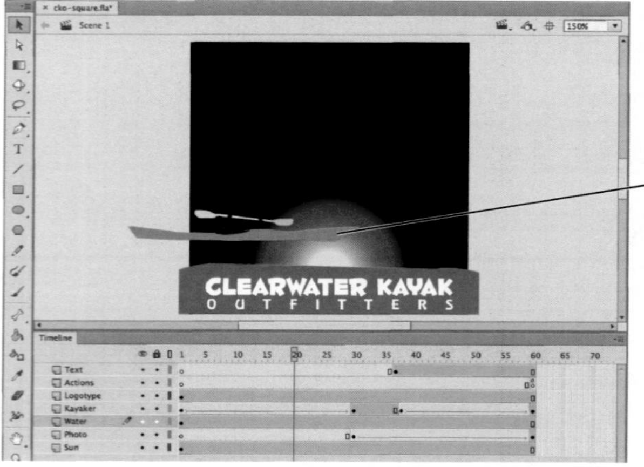

As the playhead moves, the kayaker moves back to its original position on Frame 30.

9. **Return the playhead to Frame 1 on the timeline, then click the kayaker symbol instance to select it.**

10. **In the Properties panel, note the instance's Y position.**

    In our example, the Y position is 193.60. If yours is different, you should use the exact value from your file in the following steps. The point is to make the instance's Y (vertical) position consistent in all keyframes.

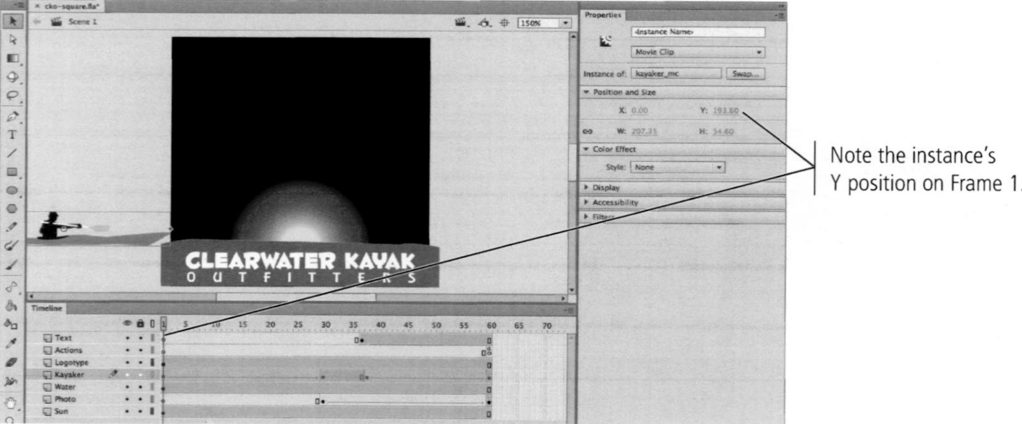

Note the instance's Y position on Frame 1.

11. **Click Frame 30 of the Kayaker layer, then click the symbol instance on the Stage to select it.**

12. **In the Properties panel, change the Y position to the same value you noted in Step 10.**

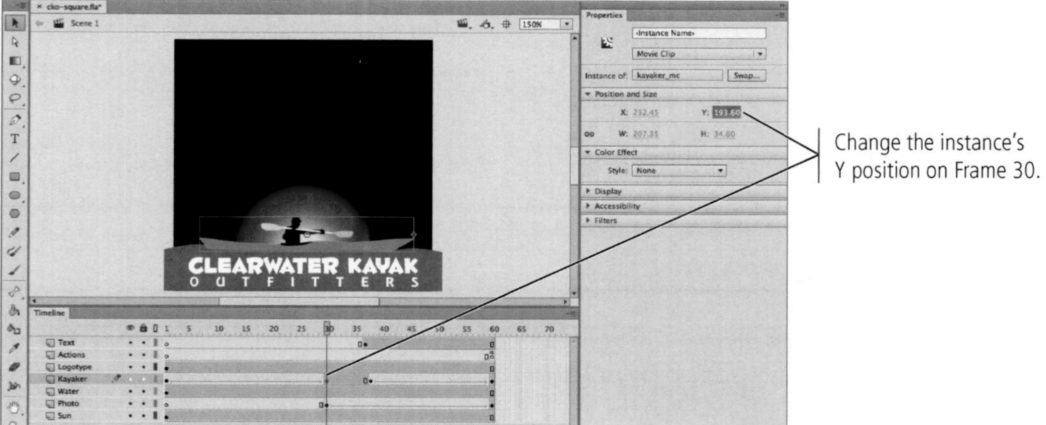

Change the instance's Y position on Frame 30.

13. **Repeat Steps 11–12 for the two remaining keyframes on the Kayaker layer.**

    When you get to Frame 60, you should notice another problem — the photo no longer fills the background area. (This was harder to see when the image was entirely or semitransparent). You now need to adjust the photo to fill the space.

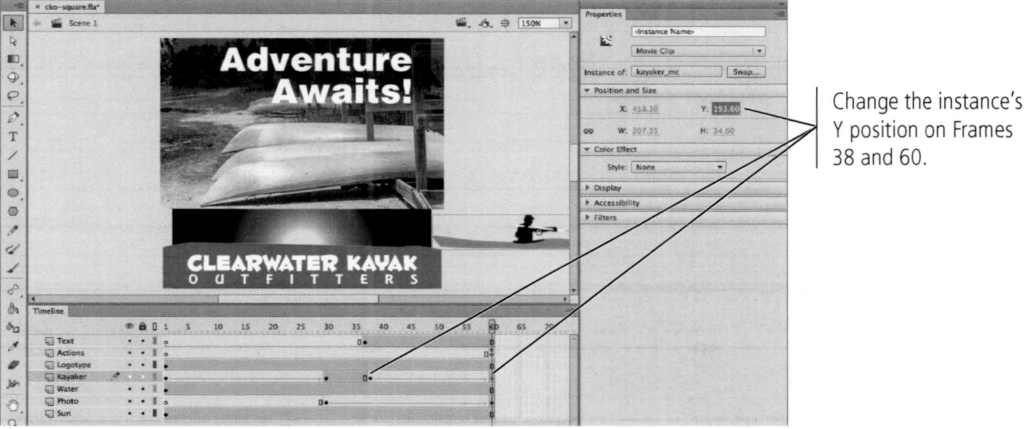

Change the instance's Y position on Frames 38 and 60.

14. **Select Frame 30 on the Photo layer.**

    The first keyframe (Frame 1) on the Photo layer is blank; the image doesn't exist on that frame, so you don't need to edit that keyframe.

    Remember, this image is actually an instance of a symbol, which you created from the original bitmap image.

15. **If necessary, use the Selection tool to nudge the photo up to cover the top of the Stage.**

16. **Choose the Free Transform tool, then move the transformation point of the selected object to the top center handle.**

17. **Using the Transform panel, scale the instance proportionally until the bottom edge is just hidden by the top edge of the water shape.**

    Be careful when you scale bitmap images, especially making them larger. Bitmap images have a fixed resolution, which means enlarging them can significantly reduce the quality.

    If you remember the first part of this project, you actually reduced the image before creating the symbol instance. Enlarging this particular instance above 100% still keeps the image smaller than the original bitmap's physical dimensions, so you should not see any significant lack of quality in this case.

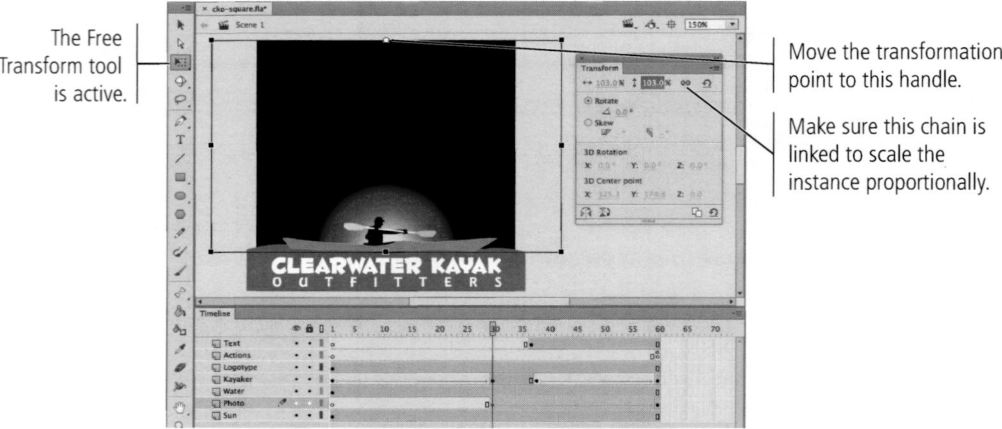
The Free Transform tool is active.
Move the transformation point to this handle.
Make sure this chain is linked to scale the instance proportionally.
CLEARWATER KAYAK
OUTFITTERS

18. **Repeat Steps 14–17 for the instance on the Frame 60 keyframe.**

    You should apply the exact same transformation on Frame 60 as you did on Frame 30. Rather than scrubbing the values in the Transform panel, you can click one of the existing values to enter the field, constrain the two dimensions, and then type the exact same value that you applied in Step 16.

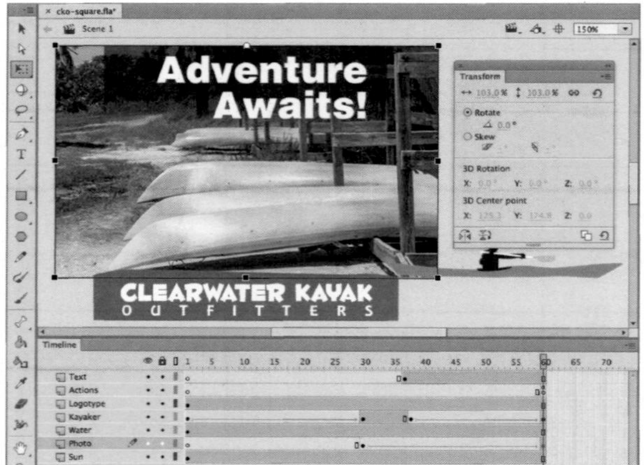
Adventure
Awaits!
CLEARWATER KAYAK
OUTFITTERS

19. **Save the file and continue to the final exercise.**

Publish the Ad Files

Exporting a document refers to publishing it in a form that can be viewed in another application. The File>Export menu has three options: Export Image, Export Movie, and Export Video.

- If you choose **Export Image**, you can save your file as a static graphic (with no animation) in formats such as GIF or JPEG.
- **Export Movie** allows you to create a file (or sequence of files) that includes animation, which can be placed into an HTML document created in another application. A number of formats are available in the File Format/Save As Type menu. Each format has distinct uses, advantages, and disadvantages.

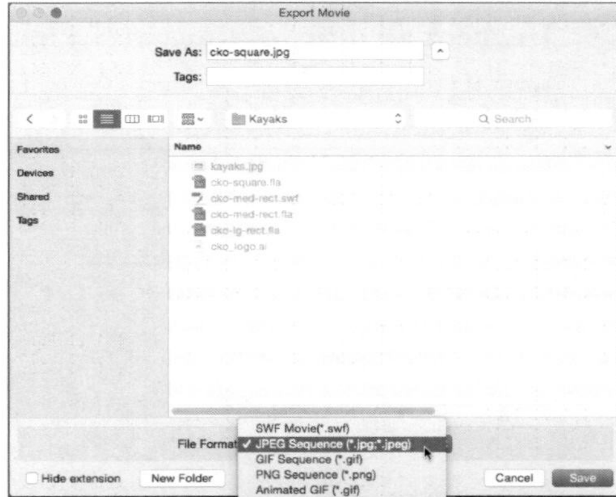

  - **SWF Movie.** A Animate movie file can be placed into an HTML file, or it can be used in another Animate application.
  - **JPEG Sequence.** Selecting this option allows the file to be exported in the JPEG format. The Match Movie option matches the size of the exported file with that of the original document. When you use any of the sequence options, each frame of the movie is exported as a separate image.
  - **GIF Sequence.** This format exports the files in GIF format, except the files are generated in a sequence for each frame animation. The animated GIF format exports a single file that contains all of the animations; this option generates a sequence of files.
  - **PNG Sequence.** This option saves the files in the Portable Network Graphics (PNG) format, which supports transparency for objects that might need to be placed on various backgrounds. You can specify options such as dimension, resolution, colors, and filters.
  - **Animated GIF.** Files exported in this format preserve all the animations in a single file. You can specify various options, such as dots per inch (dpi), image area, colors, and animation for the resulting GIF file. Setting the dpi is the same as setting the dimensions of the image; the number of times the animation needs to repeat can also be defined (0 creates an endless loop).
- If you choose **Export Video**, you will export the active file as a MOV video file, which is a QuickTime file. (The format was created by Apple Computer to work with multimedia files.)

You can also use the Publish option (File>Publish) to generate an Animate SWF file, as well as a number of other formats. When you publish a file, the resulting output is based on the active options in the Publish Settings dialog box.

1. **With `cko-square.fla` open, choose File>Publish Settings.**

   Rather than simply choose File>Publish, you are using this dialog box to first review the settings that will apply when you publish the files.

2. **In the Publish options on the left side of the Publish Settings dialog box, make sure the Animate (.swf) option is selected.**

3. **Uncheck all other options in the left side of the dialog box.**

   If the HTML Wrapper option is checked, the publish process also generates an HTML file that includes the necessary code for opening the SWF file in a browser window. Because these ads will be distributed for insertion into other sites, the HTML option is not necessary.

4. **Click Publish at the bottom of the dialog box.**

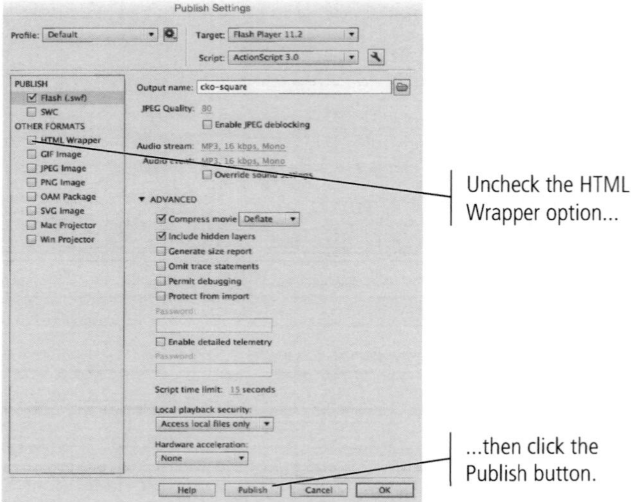

5. **When the publish process is complete, click OK to close the Publish Settings dialog box.**

6. **Save the open file (cko-square.fla) and close it.**

7. **Repeat Steps 1–6 for the other two ad files in the project.**

   Publish settings are file-specific, so you have to define these options for each file that will be published.

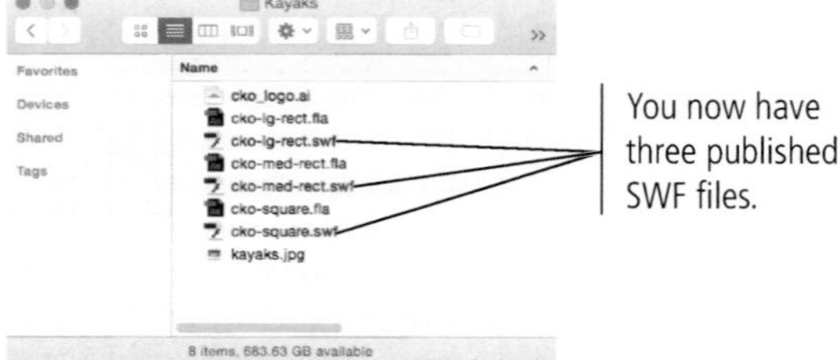

Understanding SWF Publish Settings

The Publish Settings dialog box (File>Publish Settings) contains all the necessary settings for publishing files from Animate.

- The **Profile** menu lists all available saved profiles, which save defined publish settings for easier access. You can use the attached Profile Options button to create, import, export, and manage saved profiles.
- The **Target** menu allows you to export the Animate movie to be compatible with an earlier version of the Animate Player, or different versions Adobe AIR.
- **Script** specifies which version of ActionScript is or will be used in the file. (ActionScript 3.0 is the default and only option in Animate CC.) Clicking the ActionScript Settings button opens a dialog box where you can specify the path of an external ActionScript file.

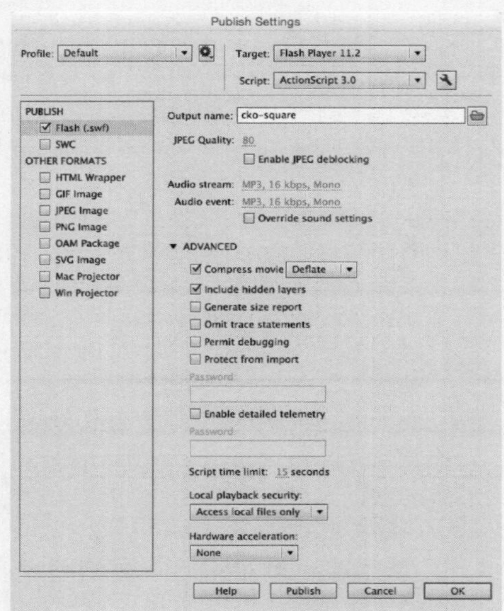

The **Publish** list on the left side of the dialog box lists the available formats that can be exported; the Animate (.swf) and the HTML Wrapper formats are selected by default. When you click a specific format in the Publish list, options related to that format appear on the right side of the dialog box.

When **Animate (.swf)** is selected in the Publish list, options on the right side of the dialog box determine how the animation is exported.

- The **Output File** field shows the default file name, based on the FLA file name, that will be used for the exported file. By default, exported files are created in the same location as the FLA file you are exporting; you can click the folder icon next to a file name to specify a different publishing location. (This is available for all publishing formats.)
- **JPEG Quality** specifies the quality of exported JPEG images. Lower values result in smaller file sizes, but also lower image quality; as the quality increases, so does the size of the file. The **Enable JPEG Deblocking** option helps smooth the appearance of JPEG files with very high levels of compression.
- The **Audio Stream** and **Audio Event** options show the current sound export settings for stream and event sounds (respectively). Clicking either link opens the Sound Settings dialog box, where you can change the compression format, quality, and bit rate options for each type of sound.

  (A streaming sound plays as soon as enough data is downloaded; the sound stops playing as soon as the movie stops. An event sound does not play until it downloads completely, and it continues to play until explicitly stopped.)
- If **Override Sound Settings** is checked, the default options in the Audio Stream and Audio Event settings override any settings that are defined for individual sound files in the file's library.
- **Compress Movie** reduces the size of the exported file, which also reduces download time. Compressed files can only be played in Animate Player 6 or later.
- **Include Hidden Layers** allows you to export hidden layer information in the exported file.
- **Generate Size Report** creates a text file with information about the amount of data in the final Animate content.
- **Omit Trace Statements** allows Animate to ignore trace options, which are ActionScript functions that display the results of certain code in the Output panel.
- **Permit Debugging** allows you to debug your SWF file and allows other users to debug your SWF file remotely. You can also define a password, which other users will have to enter in order to debug the file.
- **Protect from Import** prevents others from importing your SWF file. This option also allows you to protect your SWF file with a password. (**Password** is activated if you select the Protect from Import or the Permit Debugging option. You can specify a password that other users must enter to import the file or debug the movie.)
- **Local Playback Security** options provide security for your application. If you select Access Local Files Only, your SWF file can interact only on the local machine. If you choose Access Network Only, your SWF file can communicate with resources only on the network and not on the local machine.
- **Hardware Acceleration** options can be used to speed up the graphics performance of the exported movie.

Understanding SWF Publish Settings (continued)

HTML Wrapper options relate to publishing an Animate document on the Web. In this case, you might need an HTML file that will embed your SWF file.

- The **Template** menu contains various templates in which an HTML file can be published. Selecting a template and then clicking the Info button shows a dialog box with information about the selected template.
- If you select **Detect Flash Version**, you can use the Version fields to define which is required. Detection code is embedded in the resulting file to determine if a user has the required version. If not, a link is provided to download the latest version of the player plug-in. (Some templates do not support this code.)
- The **Size** options define the dimensions of the resulting HTML file. You can choose Match Movie to use the size of the Animate Stage, or define specific width and height (in pixels or percent).
- The **Paused at Start** option keeps the SWF file from being played unless the user clicks to initiate the movie.
- The **Loop** option causes the Animate content to repeat after it reaches the final frame, so the movie plays in a continuous loop.
- The **Display Menu** option enables a shortcut when the user Control/right-clicks the SWF file in the browser. Deselecting this option shows only About Animate in the shortcut menu.
- Selecting the **Device Font** option displays users' system fonts instead of the fonts used in the SWF file, if those fonts are unavailable in the user's system.
- **Quality** specifies the quality of the SWF content embedded in the HTML file. Auto Low gives preference to document loading rather than quality, but also tries to improve the quality of the SWF file. Auto High treats loading and quality equally; when the loading speed is reduced, quality is compromised. The remaining three options are self-explanatory; lower quality settings mean higher compression, smaller file sizes, and faster download times.
- **Window Mode** sets the value of the wmode attribute in the object and embed HTML tags. Window does not embed window-related attributes in the HTML tags; the background of the Animate content is opaque. Opaque Windowless sets the background of the Animate content to opaque, which allows HTML content to appear on top of Animate content. Transparent Windowless sets the background of the Animate content to transparent.

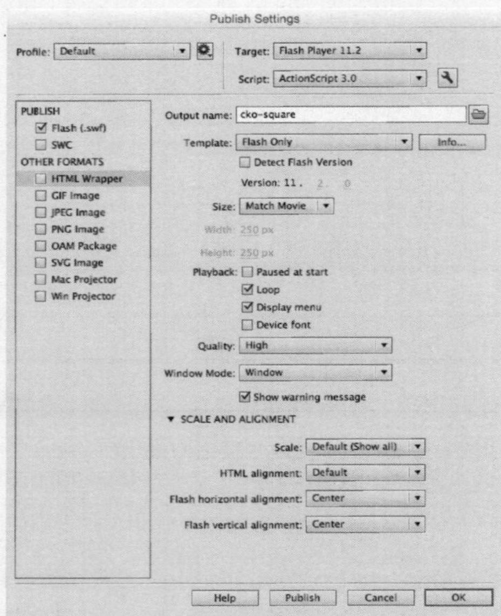

- The **Show Warning Message** option displays all warning and error messages whenever a setting for publishing the content is incorrect.
- **Scale** controls the display of Animate content when you change the dimension of the Animate content in the HTML file. Default (Show All) displays the entire document in the specified area. No Border fits the document in the specified area and maintains the quality of the SWF file by avoiding distortion. Exact Fit fits the entire SWF file in the specified area, but compromises the quality of the SWF file. No Scale prevents the Animate content from being scaled in the HTML file.
- **HTML Alignment** aligns the Animate content in the browser window. The Default option displays the SWF file in the center of the browser; you can also choose Left, Right, Top, or Bottom.
- **Animate Horizontal and Vertical Alignment** set the alignment of Animate content within the HTML file.

Project Review

fill in the blank

1. A(n) _______________ timeline functions independently of other symbols in the same file.

2. _______________ are required when an object needs to change in some way at a given point in time.

3. The _______________ can be used to scale an object proportionally with respect to the object's defined transformation point.

4. A(n) _______________ can be used if you need to change an object's color over time.

5. A(n) _______________ is identified by blue frames and an arrow in the timeline.

6. _______________ is simple text that does not change.

7. _______________ is essentially a text area that can be populated with the contents of an external file.

8. _______________ solves the potential problem of used fonts not being available on a user's computer.

9. The _______________ option allows you to change objects' size based on the edited document settings.

10. _______________ is the default extension for exported file movies.

short answer

1. Briefly explain how a movie clip symbol relates to the primary timeline of a file.

2. Briefly explain the process of creating a shape tween.

3. Briefly explain why embedding fonts in an Animate file is important.

Portfolio Builder Project

Use what you learned in this project to complete the following freeform exercise.
Carefully read the art director and client comments, then create your own design to meet the needs of the project.
Use the space below to sketch ideas; when finished, write a brief explanation of your reasoning behind your final design.

art director comments

Our agency has been hired to create a series of animated videos explaining scientific principles for children.

To complete this project, you should:

- ❑ Research the topics you are going to model and determine what (if any) data will be required to create a scientifically accurate illustration.
- ❑ Create or locate images or graphics that will result in a "kid-friendly" learning experience.
- ❑ Develop the animations so they can be placed into an existing Web site, using a 600 × 800 file size.

client comments

We would like you to create a series of videos over the next year (as the grant funds become available). The first one we want is an illustration of gravity. We're not entirely sure how it should look or function. We kind of like the legend of Isaac Newton sitting under an apple tree, when an apple fell on his head. If you could figure out how to make that work, great. If not, we're happy to consider other solutions.

As more funds become available, we're also going to want movies to illustrate other scientific principles. Our current list includes tectonic plate movement, tidal patterns, volcanic eruptions, and friction.

It will be easier to secure the secondary grants for later projects if we can include a specific plan for the different programs. Once you finish the gravity illustration (which we already have the money for), can you sketch out plans for at least two others?

project justification

Project Summary

The ability to control object shape and movement is one of the most important functions in designing animations. In this project, you used a number of basic techniques for animating object properties, including size, color, and position. As you complete the next projects in this book, you will expand on the knowledge from this chapter, learning new ways to animate multiple properties at once. The skills and knowledge from this project, however, apply to any animation — understanding frame rate, keyframes, and timeline independence are essential to being a successful animator.

This project also introduced the concept of adding text to a movie. Many Animate projects will involve some text, even if that text is eventually converted into drawing objects; you now know how to create and format text to communicate a client's message directly within an Animate file.

Finally, you learned about issues you will encounter if you need to create multiple variations of the same file —whether you need to create multiple different-sized ads or different versions for various mobile device sizes.

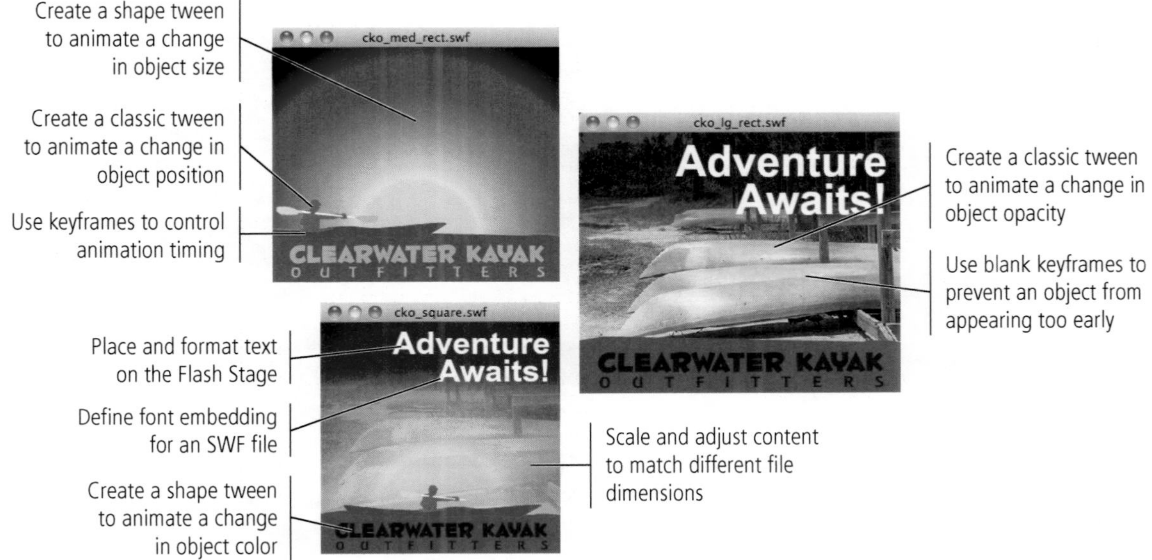
Create a shape tween to animate a change in object size
Create a classic tween to animate a change in object position
Use keyframes to control animation timing
cko_med_rect.swf
CLEARWATER KAYAK
OUTFITTERS
cko_lg_rect.swf
Adventure Awaits!
CLEARWATER KAYAK
OUTFITTERS
Create a classic tween to animate a change in object opacity
Use blank keyframes to prevent an object from appearing too early
cko_square.swf
Adventure Awaits!
CLEARWATER KAYAK
OUTFITTERS
Place and format text on the Flash Stage
Define font embedding for an SWF file
Create a shape tween to animate a change in object color
Scale and adjust content to match different file dimensions

Ocean Animation

Your client, Bay Ocean Preserve, wants to add an interactive animation to the kids' side of its Web site. As part of the Animate development team, your job is to build the required animations, and then add the necessary controls to make the buttons function as expected.

This project incorporates the following skills:

- ❑ Importing and managing artwork from Adobe Photoshop
- ❑ Importing symbols from external Animate file libraries
- ❑ Understanding the different types of Animate symbols
- ❑ Building frame-by-frame animations
- ❑ Creating motion tweens to animate various object properties
- ❑ Animating in three dimensions
- ❑ Preparing symbol instances for scripting
- ❑ Adding basic button controls to instances on the Stage

Project Meeting

client comments

Our organization focuses on natural resource conservation and habitat preservation on the central California coast. This area is home to a number of endangered species, and we work to educate people about observing those creatures without interacting and interfering with them.

We've been told that some kind of interactivity will be an important part of capturing a younger audience. Although we think cartoon fish dancing across the screen would minimize the seriousness of our message, we understand that we have to do something to make the site more interesting for children.

We were thinking about an "aquarium" screen saver we used to have, and we thought that kind of thing would be a good balance between user interactivity and pointless arcade games.

art director comments

Since the client clearly wants to avoid a cartoon look, I had the staff artist create some fish and other illustrations that are fairly realistic. I also found a good photo of a turtle that will work well with the other elements.

One of the animations — the swaying kelp forest — should play constantly, and will not be controlled by buttons.

Two animations will be controlled by the buttons. First, a fish hiding in a cave will blow bubbles. Second, a turtle will swim across the scene and get bigger, to create the effect of swimming closer.

One other animation — the organization's logo — will play as soon as the file opens, and then not again until the entire file is reset.

The programming for this isn't very complicated, so you should be able to create it with Animate's built-in Code Snippets.

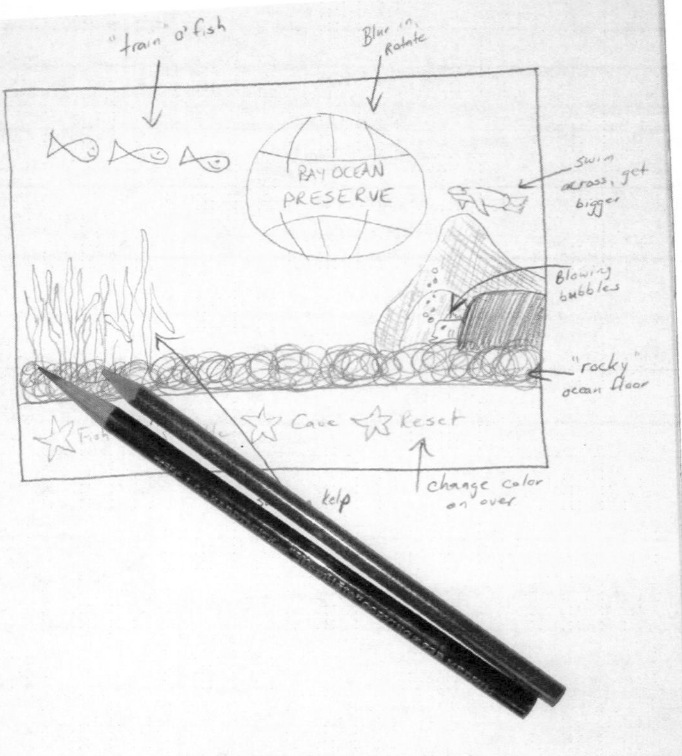

project objectives

To complete this project, you will:

- ❑ Create symbols from imported Photoshop artwork
- ❑ Import symbols from other Animate files
- ❑ Place and manage instances of symbols on the Stage, and control the visual properties of those symbols
- ❑ Control timing using keyframes
- ❑ Create animated movie clip symbols
- ❑ Generate motion tweens to animate changes in object properties
- ❑ Use the Transform panel to numerically control properties at specific points in time
- ❑ Add interactivity to button symbols

Stage 1 Importing Bitmaps and Symbols

In this project, much of the artwork was created in Adobe Photoshop — a common workflow. It's important to understand that artwork from a Photoshop file is imported into Animate as bitmap objects, which are raster images that can result in large file sizes. Fortunately, the Animate symbol infrastructure means that objects in a file's library are downloaded only once; you can use multiple instances of a symbol without increasing overall file size.

You should also keep in mind that the quality of a bitmap object is defined by its resolution. Bitmap objects can typically be reduced in size, but enlarging them much beyond 100% could significantly reduce the image quality.

Finally, it's important to realize that Animate is designed to create files that will be viewed on a digital screen. Animate recognizes the actual number of pixels in a bitmap image rather than the defined pixels per inch (ppi). If you import a 3″ × 3″ bitmap image that is saved at 300 ppi (typical of print-quality images), that image is 900 pixels × 900 pixels high. In Animate, the image is still 900 pixels × 900 pixels, but those same pixels occupy 12.5″ at a typical screen resolution of 72 ppi.

Import Adobe Photoshop Artwork

Importing a Photoshop file to the Animate Stage is very similar to importing an Illustrator file. Because of the different nature of the two applications, however, you have fewer options when you work with Photoshop files.

Note:

*Learn more about Adobe Photoshop in the companion book of this series, **Adobe Photoshop CC: The Professional Portfolio**.*

1. **Download `Aquarium_Web16_RF.zip` from the Student Files Web page.**

2. **Expand the ZIP archive in your WIP folder (Macintosh) or copy the archive contents into your WIP folder (Windows).**

   This results in a folder named **Aquarium**, which contains the files you need for this project. You should also use this folder to save the files you create in this project.

3. **In Animate, create a new Animate document for ActionScript 3.0.**

   Use the default settings for the new file.

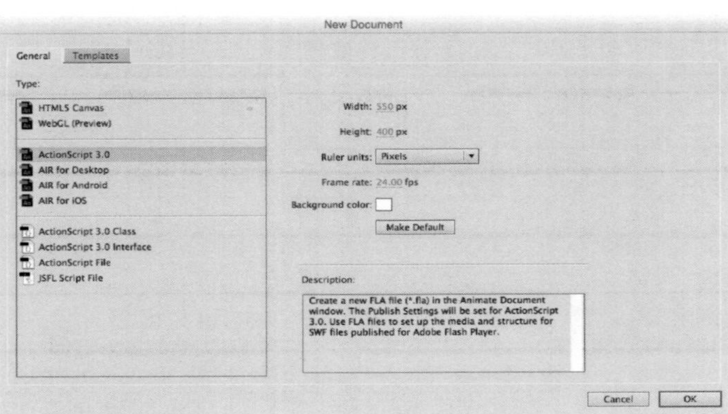

4. **Choose File>Save. Save the file in your WIP>Aquarium folder as an Animate file named `ocean.fla`.**

5. **Choose File>Import>Import to Stage. Navigate to the file `ocean.psd` in your WIP>Aquarium folder and click Open/Import.**

6. **If the button at the bottom of the resulting dialog box shows "Hide Advanced Options," click that button to show only the basic import options. Review the available options.**

   As with Illustrator, Animate recognizes individual layers in the native Photoshop file; objects on each individual layer will be imported as separate bitmap objects. Most of the options in this dialog box are the same as those for importing an Illustrator file.

7. **Check the Place Objects at Original Position and Set Stage Size... options, then click OK to complete the import process.**

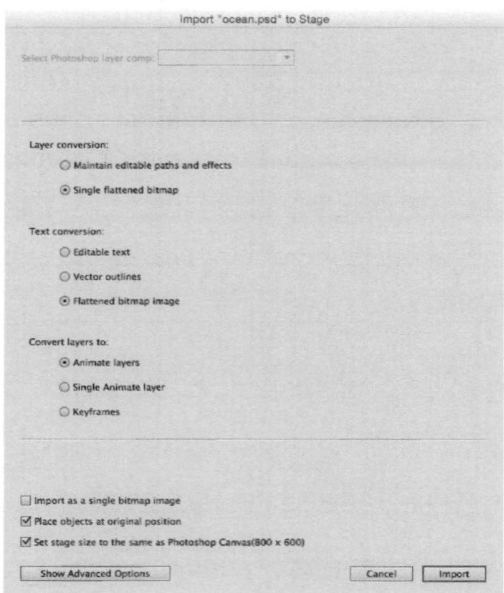

Note:

The Photoshop document area is called the canvas; the Illustrator document area is an artboard.

Note:

When artwork is created in Photoshop, each object that needs to be managed separately in Animate should be created on a separate Photoshop layer.

8. **Expand the Timeline panel until you can see all layers in the file, then choose View>Magnification>Fit in Window.**

   Layers and layer groups in the Photoshop file were imported as separate Animate layers and layer groups, as you defined in the Import to Stage dialog box. The default Layer 1 from the original file is also maintained at the bottom of the layer stack.

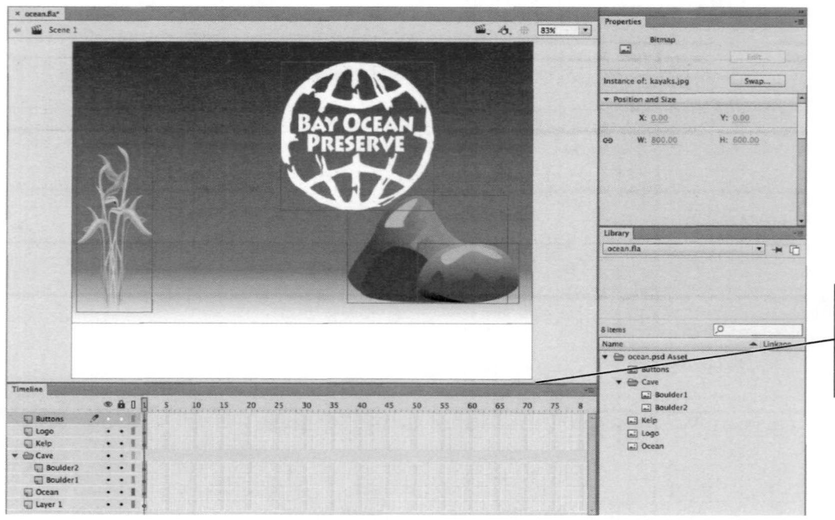

Click this line and drag up to make the panel higher (and show more layers).

9. **Select Layer 1 and click the Delete button at the bottom of the Timeline panel.**

10. **Save the file and continue to the next exercise.**

Copy Assets from External Libraries

When objects already exist in an Animate file, it is a fairly simple process to copy them from one file to another. If both files are open, you can simply copy a symbol instance from the Stage of one file and paste it into the Stage of the other file; the necessary assets are automatically pasted into the library of the second file. You can also simply open the Library panel of an external file, which enables you to access the assets in that library without opening the second file's Stage.

1. **With `ocean.fla` open, choose File>Open. Navigate to `creatures.fla` (in the WIP>Aquarium folder) and click Open.**

   When more than one file is open, each file is represented by a tab at the top of the document window. You can click any document tab to make that file active.

> *Note:*
>
> *Press Shift to select multiple consecutive items in a dialog box or panel. Press Command/Control to select multiple non-contiguous items.*

2. **In the Library panel, Shift-click to select the Fish and Turtle items in the library. Control/right-click one of the selected items and choose Copy from the contextual menu.**

The document tabs show that there are two open files.

The Library panel shows the library for the currently active file.

3. **Click the Library menu at the top of the Library panel and choose ocean.fla to display that file's library.**

Use this menu to switch between the libraries of all open files.

4. **Control/right-click the empty area at the bottom of the Library panel (below the existing assets) and choose Paste from the contextual menu.**

   The Air bitmap item is also pasted because it is used in the Fish movie clip.

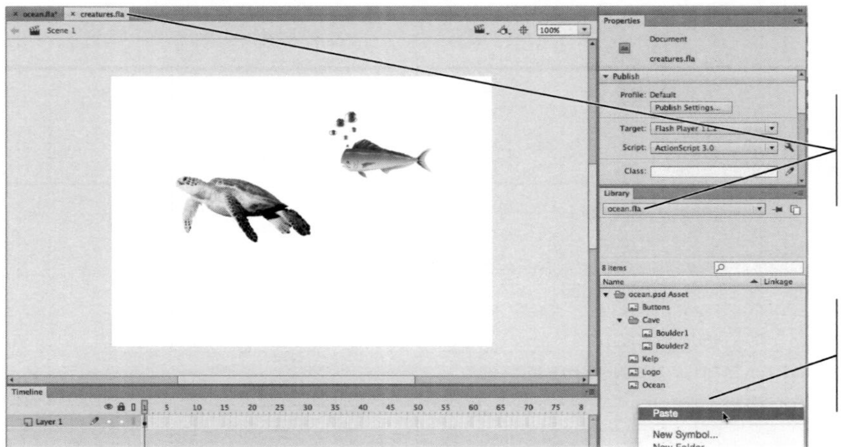

Although creatures.fla is active, the Library panel now shows the library of the ocean.fla file.

Control/right-click the empty area at the bottom of the Library panel to paste the copied items.

5. **Click the Close button on the creatures.fla document tab to close that file.**

   None of the pasted symbols is added to the Stage; they are only placed in the ocean.fla file's library.

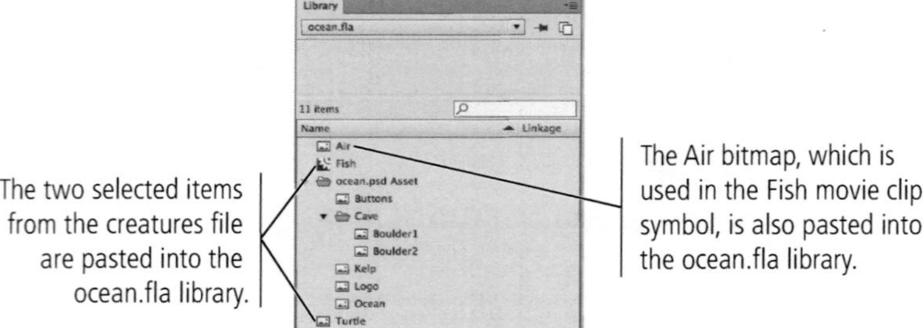

6. **With `ocean.fla` still open, choose File>Import>Open External Library.**

7. **Select `buttons.fla` (in the WIP>Aquarium folder) and click Open.**

   You can use this option to open the library of another file without opening the external FLA file. The external library opens as a separate panel; the file name is included in the panel tab.

> *Note:*
>
> *The keyboard command for opening an external library is Command/ Control-Shift-O.*

8. **Shift-click the Reset, Showcave, and Showturtle button symbols.**

9. **Click any of the selected items and drag to the ocean.fla Library panel.**

   The files don't disappear from the external library; they're simply duplicated in the ocean.fla Library panel. The Starfish bitmap object is also copied because it is used in the four button symbols.

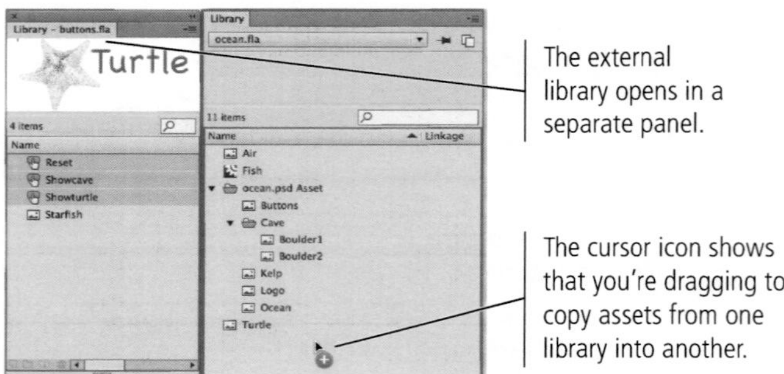

The cursor icon shows that you're dragging to copy assets from one library into another.

10. **Click the Close button of the buttons.fla Library panel to close the external file's library.**

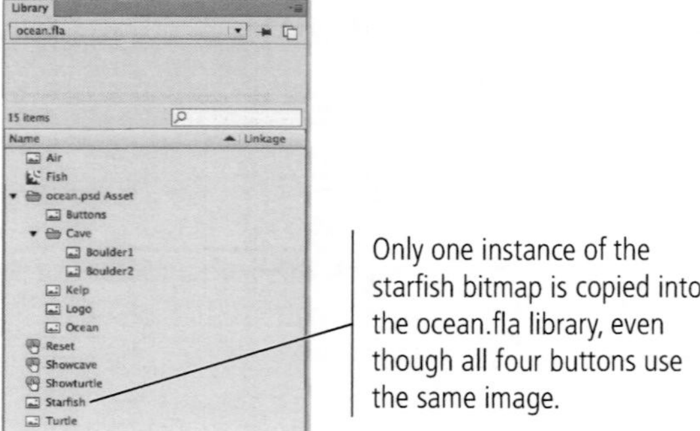

Only one instance of the starfish bitmap is copied into the ocean.fla library, even though all four buttons use the same image.

11. **Save the ocean.fla file and continue to the next exercise.**

Align Objects on the Stage

The four buttons for this project need to be placed across the bottom of the Stage, aligned to appear equally distributed across the Stage area. The Align panel makes it very easy to position multiple selected objects relative to one another.

1. **With `ocean.fla` open, select the Buttons layer to make it active.**

2. **Drag instances of the three button symbols to the middle of the Stage, arranged so they do not overlap.**

3. **Select the placed Showturtle button instance. Using the Properties panel, position the instance at X: `40`, Y: `510`.**

BAY OCEAN PRESERVE
Turtle
Reset
Turtle
Place all three button symbols anywhere on the Stage.
Use the Properties panel to precisely position the Showturtle button instance.

4. **Using the Selection tool, Shift-click to select all three button instances on the Stage.**

5. **In the Align panel, turn off the Align To Stage option and then click the Align Bottom Edge button.**

   The Align options position objects based on the selected edge. Because you used the Align Bottom Edge button, the selected objects are all moved to the bottom edge of the bottommost object in the selection.

BAY OCEAN PRESERVE
Turtle
Reset
Cave
Align Bottom Edge button
Align To Stage should not be checked.
The selected objects move to align with the bottom edge of the bottommost selected object.

6. **Select only the Reset button and set the X position to `585`.**

7. **Select the three placed button instances.**

8. **In the Align panel, click the Space Evenly Horizontally button.**

   This option calculates the overall space across the selection, then shifts the objects so that the same amount of space appears between each object in the selection. Because the buttons are different widths, this option creates a better result than the distribution options.

9. **Save the file and continue to the next exercise.**

Transform Symbols and Instances

Placed instances of a symbol are unique objects, which means they can be manipulated separately without affecting other instances of the symbol. Each instance remains linked to the primary symbol, however, so transforming the actual symbol affects all placed instances of that symbol.

1. **With `ocean.fla` open, use the Selection tool to select the Kelp object on the stage. Press the F8 key to convert the object to a symbol.**

   Remember, you can also Control/right-click the object on the Stage and choose Convert to Symbol from the contextual menu.

2. **Define the following settings in the Convert to Symbol dialog box:**

   Name: `Seaweed`

   Type: **Movie Clip**

   Registration: **Bottom center**

   Remember, the name of the actual symbol is only used internally while you develop the file. The specific names of instances on the Stage are more important, as you will see later when you add ActionScript to control the various pieces of this movie.

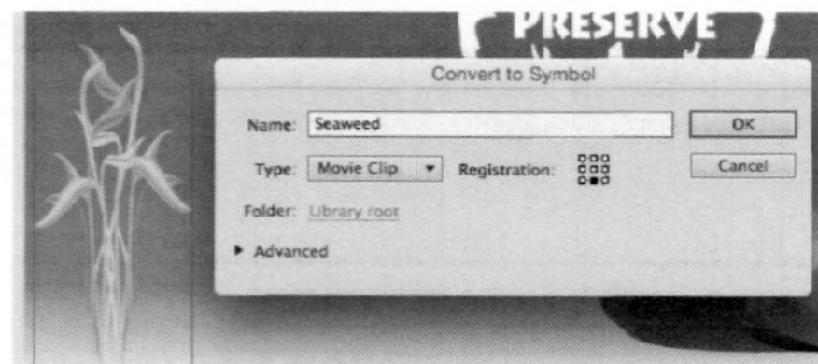

3. **Click OK to create the new symbol.**

The Properties panel now shows that the selected object is an instance of the Seaweed symbol, which has been added to the Library panel.

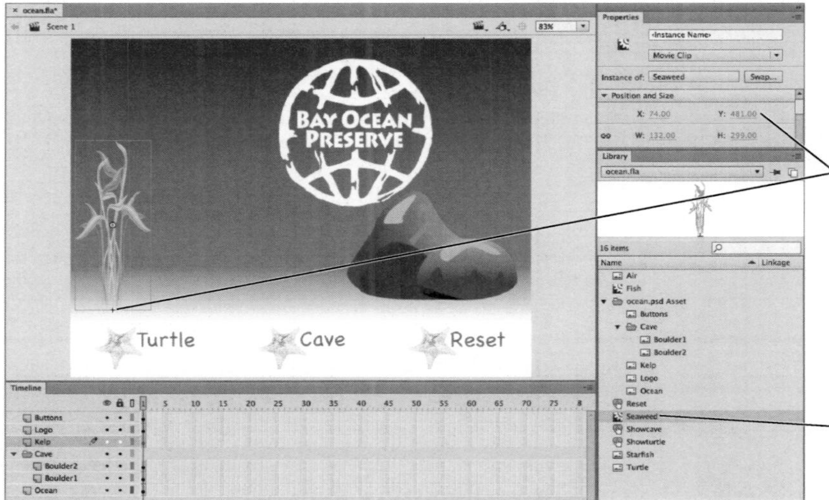

4. **Using the Selection tool, Option/Alt-click the existing instance and drag right to clone a second instance of the Seaweed symbol.**

5. **Repeat Step 4 to clone one more instance.**

6. **Deselect everything on the Stage. Choose the Free Transform tool in the Tools panel and click the middle Seaweed instance to select it.**

The Free Transform tool is used to change the size or shape of an object. Remember, all transformations are applied around the transformation point.

Note:

If the Free Transform tool is active when you click and drag to move an object, make sure you don't click the object's transformation point before you drag the object.

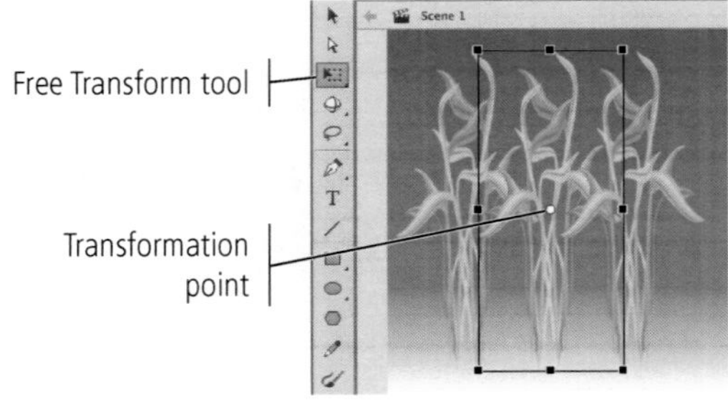

7. **Drag the transformation point until it snaps to the bottom-center bounding box handle.**

8. **Click the top-center bounding box handle and drag down to make the selected instance shorter.**

Transformations applied to individual instances have no effect on the original symbol or on other placed instances.

Note:

You can also press Option/Alt and drag a center handle to transform the object around the opposite bounding-box handle, without moving the transformation point.

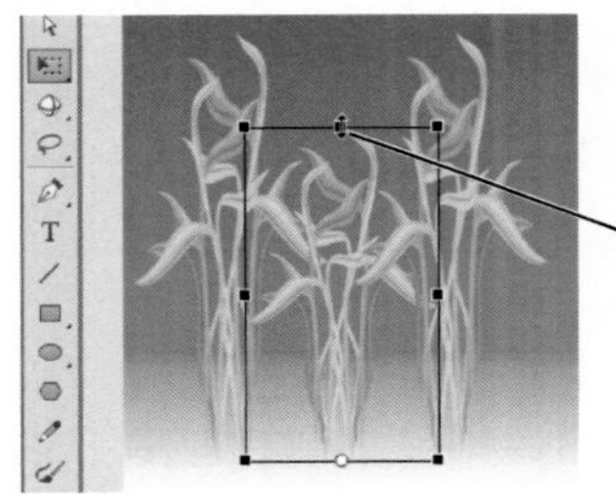

Because the bottom-center is the transformation point, dragging the top-center handle makes the instance shorter without moving the bottom of the instance.

9. **In the Library panel, double-click the Seaweed symbol icon to enter into the symbol.**

   The crosshairs in the bottom center identify the **symbol registration point**, or the location of X:0, Y:0 for placed instances; all measurements for placed instances begin at this location.

   Even though you changed the transformation point of one placed instance on the main Stage, the transformation point remains in the center of the object on the symbol Stage. The transformation point is specific to each placed object or instance.

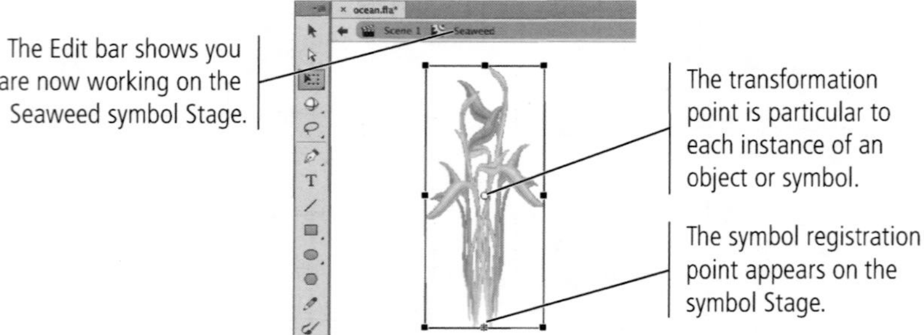

10. **With the Free Transform tool still selected, drag the transformation point until it snaps to the bottom-center bounding box handle of the object on the symbol's Stage.**

11. **Show the Transform panel (Window>Transform).**

12. **In the Transform panel, make sure the Link icon is not active and then change the Scale Height value to 80%.**

   If the Link icon shows two solid chain links, changing the height of the object would proportionally affect the width of the object (and vice versa). Because you only want to change the height, you need to break the Link icon.

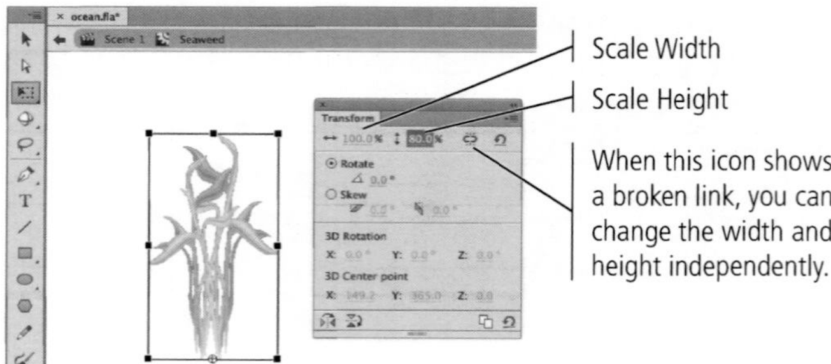

Scale Width
Scale Height
When this icon shows a broken link, you can change the width and height independently.

13. **In the Edit bar, click Scene 1 to return to the main Stage.**

   When you modify the original symbol, the changes ripple through all placed instances.

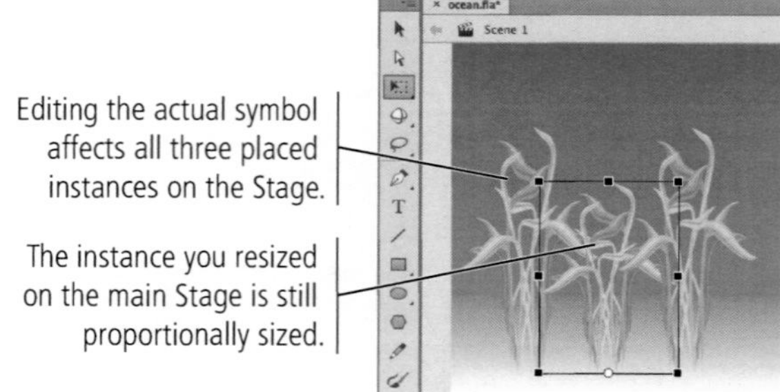

Editing the actual symbol affects all three placed instances on the Stage.
The instance you resized on the main Stage is still proportionally sized.

14. **Save the file and continue to the next exercise.**

Create a Movie Clip from Objects on Different Layers

When you imported the project artwork, the two pieces of the cave were created on separate layers — in a layer group — because you need to place a fish inside the cave, stacked between the two boulders. If the two boulders had existed on a single layer, the result would have been a single bitmap object, which could not be broken apart in Animate to accomplish the desired effect.

1. **With `ocean.fla` open, use the Selection tool to click both boulders in the right side of the Stage.**

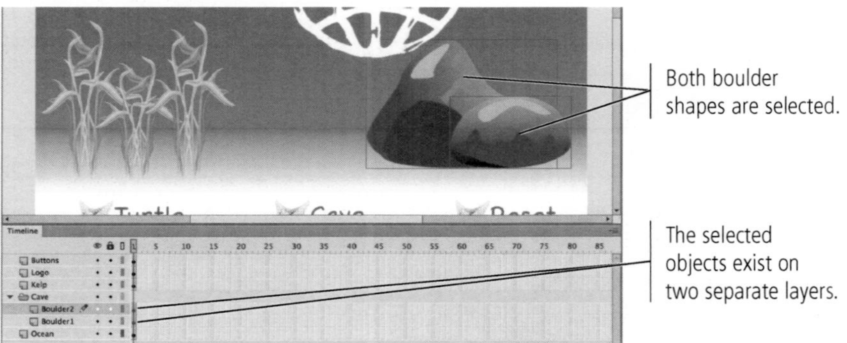

Both boulder shapes are selected.

The selected objects exist on two separate layers.

> ***Note:***
>
> *Remember, the symbol registration point marks the location of the defined X and Y values on the main Stage.*

2. **Press the F8 key to convert the two selected objects to a symbol.**

3. **Define the following settings in the Convert to Symbol dialog box:**

Name:	`cave`
Type:	**Movie Clip**
Registration:	**Bottom right**

4. **Click OK to create the new symbol.**

   The original selected objects were on two separate layers. After converting those objects into a single symbol, the new symbol instance appears on the higher layer in the layer stack (in this case, the Boulder2 layer).

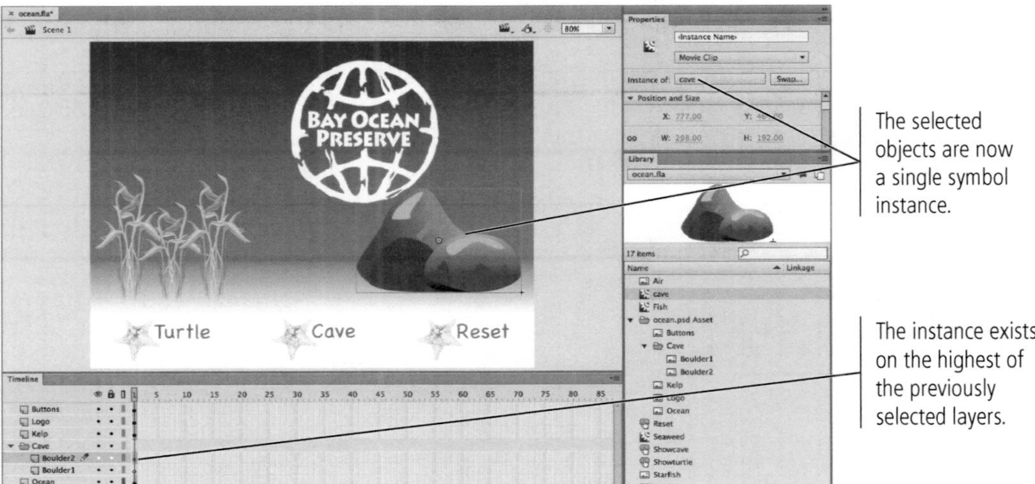

The selected objects are now a single symbol instance.

The instance exists on the highest of the previously selected layers.

5. **In the Timeline panel, change the Boulder2 layer name to `Cave`.**

6. **Drag the Cave layer above the Cave layer group.**

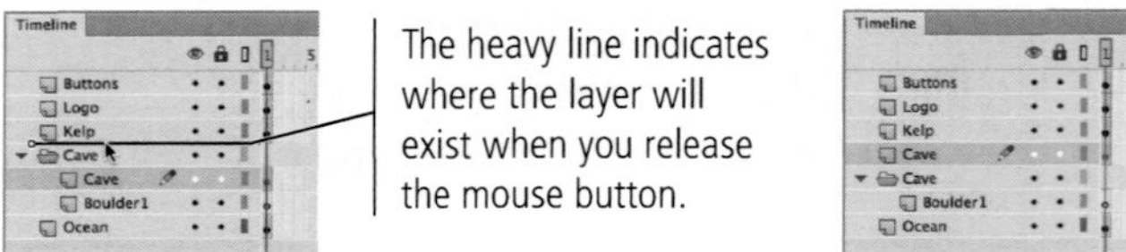

The heavy line indicates where the layer will exist when you release the mouse button.

7. **Select the Cave layer group (not the layer) and then click the Delete button at the bottom of the Timeline panel.**

8. **Read the resulting message, then click Yes.**

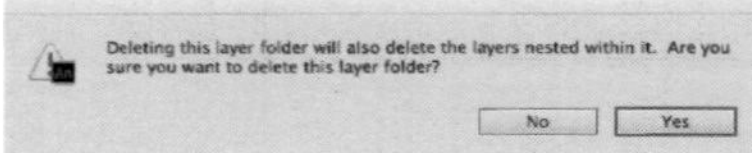

Although Steps 5–8 are not technically necessary, it is a good idea to keep your files clean by deleting unnecessary layers.

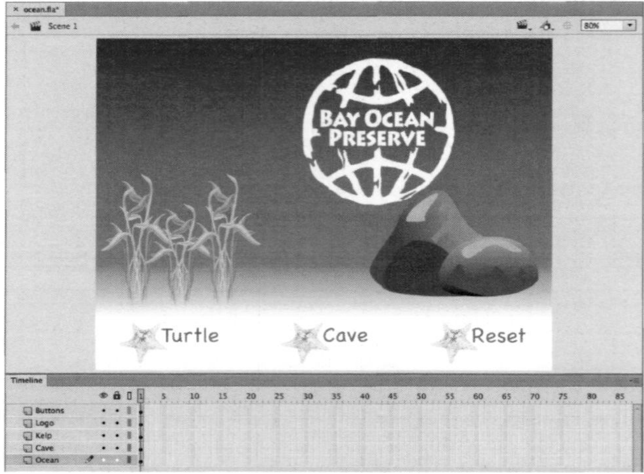

9. **Select the cave instance on the Stage. In the Properties panel, change the X position of the selected instance to `850`.**

   If the cave objects had been placed in the correct position in the Photoshop file, the imported bitmap objects would have been clipped at the Stage edge. If you create artwork in Photoshop, make sure pieces are entirely inside the Canvas edge if you don't want them clipped when they are imported into Animate.

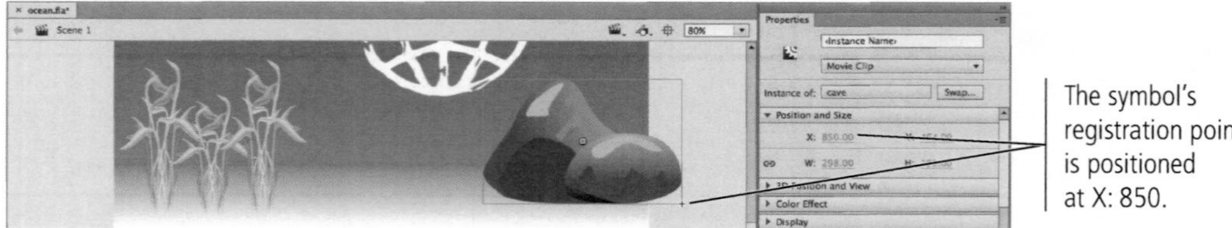

10. **Double-click the cave movie clip instance on the Stage to edit the symbol in place on the Stage.**

    Although this movie clip was created based on a layer group in the imported artwork, the layers that made up the group are not maintained in the symbol timeline.

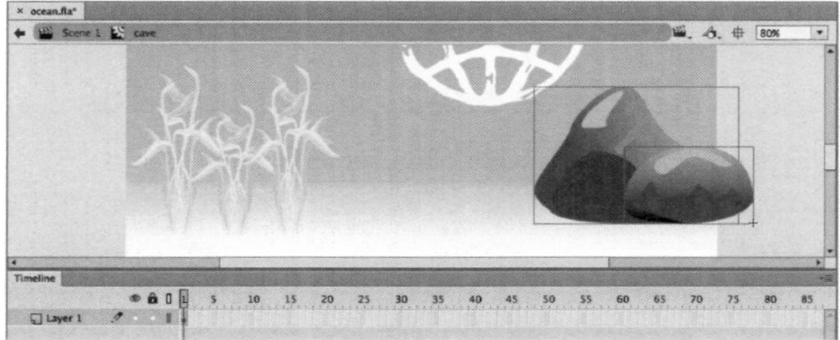

11. **Drag an instance of the Fish movie clip symbol onto the Stage, so only the head appears to the left of the front rock**

12. **With the Fish instance still selected, choose Modify>Arrange>Send Backward.**

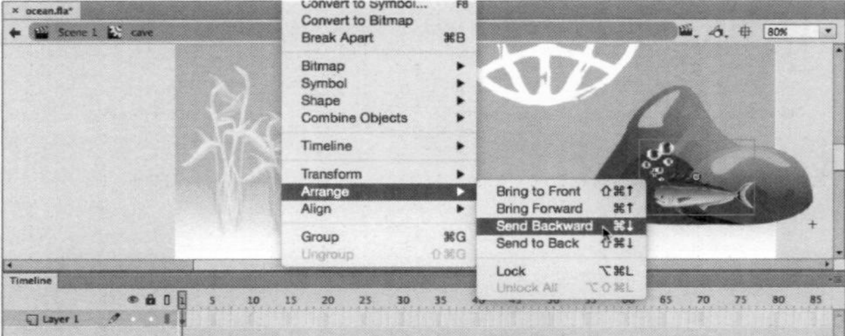

    This command moves the selected object back one step in the stacking order. The Fish instance now appears between the two boulder objects that comprise the cave symbol.

    In the second stage of this project, you will learn a number of techniques for creating animations — including making this fish blow bubbles that rise up and off the Stage.

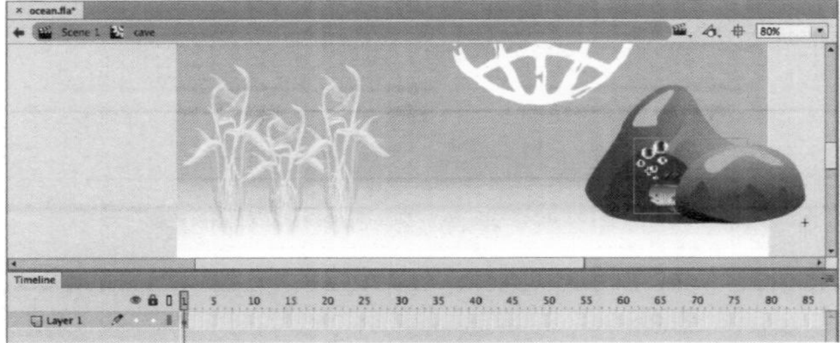

13. **Click Scene 1 in the Edit bar to return to the main Stage.**

14. **Save the file and continue to the next exercise.**

Organize Your Library with Folders

Folders make it easy to organize the assets that make up a movie, and easy to find the assets you need.

1. **With ocean.fla open, click the Library panel to activate it.**

2. **In the Library panel, change the name of the ocean.psd Assets folder to Bitmaps.**

   Changing a library folder name has no effect on placed instances of the symbols inside that folder.

3. **Select the two bitmap objects in the nested Cave folder and move them into the first-level Bitmaps folder.**

   Moving symbols to a new location in the Library panel has no effect on placed instances of the moved symbols.

4. **Select the three bitmap objects in the first level of the library and drag them into the Bitmaps folder.**

5. **Delete the nested Cave folder from the Bitmaps folder.**

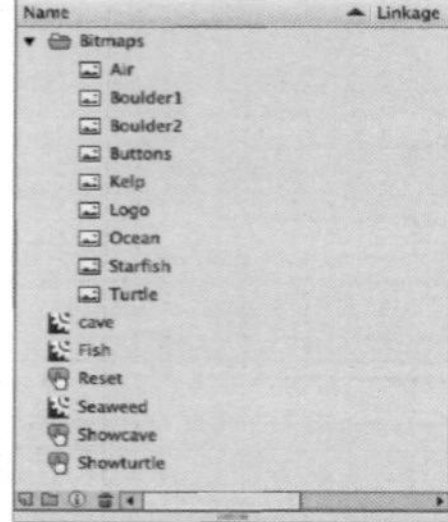

6. **Click the New Folder button at the bottom of the Library panel.**

   New folders are created at the same nesting level as the current selection. (If a nested symbol is already selected and you want to create a new folder at the first level of the library, click the empty area at the bottom of the panel to deselect any files before clicking the New Folder button.)

7. **Change the name of the new folder to Movie Clips, then drag the three movie clip symbols from the main level of the Library into the Movie Clips folder.**

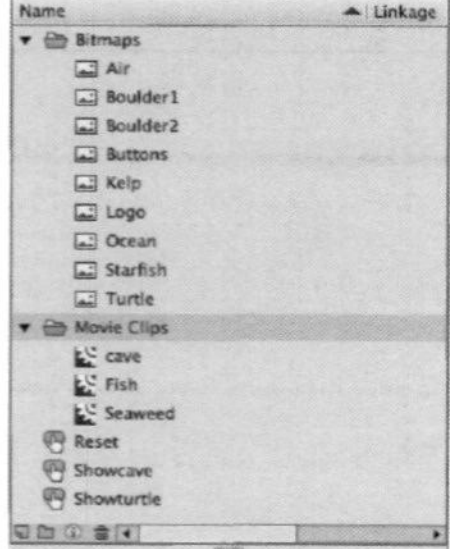

Note:

In this case, we're using simple names for the symbol folders. The names you assign to symbol (or layer) folders aren't functional; they just need to make sense to you (or other people working with your files).

8. **Create a new folder named Buttons at the first level of the library. Drag the three button symbols into the new folder.**

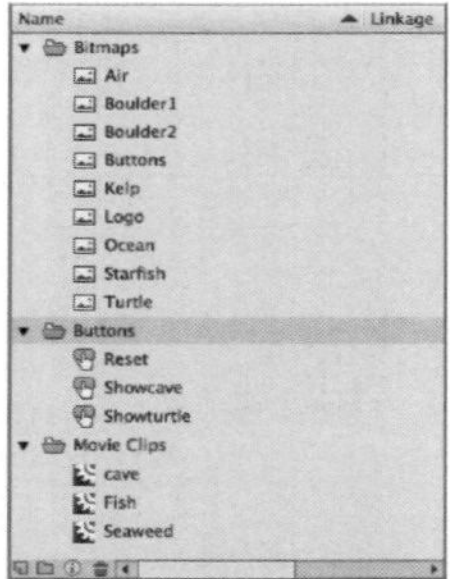

8. **Collapse the Bitmaps and Buttons folders in the Library panel**

9. **Save the file, and then continue to the next stage of the project.**

Stage 2 Animating Symbols

In Project 3: Talking Kiosk Interface, you created simple animation by swapping symbols at specific points in time; although nothing technically changed position, replacing one object with another is still considered "animation." In Project 4: Animated Internet Ads, you used classic tweening to move objects across the Stage; this technique creates smooth motion by defining the start point keyframe, end point keyframe, and path shape. In this project, you learn several different techniques for creating various types of animation, including animating specific properties of an object.

Create a Basic Frame Animation in a Movie Clip Symbol

Movie clips are animated symbols that reside on a single frame of the timeline. In its simplest form, a movie clip can include a solitary fish swimming across the ocean; at its most complex, a movie clip can include fully interactive elements in a video game. In this exercise, you create the most basic type of animation — a frame animation.

1. **With ocean.fla open, choose the Selection tool and make sure nothing is selected on the Stage.**

2. **In the Properties panel, change the FPS hot text to 15 frames per second.**

   Using 15 fps for a movie — especially one that's going to run on the Web — provides decent quality. The default 24 fps is not necessary for standard computer viewing and could create files that require too much processing power for some users.

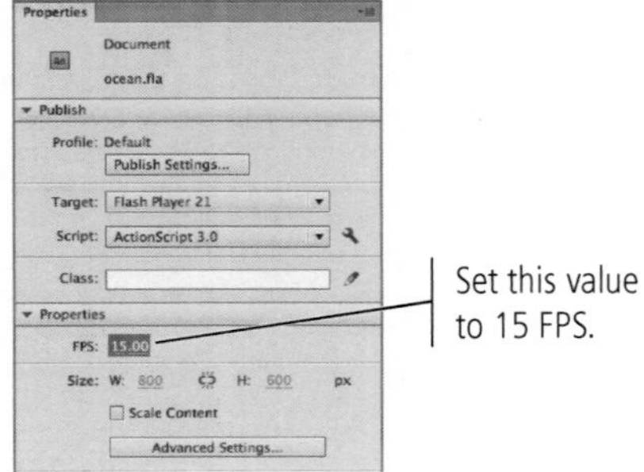

3. **On the Stage, double-click the cave symbol instance to enter into the symbol Stage (edit in place).**

4. **Double-click the placed Fish instance to enter into the nested symbol.**

   You are going to move only the bubbles, which are an instance of the Air bitmap object that is placed inside the Fish symbol. You are editing in place on the main Stage so that you can see when the bubbles are entirely outside the Stage area.

5. **In the timeline, click Frame 7 to select it, then press the F6 key to insert a new keyframe.**

   You can also Control/right-click a frame in the timeline and choose Insert Keyframe from the contextual menu, or choose Insert>Timeline> Keyframe.

   As you already know, **keyframes** are special frames where something happens to an object: it appears or disappears, changes size, moves to another position, changes color, and so on. When you add a new keyframe, regular frames are automatically added immediately before the previous keyframe; objects on the preceding keyframe will remain in place until the playhead reaches the new keyframe.

Note:

If you change an object on a regular frame in the middle of a movie, all frames between the two surrounding keyframes (or the nearest preceding keyframe and the final frame) reflect that change.

You are working on the Fish symbol, which is nested inside the cave symbol.
When you add a keyframe, regular frames are automatically added directly before it.
Scene 1
cave
Fish
BAY OCEAN
PRESERVE

6. **With Frame 7 selected in the timeline, select only the air bubbles graphic object. Using the Selection tool, drag to reposition that graphic directly above the original position.**

   When you create or select a keyframe, all objects on that keyframe are automatically selected. You can Shift-click the fish to deselect that object, leaving only the air bubbles object selected.

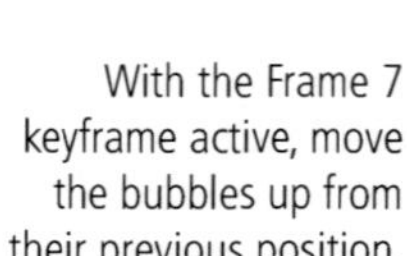

With the Frame 7 keyframe active, move the bubbles up from their previous position.

7. **Repeat Steps 5–6 six more times, adding a new keyframe every seven frames and moving the air bubbles up until they are outside the top edge of the Stage.**

   Because you're editing the symbol in place, you can see how far you need to move the bubbles until they are outside the Stage area. If you edited this symbol on its own Stage, you would have to guess about positioning, return to the main Stage to test your guess, return to the symbol to add more frames, return to the main Stage to test again, and so on.

At Frame 49, the bubbles are entirely off the Stage.

8. **Select Frame 56 on the timeline and press F5 to add a regular frame.**

   This regular frame at Frame 56 extends the timeline by half a second, which prevents the bubbles from reappearing in the fish's mouth (Frame 1) immediately after they move past the top of the Stage (Frame 49).

9. **Click the playhead above the timeline and drag left and right.**

   Scrubbing the playhead allows you to look at specific sections of a movie over time, so you can see if they work the way you expect.

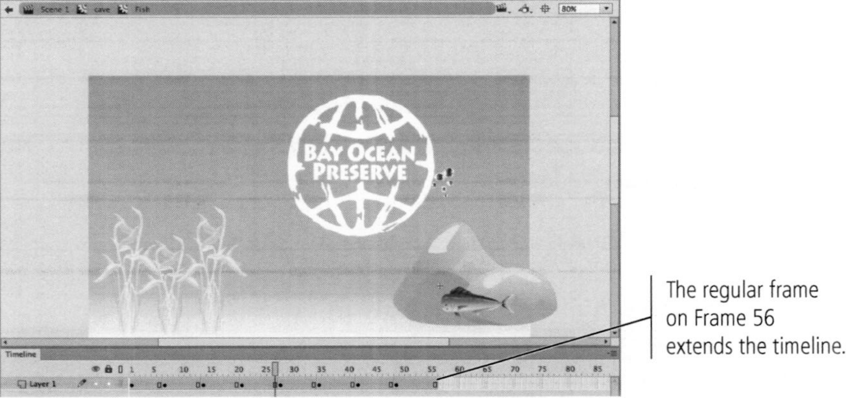

The regular frame on Frame 56 extends the timeline.

10. **Click Scene 1 in the Edit bar to return to the main Stage.**

11. **Press Command-Return/Control-Enter to test the movie.**

    You can see the air bubbles moving up in a continuous loop. Even though the primary Stage has only one frame, the movie clip's timeline continues to play as long as the movie remains open.

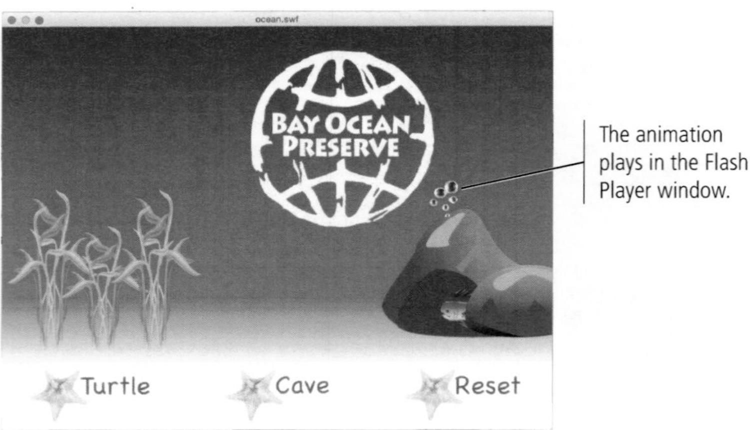

The animation plays in the Flash Player window.

> *Note:*
>
> *Remember from Project 3: Animated Internet Ads, you can't preview the animation inside a movie clip on the main Stage. You have to test the file in the Animate Player window to see the animation.*

12. **Close the Animate Player window and return to Animate.**
13. **Save the file and continue to the next exercise.**

Create a Motion Tween

Creating the appearance of continuous, fluid movement requires a slightly different position or shape (depending on what you are animating) on every frame in an animation. Rather than defining each individual frame manually — which could take days, depending on the length of your animation — you can let Animate define the frames that are in between two keyframes (the tween frames).

Animate incorporates technology that makes it very easy to define smooth animations by simply moving a symbol object around on the Stage.

1. **With ocean.fla open, create a new layer named Turtle immediately above the Logo layer. Select the Turtle layer as the active layer.**
2. **Drag an instance of the turtle bitmap image from the Library panel onto the Stage. Use the Transform panel to scale the instance uniformly to 50%, and then position it beyond the right edge of the Stage, higher than the Cave instance.**

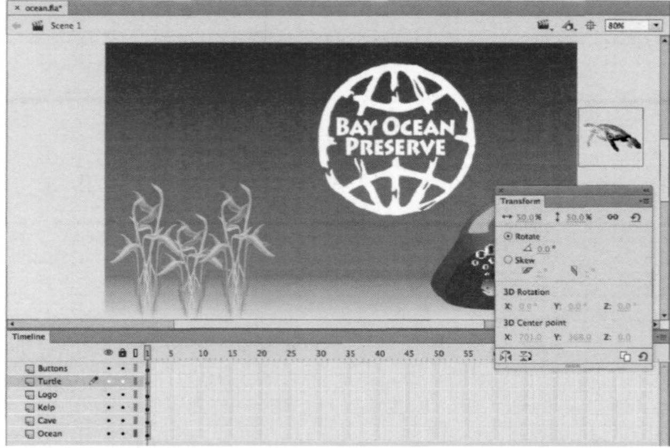

3. **Press the F8 key to convert the turtle instance to a symbol.**

4. **Define the following settings in the Convert to Symbol dialog box:**

   Name: Swimmer

   Type: Movie Clip

   Registration: Center

5. **Click the Folder:Library Root link. Select the Existing Folder radio button and choose Movie Clips in the list. Click Select to return to the Convert to Symbol dialog box, and then click OK to create the new symbol.**

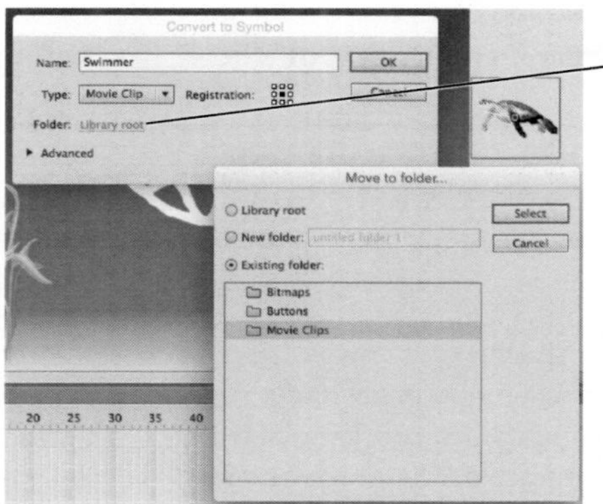

Click this link to open the Move to Folder dialog box.

6. **Click Frame 90 on the Turtle layer and press F5 to add a new regular frame.**

   Other objects on the Stage are not visible because you have not yet extended the other layers' timelines.

Note:

You can also select the frame and then choose Insert>Timeline>Frame.

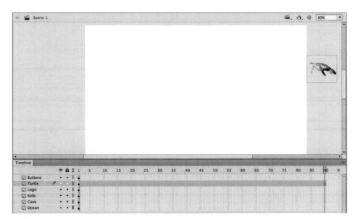

7. **Control/right-click any frame on the Turtle layer and choose Create Motion Tween.**

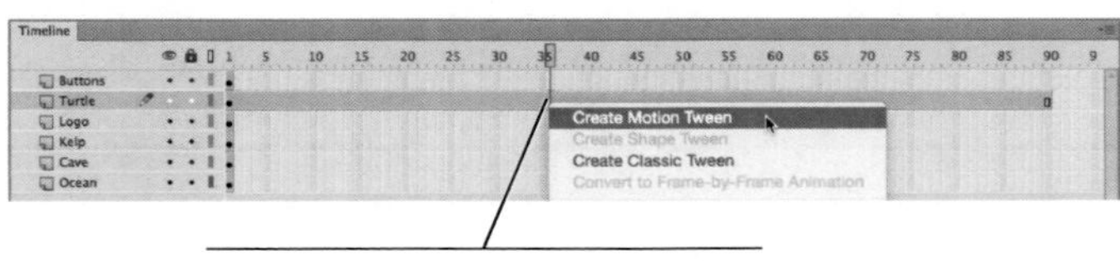

Control/right-click between keyframes to add a motion tween between keyframes (or between a keyframe and the final frame on that layer).

8. **Click Frame 90 of the Turtle layer to select that frame.**

   Animate creates a motion tween in the frames between keyframes. Because Frame 1 is the only keyframe on this layer, the motion tween is created between Frame 1 and the last frame on the layer.

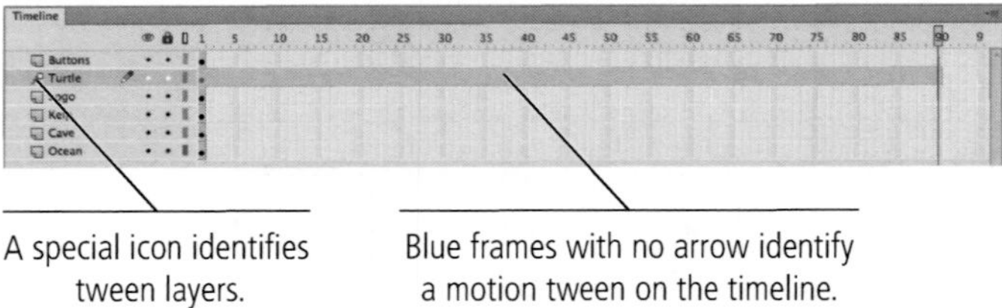

A special icon identifies tween layers.
Blue frames with no arrow identify a motion tween on the timeline.

9. **Select the Turtle image located at the right of the Stage, and drag it off the left edge of the Stage.**

   A new keyframe is automatically added on Frame 90 to mark the new position of the Swimmer symbol. A line — the motion path — shows the path of movement from the symbol's position on Frame 1 to its position on Frame 90. The small dots along the motion path correspond to the frames within the tween.

   When you edit symbols on a tween layer, the position of the playhead is crucial. When you change any property of an object on a tween layer, a property keyframe is automatically inserted at the current frame. Animate generates the tween frames based on the change in the property value between the active keyframe and the previous one.

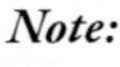

Note:

The motion path line corresponds to the color of the layer containing the path.

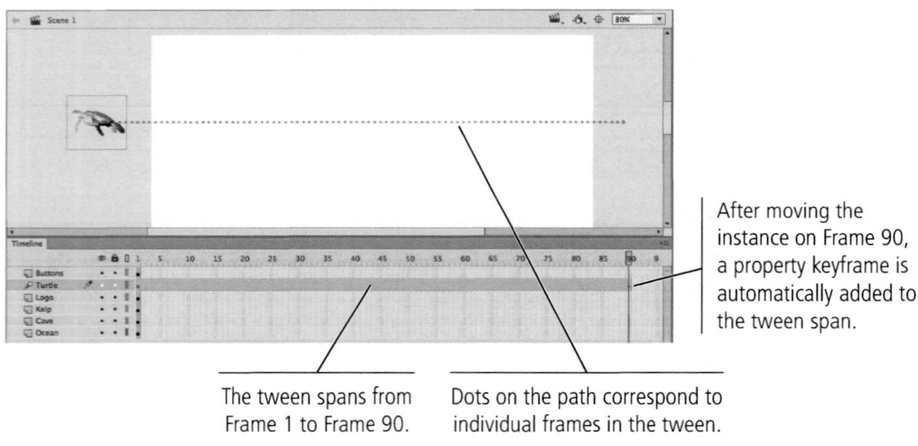

After moving the instance on Frame 90, a property keyframe is automatically added to the tween span.
The tween spans from Frame 1 to Frame 90.
Dots on the path correspond to individual frames in the tween.

10. **Click Frame 1 to move the playhead back to the beginning of the timeline, and then press Return/Enter to play the timeline on the Stage.**

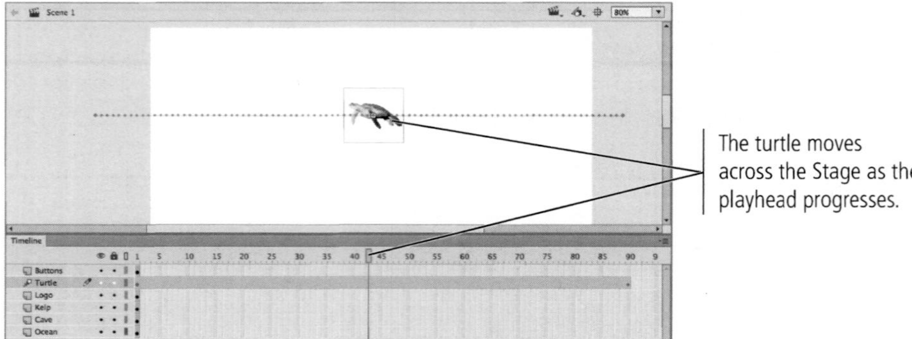

The turtle moves across the Stage as the playhead progresses.

Using Onion Skins

Onion skinning, accessed through a set of buttons at the bottom of the timeline, is a technique that allows you to view more than one frame of an animation at a time.

- Clicking the **Onion Skin** button toggles the feature on or off.
- Clicking the **Onion Skin Outlines** button turns all visible skins to outlines (or wire frames). Combining outlines and onion skins allows you to clearly see the components of your animations without fills or (true-weight) strokes.
- Clicking the **Edit Multiple Frames** button allows you to edit multiple frames at the same time: moving an entire animation, for example, or simply changing single frames within a tween. Without this feature, you would have to move objects one frame at a time. With the feature, you can see previous or subsequent frames, which often helps when you're fine-tuning an animation and you need to move an object in one frame relative to its position in other frames.
- Clicking the **Modify Markers** button allows you to select from a range of predefined skins, or turn onion skinning off. You can choose to have onion skins span two frames, five frames, or all frames. You can also manually adjust the onion skin markers and bypass these presets.

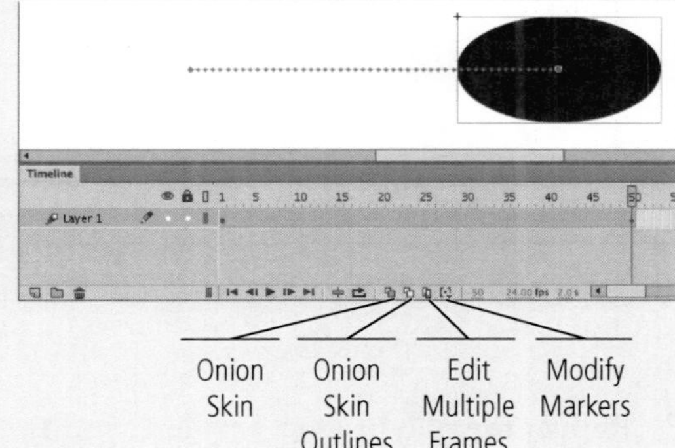

The following illustrations show a simple motion tween that moves the oval symbol across the Stage, from left to right.

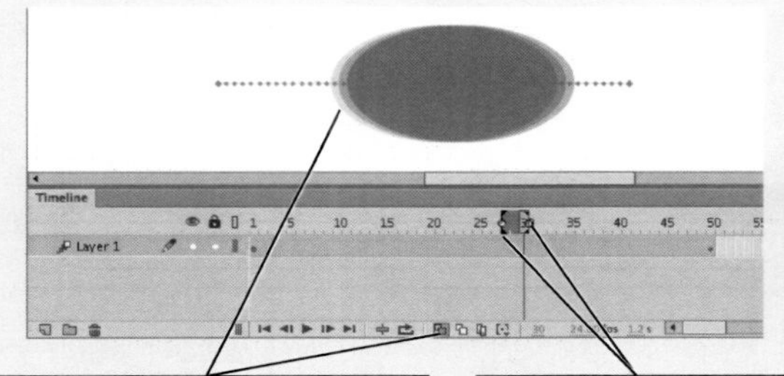

When the Onion Skin feature is active, you can see multiple frames at once (around the playhead).

These markers show the range of frames that is visible on the Stage.

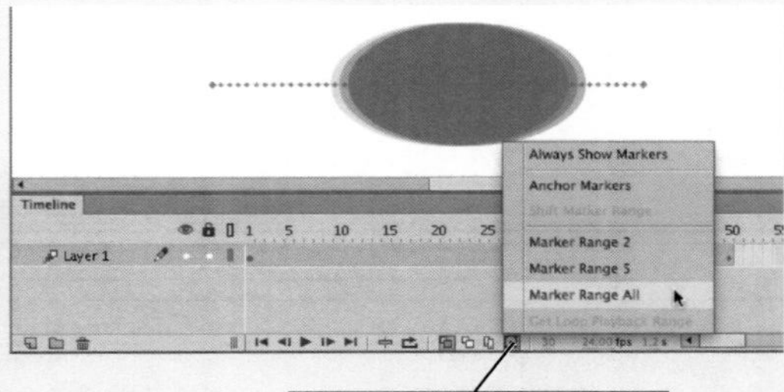

Click the Modify Markers button to show predefined skinning options.

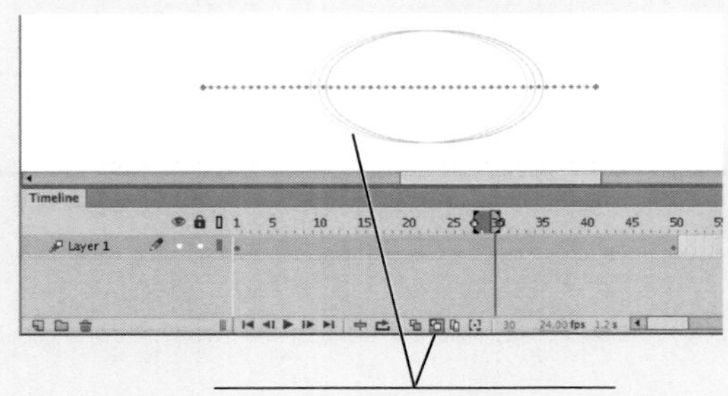

When Onion Skin Outlines is active, frames within the visible onion skin display as wireframes.

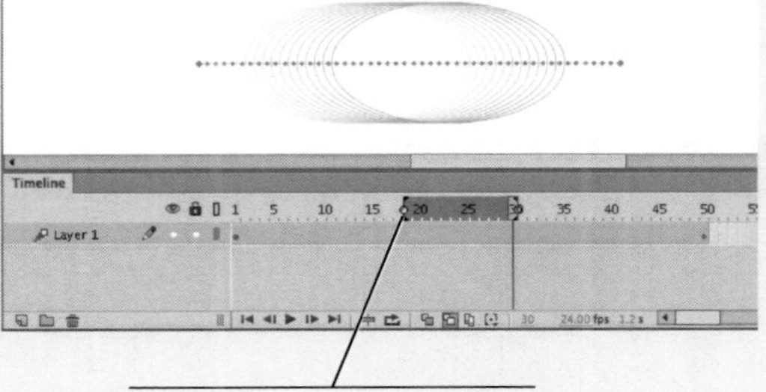

Click an onion skin marker and drag to manually change the number of visible frames.

11. Move the playhead to Frame 90, then click the turtle instance to select it. Scale the selected instance to 200% of its current size. If necessary, use the Selection tool to reposition the resized turtle so that it is entirely outside the edge of the Stage.

The term "motion path" is deceptive because you can animate much more than just motion when you apply a motion tween. By scaling the object on Frame 90, you told Animate to change both the symbol size and position as the timeline progresses.

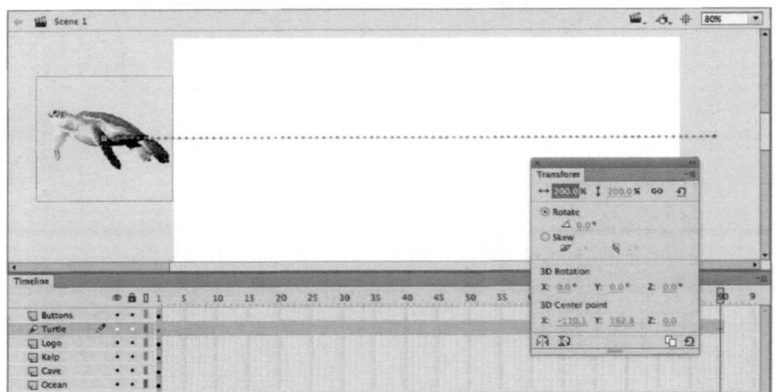

> *Note:*
>
> *Because you scaled the object to 50% before you created the Swimmer symbol, resizing this instance to 200% restores the bitmap to its original size.*

12. Return the playhead to Frame 1, and then press Return/Enter to play the timeline on the Stage.

Now the turtle gets larger as it moves across the stage, creating the effect of the turtle swimming closer. Animate automatically calculates the appropriate position and size of the symbol for all frames between the Frame 1 and Frame 90 keyframes.

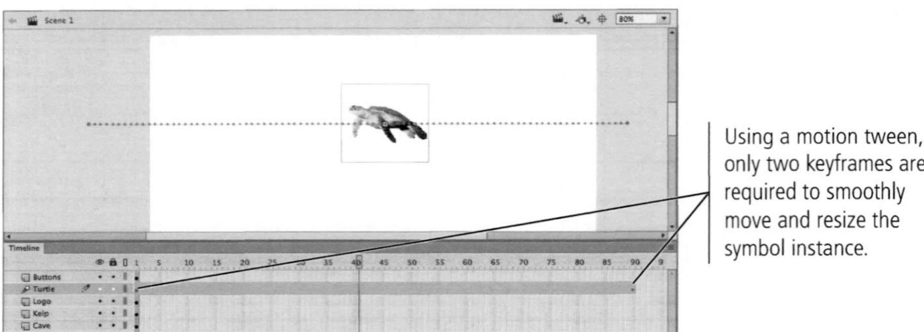

Using a motion tween, only two keyframes are required to smoothly move and resize the symbol instance.

13. Save the file and continue to the next exercise.

Controlling Animation Speed with Easing

Physical objects are subject to physical laws; in the real world, friction, momentum, and mass (among other things) affect how an object moves. A bouncing ball is a good example of these laws. If you throw a ball at the ground, how hard you throw the ball determines its beginning speed. When the ball hits the ground, it transfers energy to the ground and then rebounds, causing the ball to move away from the ground (its first bounce), at which point it is moving slightly faster than when you threw it. As the ball arcs through the bounce it slows down, then starts to drop and hits the ground again, repeating the process in ever-decreasing arcs until it finally gives up its energy and then stops. The speed of the ball changes when the energy behind the ball changes.

In animation terms, these changes in speed are called **easing**. In Animate, you can control easing in the Properties panel when a tween is selected in the timeline.

- Positive Ease values decrease the distance of movement on subsequent frames, causing the object to slow down as it moves through the tween.
- Negative Ease values increase the distance of movement on subsequent frames, causing a moving object to speed up through the tween.
- Ease values closer to 100 or –100 result in greater apparent changes in speed.

The accompanying illustrations show a simple 50-frame motion tween that moves a circle symbol across the Stage.

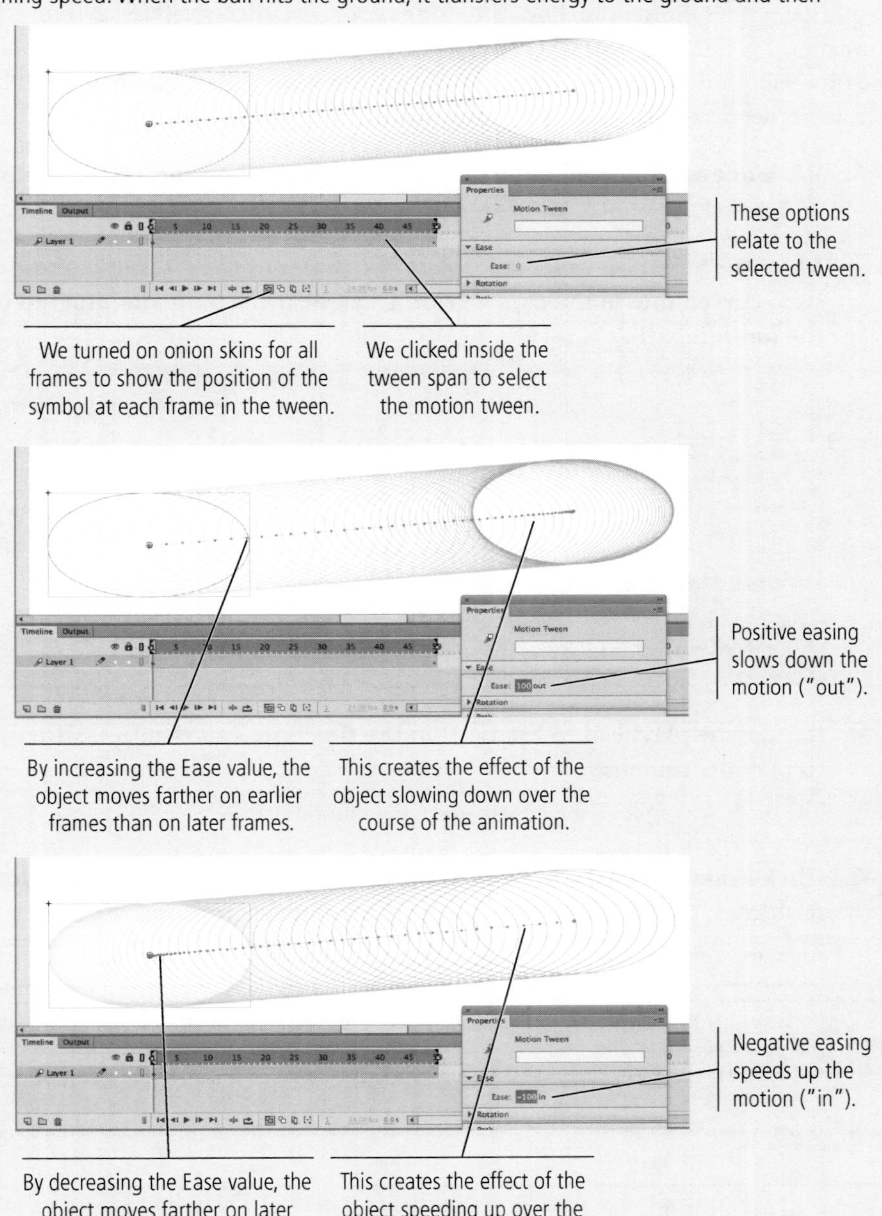

These options relate to the selected tween.
Positive easing slows down the motion ("out").
Negative easing speeds up the motion ("in").

We turned on onion skins for all frames to show the position of the symbol at each frame in the tween.

We clicked inside the tween span to select the motion tween.

By increasing the Ease value, the object moves farther on earlier frames than on later frames.

This creates the effect of the object slowing down over the course of the animation.

By decreasing the Ease value, the object moves farther on later frames than on earlier frames.

This creates the effect of the object speeding up over the course of the animation.

Edit the Shape of the Motion Path

As you learned in the previous exercise, moving an object and changing its size (or other properties) can be as simple as creating a motion tween and adjusting the symbol at specific frames on the timeline. You don't need to manually create keyframes because Animate adds them for you whenever you change the symbol at a particular point in the timeline. In this exercise, you work with the motion path line, which can be edited like any other line in Animate — giving you precise control over the course of a tween.

1. **With `ocean.fla` open, click the Swimmer symbol on the Stage to select it and reveal the related motion path.**

2. **Move the Selection tool cursor near the center of the motion path until you see a curved line in the cursor icon. Click near the path and drag up to bend the motion path.**

   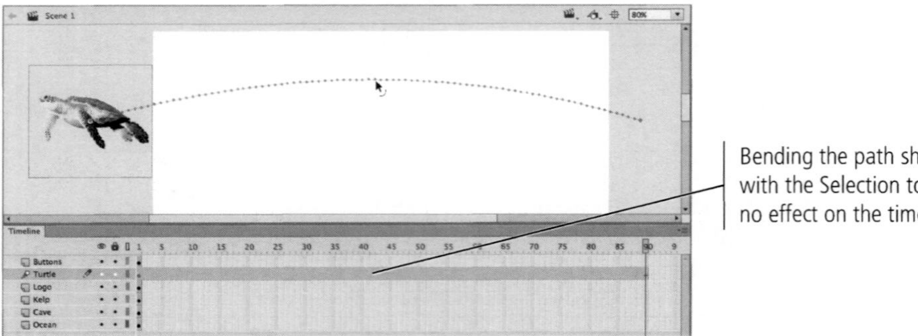

   Bending the path shape with the Selection tool has no effect on the timeline.

3. **Return the playhead to Frame 1 on the timeline, and then press Return/Enter to play the timeline.**

   The turtle now follows the new shape of the motion path.

4. **Click Frame 45 of the Turtle layer to select that frame. Using the Selection tool, click the Swimmer symbol instance and drag down.**

   Animate automatically adds another keyframe to the motion tween to mark the instance's position at that point; the motion path bends again to reflect the defined position for the turtle at the selected frame. Animate adds an anchor point to the path at the new keyframe.

   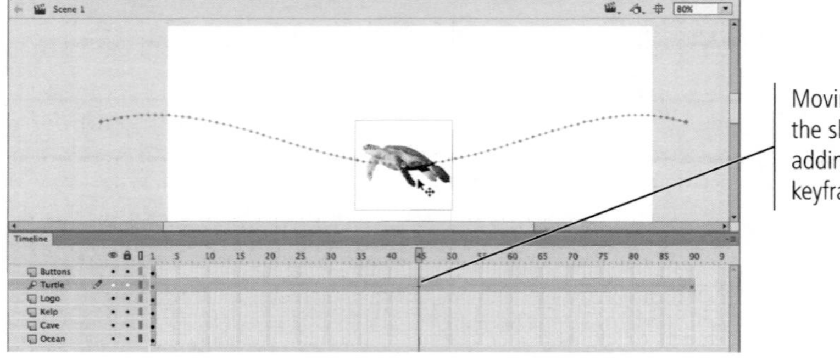

   Moving the object affects the shape of the path by adding a new position keyframe to the timeline.

5. **Choose the Subselection tool in the Tools panel, and then click the new anchor point in the middle of the path.**

   The Selection tool selects entire paths. The Subselection tool selects the anchor points and handles that make up a shape.

6. **Click the selected anchor point and drag left.**

Moving the anchor point changes the shape of the motion path, just as it does when you edit a regular Bézier curve. You can also adjust the handles of the point to change the shape of the motion path between the two connecting anchor points (the selected point and the point at the left end of the path).

When you change the position of the anchor point, notice that the number of dots (representing frames in the tween) on either side of the point remains unchanged. Because you effectively shortened the left half of the path, the same number of frames display over a shorter distance than the same number of frames to the right of the selected point. In effect, you made the turtle swim faster in the first half of the animation (moving a longer distance) and slower in the second half (moving a shorter distance).

> *Note:*
>
> *You can use the Convert Anchor Point tool to convert a smooth anchor point on a motion path to a corner anchor point, allowing you to change directions in the tween.*

Frames to the left of the repositioned keyframe are closely spaced.

The keyframe still exists on Frame 45.

Frames to the right of the repositioned keyframe are more widely spaced.

> *Note:*
>
> *By default, motion paths are created with a non-roving keyframe property, which means the anchor points along the path are attached to specific keyframes in the timeline.*

7. **Control/right-click anywhere within the motion tween (in the timeline), and then choose Motion Path>Switch Keyframes to Roving in the contextual menu.**

When you choose this option, the dots along the path redistribute to equal spacing across the entire length of the tween, and the keyframe from Frame 45 is removed from the layer timeline. The shape of the path is not affected.

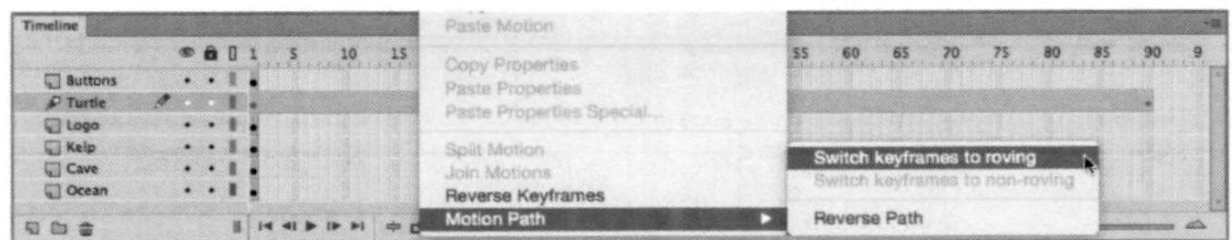

A roving-property keyframe is not attached to any particular frame in the tween. This type of keyframe allows you to create a custom-shaped motion path with consistent speed throughout the tween.

> *Note:*
>
> *If you convert keyframes to roving, frames are redistributed along the entire span of the tween. If you then convert the frames back to non-roving, the location of keyframes added to the tween is determined by the location of anchor points on the path.*

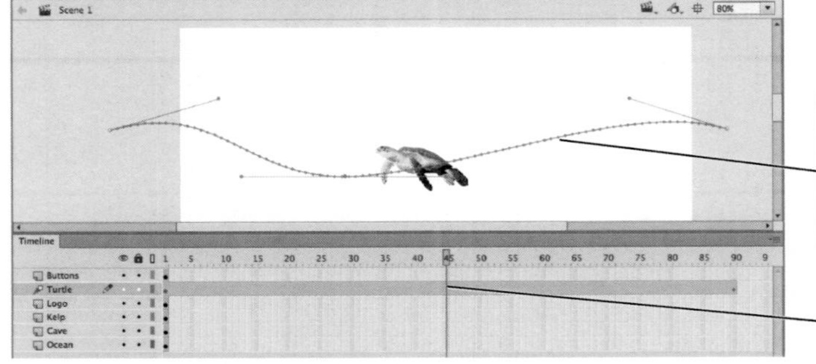

After choosing the Roving option, the frames along the path are redistributed to be equally spaced across the entire path.

The property keyframe is removed from the timeline.

8. **Save the file and continue to the next exercise.**

Motion Tween Properties and Presets

In Animate, the motion tween includes all information for the animation, including the length of the animation and specific object properties at various points along the path. A motion path is actually a specific type of object rather than simply a guide; the Properties panel shows a number of options that relate to the selected motion tween.

Because a motion tween is an actual object, you can attach any symbol to the path by simply dragging a new symbol onto the Stage when the motion tween layer is selected.

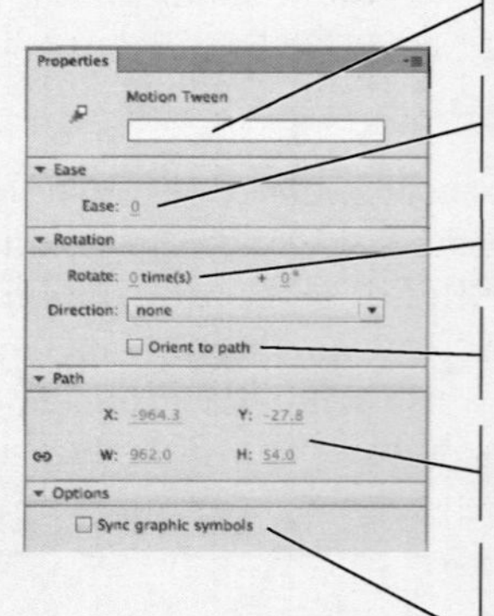

Use this field to define a name for the motion path instance.

Use Ease values to speed up or slow down an animation over time.

Use this option to rotate a symbol X number of times as it moves along the motion path.

Check this option to rotate the object so its bottom edge follows the contour of the path.

Use these options to change the position and size of the overall path.

Check this option to synchronize the number of frames in a tween within a graphic symbol to match the number of frames on the timeline where the graphic symbol is placed.

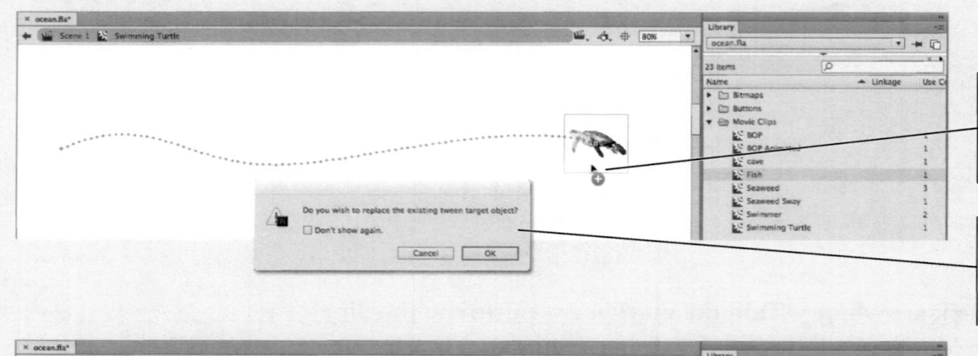

We dragged the Fish symbol onto the Stage while the motion path layer was active.

A warning asks if you want to replace the current symbol on the selected motion path.

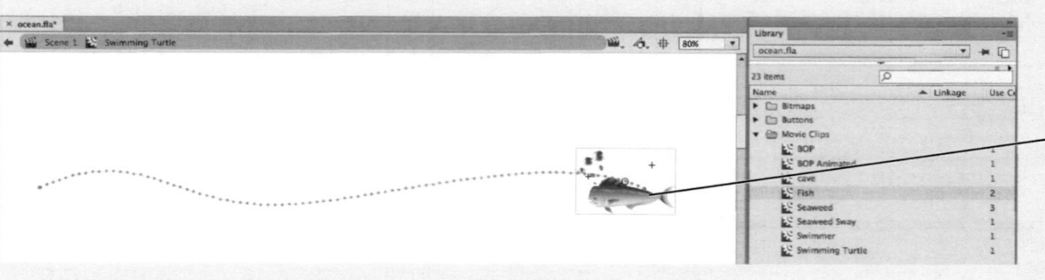

After clicking OK in the warning, the Fish symbol follows the same motion path.

Animate includes a number of predefined motion presets (Window>Motion Presets), which you can use to add common animations to your files. You can also save your own motion presets by Control/right-clicking an existing motion path and choosing Save as Motion Preset from the contextual menu. (User-defined presets are stored and accessed in a Custom folder in the Motion Presets panel. Custom presets do not include previews.)

Copy and Paste Frames

Your turtle currently swims from right to left across the Stage. When the animation loops, however, it would seem to miraculously jump back to the right and swim across again. For a more realistic effect, you are going to make a copy of the motion path animation and reverse it so the turtle swims back across the Stage before the animation loops.

1. **With `ocean.fla` open, Control/right-click anywhere in the Turtle layer motion tween and choose Copy Frames from the contextual menu.**

   You could also use the options in the Edit>Timeline submenu, but the standard Edit menu commands (and the related keyboard shortcuts) do not work when you want to copy or paste frames in the timeline.

   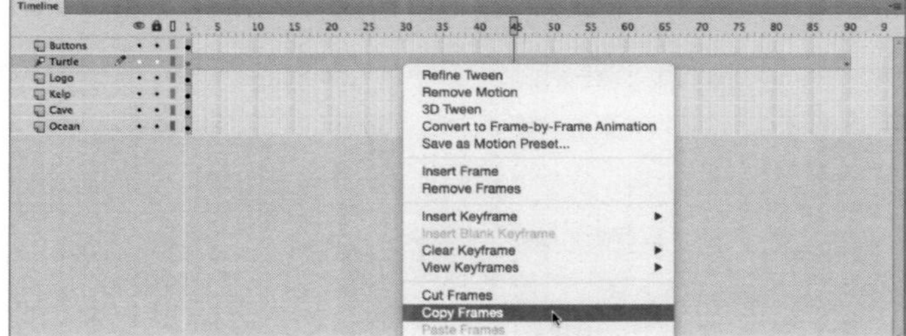

2. **Control/right-click Frame 95 of the Turtle layer and choose Paste Frames.**

   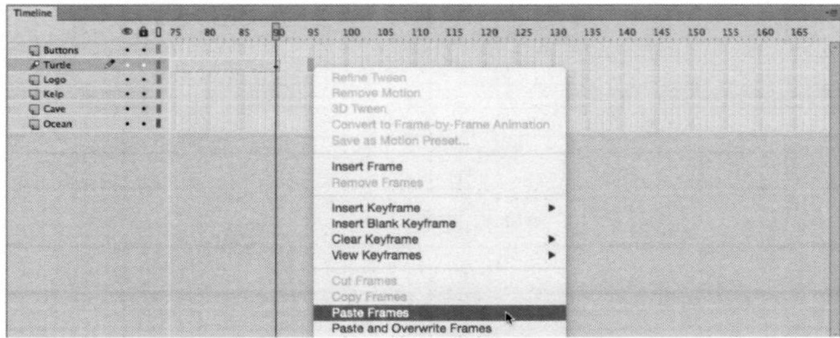

   You pasted an exact copy of the selected frames (the motion tween) — including the position of the symbol at various keyframes. In other words, the turtle is on the right at Frame 95 and on the left at Frame 184 (the end of the pasted animation).

   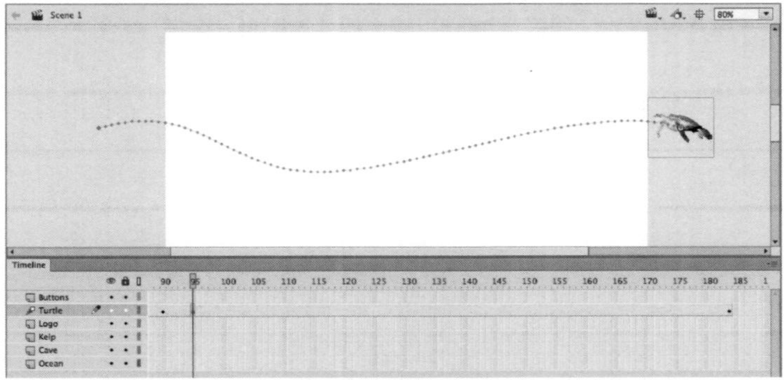

> *Note:*
>
> *You are allowing five extra frames between the time the turtle leaves and then re-enters the Stage area (ostensibly enough time for it to turn around before it swims back).*

3. **Control/right-click anywhere between Frame 95 and Frame 184 and choose Reverse Keyframes.**

   Reversing the keyframes moves the turtle to the left at Frame 95 and the right at Frame 184.

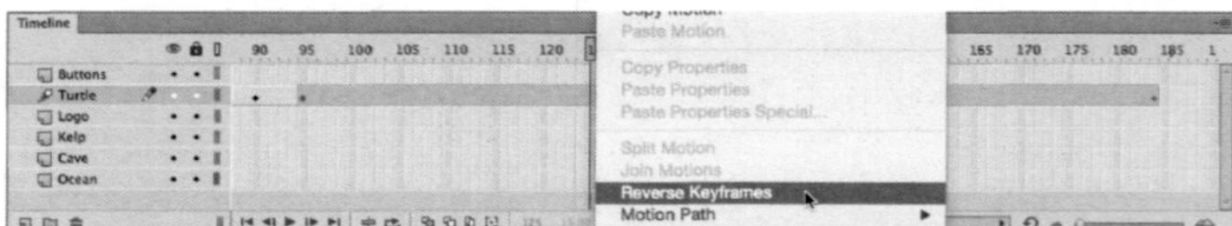

4. **Select the Frame 95 keyframe in the timeline. Click the turtle instance with the Selection tool, then choose Modify>Transform>Flip Horizontal.**

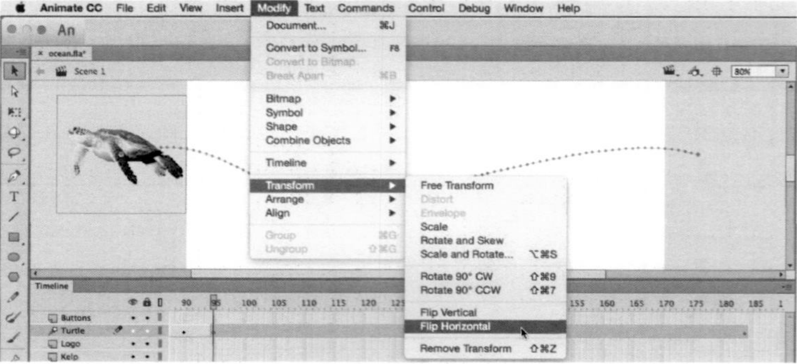

   For the turtle to realistically swim back across the Stage, you have to flip the symbol instance to face in the correct direction.

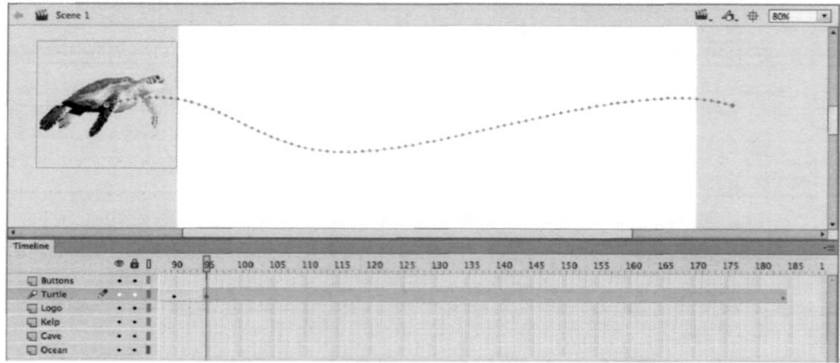

5. **Click Frame 184 to make that the active frame. With the turtle on the Frame 184 keyframe selected, choose Modify>Transform>Flip Horizontal again.**

   The turtle now faces to the right throughout the entire second half of the animation.

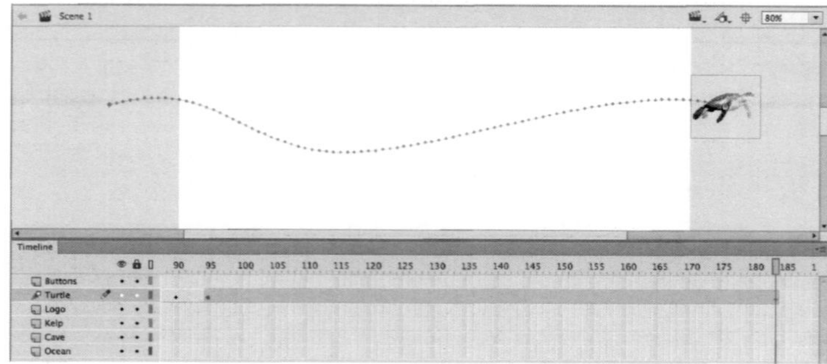

6. **Add new regular frames to Frame 184 of the remaining layers on the timeline.**

   Remember, you have to manually extend each layer so that they will all exist throughout the length of the entire animation.

7. **Click Frame 1 to reposition the playhead, then press Return/Enter to play the movie on the Stage.**

The air bubbles in the Cave movie clip instance do not move because that animation exists only inside the movie clip timeline.

8. **Save the file and continue to the next exercise.**

Define Numeric Transformations in a Tween

In addition to making changes on the Stage, you can also use various panels to define specific changes to specific properties at specific points in time. In this exercise, you use the Transform panel to animate the seaweed with a tween that creates the effect of a smooth, swaying motion.

1. **With ocean.fla open, double-click the Seaweed movie clip icon in the Library panel to enter into the symbol Stage.**

2. **In the timeline, select Frame 40 and press F5 to insert a new regular frame.**

   You can also Control/right-click the frame and choose Insert Frame from the contextual menu.

3. **Control/right-click anywhere between Frame 1 and Frame 40 and choose Create Motion Tween.**

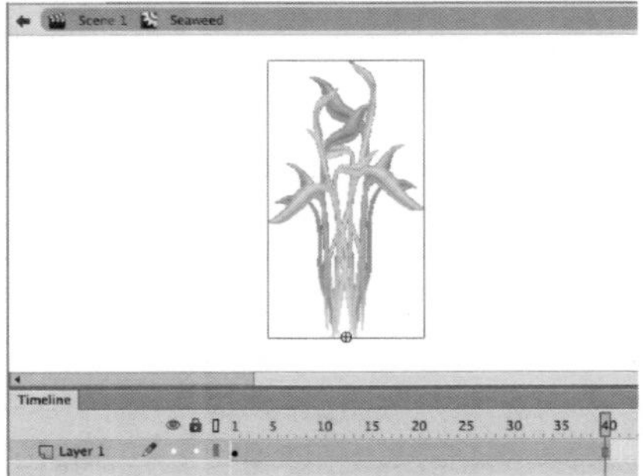

4. **Read the resulting message.**

   You created the Seaweed movie clip symbol by converting the bitmap instance on the main Stage to a symbol. However, the artwork on the symbol Stage is still a regular bitmap object. Motion tweens only work with symbol instances. As you see in the warning dialog box, Animate can automatically convert the placed bitmap instance to a movie clip symbol.

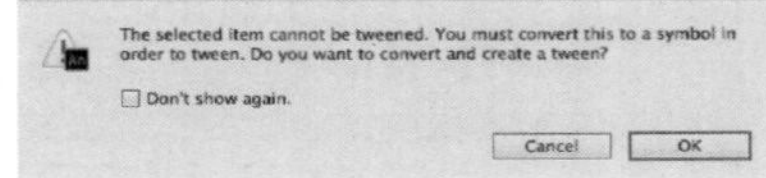

5. **Click OK in the message to create a symbol from the selected object.**

   You are not creating this tween on the main Stage because you want the animation to loop continuously regardless of the position of the playhead on the main timeline. Even though you are already inside of a symbol, you need to create a nested symbol structure for the motion tween to work properly.

6. **In the Library panel, change the name of Symbol 1 to Seaweed Sway, and then move the symbol into the Movie Clips folder.**

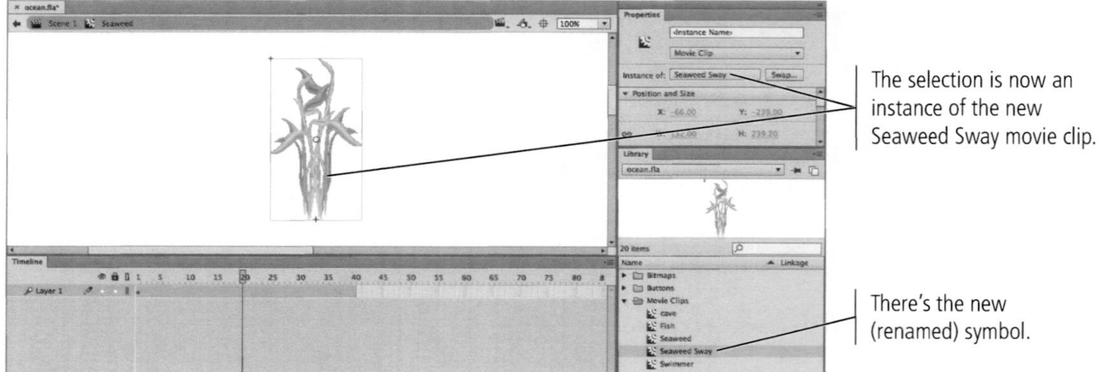

The selection is now an instance of the new Seaweed Sway movie clip.
There's the new (renamed) symbol.

7. **Choose the Free Transform tool in the Tools panel. Select the object on the Stage, and drag the transformation point to the bottom-center handle.**

8. **Select Frame 10 on the timeline. In the Transform panel, activate the Skew radio button, then change the Skew Horizontal value to 5°.**

   The concept here is the same as in the previous exercise: select the frame, and then change the object properties to what you want at that particular point in time.

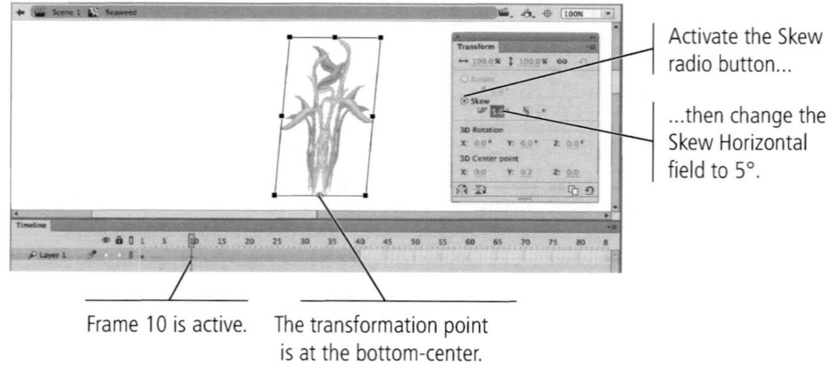

> ***Note:***
>
> *The object must be selected to change its properties. Selecting the frame in the timeline also selects the object on that frame.*

9. **Move the playhead to Frame 30 in the timeline. In the Transform panel, change the Skew Horizontal value to -5°.**

   You don't need to manually move the skew back to 0°; the tween frames do that for you.

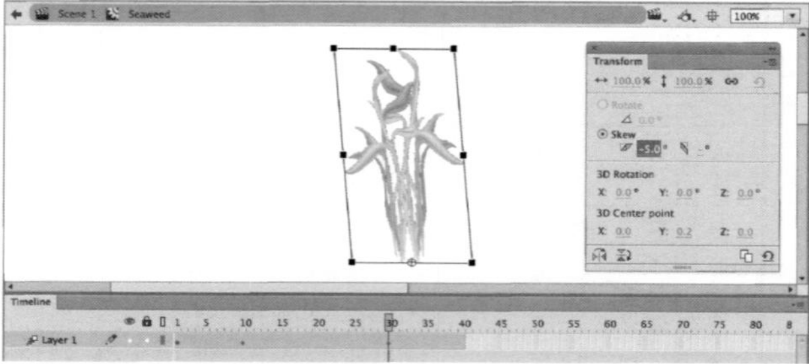

10. **Move the playhead to Frame 40 in the timeline. Make sure the symbol instance is selected on the Stage, then change the Skew Horizontal value (in the Transform panel) to 0°.**

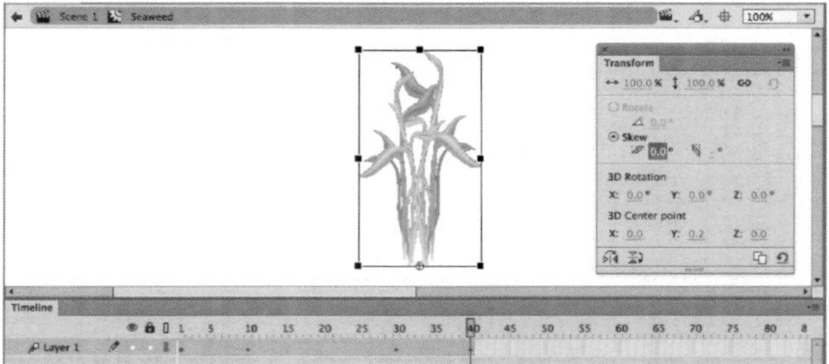

11. **Click Scene 1 in the Edit bar to return to the main Stage.**

12. **Press Command-Return/Control-Enter to test the movie in a Player window.**

    Because you created the animation inside of the Seaweed movie clip symbol, all three instances of the symbol sway continuously as long as the animation is open.

13. **Close the Player window and return to Animate. Save the file and continue to the next exercise.**

Graphics vs. Movie Clips

Both graphics and movie clips can include animation. However, there are two fundamental differences in the capabilities of the two symbol types.

First, movie clip symbol instances can be named, which means they can be addressed by code. You can write scripts to control the timeline within a movie clip symbol independently of other objects in the file. Graphic symbol instances can't be named, which means you can't affect them with code.

Second, if you create animation inside of a graphic symbol, the timeline where you place the instance determines how much of the graphic symbol's animation plays. In other words, frames in the graphic symbol must correspond to frames on the parent timeline (they are "timeline dependent").

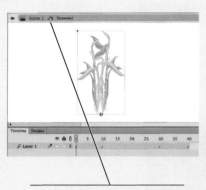

In this example, the seaweed animation was created in a graphic symbol instead of a movie clip.

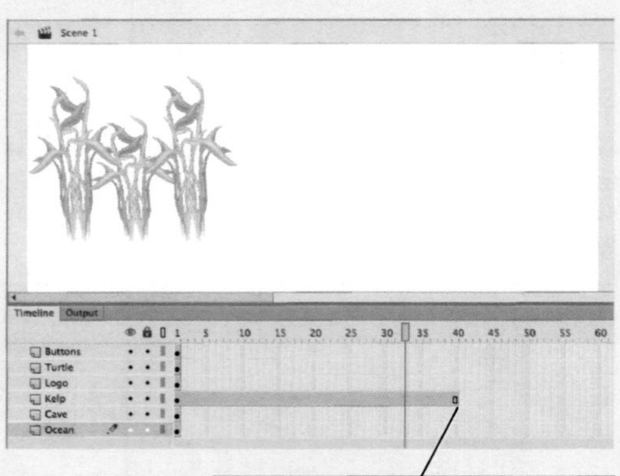

On the main Stage, playing the animation requires the same number of frames that are contained in the graphic symbol timeline.

In the example here, the 40-frame seaweed animation was created in a graphic symbol (as you can see in the Edit bar above the symbol Stage, above left). For the instances on the main Stage to play properly, you need to extend the layer containing the graphic symbol to include all 40 required frames (above right).

If the parent timeline includes more frames than the graphic symbol (as in the example on the right, where the timeline has 94 frames) the graphic symbol's timeline will play slightly less than 2.5 times before looping back to the beginning — causing a visible jump in the animation.

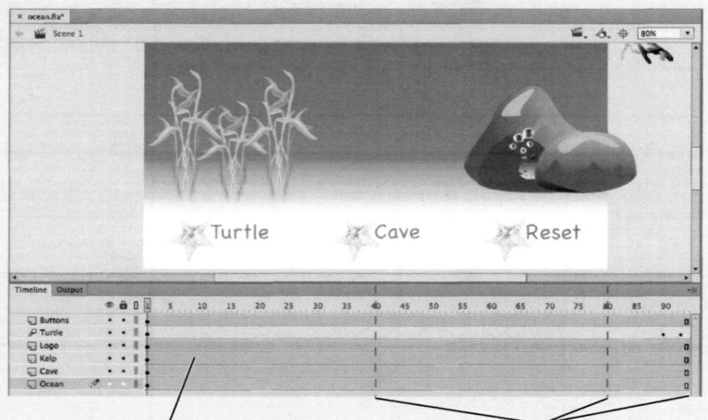

If you extend the timeline to create other animations, the graphic symbol animation repeats as long as the timeline allows.

The 40-frame seaweed animation would play 2 full times plus 14 frames before the main timeline looped back to Frame 1.

If you have a number of animations of different length, you should use movie clip symbols, which function independently of the timeline where they are placed and can loop continuously regardless of the length of other animations on the same parent timeline.

Animate Effects and Filters

In addition to changing the common symbol properties — position, size, etc. — a motion tween can be used to animate a number of other options. Effects and filters, which can add visual interest to most objects on the Stage, can also be animated to change over time. In this exercise, you are going to cause the client's logo to fade into view over time, changing from blurry to clear and fully visible.

1. **With `ocean.fla` open, use the Selection tool to select the logo instance on the Stage, then press the F8 key to convert it to a symbol.**

2. **Define the following settings in the Convert to Symbol dialog box:**

Name:	**BOP**
Type:	**Movie Clip**
Registration:	**Center**
Location:	**Movie Clips folder**

3. **Click OK to create the symbol.**

4. **Using the Selection tool, double-click the Logo instance on the Stage to edit the symbol in place. Select Frame 60 on the Layer 1 timeline and press F5 to add a new regular frame.**

   Because movie clips are self-contained animations, every movie clip in the file can last a different amount of time. You also need to be able to control this animation separately from other animations, which is why you are creating the tween inside of the symbol.

5. **Control/right-click between Frame 1 and Frame 60 and choose Create Motion Tween from the contextual menu.**

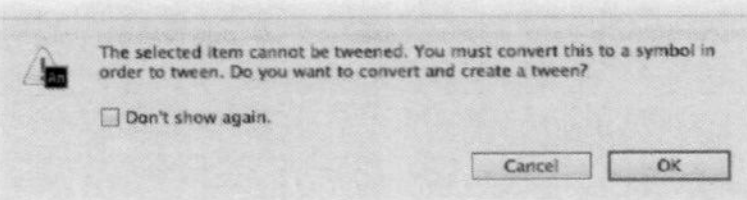

6. **Click OK in the resulting warning. Rename the new Symbol 1 as `BOP Animated`, and then move the symbol into the Movie Clips folder.**

7. **Move the playhead to Frame 1 in the timeline, and then click the symbol instance on the Stage to select it.**

8. **In the Properties panel, expand the Filters section (if necessary).**

9. **Click the + button and choose Blur from the pop-up menu.**

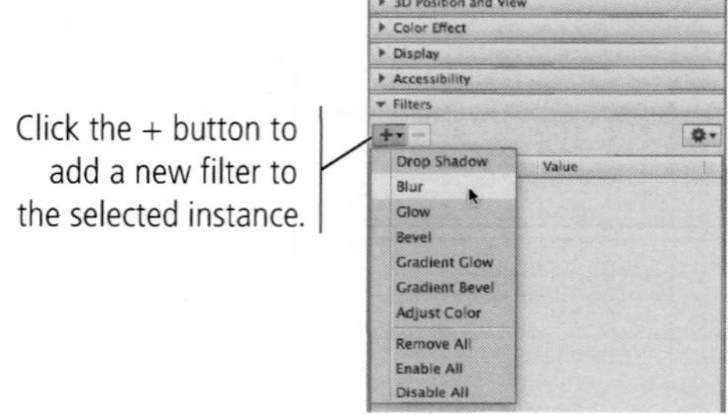

Click the + button to add a new filter to the selected instance.

10. **Make sure the Blur X and Blur Y values are linked, and then change the Blur X value to `30` px.**

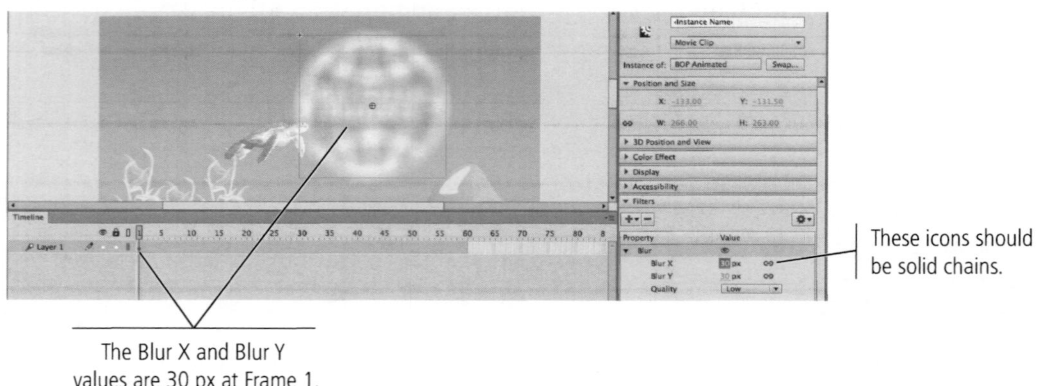

These icons should be solid chains.

The Blur X and Blur Y values are 30 px at Frame 1.

11. **In the Properties panel, expand the Color Effect section (if necessary).**

12. **Open the Style menu and choose Alpha. Drag the resulting slider all the way to the left to change the Alpha value to `0`.**

The Alpha value controls an object's opacity; a value of 0 means the object is not visible.

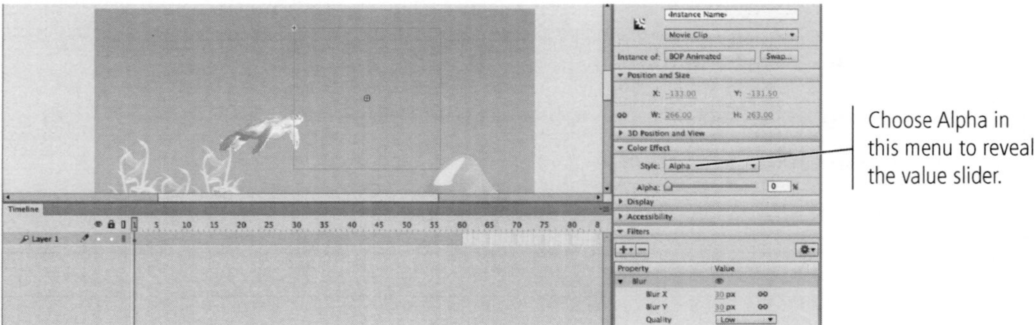

Choose Alpha in this menu to reveal the value slider.

13. **Move the playhead to Frame 30 on the Layer 1 timeline, and then click the symbol registration point on the Stage to select the symbol instance.**

Because the current Alpha value is 0, you can't see the actual object to select it; you have to rely on the registration point to select the instance on the Stage.

14. **In the Color Effects section of the Properties panel, change the Alpha value back to `100`.**

15. **In the Filters section of the Properties panel, change the Blur X value to `0` px.**

The Alpha value is back to 100.

The Blur values are back to 0.

Frame 30 is active.

16. **Return the playhead to Frame 1, and then press Return/Enter to preview the animation.**

The BOP Animated movie clip gradually becomes clearer and more visible between Frame 1 and Frame 30.

17. **Click Scene 1 in the Edit bar to return to the main Stage.**

18. **Save the file and continue to the next stage of the project.**

Stage 3 Programming Basic Timeline Control

You now have all of the pieces in place for the ocean scene, including a number of animations that play automatically when the movie opens. According to the project specs, however, most of these animations should not play until a user clicks the appropriate button at the bottom of the screen. For everything to work properly, you need to complete several additional steps to accomplish the following goals:

- Play the logo animation only once when the movie first loads.
- Play the swimming turtle when the Turtle button is clicked.
- Show the cave with the bubbly fish when the Cave button is clicked.
- Hide the cave, stop the turtle and school of fish, and replay the logo animation when the Reset button is clicked.

Convert a Motion Tween to a Movie Clip

At this point, all but the swimming turtle animations are contained inside of various movie clip symbols. In order to add code that controls the turtle animation independently of the main timeline, you need to move the symbol instance and motion tween into a symbol, and then place an instance of that symbol on the Stage.

1. **With `ocean.fla` open, click the Turtle layer name in the Timeline panel to select everything on that layer.**

   Remember, the animation on this layer includes two motion tweens. Clicking the layer name selects both tweens on the layer.

2. **Control/right-click inside the selected frames and choose Copy Frames in the contextual menu.**

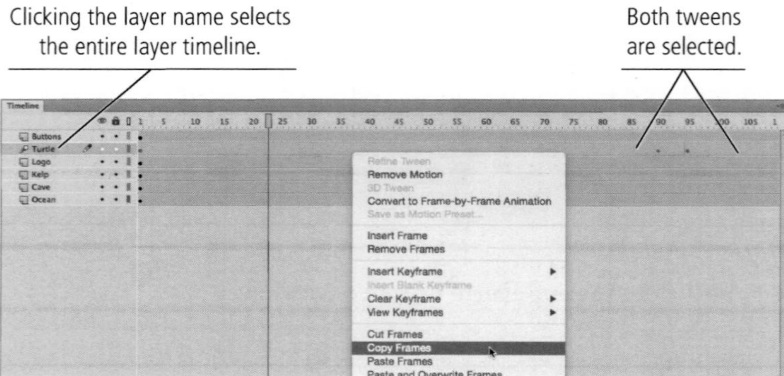

3. **Choose Insert>New Symbol. In the resulting dialog box, define the following settings:**

   Name: `Swimming Turtle`
   Type: **Movie Clip**
   Location: **Movie Clips folder**

   You are creating a new symbol, so there is no Registration option in the Create New Symbol dialog box. The new symbol Stage will include a registration point, around which you can place or create artwork.

4. **Click OK to create the new symbol.**

5. **Control/right-click Frame 1 of the new symbol's timeline and choose Paste Frames from the contextual menu.**

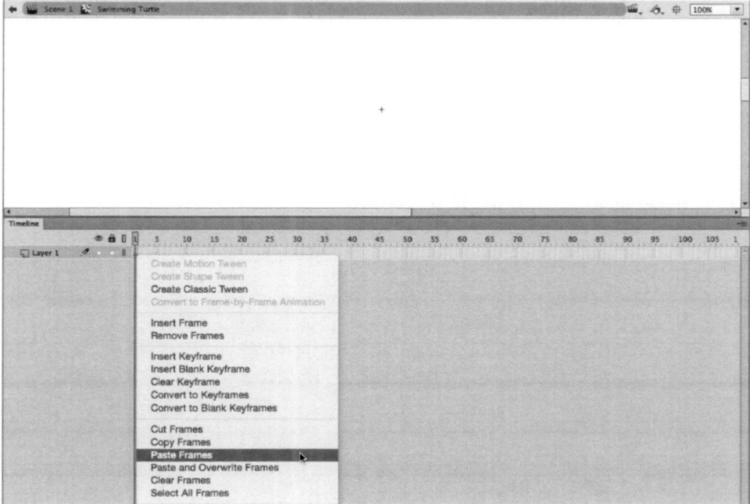

This pastes the full set of contents of the selected frames — including the turtle instance and the motion tweens — inside the symbol.

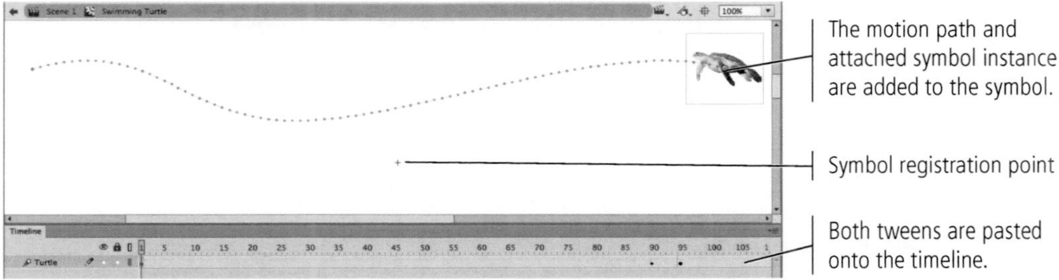

6. **Click anywhere within the Frame 1–94 tween, then choose Edit>Select All to select the motion path and the turtle symbol instance.**

This command selects both the motion path and the attached instance, so you can drag the entire piece as a single group.

7. **Use the Selection tool to drag the selection until the right end of the motion path aligns to the symbol registration point.**

The existing Swimmer symbol uses the center registration point. You're going to swap symbols, and the registration point in this symbol will align to the position of the previous one. For the tween to work as it does on the main timeline, you need to place the right end of the motion path at the registration point. (This will make more sense shortly).

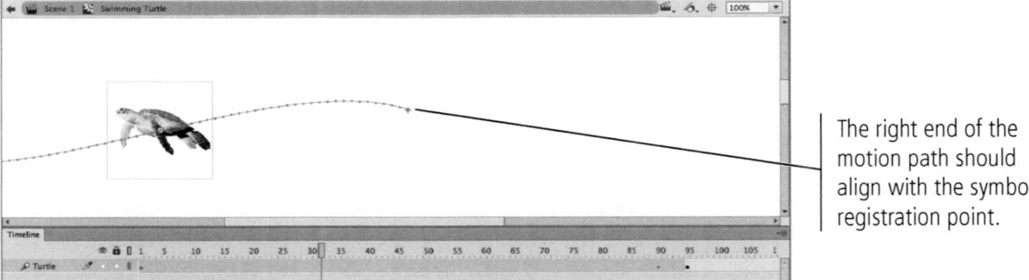

8. **Repeat Steps 6–7 for the Frame 95–184 tween.**

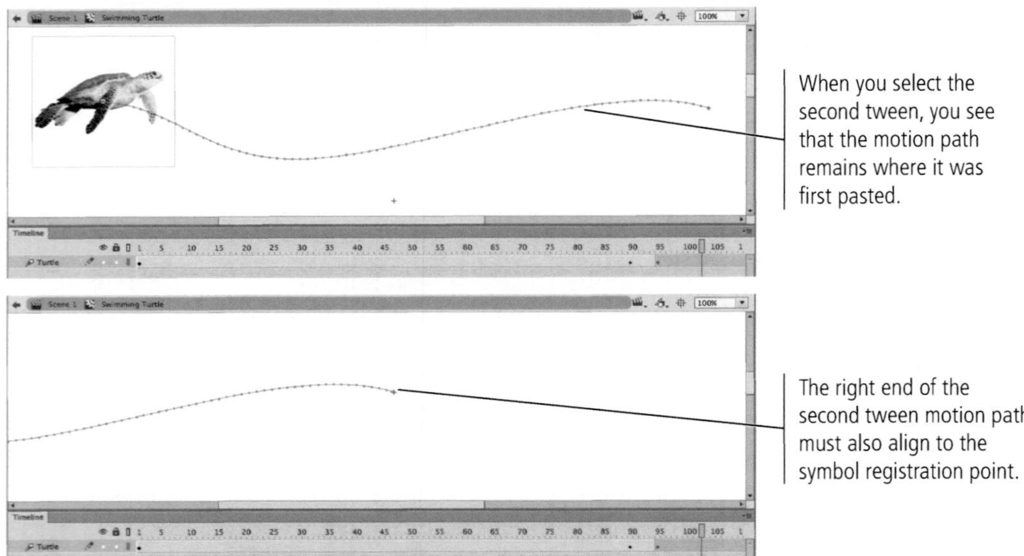

When you select the second tween, you see that the motion path remains where it was first pasted.

9. **Click Scene 1 in the Edit bar to return to the main Stage.**

10. **Control/right-click the Frame 1–94 tween on the Turtle layer and choose Remove Motion from the contextual menu.**

    The tweens now exist in the new Swimming Turtle movie clip symbol, so they are no longer needed on the main timeline.

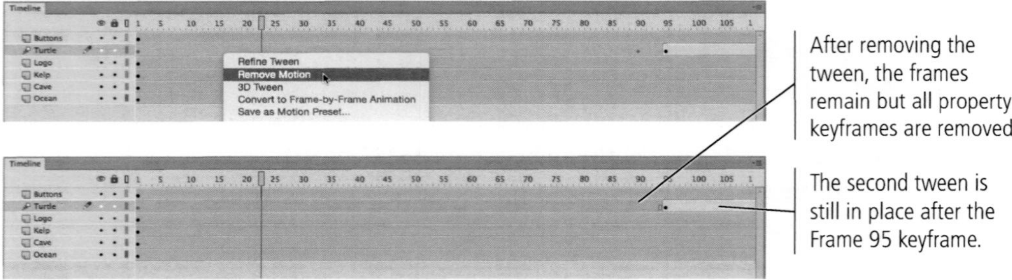

After removing the tween, the frames remain but all property keyframes are removed.
The second tween is still in place after the Frame 95 keyframe.

11. **Repeat Step 10 for the Frame 95–184 tween on the same layer.**

12. **Click Frame 2 of the topmost layer to select it.**

13. **Scroll the Timeline panel as necessary until you see Frame 184. Press Shift, then click the last frame on the bottommost layer to select all frames from 2–184 on all layers.**

Note:

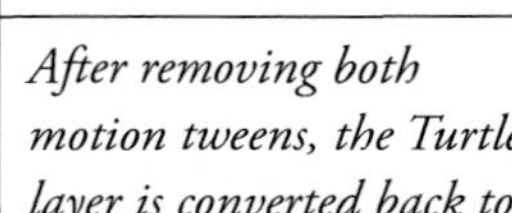

After removing both motion tweens, the Turtle layer is converted back to a regular layer.

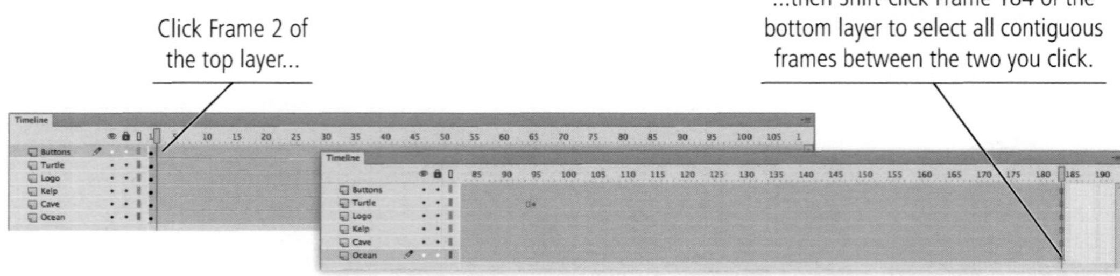

Click Frame 2 of the top layer...
...then Shift-click Frame 184 of the bottom layer to select all contiguous frames between the two you click.

14. **Control/right-click anywhere within the selected frames and choose Remove Frames from the contextual menu.**

Because all animation in this movie occurs within the timelines of various movie clip symbols, you don't need 184 frames on each layer of the main timeline. However, you can't simply press the Delete key to remove frames. You must use the contextual menu (or the related commands in the Edit>Timeline submenu).

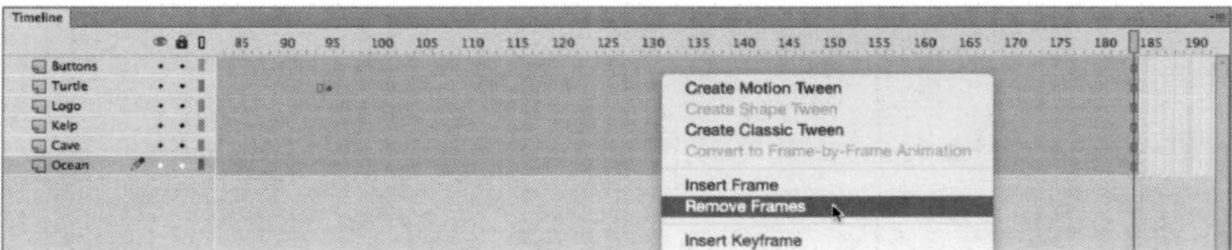

15. **Click the existing turtle instance on the Stage to select it.**

Because all of the animations are now contained within movie clip symbols, the main timeline now has only a single frame for each layer.

As you can see in the Properties panel, the selected object is currently an instance of the Swimmer movie clip. You need to replace it with the Swimming Turtle movie clip.

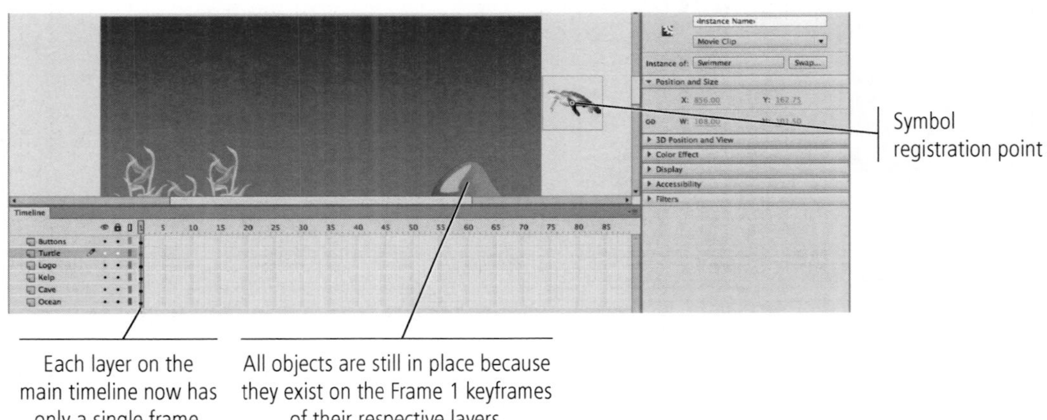

16. **In the Properties panel, click the Swap button. Choose the Swimming Turtle movie clip in the resulting dialog box and click OK.**

When you swap symbols, the registration point of the new symbol is put in exactly the same spot as the registration point of the replacement symbol — which is why you moved the right end of the motion path to align with the symbol's registration point.

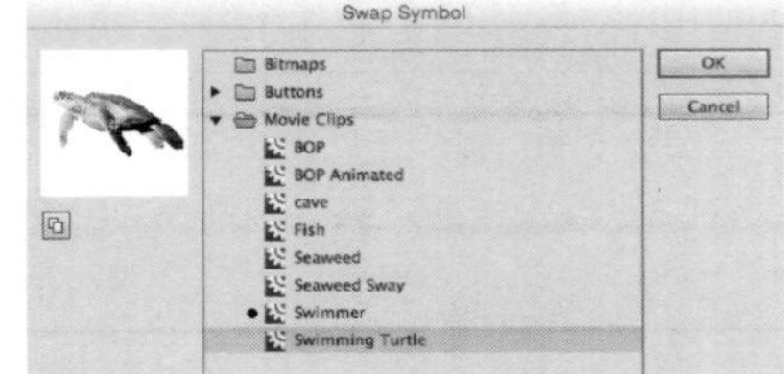

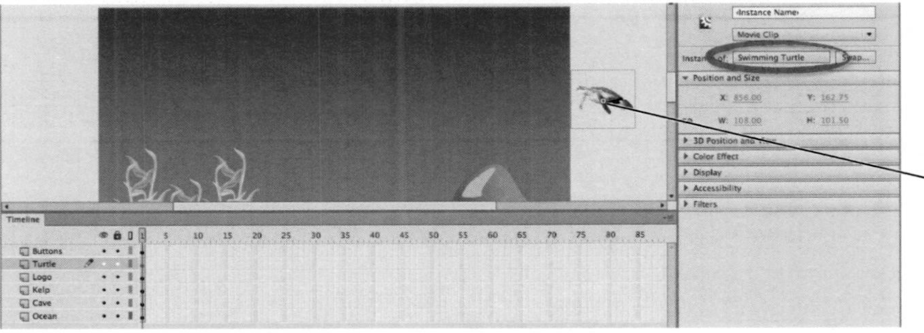

Although you can't see the motion path, you know the center of the turtle was aligned to the right end of the path at Frame 1.

17. **Save the file and continue to the next exercise.**

Prepare Symbol Instances for ActionScript

As you know, when you drag a symbol from the Library panel to the Stage, you create an instance of the symbol. **Named instances** are instances that have been assigned a unique identifier or name, which allows them to be targeted with ActionScript code.

1. **With ocean.fla open, make sure you are working on the main Stage.**

2. **Using the Selection tool, click the Swimming Turtle instance to the left of the Stage. In the top field of the Properties panel, type turtle_mc.**

Use the Properties panel to assign instance names.

3. **Define names for the rest of the placed instances as follows:**

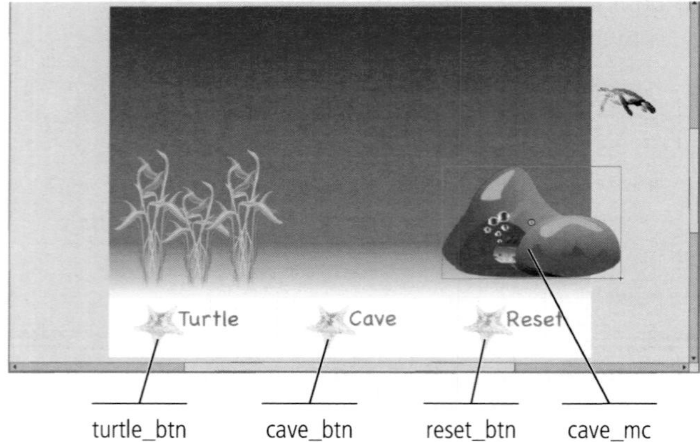
Turtle
Cave
Reset
turtle_btn
cave_btn
reset_btn
cave_mc

Note:

You don't need to name the seaweed instances because those will not be targeted with scripts.

4. **In the Timeline panel, click the Logo layer name to select the layer.**

   Remember, selecting a layer reveals the bounding boxes for all objects on the layer.

5. **Click the symbol registration point to select the logo.**

   Because the logo object has an Alpha value of 0, this is the easiest way to select the instance so you can name it.

6. **In the Properties panel, type bop_mc as the instance name.**

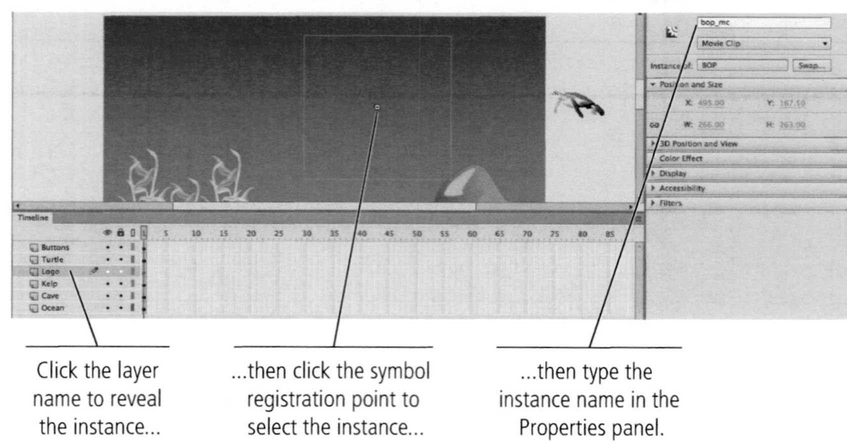
Click the layer name to reveal the instance...
...then click the symbol registration point to select the instance...
...then type the instance name in the Properties panel.

7. **Save the file and continue to the next exercise.**

Note:

The "_mc" and "_btn" naming convention is common in the world of Animate development. This convention allows programmers to easily recognize the type of a particular instance when they add scripts to the file.

Add Movie Clip Controls

If you completed Project 4: Animated Internet Ads, you saw that the Code Snippets panel makes it relatively easy for non-programmers to add basic code to an Animate movie. Items in the panel, written in plain English, automatically add whatever code is necessary to perform the listed function. In this exercise, you will use code snippets to determine what is visible when you first open the movie.

1. **With `ocean.fla` open, open the Code Snippets panel from the Window menu.**

   Different types of common commands are available, grouped into logical sets or folders.

2. **Expand the ActionScript>Actions folder in the Code Snippets panel. Move your mouse cursor over the Stop a Movie Clip item to get more information about that snippet.**

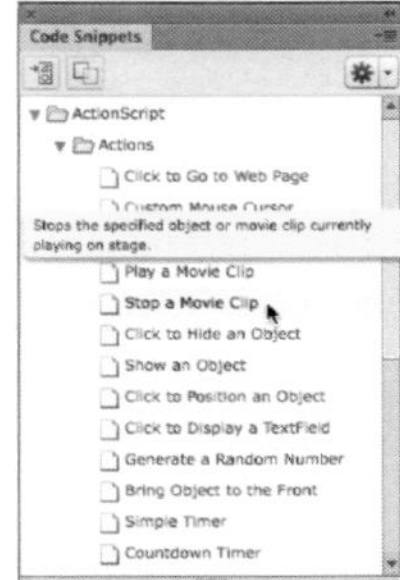

3. **Select the Swimming Turtle instance on the stage and then double-click the Stop a Movie Clip item.**

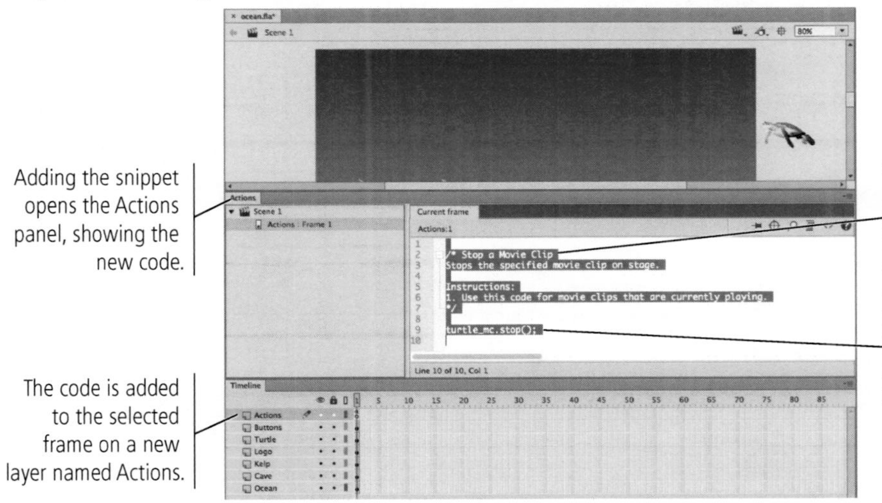

Adding the snippet opens the Actions panel, showing the new code.

The code is added to the selected frame on a new layer named Actions.

Code snippets include instructions in the form of comments, which are enclosed by /* and */.

The actual command uses dot syntax to define what instance is affected and what will happen to that instance.

It might seem that by first selecting the object, you are attaching script to that object. Instead, you are telling Animate which object you want the command to address. In ActionScript 3.0, all scripts are placed on the timeline frames rather than attached to specific objects on the Stage. In the Timeline panel, a new layer named Actions is added to the top of the layer stack. (Although not required, this separate layer for the code is a common convention among developers.)

In the Actions panel, which opens automatically when you add the snippet, you can see that the stop command has been added to Frame 1 of the Actions layer. The command references turtle_mc, which is the instance name you defined. In other words, this command stops the turtle_mc instance from playing. The instance is stopped as soon as the main timeline reaches the command; because the command is on Frame 1 of the main timeline, the instance is stopped as soon as the movie opens.

> ***Note:***
>
> *The format or syntax of the added code is called **dot syntax**: it first defines the object you are addressing, then adds a dot, then defines what you want to do to that object.*

4. **Select the Cave instance and then double-click the Stop a Movie Clip item in the Snippets panel.**

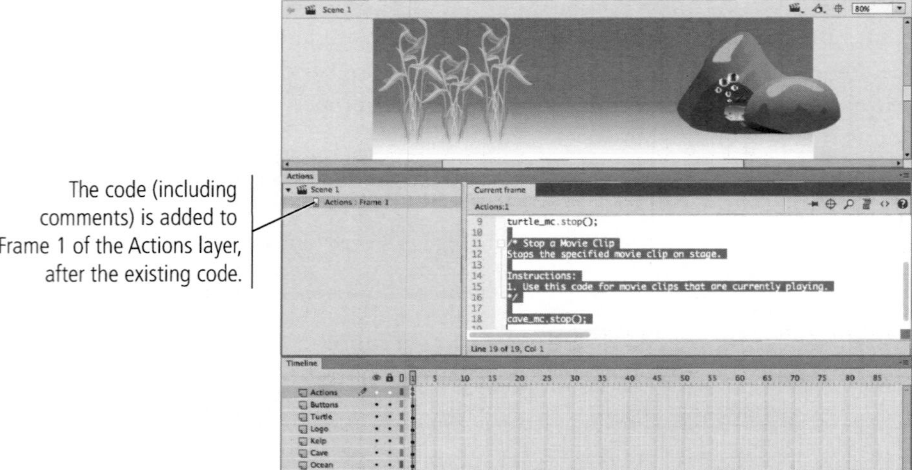

The code (including comments) is added to Frame 1 of the Actions layer, after the existing code.

5. **Select the Cave instance again and double-click the Show an Object item.**

   Unfortunately, there is no snippet to simply hide an item without requiring the user to click something. (The Click to Hide an Object item is not appropriate because you want to hide the instance as soon as the movie opens, and not as a reaction to the user's click.)

   However, the added Show an Object statement shows that the value "true" is attached to the visible property of the instance. To make the instance *not* visible, you simply have to change the property's value in the code.

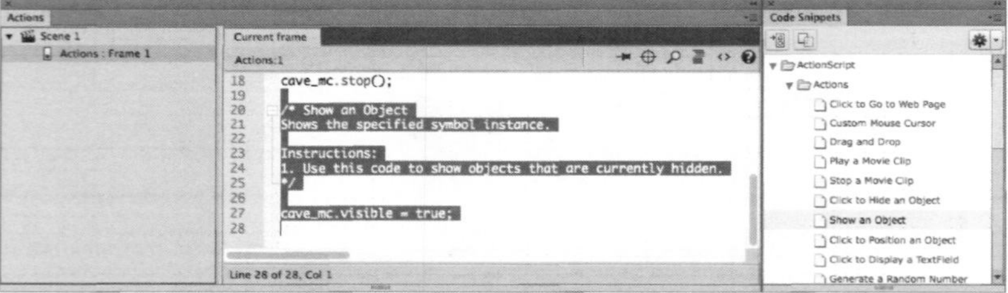

6. **In the Actions panel, change the word true to `false` on Line 27.**

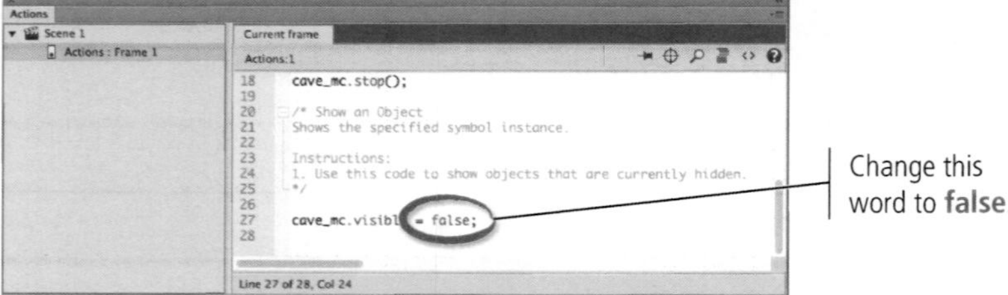

Change this word to **false**.

7. **Press Command-Return/Control-Enter to test the movie.**

   The two movie clips are stopped, and the cave is hidden. However, the logo animation still plays continuously, and you want it to play only once when the movie opens.

8. **Close the Player window and return to Animate.**

9. **In the Library panel, double-click the BOP movie clip symbol icon to enter into the symbol's Stage.**

   You can't stop the BOP instance on the main Stage because you want the animation to play one time when the movie first opens. To accomplish this goal, you need to add a stop command to the end of the movie clip timeline.

10. **Move the playhead to the last frame in the timeline, then click the logo instance on the Stage to select it.**

11. **Expand the ActionScript>Timeline Navigation folder in the Code Snippets panel, then double-click the Stop at this Frame item to add the necessary code.**

    Timeline Navigation snippets can be used to control the timeline (and thus, the playback) of specific symbols. The Stop at this Frame command affects the active timeline at the selected frame, so a specific instance is not referenced in the resulting code.

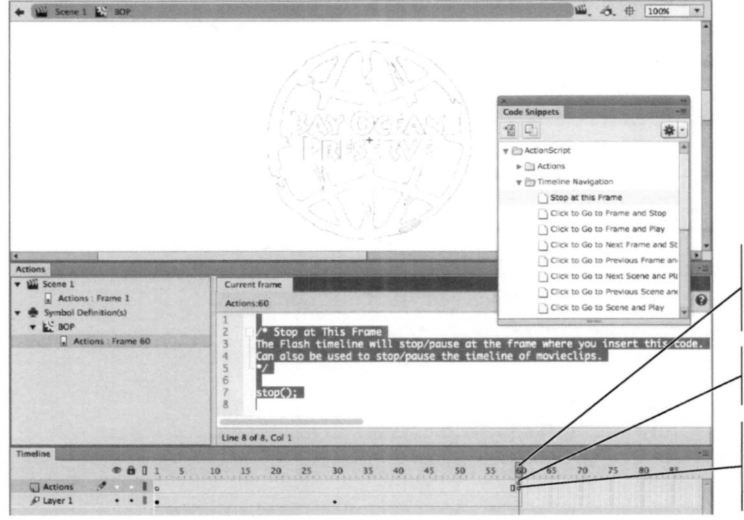

Move the playhead to Frame 60 before adding the Stop at this Frame snippet.
An Actions layer is added to the symbol timeline.
A keyframe is added at Frame 60 to contain the stop command.

12. **Click Scene 1 in the Edit bar to return to the main Stage, then press Command-Return/Control-Enter to test the movie.**

    The logo animation now plays only once and then stops.

13. **Close the Player window and return to Animate, then save the file and continue to the next exercise.**

Add Event Handlers to Buttons

As you saw in the previous exercise, ActionScript 3.0 requires code to be attached to a frame on the timeline. To affect a specific object on the Stage, you have to use the defined instance names as reference in the code. Programming a button requires more complex code called an **event handler**, with (at least) two referenced objects — the event that triggers the action, and the name of the function that is affected by the event.

The Code Snippets panel includes options for creating event handlers with the proper syntax, although defining what occurs as a result of the event might require a few workaround steps. Even using code snippets, it is helpful if you are familiar with the basics of ActionScript code.

1. **With `ocean.fla` open, expand the ActionScript>Timeline Navigation folder in the Code Snippets panel.**

2. **Select the Turtle button instance on the Stage, then double-click the Click to Go to Frame and Play item in the Code Snippets panel.**

    The added code is not attached to the selected instance; it is added to Frame 1 of the existing Actions layer, after all code that you already added.

The selected instance becomes the object that can trigger the function.

The specific trigger (CLICK) is defined inside the event listener.

This is the event listener statement.

This is the function that is called when the defined event occurs.

The function name is the same in the event listener and the defined function.

Although you do not need to know every detail of ActionScript code to use Code Snippets, there are a few important points that you should understand:

- The first line of added code defines what will happen to trigger the function (the **event listener**). Inside the parentheses, the MouseEvent.CLICK statement says that the following function will be called when the turtle_btn instance is *clicked*.
- The first line of code includes a **function name** immediately before the closing parenthesis. That same name is defined at the beginning of the following function, so the file knows which function to play when the defined button is clicked.
- The **function body** — between the two braces — defines what occurs when the event is triggered.

3. **Place the insertion point before the gotoAndPlay command inside the function body and click the Insert Instance Path and Name button at the top of the Actions panel.**

   The statement inside this function currently says "go to Frame 5 and play the timeline". Because the statement does not address a specific instance, the code will be interpreted to mean the timeline on which the code is placed (in this case, the main Stage timeline). You want the function to play the School movie clip instance, so you have to add the appropriate reference.

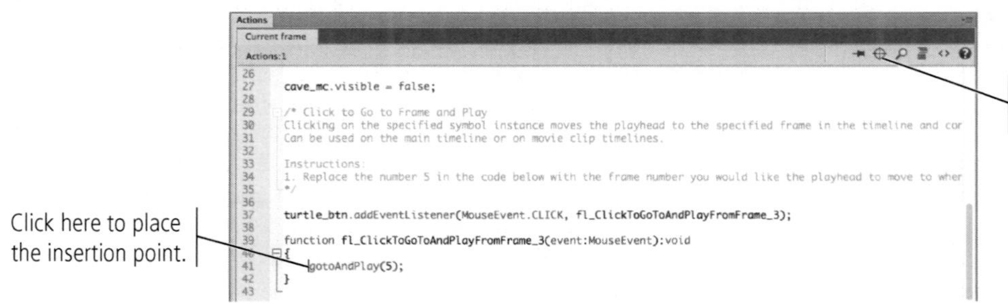

4. **Choose turtle_mc in the Insert Target Path dialog box and click OK.**

   This dialog box lists every nameable instance on the Stage, so you can choose from the list instead of trying to remember the exact name you defined for a specific object.

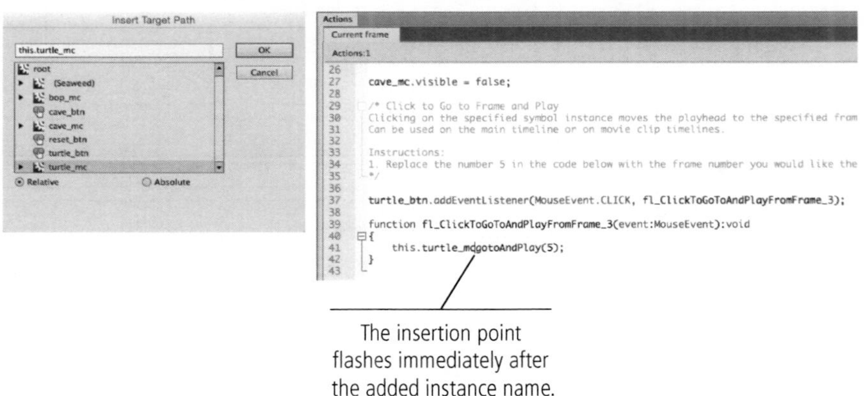

The insertion point flashes immediately after the added instance name.

   The word "this" in the instance name refers to the timeline where the code is written. The overall statement is essentially saying, "On *this* timeline, you will find something called school_mc. Tell school_mc to execute its gotoAndPlay() method."

5. **Type a period (dot) immediately after the instance name to separate it from the gotoAndPlay command.**

   Remember, dot syntax requires a period separating the different parts of code — in this case, the instance that will be affected by the gotoAndPlay command.

6. **Change the number inside the parentheses to 1.**

   This number defines the frame number of the instance that will be called when a user clicks the button. You want the instance to start at the beginning, so you are changing the frame reference to 1.

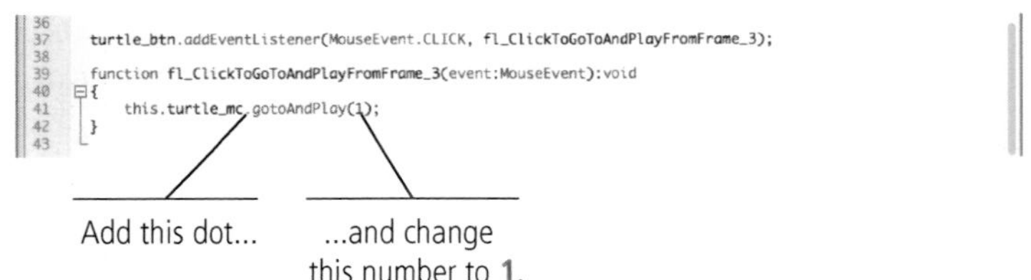

Note:

If an item in the Insert Target Path dialog box appears in parentheses, the instance is not yet named; selecting it will prompt you to define an instance name.

Note:

The word "this" is automatically included when you use the Insert Target Path dialog box. It is not strictly necessary in this case because the instances are all on the main timeline of the file you are building, but you do not need to remove it from the code.

7. **Repeat Steps 2–6 to create an event handler for the Cave button that plays the cave_mc movie clip instance from Frame 1.**

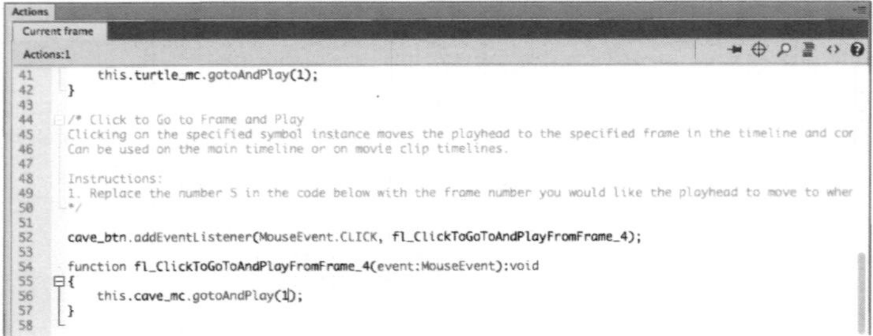

8. **Select the cave_mc instance on the Stage (not the Cave button) and double-click the Show an Object item in the ActionScript>Actions folder of the Code Snippets panel.**

   The Cave button needs to show the instance before it plays, so this button function needs two lines of code. However, the Code Snippets panel was not designed to add code inside of an existing function. The Show an Object snippet is added at the end of the existing code, *after* the function that is called when a user clicks the cave_btn instance. As a work-around, you have to add the necessary command and then paste it into the function body.

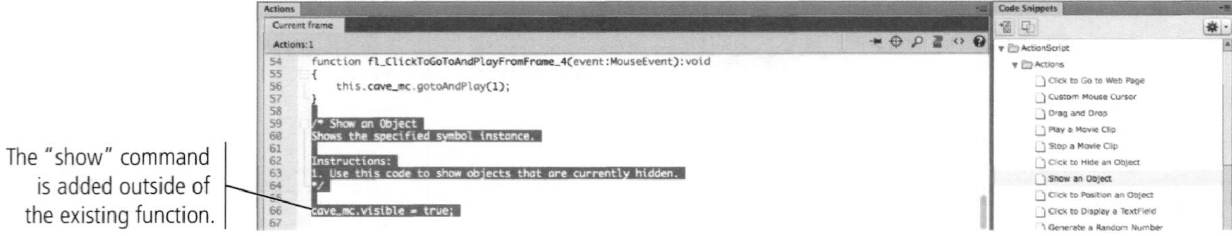

9. **Select the line of code that makes the cave_mc instance visible (Line 66 in the above example) and press Command/Control-X to cut the selected code.**

   You have to use the keyboard shortcuts to copy (Command/Control-C), cut (Command/Control-X), or paste (Command/Control-V) code in the Actions panel. The menu commands do not work while you are active in the Actions panel.

10. **Place the insertion point immediately after the opening brace in the previous function for the cave_btn instance (Line 55 in our example). Press Return/Enter to add a new line in the function body, then press Command/Control-V to paste the code that you cut in Step 9 into the function body.**

11. **Delete the extra lines of comments at the end of the code.**

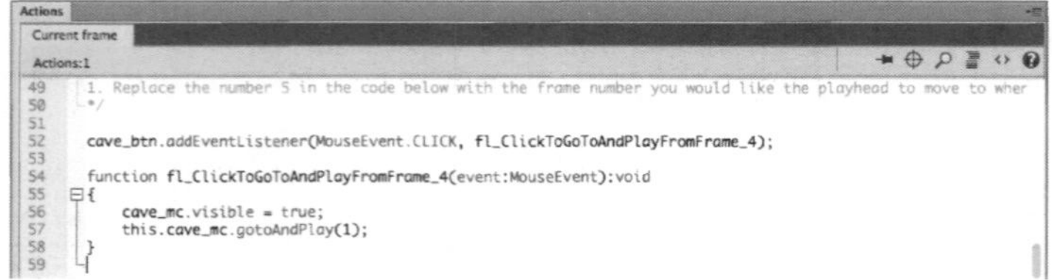

Note:

The comments are the gray lines that are surrounded by / and */. After you moved the actual code into the function body (Steps 9–10), the comments from the original code are unnecessary. Deleting them helps keep the code pane as clean as possible.*

12. **Press Command-Return/Control-Enter to test the movie.**

    Test the buttons that you just programmed. Each should play the relevant movie clip.

13. **Close the Player window and return to Animate, then save the file and continue to the next exercise.**

Combine Multiple Event Handlers in a Button

The final element of this project is the Reset button, which needs to accomplish a number of things. As the name suggests, clicking this button should restore the movie to exactly what happens when it first opens. Because the symbols in this movie are controlled with code, you need to add more code that defines what happens when this button is clicked.

1. **With `ocean.fla` open, select the Reset button instance on the Stage.**

2. **Double-click the Click to Go To Frame and Stop item in the ActionScript>Timeline Navigation folder of the Code Snippets panel.**

3. **Inside the function body, add a reference to the turtle_mc instance before the gotoAndStop command, and change the referenced frame inside the parentheses to 1.**

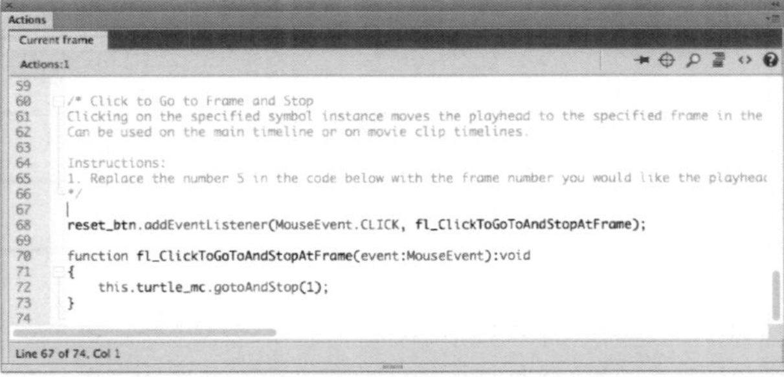

4. **Select the line inside the function body (Line 72 in our example) and copy it.**

5. **Place the insertion point at the beginning of the existing function body (Line 72) and paste the copied code two times.**

6. **Change the second line to reference the cave_mc instance.**

7. **Change the third line to reference the bop_mc instance, and change the command to `gotoAndPlay`.**

When a user clicks the Reset button, the logo animation should replay from the first frame. It will replay only once because you already added the stop command inside the movie clip's timeline.

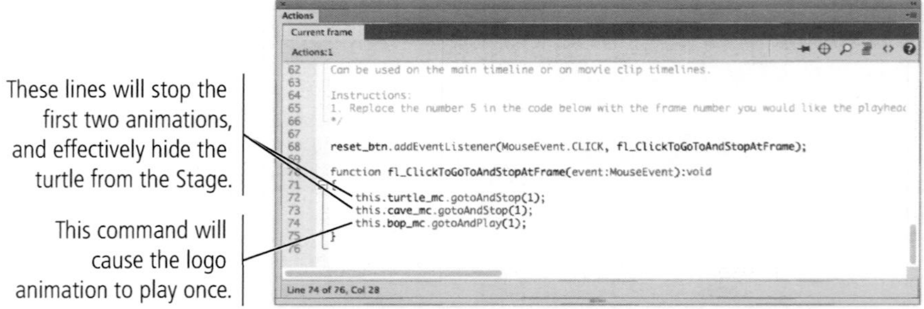

These lines will stop the first two animations, and effectively hide the turtle from the Stage.
This command will cause the logo animation to play once.

8. **Select the Reset button on the Stage again, and double-click the Click to Hide an Object item in the Actions folder of the Code Snippets panel.**

9. **In the resulting function, change the referenced instance to `cave_mc`.**

By default, this snippet hides the object that triggers the function. Because you want to hide the cave and not the Reset button, you need to change the instance name inside of the function body.

10. **Cut the function body (Line 89 in our example) from the code and then paste it inside the body of the previous function.**

In this case, it is not necessary to have two separate event handlers for the same button.

Note:

You don't need to hide the turtle instance because Frame 1 of that movie clip exists entirely out of the Stage area; it won't be visible when its timeline is reset.

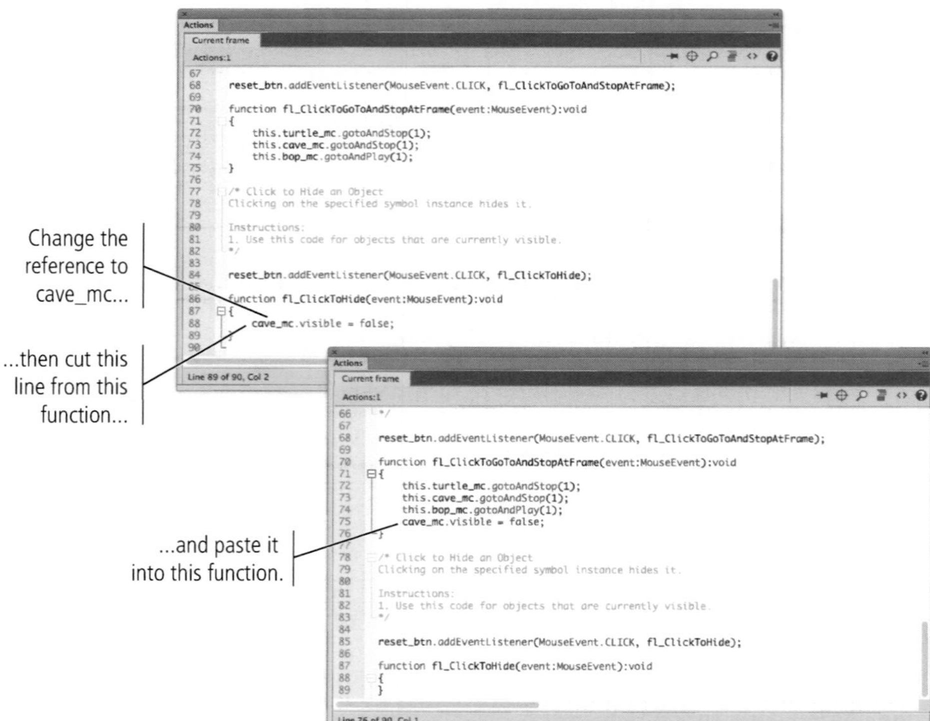

Change the reference to cave_mc...
...then cut this line from this function...
...and paste it into this function.

11. **Delete all code related to the second reset_btn event handler (Lines 78–89 in our example above).**

Because you combined this function body with the other event handler for the same button, this code is no longer necessary.

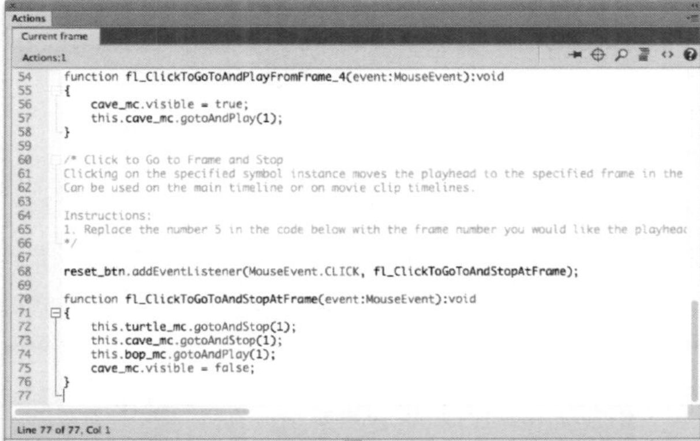

12. **Press Command-Return/Control-Enter to test the movie.**

Test the buttons that you just programmed. The Reset button should stop and hide all animations except for the swaying seaweed.

13. **Close the Player window, then save the Animate file and close it.**

Project Review

fill in the blank

1. Objects from a Photoshop file should be created on _______________ if they need to be managed separately when imported into Animate.

2. The _______________ tool allows you to scale objects dynamically on the Stage.

3. The _______________ defines the point around which object transformations are made.

4. The X and Y position of a symbol instance is based on the _______________.

5. You can use the _______________ panel to define numeric scale and skew values for the selected object.

6. Animation in a _______________ requires the same number of frames on the timeline where the instance is placed.

7. Animation in a _______________ plays regardless of the number of frames in the timeline where instances are placed.

8. _______________ is the format required by ActionScript 3 code.

9. Using ActionScript 3, code is attached to a specific _______________, and uses instance names to address specific objects.

10. In ActionScript, a(n) _______________ includes a statement defining the instance that triggers an event and the function that is called when the defined event occurs.

short answer

1. Briefly explain the concept of "tweening."

2. Briefly explain the difference between a graphic symbol and a movie clip symbol.

3. Briefly define an event handler.

Portfolio Builder Project

Use what you learned in this project to complete the following freeform exercise.
Carefully read the art director and client comments, then create your own design to meet the needs of the project.
Use the space below to sketch ideas; when finished, write a brief explanation of your reasoning behind your final design.

art director comments

The media director for the Chicago Wild Animal Park is re-branding the facility from the "City Zoo" image it has had for the past twenty years. He has hired you to create a series of animated icons for the park's new interactive Web site.

To complete this project, you should:

- ❑ Create each icon in the same shape and size, and use the same general style for each.
- ❑ Add some kind of animation to each icon. Use any combination of frame animations, shape tweens, and/or motion tweens.

client comments

We've gotten rid of the cages and created realistic natural habitats for the animals. Our main goals now are rehabilitation, preservation, and education. We're going to have educational programs and exhibits throughout the facility, but we don't want people to be scared off by the idea of learning!

We have many international visitors, so most of our collateral — including our new Web site — is based on images that can be understood in any language. Although there will be text as well, the icons should very clearly indicate what users will find when they click on any specific one (even if they can't read the words).

We need a series of six animated icons that will label the different areas of the facility. The six main sections are: the tropics, the desert, the Arctic, the forest, the ocean, and the sky. There will also be a special children's section that needs its own icon.

project justification

Project Summary

This project incorporated artwork that was created in Adobe Photoshop, which is a common development workflow. You also worked with symbols that were created in another Animate file, which is also a common collaborative process.

The second stage of this project focused on different methods of creating animation — frame-by-frame to move something in jumps, motion tweening to move objects smoothly, tweening to change only certain properties over time, and even tweening to rotate an object in three-dimensional space. To create these animations, you have also learned a number of techniques for transforming objects on the Stage; the Transform panel, the Free Transform tool, the Properties panel, and the Motion Editor panel all play valuable roles in Animate development.

Finally, you were introduced to the object-oriented model of ActionScript 3 when you added button controls using the Code Snippets panel. With very little (if any) knowledge of coding or programming, you were able to use the built-in functionality to meet the project's interactive requirements.

ocean.swf
BAY OCEAN
PRESERVE
Turtle
Cave
Reset
Animate Alpha properties and graphic filters
Define movie clip symbols to create tween animations
Import artwork from an Adobe Photoshop file
Create frame animations to move objects over time
Import symbols from an external Flash library
Add code to control the playback of various movie clip instances.

The Dreamweaver CC User Interface

Adobe Dreamweaver is an industry-standard application for building Web sites. Typical work ranges from static HTML pages with hyperlinks to complex, dynamic sites, where pages are generated on-the-fly based on individual user requests. Mastering the tools and techniques of the application can significantly improve your potential career options.

Explore the Dreamweaver Interface

Much of the Dreamweaver interface functions in the same way as the Photoshop and Flash user interface. Panels can be opened, moved, and grouped in the same manner, and you can save custom workspaces. In this exercise, you import an existing site into Dreamweaver and explore some of the options for looking at files.

1. **Download the `InterfaceDW_Web16_RF.zip` archive from the Student Files Web page.**

2. **Expand the ZIP archive in your WIP folder (Macintosh) or copy the archive contents into your WIP folder (Windows).**

   The resulting **InterfaceDW** folder contains all the files you need to complete this introduction.

3. **Launch Dreamweaver. If you see a message about syncing settings, click Disable Sync Settings.**

4. **Set up the Dreamweaver workspace so the Files and Properties panels are visible.**

5. **In Dreamweaver, click the Manage Sites link in the Files panel. If you don't see the Manage Sites link, open the Directory menu and choose Manage Sites from the bottom of the list.**

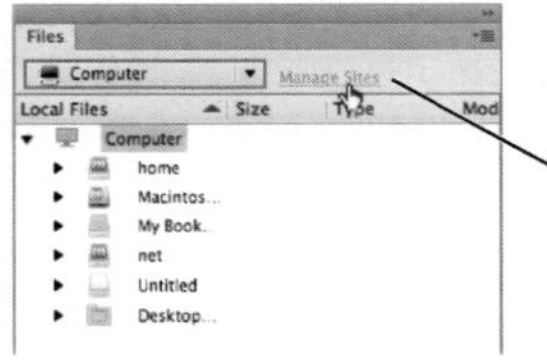

If no sites are currently open in Dreamweaver, click the hot-text link to open the Manage Sites dialog box.

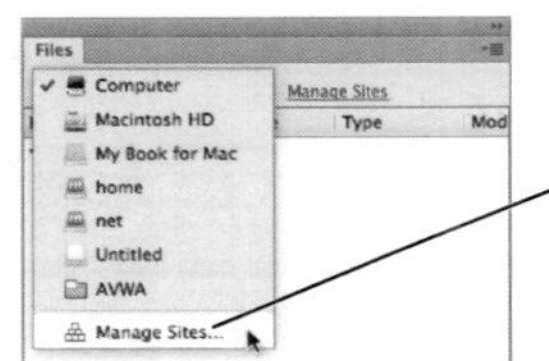

If the Manage Sites link is not available, open the Directory menu and choose the Manage Sites option.

Although Dreamweaver can be used to build individual HTML pages with no links to external files, the application is more commonly used to build entire sites. The Manage Sites dialog box is used to create new sites or import existing ones into Dreamweaver.

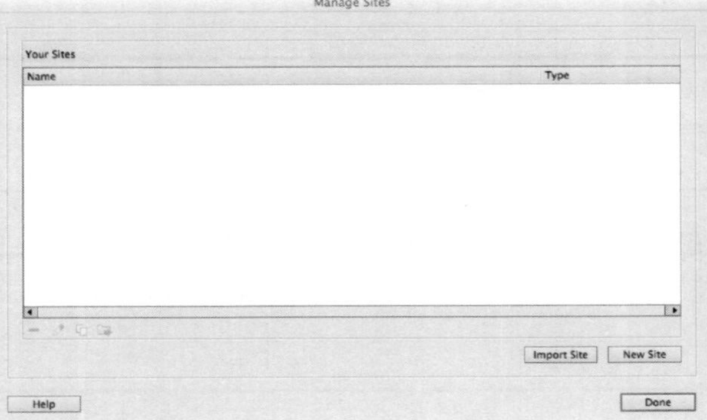

6. **Click the Import Site button in the Manage Sites dialog box. Navigate to your `WIP>InterfaceDW` folder, select `sf-arts.ste` in the list of available files, and click Open.**

   The ".ste" extension identifies a Dreamweaver site file, which stores information about the site such as URL, FTP login information, etc. By importing this file into Dreamweaver, you can work with an existing site.

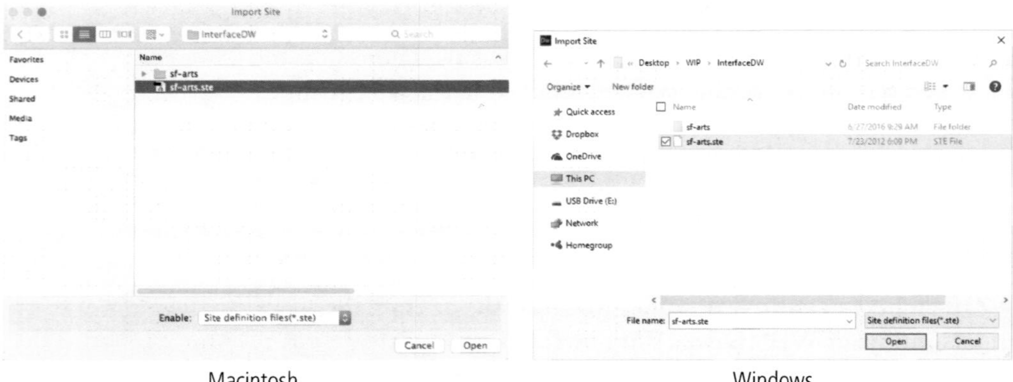

Macintosh Windows

7. **If asked to select the local root folder of the site:**

   Macintosh users: Select the `sf-arts` folder (in your WIP>InterfaceDW folder) and click Open.

   Windows users: Navigate to and open the `sf-arts` folder (in your WIP>InterfaceDW folder), then click Select.

Macintosh Windows

The **root folder** is simply the base folder that contains the files of your site. This is referred to as the "local" root folder because it is the folder on your computer system. When you upload site files to a Web server, you place the files in the remote root folder.

8. **If asked to select the local images folder for the imported site:**

   Macintosh users: Select the `images` folder in the `sf-arts` folder and click Open.

   Windows users: Navigate to and open the `sf-arts>images` folder, then click Select.

Macintosh Windows

After you identify the local images folder, files in the site are processed and then the site is listed in the Manage Sites dialog box. The name of the site (in this case, "sf-arts") is used for internal purposes only; it has no relation to the file names in the live HTML files.

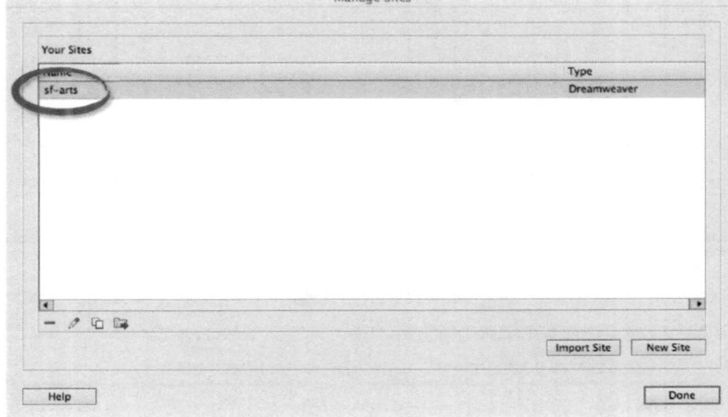

9. **Click Done to close the Manage Sites dialog box.**

   A Dreamweaver site typically includes links — from HTML pages to images, from one HTML page to another, and so on — which are the heart of interactive Web sites. When you import a site into Dreamweaver, the application processes the files in the site to identify links and other information required to maintain the integrity of the overall site.

   Depending on the number of files in a site, you might see a progress bar indicating that Dreamweaver is processing the files and creating a site cache, which helps the application manage the links between various files in the site.

10. In the Files panel, click the arrow/plus sign (+) to expand the site folder.

The Files panel provides access to all the elements that make up a Web site, including page files (whether HTML, PHP, or some other format), images, downloadable PDFs, and anything else required for the site to display properly.

On Macintosh, expanded folders show a down-facing arrow; clicking that arrow collapses the folder and changes the arrow to face to the right. You can click a right-facing arrow to expand a folder and show its contents.

On Windows, expanded folders show a "–" symbol; clicking that symbol collapses the folder and changes the "–" to a "+" symbol. You can click a "+" symbol to expand a folder and show its contents.

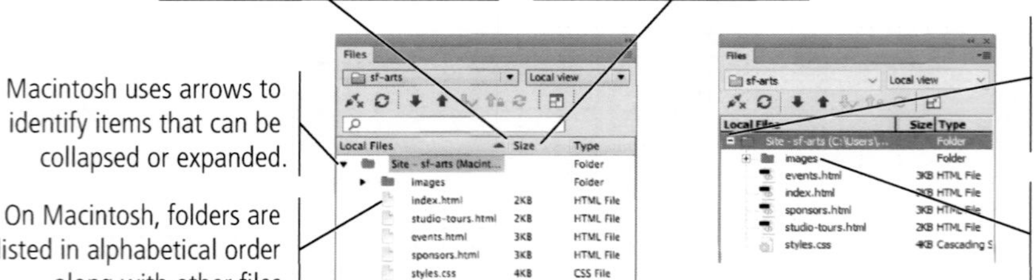

Click and drag the line between columns to make a column wider or narrower in the panel.
Click any column heading in the panel to sort the files by that category.
Macintosh uses arrows to identify items that can be collapsed or expanded.
On Macintosh, folders are listed in alphabetical order along with other files.
Windows uses "+" and "–" to identify items that can be expanded or collapsed.
On Windows, folders appear at the top of the Files list.

Customizing Dreamweaver Behavior

DREAMWEAVER FOUNDATIONS

You can customize the way many of the program's options function. The left side of the Preferences dialog box (Dreamweaver>Preferences on Macintosh or Edit>Preferences on Windows) allows you to display the various sets of preferences available in Dreamweaver. As you work your way through the projects in this book, you will learn not only what you can do with these collections of Preferences, but also *why* and *when* you might want to use them.

You can also customize the various keyboard shortcuts used to access Dreamweaver commands (Dreamweaver>Keyboard Shortcuts on Macintosh or Edit>Keyboard Shortcuts on Windows). Once you have defined custom shortcuts, you can save your choices as a set so you can access the same custom choices again without having to redo the work.

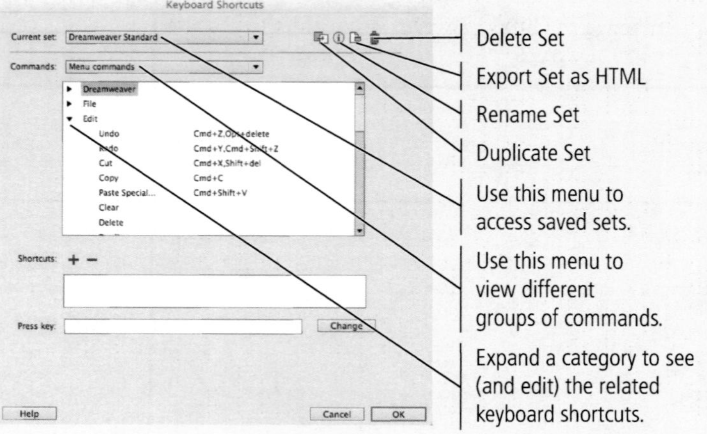

Delete Set
Export Set as HTML
Rename Set
Duplicate Set
Use this menu to access saved sets.
Use this menu to view different groups of commands.
Expand a category to see (and edit) the related keyboard shortcuts.

11. **In the Files panel, double-click the index.html file.**

Double-clicking a file in the Files panel opens that file in the document window.

For Dreamweaver to effectively monitor and manage the various links to required supporting files (images, scripts, etc.), you should only open and change site files from within the Files panel. If you open and change a file outside the context of the Files panel, Dreamweaver can't keep track of those changes, which can result in broken links.

The specific view you see in the document window depends on what view was active the last time a user opened a file.

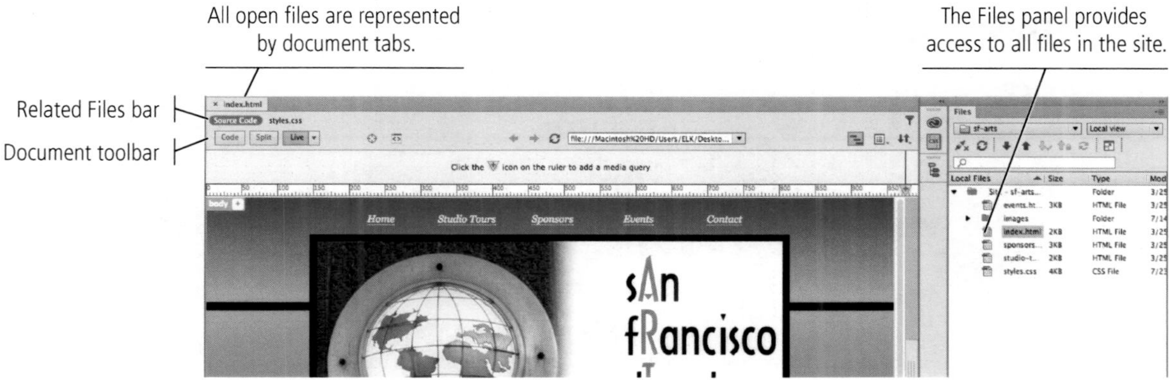

12. **If you don't see the Code and Split buttons above the document window, choose View>Toolbars>Document to toggle on the Document toolbar.**

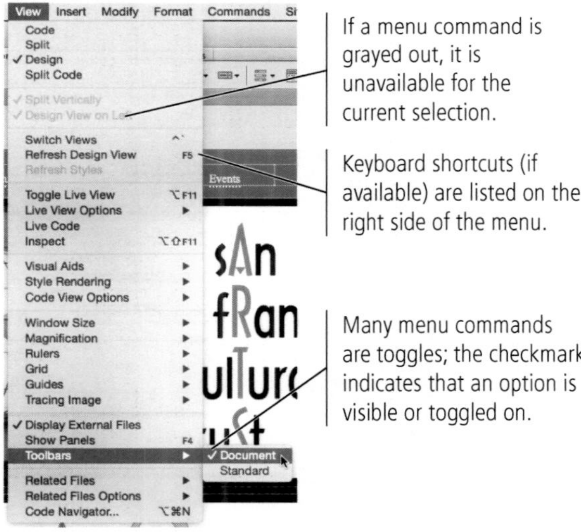

If a menu command is grayed out, it is unavailable for the current selection.
Keyboard shortcuts (if available) are listed on the right side of the menu.
Many menu commands are toggles; the checkmark indicates that an option is visible or toggled on.

13. **In the Document toolbar, look at the third button from the left. If the button does not show the word "Design", click the arrow to the right of the button and choose Design from the resulting menu.**

Design view is useful for visually-oriented site design, providing a fairly accurate visual preview of the file similar to the way it will appear in a browser window. Live view (the default) will be explained in the next exercise.

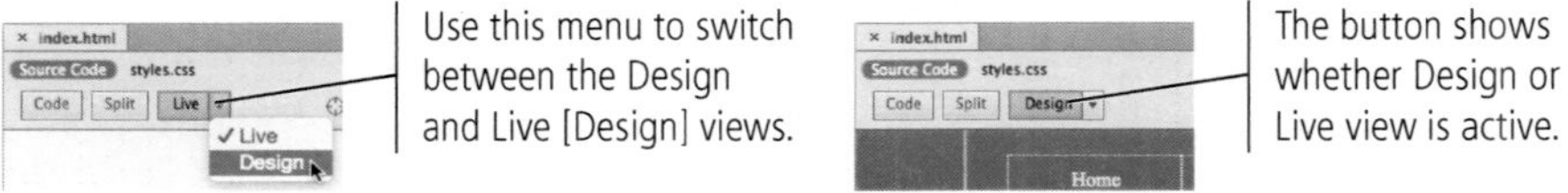

The button shows whether Design or Live view is active.

14. **Click the Design button to show only the Design view in the document window.**

Click these buttons to change which panes are visible in the document window.
Home
Studio Tours
Sponsors
Events
Contact
sAn fRancisco culTural truSt

> *Note:*
>
> *If the Application frame is not active on Macintosh, the first open file will not have a document tab. Instead, a title bar appears at the top of the one open document. When you open more than one file at a time, each open document is represented by a tab at the top of the document window.*

15. **If necessary, scroll down to show the bottom of the page. Click the "Art&Architecture" logo to select it, then review the Properties panel.**

At this point, it isn't necessary to understand what the various properties do; you learn about all these options in later projects. For now, you should simply understand that the Properties panel is context sensitive, which means the available options depend on what is currently selected.

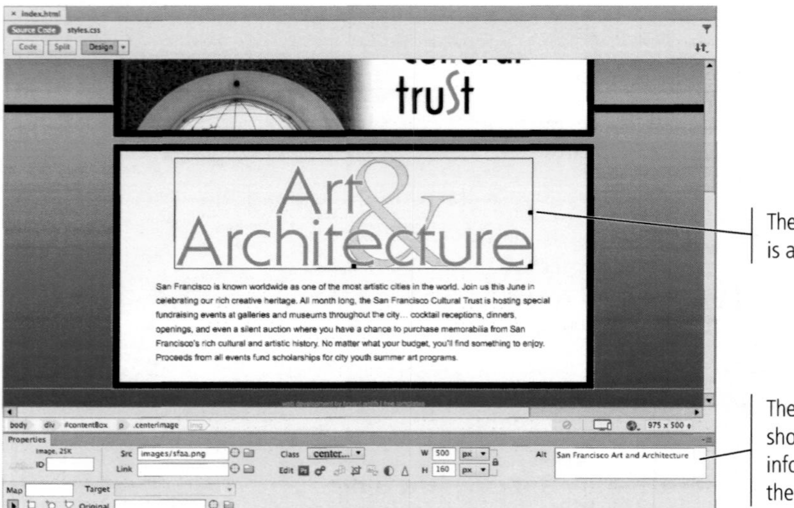
truSt
Art&Architecture
The selected object is an image.
The Properties panel shows options and information specific to the active selection.

> *Note:*
>
> *The design for this site is based on the "Barren Savannah" template by Bryant Smith. The original template was found at www.free-templates.me, one of many online sources for Web design templates that are free to use and modify to meet your specific needs.*

16. **Double-click the word "Francisco" (in the first line of text below the logo) to select the entire word, and then review the Properties panel.**

Unlike many design applications, in Dreamweaver you don't have to choose a specific tool to select objects in a document.

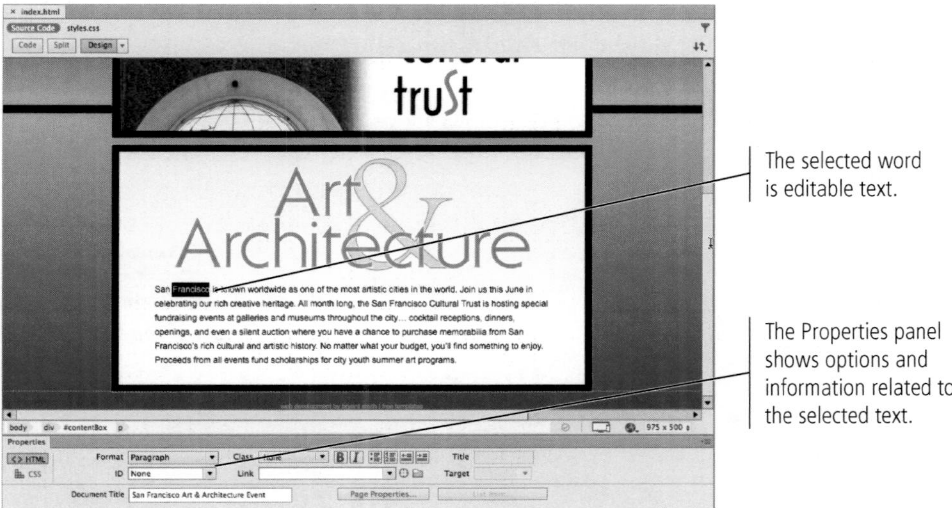

The selected word is editable text.
The Properties panel shows options and information related to the selected text.

17. **With the text still selected, click the Split button in the Document toolbar.**

Split view shows both the Code and Design view windows. When working in Split view, selecting an object in the Design view highlights the related code in the Code view.

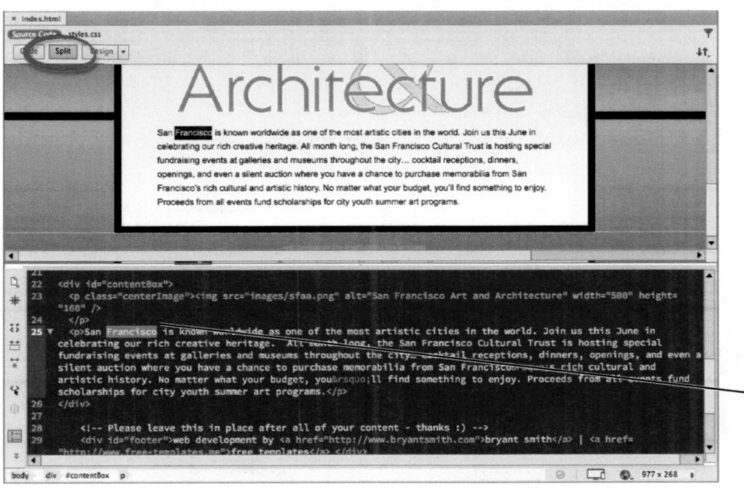

Note:

You can also choose Split Code view in the View menu, which shows the page code in two panes at the same time. This view can be useful if you need to write code in one area that specifically relates or refers to code at another point in the page.

18. **Macintosh users: Choose Dreamweaver>Preferences.**
    Windows users: Choose Edit>Preferences.

    Remember that on Macintosh systems, the Preferences dialog box is accessed in the Dreamweaver menu; Windows users access the Preferences dialog box in the Edit menu.

19. **Click Code Coloring in the category list on the left side of the dialog box.**

    In addition to customizing the workspace, you can customize the way many of the program's options function. The left side of the Preferences dialog box allows you to display the various sets of options that you can control.

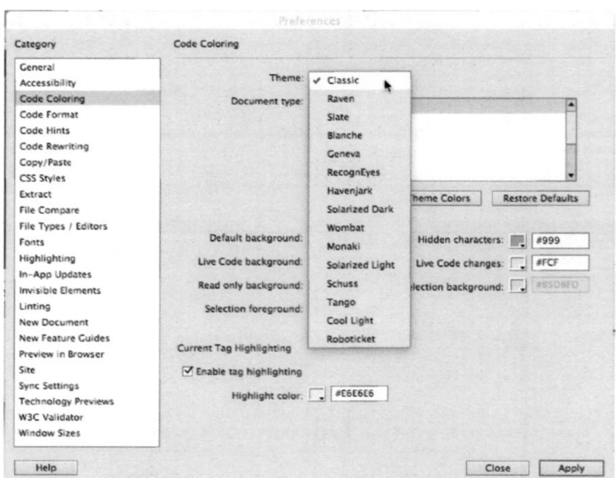

> ***Note:***
>
> *As you work your way through the projects in this book, you will learn not only what you can do with these collections of Preferences, but also* ***why*** *and* ***when*** *you might want to use them.*

20. **Choose whatever option you prefer in the Theme menu, then click the Apply button.**

    The Code Coloring preferences control the appearance of various code elements that are visible in the Code pane. The default theme, RecognEyes, displays colors text on a black background — which many argue is easier to read (and easier on the eyes) when viewing the code on a monitor. We use the Classic theme in our screen captures because the dark text on a white background is easier to read in print.

21. **When you are satisfied with the appearance of the Code pane, click the Close button to close the Preferences dialog box.**

22. **Choose View>Design View on Top to toggle that option off.**

    By default, the Split view shows the Code view on the bottom and the Design view on the top; you can reverse this orientation to suit your personal work preferences.

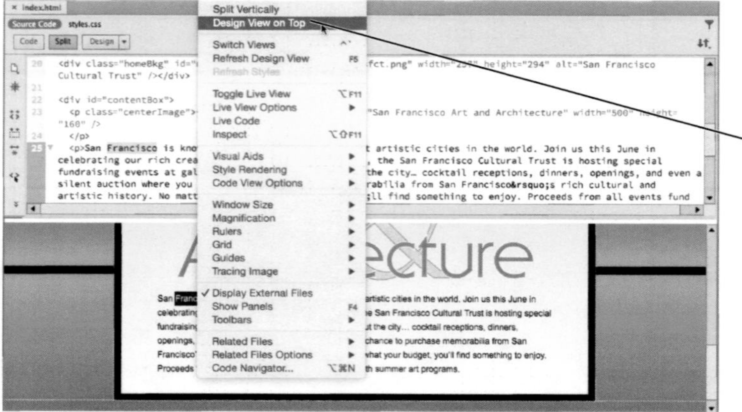

When Split Vertically is not active, you can toggle the Design View on Top command to reverse the views in the document window.

23. **Choose View>Split Vertically to toggle this option on.**

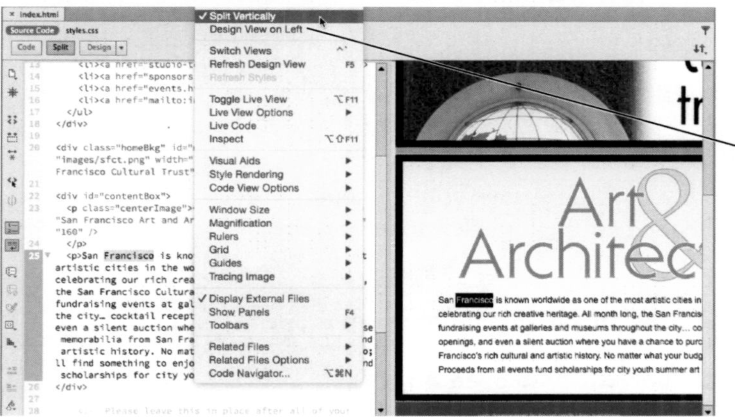

When Split Vertically is active, you can toggle the Design View on Left command to reverse the views in the document window.

24. **Click the Code button in the Document toolbar.**

    The Code view is useful for people who are familiar with writing code; this mode allows you to (temporarily) ignore the visual design and work solely on the code.

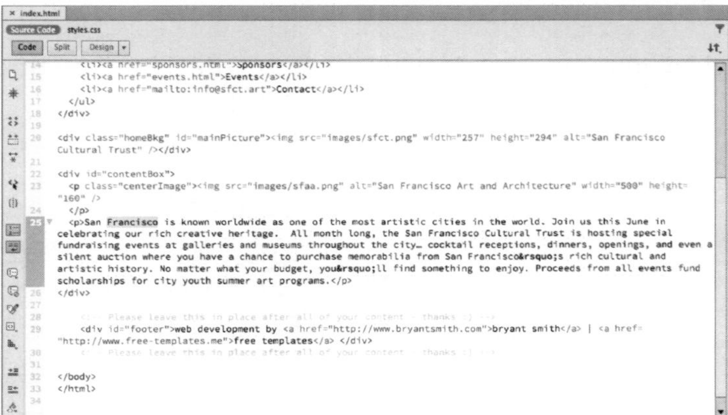

25. **Click the Design button in the Document toolbar to return to only the Design view.**

26. **Continue to the next exercise.**

Preview Files in Dreamweaver Live View

Dreamweaver's Design view does a reasonably good job of allowing you to design Web pages visually, but some common design elements, such as rollovers and multimedia files, are not enabled in the Design view. The Live view provides an internal method for checking many of these elements without leaving the Dreamweaver environment.

You can't edit pages directly in Live view. However, if you are working in Split view, you can make changes to the code and then refresh the Live view to see the effect of those changes.

1. **With the sf-arts site open in the Files panel, make sure index.html is open.**

2. **In the Files panel, double-click studio-tours.html to open that page.**

   Each open file is represented by a tab at the top of the document window. You can click any tab to make the associated file active in the document window.

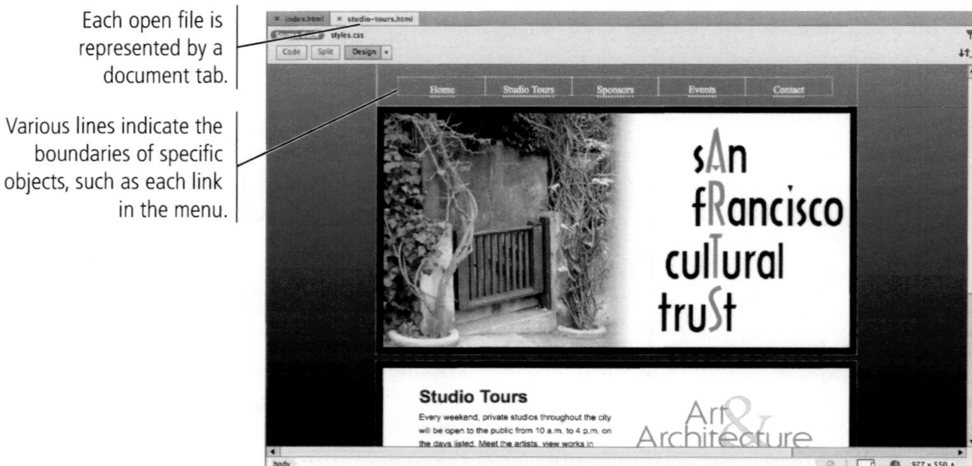

Various lines indicate the boundaries of specific objects, such as each link in the menu.

3. **Choose View>Visual Aids>Hide All.**

   Visual aids make it easier to identify the various elements (such as page divisions) used to create structure but which do not necessarily have a tangible physical appearance. While certainly useful, these visual aids interfere with the physical layout of the site so what you see in the document window is *not* what you get in the browser window.

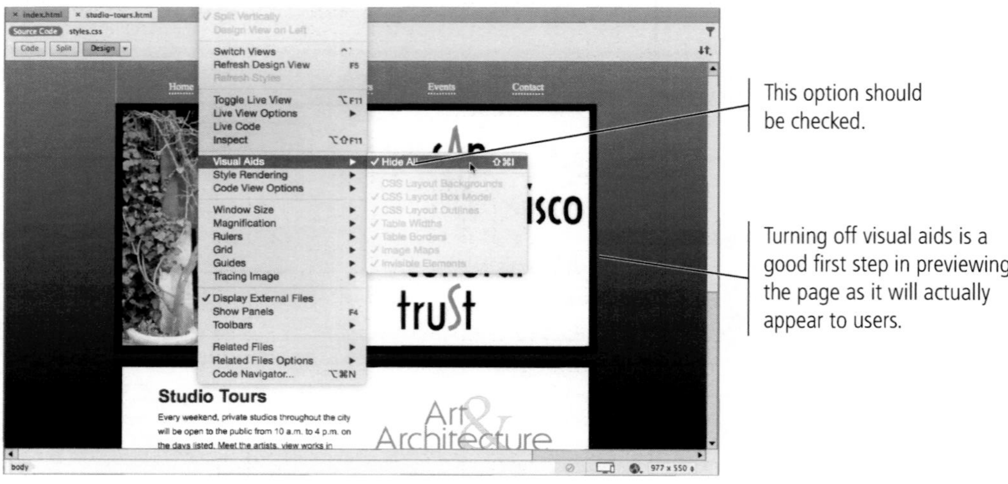

This option should be checked.
Turning off visual aids is a good first step in previewing the page as it will actually appear to users.

4. In the Document toolbar, click the arrow button to the right of the Design button in the document toolbar. Choose Live from the resulting menu.

5. Move your mouse cursor over the Events link at the top of the page.

Rollover elements do not function properly in Dreamweaver's Design view. The Live view provides a way to test interactive elements (such as rollovers) within the Dreamweaver environment.

In Live view, the rollover button displays as it would in a browser.

6. Press Command/Control and click the Events link.

One final reminder: Throughout this book, we list differing commands in the Macintosh/Windows format. On Macintosh, you need to press the Command key; on Windows, press the Control key. (We will not repeat this explanation every time different commands are required for the different operating systems.)

In Live view, pressing the Command/Control key lets you preview linked files in the local site folder directly in the Dreamweaver document window. If you click a link to an external file, you will see a "File Not Found" error message.

> **Note:**
>
> *When working in Live view, the Browser Navigation buttons in the Document toolbar function in the same way that standard browser navigation buttons work: Back, Forward, Stop/Refresh (reload), and Home (the site's index file).*

The active file does not change even though you navigated to a link in the Live view.

Use these buttons to navigate back and forward, just as you would in a browser.

7. **In the Document toolbar, open the menu to the right of the Live button and choose Design to return to the regular Design view.**

   Navigating in the Live view does not technically open the linked pages. When you return to the regular Design view, the previously active page — in this case, studio-tours.html — is still the active one.

8. **Click the Close button on the studio-tours.html tab to close that file.**

   Each document has its own Close button.

9. **Click the Close button on the index.html document tab to close that file.**

   On Macintosh systems, clicking the Close button on the document window closes all open files, but does not quit the application.

   On Windows systems, clicking the Close (X) button on the Application frame closes all open files and quits the application.

10. **Continue to the next exercise.**

Preview a File in a Browser

As you saw in the previous exercise, the Live view can be used to verify the appearance of many common Web design objects. Of course, site users will not be using Dreamweaver to view your pages, so it is always a good idea to test pages using the same method that will actually be used to display your pages — namely, the various browsers that are in common use.

Although there are some standards that govern the way browsers display Web page code, the various browsers do have some different capabilities. Different operating systems also introduce display variables, so what you see in Mozilla Firefox on a Macintosh might appear different than what you see in Firefox on Windows. As a general rule, you should test your pages on as many browsers as possible — on both Macintosh and Windows operating systems.

1. **Macintosh: Choose Dreamweaver>Preferences.**
   Windows: Choose Edit>Preferences.

   On the left side of the Preferences dialog box, click Preview in Browser to display the related options.

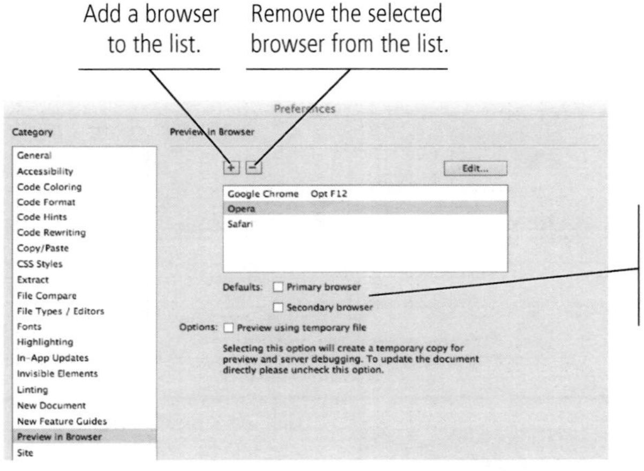

Note:

Press Option-F12/F12 to preview a page in your primary browser. Press Command/Control-F12 to preview the page in your secondary browser.

If you are using a Macintosh laptop, you also have to press the Function (FN) key to use the F key shortcuts.

2. **Review the list of browsers that are identified by Dreamweaver.**

   When installed, Dreamweaver scans your computer for available browser applications. You likely have at least one browser in this list, and probably even more than one.

3. **If a browser is available on your system but not in Dreamweaver, click the "+" button above the list of browsers.**

4. **In the resulting Add Browser dialog box, click the Browse button and identify the location of the browser you want to add.**

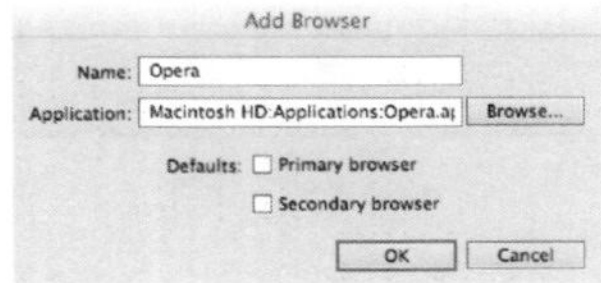

5. **Click OK to return to the Preferences dialog box.**

   The list of browsers shows the defined primary and secondary browsers, which you can invoke using the associated keyboard shortcuts. To change the defaults, you can simply select a browser in the list and check the related Defaults options.

6. **Repeat Steps 3–5 as necessary to add all available browsers to Dreamweaver,**

7. **Click Apply in the Preferences dialog box to finalize your changes, then click Close to close the dialog box.**

8. **In the Files panel, double-click the index.html file to open it.**

9. **Click the Preview/Debug in Browser button in the bottom-right corner of the document window and choose one of the listed browsers.**

Note:

Choosing Edit Browser List in this menu opens the Preview in Browser pane of the Preferences dialog box.

Preview/Debug in Browser button

Note:

A mailto: link opens a new mail message in the user's default email application. If a user does not have an email client, or has not specified one as the default option, clicking a mailto: link might open a message asking which application to use to send the email.

10. **In the resulting browser window, click the links at the top of the page to test them.**

The Contact link on the right side of the menu opens a new, preaddressed mail message in your default email application.

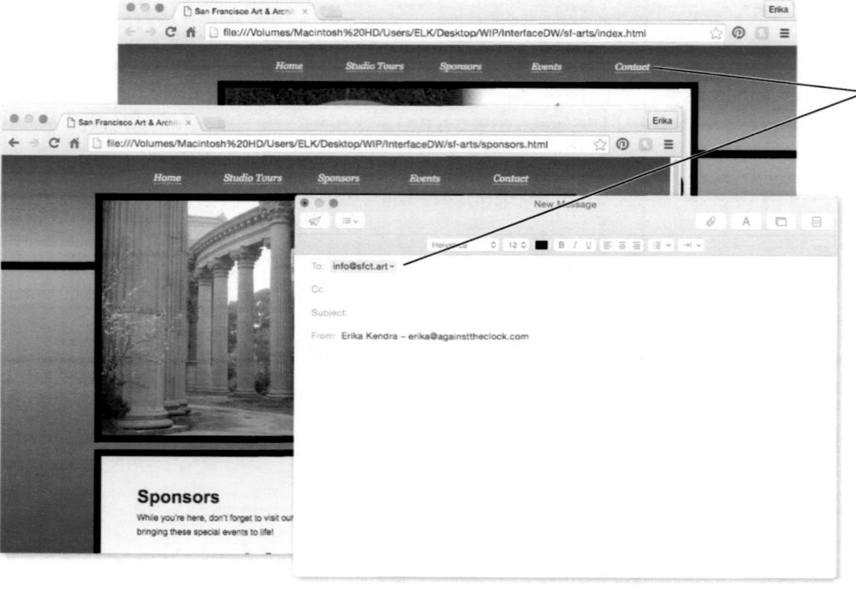

Clicking the link in a browser window correctly opens a new email message in your default email application.

11. **Close the mail message without sending.**

12. **Close the browser window and return to Dreamweaver.**

13. **Close index.html, then continue to the next exercise.**

Remove a Site from Dreamweaver

As you gain experience designing and developing Web sites, your site definition list will continue to grow. To keep your list under control, you can export site definitions and remove certain sites from the list. When you remove a site from Dreamweaver, you are not deleting the actual files and folders from your computer; you are simply removing them from Dreamweaver's view.

1. **In the Files panel, open the Directory menu and choose Manage Sites at the bottom of the list.**

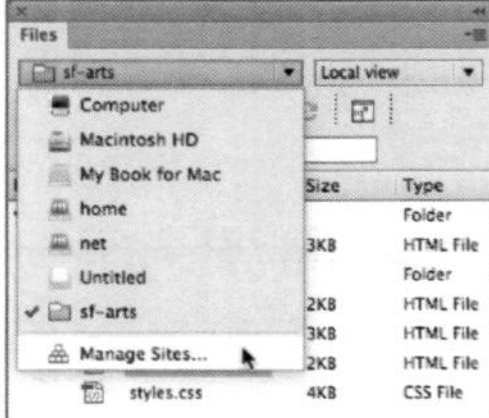

2. **In the resulting Manage Sites dialog box, select the sf-arts site in the list and click the "–" button below the list of available sites.**

   In this case, you made no changes to the site definitions or files. Because you already have an STE file with the correct information, it is not necessary to re-export the site definition.

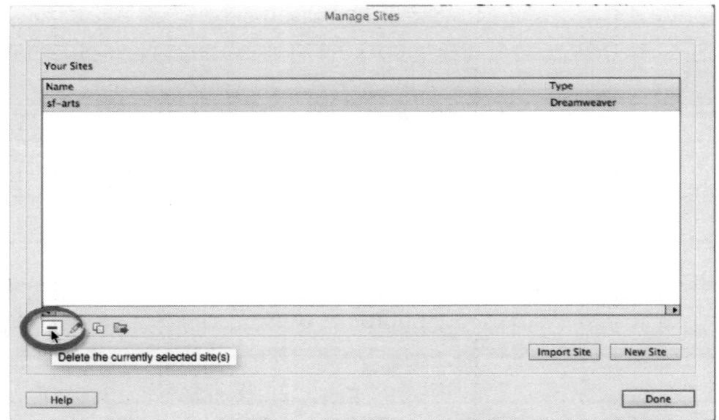

3. **Click Yes in the Warning dialog box, and then click Done to close the Manage Sites dialog box.**

   After removing the site, it no longer appears in the list of sites.

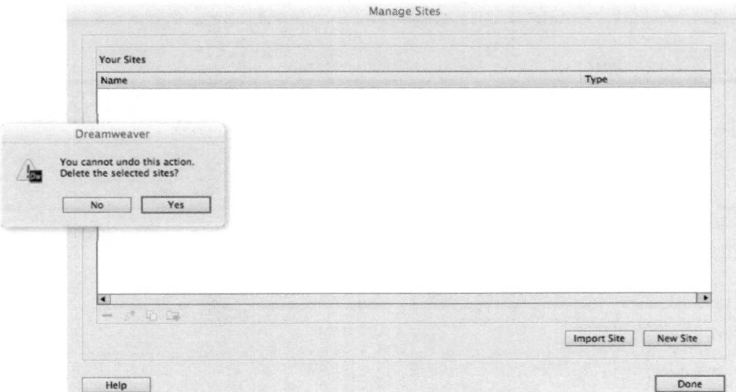

Synchronizing Settings

As part of your individual-user Adobe Creative Cloud membership, you can use the Sync Settings options to share certain custom assets between different computers. This means that you can access those same assets on any computer where you are logged in to your Creative Cloud account.

First, you must be logged into your Creative Cloud account and connected to the Internet for the sync process to work. You can open the Help menu to verify that you are signed in to your Creative Cloud account.

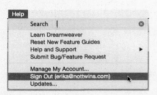

When you first launch the application, you will see a message that Dreamweaver "securely syncs your preferences and settings with Creative Cloud."

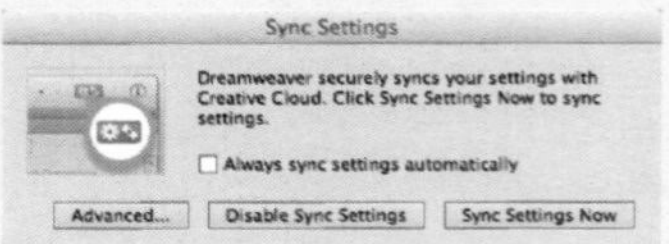

Disable Sync Settings cancels the synchronization process.

Sync Settings Now synchronizes settings using the default sync options.

Advanced opens the Sync Settings pane of the Preferences dialog box, where you can customize which assets will be synchronized (Application Preferences and/or Site Settings).

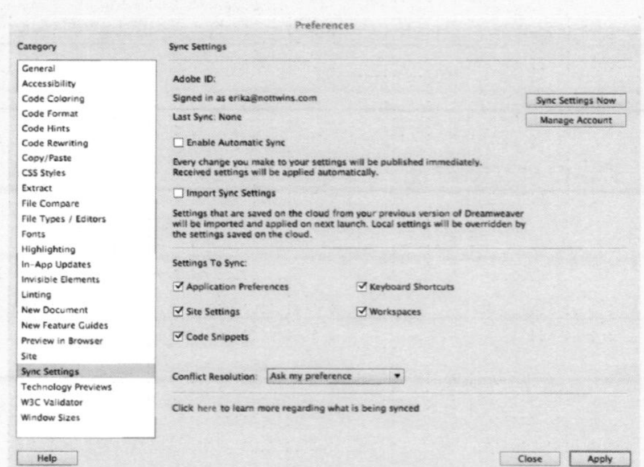

If you check the Enable Automatic Sync option, changes to the settings in your Cloud account are automatically applied whenever you use the application.

After the first launch, you might see a similar message telling you that synchronized settings are available in your Creative Cloud account.

- **Advanced** opens the Sync Settings pane of the Preferences dialog box
- **Upload Sync Settings** overwrites the settings on the Cloud with the settings from your local computer.
- **Download Sync Settings** overwrites the settings on your local computer with the settings in your Creative Cloud account.

At any time, you can use the Sync icon in the top-right corner of the user interface to initiate the sync process. (If you clicked Disable Sync Settings in the initial message dialog box, the Sync Settings Now button is disabled; you can always re-enable synchronization in the Preferences dialog box.)

Sync options are also accessible by opening the submenu for your user account (in the Dreamweaver menu on Macintosh or the Edit menu on Windows). Choosing **Sync Settings Now** initiates the sync process. Choosing **Manage Sync Settings** opens the Sync Settings pane of the Preferences dialog box.

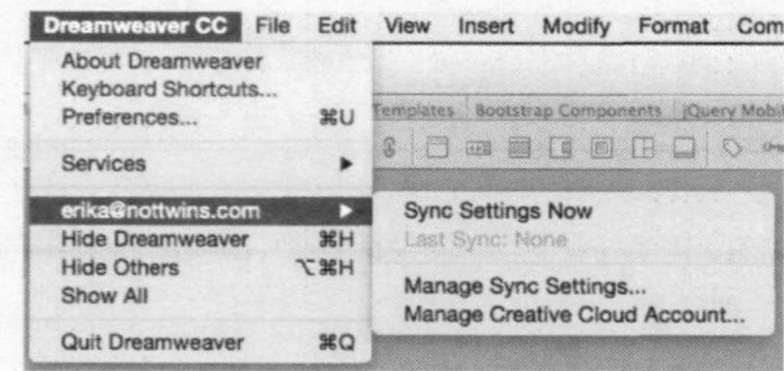

If you try to sync settings and a conflict exists between your local and Creative Cloud settings, you are asked how you want to resolve the conflict (Sync Local or Sync Cloud).

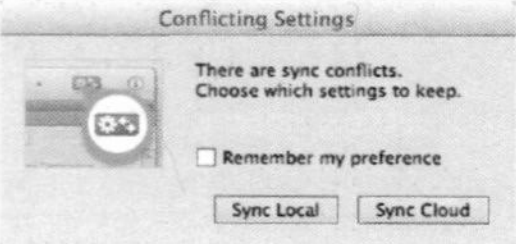

Bistro Site Organization

Your client has opened a new restaurant in a fast-growing community in Southern California. He has already designed the pages for his site, but has hired you to make sure everything works properly and then make the site available to the browsing public.

This project incorporates the following skills:

- ❑ Creating, exporting, and removing site definitions in Dreamweaver
- ❑ Moving files around in a site root folder
- ❑ Creating relative links between pages in a site
- ❑ Defining absolute links to external sites and email addresses
- ❑ Improving search engine optimization (SEO) with file names and titles
- ❑ Cloaking site files from a Web server
- ❑ Uploading files to a Web server

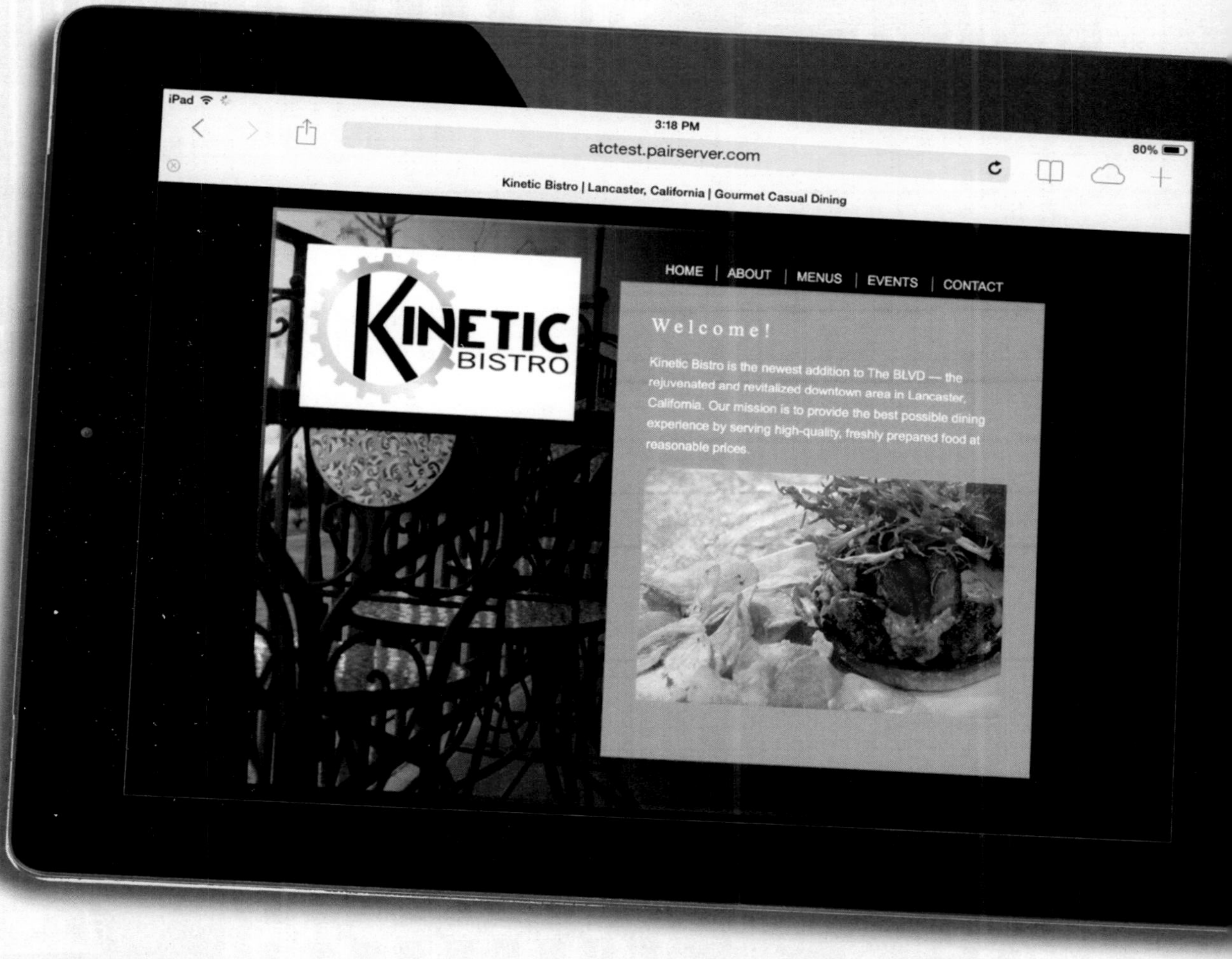

Project Meeting

client comments

I already created the pages for our site, but I don't know what links to use, and I'm not sure how to create them. I've also heard that there are certain things you should do to improve a site's search engine rating — which is obviously important for a small business like mine.

art director comments

The more pages you add to a site, the more complex it becomes, until it's almost impossible to make sense of what you have and where it is located. Web sites — even those with only a few pages — should be designed with a good organizational plan, making it easier to modify pages later.

Once you have a handle on the organization, make sure the pages link to each other properly. Visitors get frustrated very quickly when they're forced to return to the home page every time they want to jump to a different set of pages.

The last thing you should do is add page titles and change file names to give a better indication of what's on each page. Doing so will make the site more accessible to people with screen-reader software, and it will also improve the site's ratings on search engines.

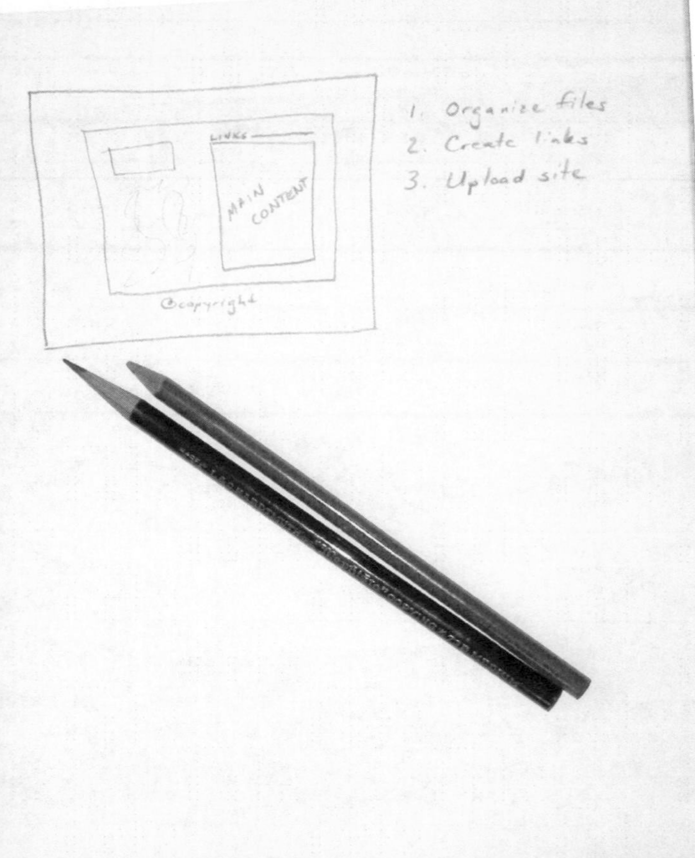

project objectives

To complete this project, you will:

- ❑ Create a Dreamweaver site definition
- ❑ Create new folders within the site root folder
- ❑ Use various methods to move files from one place to another within the site
- ❑ Create links between pages using several techniques available in Dreamweaver
- ❑ Differentiate between relative and absolute links
- ❑ Copy and paste links from one page to another
- ❑ Improve searchability and usability using page names and titles
- ❑ Cloak site files to hide them from the Web server
- ❑ Upload the site files to a server so they can be viewed online

Stage 1 Exploring Site Structure

When you start a new project that involves updating an existing site, your first task is to assess the file and folder structure. Doing so gives you a good idea of what the site contains.

A small site with only a few pages requires very little organization; in fact, you *can* place all of the files — Web pages and image files — in one folder (although even a small site benefits from a dedicated folder for images). Larger sites, however, require careful organization of file names, pages, and image files. A good site design with excellent organization speeds development now, and makes it much easier to update the site later.

Create a New Site Definition

Web sites are designed so all of the Web pages, image files, style sheets, and other resources are stored on your local drive in a base folder called the **root folder**. Other folders can be placed inside (below) the root folder to make it easier to manage and organize files.

1. **Download Kinetic_Web16_RF.zip from the Student Files Web page.**

2. **Expand the ZIP archive in your WIP folder (Macintosh) or copy the archive contents into your WIP folder (Windows).**

   This results in a folder named **Kinetic**, which contains all the files you need to complete this project.

3. **In Dreamweaver, set up your workspace so the Files, Insert, and Properties panels are visible.**

   It doesn't matter which saved workspace you start with. The primary tools you need for this project are the Files, Insert, and Properties panels. We have closed all other panels to maximize the available space in our screen shots.

4. **In the Files panel, click the Manage Sites link or open the Directory menu and choose Manage Sites from the bottom of the list.**

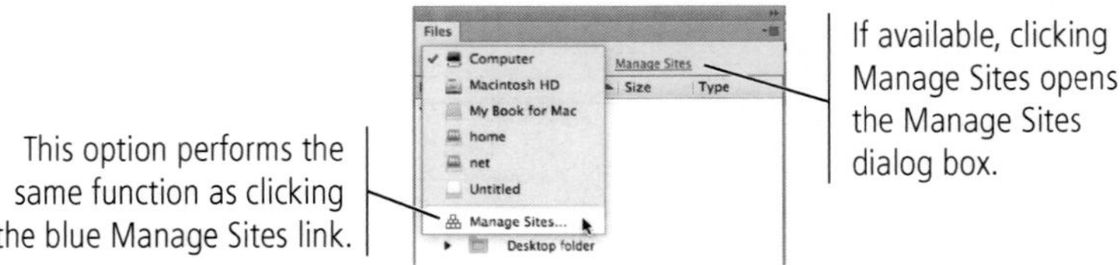

5. **Click the New Site button in the Manage Sites dialog box.**

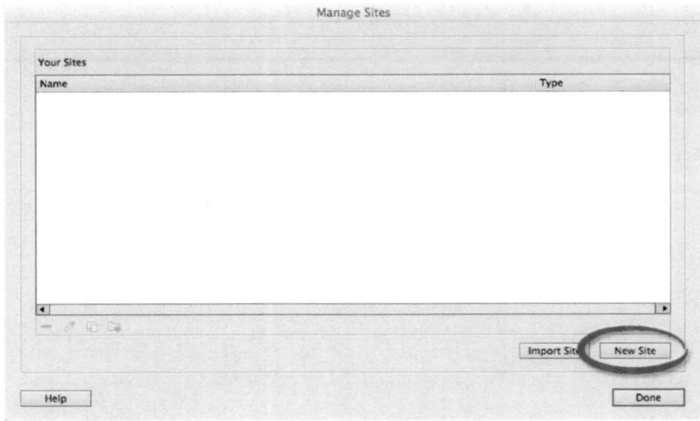

Note:

When a site is defined in Dreamweaver, the Manage Sites link at the top of the Files panel is replaced by a menu that defaults to Local view.

Note:

Ellipses in a menu or button name indicate that clicking will open a dialog box. We do not include the ellipses in our instructions.

6. **In the Site Setup dialog box, make sure Site is selected in the category list.**

7. **Type Kinetic in the Site Name field.**

   The site name can be anything that will allow you to easily recognize the project; it is only for identification within Dreamweaver. For example, you could use "Eve's site" as the site name within Dreamweaver to describe the Web site (www.evelynsmith.biz) that you are creating for your friend.

8. **Click the Browse for Folder button to the right of the Local Site Folder field. Navigate to the WIP>Kinetic folder and click Choose/Select Folder to return to the Site Setup dialog box.**

   Part of the process of defining a site within Dreamweaver is to specify a particular folder as the site root folder of the Web site. Clicking the Local Site Folder button opens a navigation dialog box where you can find the folder you want to use.

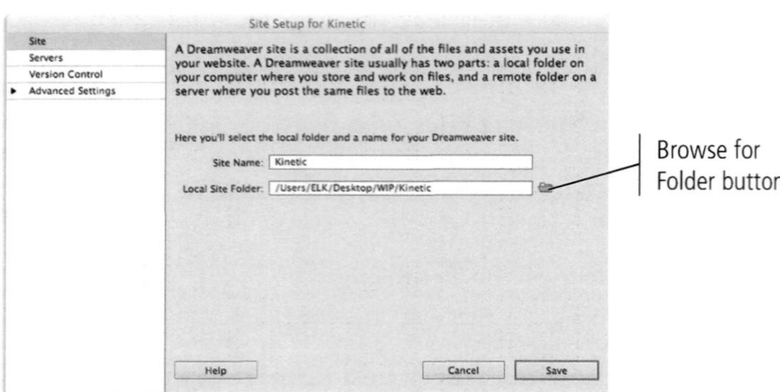

Note:

You will learn about other options in the Site Setup dialog box later in this book.

9. **Click Save to close the Site Setup dialog box.**

10. **In the Manage Sites dialog box, make sure the Kinetic site appears in the list of sites, and then click Done.**

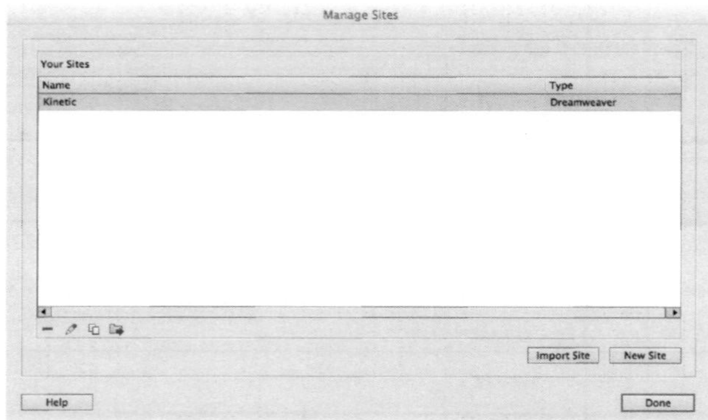

11. **Continue to the next exercise.**

Examine the Site Files

There are many files in the Kinetic site folder. The first step in organizing the files is to examine the Web page files and understand what they contain.

1. **With Kinetic showing in the Directory menu of the Files panel, expand the site folder (if necessary) and examine the files in the site.**

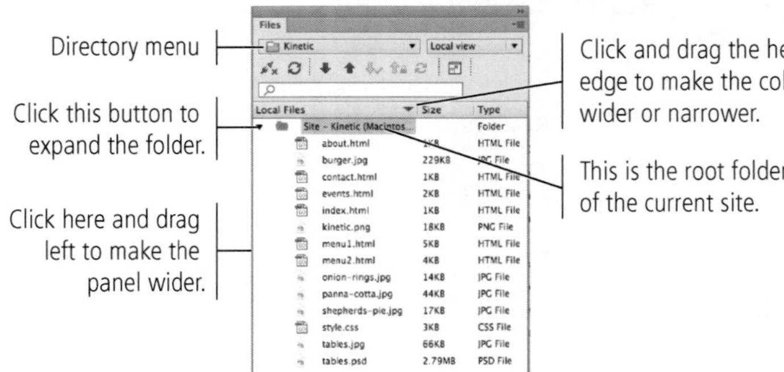

> ***Note:***
>
> *If more than one site is defined, you can switch between sites using the Directory menu of the Files panel.*

2. **Double-click index.html in the Files panel to open the file in Dreamweaver.**

   Using the options on the left side of the Document toolbar, close the Code pane (if necessary) and make the regular Design view active; the Live view should be turned off.

   All of the pages in this site use the same basic design. The links at the top of each page need to navigate between the pages. The copyright information at the bottom (in the footer area) needs to navigate to the copyright owner's Web site, which is external to your client's site.

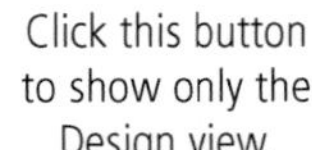

Click this button to show only the Design view.

Choose Design in this menu to show the regular Design view.

These words will be links, which will appear on every page in the site.

This should be a link to the copyright holder's Web site.

3. **Close index.html, then open contact.html.**

   As you can see, this page uses the same basic design as the index page. The specific page content also includes an email link, which you need to define so that users can click the link to send your client an email message.

HOME | ABOUT | MENUS | EVENTS | CONTACT
KINETIC BISTRO
Contact us!
These links should be the same on every page in the site.
This should be an email link to your client's email address.

4. **Close contact.html, then open menu1.html.**

   Again, the page uses the same basic layout as the other pages in the site. The top area of this page's primary content indicates that there are actually two menus — Dinner and Lunch. As you can see in the Files panel, two separate menu files exist. You will use the two headings at the top of the page to create links to each menu.

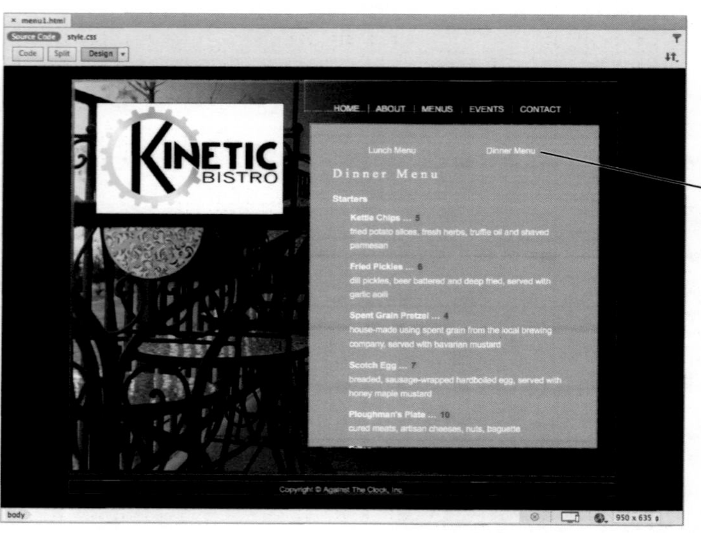

HOME | ABOUT | MENUS | EVENTS | CONTACT
KINETIC BISTRO
Dinner Menu
These words should link to the relevant menu page.

5. **Close menu1.html, then continue to the next exercise.**

> ***Note:***
>
> *The layout for this site is based on the free "Creation" template from www.templatemo.com. Photos are by Charlie Essers.*

Plan Folder Organization

When all files are dumped into the main site folder, it can be challenging to manage your work. A well-organized site is an easy-to-manage site. Ideally, organization occurs before the site is constructed, but Dreamweaver makes it easy to reorganize files and folders at any point in the process.

There are no absolute rules to follow for organizing files and folders — other than the general principle of keeping related components together, so you know where to find certain files when you need them.

1. **With the Kinetic site open in the Files panel, scroll to the top of the Files panel (if necessary). Control/right-click the site name and choose New Folder from the contextual menu.**

   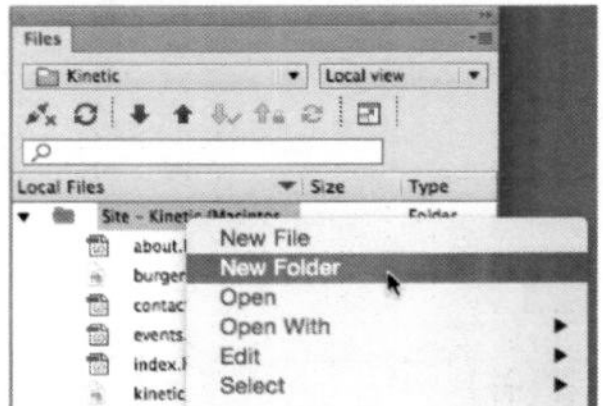

   The basic pages (home, about, contact, etc.) form the root of the site, and they should therefore appear within the root folder of the site. Other pages are better kept in folders that are named based on what they contain.

2. **Type resources and press Return/Enter to apply the new folder name.**

   If the folder name remains untitled after pressing Return/Enter, Control/right-click the untitled folder, choose Edit>Rename in the contextual menu (or press the F2 key), and retype the new folder name.

The Files Panel in Depth

DREAMWEAVER FOUNDATIONS

By default, the Files panel displays the site files on your local computer. The top of the Files panel also includes buttons that allow you to manage the files in your site:

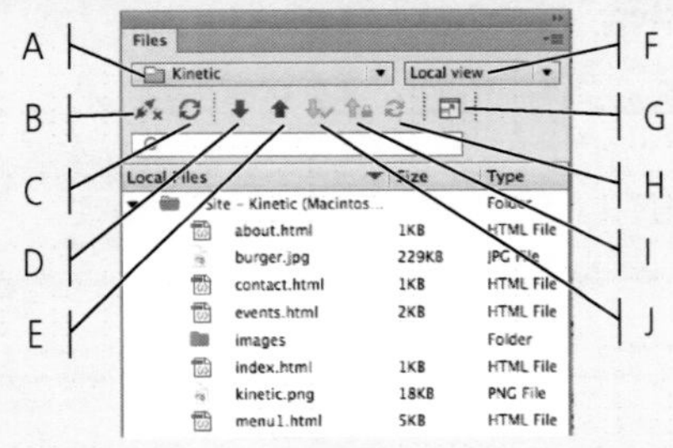

- A The **Directory menu** includes a list of available drives, sites that have been defined in Dreamweaver, and a link to the Manage Sites dialog box.
- B **Connect to Remote Server** establishes a connection with the remote server (if you defined one). Otherwise, clicking this button opens the Site Definition dialog box.
- C **Refresh** refreshes the file list that displays in the panel.
- D **Get Files from Remote Server** copies the selected files from a remote server to the local folder. If the Enable Check In and Check Out Files option is active, the copied files are available on the local site in read-only mode, which means you can't modify them. You must click the Check Out Files button to edit the files.
- E **Put Files to Remote Server** copies the selected files from the local folder to the remote server. If a new file is added to the server, and if the Enable Check In and Check Out File option is active, the file's status is Checked Out.
- F Use the **View menu** to view the files on the remote or testing servers by choosing the appropriate option from the View menu.
- G **Expand** shows both local files and the remote site (if one has been defined). The expanded Files panel has two panes; one displays the files on the remote or test server and one displays the local site files.
- H **Synchronize with Remote Server** synchronizes files between the local folder and remote server so the same version appears in both places.
- I **Check In** copies the selected files from the local folder to the remote server and makes the copied files read-only in the local folder. To edit these files, you need to select them and click the Check Out Files button.
- J **Check Out Files** copies the selected files from the remote server to the local folder and locks the files, so only the user who checked out those files can edit them.

3. **Click the Refresh button in the Files panel.**

   When the Files panel is sorted by name, folders on Macintosh are alphabetized along with all other files and folders after refreshing the file list; on Windows, folders are moved to and alphabetized at the top of the list, above individual files.

> *Note:*
>
> *Press F5 to refresh the file list in the Files panel.*

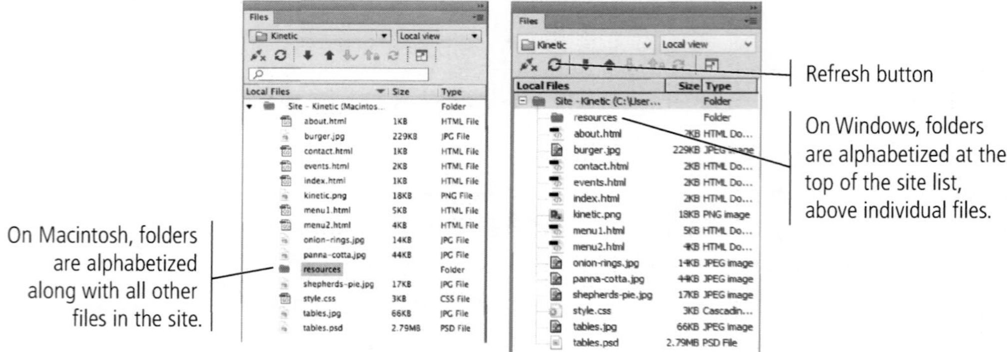
Refresh button
On Windows, folders are alphabetized at the top of the site list, above individual files.
On Macintosh, folders are alphabetized along with all other files in the site.

4. **Control/right-click the main site folder again and choose New Folder from the contextual menu.**

   You want another folder at the same level as the resources folder — in the main level of the site root — so you first have to use the contextual menu for the site root folder.

5. **Type images and press Return/Enter to apply the new folder name.**

   Web design convention dictates image files be placed in a folder named "images" for easier organization. If you have many photos in various categories, you might want to create additional nested folders inside the main images folder.

6. **Repeat Steps 4–5 to create another new folder named menus in the site root folder.**

7. **Refresh the list in the Files panel.**

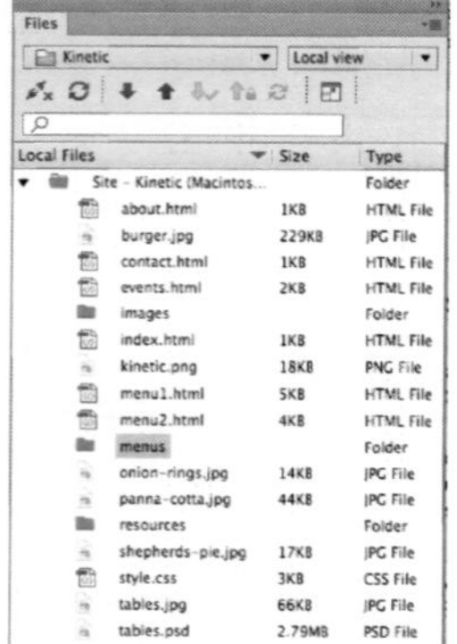

> *Note:*
>
> *You can create a new folder inside an existing folder (called nesting) by Control/right-clicking the existing folder — instead of the root folder — and choosing New Folder from the contextual menu.*

8. **Continue to the next exercise.**

Sort and Move Image Files

When you define a site in Dreamweaver, the application reads all of the pages in the site (a process that can take a few minutes in a large site), notes the links between pages, and identifies which images are used in which pages. These associations between files are stored in a cache that Dreamweaver creates when a new site is defined.

When files are moved or renamed within the site, Dreamweaver recognizes that other files are related to the moved or renamed files and prompts you to update the links in all of the affected files.

1. **With the Kinetic site open in the Files panel, click and drag burger.jpg into the images folder.**

   Make sure you drag the file directly over the name of the folder or folder icon; if you drag the file too far to the left or right, Dreamweaver will not move the file.

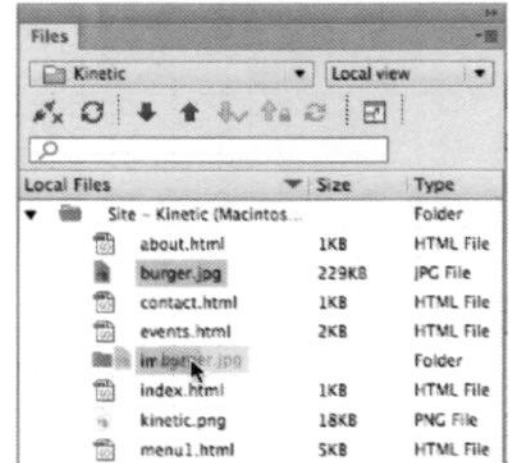

2. **When prompted, click Update to update the affected pages with the new location for the burger.jpg image file.**

   When a browser downloads a Web page, it reads the page code, requests the image files from the defined locations, and displays the images within the page. You should understand that images in Web pages are not embedded into Web pages; they are merged into the page by the browser.

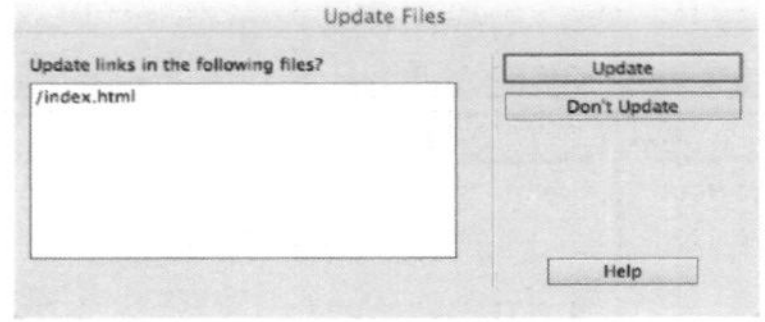

   Files being updated do not need to be open for Dreamweaver to change the required link information. If pages *are* open, links in those pages are updated, but the changes are not automatically saved; you have to manually save each open file to make the updates permanent.

   If you choose Don't Update in the Update Links dialog box, the image will not appear in the page that calls for that file. If you had moved the image file using Windows Explorer or the Macintosh Finder, Dreamweaver would not have been aware of the movement, and you would not have had the opportunity to adjust the path to the image file in pages that link to that image.

   The burger.jpg file is now stored in the main images folder. When you move files into a folder, that folder automatically expands in the Files panel.

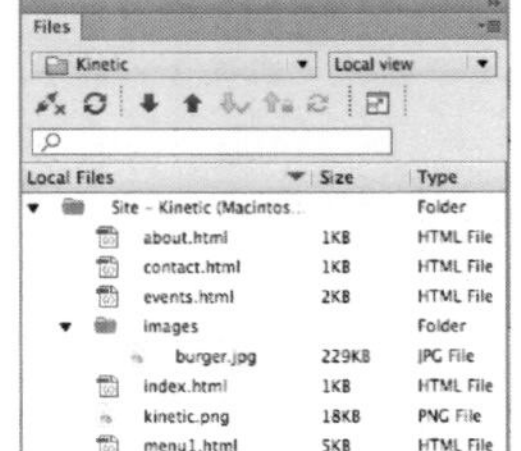

Note:

To avoid potential problems if you accidentally close a file without saving, you might want to close open files before moving or renaming files in the Files panel.

3. **In the Files panel, click the Type column heading to sort the site files by type.**

   By default, site files are sorted by name. You can sort by another criteria by clicking the column headings in the Files panel. Sorting by type allows you to easily find all of the images that are used in this site.

4. **Click the first JPG file in the list (onion-rings.jpg) to select that file. Press Shift and click kinetic.png to select all consecutive files between the first and the last ones you selected.**

   Press Shift to select multiple consecutive files in the panel. Press Command/Control and click to select multiple, nonconsecutive files.

   You can also Command/Control-click to deselect a selected file. For example, if you select a file by accident, you can deselect it by Command/Control-clicking the file name.

Note:

You can change the columns that appear in the Files panel — and the order of those columns — in the File View Columns pane of the Site Setup dialog box.

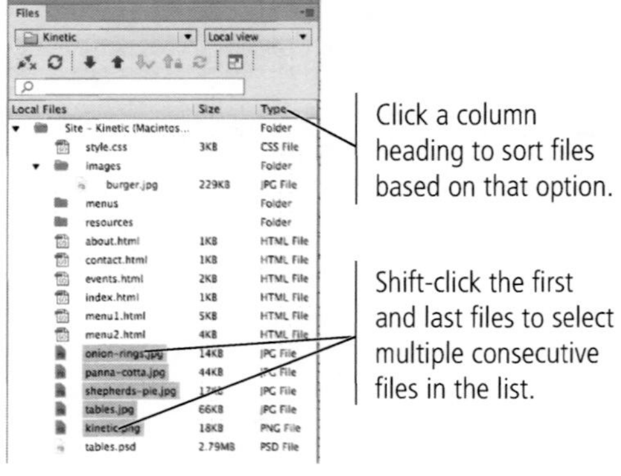

Click a column heading to sort files based on that option.
Shift-click the first and last files to select multiple consecutive files in the list.

5. **Click the icon of any of the selected files and drag the selected files into the `images` folder. When asked, click Update to update all links to all of the moved files.**

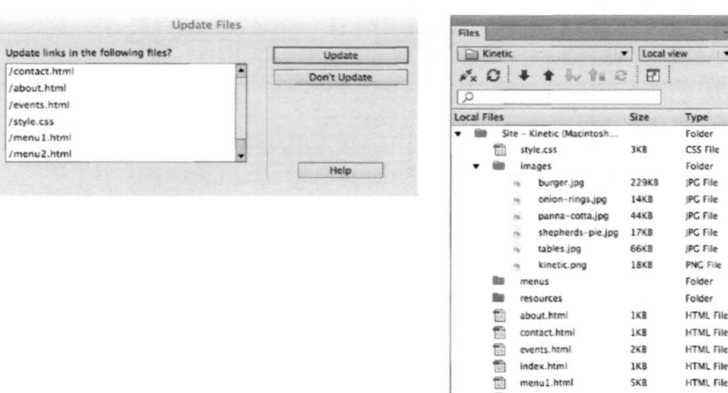

Note:

Images in Web sites typically have a GIF, JPG, or PNG extension.

6. **Click the down-facing arrow (Macintosh) or the "–" symbol (Windows) to the left of the images folder name to collapse the folder.**

7. **Click the Local Files column header to re-sort the files by name.**

8. **Select menu1.html and menu2.html, and move them into the menus folder. Update the links when asked.**

   This is a relatively small site, so nesting files into subfolders isn't strictly necessary. However, when you work with larger files, clearly organized subfolders can be extremely helpful in maintaining a site that is easy to update as often as necessary.

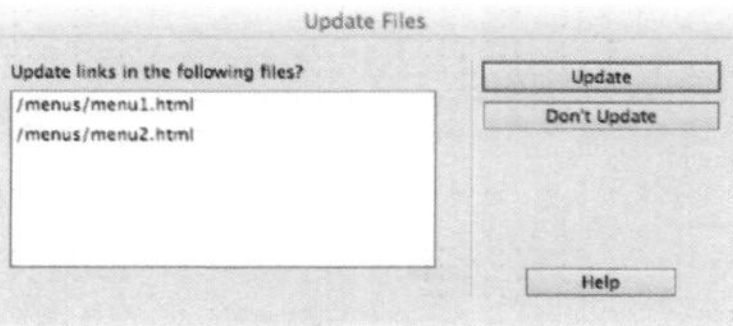

> *Note:*
>
> *You can also copy and paste files into a folder using the Edit options in the contextual menus, or using the standard keyboard shortcuts:*
>
> *Cut: Command/Control-X*
>
> *Copy: Command/Control-C*
>
> *Paste: Command/Control-V*

9. **Collapse the menus folder.**

10. **Select and move the file tables.psd into the resources folder.**

    In this case, you are not asked to update links. This is a layered Photoshop file that was used to create the background image behind the page content. It is not part of the actual Web site, but it's a good idea to keep this type of file in the site folder in case you need to make changes later. Later in this project, you will learn how to prevent this file from being uploaded as part of the site.

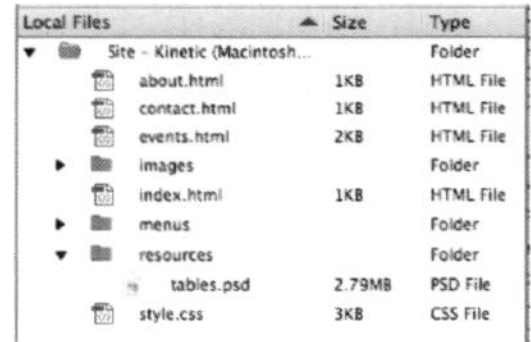

11. **Collapse the resources folder.**

    From the folder structure alone, the Web site appears to be better organized. You now know what to expect when you open each folder.

12. **Continue to the next stage of the project.**

Changing the Update Preferences

DREAMWEAVER FOUNDATIONS

As you have seen, Dreamweaver automatically asks you to update links when you move a file in the Files panel. You can change this behavior in the General pane of the Preferences dialog box.

If you choose Always in the Update Links... menu, the affected links are automatically updated without user intervention. In other words, you do not see the Update Files dialog box during the process.

If you choose Never, links are not automatically updated when you move files in the Files panel. If you do not manually correct links, they will result in an error when clicked by a user.

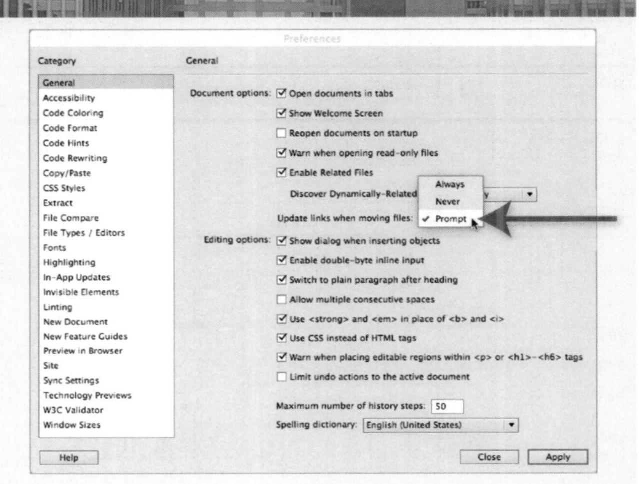

Stage 2 Organizing the Site Navigation

Hyperlinks (the official term for links) can be created to link pages on a site to other pages within the same site, or to pages on other sites. A well-designed site includes links that make it easy to get to any part of a site from any other part of a site. You should carefully plan the flow of links and connections between pages — always keeping the reader's usability in mind.

Organizing links is a simple application of a science called **information architecture**, which is the organization of a Web site to support both usability and "findability." As you organize site links, remember that your goal is to enable visitors to see a pattern in your links, which will assist them in navigating through your site. Keep the following points in mind when you plan a site's link structure:

- You can't know how visitors will enter your site. The primary site pages (home, about us, etc.) should be accessible from every page on the site.
- When linking secondary pages such as different menus for different mealtimes, don't make users constantly click the browser's Back button. Links should allow users to navigate all sibling pages (at the same level) as easily as navigating the primary structure. For example, users should be able to access the dinner menu or lunch menu in the restaurant's site without first going back to a main "Menu" page.

Using the terms "parent," "child," and "sibling" is simply a way of describing relationships between pages. A large Web site cannot provide links to all of the pages from its home page. By grouping pages, grouping groups of pages, and so on, you create relationships of equality between pages that are grouped together, as well as between groups that are grouped together.

When you plan a new site, you should create this type of flowchart to make sure you create all the necessary links that make the site as user-friendly as possible. A flowchart of the required Kinetic site link structure is shown below.

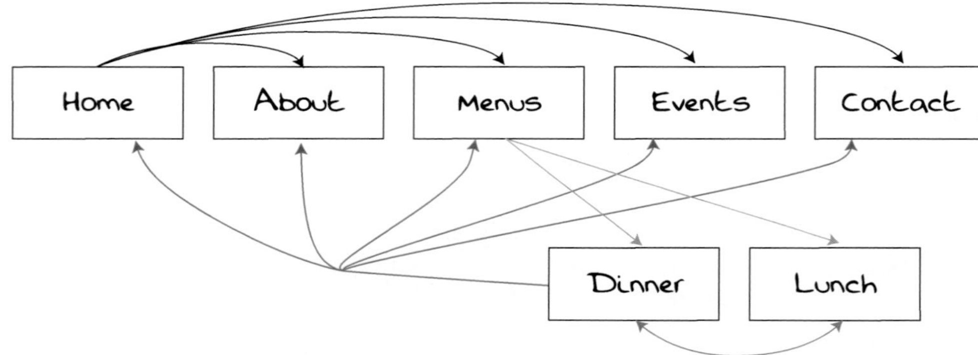

In this stage of the project, you will learn various techniques to create the necessary links on the Kinetic site pages.

Create Hyperlinks within the Site

Dreamweaver offers a number of options for creating the necessary links for any Web site structure.

- **Hyperlink Button in the HTML Insert Panel.** Clicking the Hyperlink button in the HTML Insert panel opens the Hyperlink dialog box, where you define the specific parameters of the link.
- **Insert>Hyperlink menu.** This menu command opens the same dialog box that you see when you click the Hyperlink button in the Insert panel.
- **Properties Panel Fields.** You can also simply define the specifics of a hyperlink in the Properties panel. This method offers the same options as those in the Hyperlink dialog box but does not require the dialog box interface.
- **Point to File button in the Properties panel.** To create a link using this method, simply click the Point to File button, hold down the mouse button, and drag to a file in the Files panel; Dreamweaver automatically creates a link.
- **Browse for File button in the Properties panel.** The Browse for File button opens a navigation dialog box where you can select the file that will open when a user clicks on the link.
- **Shift-Drag Method.** You can create a link directly from the document window by pressing Shift and then clicking and dragging from the link source to the destination page in the Files panel. (This method only works for text; you can't Shift-drag to create a link for an image.)
- **Quick Property Inspector in Live View.** When the Live view is active, you can use the Link button in the Quick Property Inspector, which appears attached to the selected item in the document window, to create a hyperlink.

Note:

Dreamweaver often includes several different ways to achieve the same result. You should use the method that is most efficient at the time.

1. **With the Kinetic site open in the Files panel, open index.html. Make sure the Live view is not active.**
2. **At the top of the page, double-click the word "HOME" to select it.**
3. **If your Insert panel is docked above the document window, click the HTML tab at the top of the panel.**

   If your Insert panel is docked on the right side of the screen, or if it is floating as a separate panel, choose HTML in the menu at the top of the panel.

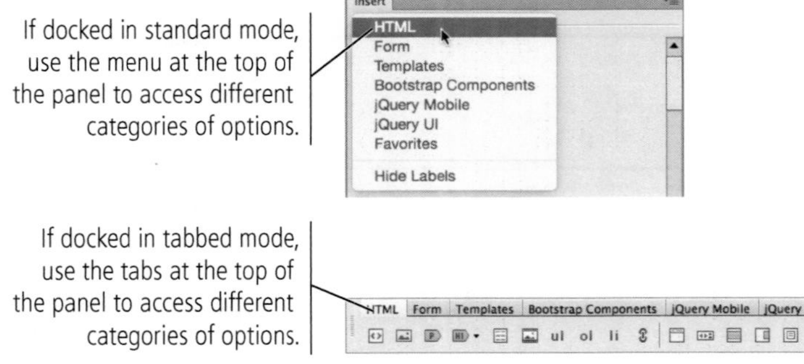

4. **Click the Hyperlink button in the HTML Insert panel.**

   The HTML Insert panel contains many of the common functions you use to create Web pages. If a different Insert panel is showing, you can return to the HTML Insert panel by choosing HTML in the panel menu.

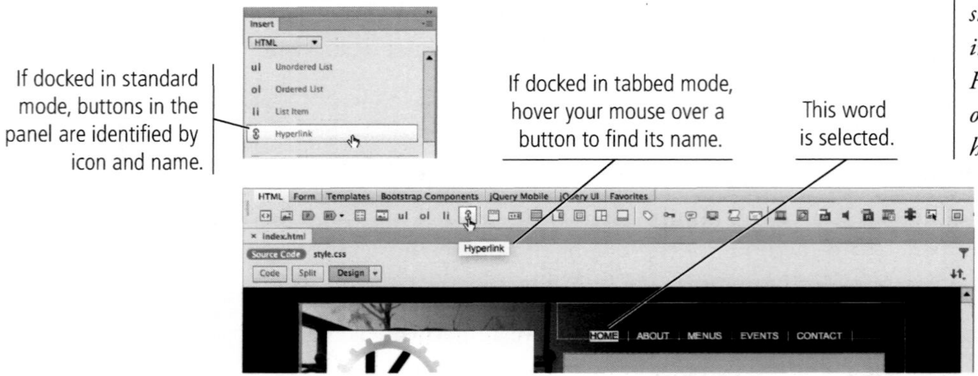

If docked in standard mode, buttons in the panel are identified by icon and name.
If docked in tabbed mode, hover your mouse over a button to find its name.
This word is selected.

> *Note:*
>
> *From this point on, we will leave our Insert panel docked on the right side of the workspace, immediately below the Files panel. Feel free to organize your workspace however you prefer.*

5. **In the Hyperlink dialog box, click the Browse button to the right of the Link field.**

   The text selected in the document appears in the Text field by default. (If an image is selected, this field defaults to be blank.)

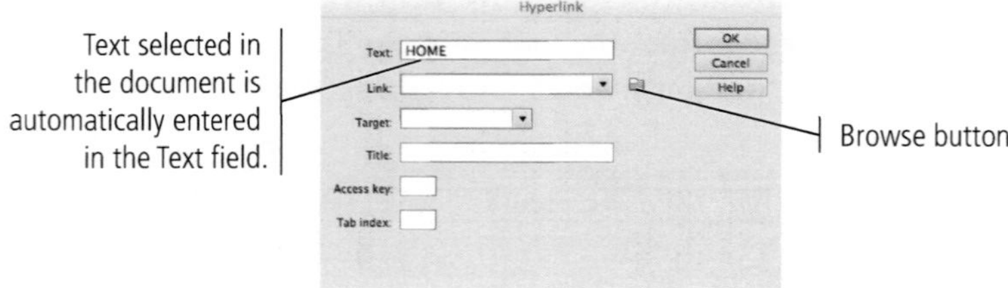

6. **Navigate to your WIP>Kinetic folder, select `index.html`, and click Open/OK to return to the Hyperlink dialog box.**

   In the Link field, you can either type the URL of a location outside the site you're building, or you can click the Browse button to select a file within the current site.

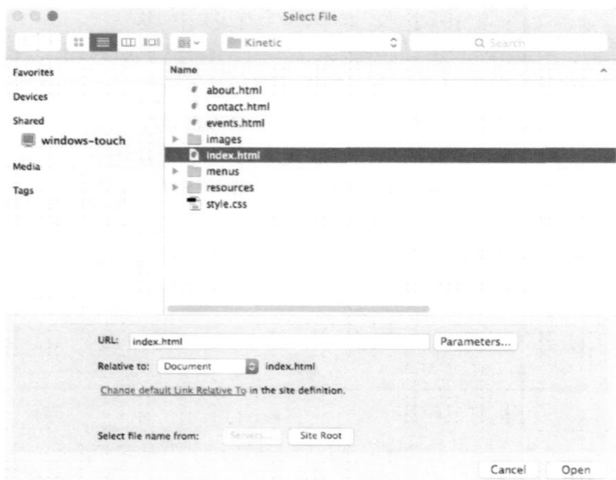

> *Note:*
>
> *Remember, when commands are different for different operating systems, we list them as Macintosh/Windows.*

The HTML Insert Panel in Depth

The HTML Insert panel contains buttons for frequently used items. For example, to insert a hyperlink, simply click the corresponding button. (Some of the terms and functions in the following descriptions will make more sense as you use those tools to complete later projects.)

- **Div** inserts sections (divisions) in a page, which are useful for inserting blocks of content that you want to format independently from other blocks. You will work extensively with div tags in later projects.
- **Image** opens a dialog box where you can define the source for the image you want to insert.
- **Paragraph** surrounds each selected paragraph with <p></p> tags, which is the proper HTML structure for a paragraph of text.
- **Heading** is used to assign predefined HTML heading levels (h1 through h6) to selected text.
- **Table** inserts an HTML table into the page.
- **Figure** inserts a properly structured HTML figure, including the appropriate tags for the figure and the figure caption.
- **Unordered List** creates a bulleted list from the selected paragraphs; each selected paragraph is automatically tagged as a list item.
- **Ordered List** creates a numbered list from the selected paragraphs; each selected paragraph is automatically tagged as a list item.
- **List Item** creates a new list item at the location of the insertion point. No ordered or unordered list is created to surround the list item.
- **Hyperlink** opens a dialog box where you can create text or image links to another file, either in the same Web site or in an external Web site.
- **Header**, **Navigation**, **Main**, **Aside**, **Article**, **Section**, and **Footer** add the related HTML5 tags to the page. You have the option to determine exactly how the tags are applied in relation to selected text, as well as defining an ID or class attribute for the resulting tag.
- **Meta** opens a dialog box where you can define a variety of page head information. When you type specific values in the name and content fields, the appropriate information is added to the page head using the following structure:

  <meta name="test" content="123">
- **Keywords** opens a dialog box where you can define keywords in the page head. The keywords are added using the following structure:

  <meta name="keywords" content="words">
- **Description** opens a dialog box where you can define a text-based description to the page head. The description is added using the following structure:

  <meta name="description" content="Text">
- **Viewport** offers a way to better control the appearance of a page on mobile devices. It sets the width of the visible area of a web page on a user's device to match the width of the device screen.
- The **Script** button can be used to add code from an external file, which will be used by the browser to perform an action when the page is accessed.
- The **Email Link** button opens a dialog box where you can create links to email addresses.
- **HTML5 Video** inserts a video element, which allows a video file to be played directly in an HTML5 page without the need for external browser plugins.
- **Canvas** inserts a canvas element, which is a container for graphics that are created directly in the page using scripts.
- **Edge Animate Composition** places a defined Edge Animate composition (OAM file) into the HTML page at the location of the cursor.
- **HTML5 Audio** inserts a audio element, which allows an audio file to be played directly in an HTML5 page without the need for external browser plugins.
- **Flash SWF** allows you to place a SWF file (created from a Flash animation). Keep in mind that SWF files require the Flash Player browser plugin to function properly.
- **Flash Video** allows you to place an FLV file, which is a video format created from Flash professional. Again, this format requires the Flash Player browser plugin to function properly.
- **Plugin** embeds a specific user-defined plugin file into the page.
- **Rollover Image** opens a dialog box where you can define the default image, as well as a different image that will appear when a user's mouse cursor enters into the image area.
- **iFrame** inserts an iFrame element, which allows you to embed one document into another.
- **Horizontal Rule** inserts a solid line across the width of the page. This can be useful for visually separating sections of text.
- The **Date** button inserts the current date and time. In the resulting dialog box, you can choose the date format, as well as an option to update the date and time whenever the file is saved.
- **Non-Breaking Space** adds a special character that prevents a line break from appearing between specific words in a paragraph.
- **Character** is used to insert special characters, such as copyright symbols and foreign currency characters.

7. **Open the Target menu and choose _self.**

   This option determines where the linked file will open:

   - **_blank** opens every linked file in a new, unnamed browser window.
   - **new** creates a new browser window with the name "_new". Every link assigned the _new target will open in that same _new browser window.
   - **_parent** is relevant if a page includes nested frames; this option opens the link in the frame or window that contains the frame with the link.
   - **_self** opens the link in the same frame or browser window as the link. This is the default behavior if you do not choose an option in the Target menu.
   - **_top** opens the link in the same browser window, regardless of frames.

8. **In the Title field, type Kinetic Bistro home page.**

   The Title field defines text that appears when the cursor is placed over the link text. Defining a descriptive title for links can help a page achieve better search engine results.

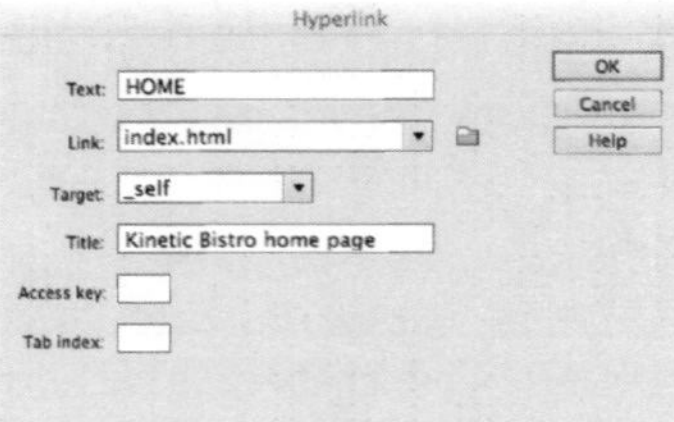

Note:

You can use the Access Key field to define a keyboard shortcut for the link and use the Tab Index field to specify the number of times a user needs to press the Tab key to select the link.

9. **Click OK in the Hyperlink dialog box to create the link.**

10. **Click the Split button in the Document toolbar to review both the design and code views at one time.**

    A Web page is basically a page full of code. A browser reads the code to determine how to treat various elements of the page. HTML code largely revolves around tags, which tell a browser how to interpret specific objects on the page.

    A hyperlink is identified by the **a** element, which starts with the opening **<a>** tag; the link destination and target are defined as attributes of that tag (**href="index.html" target="self"**). After the link text, the closing tag (**</a>**) identifies the end of the link.

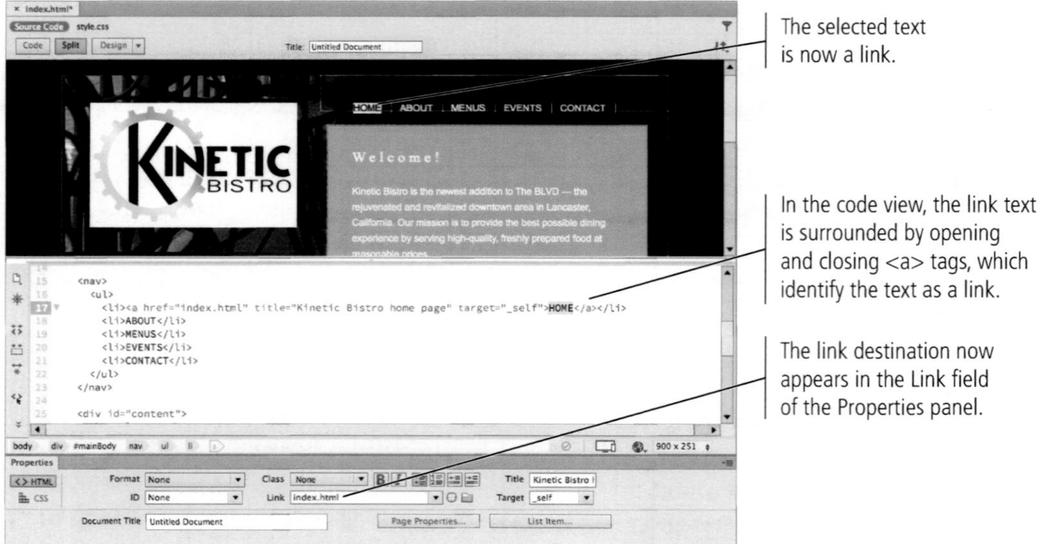

The selected text is now a link.
In the code view, the link text is surrounded by opening and closing <a> tags, which identify the text as a link.
The link destination now appears in the Link field of the Properties panel.

11. **Select the word "ABOUT" at the top of the page.**

12. **Click the Browse for File button to the right of the Link field in the Properties panel.**

    If you don't see the Properties panel, choose Window>Properties. The Properties panel's primary purpose is to review and change the properties of the selected HTML element (such as a heading, paragraph, or table cell).

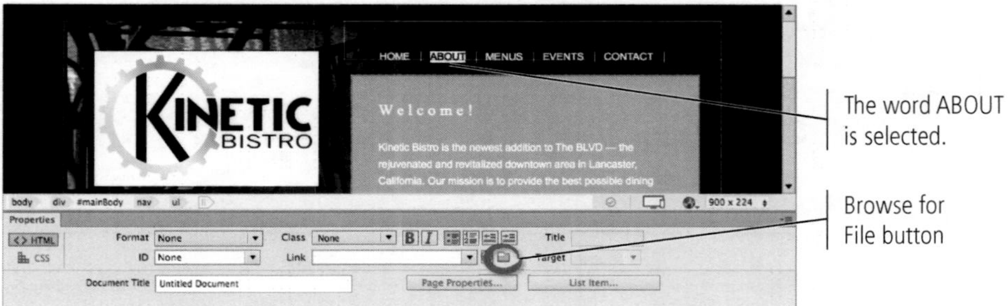

13. **In the resulting dialog box, select about.html, and then click Open/OK.**

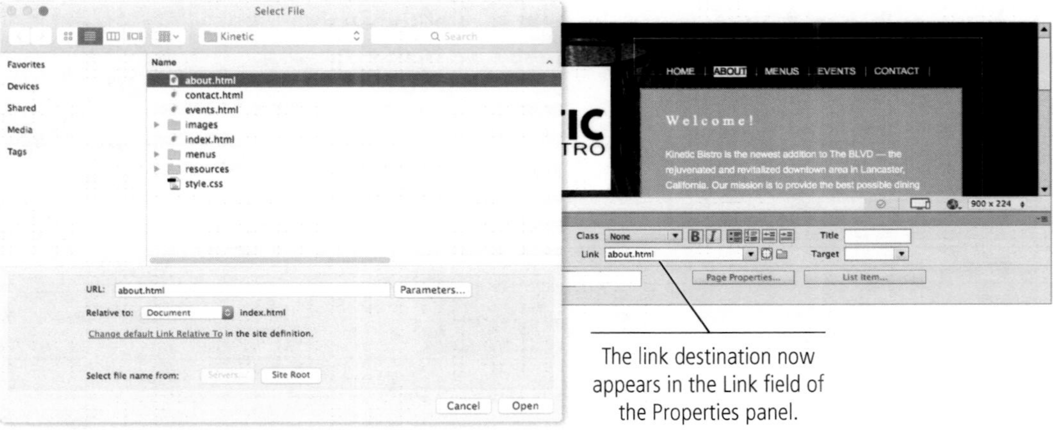

The link destination now appears in the Link field of the Properties panel.

14. **Select the word "MENUS" at the top of the page.**

15. **Expand the menus folder in the Files panel.**

    You should expand and collapse Files panel folders as necessary, depending on your available screen space. We will not repeat instructions to collapse or expand folders unless it is necessary to perform a specific function.

16. **Click the Point to File button in the Properties panel, hold down the mouse button, and drag to menus/menu1.html in the Files panel.**

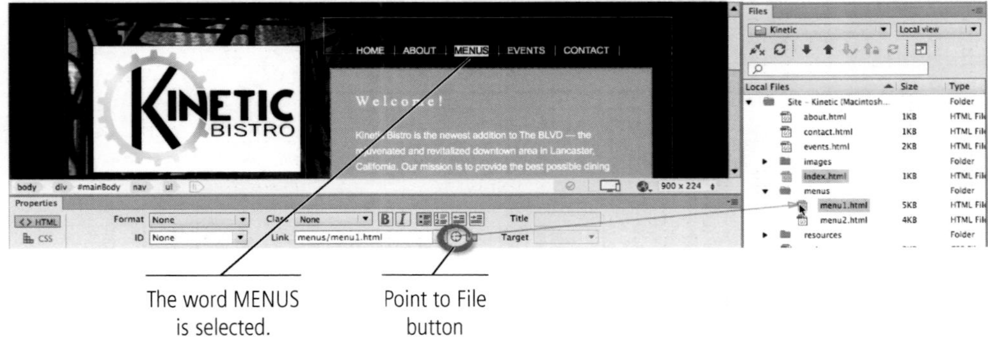

17. **Select the word "EVENTS" at the top of the page.**

18. **Press the Shift key, then click the selected text and drag to `events.html` in the Files panel.**

    You have to press the Shift key, and then click and drag to the link destination. If you try to click and drag before pressing the Shift key, this technique will fail.

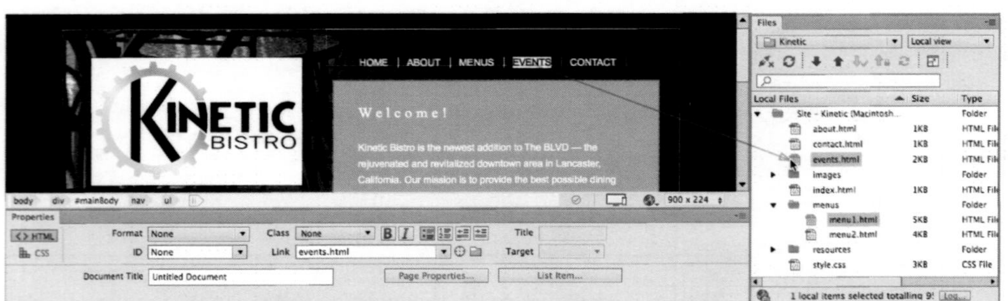

19. **Use any method you just learned to create a link from the word "CONTACT" to the `contact.html` file.**

20. **In the Document toolbar, click the arrow to the right turn of the Design button and choose Live from the menu to turn on the Live view.**

Click the arrow to open the button menu.

Choose Live in the menu to turn the Live view on.

Choose Design in the menu to turn the Live view off.

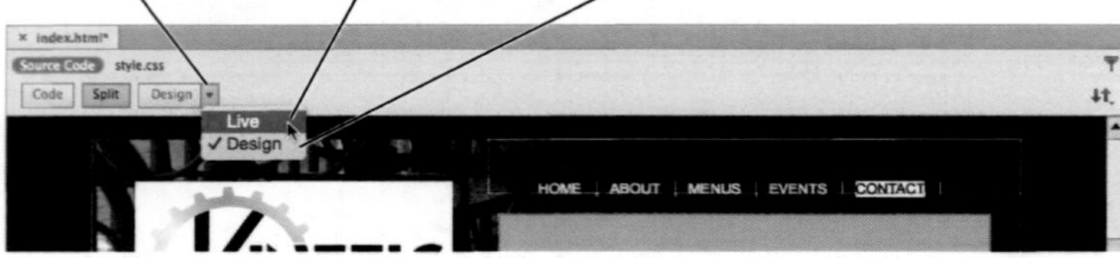

In the Live view, you can accurately see how the CSS will be rendered by Web browsers.

The button text shows whether (regular) Design or the Live view is active.

In the Live view, CSS is properly rendered and the link appears correctly on one line.

> ***Note:***
>
> *When a link to another page in the site is selected in the document, you can open the related page in Dreamweaver by choosing Modify>Open Linked Page.*

> ***Note:***
>
> *You can remove a link by selecting the linked text or object in the document and choosing Modify>Remove Link, or by simply deleting the text from the Link field in the Properties panel.*

21. **In the Design window with the Live view active, click once to select the footer paragraph at the bottom of the page.**

When the Live view is active, clicking an object in the document window shows the Element Display, which shows the active HTML element. (If an element has a defined ID or class attribute, those also appear in the Element Display. You will learn about IDs and classes in later projects.) In this case, you can see that the selected element is a **p** element — in other words, it is a paragraph.

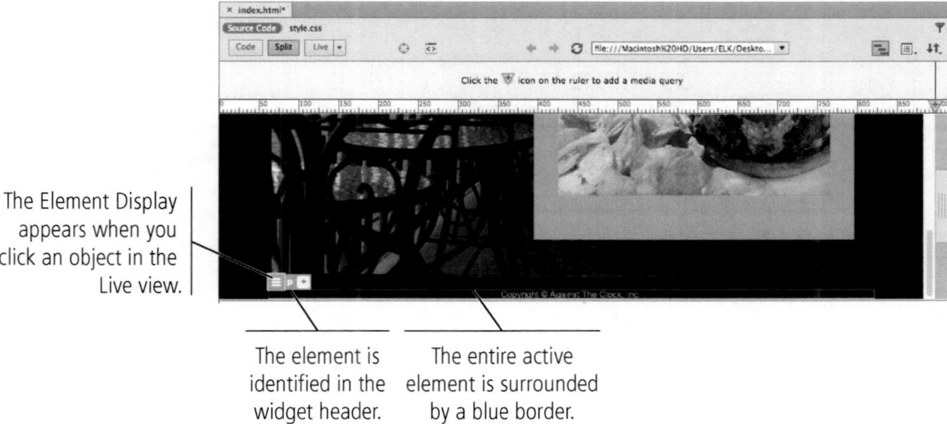

The element is identified in the widget header.

22. **Double-click the text in the selected paragraph to place the insertion point.**

You can now place the insertion point and edit text directly in the Live view. (You might have to look closely to see the insertion point in this case.)

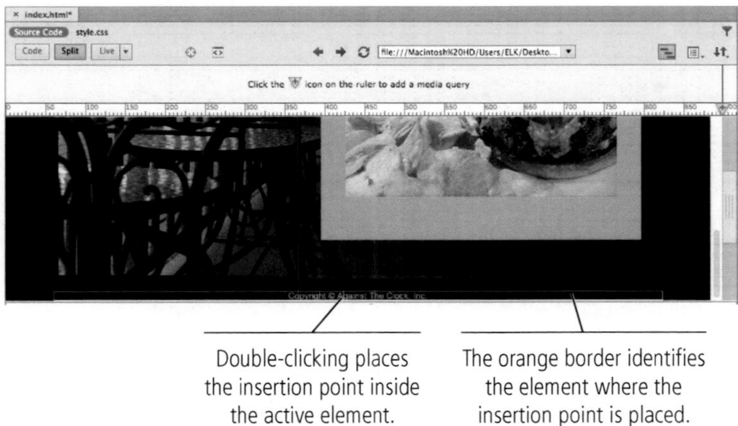

Double-clicking places the insertion point inside the active element.
The orange border identifies the element where the insertion point is placed.

23. **Double-click and drag to select the words "Against The Clock, Inc." within the active paragraph.**

In the Live view, the Quick Property Inspector shows options related to the selected text. You can use the B and I buttons to apply the **<strong>** and **<em>** tags (respectively). You can also click the Hyperlink button to define a link destination for the selected text.

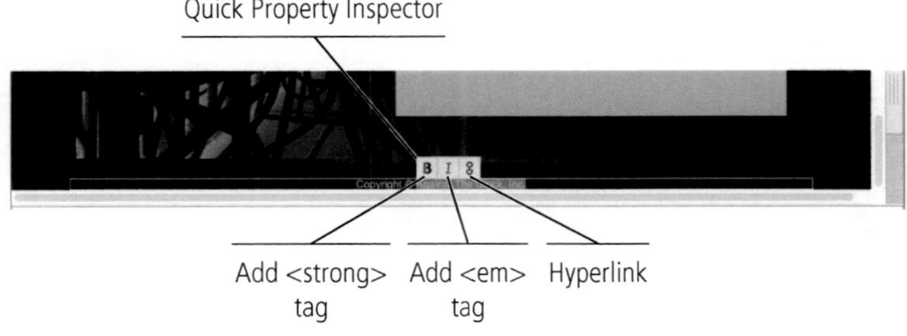

Note:

The strong and em tags are explained in Project 2: Digital Book Chapter.

24. **In the Quick Property Inspector, click the Hyperlink button. In the resulting Link field, type `http://www.againsttheclock.com` as the link destination.**

Dreamweaver can't help you create an external URL link because it's outside the site definition. You have to simply type or paste the address into the Link field.

An external **URL link** must begin with the "http://" protocol, followed by the domain name and, if relevant, the folder path and file name of the page to which you are linking.

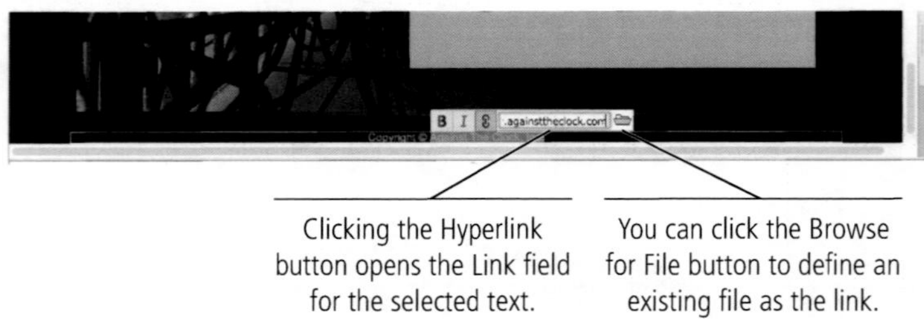

Clicking the Hyperlink button opens the Link field for the selected text.

You can click the Browse for File button to define an existing file as the link.

25. **Click anywhere else in the workspace to finalize the hyperlink you defined in Step 24.**

26. **In the Document toolbar, click the arrow to the right turn of the Live button and choose Design from the menu to turn off the Live view.**

You should become familiar with the process of turning the Live view on or off. We will not continue to repeat these specific instructions as you move throughout the projects in this book.

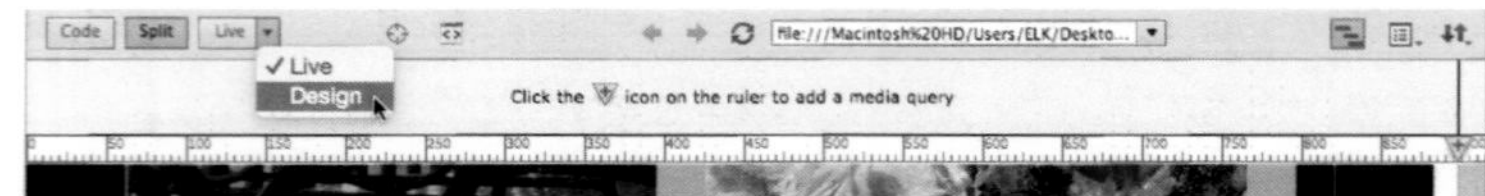

27. **Choose File>Save to save your changes, then continue to the next exercise.**

Note:

To minimize the repetitive work required, we already defined this link for you on the other pages in the site. In a professional environment, you would need to add this link to every page in the site.

Copy and Paste Links

Rather than manually creating the same links on every page, you can now simply copy and paste them from one page to another.

1. **With `index.html` open (from the Kinetic site), click in any of the text links to place the insertion point.**

The insertion point is the location where text will appear if you type.

2. **Review the Tag Selector below the document window.**

The Tag Selector, located in the status bar of the document window, shows the nesting order of HTML tags (the "path of tags") based on the current selection or the current location of the insertion point.

Note:

You will work more extensively with tags beginning in Project 7: Digital Book Chapter.

Insertion point

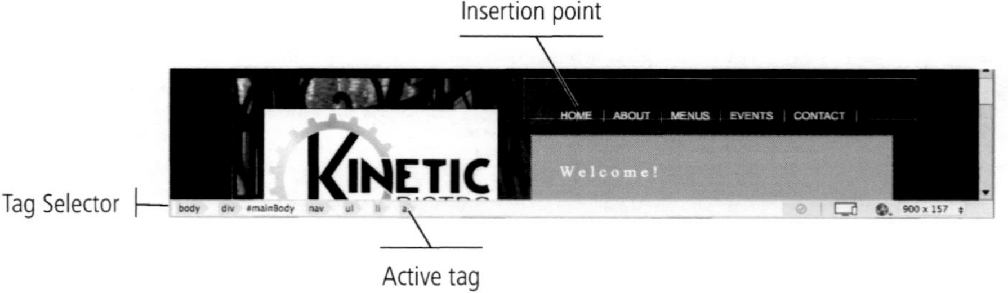

Tag Selector

Active tag

3. **Click the <ul> tag in the Tag Selector.**

   The **<ul>** tag identifies an unordered list, which is how this navigation structure was created; each link is a separate list item (using the **<li>** tag).

   Clicking a tag in the Tag Selector selects that HTML element and all of its content. In the document window, the associated content is highlighted.

4. **Choose Edit>Copy (or press Command/Control-C) to copy the selected content to the Clipboard.**

5. **Close index.html and open about.html.**

6. **Click to place the insertion point anywhere in the list of links at the top of the page, and then click the <ul> tag in the Tag Selector to select the entire unlinked list.**

7. **Choose Edit>Paste (or press Command/Control-V) to paste the copied content from the Clipboard.**

8. **Place the insertion point in any of the links and review the Tag Selector.**

   The Tag Selector now shows the **<a>** tag for the current insertion point (in our example, the EVENTS link). The Properties panel also shows the destination of the active link.

9. **Save the changes to about.html and close the file.**

10. **Repeat Steps 6–9 to paste the copied content (the links) into all HTML pages in the site root level, as well as the two HTML pages in the menus folder.**

11. **Save and close any open file, and then continue to the next exercise.**

Adjust Relative Link Paths

A **path** is the route taken through the folder structure to link one page to another. By default, Dreamweaver uses **relative paths** when creating links (the application refers to this as "relative to the document"). The alternative is to create **absolute paths** ("relative to the site"); but unless your site is running on a Web server, you can't test links that use absolute paths.

As an example, consider creating a link from index.html to about.html, both of which reside in the root folder (as shown in the figure to the right). In this case, the source and destination pages are in the same folder; the relative-path link simply states the file name of the destination page:

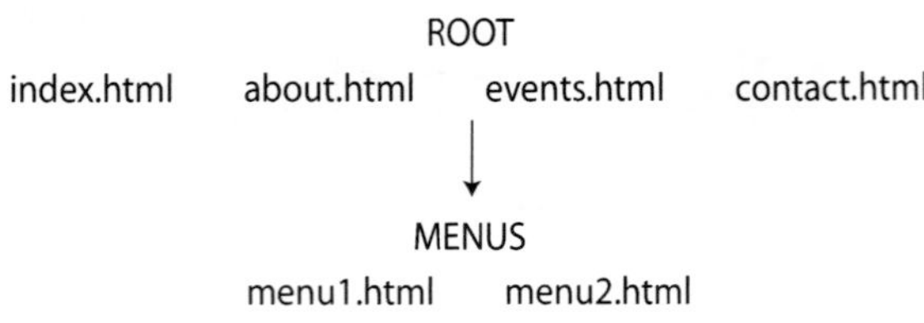

<a href="menu2.html">Link Text</a>

When you drill down into nested levels of folders, the source folder is not identified in the path; the link automatically works starting from the location of the link. To link from index.html to menu1.html, for example, you have to include the nested menus folder in the path:

<a href="menus/menu1.html">Link Text</a>

When the link is in an upward direction, the ../ notation says "go up one folder." To link from menu1.html to index.html in the site root folder means that the link needs to take the visitor up one folder level:

<a href="../index.html">Link Text</a>

Each step up in the folder structure requires another command to "go one step up" in the folder structure. If you had another level of nesting inside the menus folder, for example, a link would have to take the visitor up two folder levels to return to the main index page:

<a href="../../index.html">Link Text</a>

1. **With the Kinetic site open in the Files panel, open menu1.html.**

   In this exercise, you are going to adjust the various links so they work properly on all pages in the site.

2. **Double-click the word HOME at the top of the page to select that element.**

3. **In the Link field of the Properties panel, type ../ before the existing link. Press Return/Enter to finalize the change.**

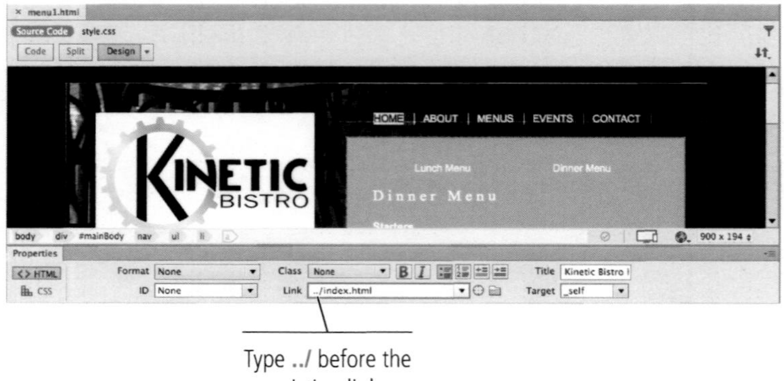

Type ../ before the existing link.

Accessing Page Content in the Menu Pages

The files for this project were created using divs (using the opening and closing <div> tags), which are simply a way to identify and format parts or sections of a page.

(You will work with divs in Project 9: Museum CSS Layout.) Although you don't need to worry about the underlying page structure for now, you might see some unusual behavior when you try to select content in the main section the menu pages when the Live view is not active.

The area that holds the actual menu content has a fixed height, but both menus have more content than will fit into the defined size. When the page is viewed in a browser, the area includes a scroll bar for users to access the content that doesn't fit.

In Dreamweaver's regular Design view, however, this scrollbar doesn't appear. Instead, the first time you click, the entire div is selected and all of the contained text is highlighted.

Double-clicking inside the area again causes the page to jump down, showing the overflow content.

If you click a third time, you can place the insertion point inside the actual text, scroll up as necessary, and then select the link text at the top of the area.

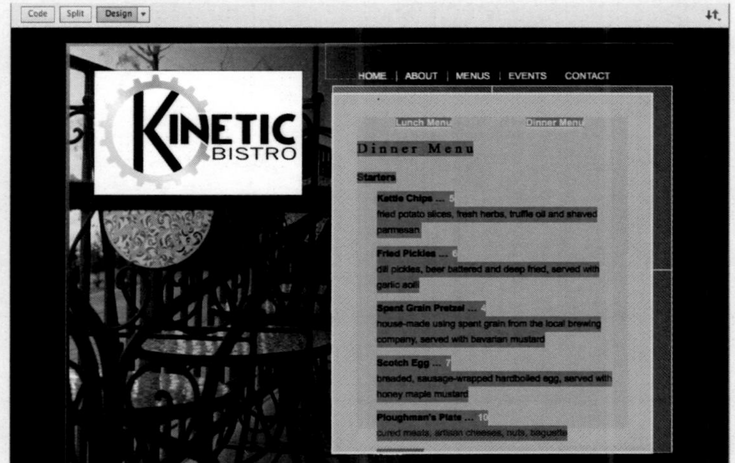

Clicking once selects the entire div that contains the menu content...

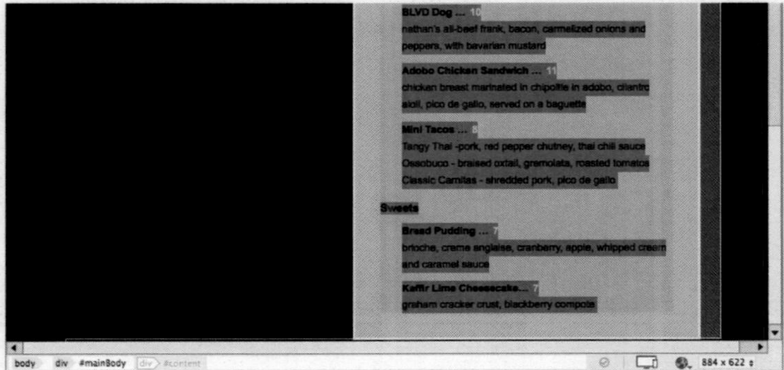

...then double-clicking jumps the page down to show the overflow content.

You can then click again to place the insertion point and select specific text.

4. **Repeat Steps 2–3 for the ABOUT, EVENTS, and CONTACT links.**

5. **Select the word MENUS at the top of the page.**

   In this case, the link is still a problem because it directs the browser to look for a folder named "menus" inside the same folder as the active page. You need to remove the folder part of the path to prevent an error if a user clicks this link from the menu1.html page.

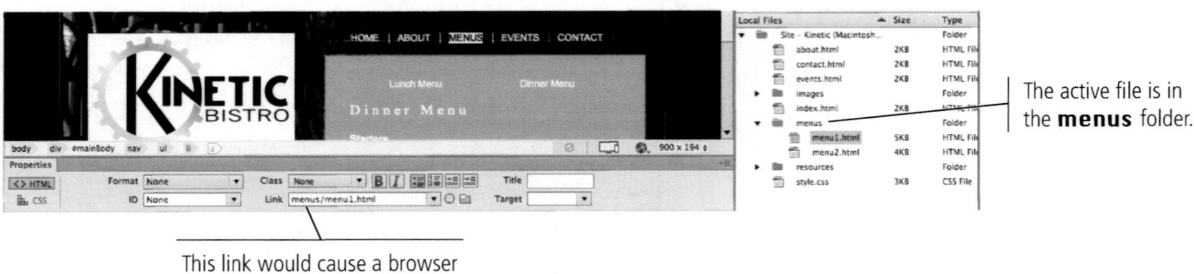

The active file is in the **menus** folder.

This link would cause a browser to look for a menus folder at the same level as the active file.

6. **In the Link field of the Properties Inspector, delete menus/ (including the forward slash) from the existing link.**

Delete the folder path from the existing link.

7. **Using any method you have learned, link "Lunch Menu" (in the main content area) to menu2.html and link "Dinner Menu" to menu1.html.**

   See "Accessing Page Content in the Menu Pages" (Page 321) for specific information about selecting the text in the main content area.

Link this to menu2.html. Link this to menu1.html.

8. **Repeat the process from Steps 1–7 to adjust the top links and add the necessary secondary links in the menu2.html file.**

9. **Save and close any open files, then continue to the next exercise.**

   You can save each file individually, or choose File>Save All to save all open files at once.

Create an Email Link

Most Web sites include one or more external links (including email links), which require the appropriate protocol to tell the browser what type of link is present.

An **email link** requires the "mailto:" protocol, followed by the appropriate email address. This instructs the browser to open a new mail message with the defined address already in the To line.

1. **With the Kinetic site open in the Files panel, open contact.html. Make sure the Live view is not active.**

2. **Select the words "info@kineticbistro.atc" in the main content area.**

3. **In the HTML Insert panel, click the Email Link button.**

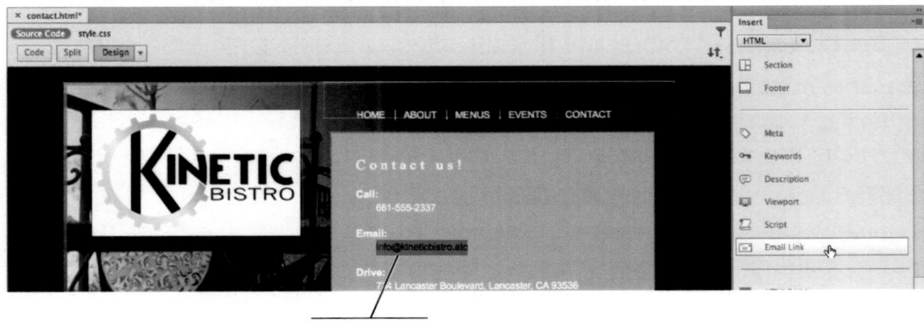

Selected text

4. **Review the resulting dialog box.**

   If you select text before clicking the Email Link icon, the Text field is completed for you. Dreamweaver also recognizes that the selected text is an email address, so the Email field is filled in for you.

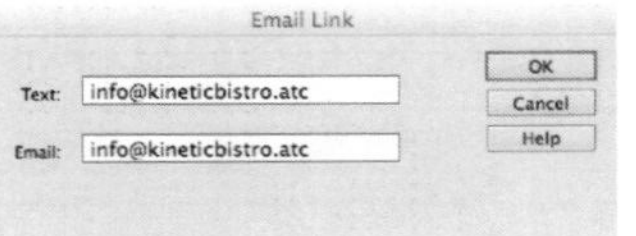

   If the selected text is not recognized as an email address, the Email field defaults to the last address that was defined in the field.

5. **Click OK to create the email link.**

6. **Review the link field in the Properties panel.**

   An email link must begin with "mailto:" followed by the address. When you use the Email Link dialog box, Dreamweaver automatically inserts the mailto: protocol.

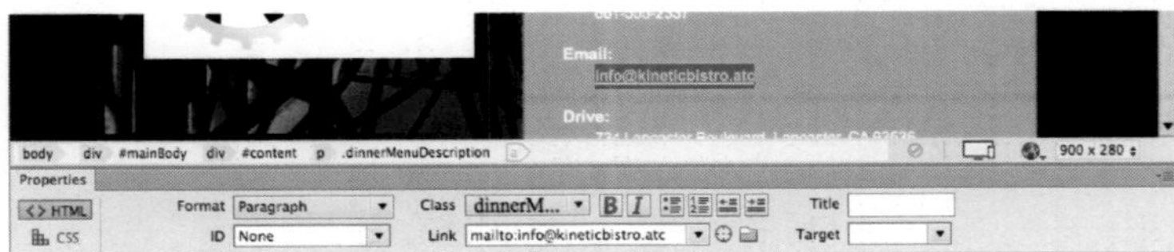

   In many cases throughout this book, we use "[company].atc" as the domain of a site. Although at the time of writing, none of the domain names we use are real, new domains are registered every day. We use the fictitious ".atc" domain to avoid inadvertently using the domain name of a real company.

   When you upload files to a server, you should use the accurate domain (.com, .gov, .edu, etc.) for the site you are building.

7. **Save the file and close it, then continue to the next stage of the project.**

> ***Note:***
>
> *You can access the same Email Link dialog box by choosing Insert>Email Link.*

Stage 3 Naming and Titling Documents

When a **Web server** (a computer that stores and delivers Web pages) receives a request for a folder but not a specific page, the Web server delivers the default page for that folder — usually named index.html or index.htm. There is no practical difference between the two extensions; most Web servers can serve files with either extension. (If you do not have an index file in that folder, the link will result in an error.)

To create links to the default page in a specific folder, you do not need to include the file name if you use the index naming convention. Both **www.kineticbistro.com/** and **www.kineticbistro.com/index.html** refer to the same page.

Rename Pages for Search Engine Optimization

Search engine optimization (SEO) is the process of improving the ranking of a Web page on search engine results pages (SERPs). Search engines certainly use the content of a page for ranking purposes, but the names of folders and files also affect rankings.

Descriptive folder and file names improve usability; you can use **m/menu1.html** for the path to the dinner menu page, for example, but **/menus/dinner-menu.html** is much easier for visitors to understand — and will improve your search engine ranking.

In this exercise, you rename the menu pages to more accurately describe what is contained in the files. As with moving files, the application recognizes when a file name has been changed and knows that links to the page must be adjusted.

1. **With the Kinetic site open, click menus/menu1.html in the Files panel to select that file.**

2. **Click the selected filename again to highlight it.**

   This highlights the existing filename, excluding the extension.

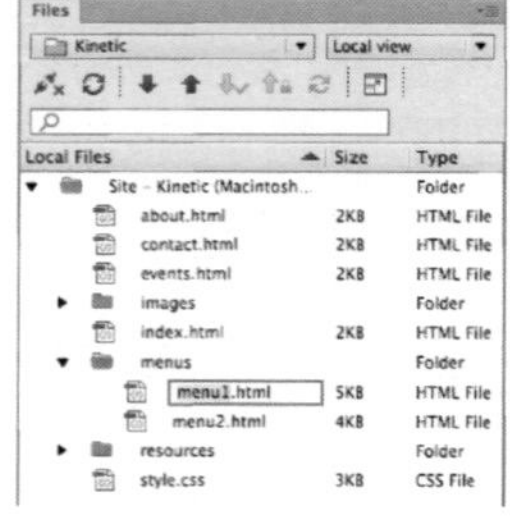

> ***Note:***
>
> *You can also Control/right-click a file in the Files panel and choose Edit>Rename to rename a specific file.*

3. **Type dinner-menu, then press Return/Enter. In the resulting dialog box, click Update to update all pages that link to this page.**

   Typing when the filename is highlighted replaces the previous file name. Pressing Return/Enter finalizes the change.

   As with moving files, Dreamweaver recognizes that all links to the renamed page need to point to the new file name.

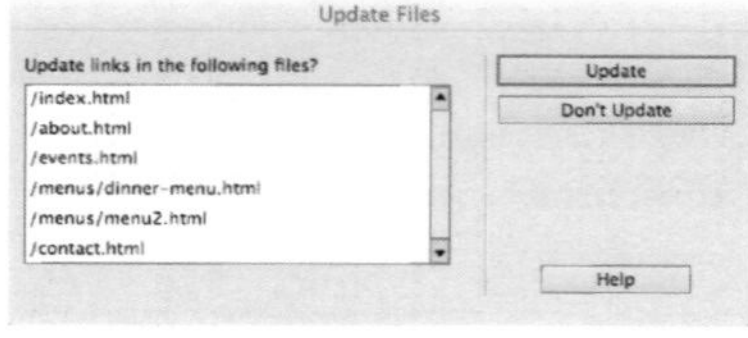

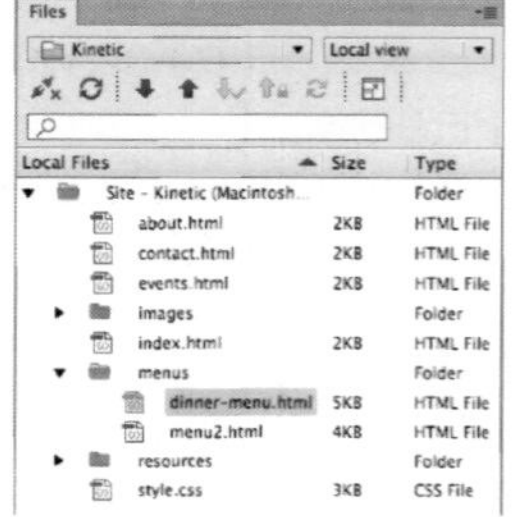

4. **Repeat Steps 1–3 to rename menu2.html as `lunch-menu.html`.**

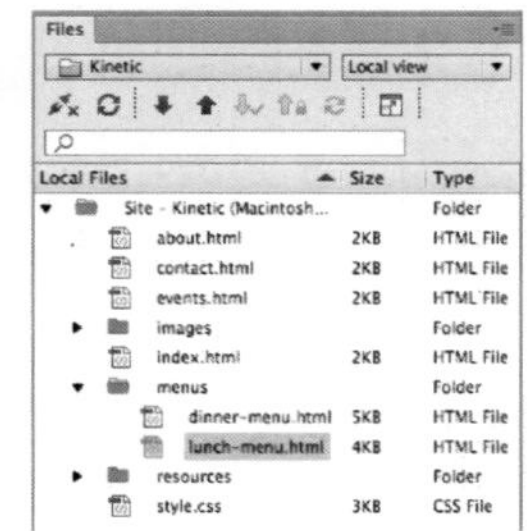

5. **Continue to the next exercise.**

Understanding Web File Naming Conventions

DREAMWEAVER FOUNDATIONS

Because different servers run on different operating systems, the safest way to name pages is to use only characters that are guaranteed to work perfectly:

- a through z (use only lowercase letters)
- 0 through 9
- Hyphen (great-site.html)
- Underscore (great_site.html)

Consider everything else to be "illegal," including:

- Spaces
- Brackets of all kinds, including ( ), [ ], { }, and < >
- Symbols, including #, @, %, ~, |, *, and &
- Quotation marks, both double (" ") and single (' ')
- Slashes, both back slashes (\) and forward slashes (/)
- Commas, periods, question marks, and exclamation points
- Uppercase characters

Some designers use **CamelCase** — uppercase letters at the beginning of each word within a file name, such as UniversalStudios.html. The problem with mixing the lettercase is that some Web server software is case-sensitive and some is not. Most Windows-based Web server software is not case-sensitive, but UNIX- and Linux-based Web server software is case-sensitive. Considering that many Web servers run on UNIX- or Linux-based computers, it's best to use only lowercase file and folder names.

Create Document Titles for Individual Pages

Appropriate document titles are an important concern for both search engines and site visitors. While the document title does not appear within the body of a Web page, it does appear in the title bar of the browser, as the default name of the page in the Bookmarks or Favorites list, and as the page name in search-engine results pages.

Page titles should be relatively short, around 70 characters or so to avoid their being truncated in various locations (such as a user's Bookmarks/Favorites list). You should separate the components of the title with some type of divider, such as a colon (:) or pipe (|) character.

In this exercise, you add document titles to the new pages to increase the pages' search engine rankings and improve usability for visitors who find the pages in search engines and bookmarks. You also learn to use the Find and Replace function, which can greatly reduce the amount of effort required to create all of the document titles.

1. **With the `Kinetic` site open in the Files panel, open `index.html`.**

2. **Click the Split button in the Document toolbar to show both the Code and Design views at one time.**

3. **Examine the Document Title field in the Properties panel.**

When you create a new page in Dreamweaver, the default title is "Untitled Document". That text appears in the Document Title field by default, and in the title element in the Code pane (wrapped in the opening and closing **<title>** tags).

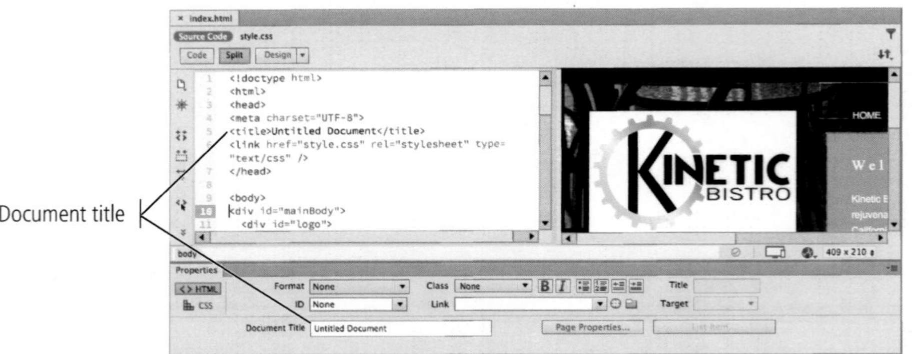

4. **Choose Edit>Find and Replace.**

5. **Open the Find In menu and choose Entire Current Local Site.**

This option allows you to affect all files in the active site. You can also search only selected text; the current (active) document; all open documents; a specific folder; or only selected files in the active site.

6. **Choose Source Code in the Search menu.**

The document title does not appear in the body of the page, so when you use Find and Replace, you must apply the change to the source code rather than the document text.

7. **In the Find field, type `Untitled Document`.**

8. **In the Replace field, type `Kinetic Bistro | Lancaster, California | `. (Include a space after the final pipe character.)**

All pages in the site will include this block of text at the beginning of the document title. Further detail about individual pages will be added to the right of this information.

Unlike file names, document titles can use mixed lettercase and include spaces and other characters. However, you should avoid both single and double quotation marks.

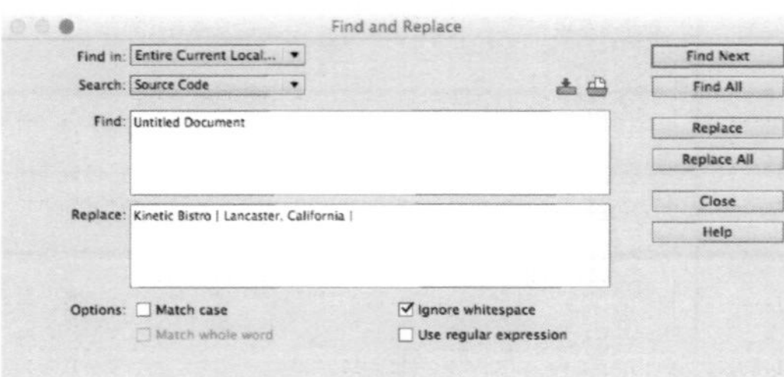

> *Note:*
>
> *When you use the Split view, feel free to arrange the pane however you prefer. We arrange them as necessary to best suit what we are trying to show in our screen captures.*

> *Note:*
>
> *Some experts disagree whether the company name should come before or after the specific page information in a title. However, putting the company name at the beginning of the page title can help with search engine results because the company name is an important keyword.*

9. **Click Replace All. When prompted to confirm whether you want to proceed with this function, click Yes.**

   Like most applications, Dreamweaver has an Undo function that allows you to undo the most recently completed actions; however, this function only works if the document is open.

   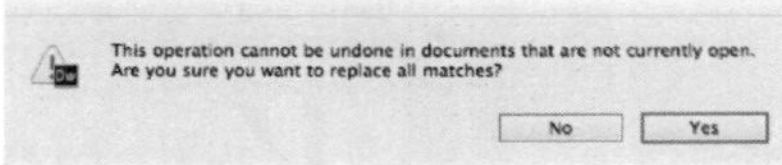

   Since you are using the Find and Replace function on the entire folder and not only on an open page, you are making changes in closed documents — which means you cannot use the Undo command.

   After completing the Find and Replace function, Dreamweaver displays the results in the Search panel.

   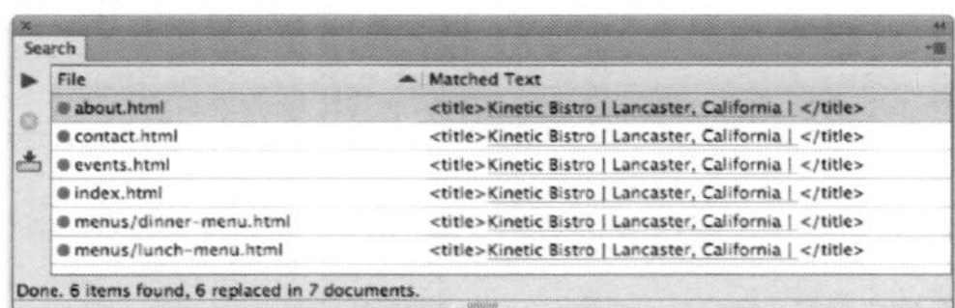

10. **Examine the title in the Properties panel and the Code pane again for the open file (index.html).**

    As a result of the Find and Replace function, the document title has been changed. The same change has been made in all pages in the site. (Because the **title** tag of the open page is active in the Code pane, the Properties panel now shows only options for that active element.)

    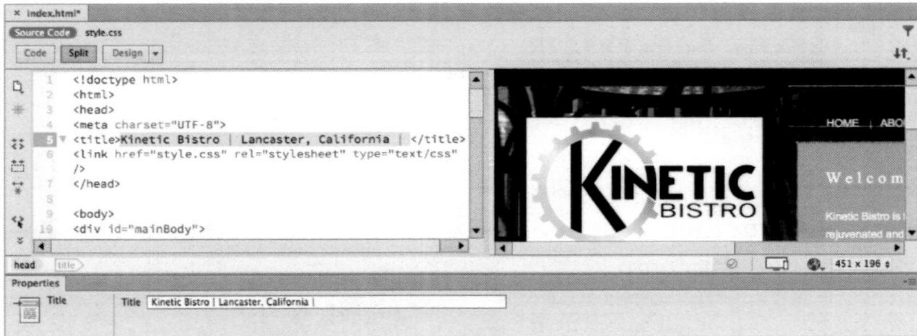

11. **Control/right-click the Search panel tab and choose Close Tab Group.**

12. **Click in the Code pane to make it active.**

    Making a specific pane active is called "bringing it into focus".

13. **Click at the end of the existing page title to place the insertion point immediately before the closing </title> tag, then type `Gourmet Casual Dining`.**

    You can edit the page title in the Document toolbar or in the Code pane. Changes in either place are automatically applied to the other.

    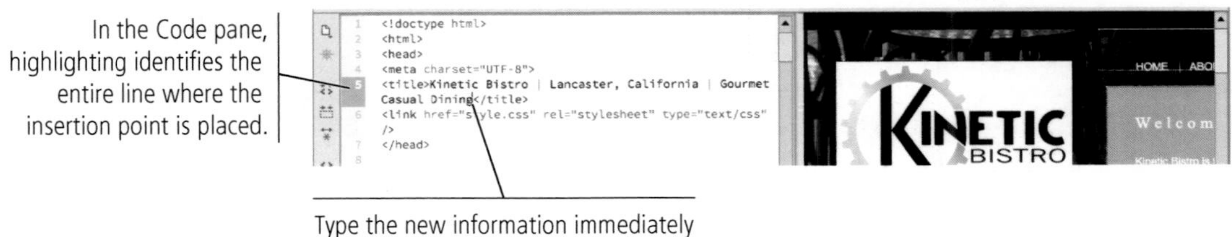

14. **Save index.html and close it.**

15. **Open about.html. Using either the Code pane or the Document Title field in the Properties panel, add Hours of Operation to the end of the existing page title.**

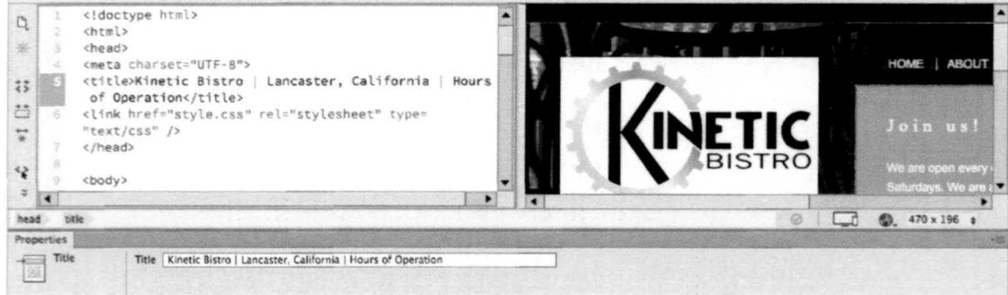

16. **Save about.html and close it.**

17. **Repeat this process (Steps 12–16) to change the page titles of the remaining pages as follows:**

File	Title
contact.html	Address and Contact Information
events.html	Special Event Facilities
menus/dinner-menu.html	Dinner Menu
menus/lunch-menu.html	Lunch Menu

18. **Continue to the final stage of the project.**

Stage 4 Making Files Public

To complete the final stage of this project — making your files accessible to the browsing public — you need to have access to some type of server.

On the inside back cover of this book, you have a code that you need to gain access to the required resource files. The same code also provides access to a six-month, free trial Web hosting account at Pair Networks (www.pair.com).

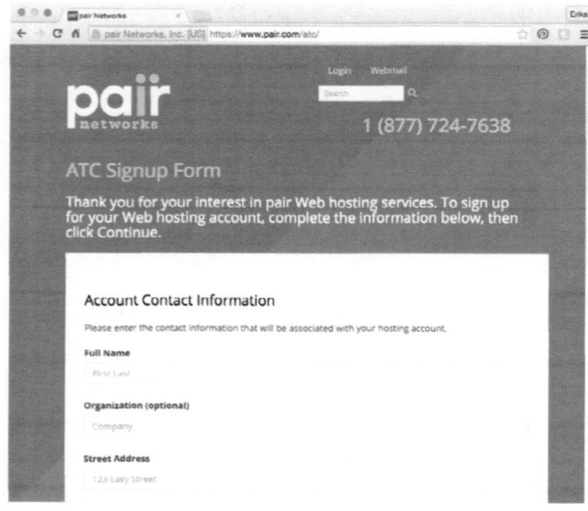

If you don't already have access to an online server, go to **www.pair.com/atc/** to sign up for your hosting account before you complete the final stage of this project. You must enter your contact information and the code from the inside back cover of your book. You should then define a user name in the last field; this will become part of the server name for your hosting account.

After you click Continue, you will receive an acknowledgement that your request is being processed. (The message warns that the setup process can take up to one business day — although it is usually about an hour. You should complete this step as early as possible.)

You will receive a confirmation email, sent to the email you defined in the Signup Form, with your username and password information. Once you receive the confirmation email, you are ready to complete the final stage of this project.

Important note: Pair Networks generously provides a free six-month trial account for Against The Clock users. If you do not cancel the account before the six months end, you will be billed a small monthly fee for the hosting account.

Note:

Pair Networks generously provides the six-month free trial hosting service exclusively for Against The Clock users. We highly recommend their service even after the free six-month trial ends for your web hosting needs.

Hide Files from the Web Server

As you saw when you created the folders for the new site, not all of the new files are meant to be uploaded to the Web server — specifically, the Photoshop file in the resources folder. (You should, however, store such files locally as source files or documentation for the work you completed.) Dreamweaver provides a very useful function — called **cloaking** — that allows you to prevent certain files from uploading. You can cloak an individual file; cloak all files with the same extension (for example, all native Photoshop files with the PSD extension); or cloak a folder, which also cloaks all files in that folder.

1. **With the Kinetic site open in the Files panel, open the Directory menu and click the Kinetic site name in the menu.**

   This opens the Site Setup dialog box for the selected site. You do not need to go through the Manage Sites dialog box to edit the settings for the active site.

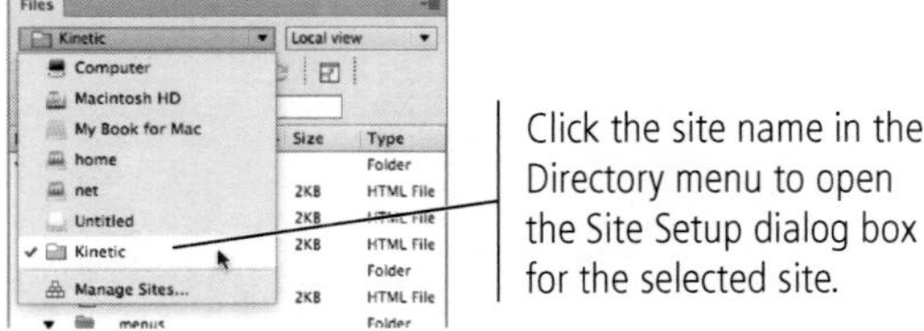

Click the site name in the Directory menu to open the Site Setup dialog box for the selected site.

2. **In the Site Setup dialog box, expand the Advanced Settings menu on the left side and click Cloaking to show the related options.**

3. **Make sure the Enable Cloaking check box is active.**

   When Enable Cloaking is checked, you can hide selected files and folders from a Web server. You can also use the Cloak Files Ending With option to hide all files with the extensions that are listed in the field.

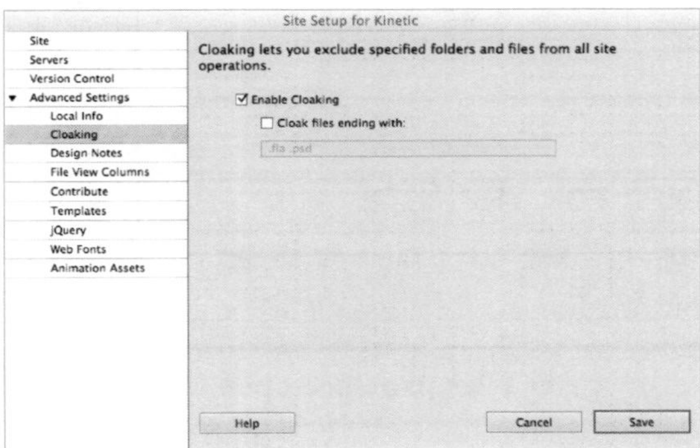

4. **Click Save to close the Site Setup dialog box.**

5. **In the Files panel, collapse all open folders and expand only the resources folder.**

6. **Control/right-click the resources folder and choose Cloaking>Cloak.**

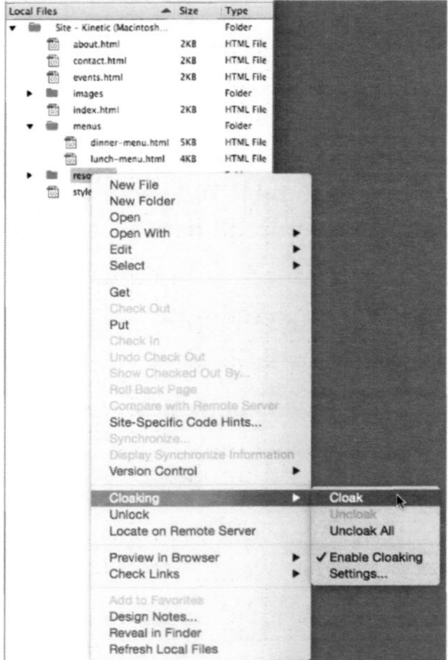

> *Note:*
>
> *You can also cloak a specific file by Control/right clicking that file in the Files panel and choosing Cloaking>Cloak.*

Notice the red slash through the resources folder icon and the icon for the file in the resources folder. The red slash refers to the cloaking function only; it does not prevent you from working with the files, adding more files, or deleting any of the existing files.

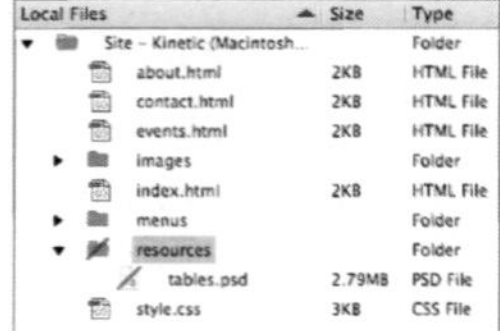

7. **Continue to the next exercise.**

Define Remote Connection Info for the Site

For Dreamweaver to manage file uploading, you first have to define the hosting server connection settings as part of the site setup information.

1. **With the Kinetic site open in the Dreamweaver Files panel, re-open the Site Setup dialog box for the site.**

2. **In the Site Setup dialog box, click Servers in the list of categories, then click the + button near the bottom of the dialog box to define a new server.**

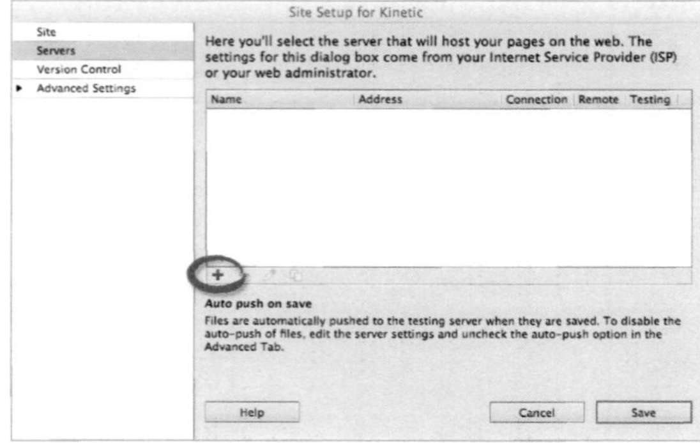

3. **In the Basic options, type a name for the server you are using.**

   This name is simply for you to identify it in Dreamweaver.

4. **Assuming you are working with a remote server, choose FTP in the Connect Using menu.**

   If you are using a local server, consult your network administrator for the settings to use.

5. **In the FTP Address field, type the hostname for your server.**

   Using our example hosting account at Pair Networks, the FTP host is the same as the server name. (If you signed up for this service, your server name was in the confirmation email that you received after signing up.) Check your hosting account documentation for your FTP hostname and account information.

6. **Type your FTP login (username) and password in the related fields.**

   These are the username and password for your hosting account. Again, this information was probably sent to you via email when you first set up the hosting account; consult your server documentation for the correct information to use.

7. **In the Root Directory field, type the location of the folder where you want the files to be placed.**

   Some hosting providers require you to place public files inside a specific folder, such as public_html or www. When users navigate to your URL, they see the index page located in the designated folder.

   Using a hosting account at Pair Networks, as in our example, public files must be placed in the /usr/home/USERNAME/public_html/USERNAME.pairserver.com/ folder (the word "USERNAME" would replaced by your personal username),

8. **In the Web URL field, type the URL at which users will access the site.**

   Dreamweaver automatically defines this URL based on your other choices in this dialog box; the default value will be "http://" plus the FTP Address plus the Root Directory. In our example, the default was http://atctest.pairserver.com/usr/home/public_html/atctest.pairserver.com/.

   You need to change the URL to the path a user would type in a browser to access your site. In our example, the address is http://atctest.pairserver.com/.

   Note that we removed the root-directory folder path from the URL; it is only required when you upload files for viewing over the Internet.

   Make sure you enter the correct information for your domain name.

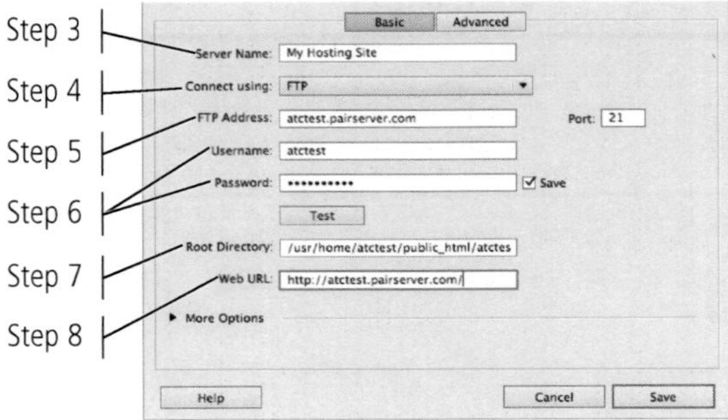

9. **Make sure the Save check box (next to the Password field) is checked, and then click Test.**

   You must receive a message stating that Dreamweaver successfully connected to the Web server. If a connection with the Web server cannot be established, check your entries to make sure your Internet connection is active, and then try again.

   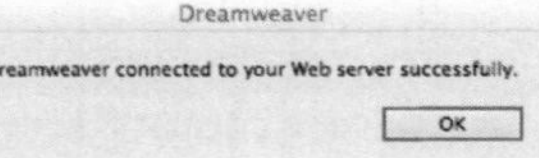

   (If you are working on a shared computer, you might want to uncheck the Save option. However, you will have to retype your username and password every time you upload files to your hosting account.)

10. **Click Save to return to the Site Setup dialog box.**

   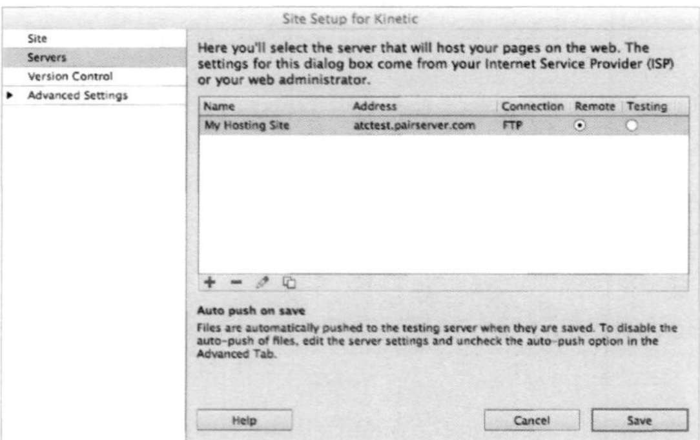

11. **Click Save to close the Site Setup dialog box, then continue to the next exercise.**

Upload Files to a Remote Site

Dreamweaver's FTP functionality makes it easy to put files into the remote site folder (defined in the Site Setup dialog box). You can even synchronize all files on the remote and local sites — which is useful when you are ready to publish the site for public Internet access.

1. **With the Kinetic site open in the Files panel, click the Expand button in the Files panel to show both the local and remote sites.**

   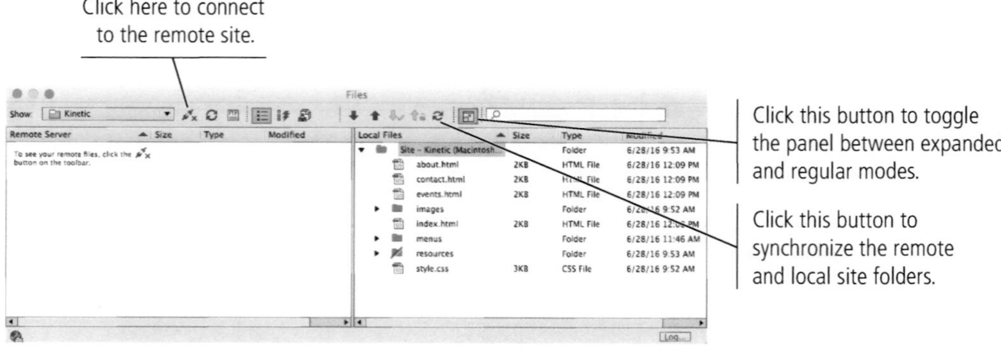

2. **Above the Remote Server pane, click the Connection button to link to and show the remote site.**

   After the connection has been made, the remote site appears in the left pane of the Files panel. (Your host account might include a number of default files.)

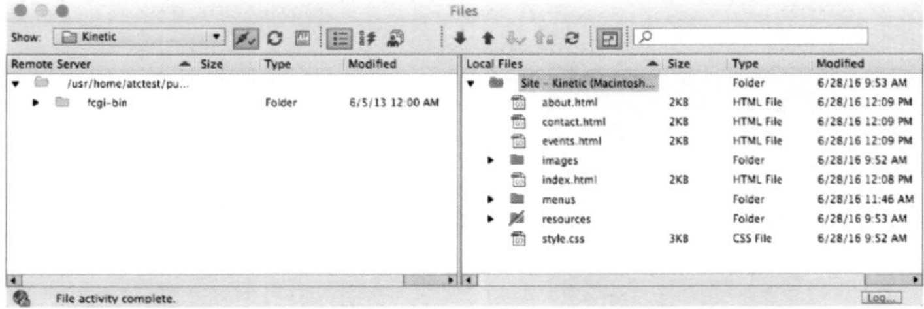

3. **Click the Synchronize button at the top of the expanded Files panel.**

4. **In the Synchronize with Remote Server dialog box, choose Entire 'Kinetic' Site in the Synchronize menu, and choose Put Newer Files to Remote in the Direction menu.**

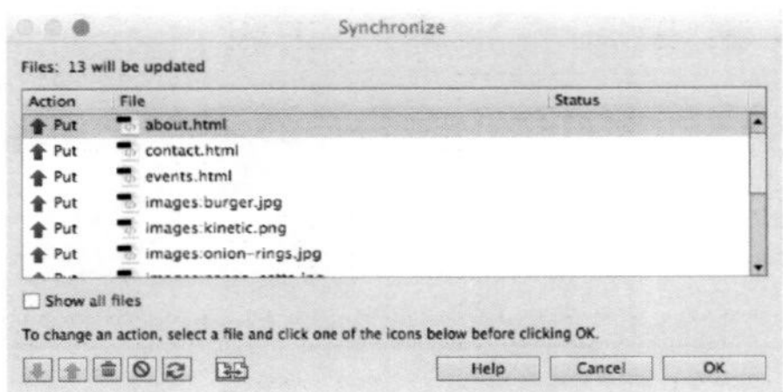

   This utility enables you to synchronize an entire site or only selected files. You can also determine which version (local or remote) to synchronize from. For example, if you accidentally delete files from your local site folder, you can choose to synchronize files from the remote site to the local site to restore the missing files.

5. **Click the Preview button.**

   After a few seconds, the Synchronize dialog box shows a list of all files that will be affected by the process. In this case, this is the first time you are uploading to the remote site, so all site files need to be put onto the remote site.

Note:

You can use the buttons at the bottom of the Synchronize dialog box to change the options for selected files in the list.

6. **Click OK to put the files onto the remote site.**

7. **In the Background File Activity dialog box, click the arrow button to the left of the word "Details."**

   When you upload files to the remote server, Dreamweaver keeps a log of affected files. The Background File Activity dialog box shows a list of each file, including any potential problems encountered during the transfer process. Clicking the Details button expands the dialog box and shows the progression of the synchronization.

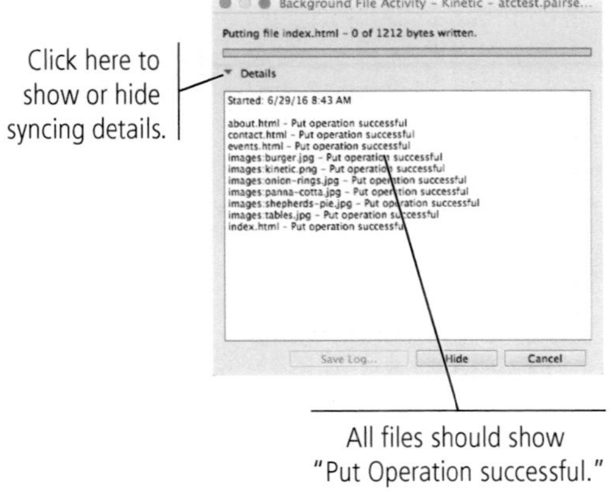

Click here to show or hide syncing details.

All files should show "Put Operation successful."

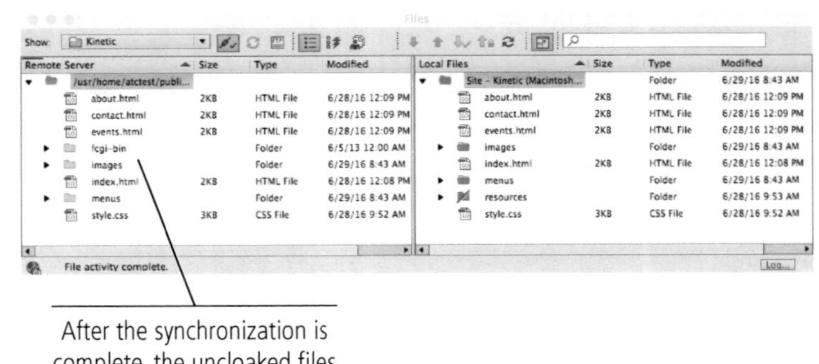

After the synchronization is complete, the uncloaked files appear in the remote site.

8. **Open a browser window. In the navigation bar, type the URL of the Kinetic home page at your domain name.**

   Type the same Web URL you defined in the Servers section of the Site Setup dialog box (see Page 331, Step 8). In our example, the complete URL is http://atctest.pairserver.com/.

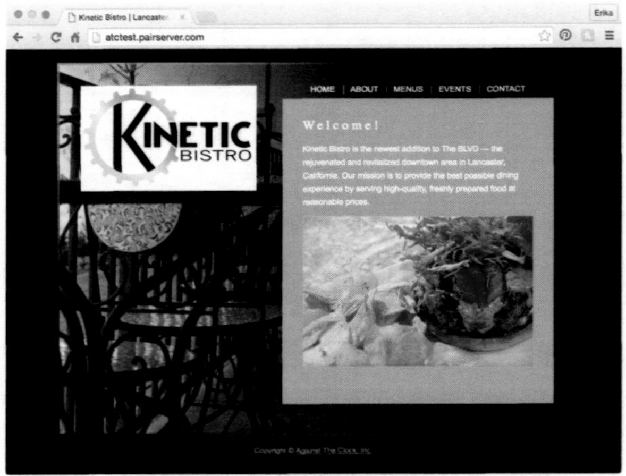

9. **Test the various links in the site.**

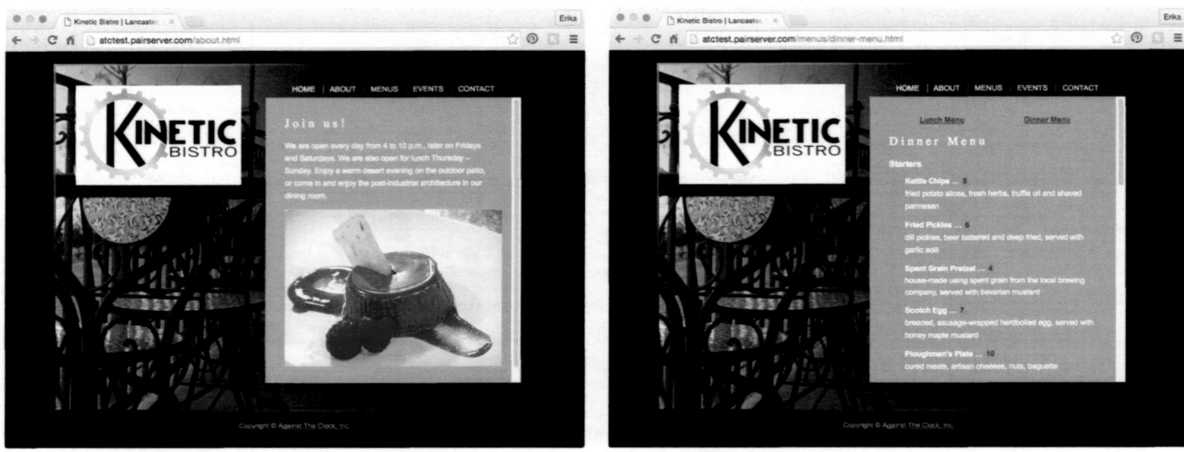

10. **Close the browser and return to Dreamweaver, then continue to the next exercise.**

Export and Remove the Site Definition

To reduce the potential for confusion, it's a good idea to remove the defined sites of completed projects, leaving only the defined sites of current projects.

As stated in the Interface chapter, removing a site from Dreamweaver does not delete the actual files and folders from your computer; it simply removes them from Dreamweaver. Rather than removing a site, however, you can export a site definition file — which you can later import to restore the same settings and options you already defined (as you did in the Interface chapter when you imported the sf-arts site).

As you work through the projects in this book, you will export and remove site definitions for completed projects, so your site list remains manageable. You should get into this habit so you can quickly reinstate site definitions if necessary.

1. **With the Kinetic site open in the Files panel, click the Collapse button in the Files panel.**

   The Files panel retains the last-used position and mode; it can be a good idea to collapse it whenever you are not interacting with files on a server.

   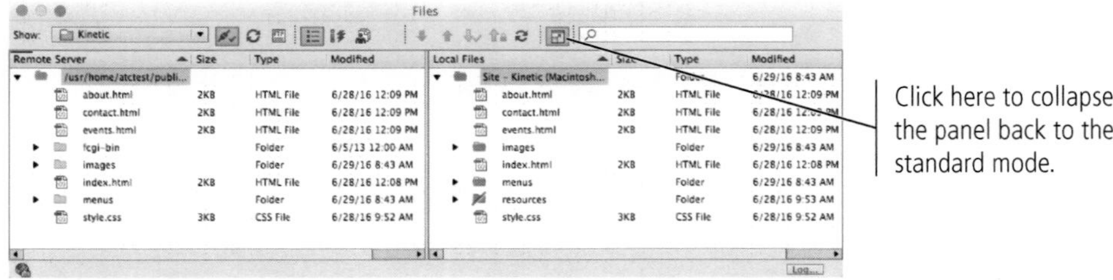

   Click here to collapse the panel back to the standard mode.

2. **Choose Manage Sites at the bottom of the Directory menu.**

   You can access this menu even when the Files panel is in expanded mode.

   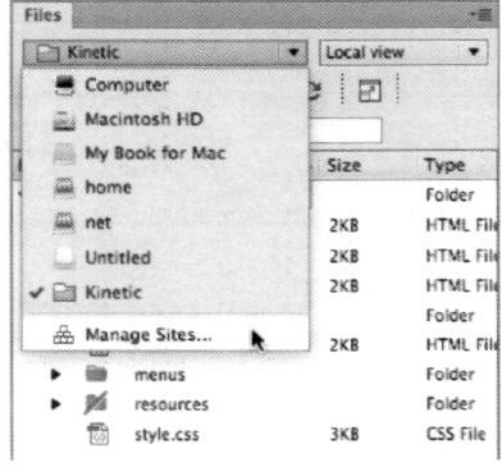

3. **In the Manage Sites dialog box, choose the Kinetic site name, and then click the Export button.**

   This function creates a ".ste" file that stores the Dreamweaver site definition settings.

   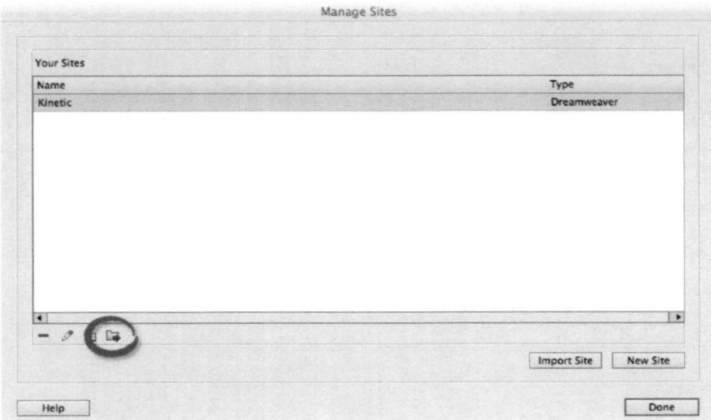

4. **Read the resulting warning. Choose the option you prefer, then click OK.**

   If you are sharing site files with other users, you might want to exclude login and password information in the site setup. Each user should have his or her own password and login information.

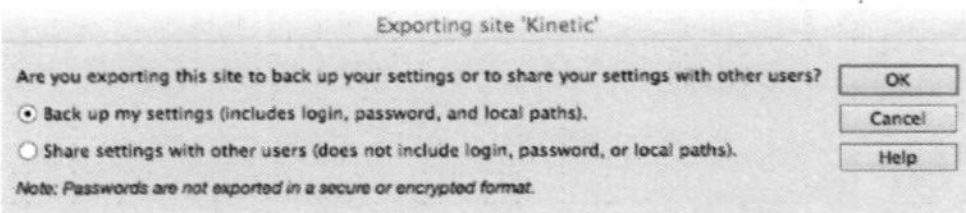

5. **Navigate to WIP>Kinetic and click Save.**

   The Export Site dialog box defaults to the current site's root folder. You can restore the site settings by importing the site definition file from this location.

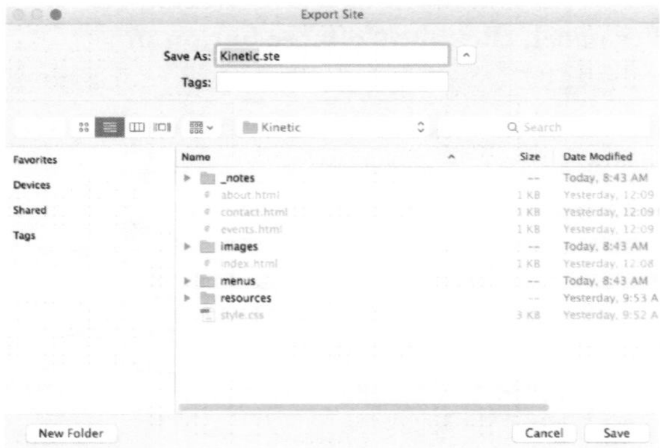

6. **In the Manage Sites dialog box, make sure Kinetic site is selected and click the "–" button to remove the site from the list.**

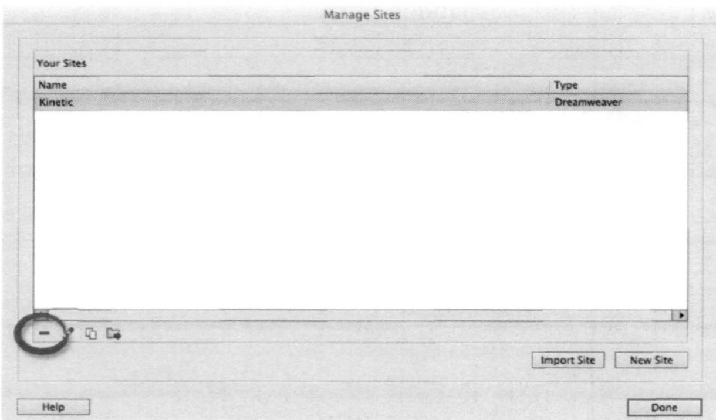

7. **Click Yes to the warning to confirm the removal of the Kinetic site definition.**

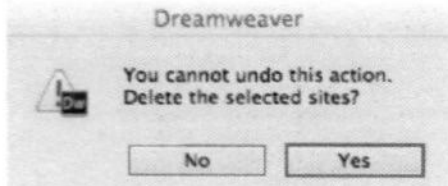

   Remember, you are not deleting the files from the site; you are simply removing the site definition from Dreamweaver.

8. **At the bottom of the Manage Sites dialog box, click Done.**

Project Review

fill in the blank

1. The _______________ extension identifies a Dreamweaver site definition file.
2. The _______________ is the primary folder that contains all files and subfolders of a Web site.
3. The _______________ is used to view and manage files that make up a site in Dreamweaver.
4. _______________ is the process of improving a page's ranking in search engine results pages.
5. A(n) _______________ is a path from one file to another, beginning from the current location and moving up or down through folder paths to the target image.
6. The notation _______________ tells Dreamweaver to move up one folder from the current location.
7. The _______________ shows the nested order of HTML tags to the currently selected object.
8. The _______________ protocol is used to define an email link.
9. _______________ is the process of hiding certain files in the site so they are not uploaded to the Web server.
10. The _______________ pane of the Site Setup dialog box defines the settings you need to upload site files through Dreamweaver's Files panel.

short answer

1. Briefly explain why it is important to define a Dreamweaver site file.
2. Briefly explain the importance of creating a site flowchart.
3. Explain three different methods for creating a link to a page in the current site.

Portfolio Builder Project

Use what you learned in this project to complete the following freeform exercise.
Carefully read the art director and client comments, then create your own design to meet the needs of the project.
Use the space below to sketch ideas; when finished, write a brief explanation of your reasoning behind your final design.

art director comments

Romana Place Town Homes is adding a photo tour to its Web site. The owner is fairly competent at building Web pages, but is having trouble finalizing the new site. Your job is to finish what he started in a professional, organized manner.

To complete this project, you should:

- ❑ Import the site files into Dreamweaver (from the **Rentals_Web16_PB.zip** archive on the Student Files Web page).
- ❑ Analyze the content of the different pages. Create a flowchart to map the direction of links from one page to another in the site.
- ❑ Organize the site folder into a clear, understandable structure.
- ❑ Create the links from one page to another throughout the entire site.

client comments

When I started working with our site files I noticed that none of the links exist anymore. I might have worked from an earlier version of the site files, but I'm not sure. Can you fix this for me? Other than the navigation in the middle of the pages, there are a number of other places where links are necessary:

- Users should be able to navigate between the different property pages without going back to the main Properties page.
- There should be a link to our main information email address (info@romanaplace.atc) on every page.
- The original design company's name in the footer should link to its Web site.

project justification

Project Summary

This project focused on two of the foundational elements of Web site design — organizing files and creating links. A well-organized site structure includes links that make it easy for users to navigate throughout the entire site. Dreamweaver makes it easy to manage the files in a site — renaming and moving them while maintaining the links between pages within the site. You also learned a number of ways to create links, whether to other pages in the site, to an external URL, or to an email address. The skills you used in this project will be required to complete virtually any site you create in Dreamweaver.

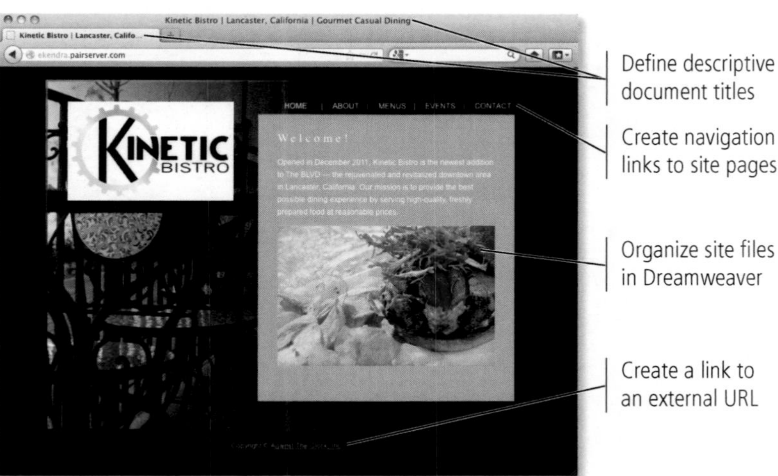
Define descriptive document titles
Create navigation links to site pages
Organize site files in Dreamweaver
Create a link to an external URL

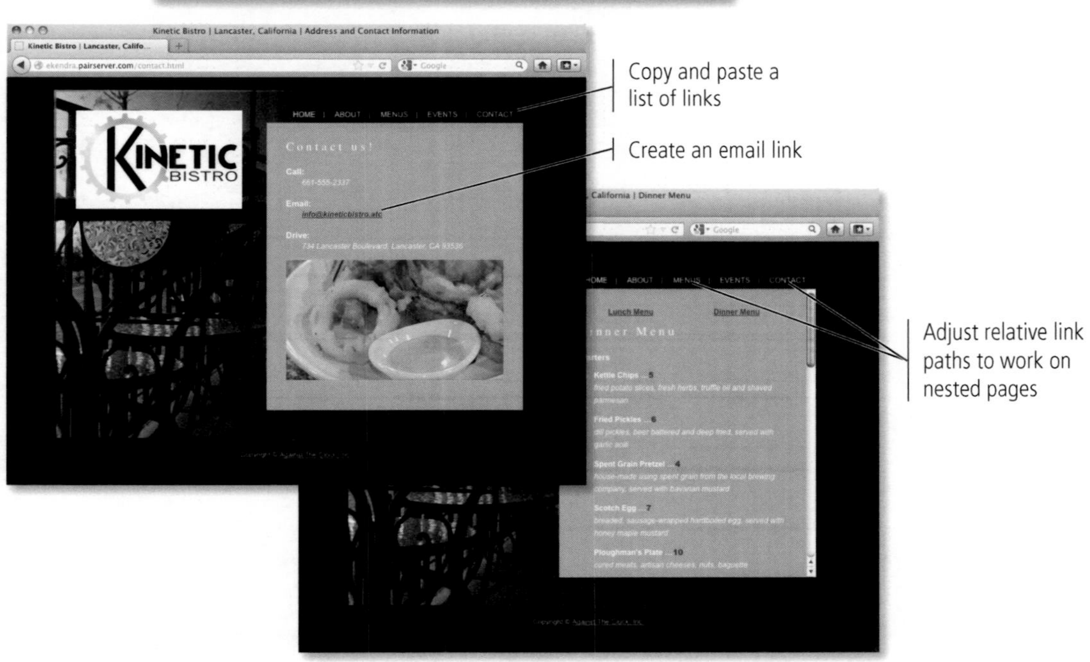
Copy and paste a list of links
Create an email link
Adjust relative link paths to work on nested pages

project 7

Digital Book Chapter

In addition to application-specific books, Against The Clock Inc. also has a series of "companion" titles that discuss the concepts underlying the use of digital software — basic design principles, type, color, and so on. You were hired to build an "excerpt" booklet of the companion titles, which ATC will use on its corporate Web site. Your task is to properly structure the content with HTML code.

This project incorporates the following skills:

- ❑ Adding text from external sources
- ❑ Working in both Design view and Code view to add appropriate HTML tags semantically
- ❑ Organizing content with appropriate heading tags
- ❑ Properly formatting block quotes and citations
- ❑ Adding special characters that work in HTML code
- ❑ Creating lists and tables within text-based content
- ❑ Attaching a CSS file to new pages

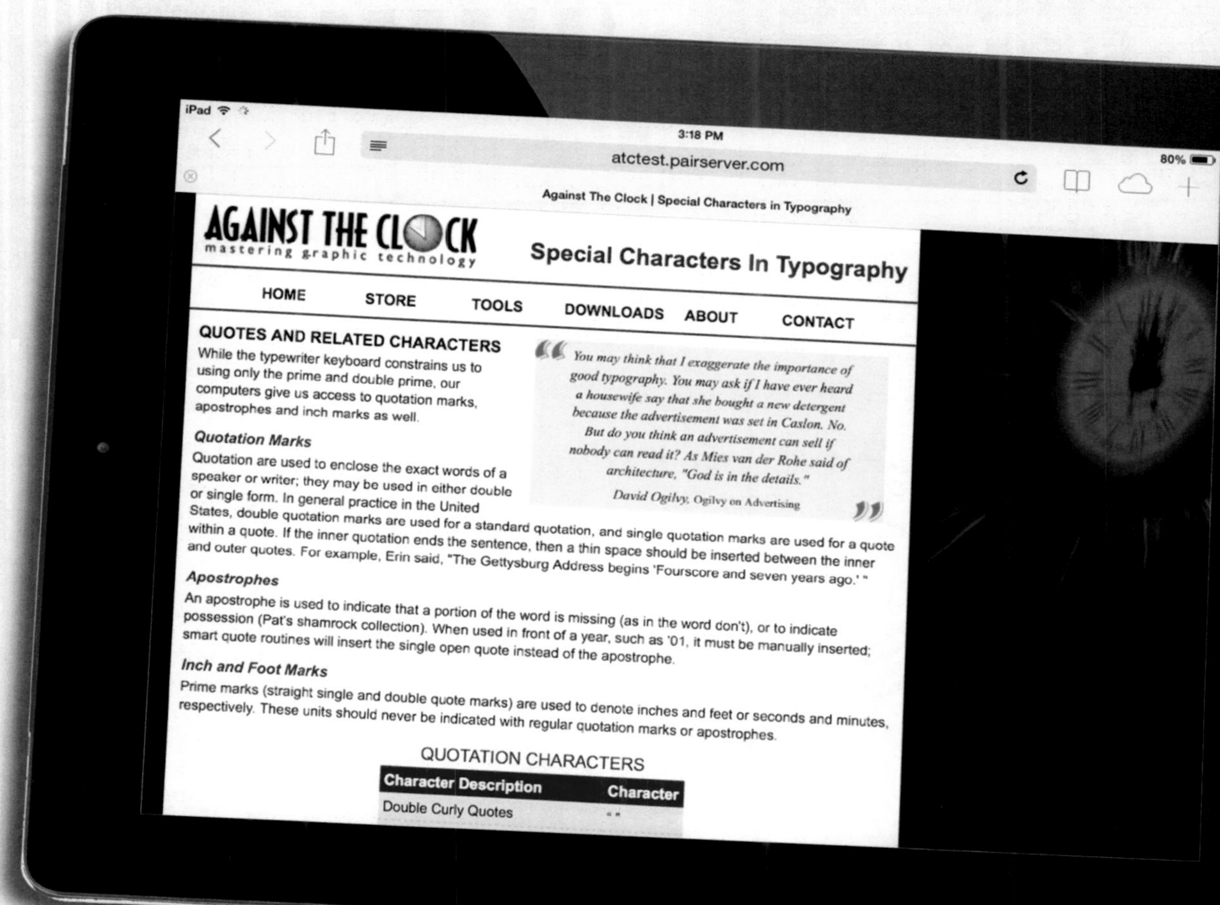

Project Meeting

client comments

We publish a series of books that are designed as companion titles to our application-specific training books (which is why it's called *The Companion Series*). The companion titles cover general topics that are important to graphic designers — basic design principles, color, writing, typography, and Web design concepts — but don't quite fit into an application-specific book.

These books have been available for several years, but we haven't done any serious marketing of the titles. When we talk to people about *The Companion Series*, they ask, "Why haven't I heard about these books before?" We're hoping the sample chapters will help get the word out about these books and dramatically improve sales.

We want to be sure of two things: first, this Web page needs to be instantly recognizable as part of our existing site, with the same layout and formatting. Second, the page must include searchable text.

art director comments

The publisher sent the text she wants to offer on the site. When you have this much text on a Web page — which isn't uncommon — it's very important to format it with the proper structural tags. If you use Heading 2 because you think Heading 1 is too big, for example, you're causing problems for search engines and anyone with screen-reader software.

As you know, the client already has a corporate Web site. To create the new page, you can use the existing CSS file that defines the appearance of the various structural elements. Once you apply the correct structural tags to the text in the new pages, you can attach the existing CSS file. This will ensure that the existing format maps to the structural tags in your new page.

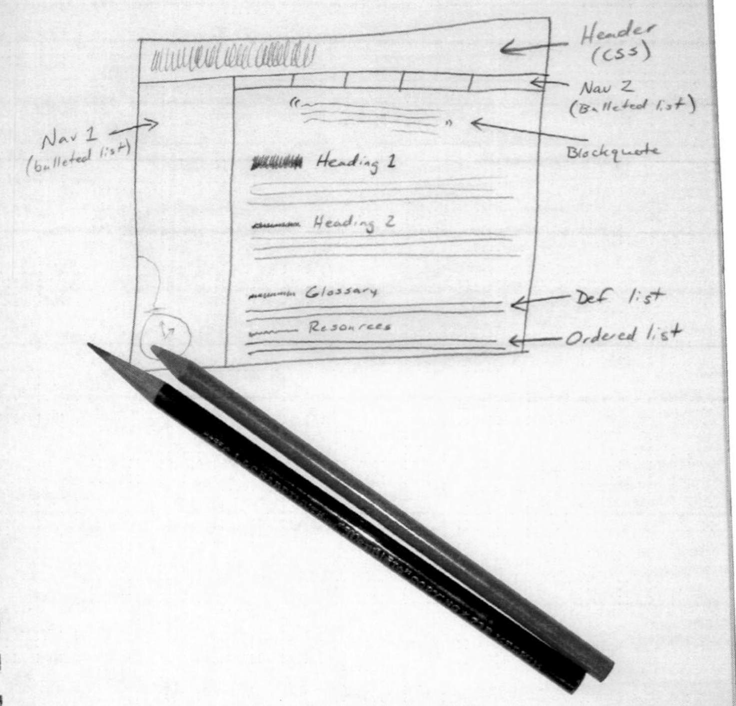

project objectives

To complete this project, you will:

- ❑ Paste text content from a text-only email
- ❑ Apply the appropriate heading and paragraph tags throughout the text
- ❑ Create block quotes and define quote citations
- ❑ Mark up abbreviations for improved usability and accessibility
- ❑ Use the correct HTML tags to show emphasis
- ❑ Add special HTML characters throughout the text
- ❑ Use a table to present well organized content
- ❑ Create ordered and unordered lists
- ❑ Attach an existing CSS file to the new page

Stage 1 Preparing the Workspace

In many Web design jobs, you need to create new HTML files in addition to working with existing files. The first step in any new project, however, is to define the Dreamweaver site, so the application can accurately manage the various files and folders that make up the site. Once the site is defined, it's relatively easy to create as many new files as necessary to complete the job.

Define the ATC Site

The procedure for defining the ATC site is essentially the same as it was for the Kinetic Site in Project 6: Bistro Site Organization.

1. **Download `Chapter_Web16_RF.zip` from the Student Files Web page.**
2. **Expand the ZIP archive in your WIP folder (Macintosh) or copy the archive contents into your WIP folder (Windows).**

   This results in a folder named **Chapter**, which contains the files you need for this project.
3. **From the Files panel, choose Manage Sites at the bottom of the Directory menu (or click the link if it is available).**
4. **In the Manage Sites dialog box, click the New Site button.**
5. **In the resulting Site Setup dialog box, type `ATC` in the Site Name field.**
6. **Click the Browse icon to the right of the Local Site Folder field, navigate to your `WIP>Chapter` folder, and click Choose/Select.**

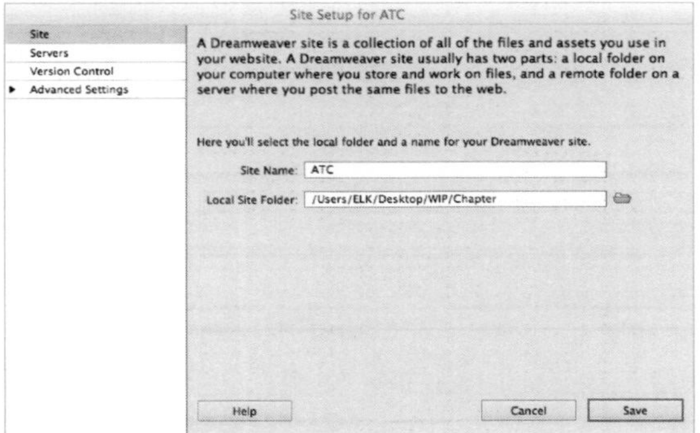

Note:

You can also choose Site>New Site to open the Site Setup dialog box.

7. **Click Save to accept the Site Setup definition.**
8. **In the Manage Sites dialog box, make sure the ATC site appears in the list of sites, and then click Done.**

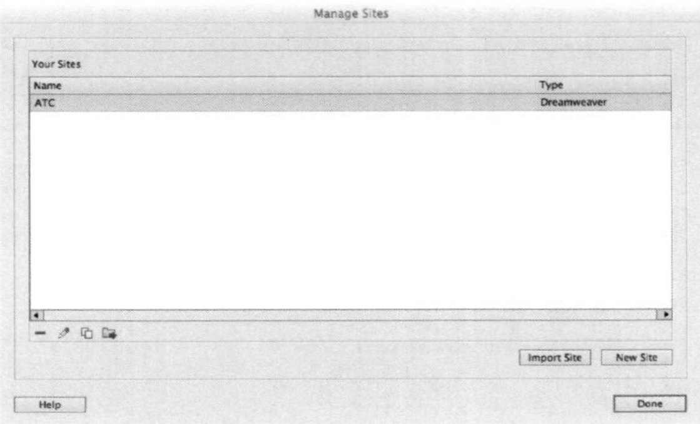

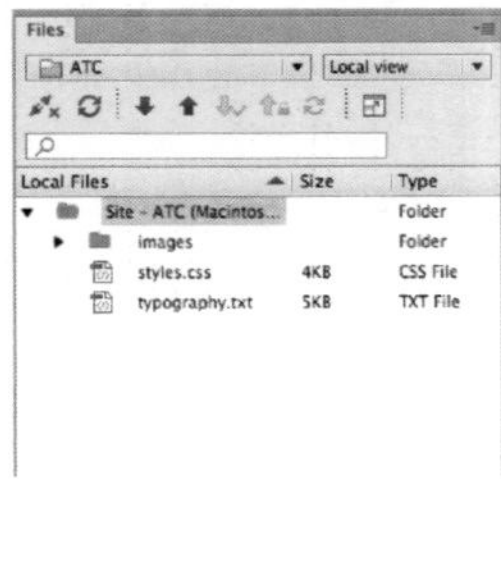

9. **Continue to the next exercise.**

Create a New HTML Document

The content for the excerpt page was sent to you by the client in an email. You need to create a new HTML page and then move the supplied text into the page so you can apply the necessary HTML structure.

HTML was created as a coding language used to apply structure (paragraphs, headings, and lists) to online documents. By 1996, the modern methods of document markup had outgrown the inflexible HTML, so the extensibility concept from XML (eXtensible Markup Language) was added to HTML 4.01 (referred to as XHTML).

HTML5, developed by World Wide Web Consortium (W3C) and the Web Hypertext Application Technology Working Group (WHATWG), is the current revision of the HTML standard and is the default document type in Dreamweaver CC. It is intended to replace both HTML 4 and XHTML.

This project explores many of the general semantic HTML mark-up issues.

> *Note:*
>
> *Extensibility means that the language can incorporate structures that don't exist in HTML. For example, HTML supports six heading levels, from 1 to 6; the extensibility principle in XHTML allows designers to create heading level 7 if necessary.*

1. **With the ATC site open in the Files panel, choose File>New.**
2. **In the New Document dialog box, choose New Document in the left pane and choose HTML in the Document Type list.**

   When you create a new HTML page, the Doc Type menu defaults to HTML5 — the current version of the standard.

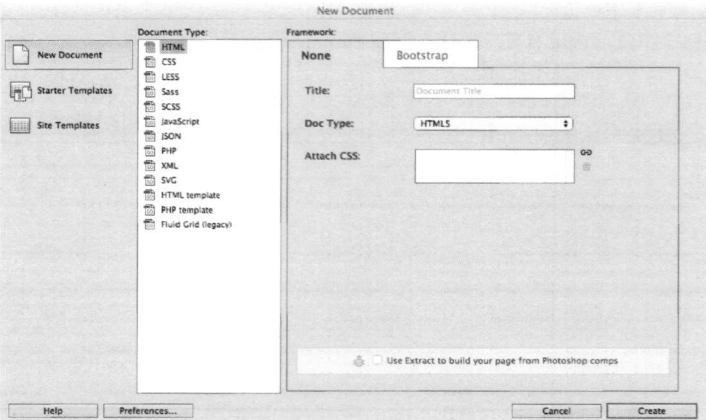

3. **Click Create to create the new blank file.**
4. **If only the Design pane is visible, click the Split button in the Document toolbar.**

   Even though the document appears to be blank in Design view, it already contains some code in the background, which you can see in Code view.

5. **Examine the code in the document window.**

   The first line — <!doctype html> — is the document type definition or DTD, which tells the browser what version of HTML is being used. For an HTML5 page — the default type in Dreamweaver CC — the doctype statement simply says "html" without a specific version number.

   Content within the **head** element — between the opening **<head>** and closing **</head>** tags — is not visible to the user (except for the content enclosed in the **<title>** tags, which appears in the title bar of a browser, as the title of a bookmark, and as the text in search engine results). Visible Web page content is created within the body section, between the opening **<html><body>** and closing **</body></html>** tags.

6. **In the Code pane, place the insertion point anywhere between the opening and closing <title> tags.**

   When certain tags are selected in the Code pane, you can use the Properties panel to change the content of the active tag.

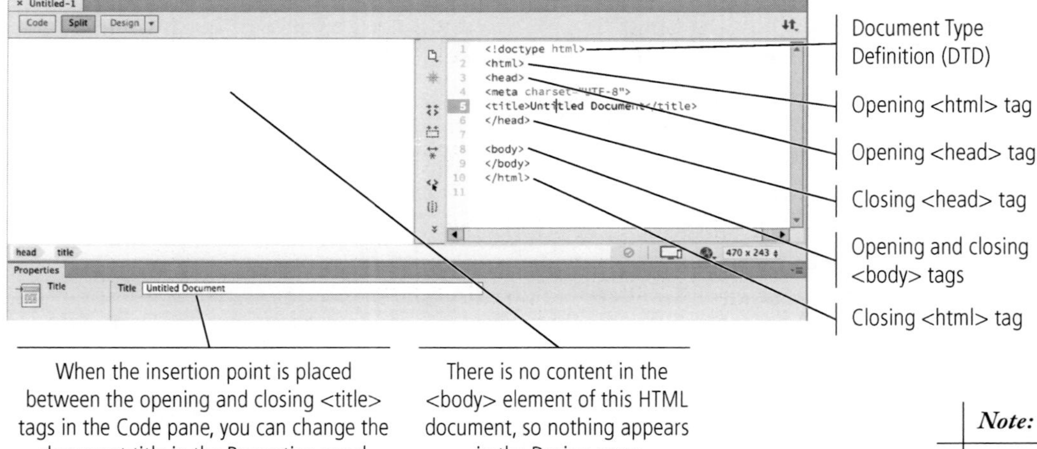

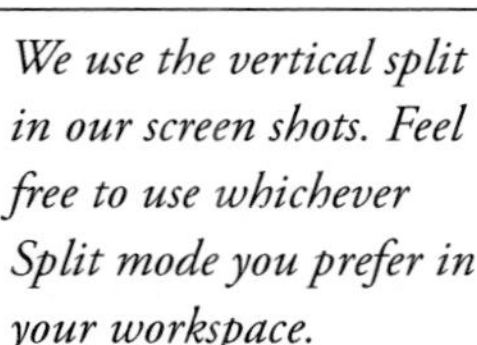

Note:

We use the vertical split in our screen shots. Feel free to use whichever Split mode you prefer in your workspace.

7. **In the Properties panel, change the Document Title field to `Against The Clock | Special Characters in Typography`. Press Return/Enter to finalize the new title.**

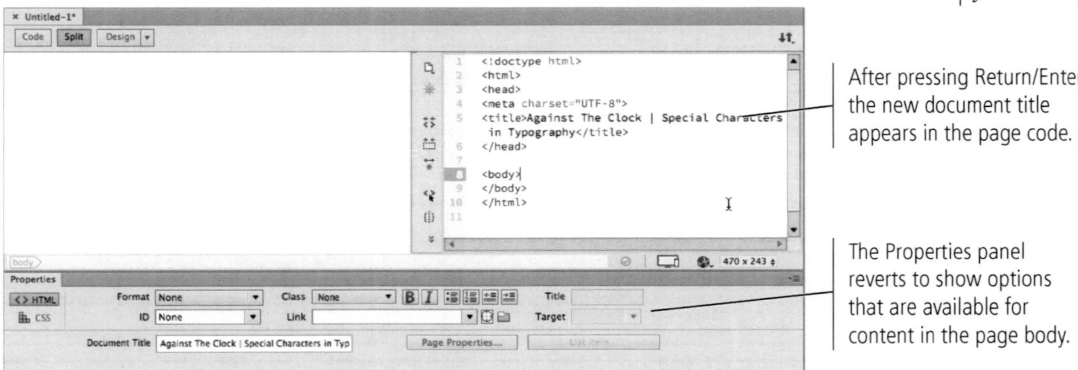

After pressing Return/Enter, the new document title appears in the page code.
The Properties panel reverts to show options that are available for content in the page body.

8. **Choose File>Save As. Navigate to your WIP>Chapter folder (the root of the ATC site) as the target location and save the document as an HTML file named `typography.html`.**

   After the file is saved, it automatically appears in the Files panel.

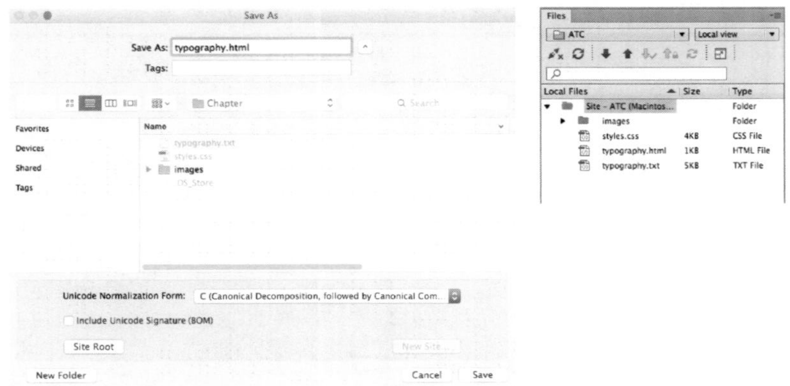

9. **Continue to the next stage of the project.**

Stage 2 Working with Semantic Markup

Many people have difficulty structuring documents — including word-processing files such as those created in Microsoft Word. Consider creating a heading; the user enters text, and then applies bold styling, increases the font size, and changes the text color. While this **local formatting** makes the text appear to be a heading, it is actually just a styled paragraph. Whether it is a Web page, a PDF file, or a word-processing document, a digital document should make use of available structures to enhance the document's usability. This is where HTML comes into play.

Properly structured HTML documents use tags semantically, to reinforce the meaning of the content and provide a wide range of benefits to users: they are more accessible, they load quickly in a browser, they reduce bandwidth costs for high-traffic Web sites, they achieve high search-engine rankings, and they are easy to style. As a Web designer, you should take full advantage of these benefits by converting the unstructured or poorly structured documents you receive from clients into properly structured HTML documents. Dreamweaver makes it easy to do this, even if you don't understand a great deal of coding and code syntax.

 Paste Text Content in Design View

HTML is a coding language that defines the structure of the elements in a page; without HTML, the content between the opening and closing **<body>** tags would be completely unstructured. Web browsers depend on the structural markup of HTML to properly display a Web page, so headings stand out from regular text and paragraphs are separated from one another. Without structure, all text on a page would appear as a single, large block of text.

> ***Note:***
>
> *Web browsers (and Dreamweaver) ignore extra spaces between words and paragraph returns between lines of text. Properly displaying Web page text requires structural markup.*

Clients often supply content as plain text without structural markup (paragraph returns do not qualify as structure). When people read text that doesn't have structural markup, they are able to make logical inferences about the intended structure — for example, they can assume that a short block of text is a heading and a long block is a paragraph. Browsers, however, can't make assumptions; they require structure to correctly display content.

Although not all lines in a text document are paragraphs (some are headings and some are list items), marking each line as a paragraph provides a starting point that you can modify later.

1. **With typography.html (from the ATC site) open in Split view, click in the Design pane to place the insertion point.**

2. **Double-click typography.txt in the Files panel to open that file.**

   Text (.txt) files only appear in Code view because there is no "design".

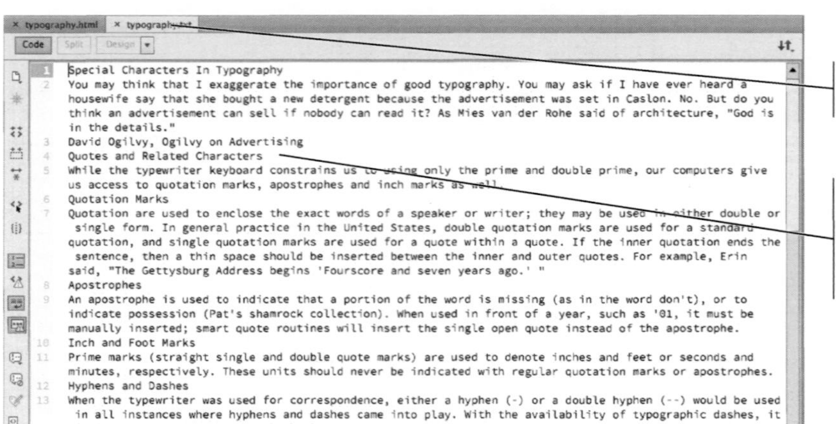

Each open file is accessible in a separate tab.

Although there are smaller and larger blocks of text, there are no codes or styles to separate headings from paragraphs.

3. **Choose Edit>Select All, and then copy the selected content to the Clipboard.**

   Choose Edit>Copy or press Command/Control-C to copy the selected text.

4. **Close typography.txt.**

5. **In typography.html, paste the copied text into the Design pane.**

   If you pasted the text into the Code pane, the line-break characters would not be included. You will use those bits of codes in the next few steps to apply the proper structure to the paragraphs of text.

> ***Note:***
>
> *Press Command/Control-A to select all content in an open file or document.*

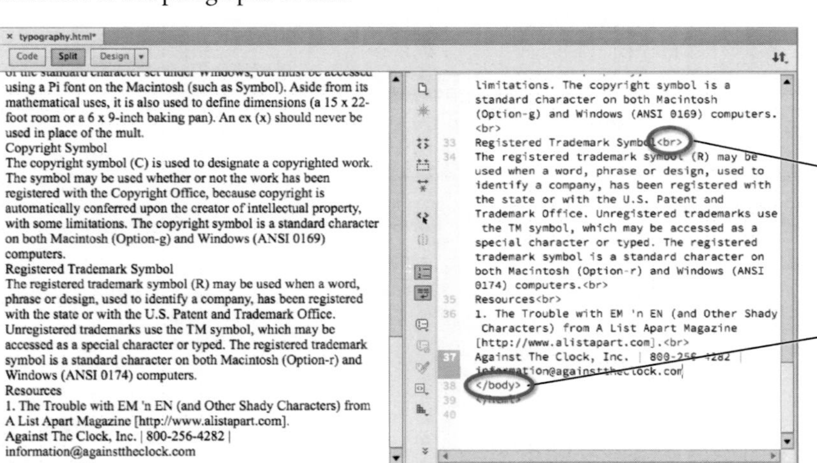

Each paragraph in the pasted text ends with the HTML5 code for a line break (<br>).

Text pasted into the Design pane automatically appears between the opening and closing <body> tags in the Code pane.

6. **Press Command/Control-A to select all the text in the Design pane, then choose Paragraph in the Format menu of the Properties panel.**

   An HTML paragraph is surrounded by opening **<p>** and closing **</p>** paragraph tags. Because the paragraphs of pasted text are separated by the code for a forced line break (**
**), the entire block of copy is treated as a single paragraph.

   When you apply the paragraph structure to the selected text, the entire block is surrounded by a single set of paragraph tags in the Code pane.

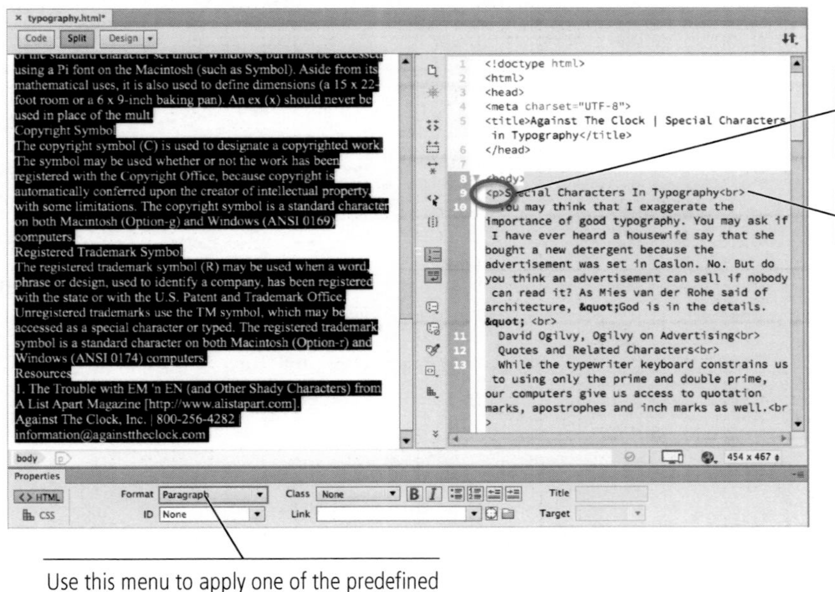

The entire selection is surrounded by a single set of paragraph tags.

The <br> tags are not removed or replaced.

Use this menu to apply one of the predefined structural tags to the selected text.

> ***Note:***
>
> *The Design pane shows text in the default font because you have not defined any other type formatting. Later in this project, you will attach a CSS file to change the formatting of various elements in the file.*

7. **Choose Edit>Find and Replace.**

   As you just saw, the line-break code only appears in the Code pane, so you want to search only the source code of the open document.

8. **Choose Current Document in the Find In menu and choose Source Code in the Search menu.**

9. **In the Find field, type <br>. In the Replace field, type </p><p>.**

   Do not press Return/Enter when typing in the Replace field because the dialog box will prematurely run the Find and Replace operation.

   Each line in the text currently ends with the line-break tag (**
) when it should end with a closing paragraph tag (</p>**). Each line should also begin with the opening paragraph tag (**<p>**), where nothing currently exists.

   Using the search and replace function, you can remove all of the line-break codes and place the necessary closing and opening paragraph tags in a single click.

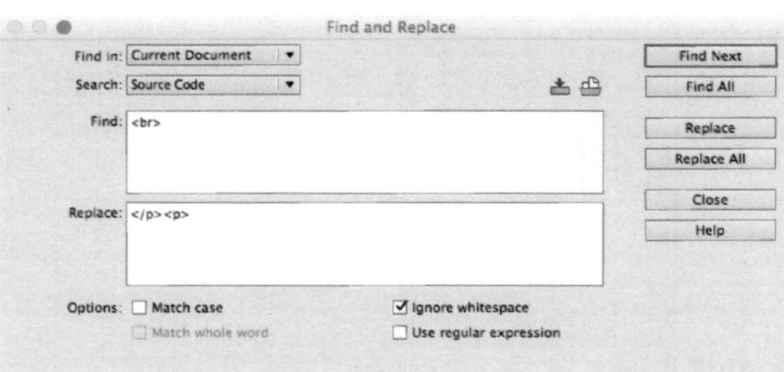

Note:

You cannot undo a Find and Replace in documents that are not open. When doing a Find and Replace that includes files that aren't currently open, you might want to back up the site's root folder outside of Dreamweaver before continuing.

10. **Click Replace All.**

Understanding Element Names, Tags, and Attributes

DREAMWEAVER FOUNDATIONS

The **element name** is the text that identifies the tag, such as meta, title, head, or body.

A **tag** consists of the element name surrounded by angle brackets, such as <html>, <head>, or <body>.

An **element** is the tag plus its containing content, such as the title element <title>Untitled Document</title>.

Container tags consist of an opening tag (<title>) and a closing tag (</title>). The closing tag is the same as the opening tag, with the addition of the initial forward slash. For example:

<title>"Weather Forecast"</title>

Empty tags (<meta />) do not have a separate closing tag. In an empty tag, the closing forward slash appears with the closing angle bracket of the tag. For example:

<img src="sun.gif" alt="sunny day" />

Attributes add properties to HTML elements. For example, the cite attribute of the <blockquote> tag allows you to identify the URL of a quotation. Attributes appear in the opening tag only; they consist of the attribute name and the attribute value in quotation marks (for example, attribute="attribute value").

When marking up a short quotation, you would type:

<q cite="http://www.useit.com/alertbox/9710a.html"> People rarely read Web pages word by word.</q>

In this example, the attribute name is cite and the attribute value is http://www.useit.com/alertbox/9710a.html.

Most attributes are optional, such as the cite attribute of the <blockquote> tag. Some attributes are required, such as the alt attribute of the <img> tag, which describes an image for visually impaired visitors.

Some HTML attributes do not require an attribute value, such as the checked attribute that allows you to preselect a check box option.

11. **Review the Search panel, and then close the tab group.**

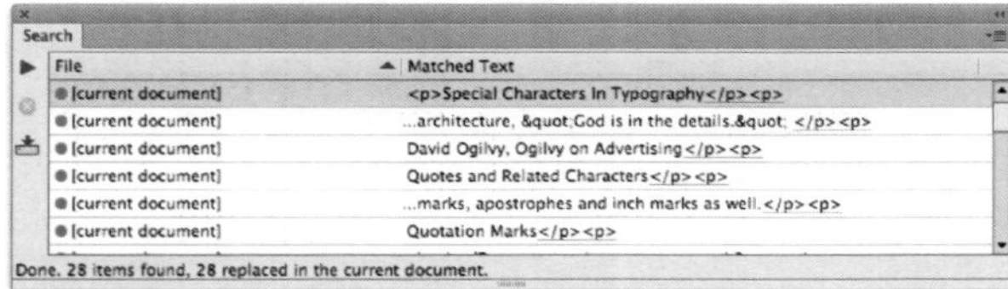

12. **Click the Refresh button in the Properties panel if necessary, then review the results in both panes of the document window.**

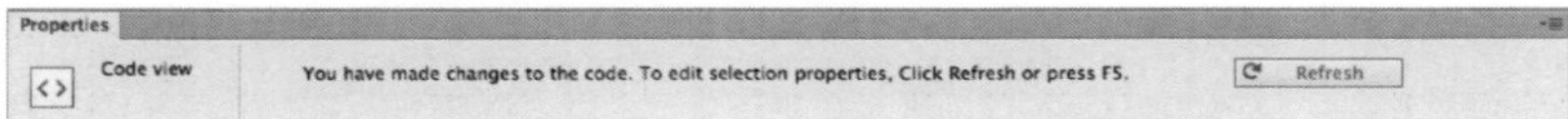

In many cases, changes in the Code pane are automatically reflected in the Design pane. If the changes do not automatically take effect (as in the case of changing the page code using the Find and Replace dialog box), you can use several techniques to manually refresh the Design view:

- Click the Refresh button in the Properties panel.
- Press F5.
- Simply click in the Design pane bring it into focus (and refresh at the same time).

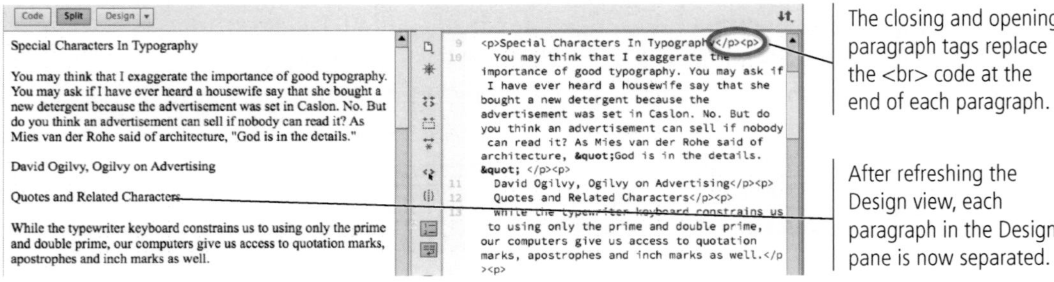

13. **Click the Format Source Code button to the left of the Code pane and choose Apply Source Formatting from the menu.**

If you split your screen horizontally, you might not be able to see all of the Code pane buttons (depending on the size of your screen). In that case, you have to click the Show More button at the bottom to access the Format Source Code button.

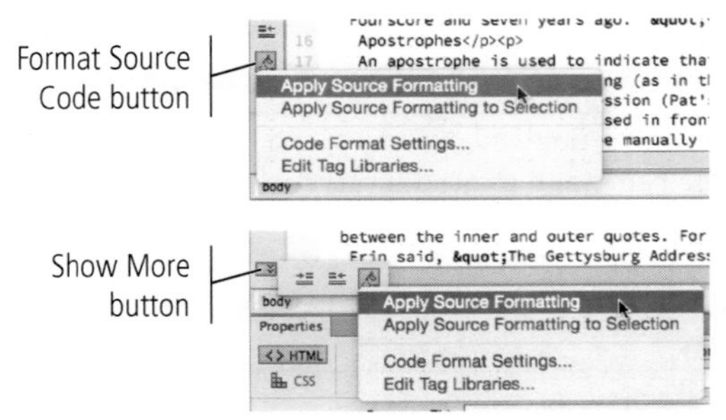

This command cleans up the code, moving the opening **<p>** tags to the beginning of each line of copy. Nothing changes in the Design pane when the tags are moved to the appropriate lines.

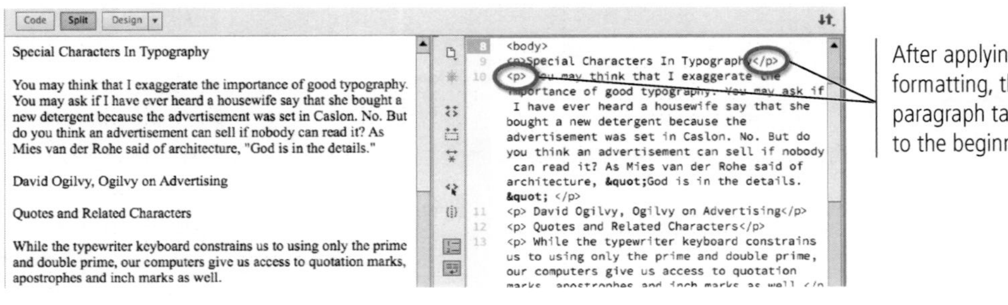

14. **Save the file and continue to the next exercise.**

Format Headings in Design View

Headings help readers find the information they need. For visual users, a heading is effective as long as it looks like a heading. This is not the case for visually impaired users who use screen-reading software; screen-reading software and some browsers enable users to skip forward and backward through headings. Also, when reviewing the content of a page and its relevance to a particular topic, search engine software uses headings and heading levels (among other criteria) to make evaluations. For these reasons, it is important to use properly structured headings rather than styled paragraphs.

Space Travel — Heading level 1
Travel to the Moon — Heading level 2
Manned Travel — Heading level 3
The Moon Base — Heading level 4
Unmanned Travel
Travel to Mars
Manned Travel
Unmanned Travel

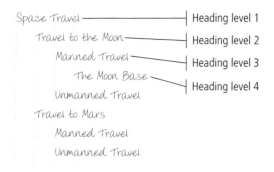

There are six predefined heading levels, **<h1>**, **<h2>**, **<h3>**, and so on to **<h6>**. Heading level 1 is the largest and most important; it should be used only once per page to describe the purpose or title of the Web page. The rest of the headings can be used multiple times, but they should be used in a branch-like pattern or hierarchy.

Many new Web designers complain that heading level 1 appears too large, so they apply heading level 2 or 3 instead. This is a mistake. In a later project, you will learn to use cascading style sheets (CSS) to define the appearance of different elements on a Web page — including different levels of headings.

The special characters described in the text in this project are divided into related groups and subgroups. Your task is to determine which heading level is appropriate for each section. In professional situations, some client-supplied copy will be well-written and well-structured, enabling you to quickly determine appropriate heading levels (called **editorial hierarchy** or **editorial priority**). Other copy will be poorly structured and difficult to decipher; in such a case, you will need to contact the author for clarification or make a best-guess assessment yourself.

1. **With typography.html (from your ATC site) open in Split view, click in the Design pane to place the insertion point in the first paragraph.**

   You should be working with the paragraph "Special Characters In Typography".

2. **In the Properties panel, open the Format menu and choose Heading 1.**

   In the Code pane, the opening and closing **<p>** tags automatically change to the **<h1>** tags that identify the paragraph as heading level 1.

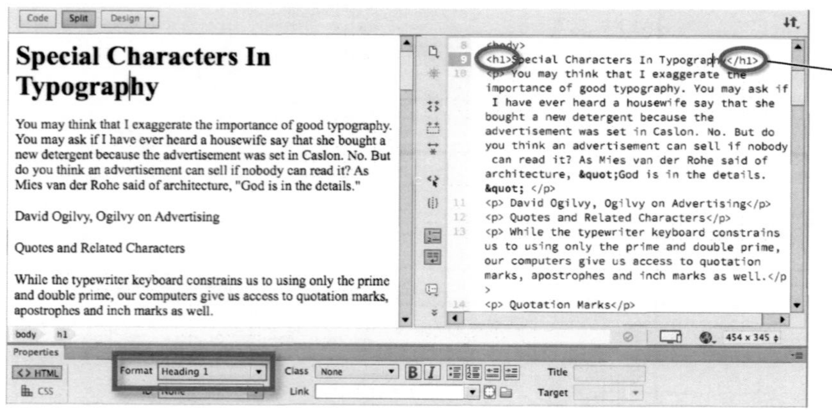

The <p> tags are replaced by the appropriate heading tags (<h1> and </h1>).

> **Note:**
>
> *If you use a mouse with a scroll wheel, move the mouse cursor away from the Format menu before you try to scroll through the document window. If the cursor is over the Formatting menu, scrolling with the mouse wheel changes the menu selection.*

3. **Move the insertion point to the "Quotes and Related Characters" paragraph and use the Properties panel Format menu to apply the Heading 2 tag.**

After choosing a format in the Properties panel, the Code pane shows that the **<p>** and **</p>** tags have been replaced with **<h2>** and **</h2>** tags, respectively.

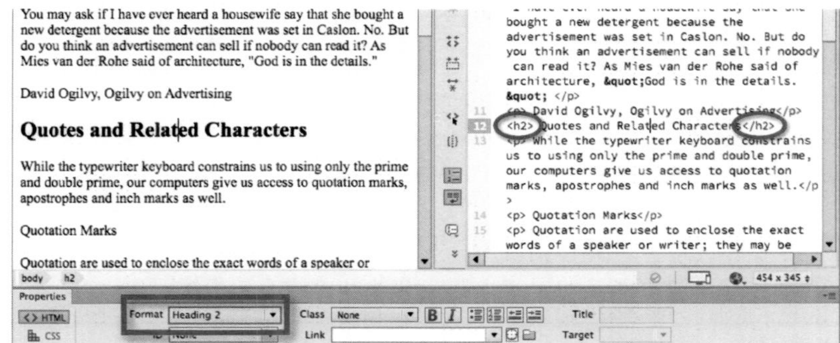

> *Note:*
>
> *When you're working in Design view, you can apply paragraph structure and heading levels by choosing from the Format>Paragraph Format menu, or in the Heading menu of the HTML Insert panel.*

4. **Using the same technique from Step 3, format "Quotation Marks," "Apostrophes," and "Inch and Foot Marks" as Heading 3.**

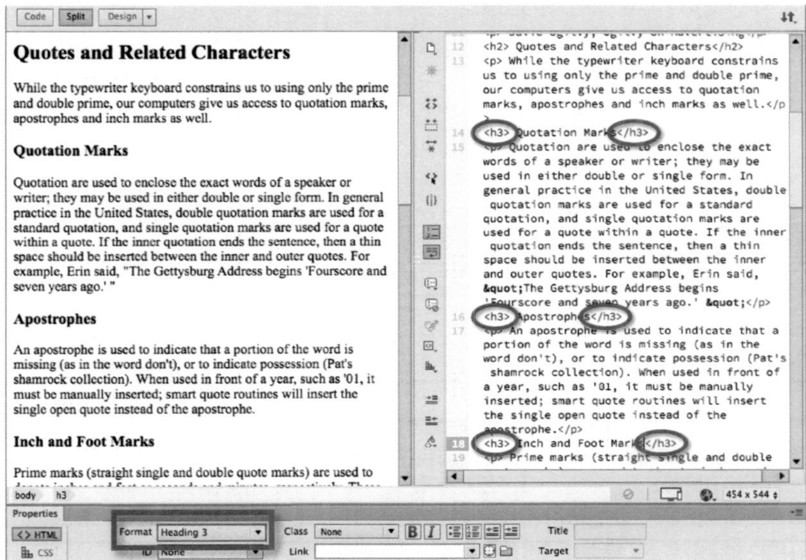

> *Note:*
>
> *You can also use keyboard shortcuts to apply common tags:*
>
> *Paragraph*
> *Command/Control-Shift-p*
>
> *Heading 1*
> *Command/Control-1*
>
> *Heading 2*
> *Command/Control-2*
>
> *Heading 3*
> *Command/Control-3*
>
> *Heading 4*
> *Command/Control-4*
>
> *Heading 5*
> *Command/Control-5*
>
> *Heading 6*
> *Command/Control-6*

5. **Apply heading levels to the rest of the document as follows:**

Line Number in the Code pane	Content	Heading Level
20	Hyphens and Dashes	2
22	Hyphen	3
24	En Dash	3
26	Em Dash	3
28	Special Characters	2
29	Multiplication Sign	3
31	Copyright Symbol	3
33	Registered Trademark Symbol	3
35	Resources	2

6. **Save the file and continue to the next exercise.**

Formatting Text with the Properties Panel

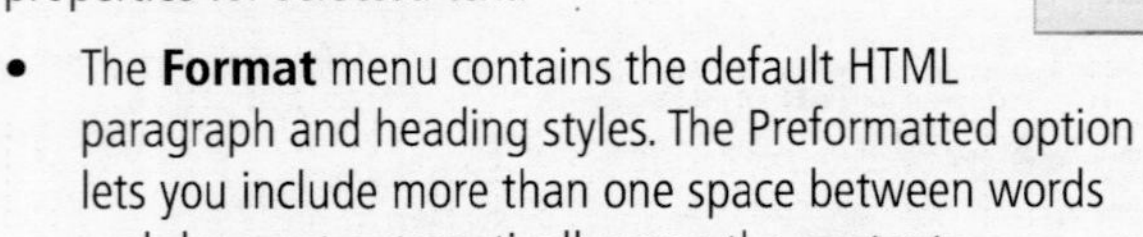

DREAMWEAVER FOUNDATIONS

You can use the Properties panel in HTML mode to view and modify a number of different properties for selected text:

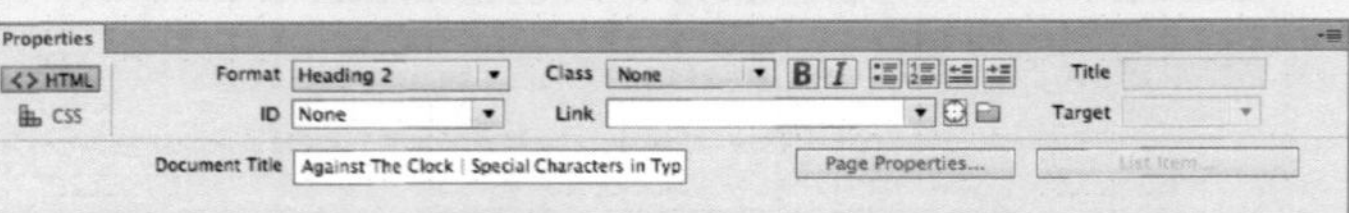

- The **Format** menu contains the default HTML paragraph and heading styles. The Preformatted option lets you include more than one space between words and does not automatically wrap the contents.
- The **ID** menu contains the list of IDs defined in the page or the attached style sheet.
- The **Class** menu contains the list of defined style classes in the related CSS.
- The **Link** field displays the URL to which the selected text is linked. You can use the Point to File and Browse for File buttons to identify link targets.
- You can use the **B** and **I** buttons to apply the <strong> and <em> tags (respectively).
- The **Unordered List** button formats selected paragraphs as items in a bulleted list.
- The **Ordered List** button arranges the paragraphs in a numbered list.
- The **Remove Blockquote** button removes the indent (and blockquote tags) from selected paragraphs.
- The **Blockquote** button indents paragraphs, wrapping those paragraphs in the opening and closing <blockquote> tags.
- The **Title** field specifies the textual tool tip for a hypertext link.
- The **Target** menu determines where a linked file opens (new window, parent frame, etc.).

Format a Blockquote and Inline Quote

The **blockquote element** formats a quotation as a block of text that is indented from the left and right margins, with extra white space above and below it. The blockquote element requires at least one paragraph element to be nested within it.

The **q element** defines a short quotation, commonly appearing inline with other text (called an "inline quote").

The **cite element** can be used to define the name of a work (book, painting, movie, etc.). This should not be confused with the cite attribute of the blockquote and q elements. The **cite attribute** defines the source of a quote; it does not have any visual effect in the browser window, but it can be used by screen-reading software.

1. **With typography.html open in Split view, make the Design pane active. Select the first and second paragraphs immediately below the heading 1 text (from "You may think..." to "...on Advertising").**

2. **Click the Blockquote button in the Properties panel to apply the blockquote element to the selected paragraph.**

   In the Design pane, the blockquote has been indented from the left and right margins. The first **<p>** tag appears after the opening **<blockquote>** tag and the second closing **</p>** tag appears before the closing **</blockquote>** tag — the **<p>** tags have been nested within the **<blockquote>** tag.

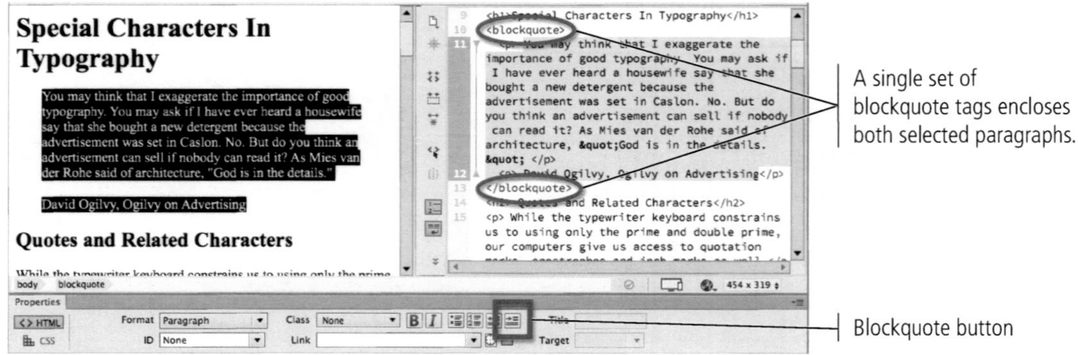

A single set of blockquote tags encloses both selected paragraphs.

Blockquote button

3. **Select "Ogilvy on Advertising" at the end of the second paragraph in the blockquote.**

   Remember, the cite element defines the source of a quote. This is the actual title of a work, not the author's name.

4. **Control/right-click the selected text in the Design pane and choose Wrap Tag from the contextual menu.**

   The Wrap Tag command opens the Quick Tag Editor, which allows you to temporarily work with code, while still working in Design view.

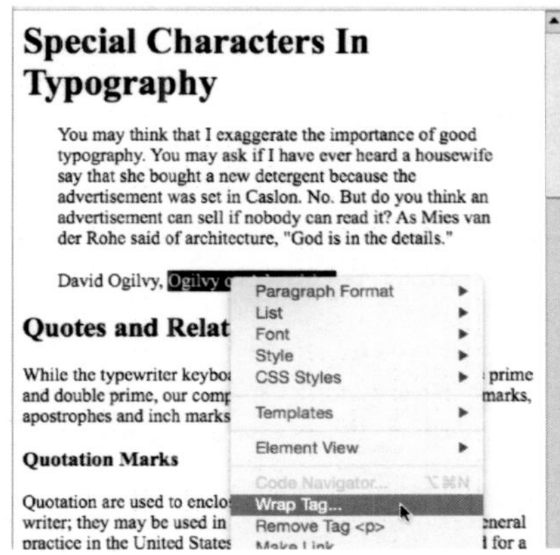

5. **Type `cit`.**

   As you type the code in the Quick Tag Editor, Dreamweaver provides Code Hints (a list of HTML tags) to assist you. As you type, the Code Hint list scrolls to the first HTML tag beginning with the letter "cit" — cite, which is the tag you want.

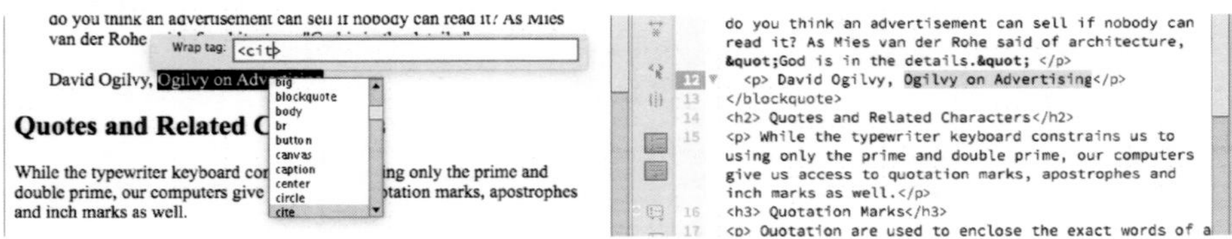

6. **Press Return/Enter to choose cite from the list of tags.**

   When a Code Hint menu is visible, pressing Return/Enter applies the item that is highlighted in the list.

Note:

You can also open the Quick Tag Editor by pressing Command/Control-T.

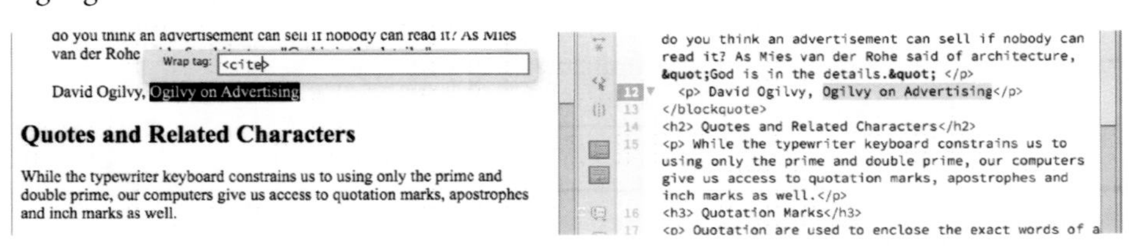

7. **Press Return/Enter again to apply the cite tags to the selected text.**

   The default appearance of the cite element text is italic. As you can see in the Code pane, using the Quick Tag Editor automatically adds the appropriate opening and closing tags, wrapped around the text that you had selected (hence the menu command "Wrap Tag").

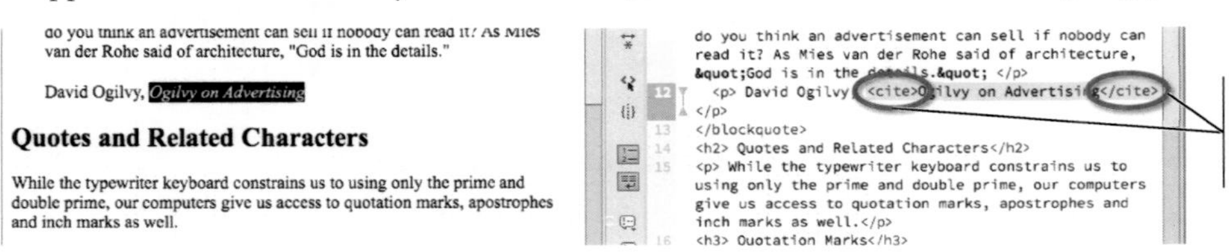

Opening and closing cite tags are added around the selected text.

8. **In the Design pane, select the words "God is in the details." (including the period and the quotation marks) at the end of the first paragraph in the blockquote.**

9. **Control/right-click the selected text and choose Wrap Tag from the contextual menu.**

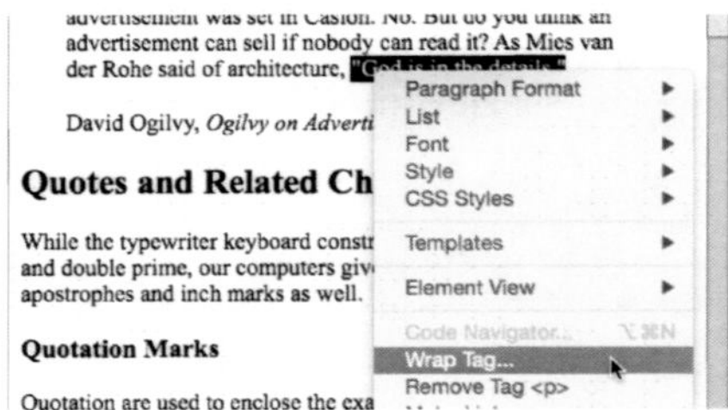

10. **In the Quick Tag Editor, type q. Press Return/Enter to accept the q tag, then press Return/Enter again to add the tag around the selected text.**

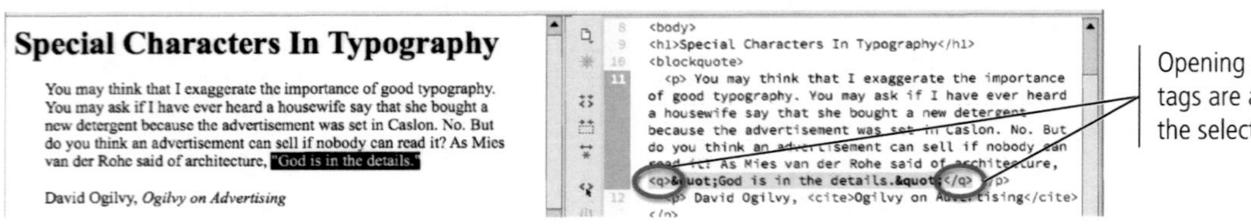

Opening and closing q tags are added around the selected text.

11. **Using the Document toolbar, turn on the Live view.**

As you can see in the Design pane, the q element adds quotation marks around the tag content. This means that the quotation marks included in the actual text are unnecessary.

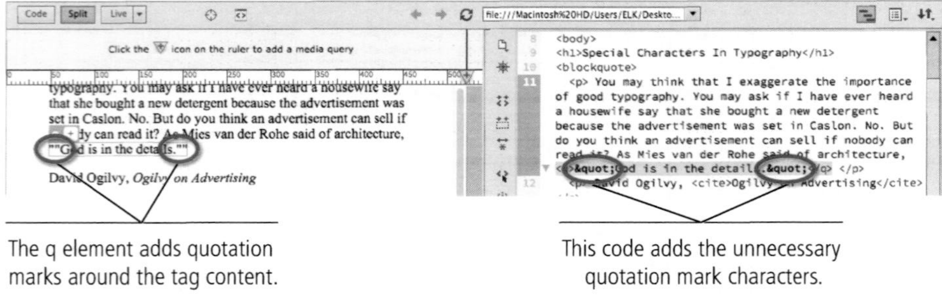

The q element adds quotation marks around the tag content.

This code adds the unnecessary quotation mark characters.

The current versions of Firefox, Safari, Opera, Chrome, and Internet Explorer automatically place quotation marks around q element text, eliminating the need to insert them as characters in the page content. However, different browsers use different types of quotes (straight quotes vs. curly quotes).

> ***Note:***
>
> *Older versions of Internet Explorer (7 or earlier) do not add the quotation marks to the tagged text.*

12. **In the Code pane, delete the code for the quote characters (")from around the "God is in the details." text.**

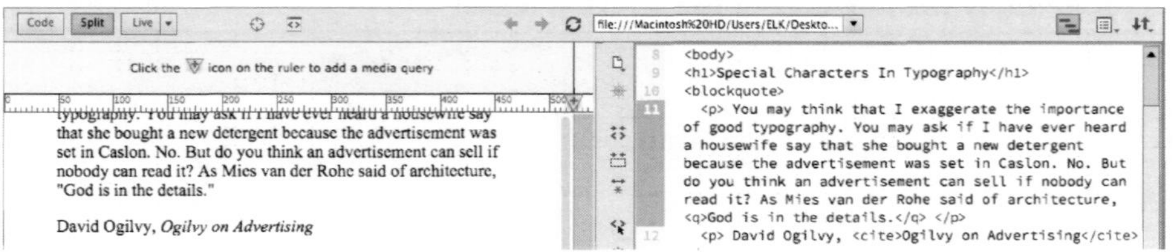

13. **Turn off the Live view, then save the file and continue to the next exercise.**

Controlling Code Hints

DREAMWEAVER FOUNDATIONS

Code hints display by default when you type code in Dreamweaver. You can use the Code Hints pane of the Preferences dialog box to control how code hints display.

The Close Tags options can be used to close tags automatically:

- If After Typing "</" is checked, the nearest open tag closes when you type the forward slash after the opening carat. This option is selected by default.
- If After Typing the Open Tag's ">" is checked, Dreamweaver automatically closes a tag as soon as it opens.
- Select Never if you don't want tags to close automatically.

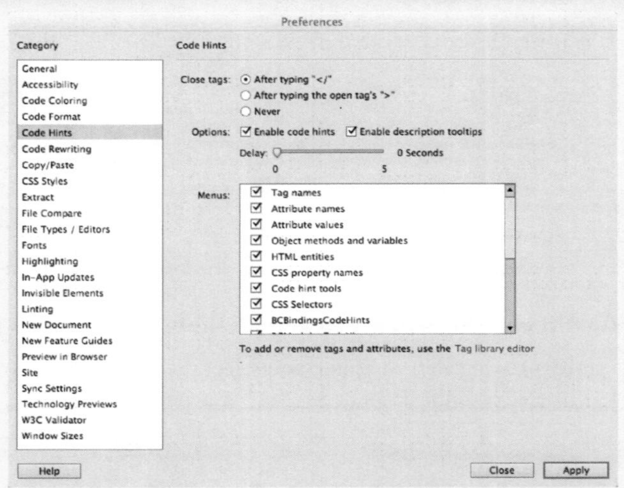

You can disable code hints by deselecting the Enable Code Hints check box. The Delay bar determines how soon code hints display when you open a tag. The Menus options list code categories for which hints can display.

Mark up Abbreviations in Code View

Both abbreviations and acronyms are shortened forms of words or phrases. If you spell out the short form (such as HTML), it is an abbreviation. If you pronounce it like a word (such as NATO), it is an acronym.

HTML 4 includes two separate elements for these words — the **abbr** element identifies an abbreviation, and the **acronym** element identifies an acronym — but the acronym element has been deprecated (removed) in HTML5, so you should get into the habit of using the abbr element for both types of words.

The title attribute plays a useful role in the **abbr** element. Any text you insert into the title attribute — for example, the full text of the abbreviation or acronym — appears as a tool tip when you hover the mouse over the titled element. People who use screen-reader software also benefit from the title attribute because the software can be set up to read the title text in place of the abbreviation.

In this exercise, you will type directly in the Code pane, using Dreamweaver's code hints to add the necessary tags and attributes.

1. **With typography.html open in Split view, select "ANSI" (in the Design pane) in the paragraph following the Copyright Symbol heading.**

   The text selected in the Design pane is also selected in the Code pane. This is a useful way to locate specific text in code (or vice versa).

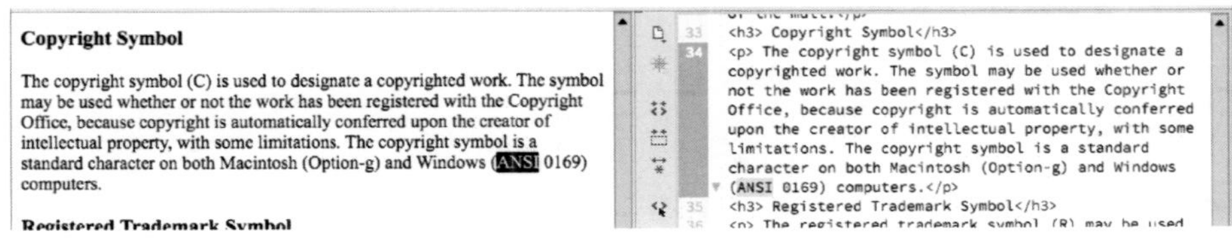

2. **Click in the Code pane to make it the active pane.**

   When working in either pane of Split view, you have to click a pane to bring it into focus (make it active) before you can make changes there.

   When you bring the Code pane into focus, the highlighted text is no longer highlighted.

3. **Place the insertion point before the previously highlighted text, and then type <ab.**

   The abbr tag is selected in the code hint list.

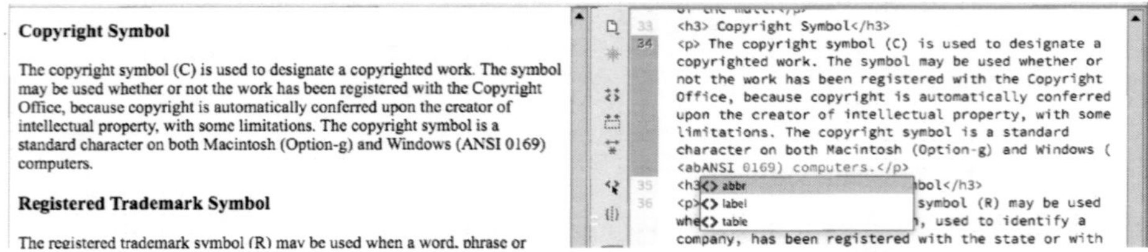

4. **Press Return/Enter to accept abbr.**

   By pressing Return/Enter, you select the **<abbr>** tag. Once you add the tag, the insertion point flashes after the tag, where you can enter attributes of the new tag.

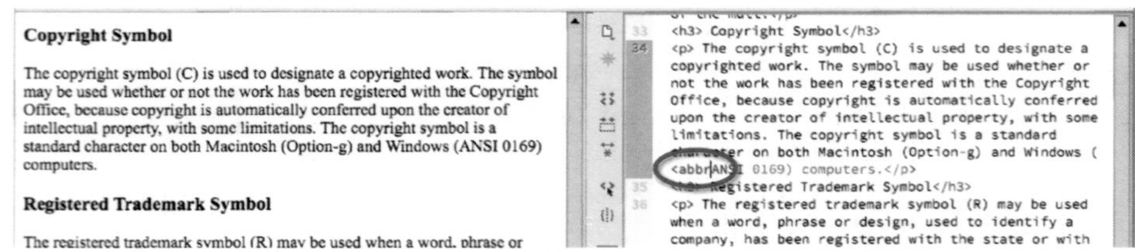

5. **Press the Spacebar, and then type t.**

   Inserting a space after the abbr element name within the tag prompts Dreamweaver to open code hints and present a list of valid attributes for the current tag.

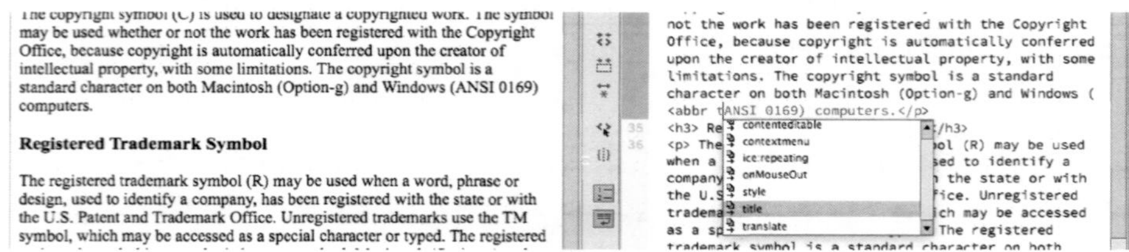

6. **Press Return/Enter to accept the title attribute.**

   When you select the attribute in the code hint list, Dreamweaver follows the attribute with =" " and places the insertion point between the two quotation marks, so you can immediately type a value for the attribute.

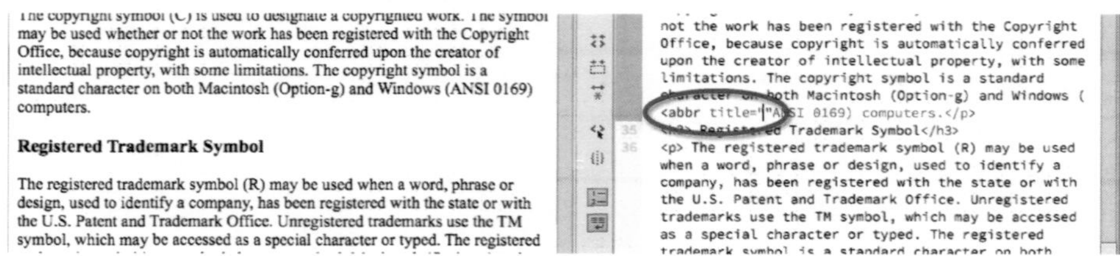

7. **Type American National Standards Institute between the quotation marks.**

   Attribute values must always be surrounded by quotation marks.

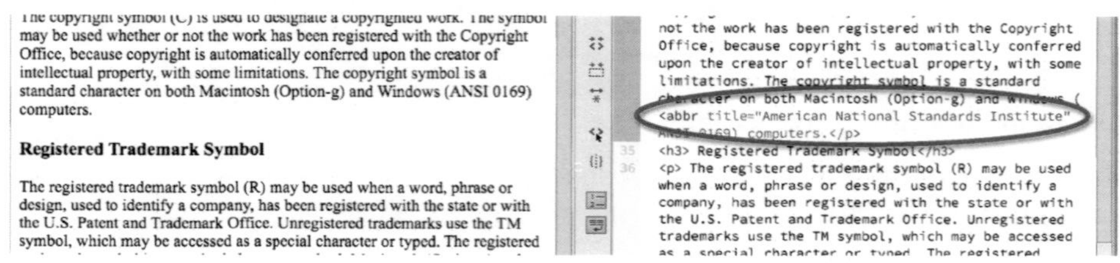

8. **Move the insertion point to the right of the closing quotation mark and type > to close the tag.**

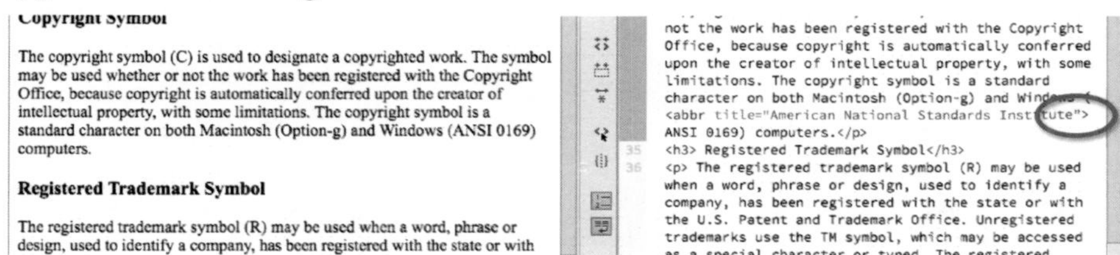

9. **Move the insertion point to the right of the text "ANSI," then type </.**

In opening tags, the HTML element name is specified between opening and closing angle brackets. In closing tags, the forward slash precedes the element name.

This step shows you another of Dreamweaver's code assistance functions, which is to automatically close the nearest unclosed tag when you type "</". In this case, Dreamweaver closes the abbr tag for you.

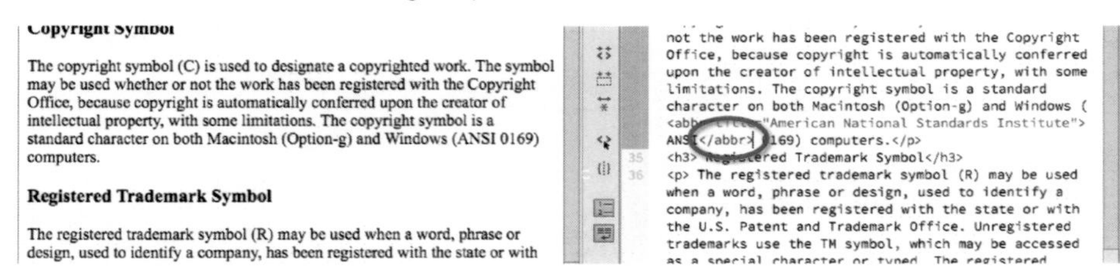

10. **Select all of the code related to the ANSI abbreviation, then choose Edit>Copy to copy the highlighted code to the Clipboard.**

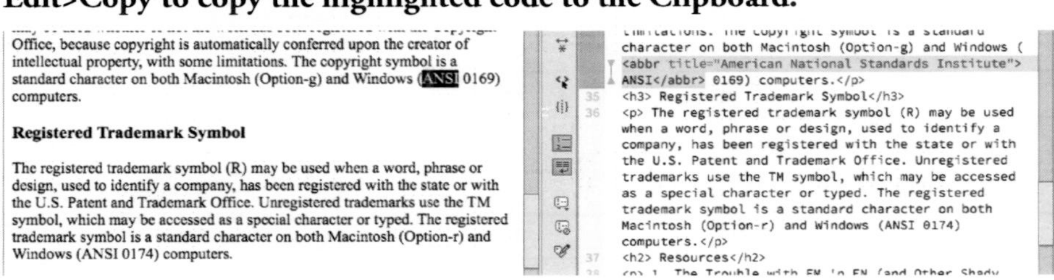

Note:

All current browsers display title text as a tool tip when the mouse hovers over the element text.

11. **In the Code pane, highlight the instance of "ANSI" near the end of line 36. Choose Edit>Paste to replace the highlighted text with the copied code (including the abbr tags and title attribute).**

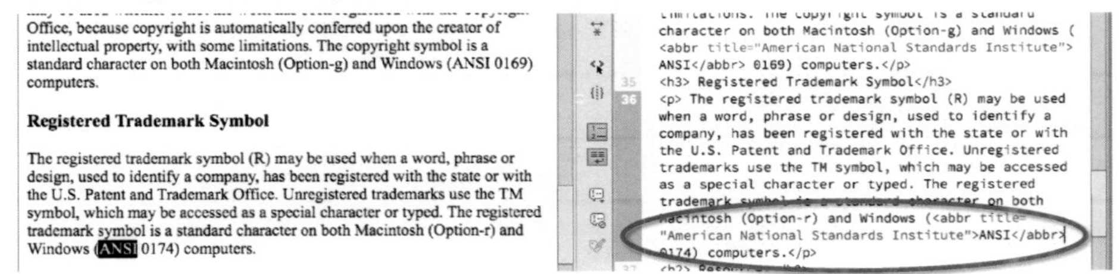

12. **Save the file, then continue to the next exercise.**

Understanding Code View Formatting

Code View Options

Code View options, which can be toggled on or off in the View menu, determine how code displays.

- Word Wrap ensures that code does not extend beyond the available width of the window. This option only affects the appearance of code in the Code pane; it does not insert actual line breaks in the code or content.
- Line Numbers shows numbers to the left of each line.
- Hidden Characters displays characters such as line-break markers, which would not otherwise display.
- Highlight Invalid Code displays incorrect code (such as a tag that has not been closed) in yellow.

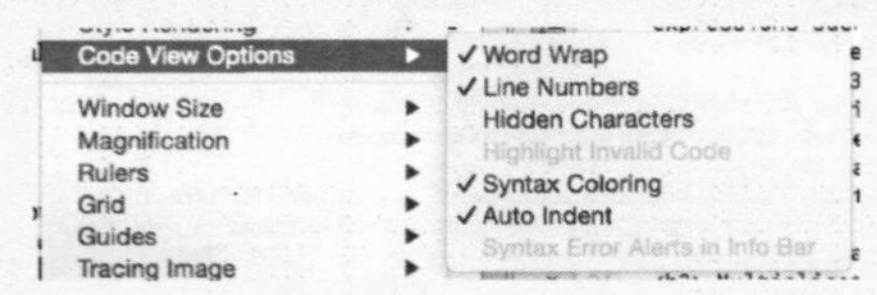

- Syntax Coloring displays the code in defined colors.
- Auto Indent indents every new line of code to the same position as the previous line. A new line is inserted each time you press Return/Enter.
- Syntax Error Alerts in Info Bar displays a yellow message bar at the top of the document window if there is a problem in your code.

Code Coloring Preferences

By default, HTML tags appear in blue. You can use the Code Coloring pane of the Preferences dialog box to change the color of specific tags (or other pieces of code).

The Document Type window lists the various types of code that Dreamweaver supports. (The code type in the active document is selected by default.) If you click the Edit Coloring Scheme button, a secondary dialog box displays a list of all possible parts of the selected code type; you can change the text and background color of any individual part.

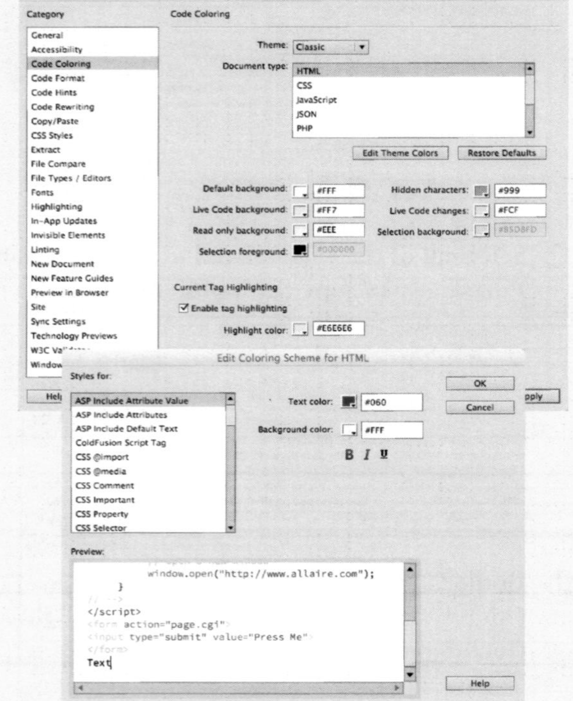

Code Format Preferences

Code Format preferences allow you to specify rules that determine how the code is structured; the sole purpose of these rules is to make it easier for you to read code.

- **Indent With** indents the text within each tag so you can easily identify each block of code. You can indent by character spaces or by tabs.
- **Tab Size** specifies the number of spaces that each tab character contains. For example, if you type "4" in this box, each time you press the Tab key, four space characters are inserted.
- **Line Break Type** ensures the line breaks inserted by Dreamweaver are compatible with the operating system of the remote server on which your site will be hosted.
- **Default Tag Case** changes the case of tags, and **Default Attribute Case** changes the case of attributes. (We highly recommend using lowercase tags and attributes.)
- **Override Case of Tags** and **Override Case of Attributes** change the case of tags and attributes to the options selected in this pane, even if a different case is defined in Tag Libraries.
- The **TD Tag** option prevents a line break or white space from being inserted directly after a <td> (table cell) tag or directly before a </td> tag. Line breaks and white spaces within the tag cause problems in older browsers.
- The **CSS** button allows you to change code formatting definitions in a cascading style sheet file.
- The **Tag Libraries** button opens a dialog box where you can define formatting options such as line breaks and indents for each tag and its associated attributes.

Format with Strong and Em Elements

Two HTML elements can be used to show emphasis — em and strong. The **em** element is used when light emphasis is needed, such as "you <em>should</em> go to your brother's game to support him." For stronger emphasis, use the **strong** element, such as "<strong>Don't</strong> touch the stove top, it is <strong>hot</strong>!"

Text marked up with the em element appears by default in italics; text marked up with the strong element appears in bold. Visually, it is the same as using the **<i>** and **<b>** tags (italic and bold, respectively), but the i and b elements are presentational — not structural — HTML. Screen-reader software changes the tone of voice when it finds em and strong element text, but not when it finds i and b element text.

> ***Note:***
>
> *Remember: b and i elements are for presentational purposes only, and strong and em elements are for structural purposes.*

1. **With typography.html open, open the Preferences dialog box (Dreamweaver menu on Macintosh or Edit menu on Windows) and show the General category.**

2. **In the Editing Options group, make sure the "Use <strong> and <em>" option is checked.**

   When this option is checked, as it is by default, Dreamweaver inserts strong or em tags when you apply bold or italic styling (respectively) through interface menus or buttons.

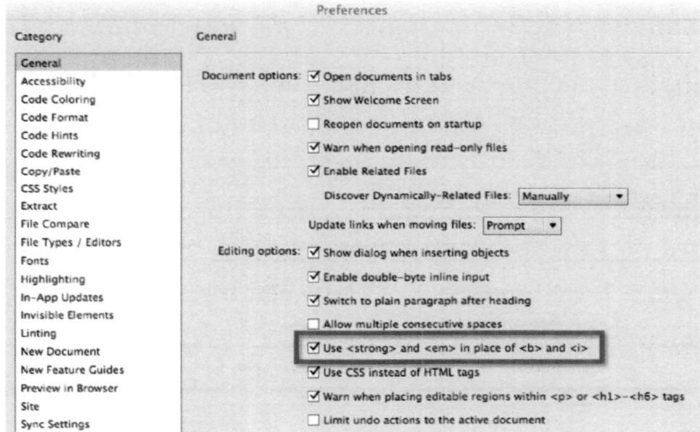

> ***Note:***
>
> *As you work through this book, remember that preferences are accessed in the Dreamweaver menu on Macintosh and the Edit menu on Windows.*

3. **Click Close to close the Preferences dialog box.**

4. **In the Design pane, scroll to the paragraph following the En Dash heading and select "not" in the fourth sentence.**

5. **Click the Bold button in the Properties panel.**

   There are no special attributes for the strong and em elements, so you can insert these elements with a single click.

6. **With the text still selected, examine the Tag Selector.**

   The selected text is formatted with the **<strong>** tag, not the **<b>** tag.

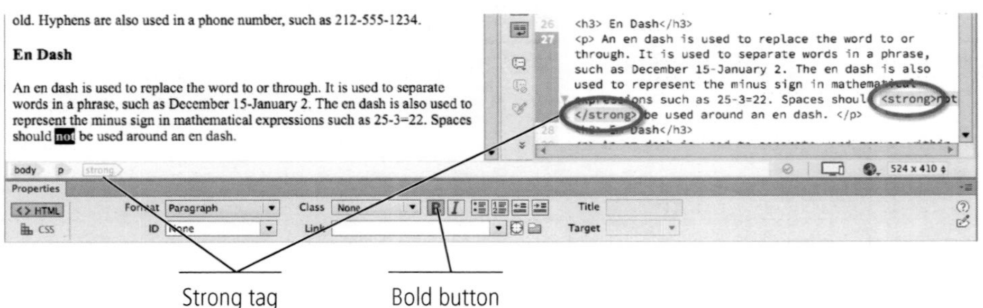

7. **In the paragraph after the Em Dash heading, select "more authority" in the third sentence and click the Italic button in the Properties panel.**

   The selected text is now formatted with the **<em>** tag.

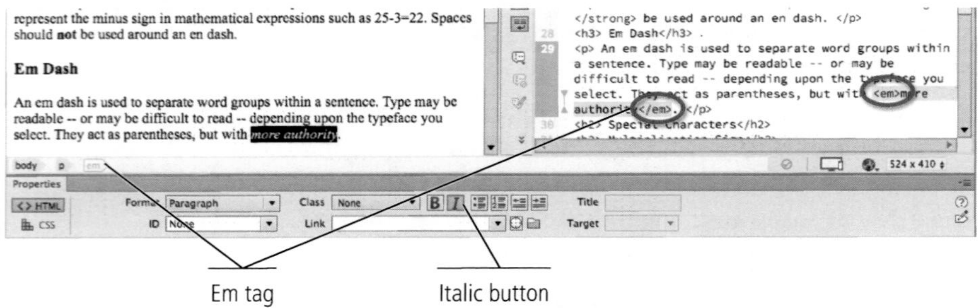

8. **Save your changes and continue to the next stage of the project.**

Stage 3 Working with Special Characters

HTML character entities are characters not directly available from your keyboard. HTML character entities can be specified in code either by name or by number. Using either method, the code begins with an ampersand (&) and ends with a semicolon (;).

- A named character entity uses a specific name for that character such as "©" for the © symbol and "™" for the ™ symbol. Some character names (such as "™") are not supported by all browsers; visitors using these browsers would see "™" in their browser window instead of the ™ symbol.
- Alternatively, you can specify a character using its numeric code, such as "¢" for ¢. (When using the numeric code, be sure to insert a "#" between the ampersand and the number.) All browsers support the numeric codes.

Insert Special Characters

In most cases, you don't need to worry about inserting the codes (named or numbered) for HTML character entities because you can select some of the most common characters from a list in the HTML Insert panel; Dreamweaver inserts the code for you.

This HTML Insert panel provides one-click access to many common structural elements — including common ones like various levels of headings, as well as headers, sections, and footers.

1. **With typography.html open in Split view, make the Design pane active. Select the hyphen between "December 15" and "January 2" in the paragraph below the En Dash heading.**

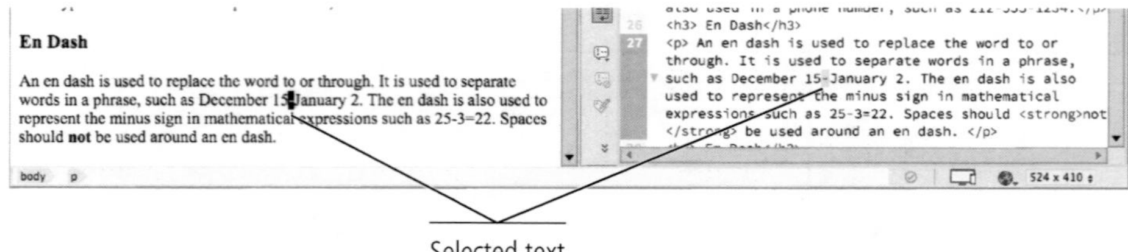

2. **With the Insert panel in HTML mode, click the arrow button to the right of the Character button icon.**

   Your button icon might appear different than the one shown in our screen shot because the button reflects the last character inserted from this list. Simply clicking the button (label or icon) — not the arrow — inserts whatever character appears on the button.

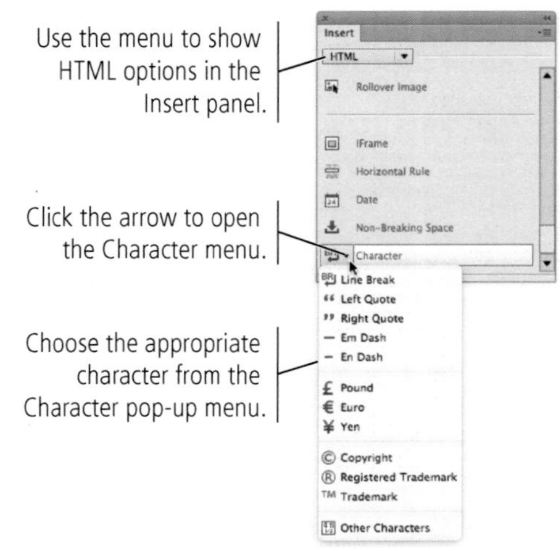

3. **Choose En Dash from the pop-up menu.**

> ***Note:***
>
> *These same characters can be inserted using the Insert>Character menu.*

4. **Select the hyphen between "25" and "3" in the same paragraph.**

   En dashes are as wide as half an em dash. As you might have read in the text of this project page, en dashes are used to replace the word "to" or "through" or in mathematical expressions of subtraction.

5. **In the HTML Insert panel, click the Character:En Dash button.**

   Because the button defaults to the last-used character, you can simply click the button to apply another en dash.

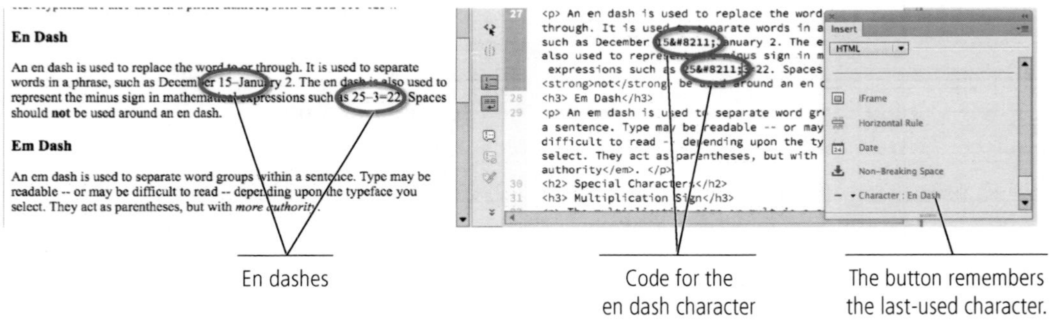

6. **Use the same techniques from Steps 2–5 to replace both sets of double hyphens with em dashes in the paragraph after the Em Dash heading.**

   The em dash is as wide as the defined type size. This dash can be used to separate part of a sentence — an aside — from the rest of a sentence. Many authors do not know how to insert an em dash; instead, they use a regular hyphen or a pair of hyphens. As there are strict grammatical rules about when to use a hyphen, an en dash, and an em dash, you should consult a professional copy editor for the proper application of these characters.

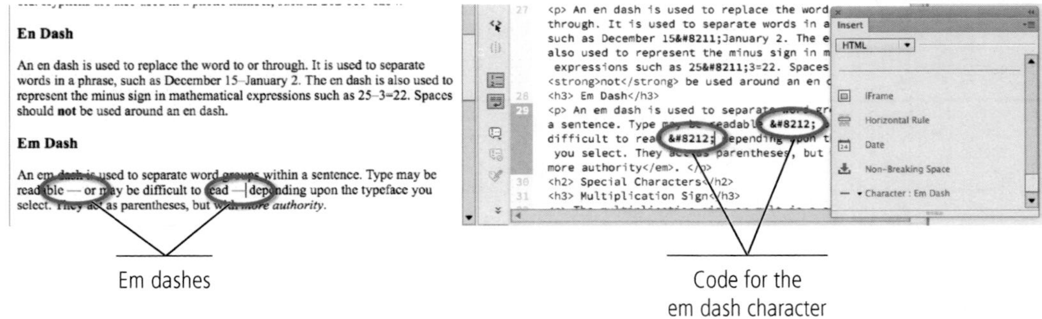

7. **Select the capital C in the first line after the Copyright Symbol heading. Use the Character menu in the Common Insert panel to replace the letter with the Copyright character.**

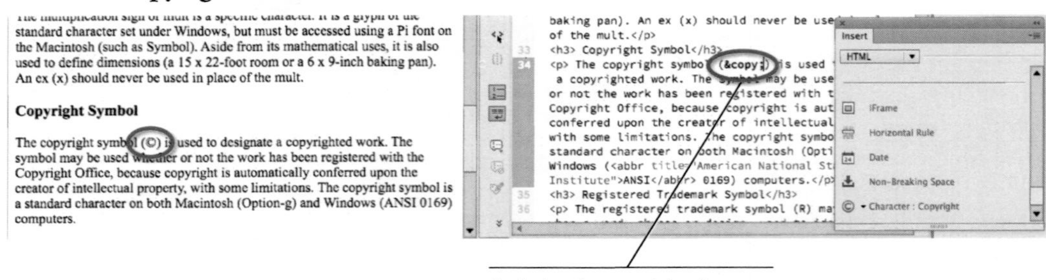

Code for the copyright character

8. **Select the capital R in the first line after the Registered Trademark Symbol heading. Use the Character menu to replace the selected letter with the Registered Trademark character.**

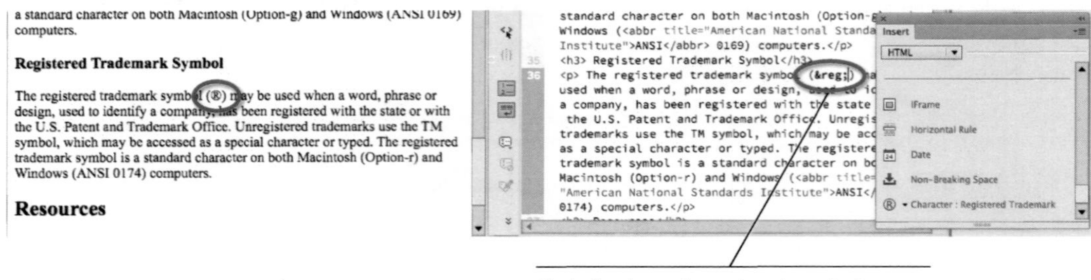

Code for the registered trademark character

9. **Select the capital TM in the same paragraph and use the Character menu to replace the selected letters with the Trademark character.**

   In the Code pane, you can see that Dreamweaver creates this character using the numeric code because some browsers do not support the name for this character.

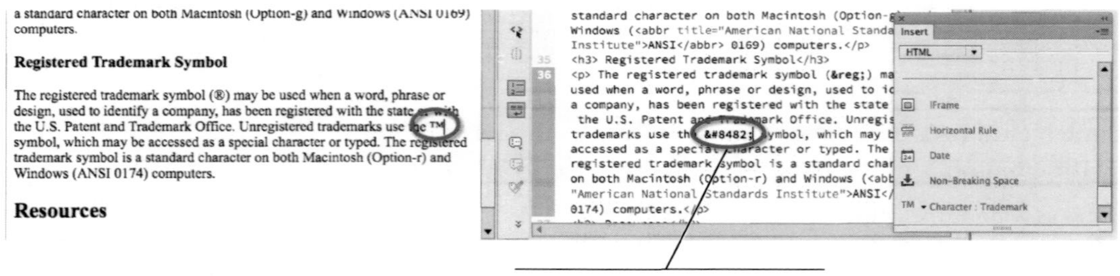

Code for the trademark character

10. **Save the changes to typography.html and continue to the next exercise.**

Create a Table of Quote Characters

Common HTML tables that are used to present data or text information consist of only three components: a caption, table header cells, and table data cells.

A caption can be used to briefly describe the contents or purpose of a table. It generally appears at the top of the table. (You can use CSS to move the caption to another position, but many browsers offer poor support for these properties.)

Table data cells make up the majority of the cells in a table. The **<td>** tag is used to mark up the table data cells.

Table header cells, using the **<th>** tag, appear at the top or left (or both) of the table; they label the contents in the regular table cells. Think about a table of the days of the week across the top and the hours of the day down the left side. If the cell at the intersection of the second row and second column contained the text "Staff Meeting," you would know that the staff meeting was scheduled for Tuesday at 10:00 a.m.

The information in table header cells is very important for people using screen-reader software. For example, when they reach the Staff Meeting cell, they can prompt the software to read the headers associated with the cell. The screen-reader would report "Tuesday" and "10:00 a.m." Without proper cell markup, the software would not be able to report the day and time of the meeting.

> ***Note:***
>
> *When tables are used for layout components of a Web page, they can become very complicated in structure, with tables within table cells (nested tables) and cells that have been merged with other cells. Tables should only be used to present tabular data.*

1. **With `typography.html` open in Split view, place the insertion point at the end of the paragraph after the Inch and Foot Marks heading. Press Return/Enter to create a new empty paragraph.**

2. **Click the Table button in the HTML Insert panel.**

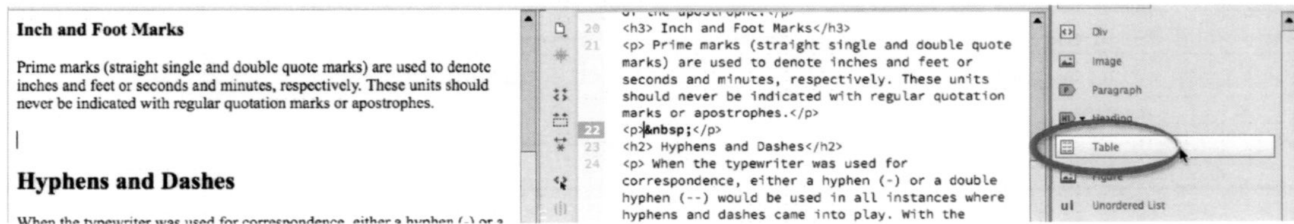

3. **In the Table dialog box:**

   - **Set both the number of rows and number of columns to 2.**
   - **Delete any values in the Table Width, Border Thickness, Cell Padding, and Cell Spacing fields.**
   - **Choose the Top Header option.**
   - **Type `Quotation Characters` in the Caption field.**

   Many Dreamweaver dialog boxes remember the last-used settings. If you or someone else used the Table dialog box before now, some of these fields might default to other values.

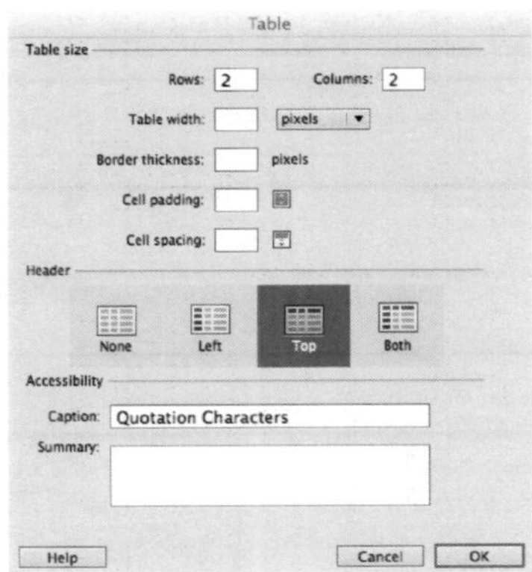

4. **Click OK to create the table.**

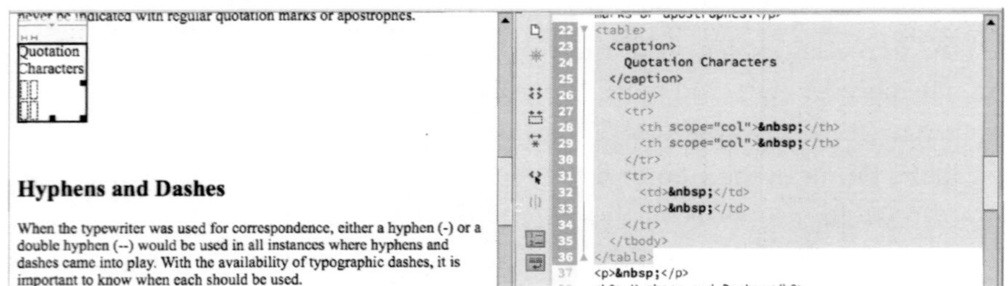

5. **Click in the top-left table cell to place the insertion point, and then type** `Character Description`**.**

6. **Press Tab to move the insertion point into the top-right cell, and type** `Character`**.**

7. **In the Code pane, review the code for the table you just created.**
    - All content that makes up the table is enclosed in opening and closing **<table>** tags.
    - The caption that you defined when you created the table is enclosed in opening and closing **<caption>** tags.
    - The body content of a table is grouped together with opening and closing **<tbody>** tags. The <tbody> element must contain one or more <tr> tags.
    - Each row in the table is enclosed in opening and closing **<tr>** tags.
    - Each header cell is identified with opening and closing **<th>** tags. The **scope="col"** attribute identifies that column as information with the heading defined in the related cell.
    - Each regular cell in the table is enclosed in opening and closing **<td>** tags. As you can see, each table row includes two <td> tags — one for each column in the row.

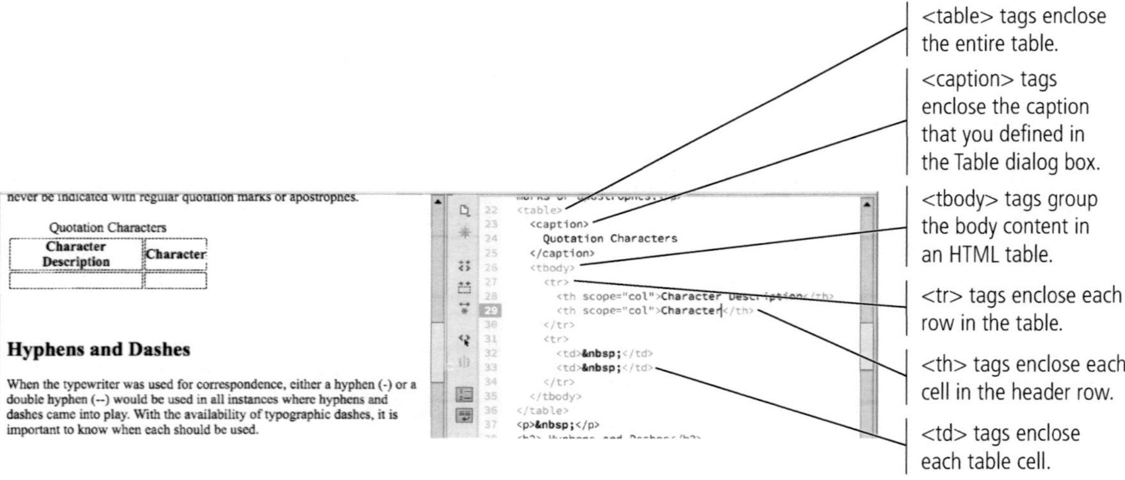
<table> tags enclose the entire table.
<caption> tags enclose the caption that you defined in the Table dialog box.
<tbody> tags group the body content in an HTML table.
<tr> tags enclose each row in the table.
<th> tags enclose each cell in the header row.
<td> tags enclose each table cell.

8. **Save the file and continue to the next exercise.**

More about Working with HTML Tables

When HTML tables were first conceived, they were intended to allow Web content developers to more clearly present tabular text — primarily charts of data — in a Web page. It wasn't long, however, before visually oriented designers figured out how to use HTML tables to combine graphic elements on a Web page just as they assemble graphics on the printed page. As a result, a significant number of Web pages were (and still are) designed with tables.

HTML tables were never intended as a graphic design tool. The overall page code that results from this method is extremely long and complex, which results in longer download times (still a significant problem for many users). The complexity of table-based page code also makes it more time consuming to make changes.

Another problem with table-based design is that the resulting code mixes content with purely presentational elements. This makes it very difficult (if not impossible) for accessibility software and search engines to separate the content from the structure, which means that table-based pages might not rank as high as a similar page designed without tables.

To solve the problems with table-based design, cascading style sheets (CSS) provide a way to separate content from presentation. CSS-based layout, which you will see in action at the end of this project, is the recommended method of standards organizations such as the World Wide Web Consortium (www.w3c.org). HTML tables should only be used to present tables of data.

Tables in Design View

When you do work with HTML tables, you have a number of options in the Properties panel, depending on whether the entire table or only specific cells are selected. Keep in mind that all table properties are better defined using CSS, which is why we are not explaining all of these options here.

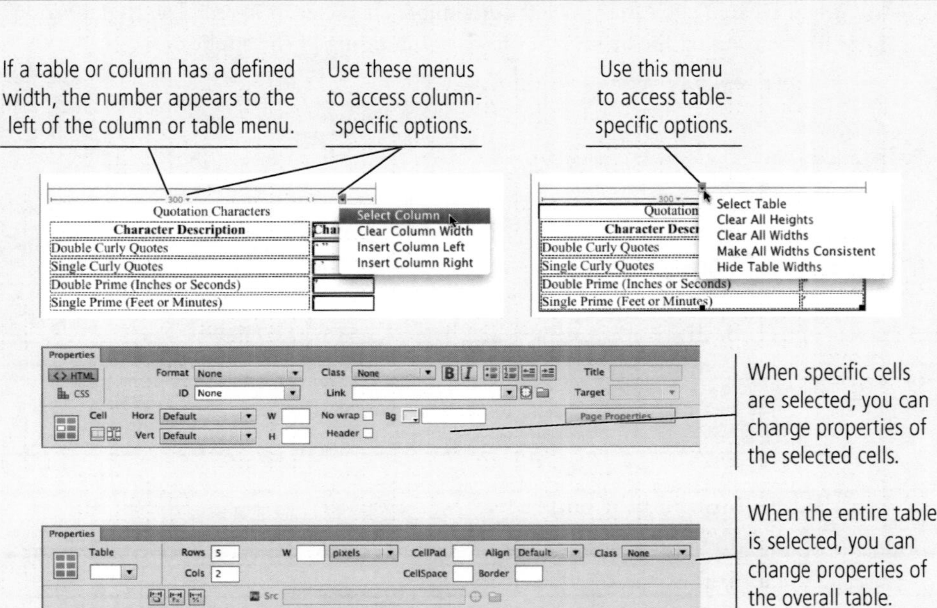

The Modify>Table Menu

- **Merge Cells** combines selected adjacent cells, so they are treated as a single cell.
- **Split Cell** creates multiple cells in a single cell, without affecting other cells in the same row or column.
- **Insert Row** adds a row above the current selection.
- **Insert Column** adds a column left of the selection.
- **Insert Rows or Columns** opens a dialog box where you can add a specific number of rows or columns. You can also choose where to add the new cells relative to the current selection.
- **Delete Row** removes the row of the active cell.
- **Delete Column** removes the column of the active cell.
- **Increase Row Span** merges the current cell with the cell below it.
- **Increase Column Span** merges the current cell with the cell next to it on the right side.
- **Decrease Row Span** splits two or more previously merged or spanned cells into two cells from the bottom.
- **Decrease Column Span** splits previously merged or spanned cells into two cells from the right.
- **Clear Cell Heights** removes all defined numeric row height values from the selected table.
- **Clear Cell Widths** removes all defined numeric column width values from the selected table.
- **Convert Widths to Pixels** and **Convert Widths to Percent** allow you to change defined widths from a percentage of the available space to a specific number of pixels, and vice versa.
- **Convert Heights to Pixels** and **Convert Heights to Percent** allow you to change defined heights from a percentage of the available browser space to a specific number of pixels, and vice versa.

Use the Insert Other Character Dialog Box

Although a few special characters are available directly in the Characters menu of the HTML Insert panel, there are many more characters available than those in the list. A number of common special characters are available in the Insert Other Character dialog box, which is accessed at the bottom of the Characters menu. Still others (many, in fact) are only available by typing the necessary code in the Code pane.

1. **With `typography.html` open, click in the lower-left empty cell of the table that you created in the previous exercise. Type `Double Curly Quotes`.**

2. **Press Tab to move to the right cell, and then choose Left Quote from the Character menu in the Common Insert panel.**

3. **Press Space, and then choose Right Quote from the Common Insert panel Character menu.**

   You might have to click after the left curly quote character to re-establish the insertion point before pressing the Space bar. This is a minor bug in the application.

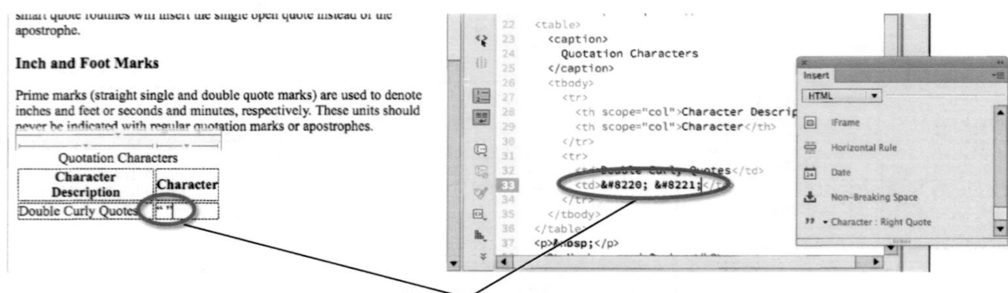

Numeric codes for the special characters are automatically added in the Code pane.

4. **Press Tab to insert a new table row.**

   Again, you might have to click after the right curly quote character to re-establish the insertion point before pressing the Tab key.

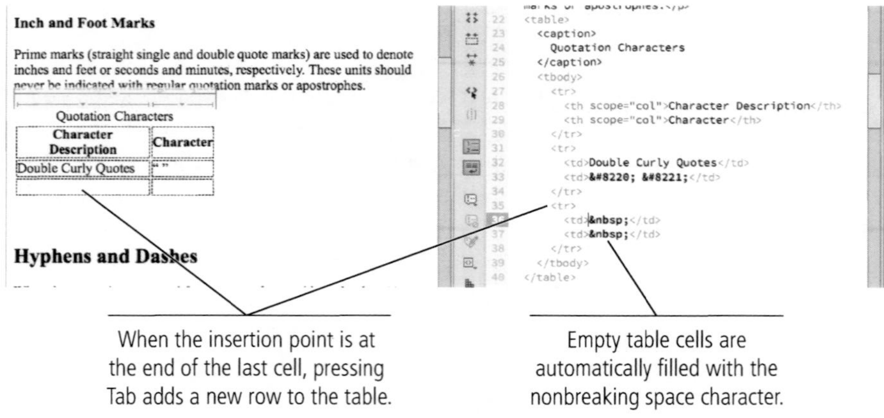

When the insertion point is at the end of the last cell, pressing Tab adds a new row to the table.

Empty table cells are automatically filled with the nonbreaking space character.

5. **In the left cell, type `Single Curly Quotes`, then press Tab to move the insertion point into the right cell.**

6. **Using the HTML Insert panel, open the Character menu and choose Other Characters from the bottom of the list.**

   You can use the Other Characters option to find special characters that aren't included in the default list. This option opens the Insert Other Character dialog box, where you can select a specific character, or type the appropriate code in the field at the top of the dialog box.

7. **In the resulting dialog box, click the Single Left Curly Quote character and then click OK to insert that character into the active table cell.**

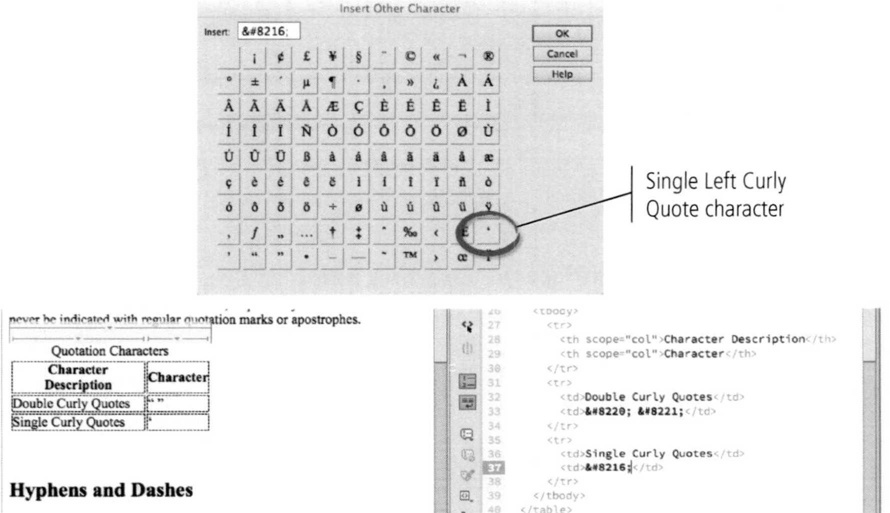

Note:

As you add content into the table, the column width changes to accommodate cell content. The specific appearance of the table will be determined by cascading style sheets when you attach an external CSS file later in this project.

8. **With the insertion point after the quote, press Space and then click the Character:Other Characters button to reopen the dialog box.**

   In this case, the button remembers the last-used option (opening the dialog box) but not the last-used character. Clicking the button opens the Insert Other Character dialog box.

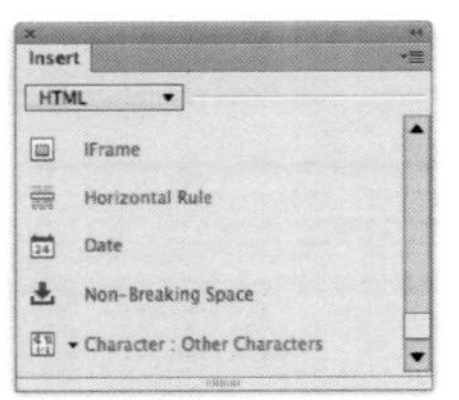

9. **Click the Single Right Curly Quote character and then click OK to insert that character into the table cell.**

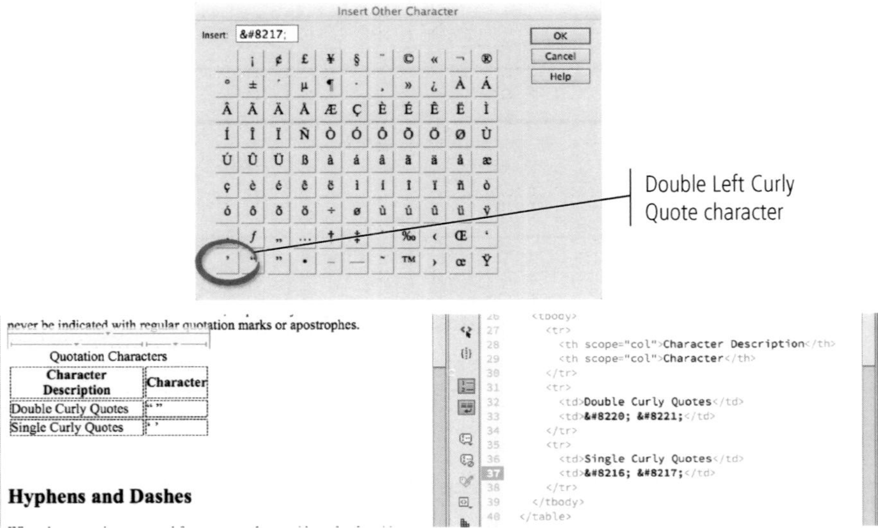

10. **Press Tab to insert another table row. Type Double Prime (Inches or Seconds) in the left cell of the new row.**

11. **Move the insertion point to the right cell of the new row, then click the Code pane to make it active.**

12. **In the Code pane, delete the code for nonbreaking space. Type ″ (with a capital P) and then refresh the Design view.**

    Remember: After typing in the Code pane, the Properties panel shows a Refresh button. You can click that button; press F5; or click in the Design pane to bring it into focus,

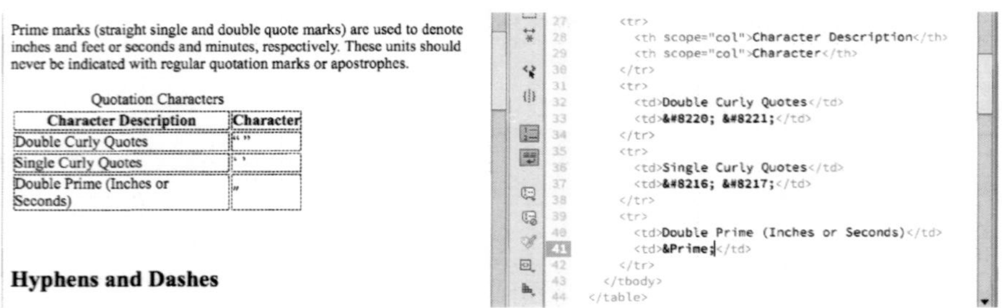

13. **Click in the Design pane to bring it into focus. Place the insertion point after the prime character, then press Tab to insert another table row.**

14. **Type Single Prime (Feet or Minutes) in the left column, then move the insertion point to the right cell.**

15. **Click the Code pane to make it active. Replace the nonbreaking-space code with ′ (with a lowercase p) and then refresh the Design view.**

    The single- and double-prime codes are almost the same; capitalization makes the difference between the two characters.

Note:

To find the necessary code for special characters, look for online sources such as http://www.w3schools.com/html/html_entities.asp.

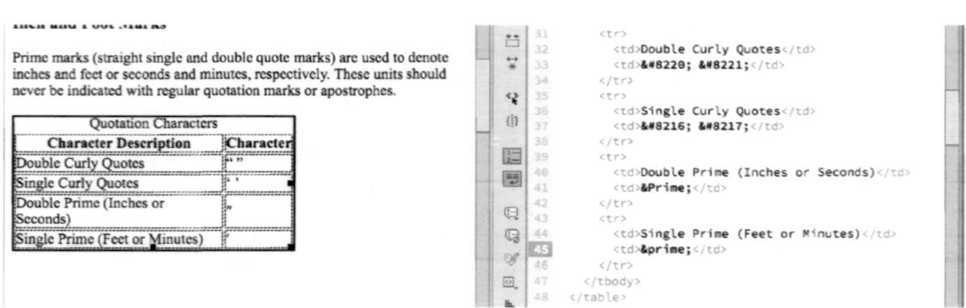

16. **Save the file and continue to the next exercise.**

Insert Special Characters in Code

The multiplication sign is a seldom-used character; it doesn't even appear in the Insert Other Character dialog box. To insert this character, you can type code directly in the Code pane, or you can use the Insert field in the Insert Other Character dialog box.

There are many lists of HTML character entities on the Internet. Use your favorite search engine to search for "HTML characters." Some Web pages have more characters than others; for very unusual characters, you might need to check a few sites until you find the code you need. Also, make note of both the name and the numeric code because some browsers support one but not the other (test both in your browser).

1. **With `typography.html` open in Split view, use the Design pane to scroll to the paragraph following the Multiplication Sign heading.**

2. **Select the letter "x" between 15 and 22.**

3. **Click the Code pane to bring it into focus, and then delete the selected letter "x".**

4. **Type `&tim` and press Return/Enter to choose × from the code hint list.**

   The code hints help you insert named character entities, but not numeric character codes.

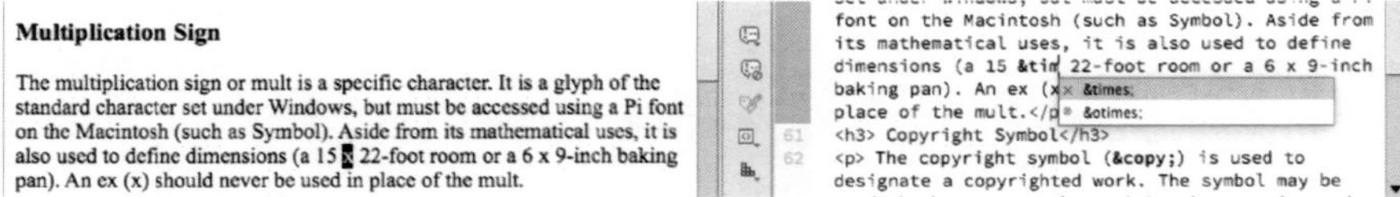

5. **Refresh the Design view.**

6. **In the Design pane, compare the appearance of the mult (multiply) character and the letter "x".**

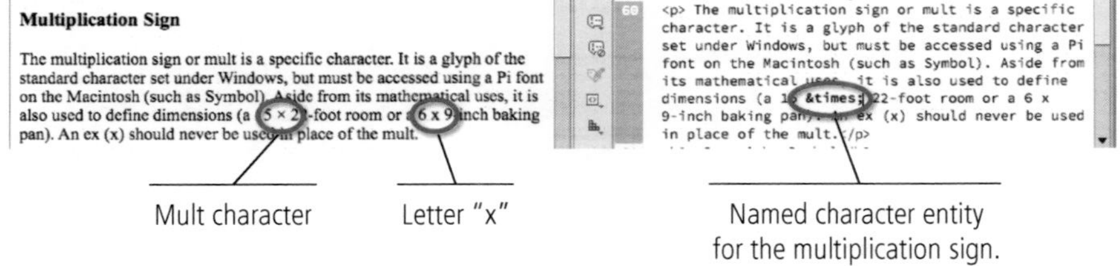

7. **Select the letter "x" between 6 and 9 in the same sentence.**

8. **In the Code pane, replace the selected character with `×` and then refresh the Design view.**

   This is the numeric code for the mult character. Dreamweaver's code hints for character entities in Code view do not support numeric codes for characters.

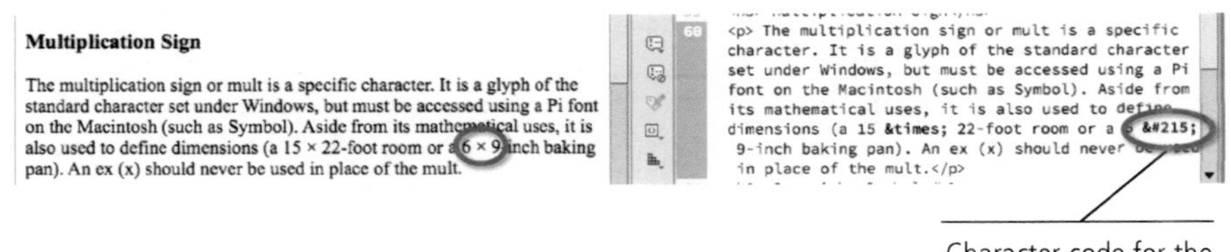

9. **Save the file, then continue to the next stage of the project.**

> *Note:*
>
> *The current versions of Firefox, Safari, Opera, and Chrome all support both the named and numeric character codes. Older versions, however, might show the characters "**×**" instead of the actual mult character.*

Stage 4 Creating Lists

There are two common types of lists: ordered (numbered) lists and unordered (bulleted) lists. The two types are very similar in structure. In this stage of the project, you will create an ordered list of references and an unordered list that becomes navigation links in the final Web page.

Create an Ordered List of Web Resources

Ordered lists are commonly called numbered lists, although they are not always numbered. You can use Roman numerals (i, ii, iii or I, II, III) or letters (a, b, c or A, B, C).

The purpose of ordered lists is to show a sequence of steps or hierarchical order. If these purposes do not apply to the content of a list, you should use an unordered (bulleted) list instead.

1. **With typography.html open, select the numbered paragraph at the bottom of the page (under the Resources heading).**

2. **Click the Ordered List button in the Properties panel.**

   The **<ol>** tags surround the entire ordered list, identifying where the list starts and ends. Each list item within the list is surrounded by **<li>** tags.

   In the Design pane, the list as a whole is indented from the left edge of the page, and the space between list items is reduced. These presentation properties clearly identify that the text is part of a list, and not part of a regular paragraph.

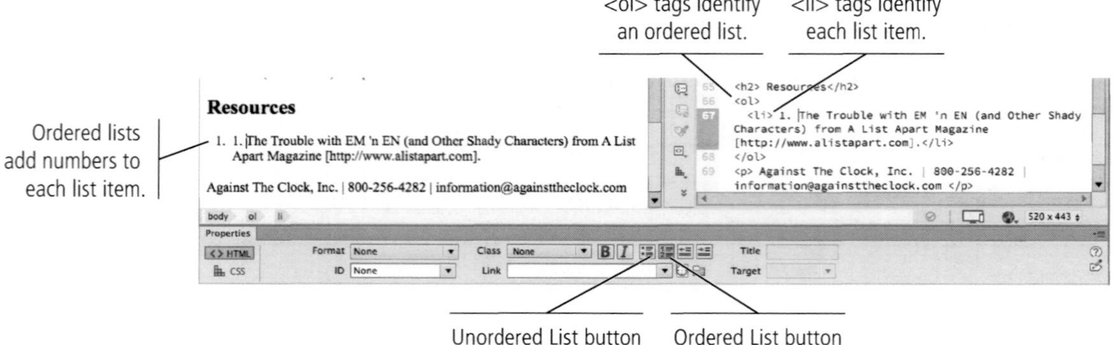

3. **In the Design pane, delete the redundant number from the beginning of the list item.**

   One of the presentation properties of an ordered list is that each list item is automatically numbered. If you receive content from an outside source, the number might already be typed at the beginning of each list item (as is the case in this project); you should remove the original number from the text of each list item.

4. **Click at the end of the text in the numbered list item and press Return/Enter.**

   When you press Return/Enter at the end of a list item in the Design pane, Dreamweaver automatically creates a new numbered list item for you. (You have to work in the Design pane to automatically add the new list item. Pressing Return/Enter in the Code pane simply adds white space in the code.)

5. **Type `HTML entities and other resources at W3schools.com.` as the new list item, but do not press Return/Enter.**

6. **In the first list item, select the URL in the square brackets and cut it to the Clipboard (Edit>Cut or Command/Control-X).**

7. **Delete the two square brackets and the space before them.**

8. **Select "A List Apart Magazine," click in the Link field of the Properties panel, paste the copied URL, and press Return/Enter.**

   A link is identified by **<a>** tags. The **href** attribute defines the link destination, or the page that will open when a user clicks the link text.

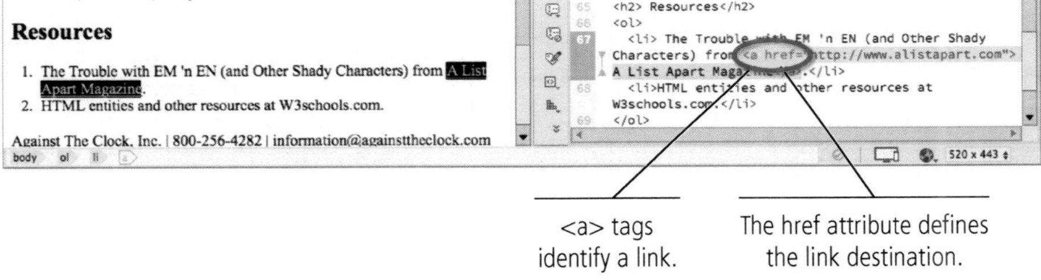
<a> tags identify a link.
The href attribute defines the link destination.

9. **Click to place the insertion point in the link.**

   Placing the insertion point removes the highlighting that was applied to the text in the previous step. You can now see the default presentational properties of the <a> tag — blue, underlined text.

10. **In the second list item, make "W3schools.com" a link to `http://www.w3schools.com`.**

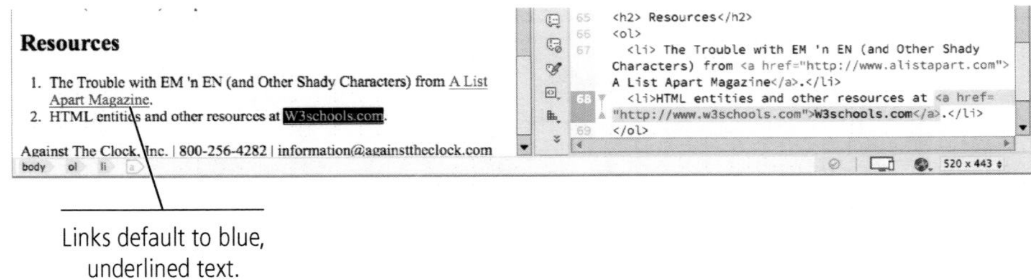
Links default to blue, underlined text.

11. **Save the file and continue to the next exercise.**

Create an Unordered List of Navigation Links

A navigation bar is simply a list of links. It is common practice among Web design professionals to mark up a navigation bar as a list of links; after CSS has been applied, however, the list takes on an all-new appearance. In this exercise, you use the unordered list format to create a navigation bar.

1. **With typography.html open, place the insertion point at the end of the last list item in the Resources section in the Design pane.**

2. **Press Return/Enter twice.**

   Pressing Return/Enter once creates the next list item — in this case, #3.

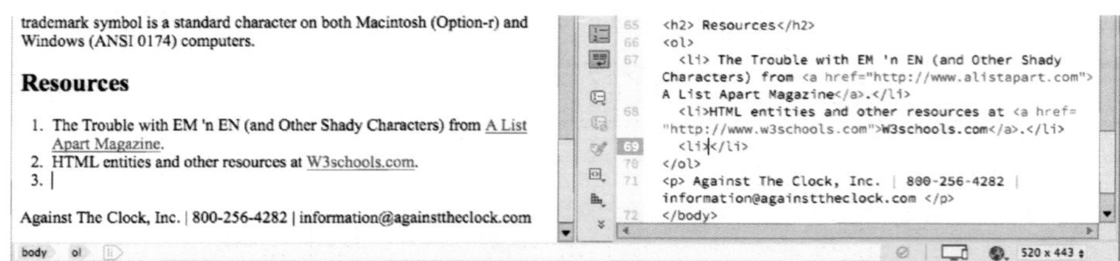

If you press Return/Enter again (before typing anything else), Dreamweaver recognizes that you want to escape from the ordered list, deletes the last empty list item, and moves the insertion point into an empty paragraph below the ordered list.

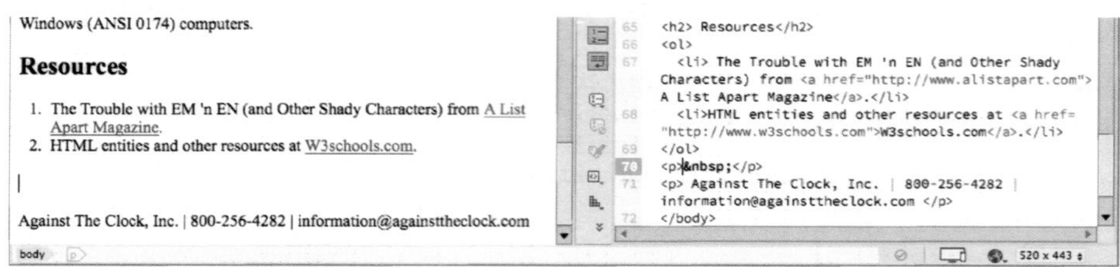

3. **Click the Unordered List button in the Properties panel.**

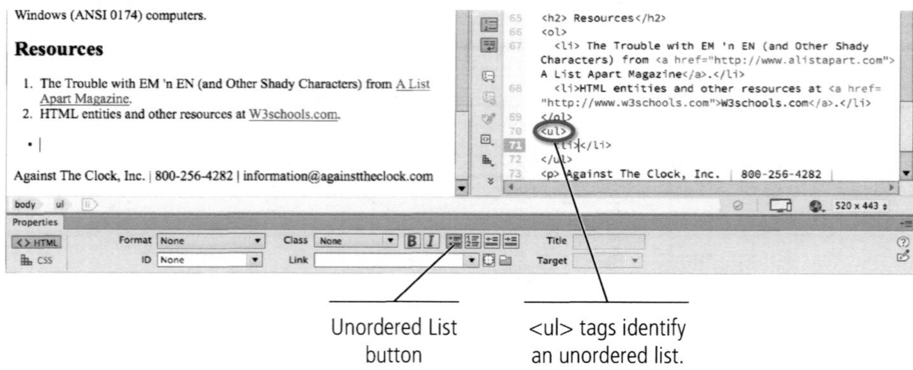
Unordered List button
<ul> tags identify an unordered list.

4. **Add six list items: Home, Store, Tools, Downloads, About, and Contact. Press Return/Enter after each item, but not after the final list item.**

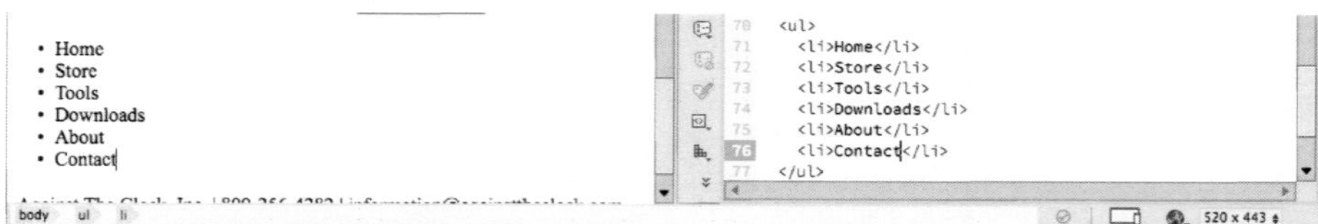

5. **Highlight the word "Home" in the Design pane. In the Properties panel, type # in the Link field, the press Return/Enter to finalize the new link.**

   Using the # character in the Link field turns the selected text into a link without defining a specific destination. For the purposes of this project, the important thing is that the text of each list item be tagged as a link.

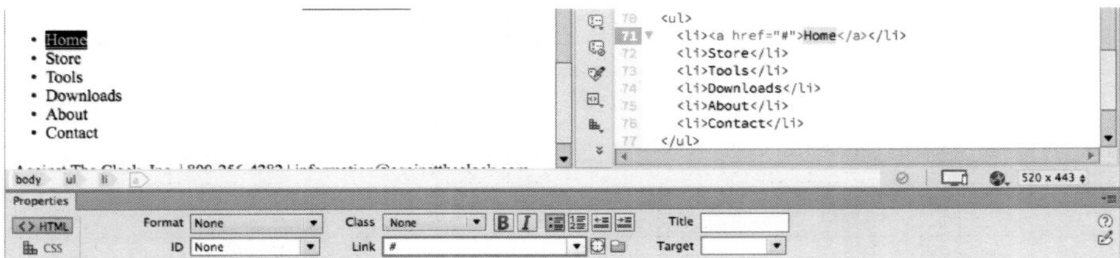

6. **Repeat Step 5 for each item in the list.**

7. **Save the changes and continue to the next stage of the project.**

Stage 5 Attaching an External CSS File

As you might have noticed, we paid particular attention to the tags that were applied to various structural elements through this project. Rather than simply accepting the default presentational properties, you can use cascading style sheets (CSS), which contain instructions that tell a browser how to format those various elements.

As you complete the rest of the projects in this book, you will work extensively with CSS to format both pages and specific page content. In this project, you are going to attach the client's existing CSS file to your page, so the appearance of your page matches the rest of the client's Web site.

Add Tags and Element IDs

Although we will not discuss the finer details of CSS at this point, the following exercises will make more sense if you understand that a CSS file includes **selectors** (rules) that define the appearance of different tags. For the formatting to correctly map to content, you need to apply the appropriate tags to various elements.

In HTML 4, the div element was commonly used to identify different areas or divisions of a page. The ID attribute was attached to various div elements to clearly identify different areas — for example, div#header, div#nav, and div#footer. HTML5 includes new header, nav, section, and footer elements that allow the same kind of page structure without the need to define and identify multiple divs on a page.

1. **With typography.html open in Split view, click in the level 1 heading in the Design pane to place the insertion point.**

2. **In the Design pane, click the <h1> tag in the Tag Selector to select the entire level 1 heading (including the related tags).**

3. **With the Insert panel in HTML mode, click the Header button.**

   HTML5 includes a number of elements that identify common elements of Web pages. This button adds the **<header> </header>** tags to identify the header element.

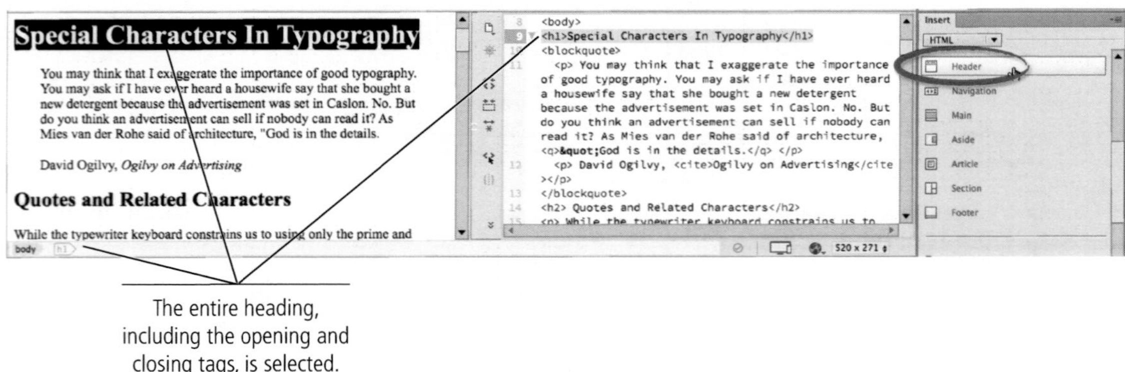

The entire heading, including the opening and closing tags, is selected.

4. **In the resulting dialog box, choose Wrap Around Selection in the Insert menu.**

   You can use the Insert dialog box (in this case, the Insert *Section* dialog box) to determine where the new element will be placed in relation to the selection. The Insert menu defaults to Wrap Around Selection because content is currently selected in the document. You can also use this dialog box to define a class or ID attribute for the resulting element.

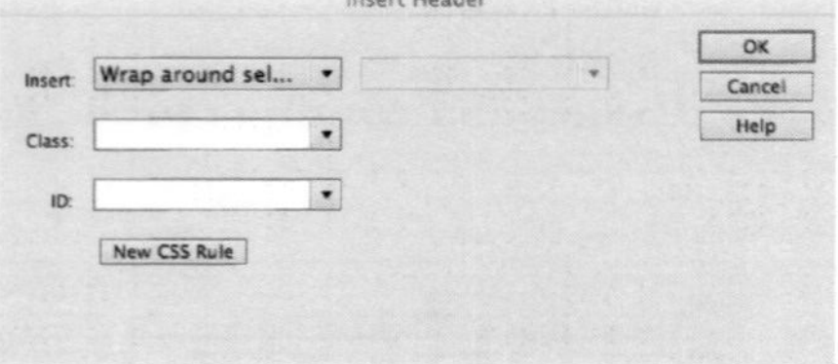

   You want the header element to include the <h1> tags, so you are wrapping the new tag *around* the current selection.

5. **Click once in the level 1 heading to place the insertion point but deselect the paragraph.**

   The boundaries of the header element are marked by a thin gray or dotted line in the Design pane. (If you don't see this border, you can turn on CSS Layout Outlines in the View>Visual Aids menu.)

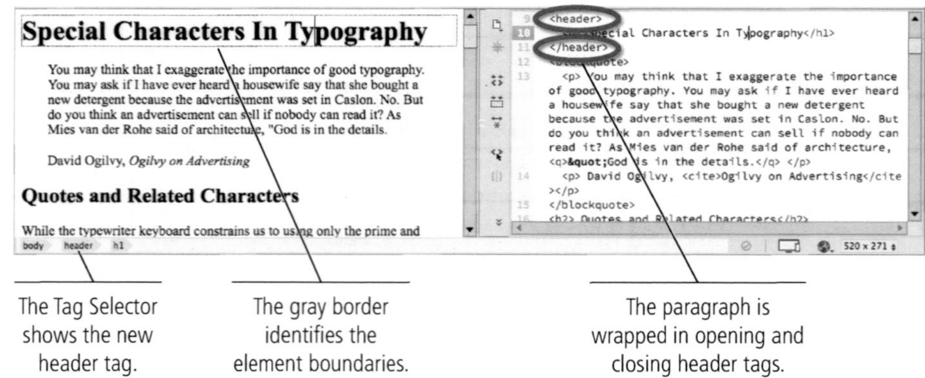

The Tag Selector shows the new header tag.

The gray border identifies the element boundaries.

The paragraph is wrapped in opening and closing header tags.

6. **In the Design pane, place the insertion point anywhere in the last paragraph. Click the <p> tag in the Tag Selector to select the entire last paragraph.**

7. **Click the Footer button in the HTML Insert panel. In the resulting dialog box, choose Wrap Around Selection in the Insert menu, then click OK.**

   The footer element identifies the footer area of the page.

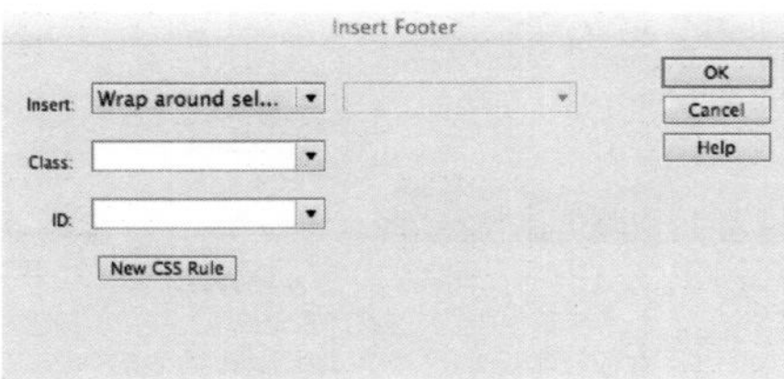

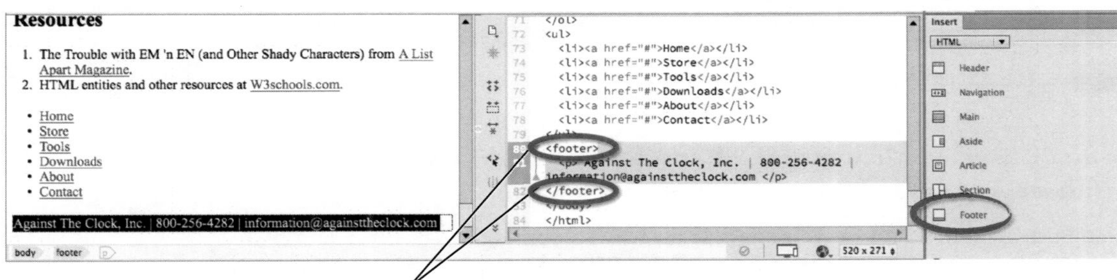

The paragraph is wrapped in opening and closing footer tags.

8. **In the Design pane, place the insertion point anywhere in the unordered list near the bottom of the page. Click the <ul> tag in the Tag Selector to select the entire unordered list.**

9. **Click the Navigation button in the HTML Insert panel. In the resulting dialog box, choose Wrap Around Selection in the Insert menu, then click OK.**

   The nav element identifies an area that includes navigation links.

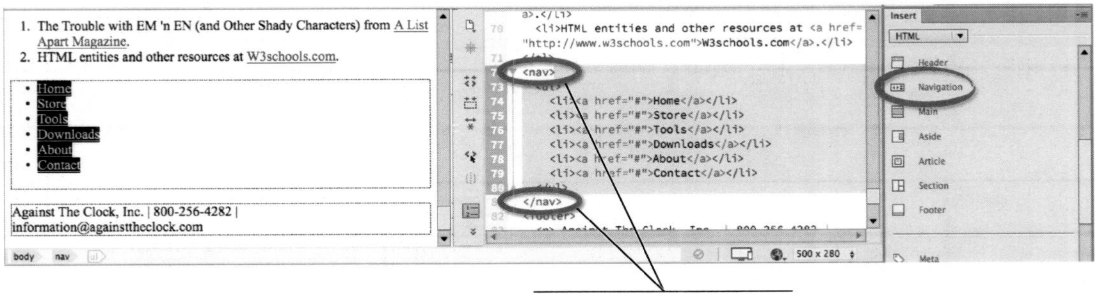

The list is wrapped in opening and closing nav tags.

10. **Switch to Design view and select all the text from the blockquote (at the top of the page) to the last numbered list item under the "Resources" heading.**

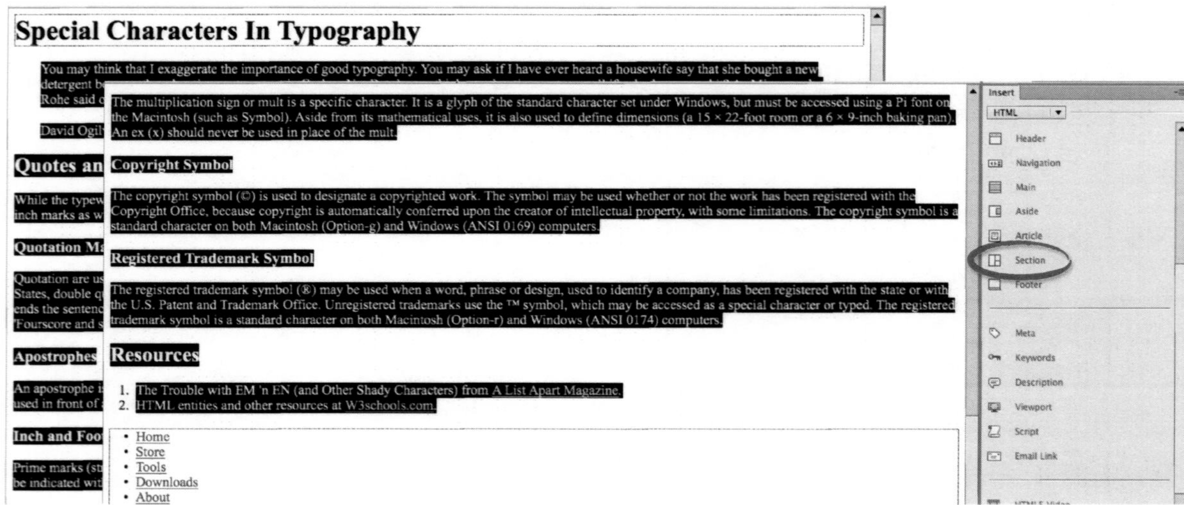

11. **Click the Section button in the HTML Insert panel. In the resulting dialog box, choose Wrap Around Selection in the Insert menu.**

The section element identifies (as you might imagine) a section of the page. By adding an ID attribute, you are uniquely identifying this section as distinct from other sections.

12. **Type excerpt in the ID field, then click OK.**

The ID attribute has no effect on the structure of content, but simply identifies it for the purposes of CSS styling. This allows you to define different appearances for the same elements in different sections. For example, **<p>** tags in a section named "content" can have a different appearance than **<p>** tags in a section named "excerpt".

The ID you are assigning (excerpt) has defined formatting in the CSS for this site. When you later attach the CSS file to this page, the appropriate formats will be applied only to content within a section tag that is identified (through the ID attribute) as an excerpt.

> ***Note:***
>
> *The most important issue is to use the exact same ID for an element as the ID defined in the CSS file that will format the appearance of the different elements. In this case, we are telling you what IDs to use based on the IDs that exist in the CSS file that you will attach to the HTML file; in a professional environment, you would have to examine the CSS styles yourself to determine which IDs are available.*

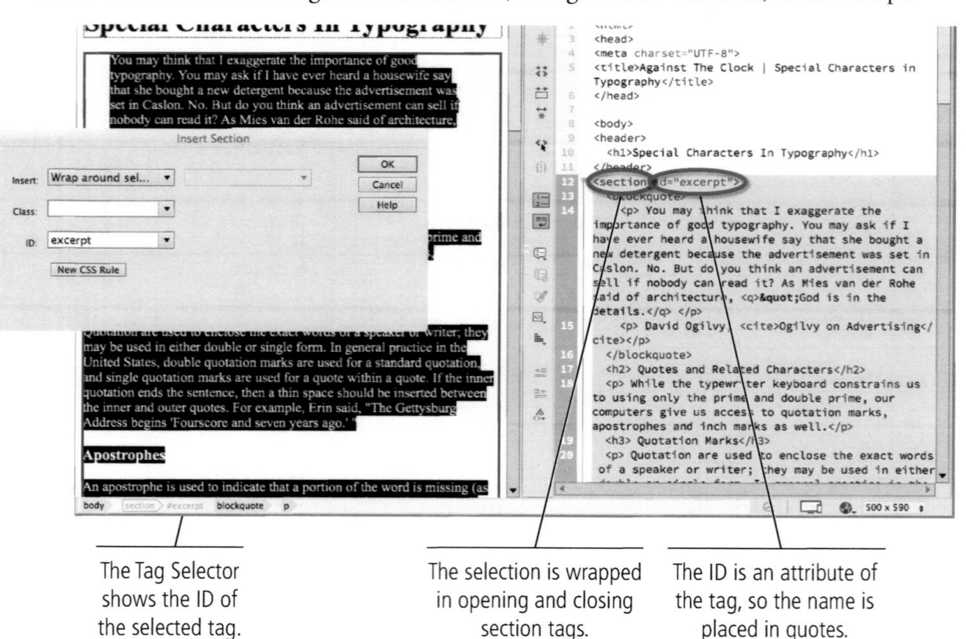

The Tag Selector shows the ID of the selected tag.

The selection is wrapped in opening and closing section tags.

The ID is an attribute of the tag, so the name is placed in quotes.

13. **Save the file and continue to the next exercise.**

Attach the CSS File

To make this page more visually pleasing to ATC site visitors — and to be consistent with the rest of the ATC site — you need to attach the CSS file already used for other pages in the client's site.

The CSS file, which is a set of instructions on how to display the Web page, is separate from the HTML document. When a browser downloads an HTML file, it examines the code for external files required to display it, such as images and CSS files. The browser then downloads the external files and merges them into the display of the Web page. In the case of a CSS file, the browser reads the instructions, and then applies the styles to the page.

After attaching the style sheet to the page, and depending on what the CSS file defines, you might see a dramatic difference in the appearance of the page. Not only will text styling change, but the layout will change too — even to the point of moving some page components to new locations.

1. **With `typography.html` open, turn on the Live view and hide the Code pane.**

2. **Open the CSS Designer panel. Make sure the All button is active at the top of the panel.**

   Remember, all panels can be opened from the Window menu. If a panel is already available in the dock, you can click the relevant panel tab or button to show that panel.

3. **In the Sources section of the panel, click the Add CSS Source button and choose Attach Existing CSS File from the resulting menu.**

   If no CSS file is attached to an HTML file, you can also click the Add a CSS Source button in the Sources section of the panel.

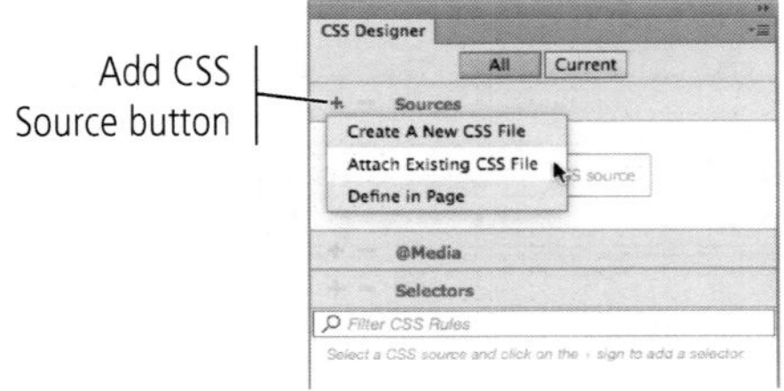

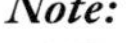

Note:

For now, don't worry about the specifics of how the CSS file formats these elements. You will spend considerable time learning about CSS in the remaining projects of this book.

4. **In the Attach Existing CSS File dialog box, click the Browse button.**

5. **In the resulting Select Style Sheet File dialog box, navigate to `styles.css` in the root folder of the ATC site (WIP>Chapter). Click Open/OK to return to the Attach Existing CSS File dialog box.**

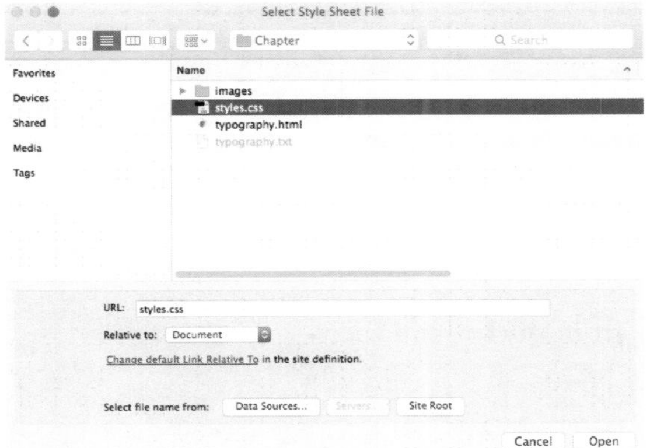

6. **Click OK in the Attach External Style Sheet dialog box to apply the CSS file.**

   Even without the CSS, the text content in this page was very readable. By attaching a CSS file that defines the appearance of various tags and IDs, the page is now visually attractive in addition to being properly structured.

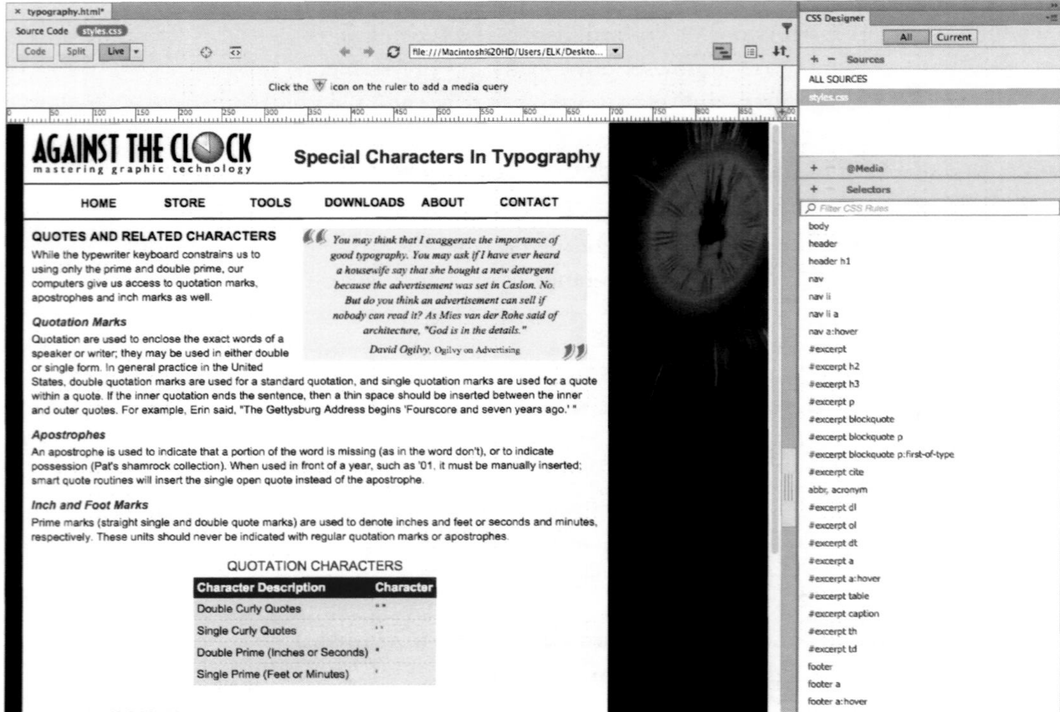

7. **Save and close typography.html.**

8. **Choose Manage Sites from the bottom of the Directory menu in the Files panel.**

9. **In the Manage Sites dialog box, choose the ATC site name, and then click the Export button. Navigate to your WIP>Chapter folder and click Save to create the ATC.ste file.**

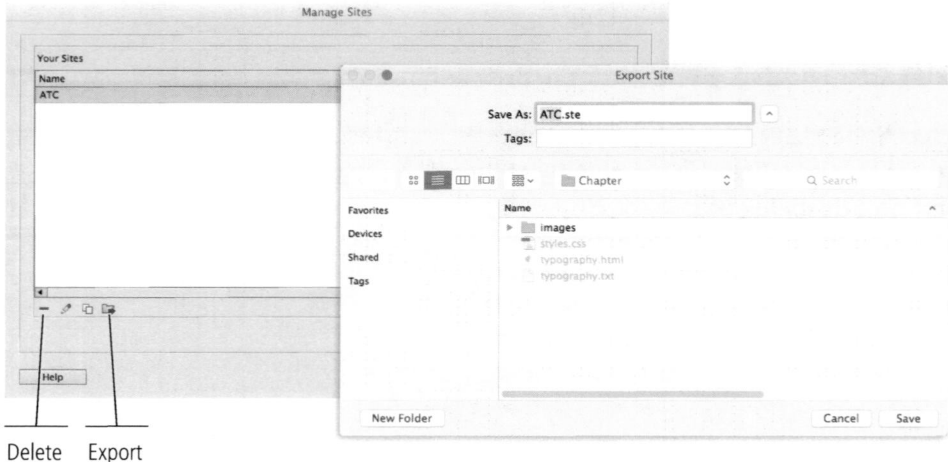

10. **In the Manage Sites dialog box, remove the ATC site from the list and then click Done to close the Manage Sites dialog box.**

Learning about HTML5 Tags

A complete list of HTML5 tags is available at www.w3schools.com/tags/default.asp.

You can click any tag in the list to find out more about its use, as well as important information about browser support for each tag.

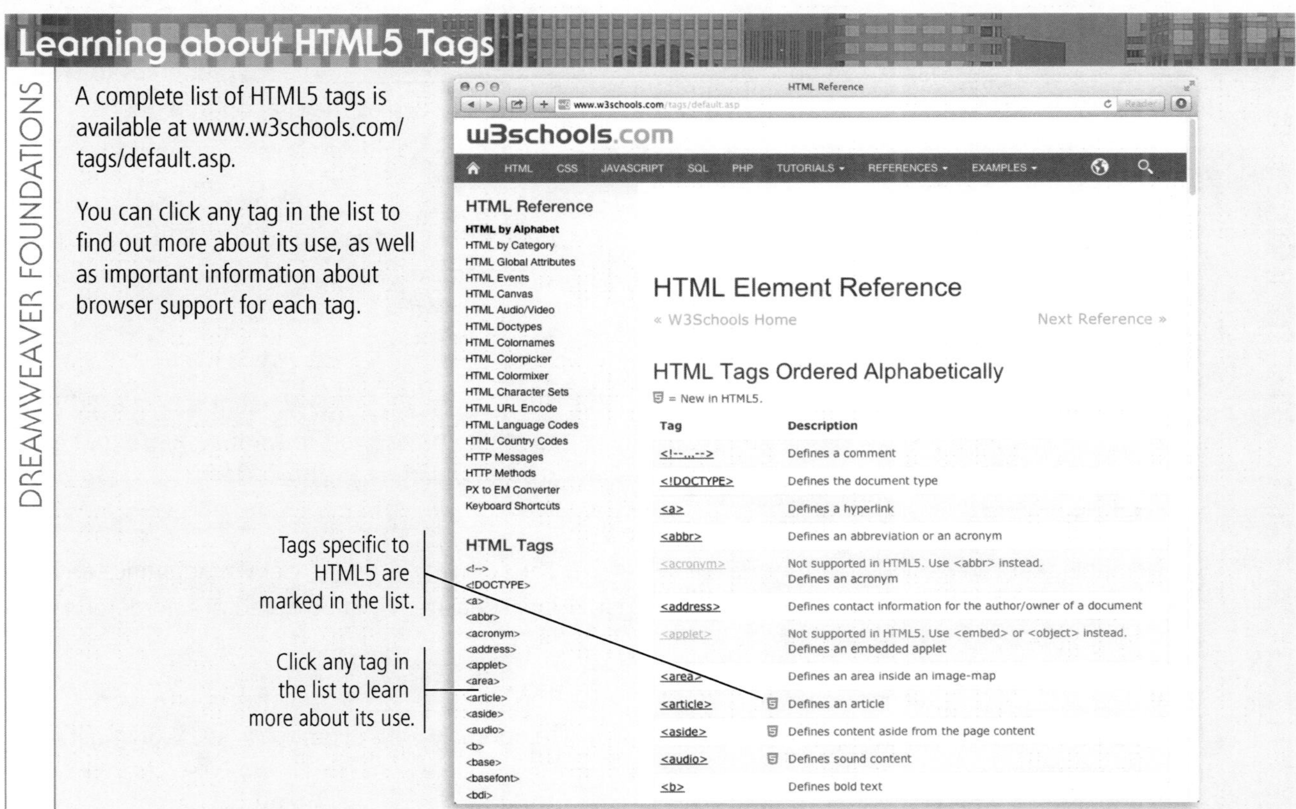

Project Review

fill in the blank

1. The _______________ tag marks up individual paragraphs in a story.

2. Each HTML page should have only one _______________ element.

3. All visible content of a Web page is contained within the opening and closing _______________ tags.

4. _______________ appear when you begin typing in the Code pane, showing a list of tags or elements that can be added at the current insertion point.

5. A(n) _______________ tag includes both opening and closing tags, such as <title>text</title>.

6. A(n) _______________ adds properties to HTML elements, such as the citation of a quote.

7. The _______________ element is used to mark up text that is indented on the right and left, with extra white space above and below the affected text.

8. The _______________ element is best used to mark up the short form of a phrase that is spoken as letters, such as HTML.

9. The _______________ element identifies an individual item in an ordered or unordered list.

10. The _______________ allows you to work temporarily with code, while still working in Design view.

short answer

1. Briefly explain the importance of properly structuring an HTML document.

2. Briefly explain the difference between an ordered list and an unordered list.

3. Briefly explain the importance of div tags for formatting an HTML page.

Portfolio Builder Project

Use what you learned in this project to complete the following freeform exercise.
Carefully read the art director and client comments, then create your own design to meet the needs of the project.
Use the space below to sketch ideas; when finished, write a brief explanation of your reasoning behind your final design.

art director comments

The owner of Against The Clock has received a number of positive comments — and new sales — because of the *Typography Companion* sample chapter that you created for her to post on her Web site. She would like to add another page with a sample from the *Color Companion* from the same series.

To complete this project, you should:

- ❑ Use the ATC site folder that you already created for the new page.
- ❑ Create a new HTML page and copy the text from **ColorCh3.txt** into the file. (The file is in the **Books_Web16_PB.zip** archive on the Student Files Web page.)
- ❑ Mark up the page text with proper structural tags.
- ❑ Create header and footer elements and attach the same CSS file that you used in the type chapter.

client comments

We've had such a positive response from the type chapter that we also want to include a sample from the *Color Companion*. If we get the same increase in sales leads from this chapter, we'll probably go ahead and do online samples for all of our books.

In addition to the text file for the *Color Companion* chapter, we've sent you a PDF file of the printed chapter so that you can more easily see the different text elements — headings, lists, italics, special characters, and so on. You can just ignore the images and sidebars in the printed chapter; we don't need those in the online sample. There is, however, a table near the end of the file that we would like you to include in the online version.

At the end of the text file, we added in the glossary terms that we think are important for this chapter. There aren't any resources, so you can leave out that section.

project justification

Project Summary

No matter how you receive content for a Web page, you will likely need to correct the formatting with the appropriate HTML tags. In this project, you learned how to use HTML tags and elements to semantically structure and mark up a document, so all visitors can successfully access and use a Web page. You also learned that by applying ID attributes, <div> tags, and using CSS, you can turn a plain HTML document into a visually pleasing and highly structured Web page.

The Web pages that you create for clients will seldom be as text-intensive as this page, but now that you have a solid understanding of how to work with HTML structures, from both Design view and Code view, you are ready to format any content you receive from a client — regardless of its condition.

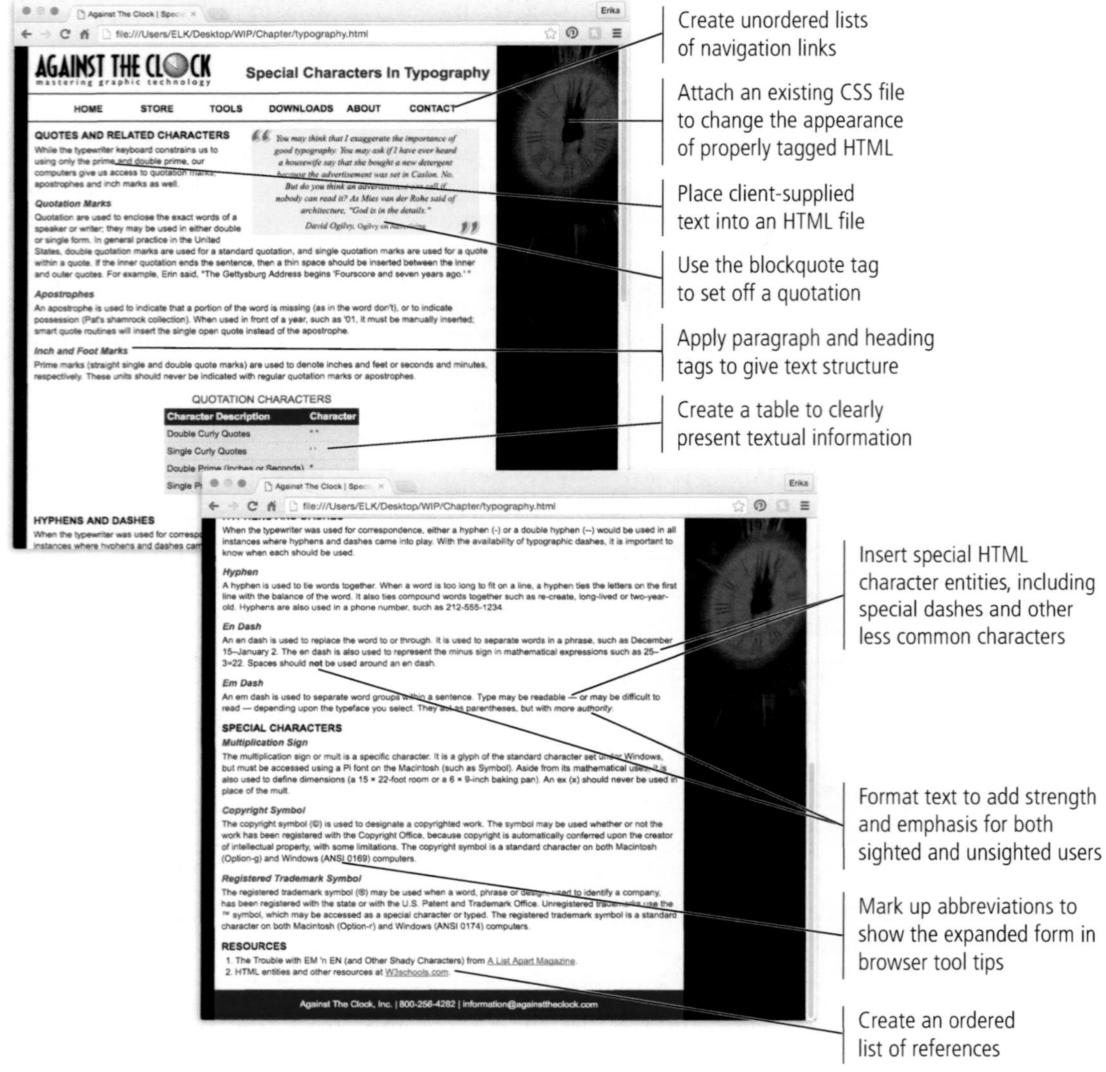

Create unordered lists of navigation links
Attach an existing CSS file to change the appearance of properly tagged HTML
Place client-supplied text into an HTML file
Use the blockquote tag to set off a quotation
Apply paragraph and heading tags to give text structure
Create a table to clearly present textual information
Insert special HTML character entities, including special dashes and other less common characters
Format text to add strength and emphasis for both sighted and unsighted users
Mark up abbreviations to show the expanded form in browser tool tips
Create an ordered list of references

Photographer's Web Site

Your client is the owner of Crowe Photography, an art studio in central California near San Francisco. Your company has been hired to create a new Web site, starting with the approved home page design.

This project incorporates the following skills:

- ❑ Using various methods to add static images into a Web page
- ❑ Assigning alt tags to images for improved usability
- ❑ Manipulating images in a Web page
- ❑ Extracting content and styles from a native Photoshop file
- ❑ Working with CSS to define various element properties

Project Meeting

client comments

We want our new site to be very basic. The primary purpose is to highlight our photography business and make it easy for potential clients to find us.

There should be several secondary pages: a blog, a page with reviews from various media, an "about us" page with our bios and credentials, a dynamic calendar with events we participate in, and an interactive gallery of photos.

We haven't finished writing and gathering the content for the secondary pages, but we want to get started on the home page as soon as possible. I sent our logo to the art director, as well as three photos that she decided to use in the home page design.

art director comments

We've been working on the design for this project for several weeks, and the client just approved the layout comp that our artist created in Photoshop.

I assigned the HTML structural composition to another Web designer, but she has other projects that need to take priority so your job is to complete the home page. Once you're finished, you'll hand it off to a developer to create the secondary pages and the required interactive elements when the client provides the content.

A few of the images you need have been saved in the project folder, but most of the assets you need are only available in the Photoshop file. Fortunately you can use Dreamweaver to access what you need to complete the project in a relatively short time.

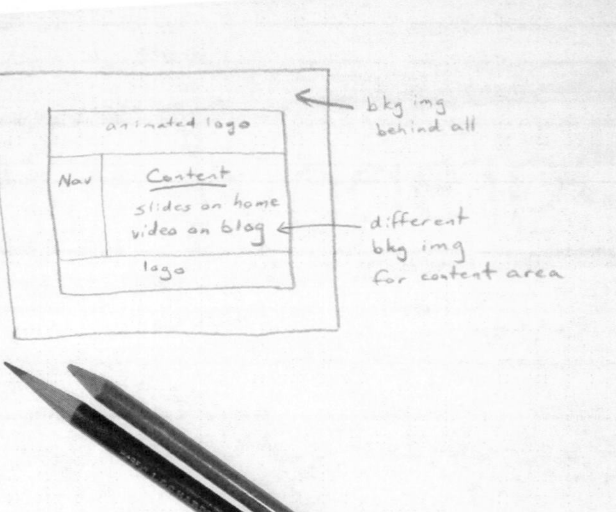

project objectives

To complete this project, you will:

- ❑ Use multiple techniques to add images to Web pages
- ❑ Resize images to fit page areas
- ❑ Resample images to reduce download time
- ❑ Load a Photoshop file into your Creative Cloud account
- ❑ Extract text, images, and styles from a supplied Photoshop file
- ❑ Use CSS to control the appearance of various page elements

Stage 1 Placing Static Foreground Images

Important note: This project requires an individual user subscription to the Adobe Creative Cloud service. If you are working on a machine with a device license, you will not have access to the Extract functionality needed to complete the project. An alternate project, which does not require an individual user CC account, is available on the Student Downloads page.

As with many tasks, Dreamweaver offers a number of methods for inserting images into an HTML page. The variety of available options means you can choose whichever method best suits your personal working style and space. Before you begin placing objects in a page, however, you should understand the basics of images that will be used for Web design.

Image Bit Depth

Bit depth refers to how many bits define the color value of a particular pixel. A **bit** is a unit of information that is either on or off (represented as 1 and 0, respectively).

- 1 bit has 2 states or colors
- 8 bits allow 256 possible colors (2^8 or 2×2×2×2×2×2×2×2=256)
- 24 bits allow 16,777,216 possible colors (2^{24}).

Image Formats

Four primary formats are used for images and graphics on the Web:

- **GIF** (Graphics Interchange Format) is best used for graphics with areas of solid color, such as logos.

  The GIF format supports 8-bit color, or 256 possible values. To create the illusion or more possible colors, the format supports dithering, in which pixels of varying colors are interspersed in areas where colors transition from one to another.

  This format supports index transparency, in which specific colors in the image can be defined as transparent areas, as well as simple frame-by-frame animation. It is largely falling out of use in favor of the PNG format for graphics.

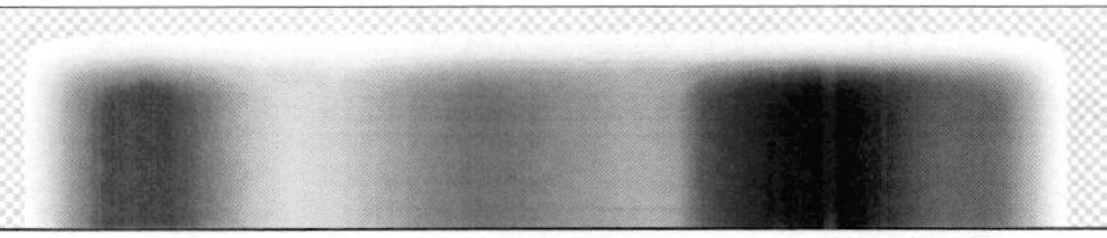

The GIF format supports 8-bit color and index transparency, which does not allow smooth color transitions or smooth fading of edges into a background.

The JPEG format supports 24-bit color but not transparency, allowing smooth color transitions but not fading of edges into a background.

The PNG-8 format supports 8-bit color and index transparency, which does not allow smooth color transitions or smooth fading of edges into a background.

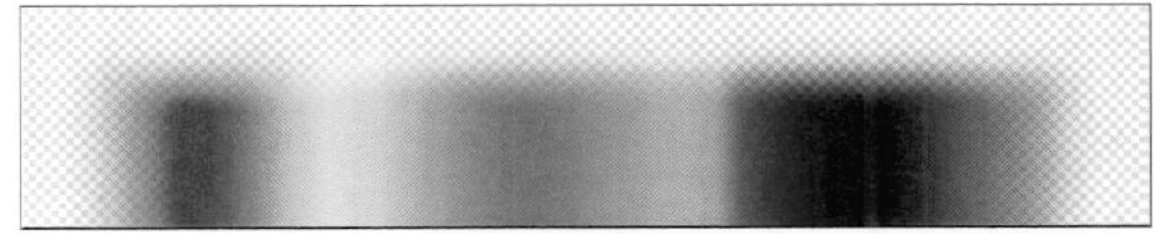

The PNG-32 format supports 24-bit color and alpha transparency, allowing smooth color and transparency transitions.

- **JPEG** (Joint Photographic Experts Group). This format supports 24-bit color, is used primarily for continuous-tone images with subtle changes in color, such as photographs or other images that are created in Adobe Photoshop. In an RGB photograph, three color channels define how much of each primary color (red, green, and blue) makes up each pixel. Each channel requires 8 bits, resulting in a total of 24 bits for each pixel (called **true color**). The format does not support transparency.

  The JPEG format incorporates **lossy compression**, which means that pixels are thrown away in order to reduce file size. When areas of flat color are highly compressed, speckles of other colors (called artifacts) often appear, which negatively impacts the quality of the design.

- **PNG** (Portable Network Graphics) has two common variants, PNG-8 and PNG-32.

  PNG-8 has 8 bits, which means it can support 256 colors in an image. Although the PNG-8 format incorporates algorithms to better reflect color transitions and colors that are not included in the file's color table, it is still only an 8-bit color format so should not be used for true-color images such as photographs. Like the GIF format, it is more appropriate for logos and other graphics that do not use a large number of colors or smooth tone changes.

  PNG-32 supports 24-bit color, which means the format can be used for photographic and other images with a large range of color. PNG-32 also supports alpha transparency, in which each pixel can have a degree of transparency (the "alpha value") in addition to the three color channel values. In other words, PNG-32 supports smooth transitions from opaque to transparent. (The "32" designation comes from 24 bits for the color definition plus 8 bits for the transparency information.)

  Both variations of the PNG format use lossless compression, which means no image data is thrown away. This results in better-quality images, but also larger file sizes than can be accomplished using a lossy compression algorithm.

- **SVG (Scalable Vector Graphics)** are made up of mathematically defined lines called **vectors** (unlike **raster images**, which are made up entirely of pixels). Vector graphics are completely **scalable** without affecting their quality.

Review the Existing Project Status

This project involves working with files that have already been created by another designer. The best way to start this type of job is to evaluate the existing work before you jump in to complete the required tasks.

1. **Download Crowe_Web16_RF.zip from the Student Files Web page.**

2. **Expand the ZIP archive in your WIP folder (Macintosh) or copy the archive contents into your WIP folder (Windows).**

   This results in a folder named **Crowe**, which contains the files you need for this project.

3. **Create a new site named Photography, using the WIP>Crowe folder as the site root folder.**

   The procedure for defining this site is the same as for the sites you created in previous projects (except for the path, which is unique for every project). If necessary, refer to the first exercises in Project 6: Bistro Site Organization for more detailed instructions.

4. **With the Photography site open in the Files panel, double-click index.html to open the file.**

5. **Review the page contents in the Live view.**

   This is a fairly simple page, with several places marked to add various content. As you complete this project, you will use a number of techniques to place and manage images and other media to add visual interest.

   In the first stage of this project you will use a variety of techniques to add content that was provided with the basic HTML file. In the second stage of the project you will extract content from a Photoshop file that shows the finished and approved page design.

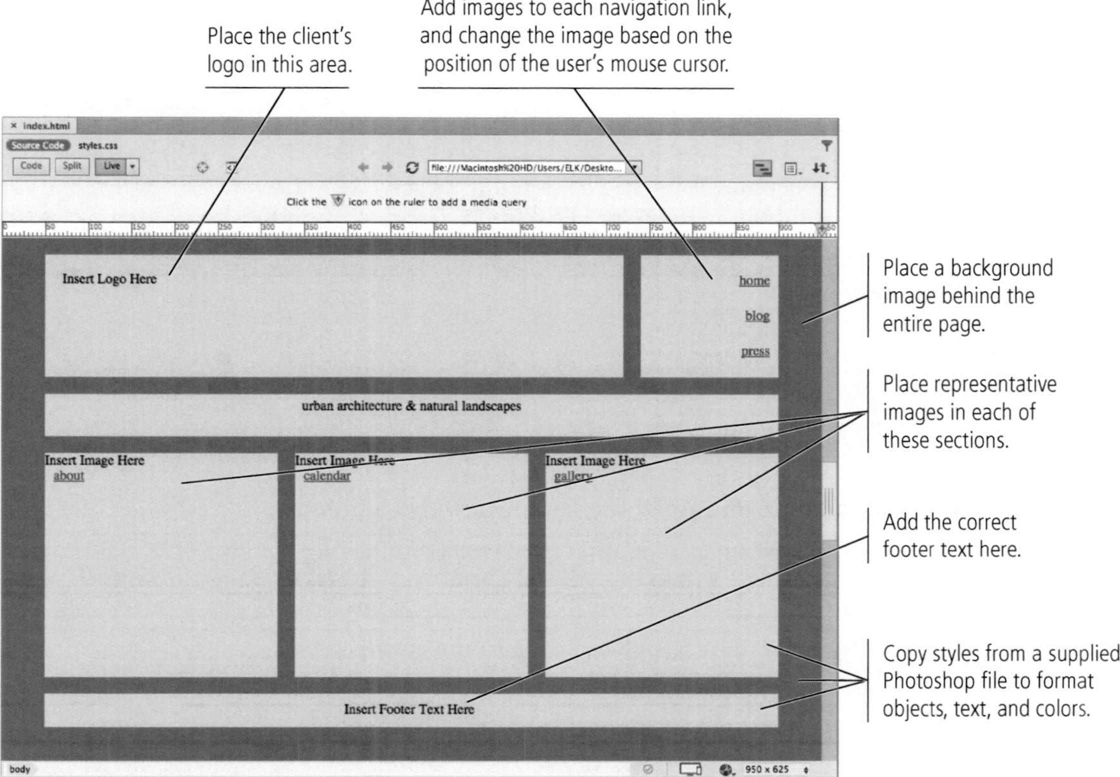

6. **Continue to the next exercise.**

 Place an Image in the Regular Design View

Dreamweaver provides many ways to insert images into Web pages, one of which is to simply drag an image file from the Files panel to a specific location on the page. (This method only works in the regular Design view; you cannot drag an image from the Files panel when the Live view is active.) In this exercise, you will use this basic technique to place an image in the client's home page.

1. **With index.html open (from the Photography site folder), turn off the Live view if necessary to make the regular Design view active.**

2. **Click the Split button in the Document toolbar to show both the Design and Code views.**

   In this project we use the horizontal split view to maximize the line length that is visible in both panes. Feel free to use whichever method you prefer.

3. **In the Design view, select the words "Insert Image Here" in the left rectangle in the third row of the layout.**

4. **Delete the selected text from the Design view.**

   When you delete the placeholder text, the code for a nonbreaking space (** **) is automatically added as a placeholder inside the **<p>** tags.

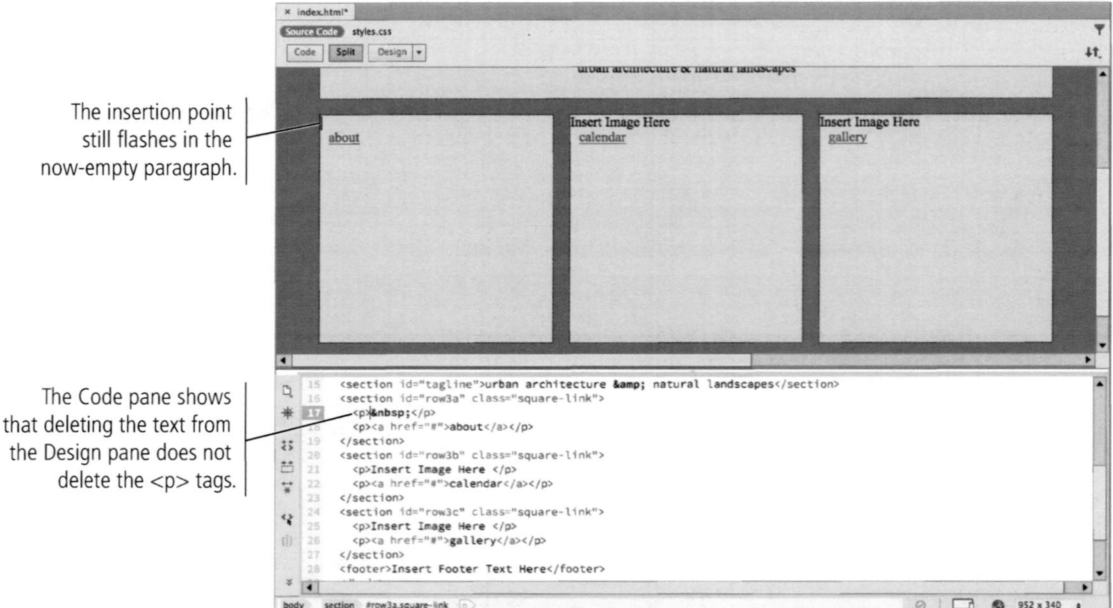

5. **In the Files panel, expand the site `images` folder and review the contents.**

   These four images have been provided by the client. You will insert them in various places on the client's new home page.

6. **Click the file `windmill.jpg` in the Files panel and drag to the empty paragraph (where you deleted the text in Step 4).**

   When the regular Design view is active, you can drag any image from the Files panel to a specific position in the layout. (This method does not work when the Live view is active.)

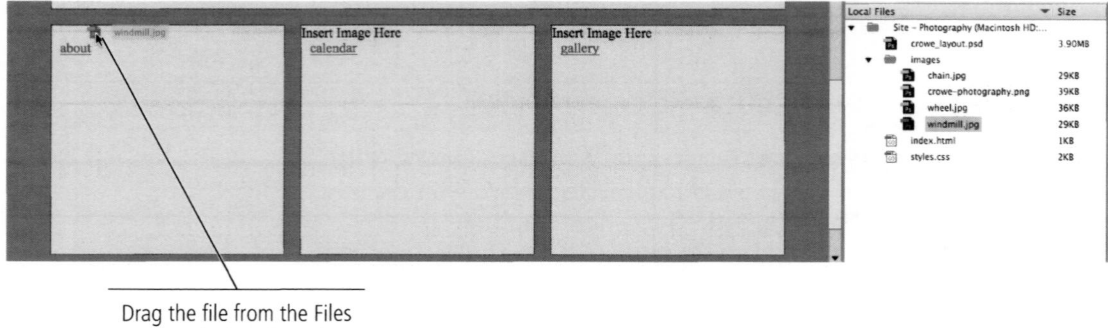

Drag the file from the Files panel to the location where you want to place the image.

7. **With the image selected in the Design view, type About Us Link in the Alt field of the Properties panel. Click the image in the Design pane to finalize the change.**

8. **With the placed image selected in the Design pane, examine the Tag Selector and the Code pane.**

   The **<img>** (image) tag appears inside the opening and closing **<p>** tags.

   Some attributes of the **<img>** tag are automatically populated based on information saved in the image file:

   - The **src** attribute defines the file name and location of the image.
   - The **width** and **height** attributes are automatically populated based on the file's physical dimensions.
   - The **alt** attribute is the alternate text; this is the text that appears in place of an image if image display is disabled in a browser, or that is read by screen-reader software. The alt text is also indexed by search engines, which allows them to show your site's images in the search engine image gallery.

     When you place an image, Dreamweaver automatically creates an empty alt attribute in the <img> tag; if you do not add text in the Alt field of the Properties panel (or directly in the Code pane), the attribute remains empty.

Note:

The alt attribute is commonly misnamed the alt tag; it is not an HTML tag but an attribute of a tag.

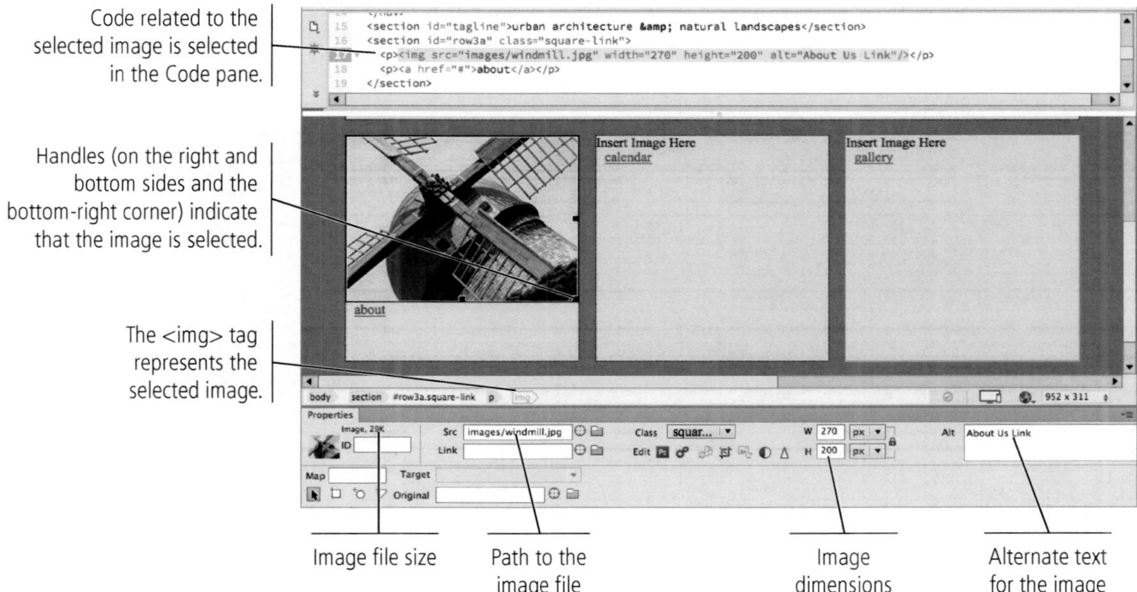
Code related to the selected image is selected in the Code pane.
Handles (on the right and bottom sides and the bottom-right corner) indicate that the image is selected.
The <img> tag represents the selected image.
Image file size
Path to the image file
Image dimensions
Alternate text for the image
<section id="tagline">urban architecture & natural landscapes</section>
<section id="row3a" class="square-link">
<p><img src="images/windmill.jpg" width="270" height="200" alt="About Us Link"/></p>
<p><a href="#">about</a></p>
</section>
Insert Image Here
calendar
Insert Image Here
gallery
about

9. **Save the file and continue to the next exercise.**

Place an Image with the Insert Panel

In the last few upgrades to the software, the Dreamweaver Live view has been significantly enhanced. You can now access many of the editing features that were previously only available in the regular Design view, so you can immediately see the results in the document window. In this exercise, you will use the buttons in the HTML Insert panel to add a new image element to the page in the Live view.

1. **With `index.html` open, click the Design button in the Document toolbar to close the Code pane, then make the Live view active.**

2. **Click once to select the "Insert Image Here" paragraph in the middle rectangle in the third row of the layout.**

   When the Live view is active, clicking an object in the document window shows the Element Display. The blue tag shows the specific element, as well as any ID or class attributes that have been defined for that element. (You will learn much more about IDs and classes in later projects.) In this case, you can see that the selected element is a **p** element — in other words, it is a paragraph.

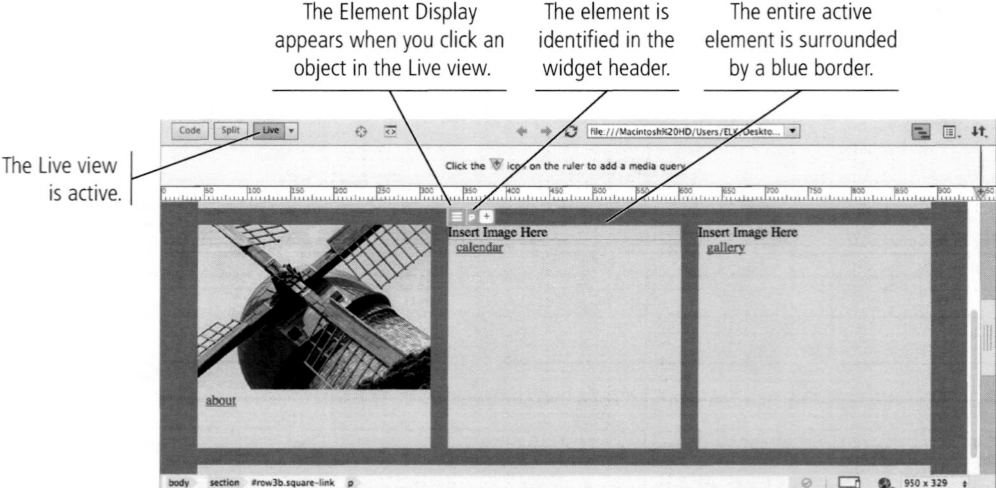

3. **Double-click the text in the selected paragraph to place the insertion point.**

   Remember, you can place the insertion point and edit text directly in the Live view.

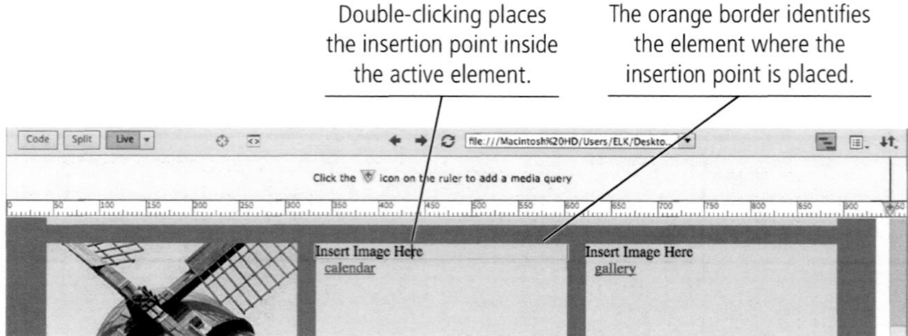

4. **Click and drag to select all the words in the active paragraph element.**

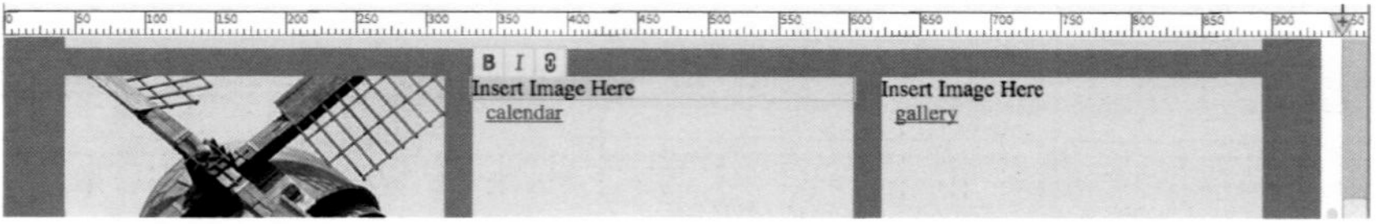

Note:

As you work with Dreamweaver, you will occasionally see pop-up messages with tips about using various aspects of the software. You can close these messages by clicking the "X" button in the top-right corner.

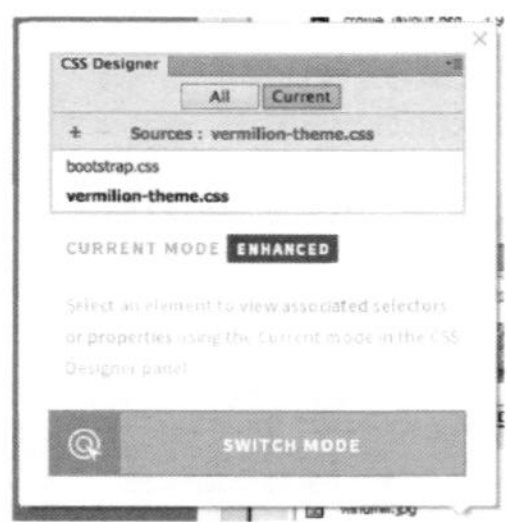

5. **Press the Delete key to remove the selected text from the Design pane.**

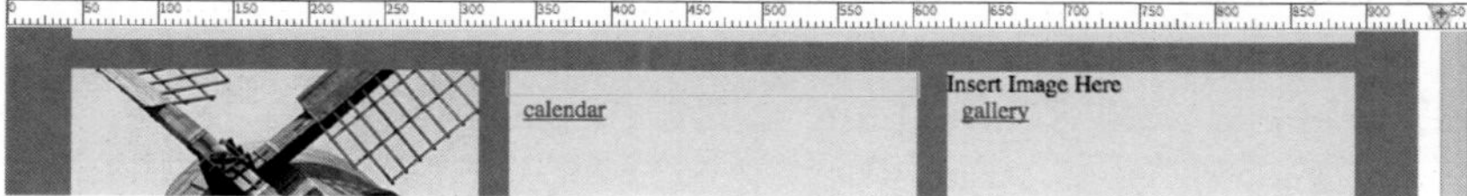

6. **Click away from the active element to exit the text-editing mode (unplace the insertion point).**

   You cannot use the Insert panel buttons when the insertion point is placed in the Live view. When you click away from the element to unplace the insertion point, the actual element — in this case, the p (paragraph) element — becomes the active selection.

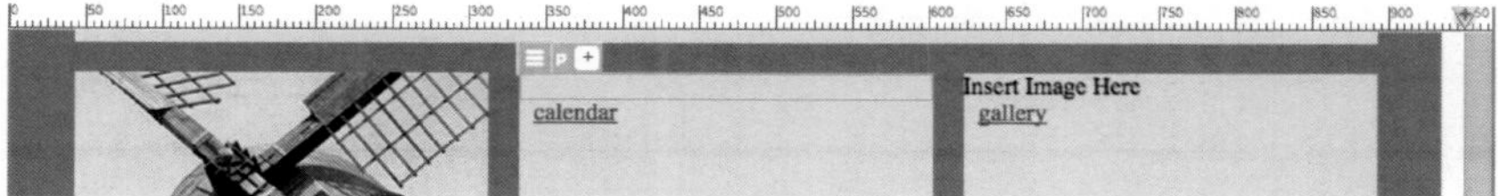

7. **Open the Insert panel and, if necessary, switch the panel to the HTML options.**

8. **With the p element selected, click the Image button in the HTML Insert panel.**

   Because an element is selected in the Live view, clicking this button results in the Position Assistant over the selected element, which you can use to determine where the image will be placed relative to the selected element — Before, After, or Nest inside. (The Wrap option is not available in this case because you can't wrap an image around another object).

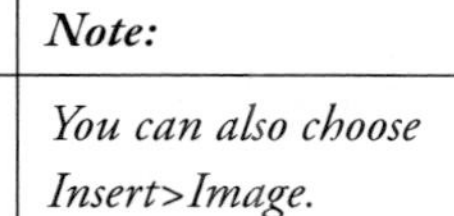

Note:

You can also choose Insert>Image.

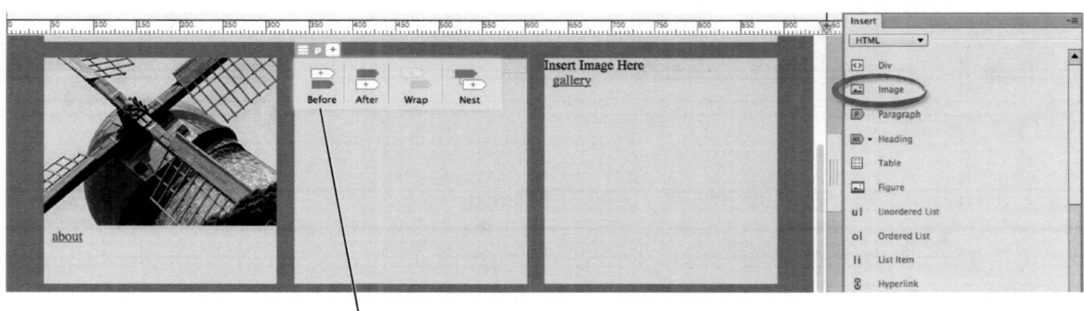

Use these buttons to place the image relative to the selected element.

9. **Click the Nest button in the Position Assistant.**

   You want to place the image inside the paragraph, so you are using the Nest option.

10. **In the Resulting dialog box, navigate to the file `chain.jpg` (in the site `images` folder) and click Open/OK.**

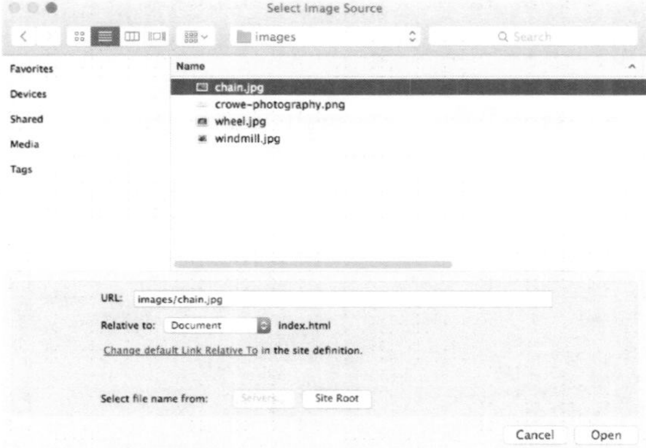

11. **With the image selected in the Design pane, click the Edit HTML Attributes button on the left side of the Element Display.**

12. **Type `Calendar Link` in the alt field and press Return/Enter to finalize the new alt attribute.**

    You can use this pop-up window to change various attributes of a placed image without using the Properties panel or Code pane.

13. **Press the ESC key to close the HTML Attributes pop-up window.**

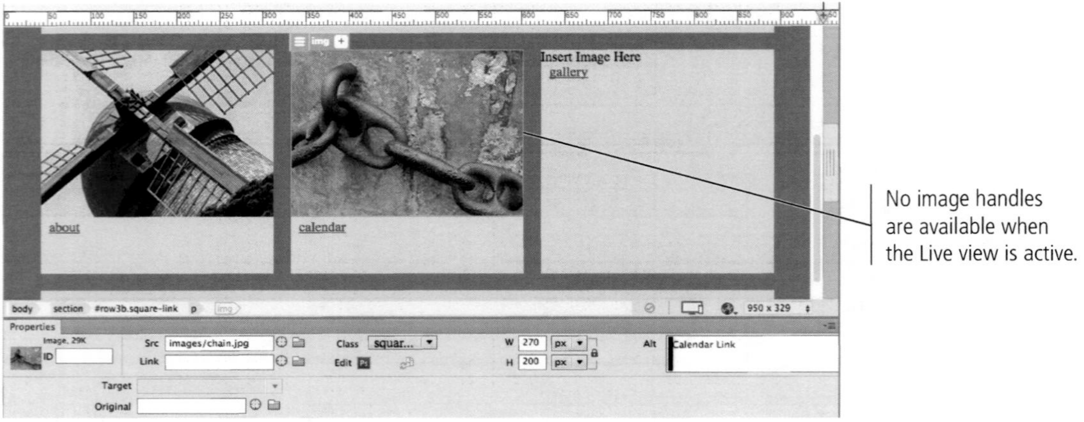

14. **Save the file and continue to the next exercise.**

Drag and Drop an Image from the Insert Panel

When the Live view is active, you can drag a button from the HTML Insert panel to place a new element in the page; on-screen guides determine where the element will be placed. In this exercise, you will use this method to place an image in the page.

1. **Make sure `index.html` is open and the Live view is active.**

2. **Select and delete the words "Insert Image Here" from the right rectangle in the third row of the layout.**

3. **Click away from the empty element to unplace the insertion point.**

4. **Click the Image button in the HTML Insert panel and drag to the empty paragraph element.**

   When you drag elements within or into the Live view, visual indicators identify where the element you drag will be placed when you release the mouse button. A green two-headed arrow indicates that the dragged element will be placed in line with other elements; the line shows exactly where (before or after) the element will be placed. A blue rectangle inside another element indicates that the dragged one will be placed inside of the element to which you drag (referred to as **nesting**).

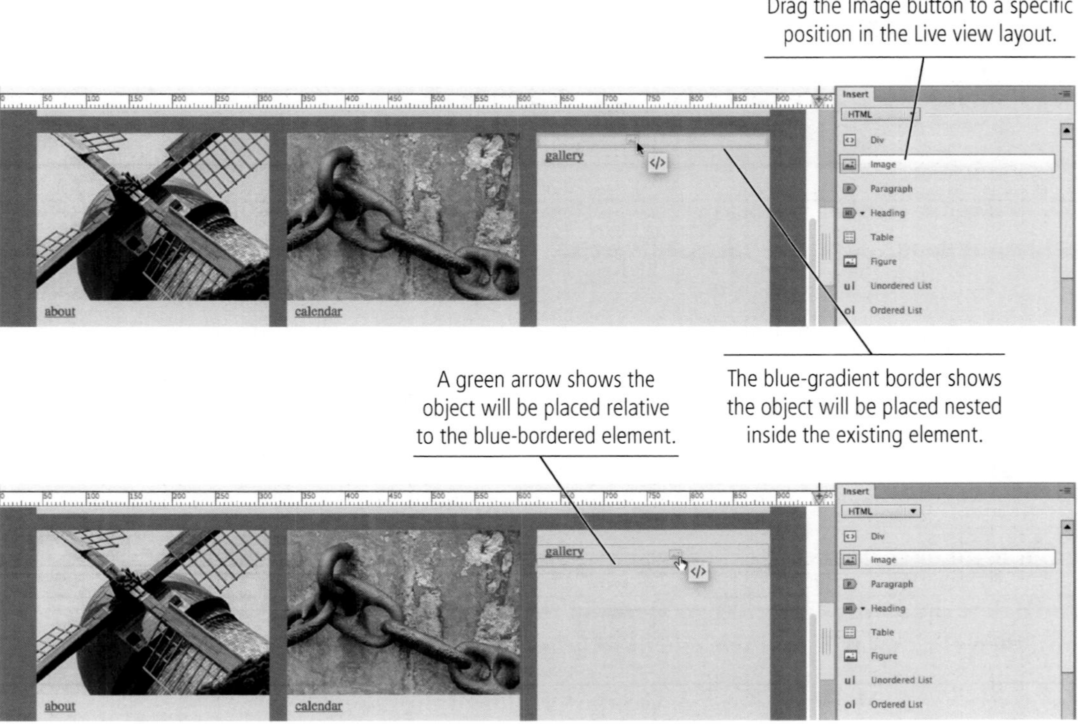

5. **When a blue border appears inside the paragraph element, release the mouse button.**

6. **In the resulting Select Image Source dialog box, navigate to `wheel.jpg` (in the site `images` folder) and click Open/OK.**

   Using the drag-and-drop method, you have to determine which image you want to place when you release the mouse button.

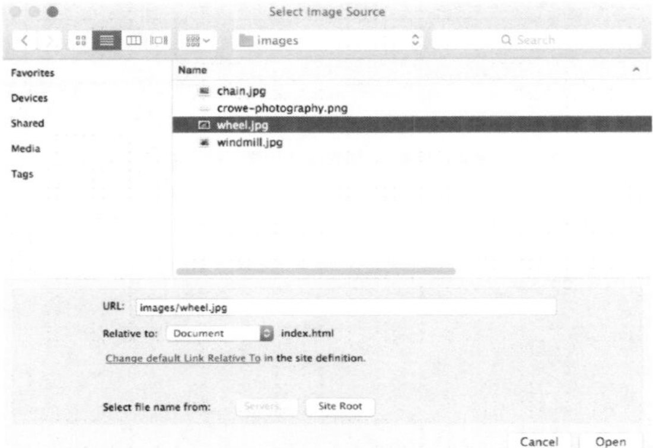

7. **Using the pop-up HTML attributes window, define `Gallery Link` as the alternate text for this image.**

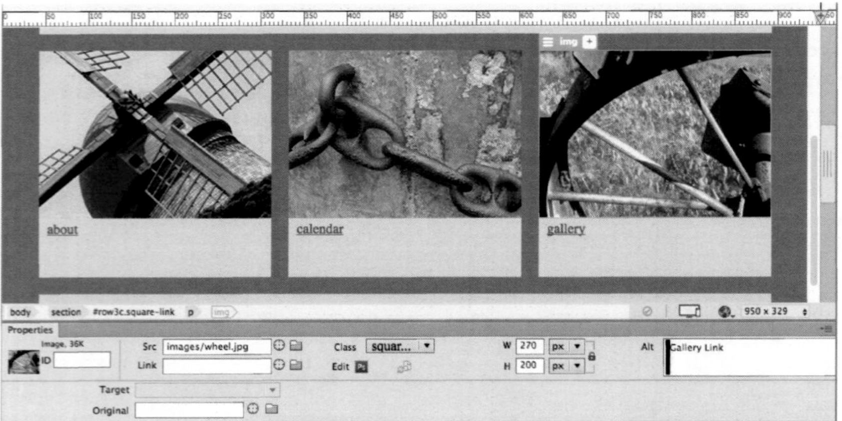

8. **Save the file and then continue to the next exercise.**

Insert an Image with the Assets Panel

The Assets panel allows you to sort the various assets in a site by type rather than by their location within the site folder structure. It also offers yet another way to insert an image into a Web page. In this exercise, you will use the Assets panel to add the client's logo to the page.

1. **With `index.html` open, make sure the Live view is active.**

2. **Select and delete the words "Insert Logo Here" in the top-left rectangle in the layout, then click away from the element to unplace the insertion point.**

3. **Open the Assets panel (Window>Assets). On the left side of the Assets panel, click the Images button to show all images in the site.**

   The Assets panel displays a thumbnail of the selected image at the top of the panel.

4. **Click the Refresh Site List button at the bottom of the Assets panel to make sure all images are visible.**

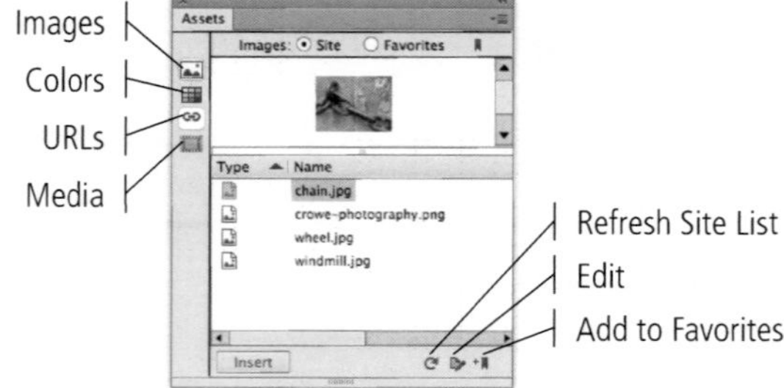

5. **Select `crowe-photography.png` in the panel.**

Note:

Do not double-click the image in the Assets panel or Files panel to insert it. Double-clicking an image in either panel prompts Dreamweaver to open the file in an image-editing application.

6. **With the empty header element selected from Step 2, click the Insert button at the bottom of the Assets panel.**

You can also drag an image from the Assets panel to the layout. If the Live view is active, on-screen guides identify where the dragged image will be placed. If the regular Design view is active, simply drag from the panel to a location indicated by the flashing insertion point.

7. **Click the Nest button in the resulting Position Assistant.**

8. **Define `Crowe Photography` as the alternate text for the placed image.**

9. **Save the file and continue to the next exercise.**

Resize and Resample an Image

As you can see in the Live view, the placed logo is much too large to fit in the defined space. In this exercise, you will adjust the image to fit the space.

1. **With `index.html` open, turn off the Live view.**

   When the Live view is active, you can only use the Properties panel to change the dimensions of a placed image.

The Live view is active.
You can use the W and H fields to change the image dimensions.

2. **Click the placed logo to select the image (if necessary).**

When the Live view is not active, the bottom center, right center, and bottom-right corner of a selected image show control handles, which you can drag to resize the height of the placed image. (You might not be able to see the right edge of the image depending on the size and arrangement of your workspace).

The Live view is not active.
crowe photography
urban architecture & natural landscapes
Src images/crowe-photog
Alt Crowe Photography
You can use the W and H fields to change the image dimensions.
You can drag the image handles to resize the image in the document window.

3. **In the Properties panel, make sure the lock icon to the right of the W and H fields is locked. If the icon is unlocked, click it to make it locked.**

When the icon is locked, changing one dimension applies a proportional change to the other dimension; in other words, changes to the image dimensions maintain the original width-to-height aspect ratio.

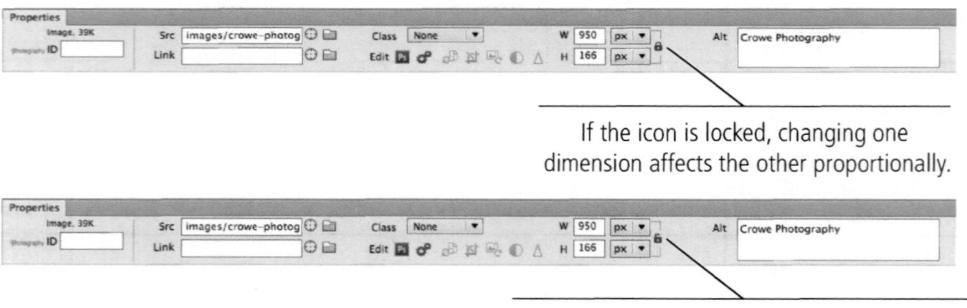
If the icon is locked, changing one dimension affects the other proportionally.
If the icon is unlocked, changing one dimension has no effect on the other dimension.

4. **Highlight the current value in the W field. Type `550`, then press Return/ Enter to finalize the change.**

   In the Properties panel, the image dimensions appear in bold, indicating that the image has been resized.

   Two additional buttons are now available to the right of the W and H fields. Clicking the **Reset to Original Size button** restores the original image dimensions regardless of how many times you have changed the image size in the page or in the Properties panel.

   Clicking the **Commit Image Size button** changes the placed image file to match the current image dimensions on the page.

Note:

You can usually reduce an image without losing quality, but enlarging an image beyond its original size can result in a significant loss of image quality.

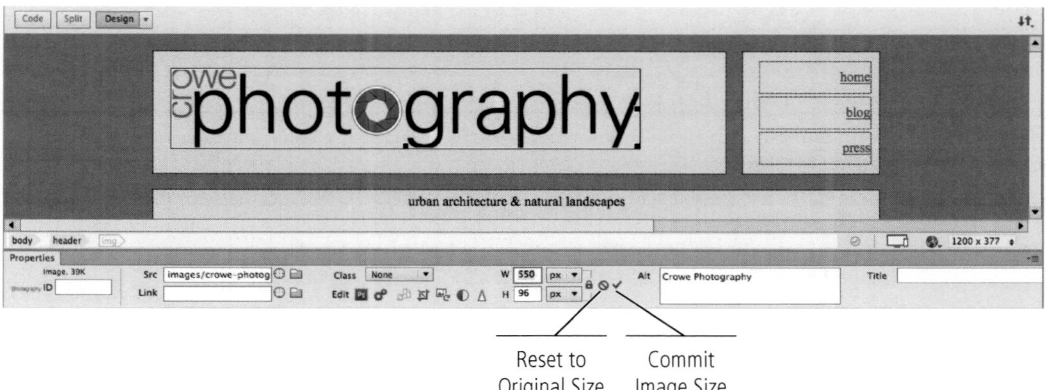

5. **Click the bottom-right image handle, press Shift, and drag down and right. When the H field shows the height of 110, release the mouse button.**

   If an image extends outside the edge of the element in which it is placed (as is the case for this logo), you will not be able to use the control handles to resize the image. Instead, you have to use the Properties panel.

   You can drag any of the handles to resize the image in only one direction (by dragging the side handles) or in both directions at once (by dragging the corner handle).

   Keep in mind that manually resizing the image using these handles does not honor the Lock icon in the Properties panel. If you drag either of the side handles, or the corner handle without pressing Shift, the lock icon in the Properties panel is automatically unlocked. By pressing Shift while dragging the corner handle, you constrain the resizing process and maintain the image's original aspect ratio.

Note:

Pressing Shift while dragging a side handle does not maintain the image's aspect ratio. You have to Shift-drag the corner handle to resize the image proportionally.

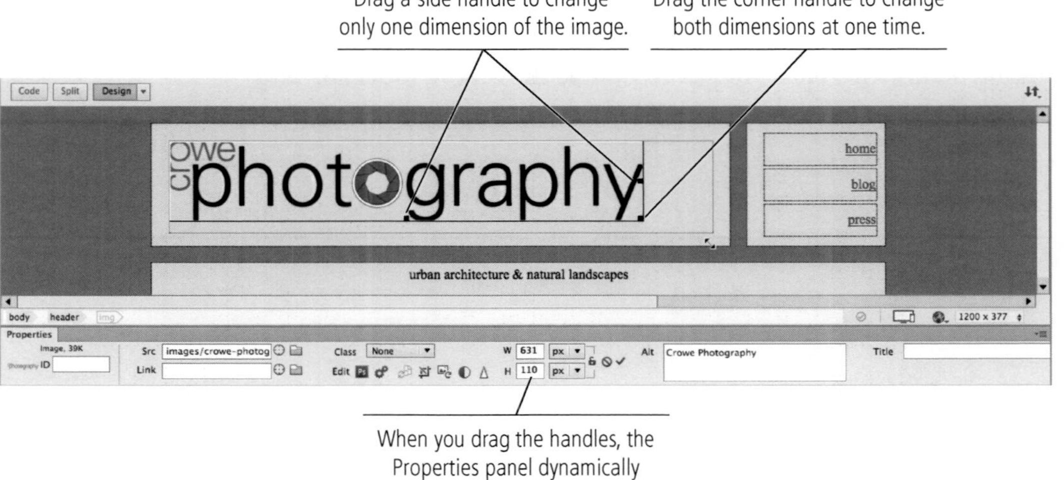

Drag a side handle to change only one dimension of the image.
Drag the corner handle to change both dimensions at one time.
When you drag the handles, the Properties panel dynamically changes to show the adjusted size.

6. **In the Files panel, expand the `images` folder if necessary.**

7. **Control/right-click the `crowe-photography.png` file, and choose Edit>Duplicate from the contextual menu.**

   It's a common mistake to insert a large image into a Web page, and then simply resize the image to take up less space on the page. The problem with resizing is that, while the image will *appear* smaller, the file size ("weight") remains the same. Users might need to wait a considerable length of time to download the large image file.

   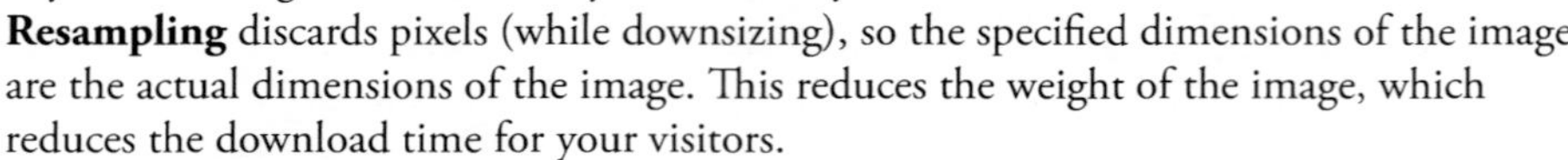

   Instead of simply resizing, you should also resample any resized images to include only the necessary data. **Resampling** discards pixels (while downsizing), so the specified dimensions of the image are the actual dimensions of the image. This reduces the weight of the image, which reduces the download time for your visitors.

   In the next few steps, you are going to resample the image that you placed into the index.html page. However, you should understand that resampling in Dreamweaver permanently changes the image file. Before you make this type of change permanent, it is a good idea to create a copy of the image file, so you can still access the original file if necessary.

8. **In the Files panel, click the original `crowe-photography.png` file once to select it, then click the file name again to highlight the file name.**

   Make sure you don't rename the one that has "Copy" in the file name; that file is the original-size logo. You want to rename the image file that you placed into the header and decreased to a smaller physical size.

9. **At the end of the current file name, type `-small`, then press Return/Enter to finalize the new file name.**

   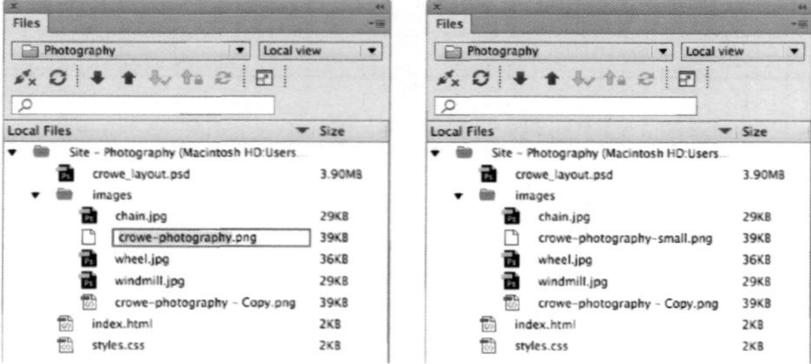

10. **In the resulting dialog box, click Update to update the link in index.html to the new file name.**

    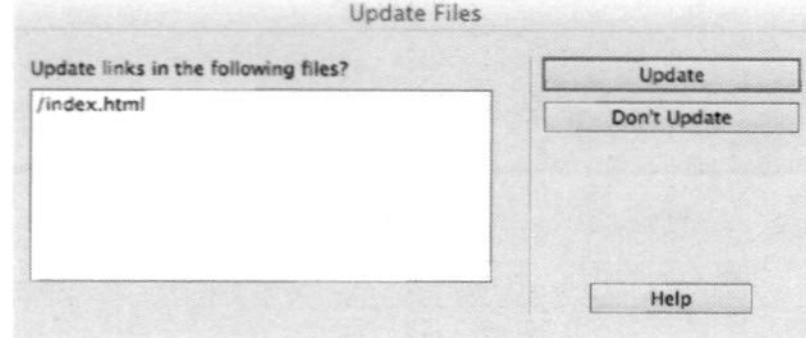

11. **With the image selected on the page, click the Commit Image Size button to the right of the W and H fields.**

> ***Note:***
>
> *You could also click the Resample button to accomplish the same effect.*

12. **Click OK to acknowledge the warning.**

As we explained earlier, resampling in Dreamweaver permanently changes the image file; the resized dimensions become its (new) actual size. After resampling, the Reset to Original Size button is no longer visible, and the Resample button is not available.

The action you are about to perform will permanently alter the selected image. You can undo any changes you make by selecting Edit > Undo.

> ***Note:***
>
> *If another user clicked the "Don't show me this message again" option, you won't see this warning.*

Also note the file size of the resampled image; it was originally 39 KB, and now (after resizing and resampling) it's around 23 KB.

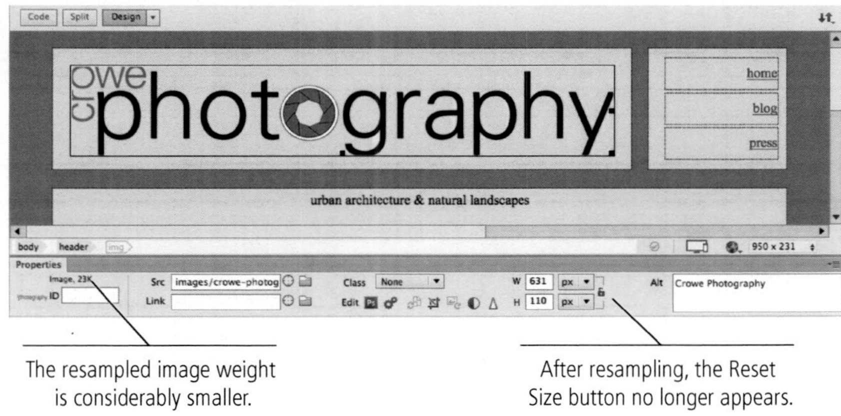

The resampled image weight is considerably smaller.
After resampling, the Reset Size button no longer appears.

13. **Save the file and continue to the next stage of the project.**

The Image Properties Panel in Depth

When an image is selected in the document window, the Properties panel not only displays properties (attributes) of the image, but also provides access to a number of image-related functions.

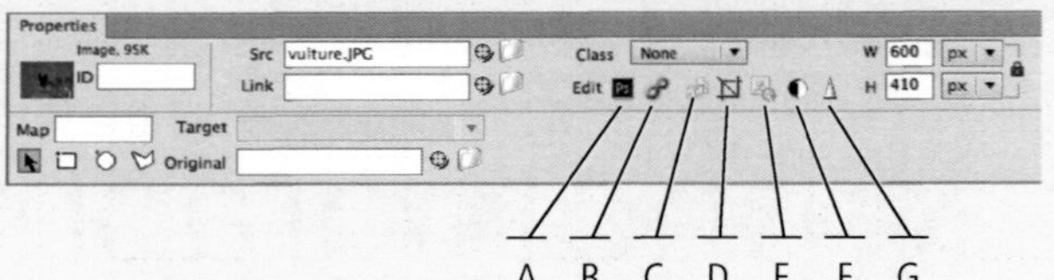

A. Edit opens the image file in its native application. GIF and JPG files open in Photoshop; PNG files open in Fireworks (assuming you have those applications).

B. Edit Image Settings opens a dialog box where you can change a variety of options for the selected file format. You can also use the Format menu to change the format of the selected image; if you change the format, you will be asked where you want to save the new file.

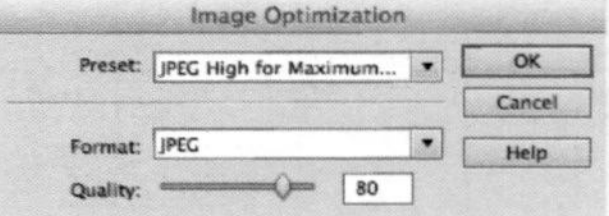

C. Update From Original can be used to make sure an inserted Photoshop image in the HTML file is the most recently saved version of the image.

If you insert a native Photoshop (PSD) file into a page, Dreamweaver converts it to a file that is appropriate for Web browsers; the Edit Image Settings dialog box automatically appears, so you can define the settings for the generated image.

The original link to the PSD file is also maintained; if the PSD file is changed, Dreamweaver notifies you that the image must be updated to the most recent version.

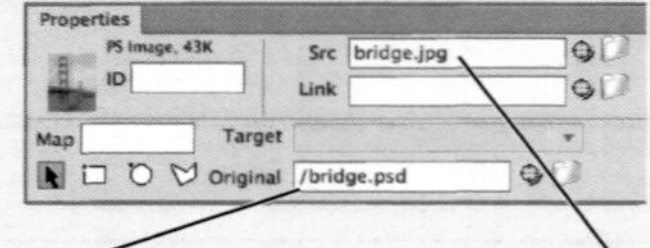

When you place a native Photoshop file, Dreamweaver stores a link to the original file.

The actual image in the page is converted to a Web-friendly format.

An icon appears in the top-left corner of a placed Photoshop file. Moving your mouse over the icon shows whether the image reflects the most-recently saved version of the Photoshop file.

Although Dreamweaver is not an image-editing application, you can use it to perform some basic image-editing functions. These tools can't replace Adobe Photoshop, but they are well suited for making quick adjustments to an image from directly within the Dreamweaver application.

D. The **Crop tool** can be used to remove unwanted areas of an image. When you click the Crop tool, the lighter area shows the area that will be included in the cropped image; you can drag any of the eight handles around the edge of the crop area to change the area. Pressing Return/Enter finalizes the crop; pressing ESC cancels the crop and restores the original image.

Drag any of the handles to change the area that will be included in the cropped version.

The lighter area shows what will remain after the crop has been applied.

E. The **Resample tool** changes the number of pixels in an image to exactly match the size of the selected instance in the page. This has the same effect as clicking the Commit Image Size button after resizing an image in the Design pane.

F. Brightness and Contrast can be used to change those properties in a selected image.

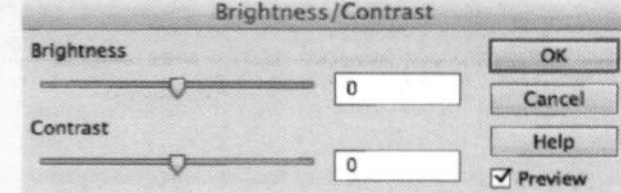

G. The **Sharpen** option can be useful for restoring some detail after resizing/resampling (especially upsizing). Keep in mind, however, that oversharpening can often produce worse results than what you start with.

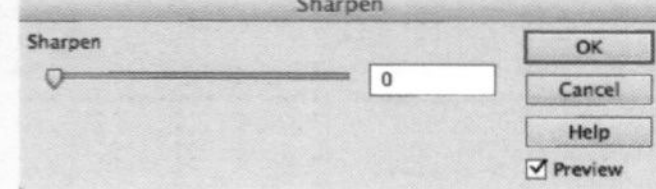

Remember: All of the Dreamweaver image-editing tools permanently modify the edited file. If you use any of the image-editing buttons, you see a warning that the changes permanently affect the file (unless someone has checked the Don't Show ... option in the dialog box). Always keep a backup image, so if you over-edit, you can replace the backup image and start over.

Stage 2 Extracting Photoshop Assets

The "look and feel" of a Web site is often created in an image-editing application such as Adobe Photoshop, while the structure and code are created in Dreamweaver. Using the Extract tools that are part of an individual-user subscription to the Adobe Creative Cloud, integrating assets that are defined in Photoshop is now far easier than ever before.

Verify your Adobe ID in Dreamweaver

In the next exercise you are going to use the Extract tools that are part of your Adobe Creative Cloud subscription services. For that process to work, you must have an active internet connection and be signed in to your Creative Cloud account in Dreamweaver.

Important note: For the Extract functions to work properly, your user ID must be associated with a paid individual-user Creative Cloud subscription account. This service is not available if you have only a free Adobe ID, and is not available if you are using a computer that has a device license instead of an individual-user license.

In this exercise, you will verify that you are signed in to your Adobe Creative Cloud account.

1. **In Dreamweaver, open the Help menu.**
2. **If you see an option to Sign In, skip to Step 5.**

3. **If you see an option to Sign Out, verify that the listed email is the Adobe ID linked to your Creative Cloud account.**

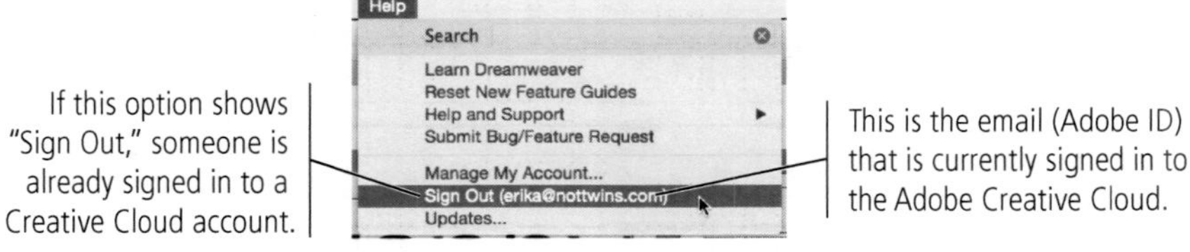

If this option shows "Sign Out," someone is already signed in to a Creative Cloud account.
Help
Search
Learn Dreamweaver
Reset New Feature Guides
Help and Support
Submit Bug/Feature Request
Manage My Account...
Sign Out (erika@nottwins.com)
Updates...
This is the email (Adobe ID) that is currently signed in to the Adobe Creative Cloud.

4a. **If the email address listed in the Help menu is yours, continue to the next exercise.**

4b. **If the email in the menu is not yours, choose the Sign Out option. Read the resulting message and then click Sign Out.**

If you sign out of any Adobe CC application, this message informs you that you are also signing out of *all* Adobe CC applications.

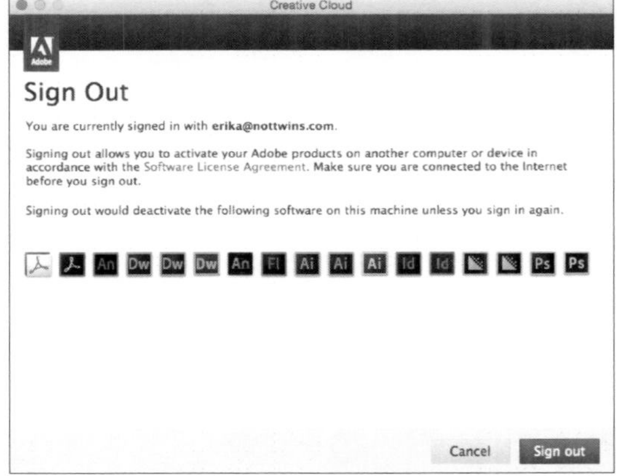

5. **In Dreamweaver, choose Help>Sign In.**

6. **Read the message in the resulting dialog box, then click Sign In Now.**

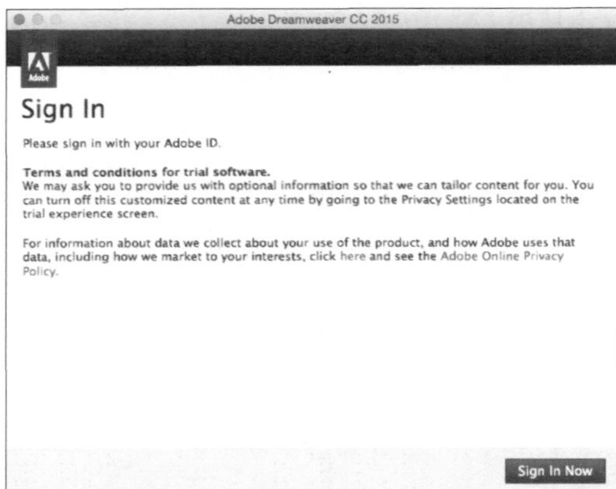

7. **In the Sign In screen, enter your Adobe ID and password, then click Sign In.**

8. **Read the message in the final screen, then click Continue.**

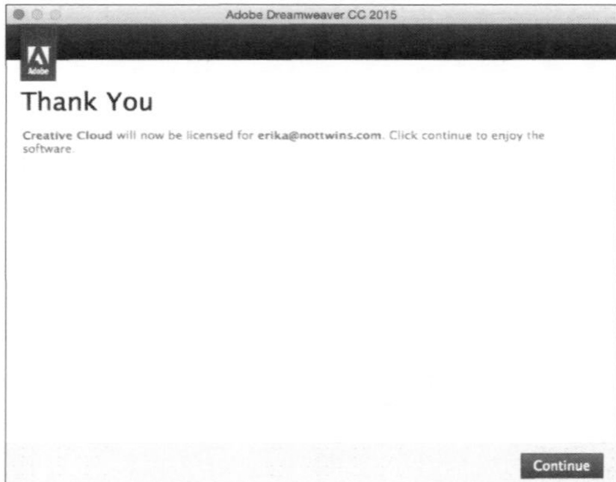

9. **Continue to the next exercise.**

Load a Photoshop File into your Creative Cloud Account

The structure of this Web page, which you saw as gray rectangles when you first opened the index.html page, was defined in Dreamweaver using CSS. The overall design, however, was created in an Adobe Photoshop file that was provided with the resource files for this project. In this exercise you, will upload the provided Photoshop file to your Creative Cloud account so that you can extract the assets that are defined in that file.

1. **With the Photography site open in the Files panel, open the file `index.html` if it is not already open**

   A file must be open in Dreamweaver before you can access the Extract panel functionality.

2. **Using the Document toolbar, activate the Live view and hide the Code pane (if necessary).**

3. **Open the Workspace switcher in the Application/Menu bar and choose Extract.**

4. **Open the Workspace switcher again and choose Reset 'Extract'.**

   The default Extract workspace places the Extract panel on the left side of the screen. Other panels — including the Files and CSS Designer panels — are available in an iconized dock column on the right side of the screen.

   Throughout the rest of this project (and in the rest of this book), we tell you what panels to use at various points. Our screen captures show only the panels most relevant to the immediate discussion. Feel free to arrange the workspace in any way that best suits your working environment.

   The Creative Cloud Extract service offers an in-app method for accessing the images, text, colors, and styles that have been created in a Photoshop file directly in Dreamweaver — which makes it relatively easy to translate a designer's vision into a functioning Web page.

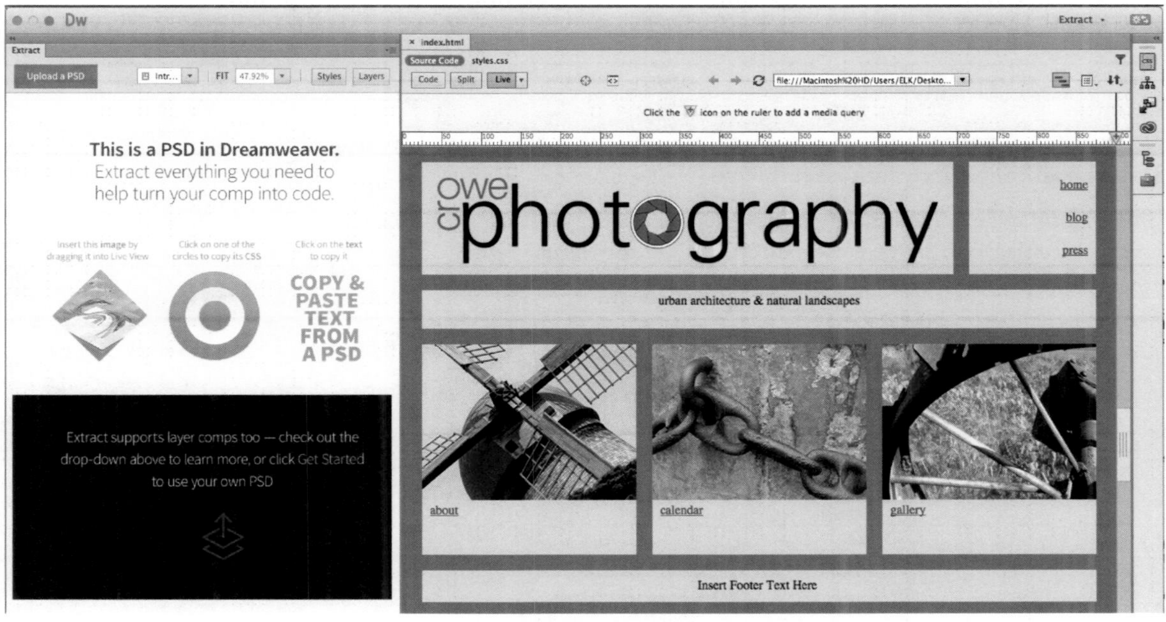

5. **Click the Upload a PSD button at the top of the Extract panel.**

6. **In the resulting navigation dialog box, navigate to the `crowe-layout.psd` file in your WIP>Crowe folder.**

   This file was created by another designer. It includes the images and text that you need to complete the Crowe Photography home page. It also shows the formatting that should be used for various elements, such as the applied font and type sizes, element backgrounds, and colors.

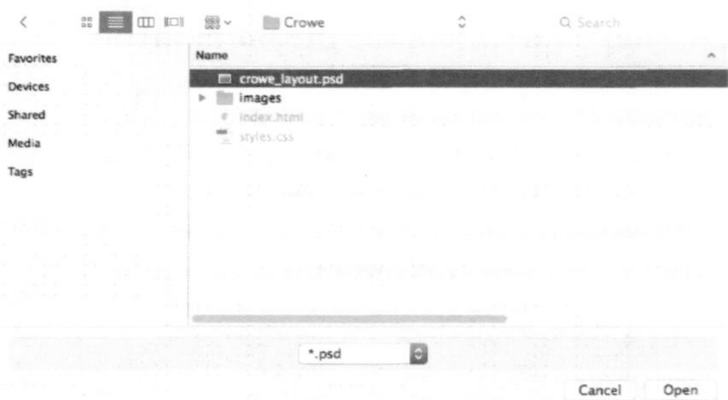

7. **Click Open.**

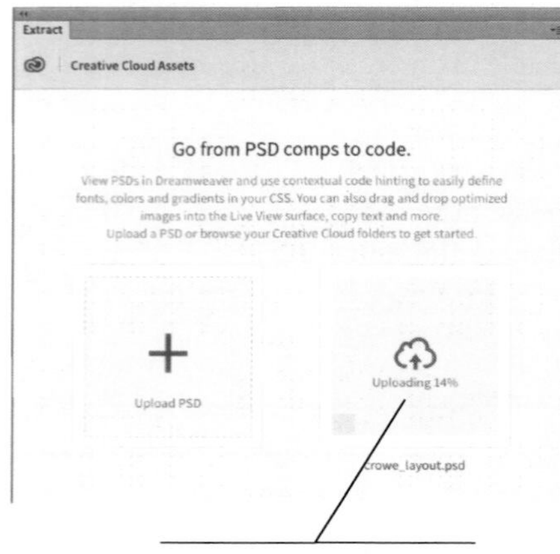

The new thumbnail shows the progress of the upload.

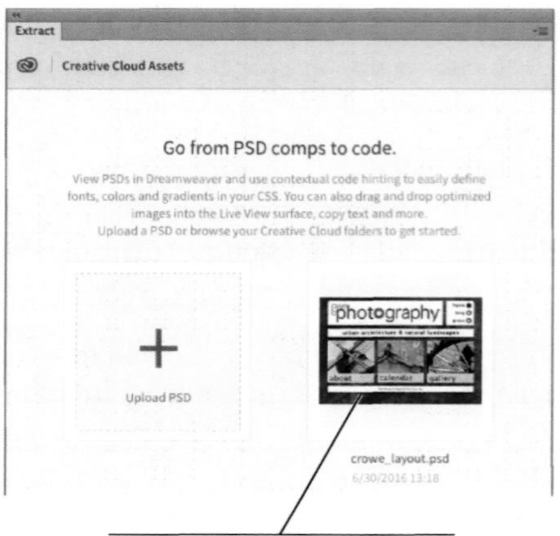

When the upload is complete, a thumbnail of the file appears.

Note:

Files that you upload are stored in your Creative Cloud account; you can manage those files using the Assets>Files tab of the Adobe Creative Cloud app.

8. **When the upload process is complete, double-click the crowe-layout.psd thumbnail in the Extract panel.**

   This opens the file in the Extract panel, which means you can now access the various file assets — images, type styles, etc. — directly in Dreamweaver.

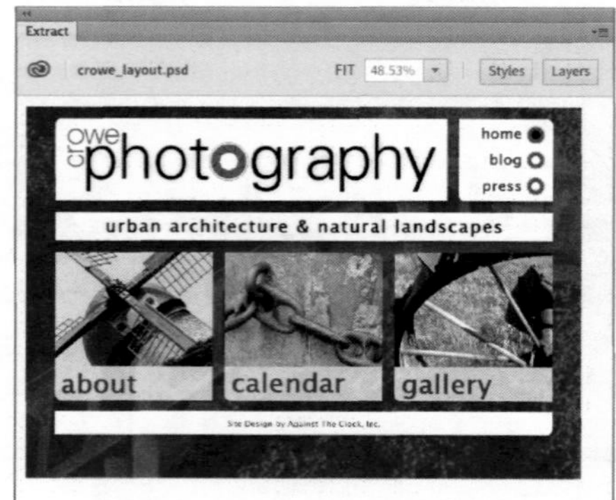

Note:

You can click the Creative Cloud icon in the top-left corner of the panel to return to the list of uploaded files.

9. **Continue to the next exercise.**

Extract Text and Images from a Photoshop File

The Photoshop file that you uploaded in the previous exercise defines the appearance and content of the various elements in the HTML page. In this exercise you will extract content that will be required to complete the Web page design in Dreamweaver.

1. **With index.html open from the Photography site, make sure the Live view is active.**

2. **With the Photoshop file that you uploaded in the previous exercise open in the Extract panel, expand the panel as large as possible so you can clearly see the elements in the file.**

3. **Move your mouse cursor different areas of the preview.**

   In the Extract panel, a black border identifies distinct elements (layer content) in the Photoshop file. As you move your mouse cursor over various parts of the preview, you can see which element would be selected if you click.

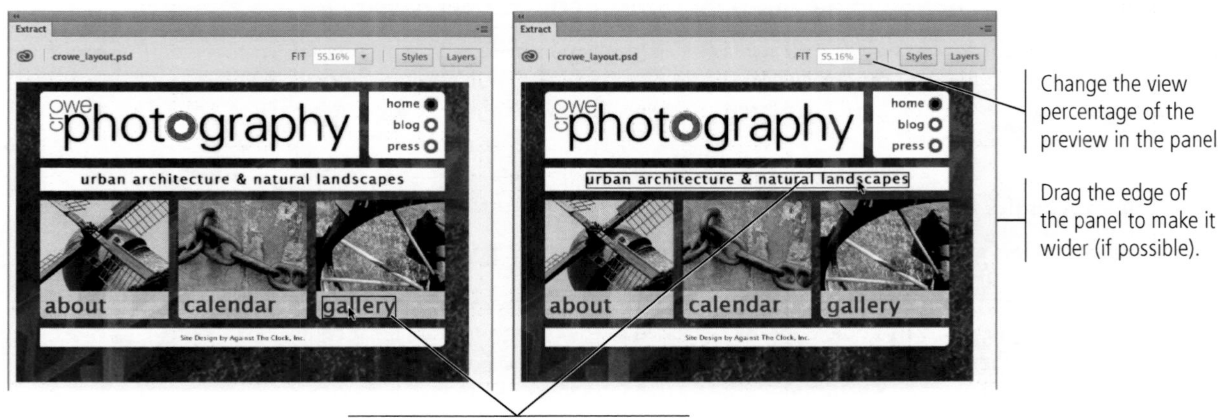

Drag the edge of the panel to make it wider (if possible).

4. **Click the text element in the bottom row of the preview to select it.**

   When you select a specific element in the panel preview, a pop-up window presents options that can be extracted for the selected element.

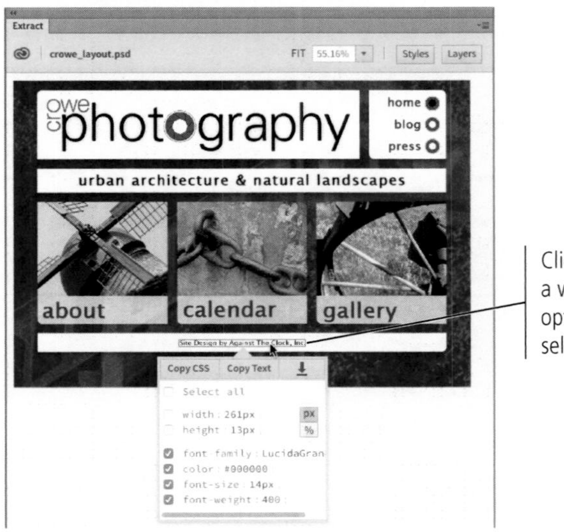

Click an item to open a window with extract options for the selected layer content.

5. **Click the Copy Text button in the pop-up window.**

> ***Note:***
>
> *Feel free to dock or float panels however you prefer as you work through the projects in this book.*

6. **Select and delete the words "Insert Footer Text Here" from the bottom rectangle in the layout.**

Delete the placeholder text from this area.

7. **With the insertion point in the now-empty paragraph, choose Edit>Paste (or press Command/Control-V).**

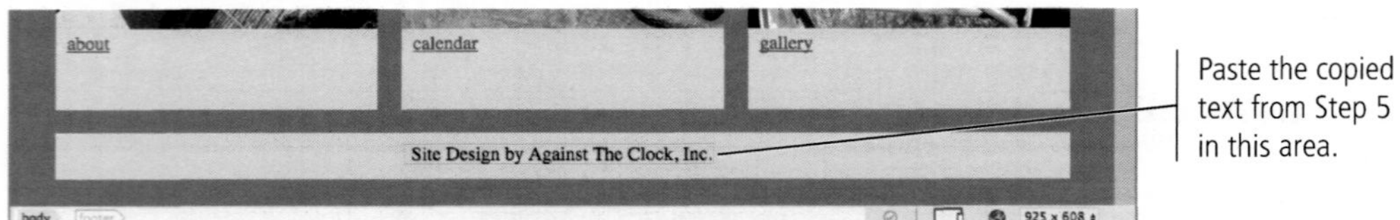

Paste the copied text from Step 5 in this area.

8. **Click the Layers button in the top-right corner of the Extract panel.**

   These buttons allow you to review all the layers and layer groups that have been saved in the Photoshop file. You can expand layer groups to review the sublayers in those groups, show or hide individual layers, and select specific layers to more easily extract the information they contain.

9. **Click the stairs layer in the list to select it.**

   When you select a layer, the available extract options appear in a pop-up window (just as when you selected a specific element in the preview image).

   As the preview suggests, this image should be added as the background image for the entire page. Rather than copying the image's dimensions, you are going to extract the image from the Photoshop file into the site's images folder so you can use the image directly in Dreamweaver.

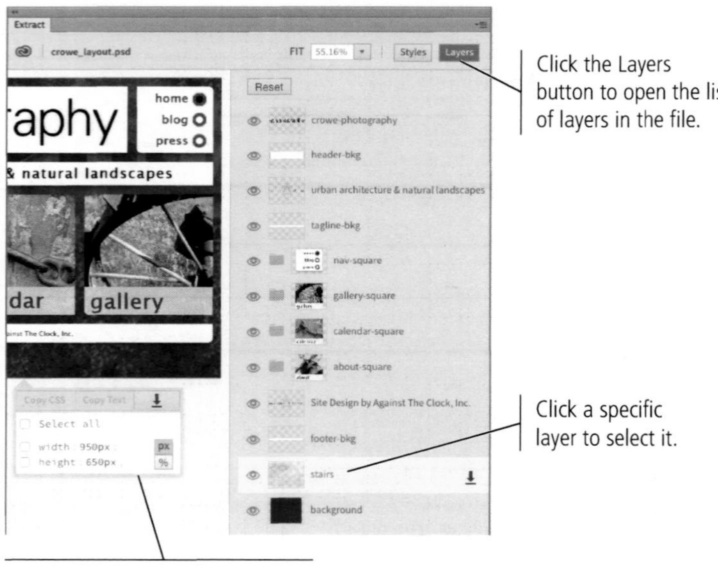

Click the Layers button to open the list of layers in the file.

Click a specific layer to select it.

The pop-up window identifies the selected layer content and presents extract options for that content.

10. **Click the Extract Asset button either on the layer list or on the pop-up window.**

11. **In the resulting pop-up window, click the Browse for Folder button to the right of the Folder field. Navigate to the images folder in your WIP>Crowe folder, then click Open/Select Folder.**

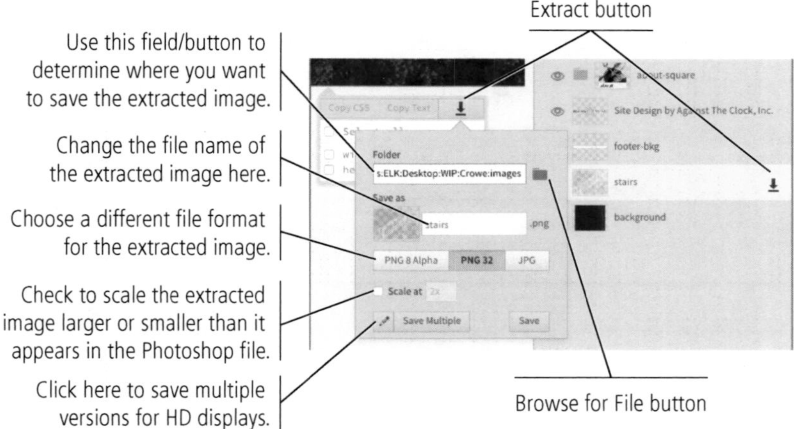

Extract button
Use this field/button to determine where you want to save the extracted image.

Click here to save multiple versions for HD displays.

12. **Make sure the PNG 32 button is active, then click Save.**

    This layer is semi-transparent, allowing the background layer color to show through the image pixels. To incorporate that transparency into the extracted image, you must use the PNG 32 format (the default format).

    When the Extract process is complete, you see a message that the asset has downloaded successfully.

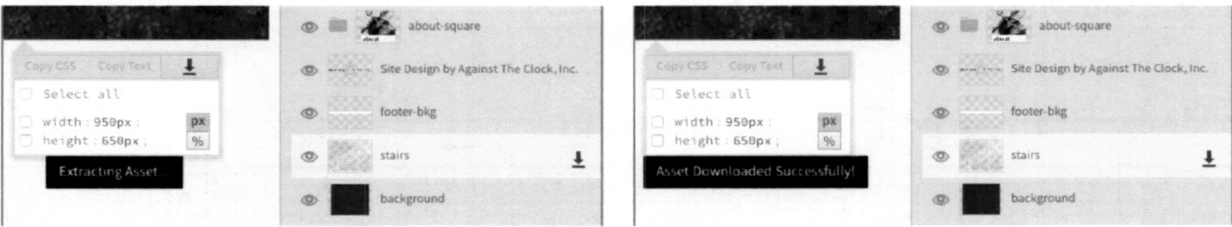

13. **Click the folder icon to the left of the nav-square layer to expand that layer.**

    The layer group includes three image layers, one for each item in the list. The "open" icon should be the default image for each navigation link; the "closed" icon should appear when the user's mouse moves over that link. For now you need to extract the required images so you can later use CSS to define the link backgrounds and change the image from "open" to "closed" when the user's mouse cursor moves over a specific link.

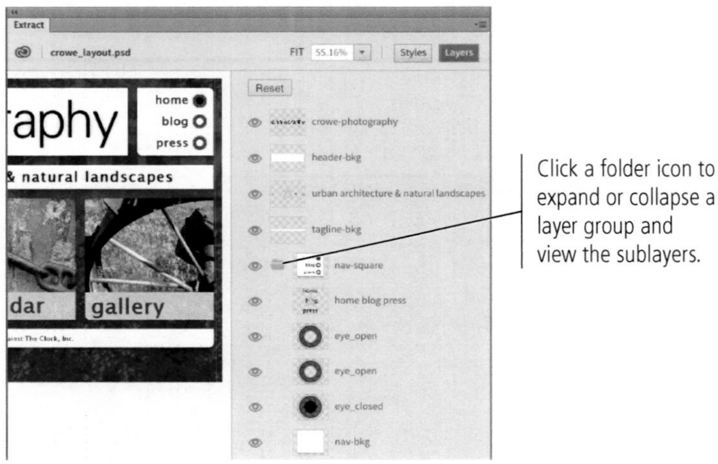

Click a folder icon to expand or collapse a layer group and view the sublayers.

14. **Repeat Steps 9–12 to extract the eye-open and eye-closed images as PNG 32 files into the site images folder.**

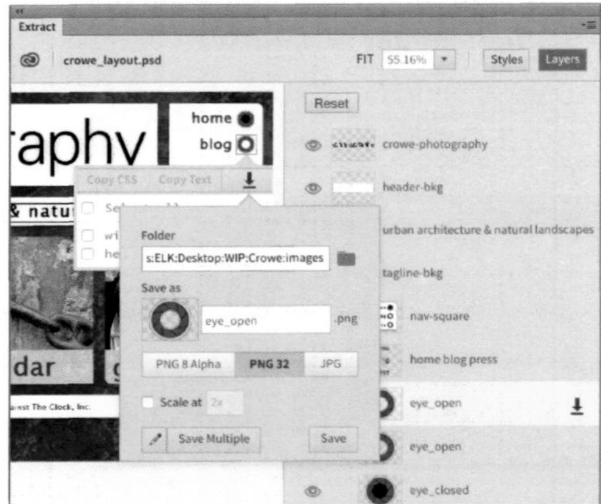

Note:

The Layers list floats over the image preview in the Extract panel. You should make the panel as wide as possible so you can see both the preview and the layers list.

15. **In the Files panel, expand the images folder. If you don't see the three extracted files, click the Refresh button at the top of the panel.**

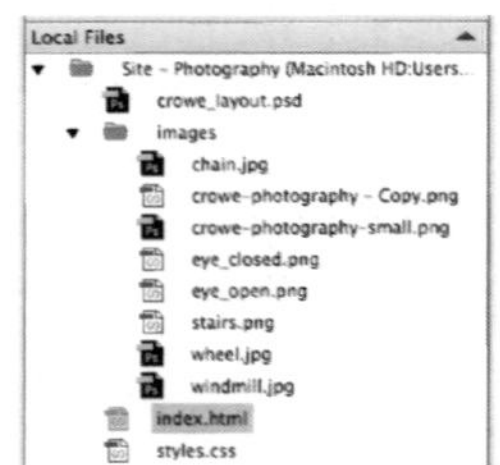

Note:

You can also drag an image from the Extract panel to the document window. When you release the mouse button, the file is extracted using the default settings and the image is placed at the location to which you drag.

16. **Save the HTML file and continue to the next exercise.**

Format the Page Body with Extracted Assets

In the previous exercise you extracted text from a Photoshop file and placed it into your HTML page. You also extracted images from a Photoshop file, one which you will use in this exercise to define the appearance of the overall page background. (You will use the other images later to create different states for the links at the top of the page.)

1. **With index.html open, click the Crowe Photography logo in the top-left rectangle on the page.**

2. **Review the Tag Selector in the bottom-left corner of the document window.**

   The Tag Selector shows the "path of tags", or the nested order of tags to the active selection.

<body>	identifies the basic page, where all visible content is contained
<header>	identifies the HTML header element
<img>	identifies the placed image.

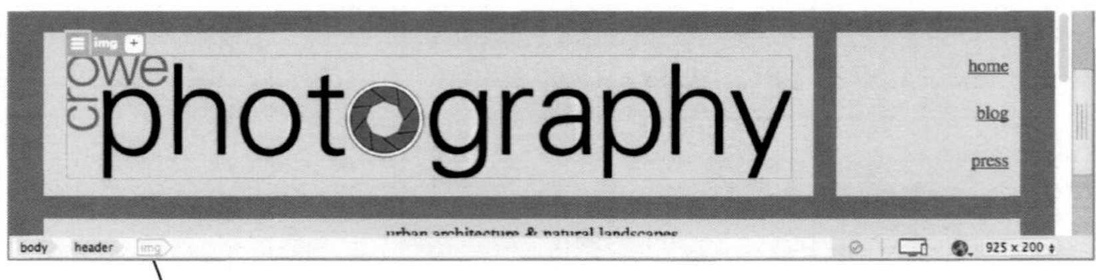

The Tag Selector shows that this img element is in the header element, which is inside the body element.

3. **Open the CSS Designer panel (Window>CSS Designer).**

The CSS Designer panel is divided into four sections:

- **Sources** lists the locations and files containing CSS styles that affect the active site.
- **@Media** lists media queries, which can be used to define different styles depending on the size of the device being used to display a site.
- **Selectors** are the items that define the properties of specific elements. If you have an object selected in the Design pane, only selectors related to the active selection appear in the list. When a specific selector is active in the panel, the relevant Source and Media options appear bold in those sections of the panel.
- **Properties** are the rules that define the specific appearance of the selector for which they are defined.

You can click and drag the lines between sections in the panel to expand a specific section. Clicking a section heading minimizes that section, so only the heading is visible in the panel; you can click a minimized section heading to re-expand that section. (The + and – buttons on the left side of each section heading are used to add or remove items from the panel; these buttons do not collapse or expand the various section.)

If you expand the width of the CSS Designer panel far enough, the Properties section moves to the right, creating a second column within the panel.

4. **If necessary, click the All button at the top of the panel.**

The CSS Designer panel defaults to Current mode, in which the panel show only selectors related to the element that is selected in the document window. If you click the All button at the top of the panel, all selectors in the CSS file appear in the Selectors list.

5. **Click the body selector in the Selectors section of the panel.**

Selectors beginning with a # character are **ID selectors**. These apply only to the element that is identified with the matching **ID attribute**. It is important to realize that an ID can only apply to a single element on the page.

Selectors beginning with a . (period) character are **class selectors**. These apply to any element that has the matching class attribute. A single **class attribute** can be applied to multiple elements on the same page, which means you can define the same properties for various elements at the same time.

In the following example, three section elements have a defined ID attribute and a defined class attribute. The ID attribute for each section is unique, but the same class has been applied to all three.

<section id="row3a" class="square-link">content here</section>

<section id="row3b" class="square-link">content here</section>

<section id="row3c" class="square-link">content here</section>

Selectors that do not begin with a # or . character are HTML **tag selectors**. These apply to the specific HTML elements that match the selector name. For example, the section selector applies to all section elements on the page, regardless of any applied ID or class attributes. The section element is enclosed in the opening and closing **<section></section>** tags.

The body selector applies to the body element (the overall page background), which is enclosed in the opening and closing **<body></body>** tags. All visible elements are contained within the body element.

Note:

For the sake of readability, we identify selector names in red in the exercise steps.

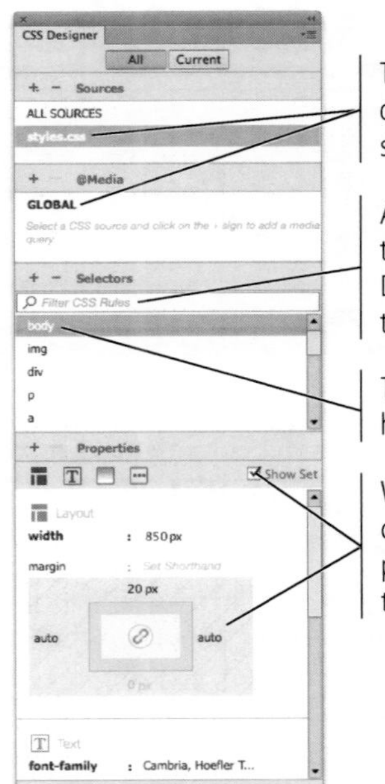

The source and media query of the active selector appear in **bold**.

All selectors related to the active selection in the Design pane are listed in the Selectors section.

The active selector is highlighted in the list.

When Show Set is checked, only defined properties appear in the Properties section.

5. **In the Properties section of the panel, uncheck the Show Set option.**

   When the Show Set option is checked in the Properties section of the panel, only defined properties appear in the Properties pane. If this option is not checked, all available properties are listed; properties that appear grayed out are not defined for the active selector.

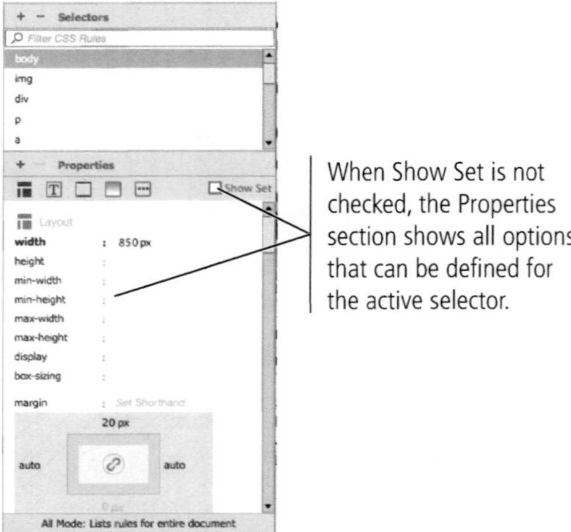

When Show Set is not checked, the Properties section shows all options that can be defined for the active selector.

6. **With the Photoshop file that you uploaded open in the Extract panel, click the Styles button in the top-right corner of the Extract panel.**

   The Styles list shows all fonts, colors, and gradients that are used in the Photoshop file.

7. **Click the blue swatch in the Colors section of the list, and note the color value in the pop-up window.**

   When you select a specific element in the Styles list, arrows in the preview image identify which elements use the selected color. The color definition appears highlighted in a pop-up window.

Click the Styles button to show the fonts, colors and gradients that are used in the Photoshop file.

Click a color swatch to show the color definition.

Arrows in the preview identify the elements that use the selected color.

8. **With the body selector selected in the CSS Designer panel, click the Background button at the top of the Properties section.**

   When Show Set is not checked, the Properties section includes a large number of options that can be defined for the active selector. You can simply scroll through all of the available options, or you can use these buttons to quickly jump to specific categories of properties.

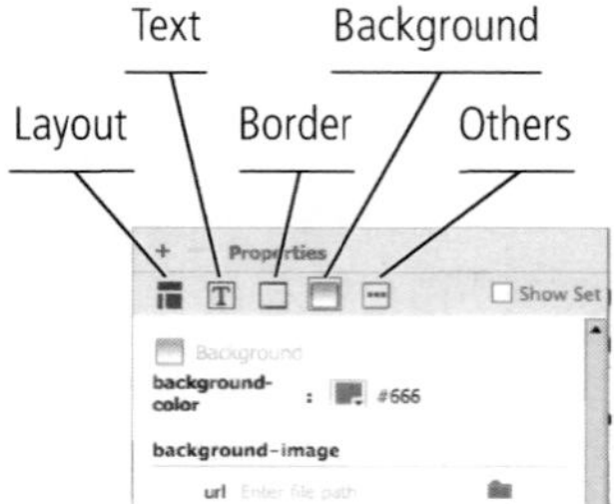

9. **Click the existing background-color value to highlight it, then type `rgb(0, 67, 102)` — the value you noted in Step 7 — as the new color.**

You might be able to copy and paste the color value from the pop-up window in Step 7 to the CSS Designer panel in Step 9. However, there is a bug in the software that prevents users on certain operating systems from using the copy-and-paste method.

Click the existing value to highlight it.

Type the value noted from the Extract panel as the new background-color value.

10. **Press Return/Enter to finalize the new background-color value.**

11. **In the CSS Designer panel, click to the right of the url option to highlight that field and then click the attached Browse button.**

The CSS Designer panel provides available properties whenever possible. In this case, you have to define a file, so you are presented with a text field and a Browse button, which you can use to define the image you want to use as the background.

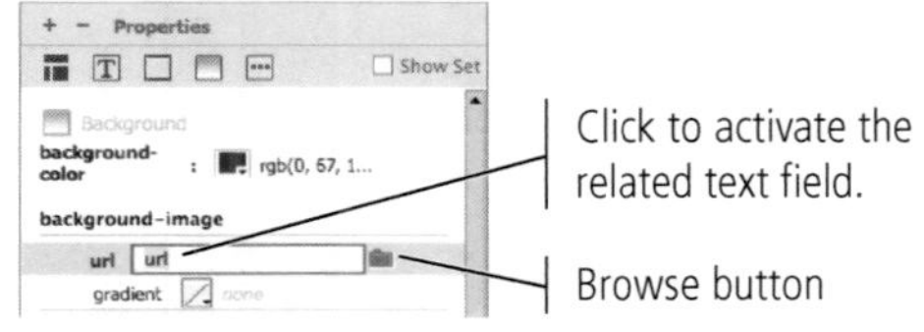

Click to activate the related text field.

Browse button

Note:

You might have to perform this step twice to open the navigation dialog box due to an apparent bug in the software.

12. Navigate to the Photography site images folder, select stairs.png, and click Open/OK.

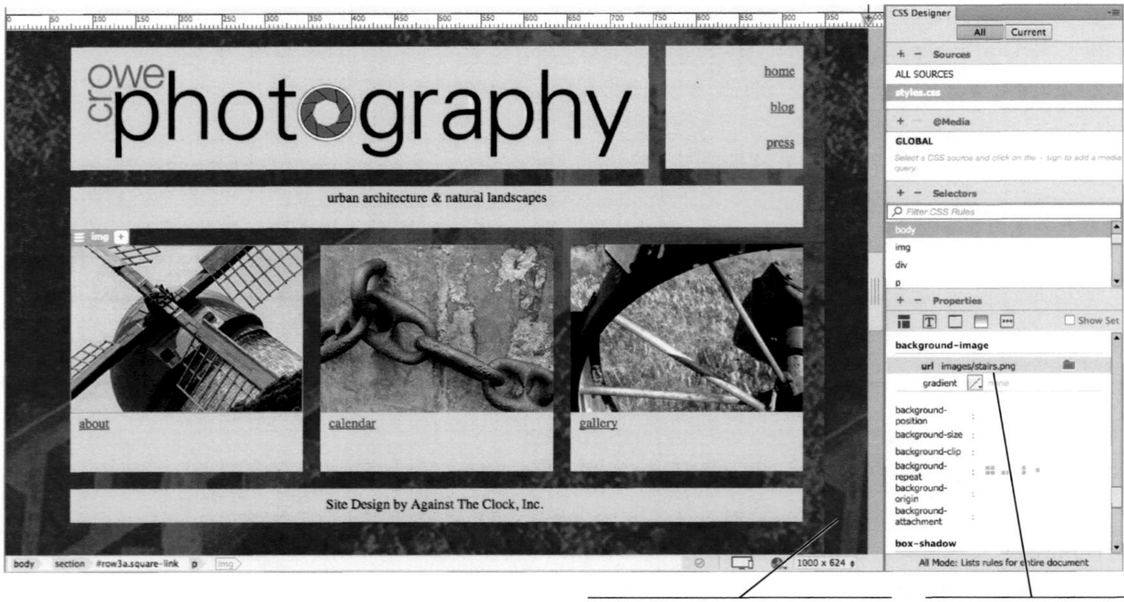

By default, background images tile both horizontally and vertically.

The defined value now appears in the panel.

13. Click the no-repeat button for the background-repeat option.

Unless you specify otherwise, a background image will repeat (tile) across and down until the background of the element is completely filled with the background image.

The CSS **background-repeat** property has four options: repeat (the default), repeat-x (horizontally only), repeat-y (vertically only), and no-repeat (the background image appears only once in the top-left corner of the element).

Again, the panel provides the available options; the button icons suggest the values that will be defined.

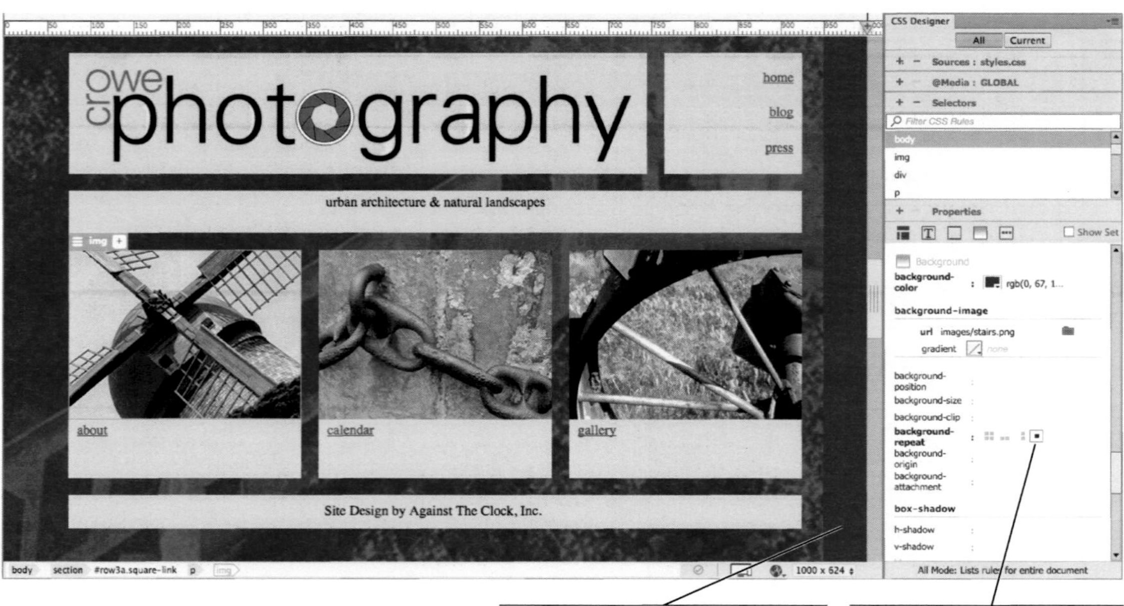

Using the no-repeat option, the background image appears only once.

The background-repeat options are available as buttons.

14. **Click the background-size value, and choose cover from the pop-up menu.**

In this case, the panel offers a menu with the available values for this property.

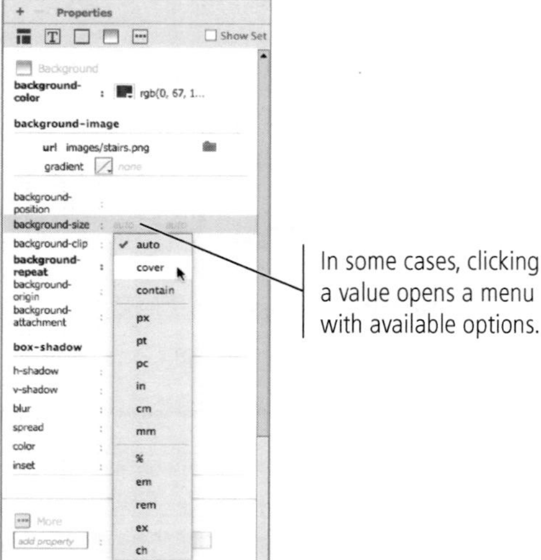

In some cases, clicking a value opens a menu with available options.

Using the cover value for the **background-size** property, the image will enlarge or shrink to fill the available window width.

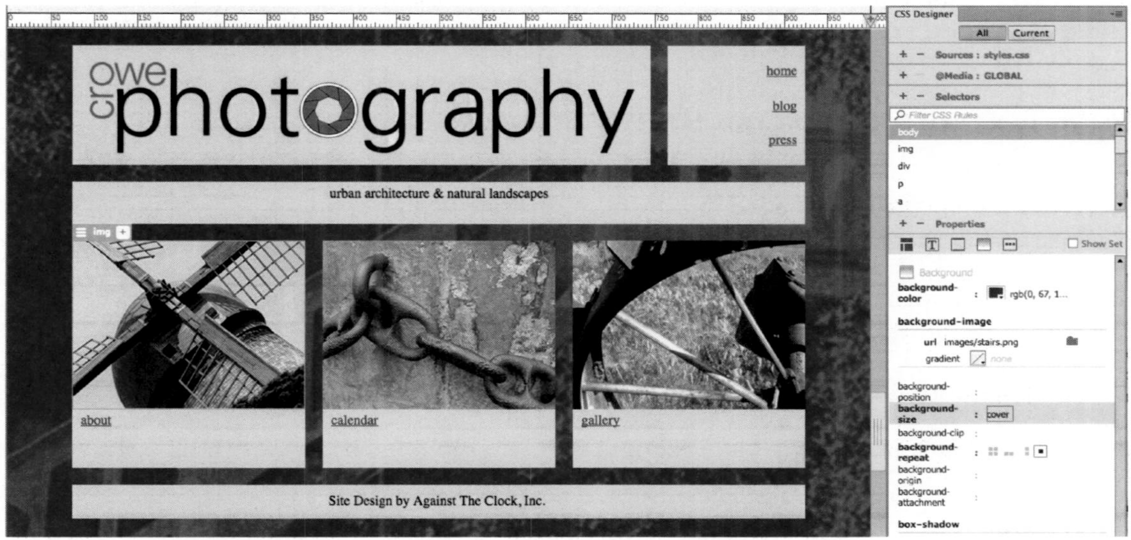

15. **Look at the top of the document window.**

Although you made changes that affect the appearance of the index.html file, the document tab does not show an asterisk — in other words, the HTML document has not been changed. You do not need to save it before continuing.

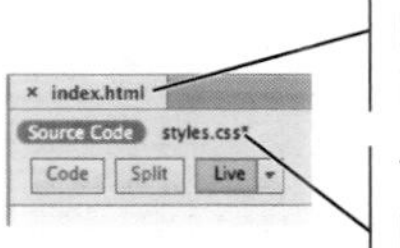

The index.html file has not been changed in this exercise.

The styles.css file has been changed in this exercise.

All changes in this exercise were made to the CSS file that is linked to the open HTML file. The Related Files bar below the document tab shows an asterisk next to styles.css, indicating that the CSS file has been changed and so should be saved.

16. **Click styles.css in the Related Files bar, then choose File>Save.**

    When you click one of the related files in the bar, the document window automatically switches to Split view and the file you clicked is displayed in the Code pane.

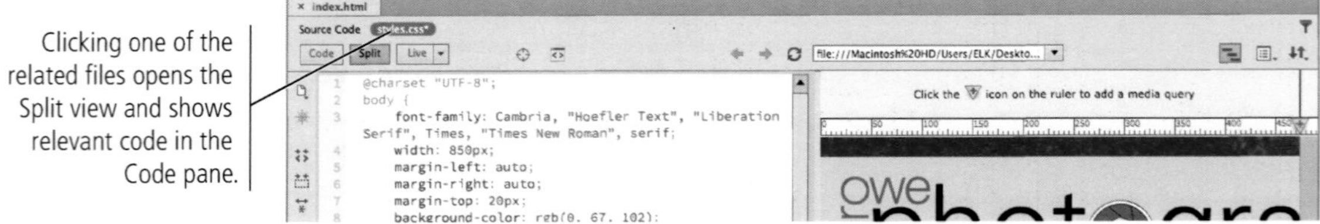

17. **Click Source Code in the Related Files bar to return to the main HTML file.**

    Clicking the Source Code button restores the active page's HTML code to the Code pane.

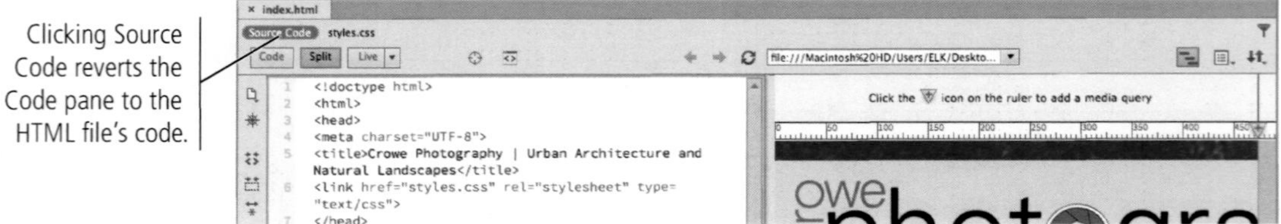

Clicking Source Code reverts the Code pane to the HTML file's code.

18. **Click the Live button in the Document toolbar to close the Code pane, then continue to the next exercise.**

 Format Text with Extracted Styles

In the previous exercise you copied the actual text that was created in a Photoshop file. In this exercise you will use the Extract panel to copy the formatting that is applied to text in various parts of the design.

1. **With `index.html` open, make sure the Photoshop file you uploaded is open in the Extract panel.**

2. **Click the Styles button in the Extract panel to show the list of available styles.**

3. **Expand the LucidaGrande font.**

   This list shows that only one font is used in the design, although every font size is listed separately. You are going to change the font property in the body tag selector to effectively change the font that is applied in all nested elements.

4. **Click the 14px option to show where that type size is used in the design.**

   When you select a specific font size in the list, you see the font-family and font-weight properties that apply to the selected size.

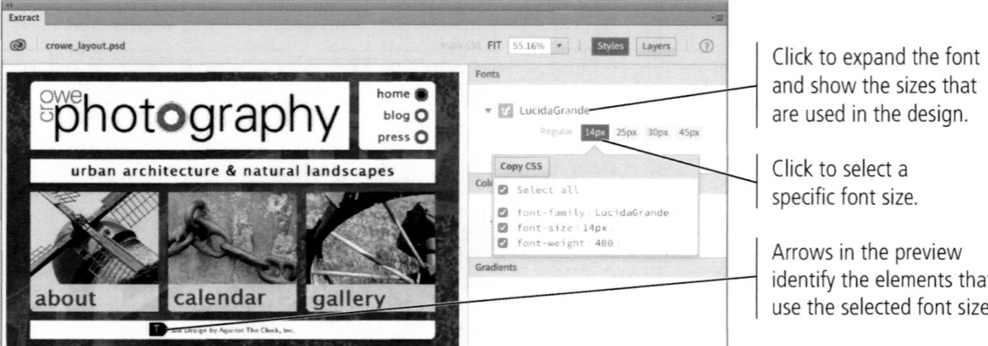

5. **Click the Copy CSS button in the pop-up window.**

6. **Control/right-click the body selector in the CSS Designer panel and choose Paste Styles in the contextual menu.**

Because every visible element on the page is contained within the HTML body element, text in every element now adopts the new type properties (font-family, font-size, and font-weight).

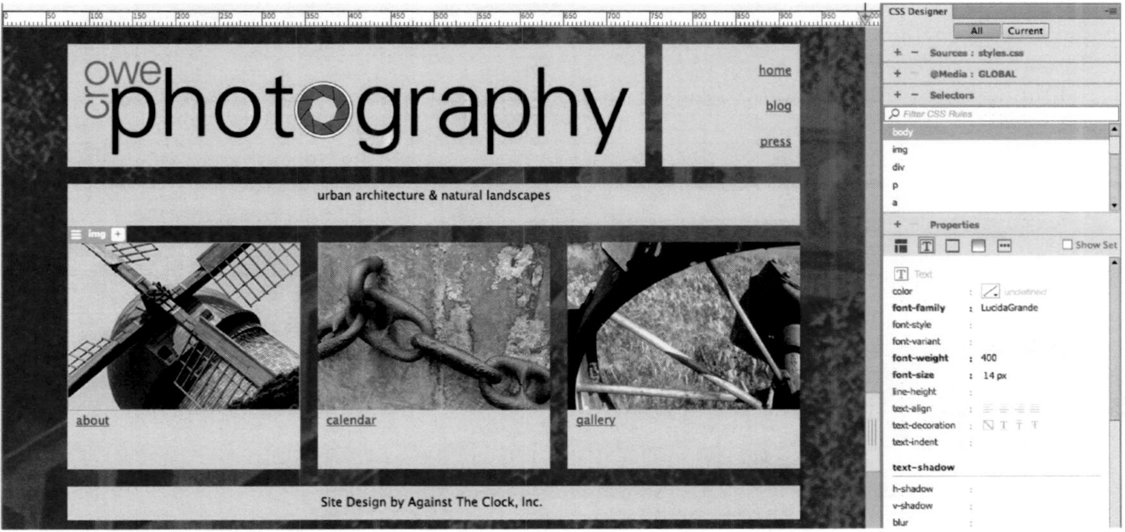

If you are using a Windows computer, you should notice that the font does not change. The Lucida Grande font is default font on the Macintosh operating system; on Windows, the Lucida font family has slightly different names, so Windows computers can't display the exact font that is defined in the body selector's font-family property.

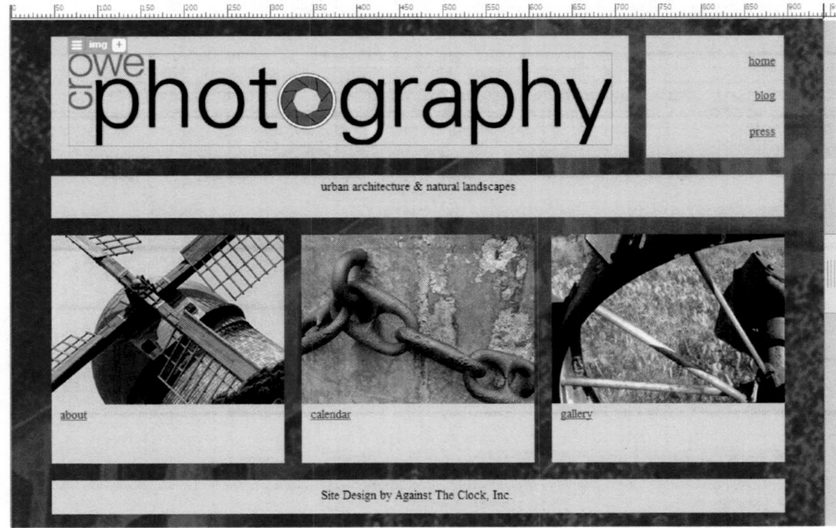

Note:

Some Macintosh users might also notice this issue if certain fonts have been removed from your default operating system configuration.

7. **With the body selector active in the CSS Designer panel, click the Text button at the top of the Properties section to show those properties in the panel.**

8. **Click the existing font-family value to open the menu of available font stacks. Choose the option that begins with Lucida Grande and ends with "sans-serif".**

   A **font stack** (also called a **font family**) is a sequence of fonts that can be used to display content. When a browser opens a page, it goes through the various fonts in the list until it finds one that can be used on the active device. If none of the fonts in the list area available on a user's computer, the text will be displayed in the default font that is defined for the style at the end of the list — in this case, whatever the user chose as the default sans-serif font on the computer being used to display the page.

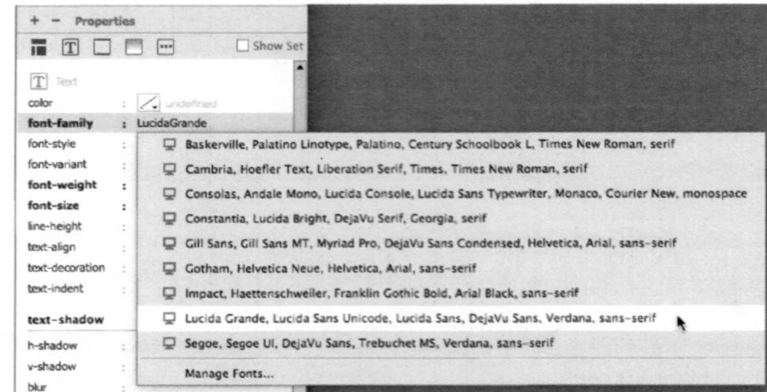

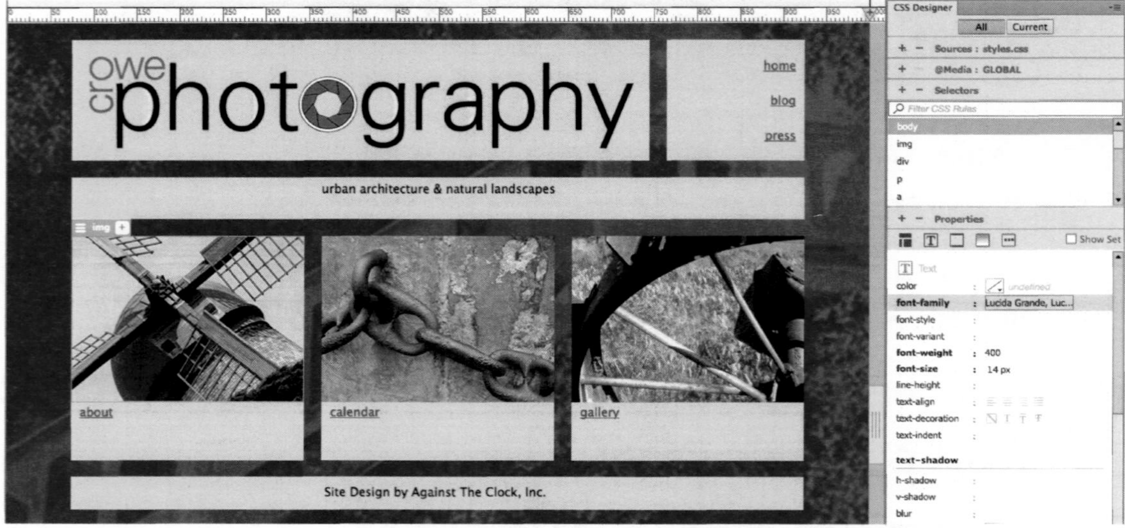

9. **In the document window, click the tagline text to select that element. Review the Tag Selector at the bottom of the document window.**

   This paragraph exists in a section element with the ID attribute of "tagline". If you apply the copied font size to the section tag selector in the CSS Designer panel, the change would apply to all text in any section element on the page. Instead, you want the new font-size property to apply only to text in this element, so you will edit the ID selector that applies to this specific section element.

> ***Note:***
>
> *You will format the navigation links in a later exercise.*

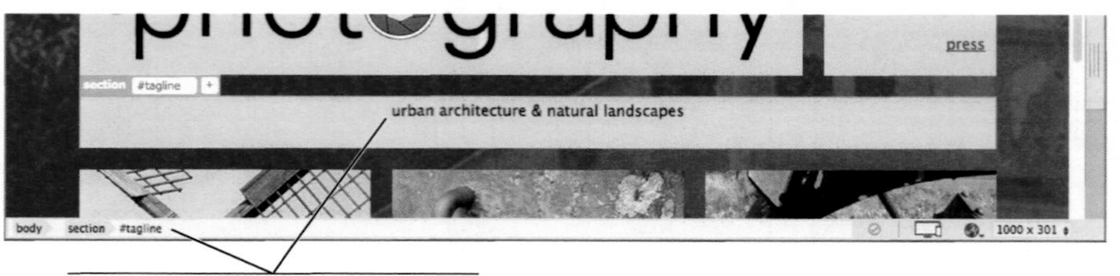

This text exists in a section element with the ID attribute of "tagline".

10. **In the Extract panel, click 30px item in the font-size list to select it.**

11. **In the pop-up window, uncheck the font-family and font-weight properties, then click the Copy CSS button.**

    These are the same as the properties you pasted into the body selector, so you don't need to include them in the selector for the nav paragraphs.

Uncheck the font-family and font-weight properties.

12. **Control/right-click the #tagline selector in the CSS Designer panel and choose Paste Styles.**

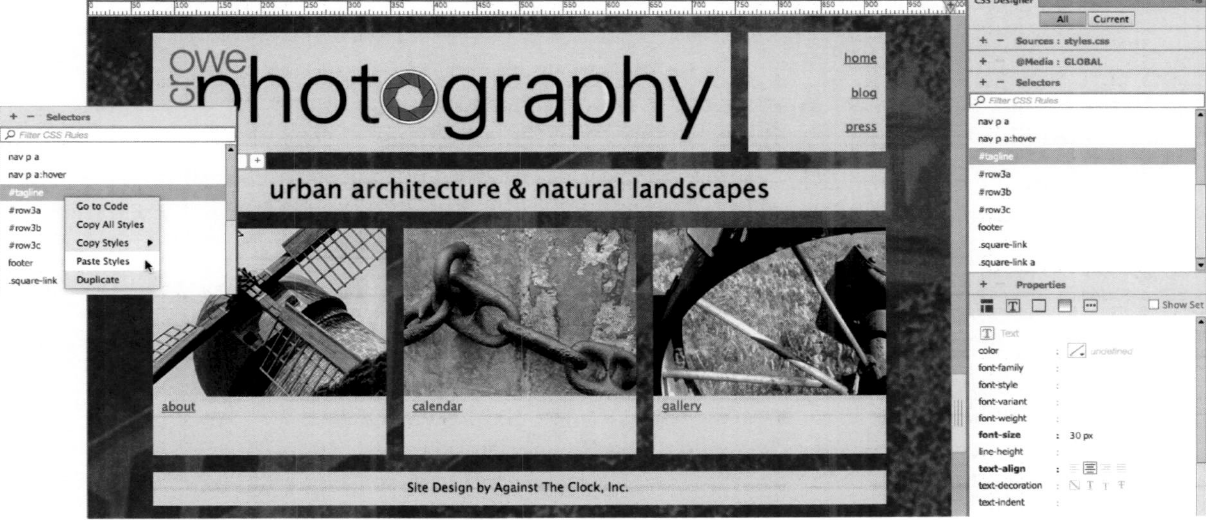

13. **Choose File>Save All.**

    This command saves all files that are related to the active site, including the CSS file that you have been editing by defining CSS properties.

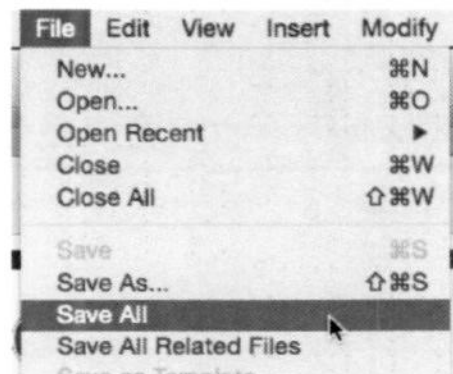

14. **Continue to the next exercise.**

Format Element Backgrounds with Extracted Styles

As you can see in the Extract panel, different elements on the page should have different background properties — white background color, an applied drop shadow, and rounding on various corners. In this exercise you will extract settings from the Photoshop file to properly format the backgrounds of various elements in the page.

> *Note:*
>
> *Every element in an HTML file can have distinct background settings.*

1. **With index.html open, click to select the logo in the top-left section of the page.**

2. **With the logo selected in the page, review the Tag Selector again.**

   The logo image is placed inside the header element, which is enclosed in the opening and closing **<header></header>** tags. To change the background properties for this element, you will edit the header tag selector in the CSS file.

The img element is placed inside the header element.

3. **In the Extract panel, click Layers button to show the list of layers in the uploaded file.**

   The designer of this file provided meaningful names for the various layers in the file, so you can easily see which layer translates to which element in the HTML page. As a general rule, you should use meaningful names when you define elements in a file — whether layers in a Photoshop file or elements in an HTML file.

4. **Click the header-bkg layer to select it in the Extract panel.**

   When you click the layer in the Extract panel, a pop-up window shows the three aspects of this element that you need to apply to the related element in the HTML page. Any properties and styles applied in the Photoshop file that can be translated to CSS are listed in the pop-up window.

   Because Photoshop does not incorporate settings that accurately map to element size and positioning, the width and height properties are not checked by default.

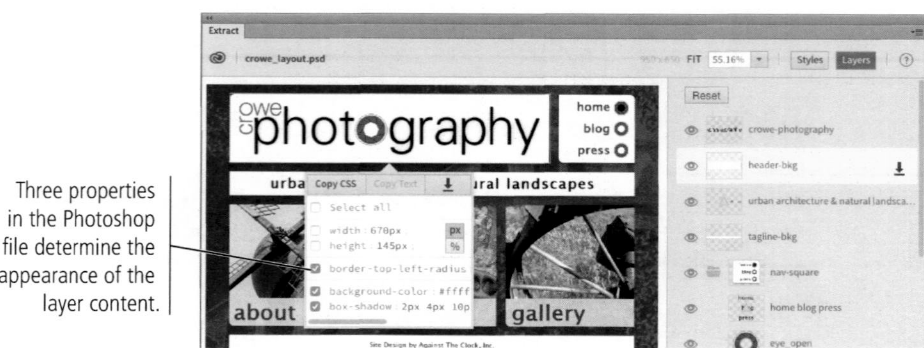

Three properties in the Photoshop file determine the appearance of the layer content.

5. **With the bottom three properties selected in the list, click the Copy CSS button in the top-left corner of the pop-up window.**

6. **In the CSS Designer panel, Control/right-click header in the Selector list. Choose Paste Styles in the contextual menu for the header element.**

   Remember, you want to apply these settings to the header element on the page, so you are pasting the copied properties into the header HTML tag selector in the CSS file.

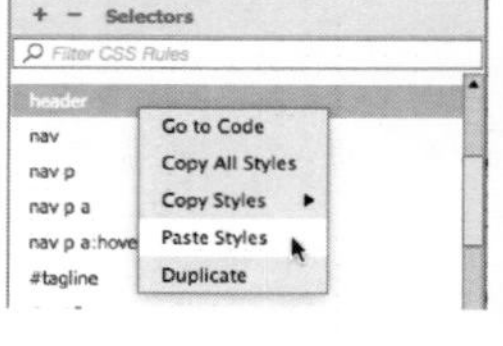

7. **Repeat this process to copy the CSS styles from various Photoshop layers to the corresponding elements in the HTML page.**

Layer	CSS Selector
tagline-bkg	#tagline
nav-bkg (in the nav-square folder group)	nav
footer-bkg	footer

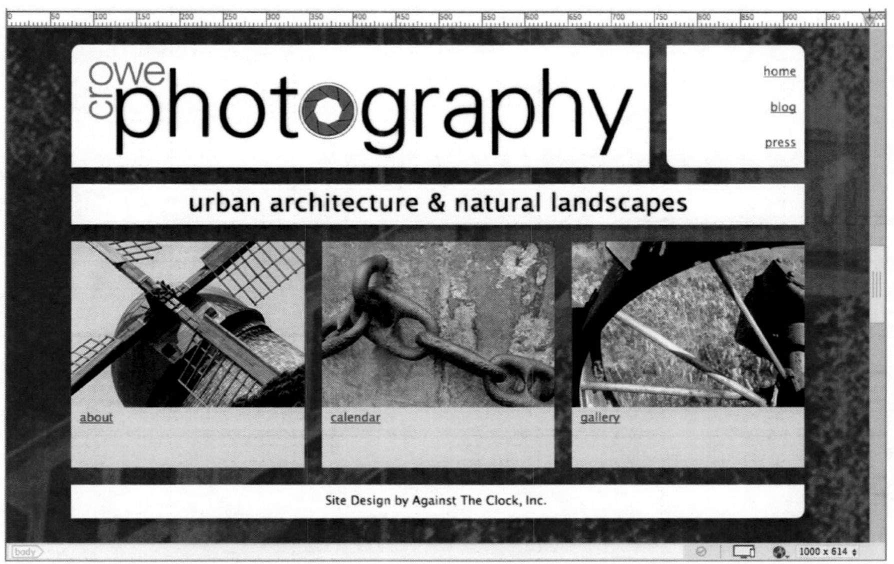

8. **Click in the document window to select the word "about" in the left rectangle of row three.**

   The Tag Selector shows that this word is a link, which is in a paragraph, which is in a section element. The section element has both defined ID attribute (#row3a) and class attribute (.square-link).

This p element is inside a section element with the ID attribute "row3a" and the class attribute "square-link".

9. **Click in the document window to select the word "calendar" in the middle rectangle of row three.**

   Again, the Tag Selector shows that this word is a link, which is in a paragraph, which is in a section element. The section element has both defined ID attribute (#row3b) and class attribute (.square-link).

This p element is inside a section element with the ID attribute "row3b" and the class attribute "square-link".

   Each section element in this row has a different ID attribute, which allows each to have different layout properties. All three sections in the row have the same applied class attribute, however, which means you can change the background properties of all three sections by changing properties in the related class.

10. **In the Layers pane of the Extract panel, expand the gallery-square layer group and select the square-link-bkg sublayer.**

11. **Click the Copy CSS button in the pop-up window for the selected layer.**

    When multiple layers overlap in a Photoshop file, it can be difficult to use the Preview to select exactly what you need. The Layers list makes it much easier to select the exact layer or sublayer that you need.

12. **Control/right-click the .square-link selector in the CSS Designer panel and choose Paste Styles in the contextual menu.**

Because the .square-link class is applied to all three sections in the row, the pasted properties now apply to all three elements.

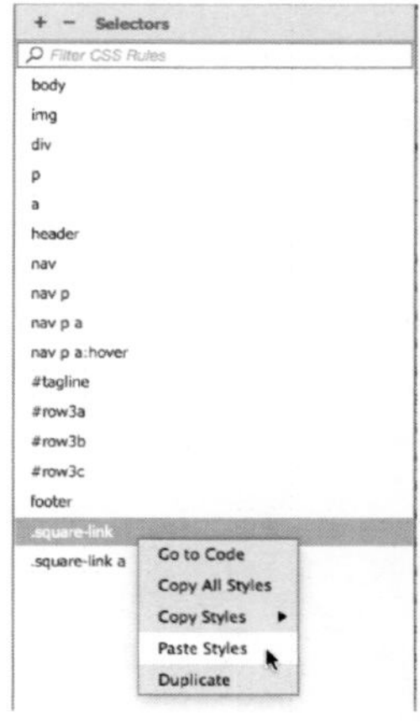

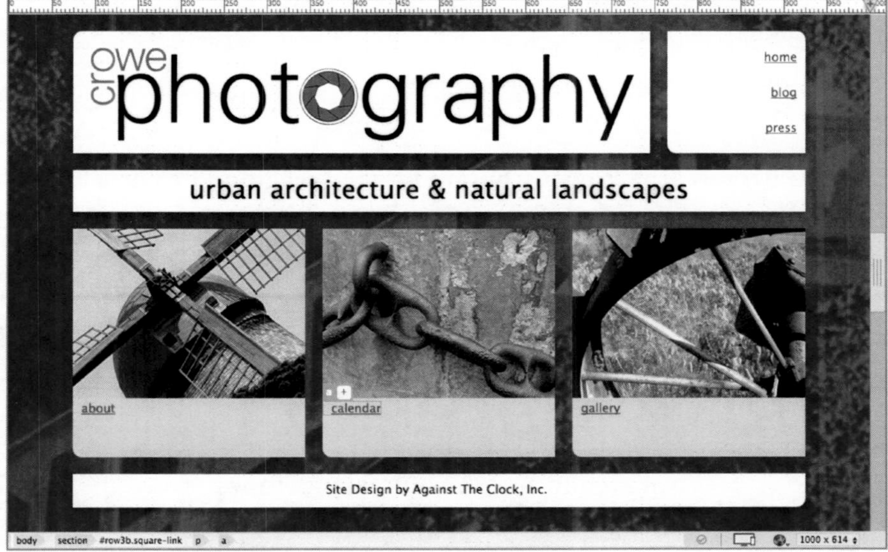

Although the background color of the .square-link class selector is semi-transparent, you might notice that the background of the three section elements is not showing the underlying background image.

13. **In the Selectors section of the CSS Designer panel, click the #row3a ID selector, and click the Show Set option in the Properties section.**

It is important to understand that more than one CSS selector might affect the appearance of a single element in the HTML page. In this case, properties applied to each of the following selectors affect the appearance of the elements in the third row:

body	defines a background color and a semi-transparent background image
section	
#row3a	defines a non-transparent background color
.square-link	defines a semi-transparent background color
p	
a	

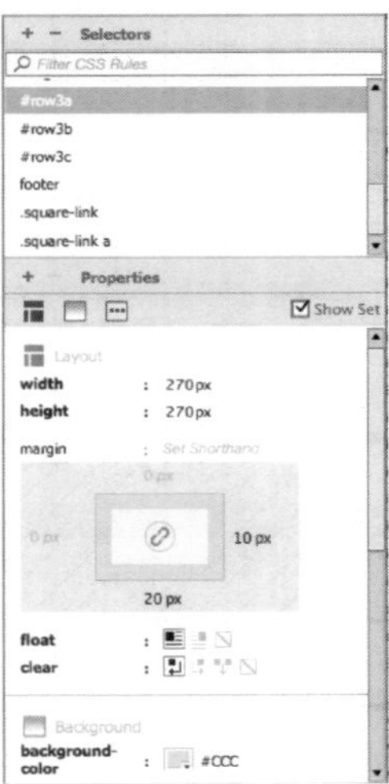

The gray (#CCC) that is defined as the background color of the #row3a ID selector shows through the semi-transparent background of the #square-link selector, instead of the background image that is defined in the body tag selector. To achieve the desired effect, you have to remove the background-color property of the ID selector.

14. **In the CSS Designer panel, move the mouse cursor over the background-color property.**

When the cursor moves over a specific property, two icons appear to the right of the defined value. You can click the Disable CSS Property icon to disable the property (the code stays in the CSS file, but is disabled using comments), or click the Remove CSS Property icon to permanently delete the property's code from the selector.

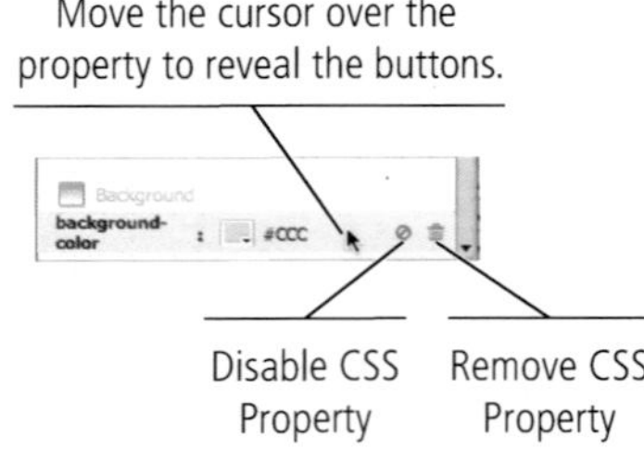

15. **Click the Remove CSS Property button for the background-color selector.**

Now that the ID selector has no defined background color, you can see the background image of the body selector through the background color of the .square-link element.

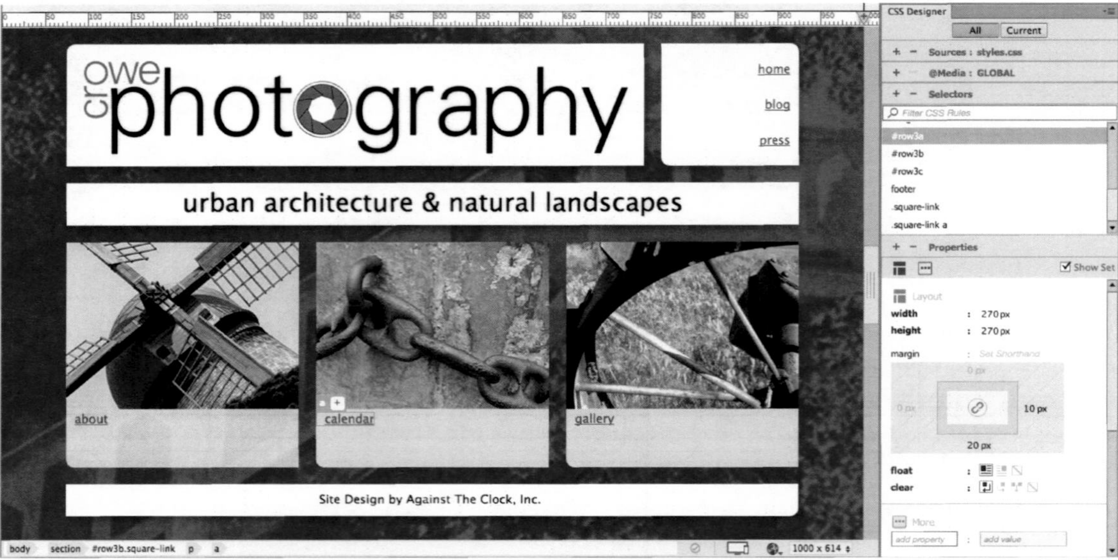

16. **Repeat Steps 13–15 for the #row3b and #row3c ID selectors.**

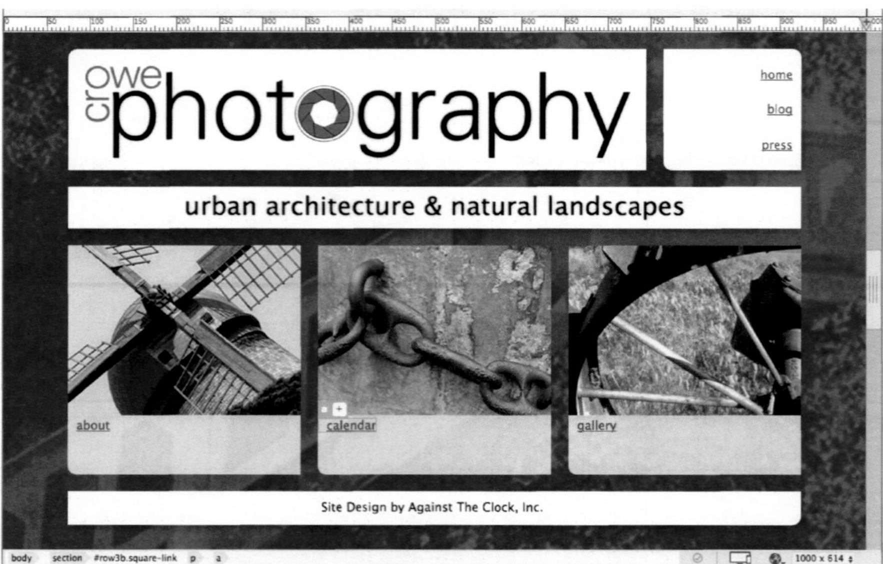

17. **Save all files and continue to the next exercise.**

Format Navigation Links with Extracted CSS

The final required tasks for this project involve formatting links in various areas of the page. In this exercise you will work with descendent selectors, which allow you to define properties that affect only very specific elements on the page.

1. **With index.html open, click to select any of the paragraphs in the nav div.**

The Tag Selector shows the path of tags that applies to the selected element. Working in reverse order:

- This element is a link (**<a>**),
- which is contained in a paragraph (**<p>**),
- which is contained in the nav element (**<nav>**),
- which is contained in the page body (**<body>**).

2. **In the document window, click to select the "about" paragraph in the left square in the third row of the layout.**

Again, the Tag Selector shows the path of tags that applies to the selected element. Working in reverse order:

- This element is a link (**<a>**),
- which is contained in a paragraph (**<p>**),
- which is contained in a section element with the ID attribute of "row3a" and the class attribute of "square-link" (**<section#row3a.square-link>**),
- which is contained in the page body (**<body>**).

Both of these elements are links, which means you can change their properties by editing the basic a tag selector.

3. **Select the a tag selector in the Selectors section of the CSS Designer panel.**

   By default, link text (defined using the <a></a> tags) appears underlined and in blue.

4. **In the Properties section of the panel, uncheck the Show Set option and then click the Text button to scroll to those properties.**

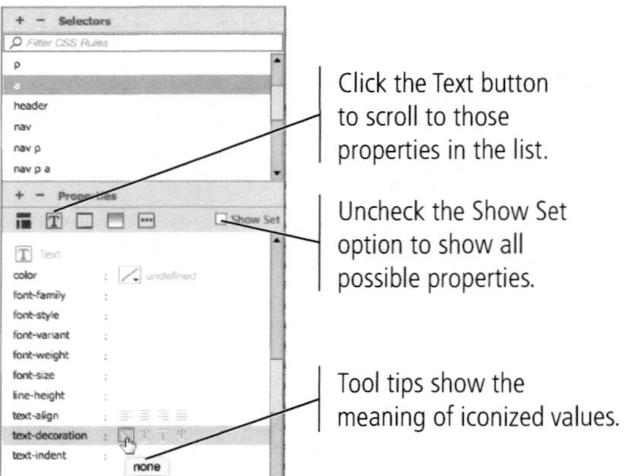

5. **Locate the text-decoration property and click the none button.**

   Because this selector applies to all links in the page, the links in the nav element and the three squares are no longer underlined.

Understanding Hexadecimal Color Codes

DREAMWEAVER FOUNDATIONS

The RGB color model describes colors using values for red, green, and blue respectively. Each color can be assigned a value from 0 (none of that color) to 255 (full strength of that color), for a range of 256 values.

Black has zero values for all three colors, so it is represented as 0, 0, 0. White has full values for all three colors, so it is represented as 255, 255, 255. The hexadecimal system is a numeric system that uses 16 numerals from 0–9 plus A–F (11 is represented by A, 12 by B, up to 15 by F). Since 256 = 16 × 16, in hexadecimal code, 256 = F × F.

The range of 256 values for each color is from 0 to FF (by convention, the first 16 values from 0 to F are given a leading zero: 00 to 0F). Since RGB requires a value for each of the three colors, you will see hexadecimal color values such as #EE04F3, #40896C, and #E843A0.

When both digits for a particular color value are the same, you can abbreviate the code to only three digits. For example, the full code for black is #000000, but it can be abbreviated to #000.

In Web design, the hexadecimal color code must be preceded by the "#" sign (called the hash, pound, or octothorpe character). By convention, the letters should be uppercase, but neither Dreamweaver nor browsers differentiate between #EE04F3, #ee04f3, or #eE04f3.

6. **In the CSS Designer panel, click the swatch for the color property to open the color picker.**

   The **background-color** property affects the background of an element. The **color** property affects the color of text in the element.

7. **Choose the Eyedropper tool in the bottom-right corner of the color picker.**

8. **Move the mouse cursor over the blue area in the placed logo image, then click to sample the logo color as the new color for the a selector.**

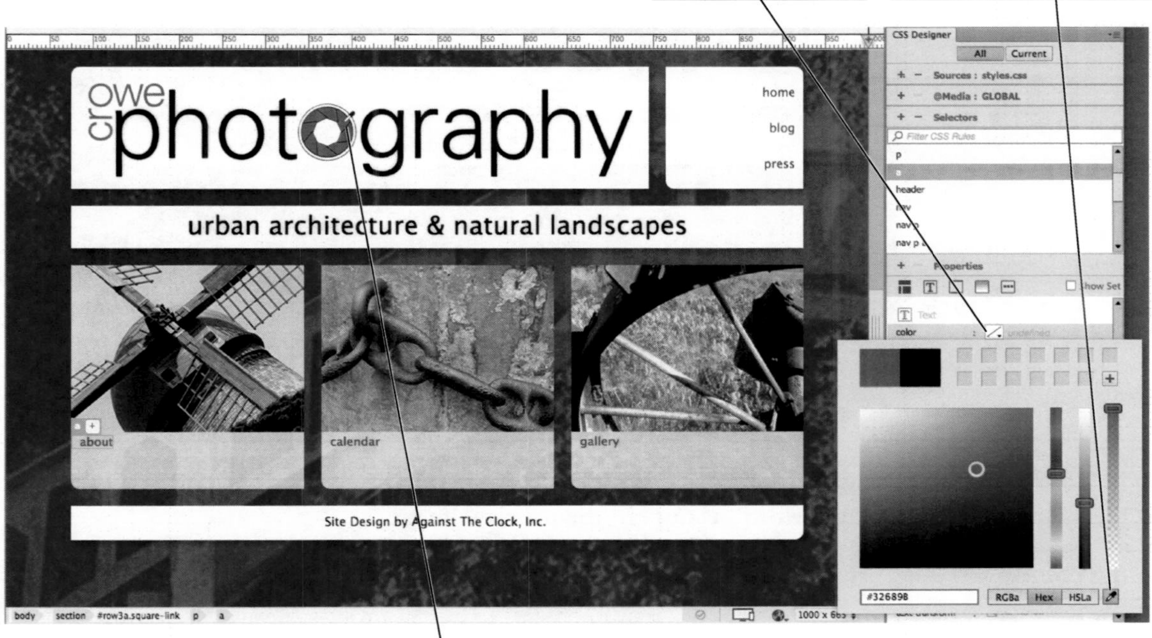

9. **Press Return/Enter to finalize the new color for all links on the page.**

10. **In the Extract panel, click to select the links in the top-right corner of the file. In the pop-up window, uncheck all but the font-size property and then click the Copy CSS button.**

    The unchecked properties are the same as the properties you pasted into the body selector, so you don't need to include them in the selector for the nav paragraphs.

11. **Control/right-click the nav p a selector in the CSS Designer panel and choose Paste Styles.**

This is called a **compound selector** or **descendant selector**. It applies only to links (using the <a> tags) which are in paragraph elements (using the <p> tags) in the nav element (using <nav> tags). Links in other elements are not affected by the properties in this selector.

Properties in this compound selector apply only to links in the nav element.

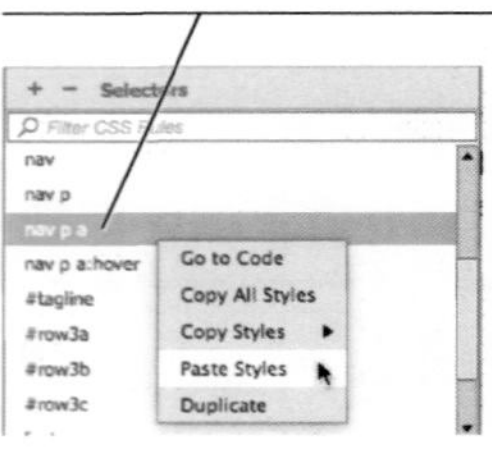

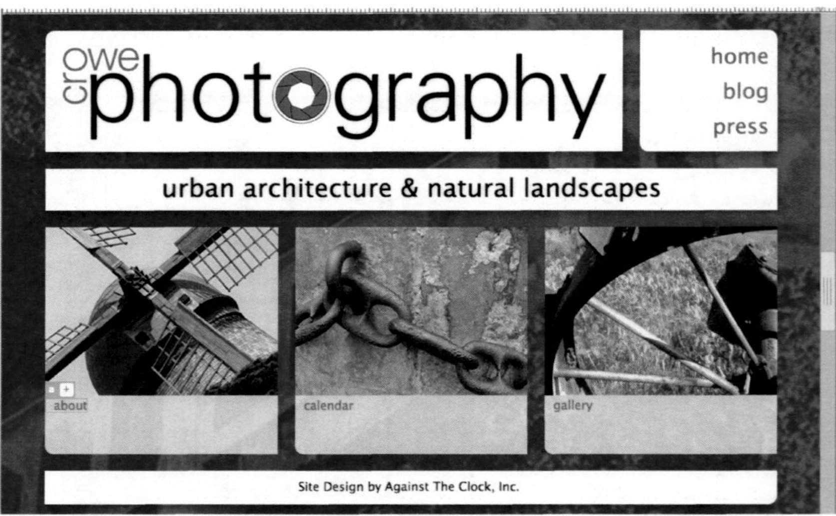

12. **In the Extract panel, click the word "about" in the preview image.**

13. **In the pop-up window, uncheck all but the font-size property, then click the Copy CSS button.**

Again, the other properties have already been applied through the body selector; you don't need to include them in the selector for the square links.

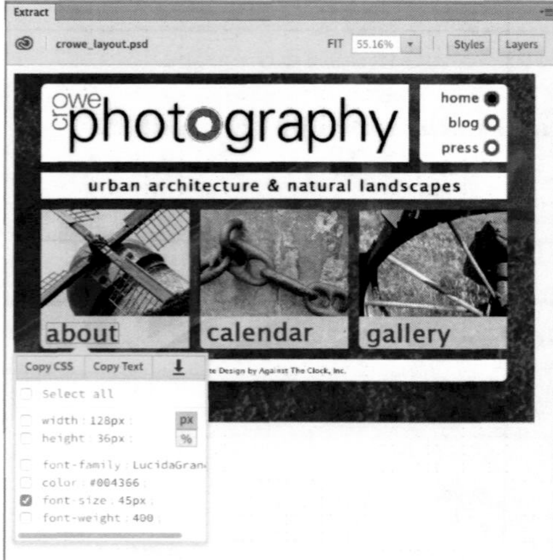

14. **In the CSS Designer panel, Control/right-click the .square-link a compound selector and choose Paste Styles in the contextual menu.**

    Because the .square-link class is applied to all three section elements in the third row, changing this class changes the appearance of links in all three elements.

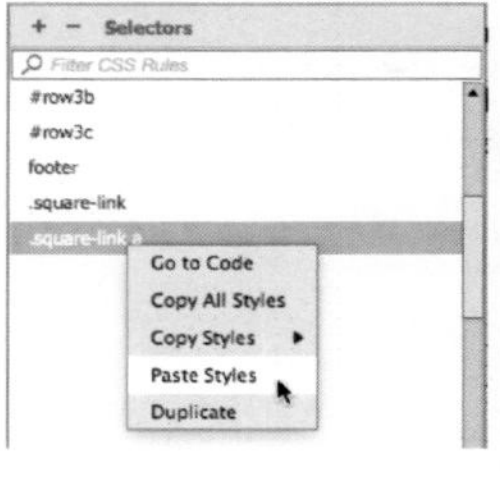

15. **Choose File>Save All, then continue to the next exercise.**

Define Background Images for Navigation Link States

As you saw in a previous exercise, one advantage of CSS is that you can define different background properties for every identified element. In this exercise, you will use this capability to create a background image for each link in the nav element, and change that background image based on the position of the user's mouse cursor.

1. **In the open index.html file, click to select any of the links in the nav element.**

2. **In the CSS Designer panel, locate and select the nav p a compound selector.**
3. **In the Background category of properties, define eye-open.png (from the main site images folder) as the background image url.**

    As we explained earlier, a background image repeats (tiles) across and down until the background of the element unless you specify otherwise. Each link in the nav element shows the background image tiled down and across, originating in the top-right corner.

Click to jump to the Background options.

4. **Choose no-repeat for the background-repeat property.**

5. **Click the "%" option for the first background-position value (X), and choose right from the pop-up menu.**

The CSS **background-position** property allows two values: X (horizontal) position and Y (vertical) position. The panel lists both on the same line, X then Y.

You can define positions relative to the containing element (left, right, etc.) or use specific measurements such as "5 pixels" to position a background image.

Remember, these properties define the horizontal (X) and vertical (Y) positions of the background image *relative to the containing element.*

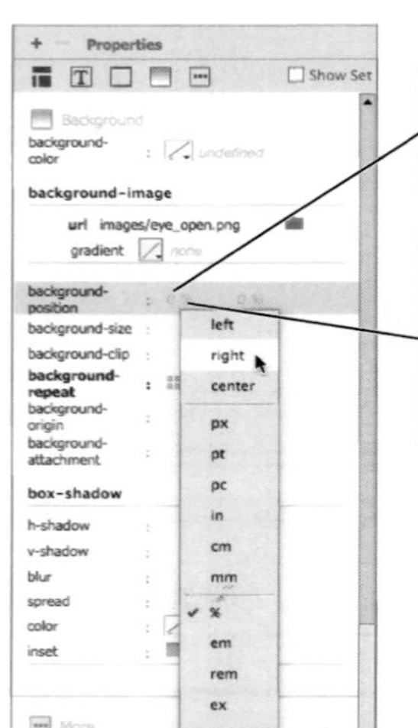

Click the number and type to define a specific numeric value.

Click the measurement to open a menu to change the active unit of measurement or to choose a fixed position relative to the document.

6. **Click the "%" option for the second background-position value (Y), and choose center from the pop-up menu.**

7. **Click the Layout button at the top of the Properties section of the CSS Designer panel.**

8. **Highlight the right-padding value and type `40`. Press Return/Enter to apply the change.**

   Padding is the extra space between the element content and the element edge. Background colors and images extend into the padding.

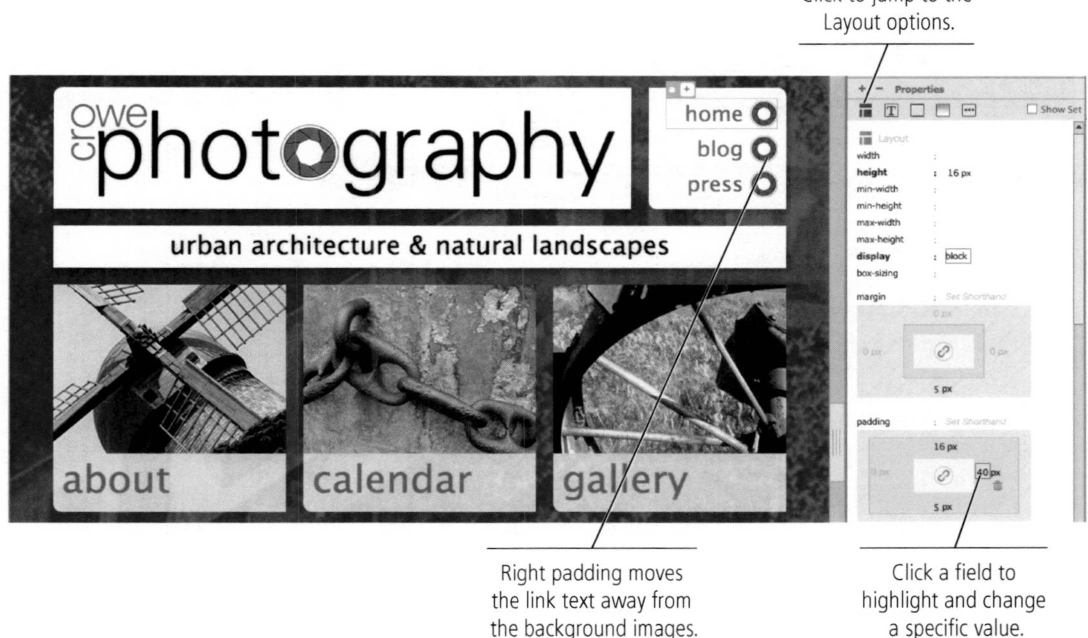
Click to jump to the Layout options.
Right padding moves the link text away from the background images.
Click a field to highlight and change a specific value.
crowe photography
home
blog
press
urban architecture & natural landscapes
about
calendar
gallery

9. **Select the nav p a:hover selector in the CSS Designer panel.**

   The "hover" selector defines the **mouseover state** for a particular link, which determines what happens when the user moves the mouse cursor over the link.

10. **In the Background properties, define `eye-closed.png` as the background image. Set the background-repeat property to no-repeat, define right as the X background-position, and define center as the Y background-position.**

    The **:hover** pseudo-class only applies when the mouse cursor hovers over a link; it does not apply when the mouse cursor is away from the link.

The :hover pseudo-class defines the appearance when a user's mouse hovers over the element.
crowe photography
home
blog
press
urban architecture & natural landscapes

11. **With the Live view active, move your mouse cursor over the navigation links to test the hover effect.**

The **:hover** pseudo-class is a dynamic effect that Dreamweaver's Design pane cannot display. To see the effect, you must view the page in a browser or switch to Live view.

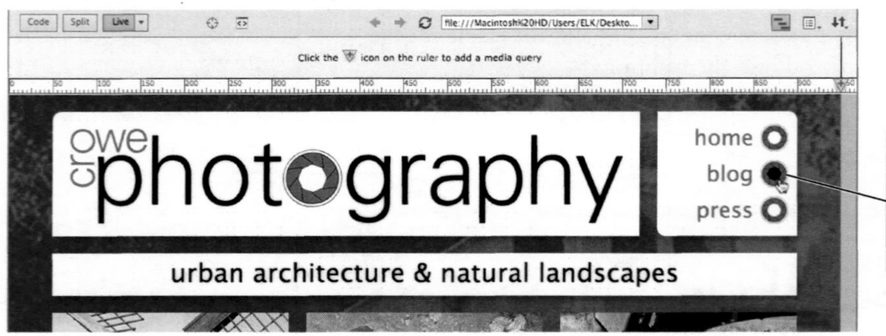

As you move your mouse cursor over a link, the :hover pseudo-class is activated and swaps the "open eye" icon with the "closed eye" icon.

12. **Save all files, then close index.html.**

13. **Export a site definition named Photography.ste into your WIP>Crowe folder, and then remove the Photography site from Dreamweaver.**

If necessary, refer back to Project 6: Bistro Site Organization for complete instructions on exporting a site definition or removing a site from Dreamweaver.

Project Review

fill in the blank

1. The _______________ attribute of the <img> tag is required to make images accessible for all Web users.

2. The _______________ attribute defines the specific file that will appear in the <img> tag location.

3. The _______________ property of CSS can be used to tile a single background image horizontally, vertically, or both throughout the entire document window.

4. _______________ is the process of cutting out/off portions of an image.

5. The _______________ format supports continuous-tone color but not transparency; it is best used for photographs.

6. The _______________ format supports index transparency but not a large gamut of color; it is best used for graphics and artwork.

7. In CSS, a(n) _______________ selector defines the appearance of specific HTML tags such as <body> or <header>.

8. In CSS, a(n) _______________ selector defines the appearance of the one element on the page that has the matching attribute, such as #row3a.

9. In CSS, a(n) _______________ selector defines the appearance of all elements on the page that have been identified with the matching attribute, such as .square-link.

10. In CSS, a(n) _______________ selector defines the appearance of specific elements within other specific elements on the page, such as nav p a.

short answer

1. Briefly describe three image file formats that might be used on the Web, including advantages and disadvantages of each.

2. Briefly explain the importance of resampling, relative to resizing images in Dreamweaver.

3. Briefly explain the advantages to using CSS to define background colors and images.

Portfolio Builder Project

Use what you learned in this project to complete the following freeform exercise.
Carefully read the art director and client comments, then create your own design to meet the needs of the project.
Use the space below to sketch ideas; when finished, write a brief explanation of your reasoning behind your final design.

art director comments

You have been hired by the National Aeronautics and Space Administration (NASA) to design a new site that presents general information of interest to the public at large.

To complete this project, you should:

- ❑ Design a consistent, easily-navigable layout that provides prominent links between the five pages in the site.
- ❑ Create a logo treatment for the new site. Include that logo on every page in the site.
- ❑ Create representative icons for the main heading of each page.
- ❑ Identify and download images you want to use from the NASA on the Commons Web page (https://www.flickr.com/photos/nasacommons).

client comments

We want to create a new Web site called NASAview, which should be a simple, easy-to-navigate site that includes only the most common things that the general public finds of interest.

The main page should link to secondary pages for each of the four site categories:

- About NASA
- History of U.S. Space Travel
- Upcoming Events and Exhibits
- Image Galleries

We haven't written the text content yet, so just use placeholder text for the headings and body copy.

NASA images generally are not copyrighted, although we occasionally use copyrighted material by permission. Those images are marked copyright with the name of the copyright holder; please don't use those images in the new site design.

project justification

Project Summary

When you prepare the design for a site, you need to determine which images will carry content (they must be placed in the foreground using the **<img>** tag), and which images will appear in the background. Appropriate alt text — which enables visually impaired visitors, users who have disabled the display of images, and search engines to use the content of your pages — is required for all foreground images.

Dreamweaver also provides image-editing tools that enable you to crop, resize, resample, and sharpen images. Although these tools do not replace full-featured image-editing applications such as Photoshop, the Dreamweaver tools enable you to complete simple editing tasks quickly and easily, without requiring another application.

The Extract utility, available to individual-user Creative Cloud subscriptions, provides an easy interface for translating Photoshop page comps into functional HTML and CSS code. By editing various CSS properties, you have virtually unlimited options for controlling the appearance of different sections of a page.

file:///Volumes/Macintosh%20HD/Users/ELK/Desktop/WIP/Crowe/index.html
crowe photography
home
blog
press
urban architecture & natural landscapes
about
calendar
gallery
Site Design by Against The Clock, Inc.
Use CSS to change the appearance of different link states
Use CSS to define background properties for different elements
Extract content from a provided Photoshop file
Extract element styles from a provided Photoshop file
Use a variety of techniques to place foreground images
Resize and resample a placed image

Museum CSS Layout

The Getty Foundation hired you to build a new Web site to provide area visitors with information about the various art collections being displayed at their facilities. The client wants a Web site that can be quickly and easily updated and modified. In addition, the site should project a consistent look and style across all pages. To fulfill these requirements, you will create and apply a cascading style sheet for the Web site.

This project incorporates the following skills:

- ❑ Creating and linking an external CSS file
- ❑ Understanding the CSS box model
- ❑ Creating a layout with HTML elements
- ❑ Working with templates to improve workflow and maintain consistency
- ❑ Editing CSS rules to adjust the page layout
- ❑ Defining HTML tag selectors, ID selectors, and compound selectors to control the appearance of page content

Project Meeting

client comments

We want to create a new Web site to provide a brief decription of permanent and traveling exhibits at our museums.

We have a site already, but we can't figure out how it was built, so it's extremely difficult to change even a comma. We called the site designer, but he can't work us into his schedule for more than a month — and we don't have the time to wait.

The new site should be very easy to manage and, more importantly, easy to change — whether it's a comma or the entire site layout.

art director comments

When a site is properly designed, the HTML file stores the page content, while the cascading style sheet (CSS) file defines the appearance of page elements. This makes it easier to find and change content, since the HTML code isn't cluttered with formatting instructions.

You're also going to use template files, which are an excellent tool for maintaining consistency across multiple pages of a site. The template defines the overall page structure, including common elements such as navigation links and editable areas where content varies from one page to another. If you make changes to common elements in the template file, those changes automatically appear in pages where the template is applied.

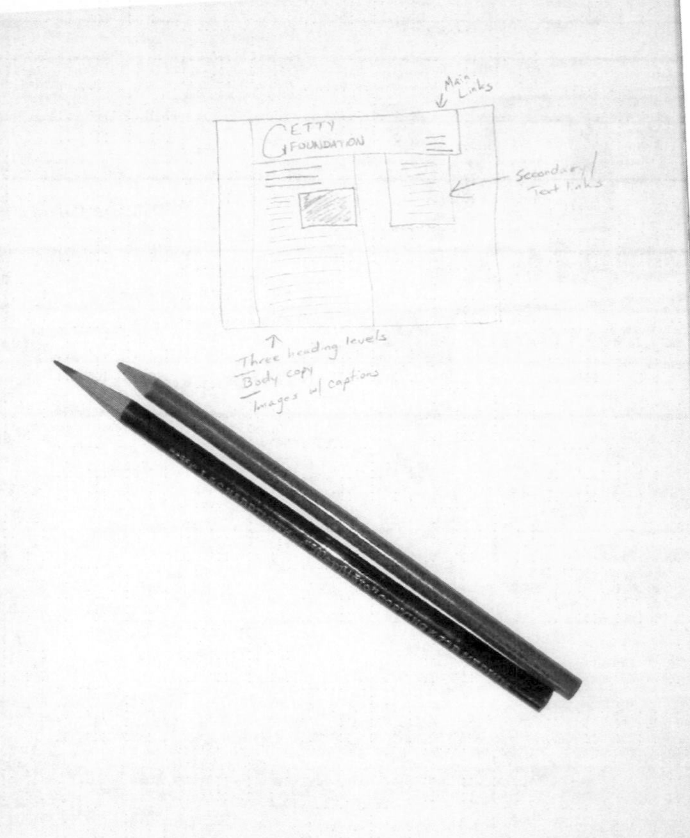

project objectives

To complete this project, you will:

- ❑ Create and link an external CSS file
- ❑ Create ID selectors
- ❑ Create a layout with HTML elements and CSS selectors
- ❑ Use the float property to control nested elements
- ❑ Use margins and padding to affect element placement
- ❑ Define properties for the body tag
- ❑ Create a template file
- ❑ Define named anchors
- ❑ Create figure tags to contain images and captions
- ❑ Define HTML tag selectors
- ❑ Create compound tag selectors
- ❑ Create pseudo-class selectors

Stage 1 Creating Layouts with Style Sheets

A **cascading style sheet** (CSS) is a collection of formatting rules that controls the appearance of different elements in a Web page. Formatting instructions are stored in **rules**, which consist of two parts: a **selector** (basically, naming the element to be formatted) and **attributes** (such as font, color, width, height, etc.) that will be applied to the selected element.

The following example shows the proper syntax for a CSS rule; **p** is the selector, **font-size** is the attribute, and **14px** is the attribute value:

```
p {
   font-size: 14px;
}
```

There are three types of styles: inline, embedded (or internal), and external. To make the best use of styles, you should have a clear understanding of these different types — including when each is best suited to a specific goal.

An **inline style** applies directly and instantly to an individual element within a tag, affecting only that single element of the HTML page. For example, if you apply a font size and color to a paragraph, the inline style looks like this:

```
<p style="font-size: 10px; color: blue">Paragraph content goes here.</p>
```

An **embedded or internal style sheet** is added directly in an HTML page, within style tags; this type of style affects only the particular HTML page in which it is placed. The following code for an embedded style sheet includes a style that defines the formatting of all h1 elements:

```
<style type="text/css"
<!--
h1 {
   font-size: 24px;
}
-->
</style>
```

> ***Note:***
> *The set of <!-- and --> tags prevents a few older browsers from displaying the style rules.*

An **external style sheet** is saved as a separate file (with the extension ".css"). HTML files include links to the external CSS files, which are uploaded to the Web server along with the Web site pages. External CSS files offer several advantages:

- A single CSS file can be attached to multiple HTML pages at one time, applying the same rules to elements in different pages. Changes to the styles affect all HTML pages that are linked to that CSS file, which makes it easier to maintain consistency across all pages in a site.
- Different types of styles can control the appearance of general HTML elements; specific individual elements that are identified with a unique ID attribute; all elements that are identified with a specific class attribute; and even elements only within a certain area of a page.
- External styles separate page formatting (CSS) from structure and content (HTML). This helps to reduce file size and server processing time, as well as making it easier for designers and coders to more easily find exactly what they are looking for.

Prepare the Site Files

In this exercise, you will import the client's provided files, then create the HTML and CSS files that you need to complete the project.

1. **Download Museum_DWCC16_RF.zip from the Student Files Web page.**

2. **Expand the ZIP archive in your WIP folder (Macintosh) or copy the archive contents into your WIP folder (Windows).**

   This results in a folder named **Museum**, which contains the files you need for this project.

3. **Create a new site named Museum, using the WIP>Museum folder as the site root folder.**

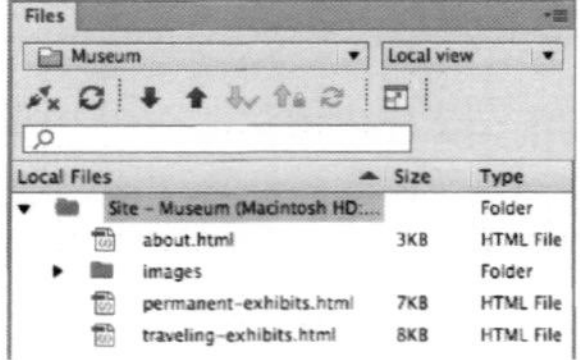

4. **With the Museum site open in the Files panel, choose File>New. Using the New Document dialog box, create a new, blank HTML5 page.**

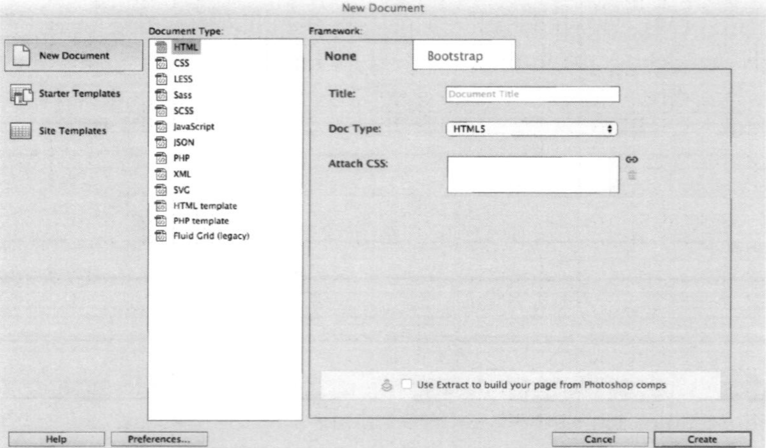

5. **Choose File>Save. Save the new page as an HTML file named design.html in the root folder of the Museum site.**

6. **With design.html open, open the CSS Designer panel. Make sure the All button is active at the top of the panel.**

7. **In the Sources section of the panel, click the Add CSS Source button and choose Create a New CSS File.**

   You can also create a new CSS file in the New Document dialog box. Simply choose CSS in the Document Type window and click Create.

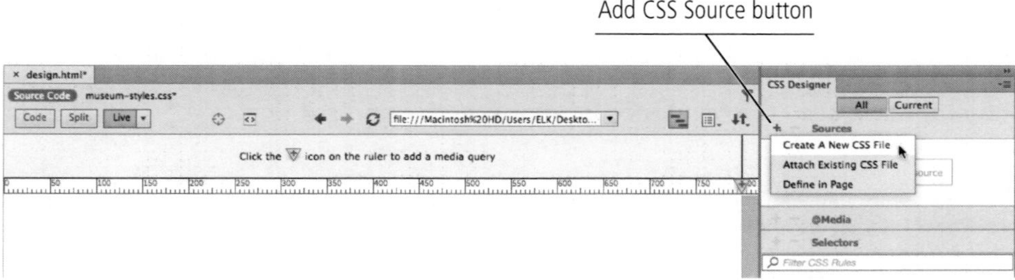

8. **In the resulting dialog box, type `museum-styles.css` in the File/URL field.**

   The name you define will be used for the new CSS file that is created. By default, the CSS file is placed in the root folder of the active site; you can click the Browse button if you want to create the file in another location.

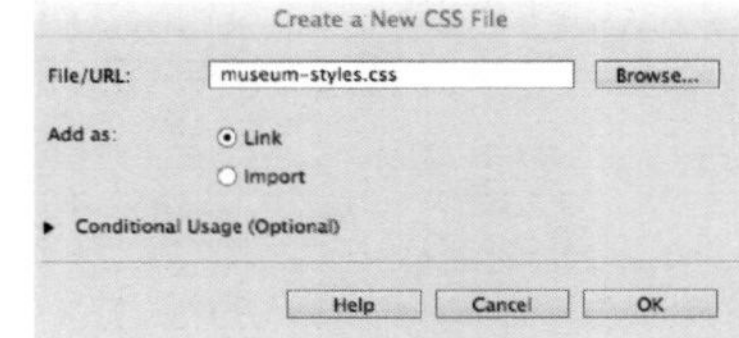

9. **With the Link option selected, click OK to create the new CSS file.**

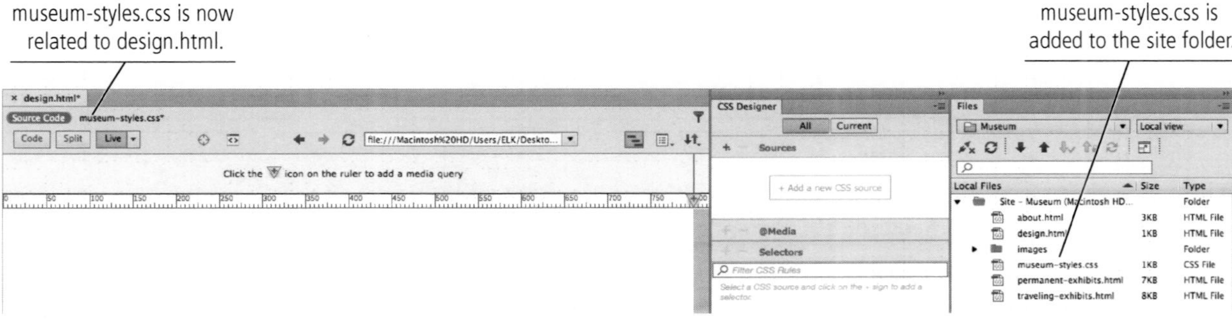

museum-styles.css is now related to design.html.
museum-styles.css is added to the site folder.

10. **Click the Split button in the Document toolbar, and review the page source code.**

    Using the Link option, the CSS file is connected to the HTML page using the **<link>** tag in the HTML page's header information. When a user opens the HTML page, the browser merges the instructions in the linked CSS file with the information in the HTML file to present the final page design.

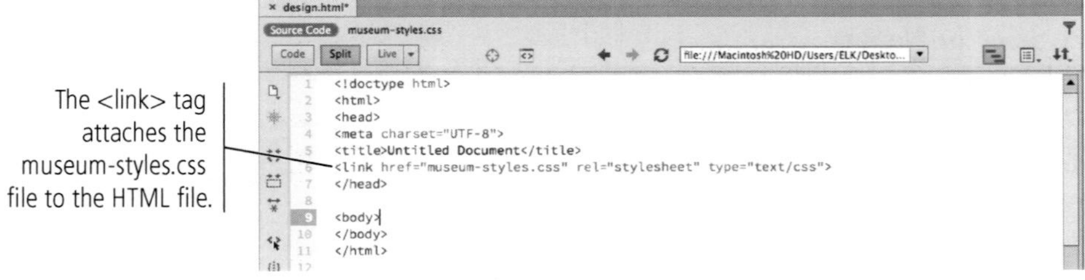

11. **Choose File>Save All, then continue to the next exercise.**

    The Save All command saves any open HTML page, as well as any linked files such as the CSS file that you created in this exercise.

Define a New Element and Tag Selector

HTML includes a large number of elements that are specifically designed to create common page elements — headers (usually) at the top of the page, footers at the bottom, navigation (nav) areas with lists of links, and so on. In this and the next exercise, you are going to use several of these elements to create the basic page structure for the museum's Web site.

1. **With design.html open, make sure the regular Split view is active and the Live view is turned off.**

   You are going to work in the regular Design view in this exercise. In later exercises, you will use other methods in the Live view to add elements to the page.

2. **Click the Header button in the HTML Insert panel.**

   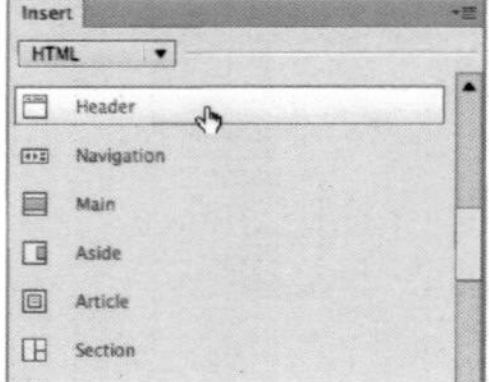

3. **In the resulting dialog box, click the New CSS Rule button.**

   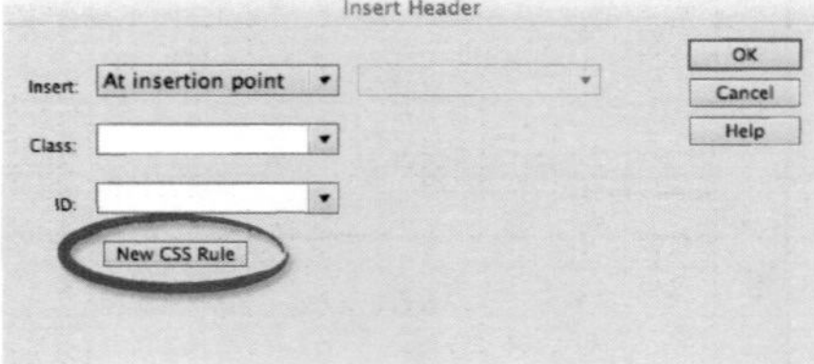

4. **Choose Tag in the Selector Type menu.**

   In the New CSS Rule dialog box, you can define the type and name of a selector, as well as where to create the rule (in the attached external CSS file or embedded in the active HTML file).

   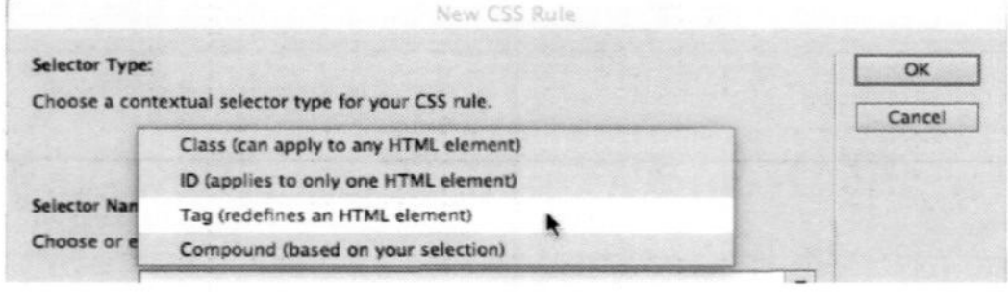

   A tag selector applies to all elements using that tag, such as every paragraph that is structured with <p> tags.

5. **Choose header in the Selector Name menu.**

   When you choose Tag in the Selector Type menu, the Selector Name menu includes a large number of available HTML tags. You can open the menu and choose the tag you want, or simply type the tag name in the field.

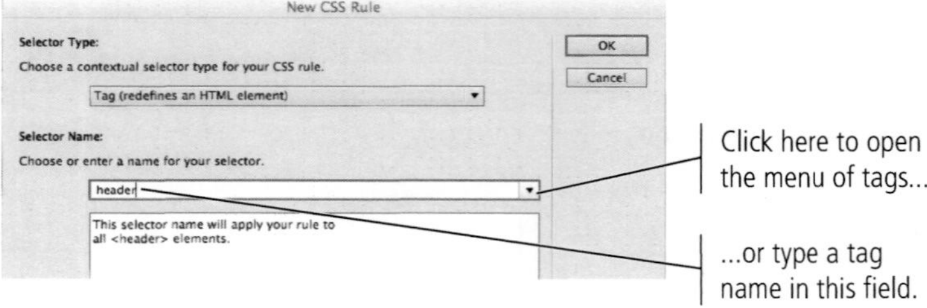

5. **In the Rule Definition menu (at the bottom of the dialog box), choose museum-styles.css.**

   If you choose This Document Only, the resulting CSS style will be created in the active HTML file's header information; the style will not be available for other files in the site.

   Because you want to use these styles in multiple files, it is best to place them in the separate CSS file and link each HTML file to that file.

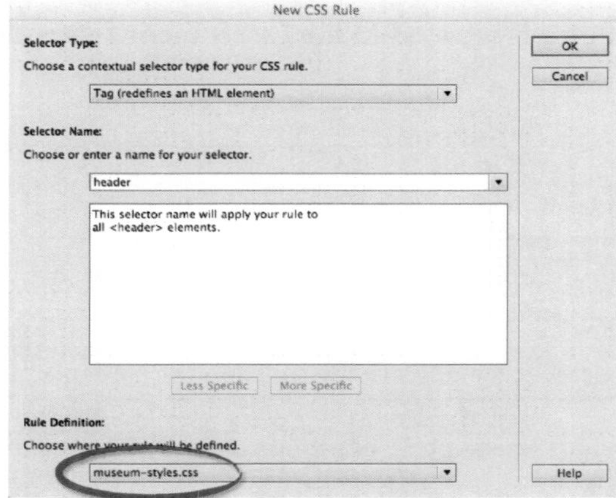

6. **Click OK to open the CSS Rule Definition dialog box.**

   This dialog box includes nine categories of options. Many properties that can be saved in a CSS rule are available in the various panes of this dialog box.

7. **Click Background in the Category list. Type #FFF in the Background-color field, or click the related swatch and use the pop-up color picker to define white as the background color.**

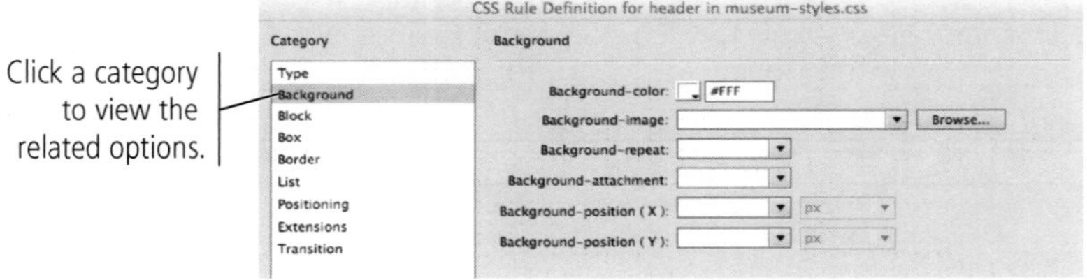

8. **Click Box in the Category list. Type 930 in the Width field, and make sure px (pixels) is selected in the related menu.**

   If you do not define a specific width or height, elements fill the containing element horizontally; their height expands automatically as content is added.

9. **In the Padding area, leave the Same for All option checked. Type 10 in the Top field, and make sure px is selected in the related menu.**

10. **In the Margin area, uncheck the Same for All check box. Type 0 in the Top and Bottom fields, and make sure px is selected in the related menus.**

11. **Type auto in the Left and Right fields.**

    The **auto** value allows the element to be centered within its parent container (in this case, the body element of the HTML page).

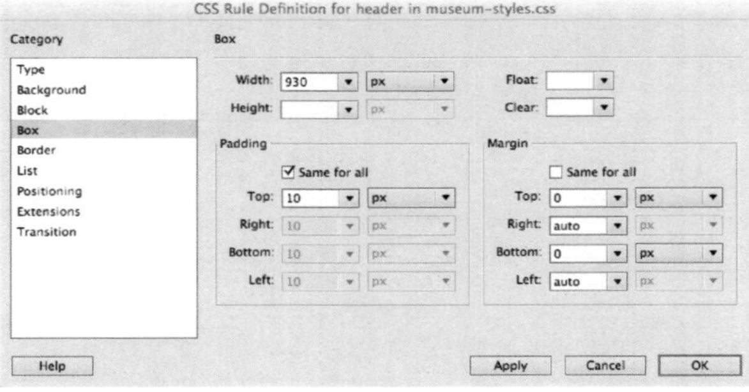

12. **Click OK to return to the Insert Header dialog box.**

13. **Make sure At Insertion Point is selected in the Insert menu, then click OK to return to the HTML page.**

    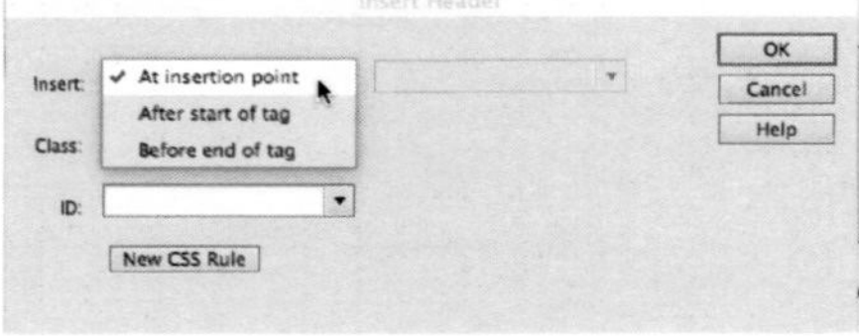

    Different options are available in this menu depending on what is selected in the document. Because nothing exists in the file yet, the insertion point is assumed to be placed at the beginning of the document body — that is where the new element will be added.

    After clicking OK, the new element is automatically added to the page; placeholder content is added inside the element. The top edge is slightly indented because Dreamweaver automatically adds several pixels of padding around the content of a new page. (Some browsers do the same.)

    In the document tab, an asterisk indicates that the HTML file has been edited. In the Related Files bar, an asterisk indicates that the museum-styles.css file has been edited.

    In the CSS Designer panel, the Selectors section shows the new header selector.

14. **Review the page code in the Code pane.**

    Adding elements adds to the page's HTML code. Those elements, however, are very short — they simply identify each element and add some placeholder content. In the page code, there is no mention of background images, borders, or other attributes that make up the page layout. Those attributes are controlled by editing the selectors applied to each element within the CSS file.

The asterisks tell you the files have been modified since they were last saved.

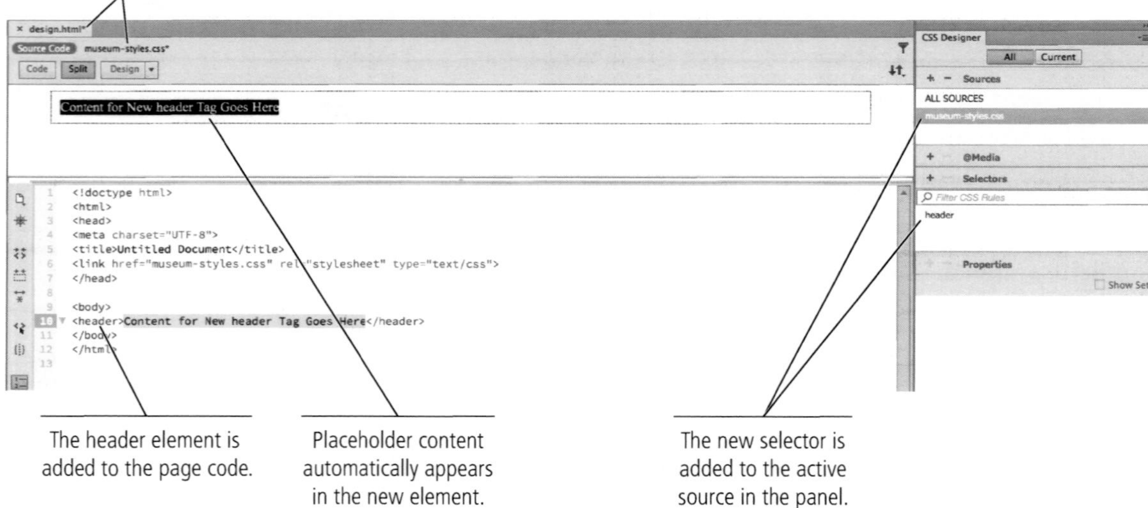

15. In the Design pane, click the edge of the header element to select it.

When an element is selected in the page in the regular Design view, you can see various aspects of the CSS box model in the design pane. If you don't see the margin area, make sure CSS Layout Box Model is toggled on in the View>Visual Aids menu.

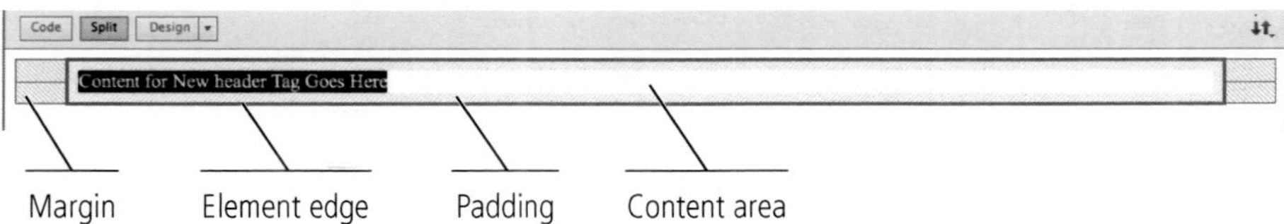

16. In the Related Files bar, click museum-styles.css to show that file in the Code pane.

Clicking the CSS file name in the Related Files bar automatically switches the document window to Split mode if the Code pane is not already visible; the CSS file code is displayed in the Code pane.

You can now see the code for the new rule you defined. Properties and values for the selector are contained within curly brackets; each property is separated by a semicolon.

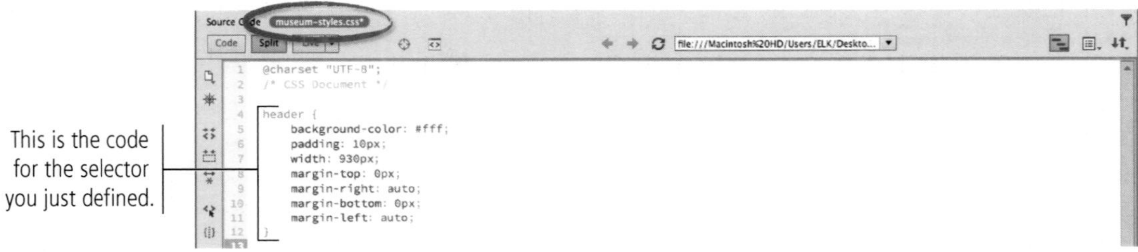

17. Choose File>Save All, then continue to the next exercise.

Add a Div Element in the Live View

There are many different methods for adding new elements to a page. In the last exercise, you used the buttons in the HTML Insert panel to add a new element and define the related CSS selector at the same time. In this exercise you use the Live view to add a new div element, then define the CSS for that element separately.

1. **With design.html open, show the page source code in the Code pane and turn on the Live view.**

2. **Click to select the existing header element, then click the Div button in the HTML Insert panel.**

   A **<div>** tag is simply a container, identifying a division or area of a page. Although the HTML5 elements such as header and section have largely replaced the div element in modern design, you can (and will) still find uses for a non-specific container.

   In this case, you are creating a div element simply as a parent container for the two main content areas of the page (which you will create later).

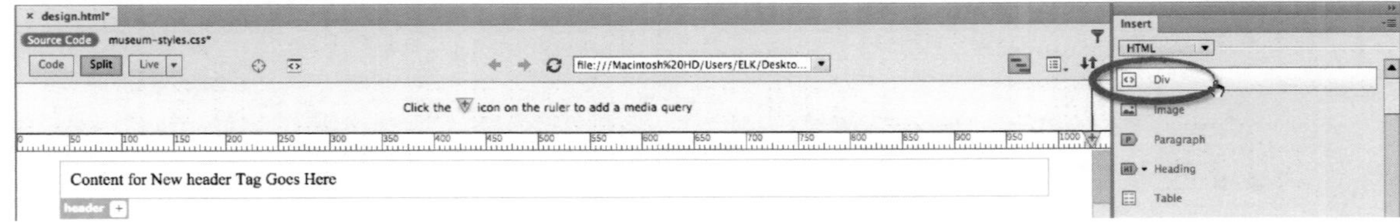

3. **Click the After button in the Position Assistant.**

   When the Live view is active, the Position Assistant determines where new elements are placed in relation to the current selection.

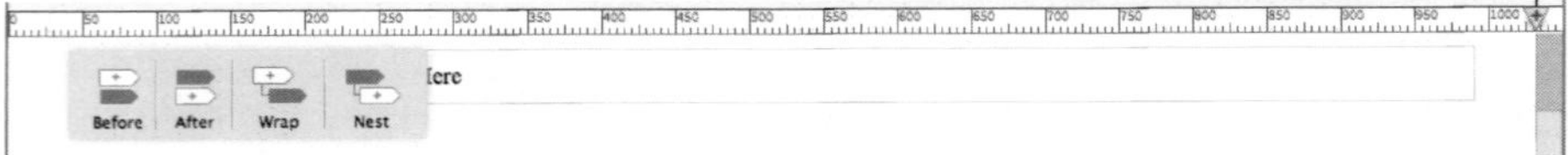

   The new div element appears in the Design pane after the previously selected header element. The box model that you saw in the regular Design view does not appear when the Live view is active; only the element boundary is visible as a thin blue line when the element is selected.

4. **With the new div selected in the Design pane, click the + button in the Element Display.**

   The div element is a fairly generic container. If you define CSS for the basic div tag, your changes would affect every div element on the page. Instead, you are going to assign this element a unique ID attribute to better identify it in the page and CSS code.

Click the + button to open the Class/ID field.

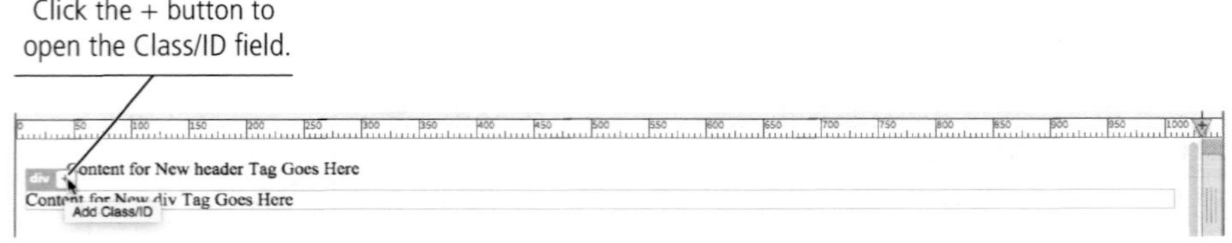

> ***Note:***
>
> *Each element on a page can have a different identity (defined using the ID attribute), and each ID can be used only once on a page.*

5. **In the resulting field, type `#page-content`, then press Return/Enter.**

   ID selectors always begin with a # character; make sure you type it in the field when you assign the new ID attribute.

Type an ID or class attribute in the field.

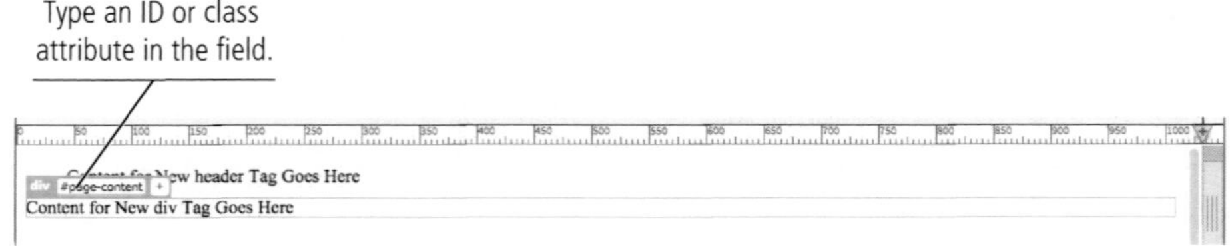

> ***Note:***
>
> *CSS Selector names are case-sensitive.*

6. **Make sure museum-styles.css is selected in the resulting Select a Source menu, then press Return/Enter.**

   Dreamweaver recognizes that a CSS selector does not yet exist for this ID, so it will create one for you. You are asked to determine where the new selector should be saved.

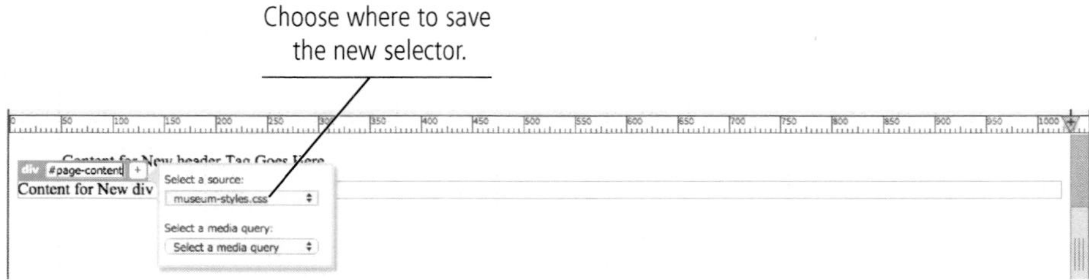

7. **In the CSS Designer panel, click to select the new #page-content selector.**

8. **At the top of the Properties section, make sure the Show Set option is <u>not</u> checked.**

9. **Click the Layout button to jump to those properties in the panel.**

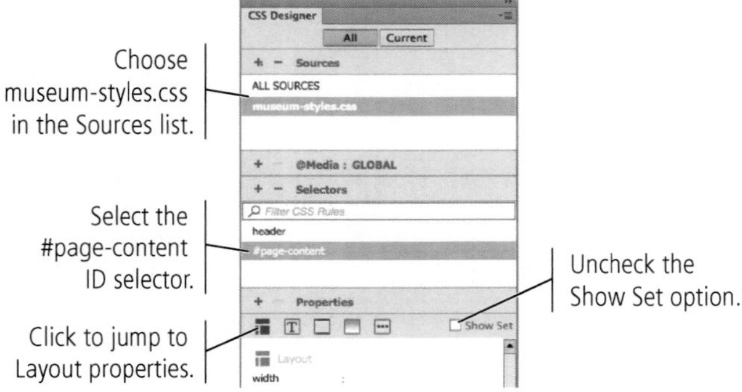

10. **In the Layout properties, click the width property value and choose px from the resulting menu. In the resulting field, type `950`.**

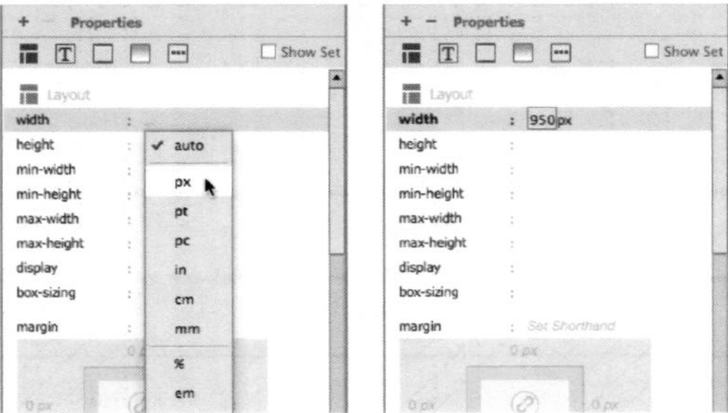

11. In the Margin settings, make sure the lock icon is not active, then define the following margins:

Top:	**0px**
Left:	**auto**
Bottom:	**0px**
Right:	**auto**

The lock is not active.

The lock is active.

When the lock icon is active, all four fields are connected and have the same value; changing any one of the values applies the same setting to the other three. If you want to define different values for different sides, you have to turn off the lock option.

Remember, setting the right and left margins to auto centers the element horizontally in its parent container.

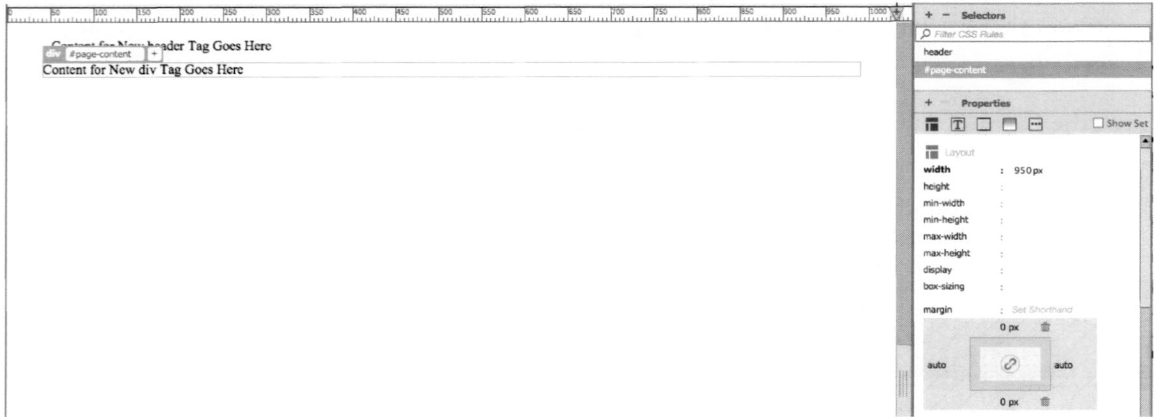

12. At the top of the Properties section, click the Border button to jump to those properties in the panel.

13. Click the Top tab to define border options for only the top edge.

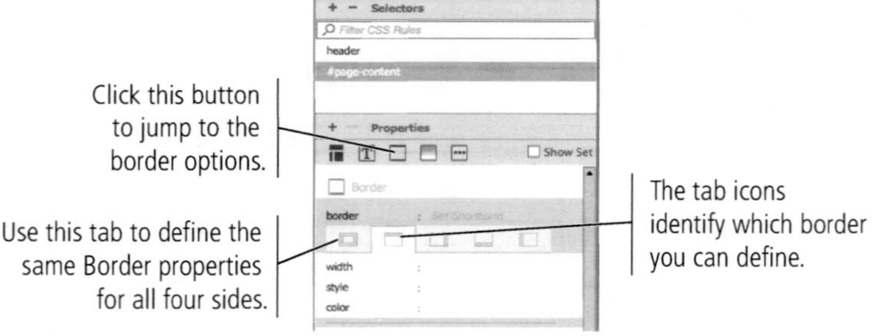

14. Define the border-top width property as 8 px.

The width menu here functions in the same way as the width menu that you used to define the box width: click the value and choose px from the menu, then type the value in the resulting field.

15. **Open the style menu and choose solid.**

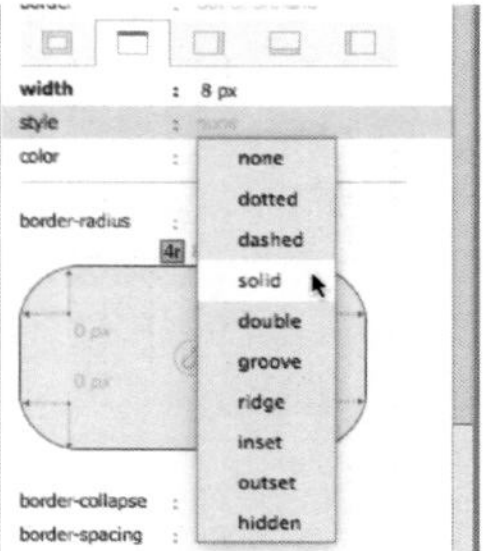

16. **Click the color swatch to open the Color picker. Type `#54210F` in the hexadecimal value field, then press Return/Enter to finalize the new border color.**

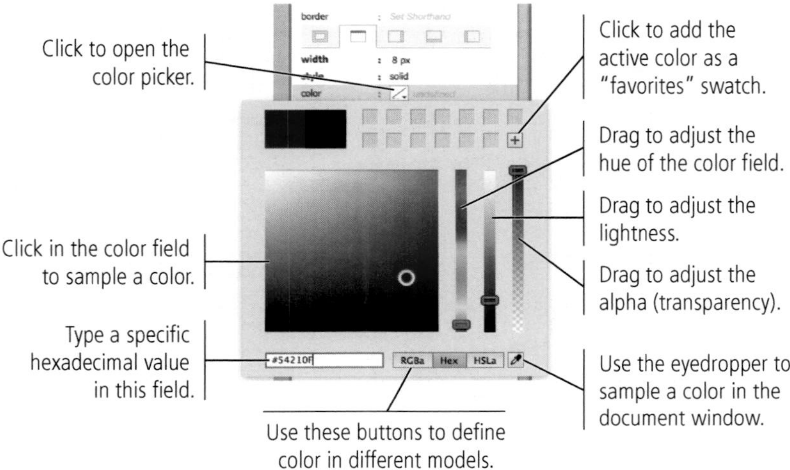

17. **Show the museum-styles.css file in the Code pane.**

All three defined options for the border-top property (width, style, color) are combined into a single property statement.

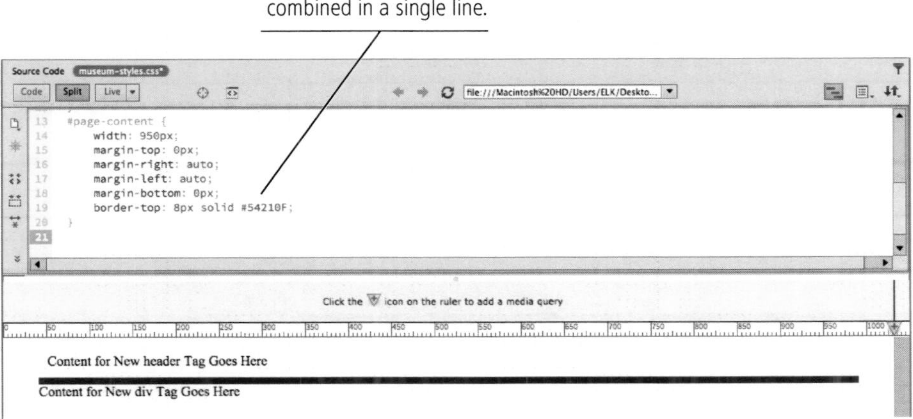

18. **Choose File>Save All, then continue to the next exercise.**

Understanding CSS Shorthand

In many cases, you will define more than one value for the same CSS property. In the previous exercise, for example, you defined the width, style, and color of the border-top property. In the Code pane, you can see that all three values are combined into a single CSS statement:

```
border-top: 8px solid #54210F;
```

This type of combining properties into a single line is referred to as **shorthand**. Without shorthand, you would require three separate lines in the selector:

```
border-top-width: 8px;
border-top-style: solid;
border-top-color: #54210F;
```

Combining the three properties into a single line saves space and makes the overall CSS code less complex.

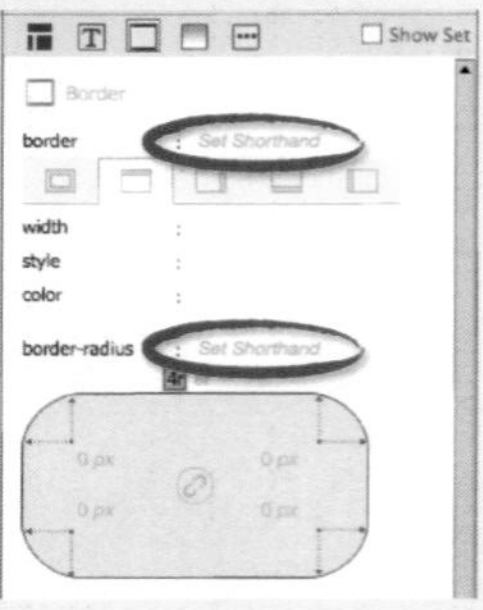

The CSS Designer panel includes a number of Set Shorthand fields that allow you to define properties without interacting with the panel's various menus and field.

Keep in mind, if you decide to type in the Set Shorthand fields, most CSS property:value pairs have very specific rules; you must use the proper syntax to accurately define those values. (For example, do not include a space between a number and unit of measurement.)

Drag and Drop to Create a New Element

Dreamweaver's Live view enables a drag-and-drop method of adding elements to a page. On-screen prompts allow you to define exactly where you want elements to exist, making it easy to create the proper code using only visual tools.

1. **With design.html open, click the footer button in the HTML Insert panel and drag onto the Live view.**

2. **When a green line appears below the div#page-content element, release the mouse button.**

   When you drag to add elements in the Live view, visual indicators identify where the new elements will be added in relation to existing elements. A thin blue line highlights the active element, and the green double-headed arrow determines whether the new element will be added above or below the highlighted element.

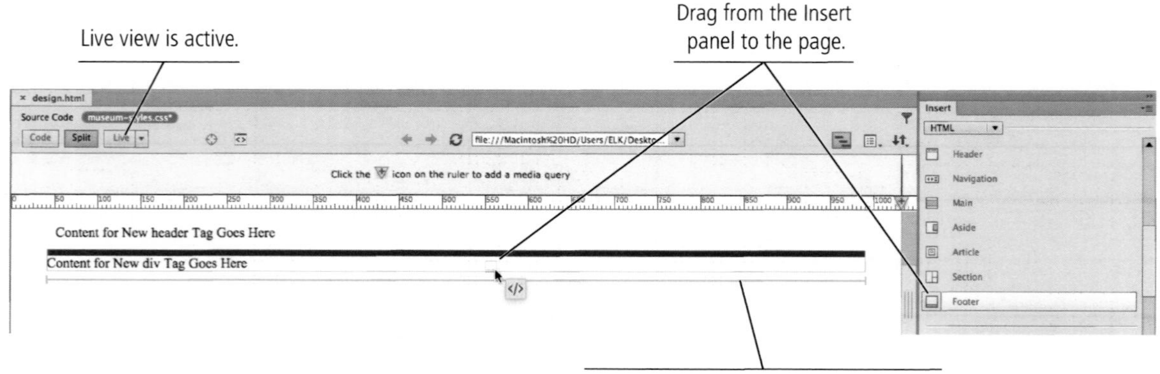
Live view is active.
Drag from the Insert panel to the page.
The green line indicates the element will be placed after the blue highlighted one.
Content for New header Tag Goes Here
Content for New div Tag Goes Here
Header
Navigation
Main
Aside
Article
Section
Footer

3. **Make sure the CSS Designer panel is displaying the All mode.**

   Current mode must be turned off to add new selectors using the panel.

4. **In the CSS Designer panel, click to select museum-styles.css in the Sources section.**

5. **Click the Add Selector button in the Selectors section of the panel.**

   Clicking this button automatically creates a descendant selector, with the entire path to the currently selected element. In this case, the new footer element is inside the body element (i.e., the body element is the immediate parent of the footer element), so "body footer" is the default selector name.

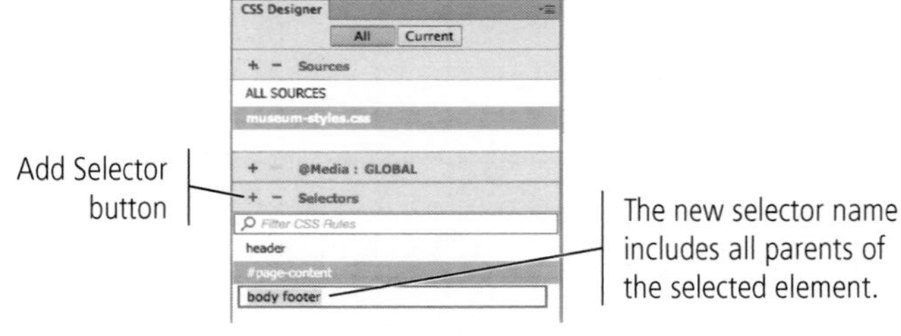

   This type of descendant selector allows you to define different settings for the same type of element in different areas of the page. Since you will only use one footer element in the client's design, the parent is not necessary in this selector name.

6. **Press the Up Arrow key once to remove the parent ("body") from the selector name, then press Return/Enter to finalize the new name.**

   Depending on the active selection, the selector name might have more than one parent in the path to the active tag. Each time you press the Up Arrow key, the first parent in the list is removed.

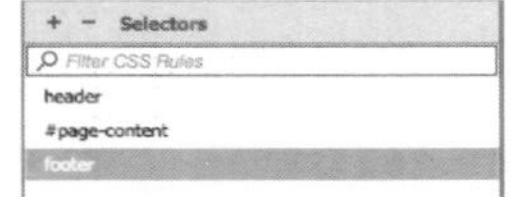

> *Note:*
>
> *You can also press the Down Arrow key to add the parents back into the selector name.*

7. **In the Properties section of the panel, show the Layout properties.**

8. **Open the Width menu and choose %, then type `100` as the percentage.**

   If you use percentage as the width measurement, you are defining the element's width as a percentage of the width of its parent container. In this case, the footer element will occupy the same horizontal width as the overall page (the body element).

9. **Define `10px` top and bottom margins.**

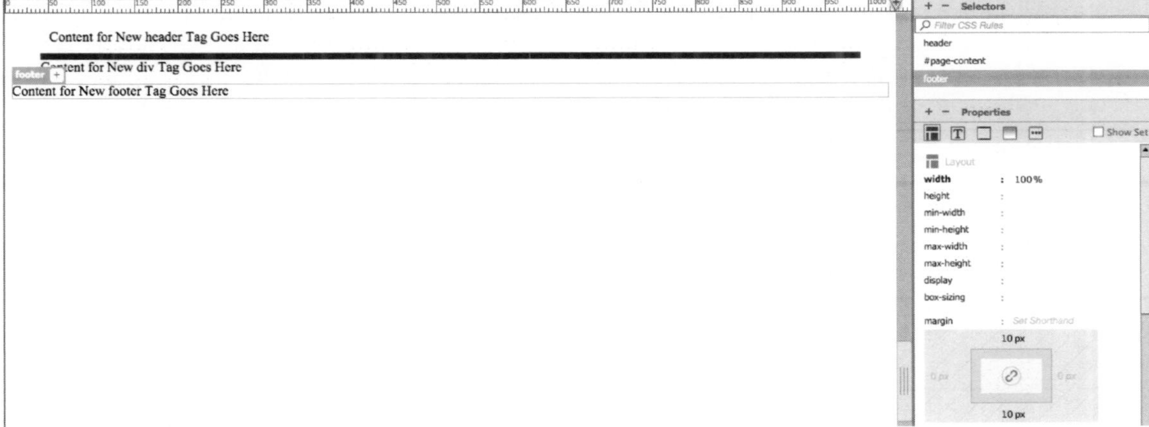

10. **Show the Text properties in the CSS Designer panel. Locate the text-align property and choose the center value.**

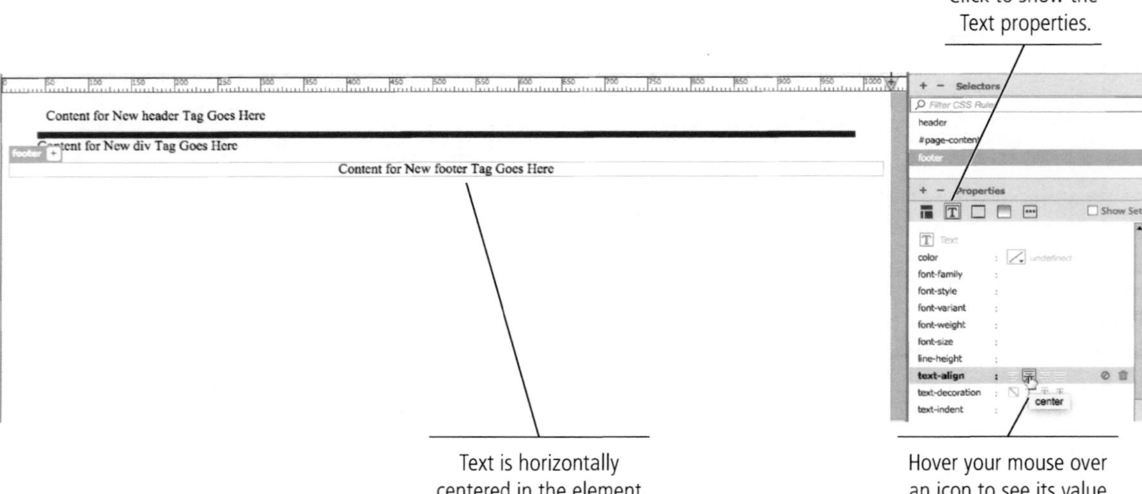

11. **Choose File>Save All, then continue to the next exercise.**

Create New Selectors using the CSS Designer Panel

The CSS Designer panel offers a lot of flexibility for creating and managing selectors. In this exercise, you will define several new selectors, which will later apply to new elements when you add them to the layout.

1. **With design.html open, click museum-styles.css in the Sources section of the CSS Designer panel.**

2. **In the Selectors area of the panel, click the Add Selector button.**

3. **With the new selector's name highlighted, type n.**

   You don't have to accept any part of the default name for a new selector. You can simply type while the name is highlighted to change the selector name.

   When you type a new selector name in the panel, Dreamweaver automatically presents a menu of known selectors that match the characters you type. In this case, a large number of tag names include the "n" character; "nav" is highlighted because it is the first (and only) name that begins with the character you typed.

Note:

Your changes in the following steps do not affect the HTML files; you are only changing the CSS file that is linked the HTML file.

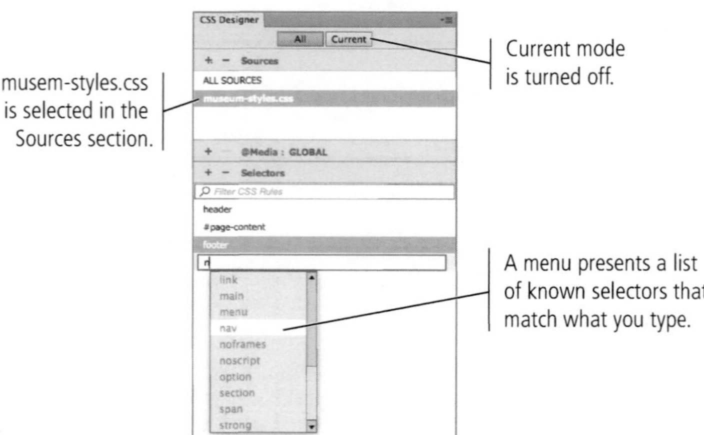

4. **With nav selected in the menu, press Return/Enter to accept the selected menu item, then press Return/Enter again to finalize the new selector.**

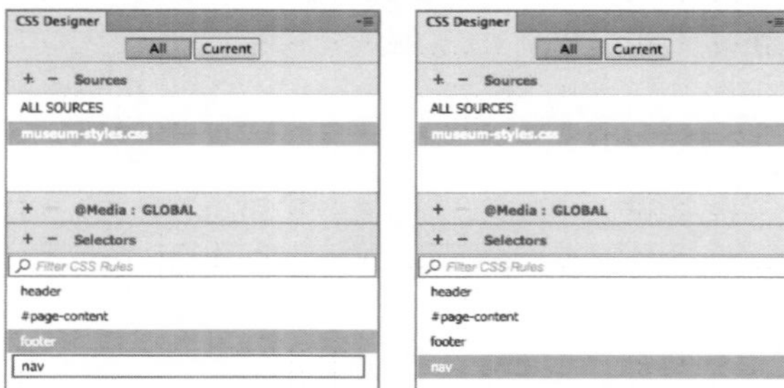

5. **In the Properties section of the panel, define a `200px` width value and `10px` padding on all four sides.**

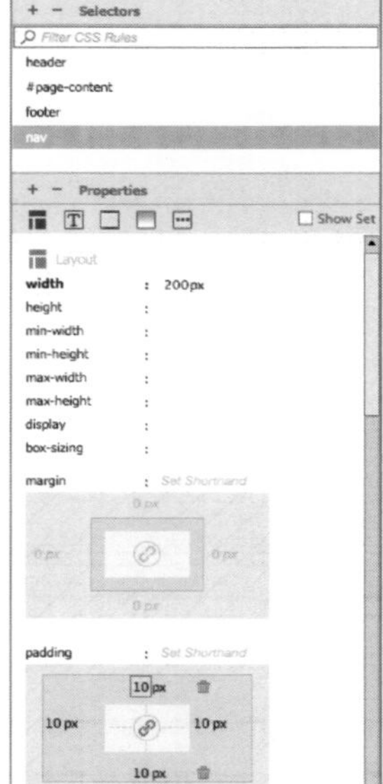

> *Note:*
>
> *There are hundreds of available CSS properties. http://w3schools.com/cssref/css_selectors.asp is an excellent source of information about each property — including proper names, browser compatibility, and possible values.*

6. **Click the Add Selector button again. Type `#main-copy` as the new selector name, then press Return/Enter to add the new selector.**

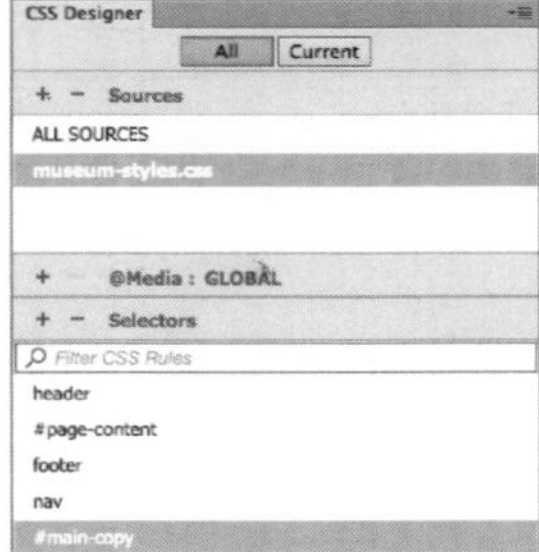

> *Note:*
>
> *Remember: ID selectors always begin with the # character.*

7. **Define the following settings for the new selector:**

width:	**500px**
min-height:	**200px**
padding (all four sides):	**20px**
margin-right:	**50px**

By default, elements collapse to the smallest possible height required to contain their content. By setting the **min-height** property, you prevent an element from collapsing entirely if you delete all the element's content.

Note:

Elements also expand as high as necessary to display all their content unless you define a specific height and restrict the overflow content.

8. **Repeat this process to create another new ID selector named #sidebar, using the following properties:**

width:	**350px**
min-height:	**200px**

9. **Show the museum-styles.css file in the Code pane.**

Because you selected museum-styles.css in the Sources section of the panel, the new selectors are added to that file. You can see the new selectors in the Code pane as long as the museum-styles.css file is showing in that pane.

Nothing has been added to the HTML file, as you can see in the Design pane. The asterisks show that the CSS file has been modified, but the HTML file has not changed.

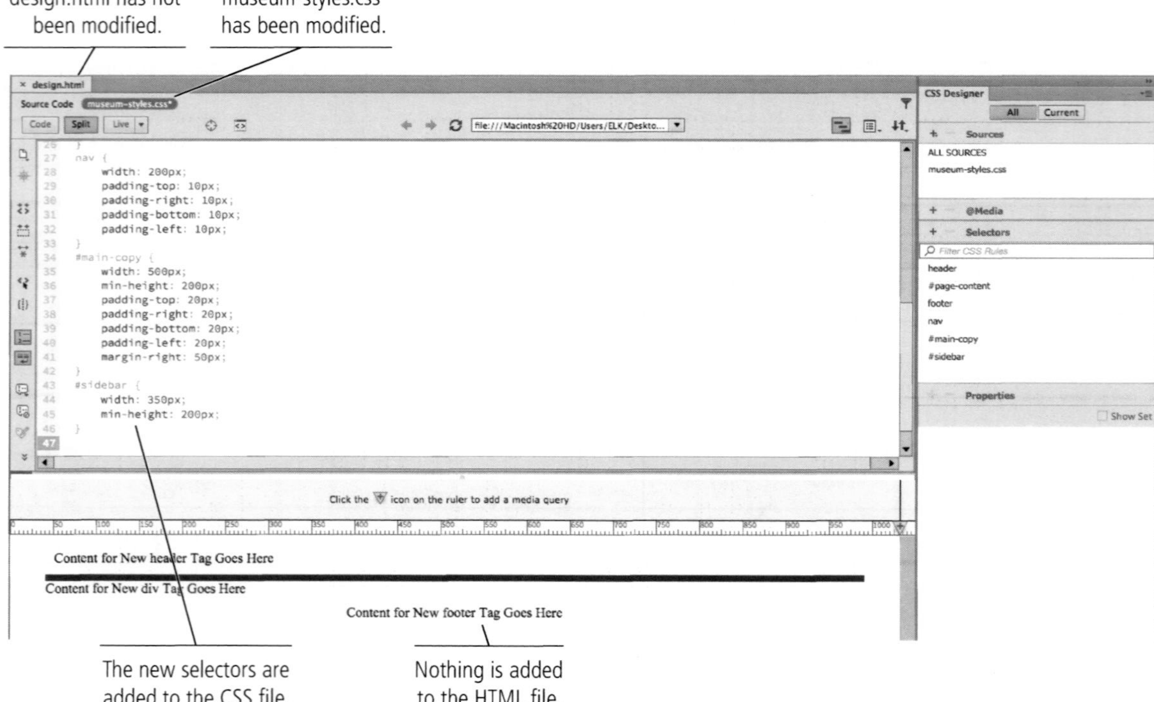
design.html has not been modified.
museum-styles.css has been modified.
The new selectors are added to the CSS file.
Nothing is added to the HTML file.
Content for New header Tag Goes Here
Content for New div Tag Goes Here
Content for New footer Tag Goes Here

10. **Click in the Code pane to make it active, then choose File>Save.**

The Save command (and its shortcut, Command/Control-S) saves the active file wherever the insertion point is placed. By clicking in the Code pane to place the insertion point in the museum-styles.css file, you are saving the CSS file and not the HTML file. (The HTML file did not change in this exercise.)

11. **Continue to the next exercise.**

Create and Manage Nested Elements

The Museum site's basic page structure requires three additional elements, which will be nested inside the ones you already created. In this exercise, you use several techniques for creating nested elements.

1. **With design.html open, show the page source code in the Code pane.**

2. **In the HTML Insert panel, click the Navigation button and drag into the document window. When a blue border outlines the header element, release the mouse button.**

   If you drag an element into an existing element, a heavy blue border identifies the active element. The new element will be nested inside the highlighted one.

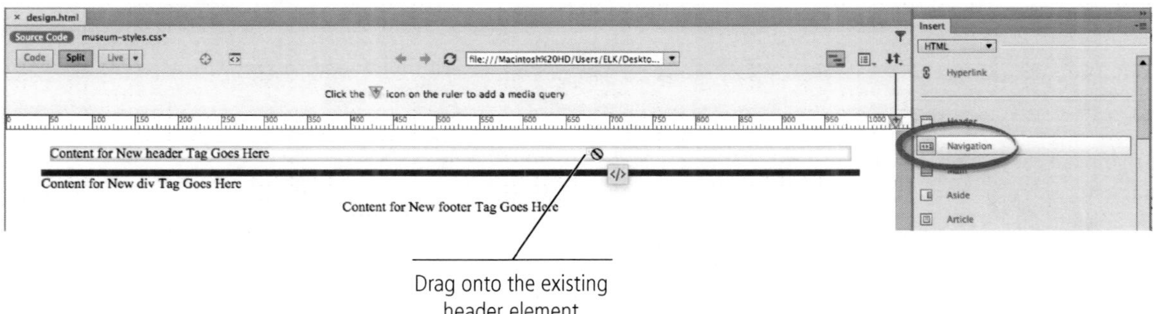

Drag onto the existing header element.

3. **Review the page's source code in the Code pane.**

   Nested container elements should always appear before other content in the containing element. As you can see, Dreamweaver properly places the nav element code before the header element's placeholder text.

   Because you defined width and padding properties for the nav selector in the previous exercise, those properties automatically apply to the newly placed nav element.

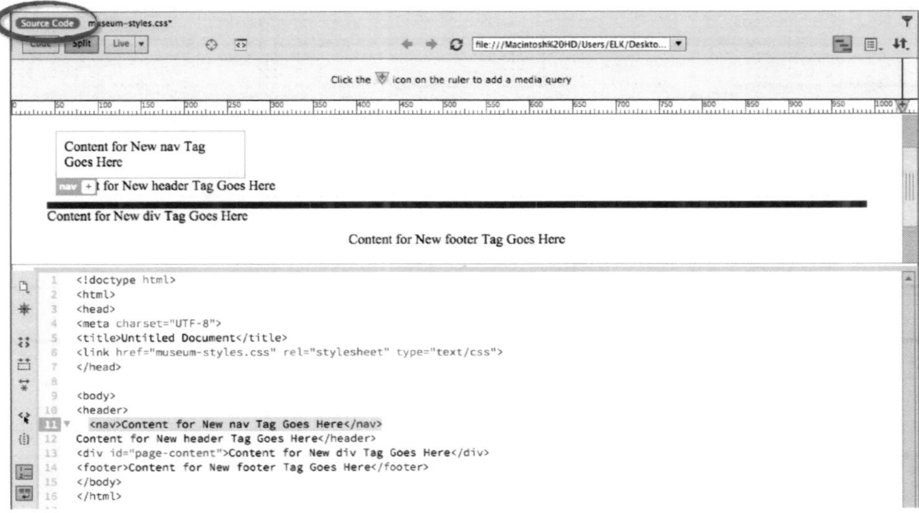

4. **Click the Section button in the HTML Insert panel and drag into the document window. When the mouse cursor is not over any existing element, release the mouse button.**

If you drag an element into an empty area of the page (below other elements), the body element is highlighted. The new element will be added at the top of the page hierarchy.

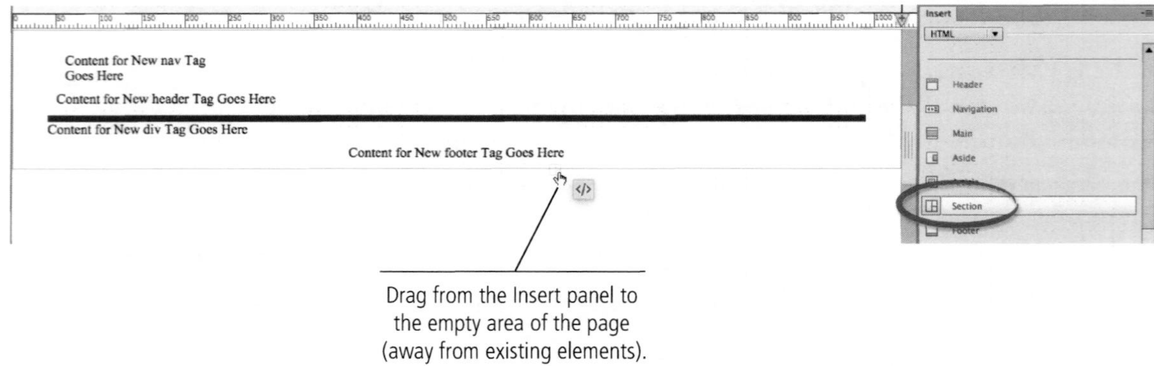

Drag from the Insert panel to the empty area of the page (away from existing elements).

As you can see in the Design pane, the element is added above the existing header element. The page code shows the position of the new section element, at the beginning of the element hierarchy.

The new section element is added to the page, above the header element.

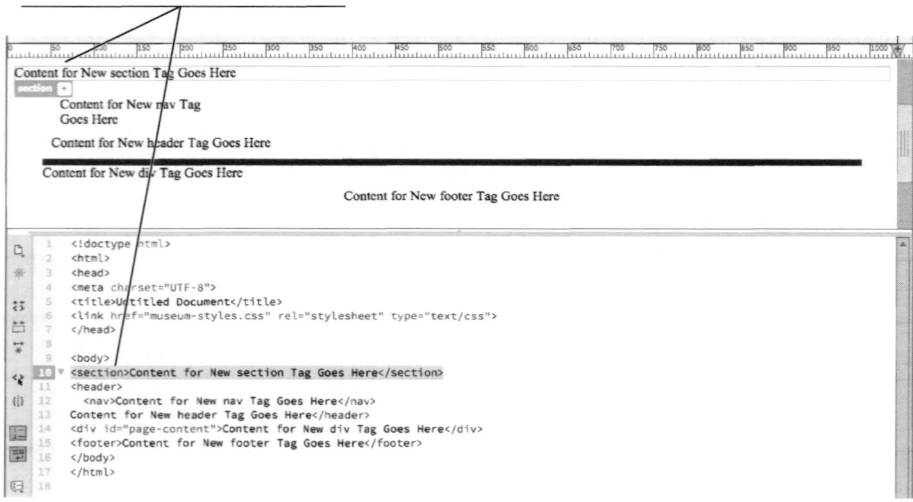

5. **Click the Add Class/ID button (the + button) in the Element Display. In the resulting field, type #.**

The resulting menu shows all available selectors that match the characters you type. (Remember, ID selectors always begin with the # character.)

You can use the Arrow keys to navigate items in the resulting menu, or double-click an option in this menu to accept it.

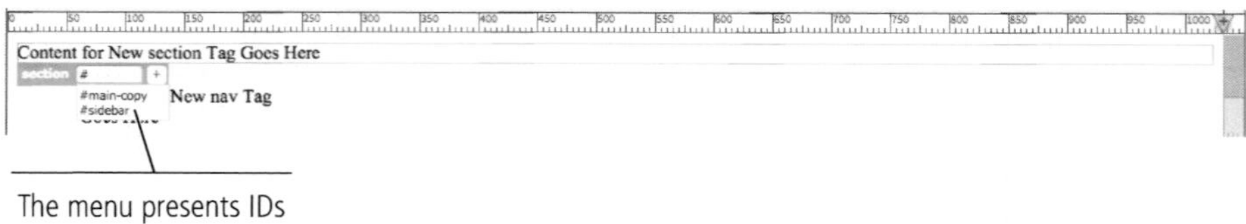

The menu presents IDs that match your typing.

6. **Click #main-copy in the menu to apply that ID to the active element.**

   Remember, the #main-copy selector defines a width of 500px and minimum height of 200px, so the section element now shows those dimensions in the document window.

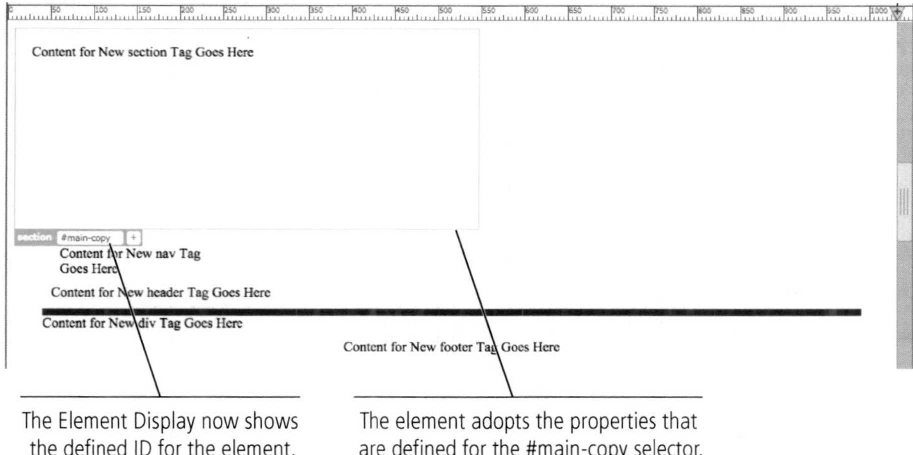

7. **Open the DOM panel (Window>DOM).**

   DOM is short for document object model. The DOM panel shows the overall structure of elements in your document. The elements appear in the same order as what you see in the document window. You can simply review your page content, or drag items in the panel to rearrange the various elements.

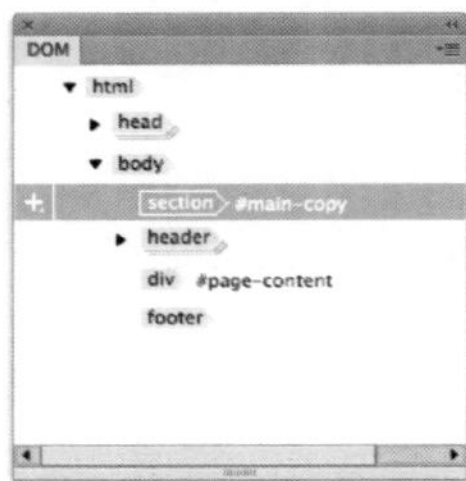

8. **In the DOM panel, drag the section#main-copy element onto the div#page-content element. When you do not see a green line in the panel, release the mouse button.**

   When you drag elements in the panel, a green line shows where the element you are dragging will be placed in the hierarchy. If you want to nest one element into another, make sure the intended parent is highlighted but no green line appears.

   When you release the mouse button, you can see the section#main-copy element has moved into the div#page-content element.

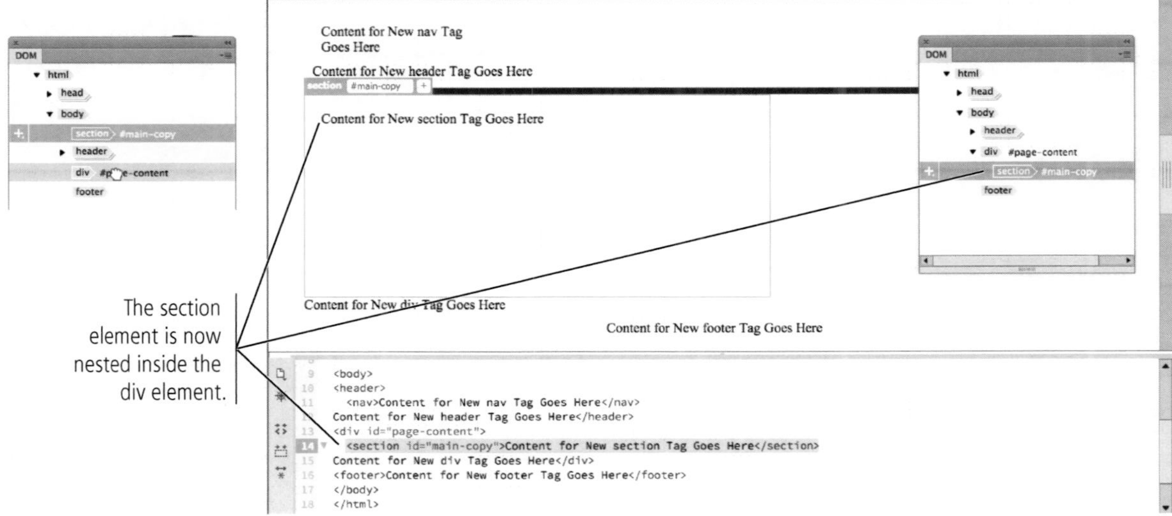

9. **Click to select the nested section element in the panel.**

10. **Click the + button to the left of the section element and choose Insert After in the pop-up menu.**

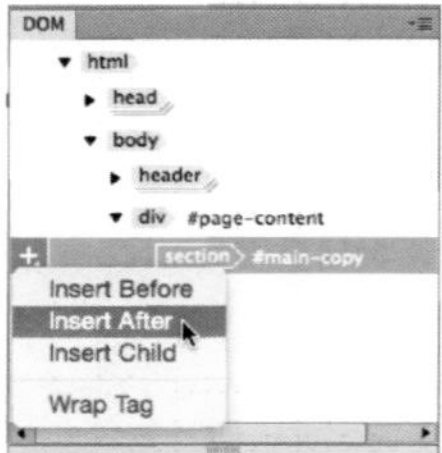

11. **With the word "div" highlighted, type `sec`.**

    The new element defaults to be a div element, but you can type a different element name in the field to change it.

    As you type, code hints present a list of options that match the characters you type. As soon as you type the "c", "section" is the only available option in the menu.

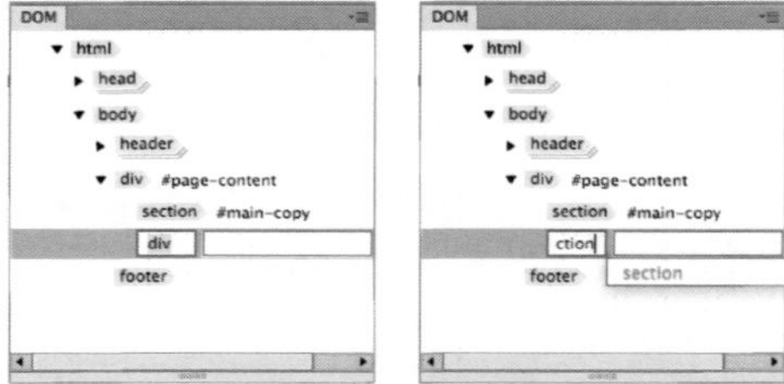

12. **Press Return/Enter two times to finalize the new element as a section instead of a div.**

13. **Double-click to the right of the section tag in the panel. In the resulting field, type `#`, then select #sidebar from the pop-up menu.**

    The menu shows all available selectors that match the characters you type. You can use each ID only once on any given page; because the #main-copy ID has already been used on this page, it is no long available and does not appear in the list.

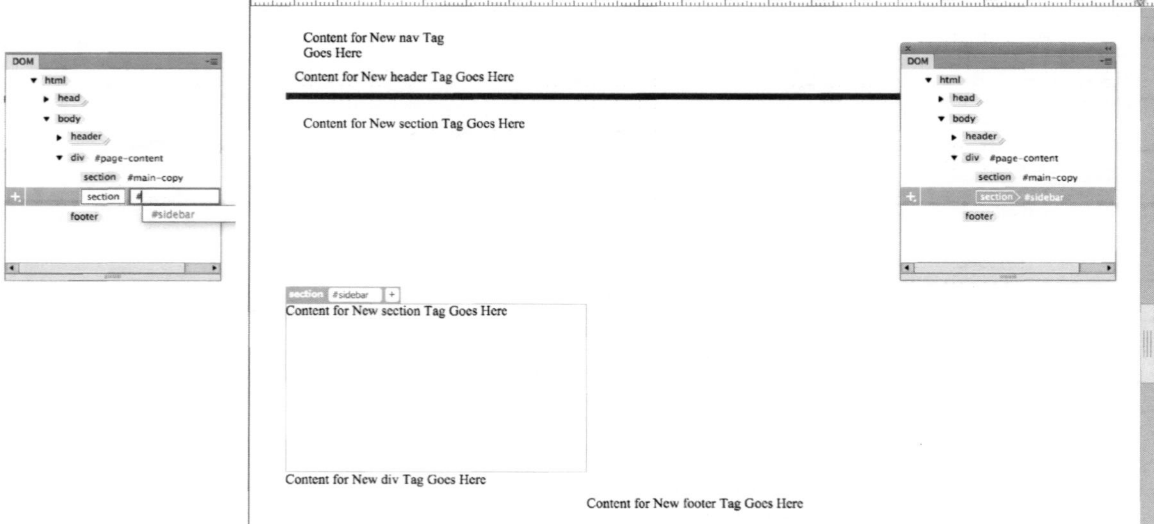

14. In the Code, select and delete the placeholder content in the page-content div.

This div exists to contain the other two elements, so you don't need the placeholder text.

If you delete the text in the Live view, Dreamweaver leaves a nonbreaking space character in place of the deleted text. By deleting the text in the Code pane, you avoid the unwanted character.

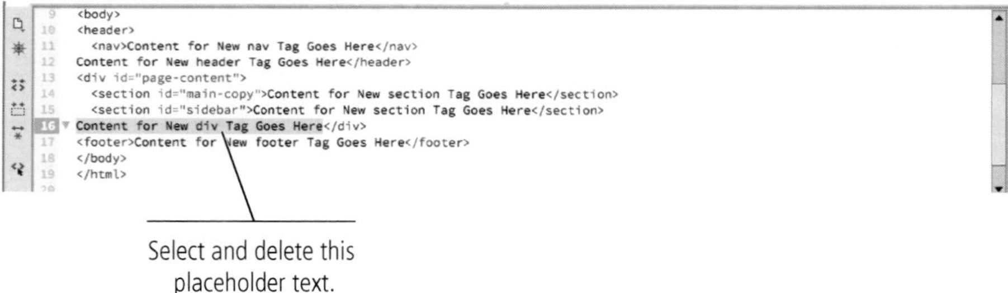

15. Choose File>Save All, then continue to the next exercise.

Control Element Float Position

The nav element should appear on the right side of the header element. Inside the div#page-content element, the main-copy section and sidebar section should appear in the same "row." As you can see in your current layout, several elements do not yet appear in the correct position.

Nested elements automatically align based on the horizontal alignment properties of the containing element. If no specific alignment is defined, the nested elements align to the left side of the container and each appears in sequential order.

1. With design.html open, show only the Design view and turn off the Live view.

When the Live view is turned off, visual aids make it easier to see the boundaries of various elements on the page.

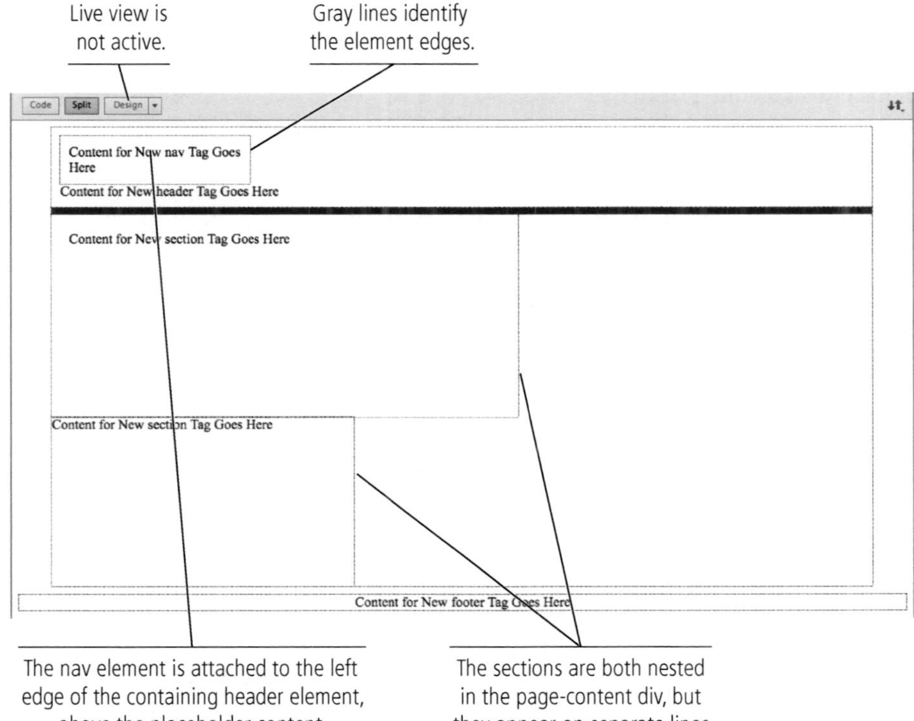

2. **Click the Current button at the top of the CSS Designer panel to turn that mode on.**

3. **Click the edge of the nav element in the document window to select it.**

   When Current mode is active, the panel shows only selectors that affect the active selection in the document. In this case, the active element is contained inside the header element, so the selected element can be affected by both the header and nav selectors.

4. **With the nav selector selected in the CSS Designer panel, check the Show Set option in the Properties section.**

When Current mode is active, the panel shows only selectors related to the active selection.

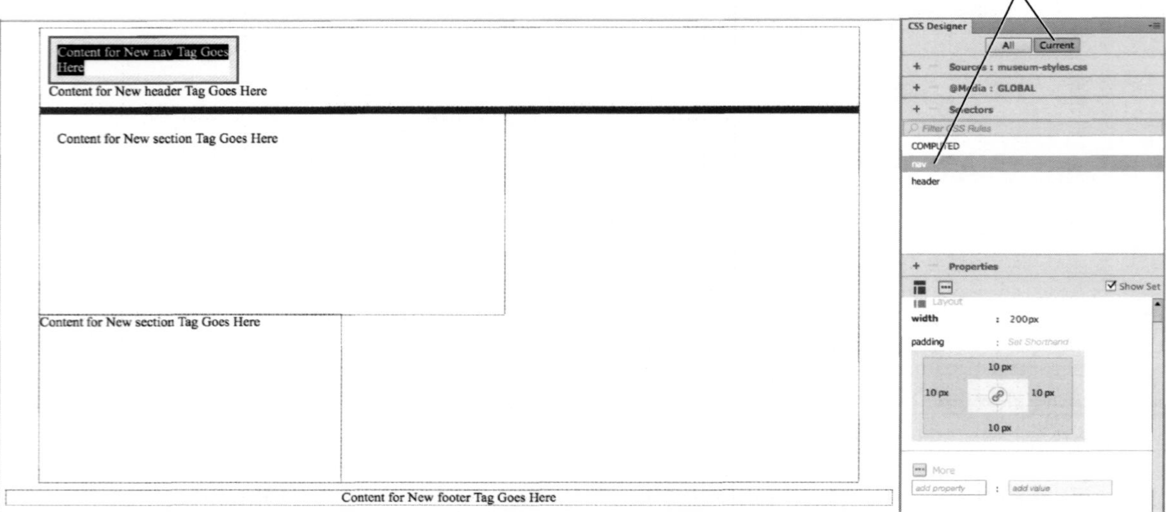

5. **Click in the Add Property field at the bottom of the Properties section and type flo.**

   You can use the "More" section of the panel to add any new property to the active selector. (Many are not available in the other sections of the panel.) Simply type the property name to add the property you want.

   Type in the field to show available properties with the characters you type.

   Choose a specific property in this menu to add it to the selector.

   Typing in the field presents a menu of all available properties that contain the characters you type. You can also use the arrow keys to navigate the resulting menu, and press Return/Enter to add the highlighted property.

6. **Click float in the resulting menu to add it as a new property.**

   After you define the property you want to add, the secondary menu presents the possible values for that property.

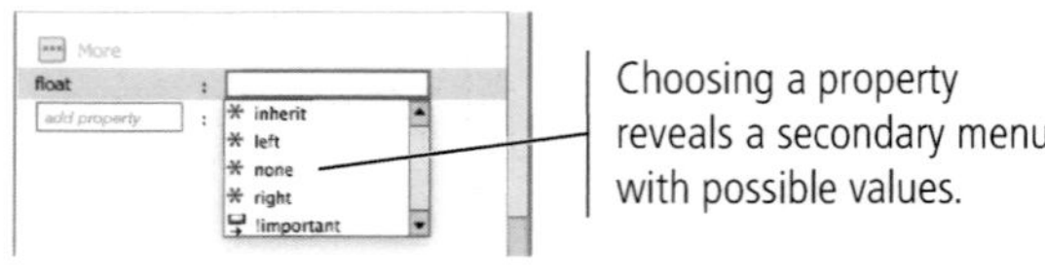

Choosing a property reveals a secondary menu with possible values.

7. **Click right in the menu of values to select it.**

The CSS **float** property allows you to intentionally attach an element to the left or right edge of the containing element, and allows other content to sit beside or wrap around that element. This gives you greater flexibility when creating complex layouts.

The nav element now properly aligns on the right side of its immediate parent container (the header element).

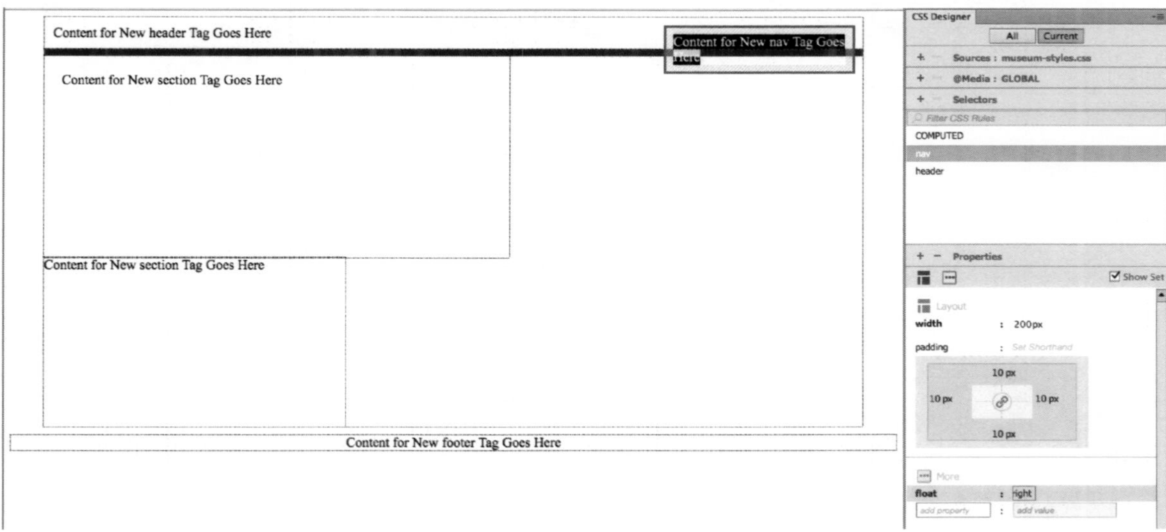

8. **Repeat the process from this exercise to define float values as follows:**

#main-copy	**float:left**
#sidebar	**float:right**

Note:

You will fix the issue with the nav element height in the next exercise.

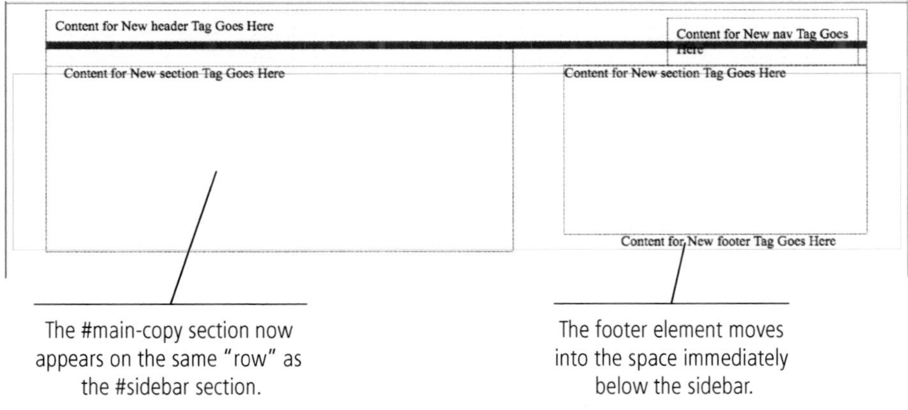

The #main-copy section now appears on the same "row" as the #sidebar section.

The footer element moves into the space immediately below the sidebar.

9. **Assign the left float value to the footer selector.**

When the footer element had no defined float property, it moved into an unpredicted position to the right of the main-copy section; to solve the problem, you are assigning a specific float property to the footer element to attach it to the left edge of its parent container (the body element).

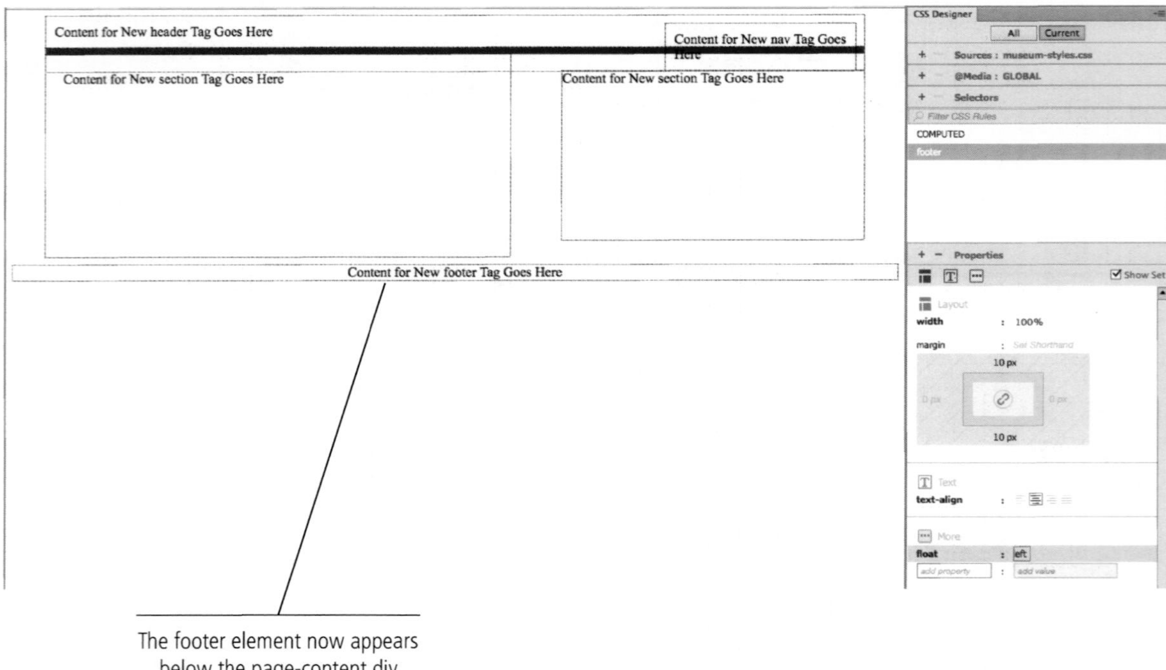

The footer element now appears below the page-content div.

10. **Choose File>Save All, then continue to the next exercise.**

 Work with the CSS Box Model

When you design layouts using CSS, think of any element as a box made up of four parts: margin, border, padding, and content. The object's overall size — the amount of space it occupies on the page — is the sum of the values for these four properties:

- The **margin** is outside the box edges; it is invisible and has no background color. Margin does not affect content within the element.
- The **border** is the edge of the element, based on the specified dimensions.
- The **padding** lies inside the edge of the element, forming a cushion between the box edge and the box content.
- The **content** lies inside the padding. When you define the width and height for an element, you define the content area.

```
#box {
    width: 200px;
    margin: 20px;
    margin-left: 100px;
    padding: 20px;
    padding-right: 100px;
    border: 10px solid #096;
}
```

Content for id "box" Goes Here

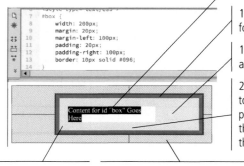

200-pixel width defines the actual content area.

10-pixel border is on all four sides of the box.

100-pixel right padding is added inside the box edge.

20-pixel padding is applied to the other three edges (the padding-right value overrides the padding value for only the right edge).

100-pixel left margin is added outside the box edge.

20-pixel margins are applied to the other three edges (the margin-left value overrides the margin value for only the left edge).

1. **With design.html open, make sure the Live view is turned off.**

2. **Drag the file getty-logo.png (from the site images folder) into the header element. Using the Properties panel, define The Getty Foundation as alternate text for the placed image.**

   Unless you define otherwise, HTML elements always expand to whatever height is necessary to show all content. When you place this image, the header element automatically expands to the height necessary to accommodate the logo.

Note:

Remember, to define alternate text, you can select the image in the Design pane and then type in the Alt field of the Properties panel.

3. **Select and delete the placeholder text from the header element.**

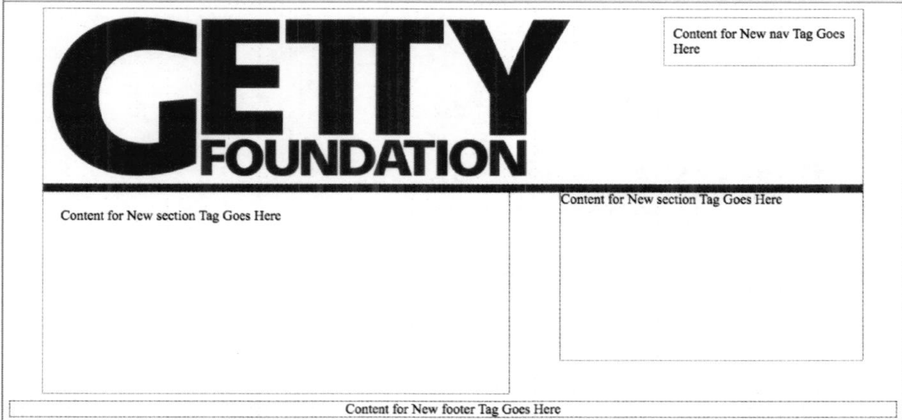

4. **Delete the placeholder text from the nav element, then type the following in the nav element:**

   About the Getty [Return/Enter]

   Traveling Exhibits [Return/Enter]

   Permanent Exhibits

5. **In the CSS Designer panel, use the Add Property field to define a 50px margin-top value for the nav selector.**

   As you can see from the gray element edges, the increased top margin aligns the bottom edge of the nav element to the bottom edge of the placed logo.

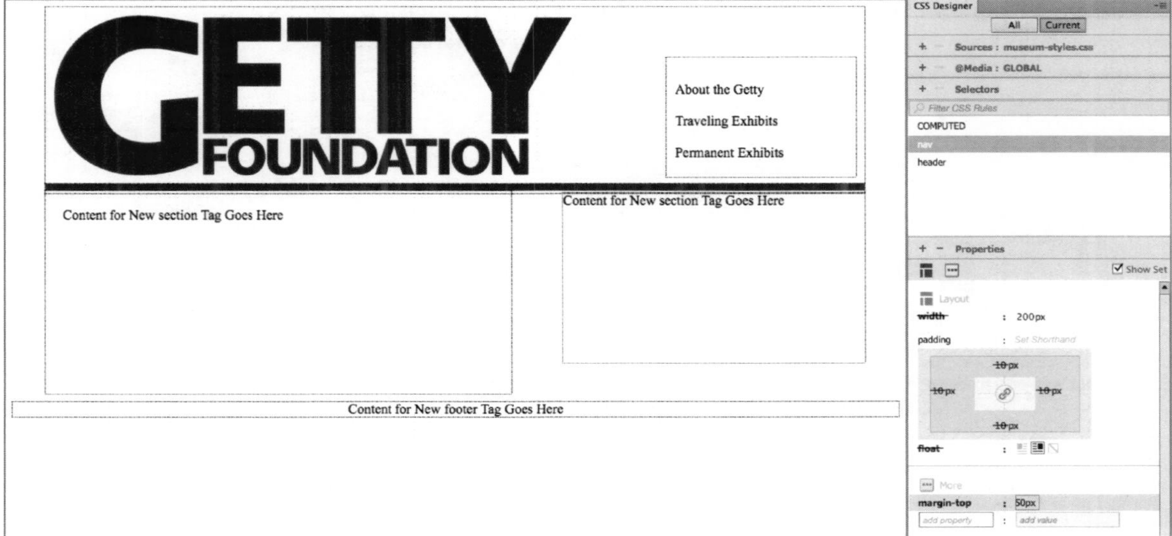

6. **Click to select the section#sidebar element in the layout.**

7. **With the #sidebar selector active in the CSS Designer panel, uncheck the Show Set option and navigate to the Background properties.**

8. **In the background-image options, define parchment.png (from the site images folder) as the background image, and choose the no-repeat option.**

   Some users will see the bottom edge of the parchment in the sidebar (as shown in our screen shot here), while others might see the edge cut off. The next few steps illustrate the problem of relying solely on the regular Design view when working with CSS.

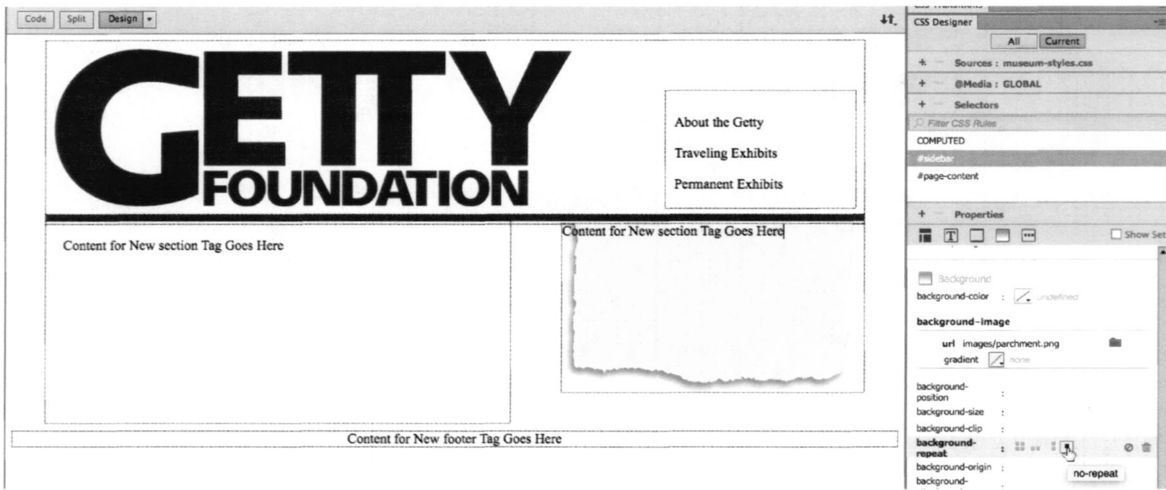

9. **Turn on the Live view.**

   Although the regular Design view makes it easier to see the CSS layout structure (including the element boundaries), it does not always accurately depict CSS. When the Live view is active, you get a better idea of exactly what will appear when a browser renders the CSS.

   As you can see, the parchment image is bluntly cut off at the bottom of the section#sidebar element. Background images default to begin at the top-left corner of their containing element.

   This section element has a defined min-height property, so it will always be at least 200px high — but it will expand as high as necessary to contain the element content. Since you don't know exactly how high the element will be, you can avoid the cutoff problem by changing the positioning of the background image.

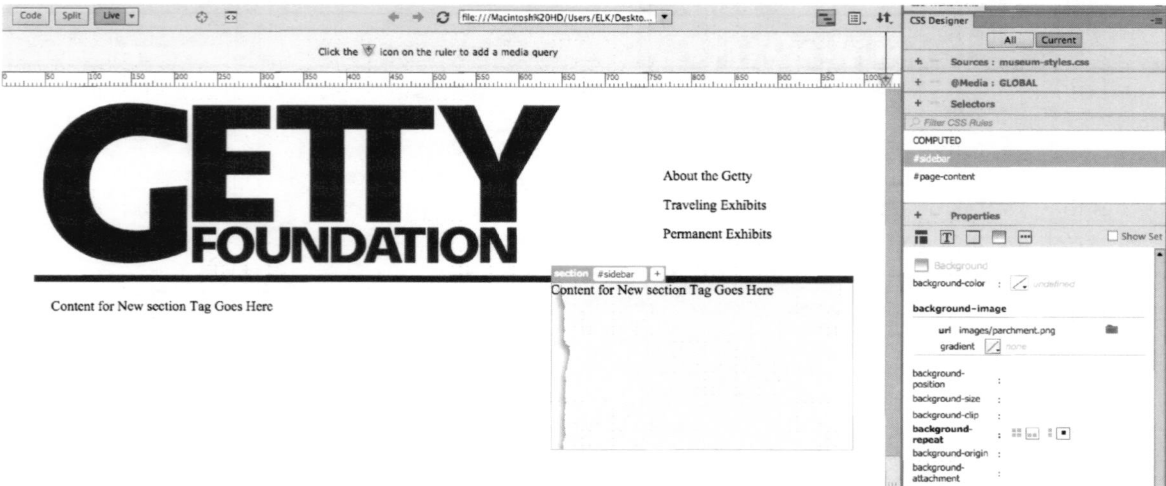

10. **Choose center in the first background-position menu, and choose bottom in the second background position menu.**

These settings tell the browser to align the bottom edge of the background image to the center bottom edge of the container. The torn-off edge of the parchment will always appear at the bottom, even when the element expands to contain various content.

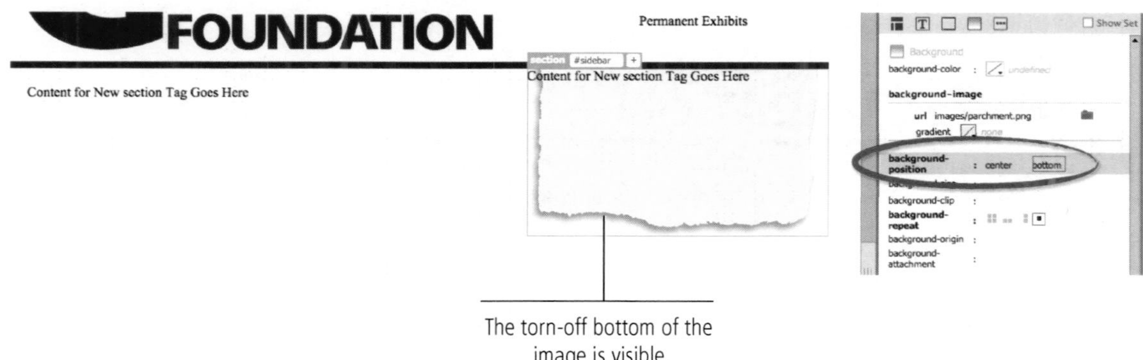

The torn-off bottom of the image is visible.

You might notice another problem. Placeholder content in the section#sidebar element runs directly into the element edge. In the CSS box model, padding defines a distance at which content exists from the element edge; you can use this property to fix the problem.

11. **Define the following padding values for the #sidebar selector:**

padding-top:	**10px**
padding-right:	**30px**
padding-bottom:	**30px**
padding-left:	**30px**

The background image extends into the padding area because the padding is part of the actual element area. Margin values are added outside the element; background images do not extend into the margin area.

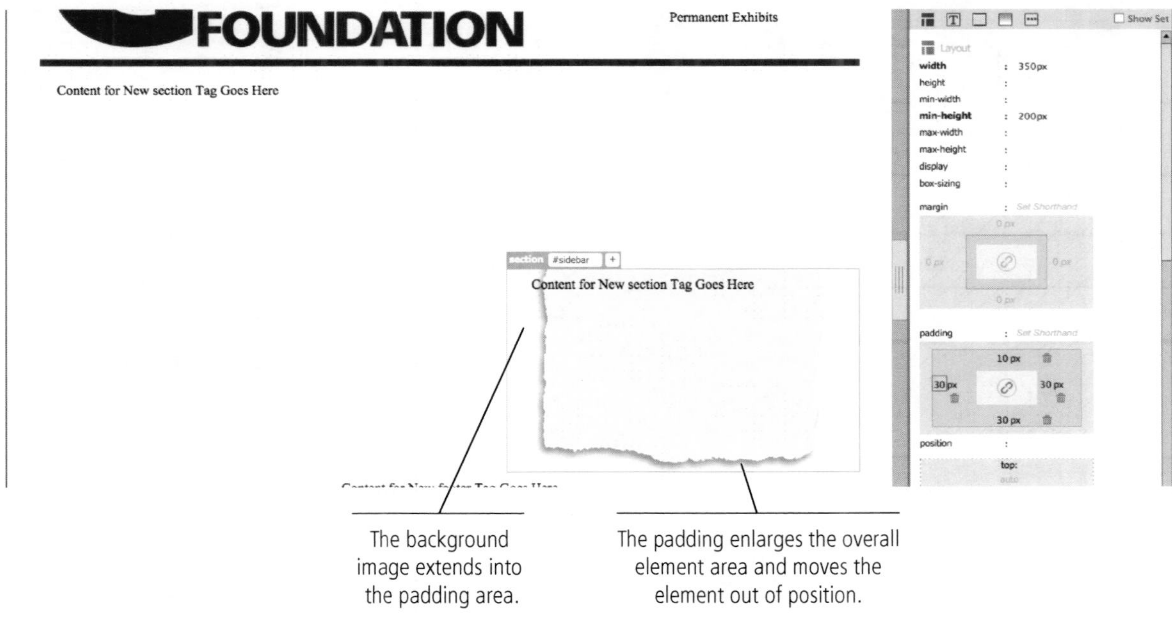

The background image extends into the padding area.

The padding enlarges the overall element area and moves the element out of position.

It is important to realize that both padding and margins affect the overall size of the element. The section#sidebar element is now 410 pixels wide (350 defined width + 30 left padding + 30 right padding). With that width, it no longer fits on the same "row" as the section#main-copy element.

12. **Subtract 60 from the width value of the #sidebar selector.**

    To change the existing property values, simply click the value to highlight it and then type the new value.

    When you change margins and/or padding, you often have to make a proportional change to the width and/or height properties if you want the element to occupy the same overall space. After changing the width, the section#sidebar element moves back into place.

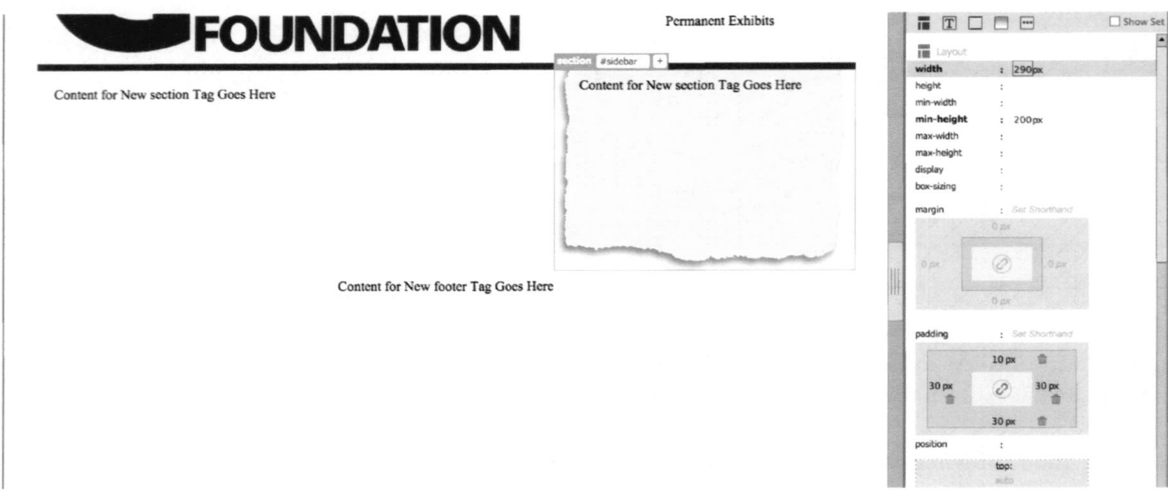

13. **Click to select the section#main-copy element in the layout.**

14. **In the CSS Designer panel, make sure #main-copy is selected and show the Background properties.**

15. **Click the background-color swatch to open the color picker, then choose the Eyedropper tool in the bottom-right corner.**

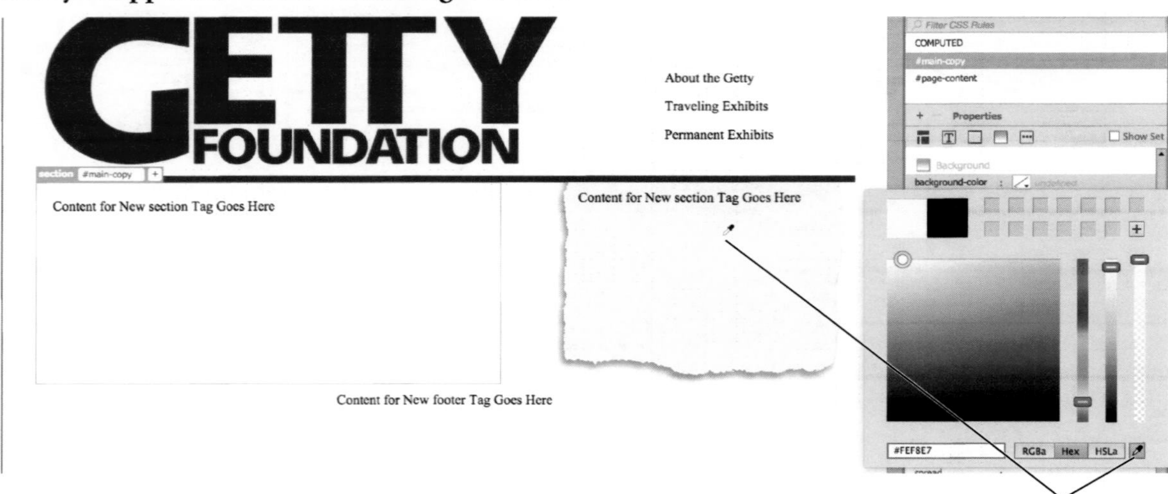

Click the eyedropper to sample color from an existing page element.

16. **Move the cursor over a medium-yellow shade in the parchment image. Click to select the color, then press Return/Enter to finalize the new background-color property.**

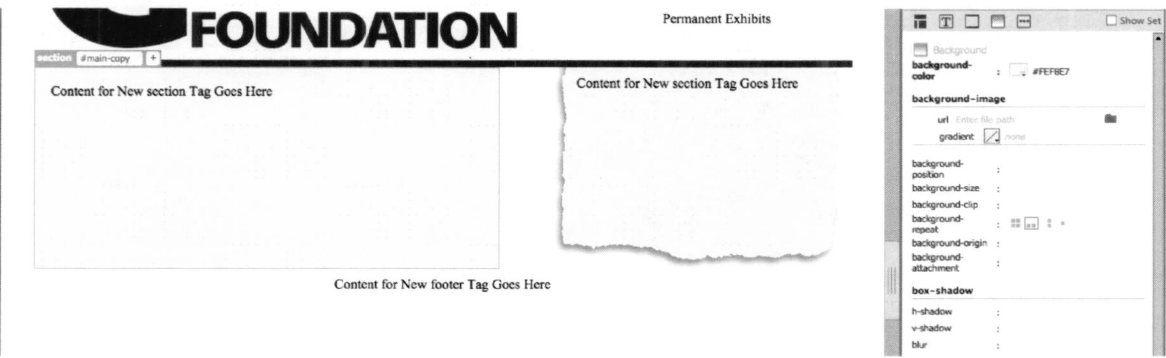

17. **Choose File>Save All, then continue to the next exercise.**

Define Properties for the <body> Tag

The **<body>** tag surrounds all visible content in a Web page. Because **<body>** is an HTML tag, you have to create a tag selector to define properties for the body element.

1. **With `design.html` open, click All at the top of the CSS Designer panel to turn off the Current mode.**

2. **Click museum-styles.css is the Sources section of the CSS Designer panel, then click the Add Selector button in the Selector section of the panel.**

3. **Type `body` as the new selector name, then press Return/Enter two times to finalize the selector.**

4. **In the Layout properties, click to highlight the Set Shorthand field for the margin property. Type `0px`, then press Return/Enter to finalize the new value.**

   When you define values for a CSS property, do not include a space between the number and the unit of measurement.

5. **Turn on the Lock icon in the center of the padding proxy to make all four padding values the same. Highlight the top padding field and type `0px` to define a zero-pixel padding.**

   Because you linked all four padding fields by clicking the lock icon, changing one value changes the other three as well.

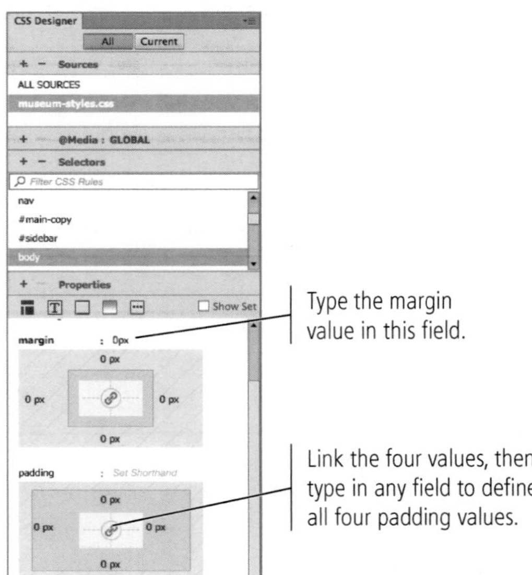

6. **Review the new selector in the code of the museum-styles.css file.**

   The margin, which you defined using the Set Shorthand field, only occupies one line; the **margin** property without specific sides defined applies to all edges of the element.

   The various fields in the Properties panel defined separate properties for each margin (**padding-top**, **padding-right**, **padding-bottom**, and **padding-left**).

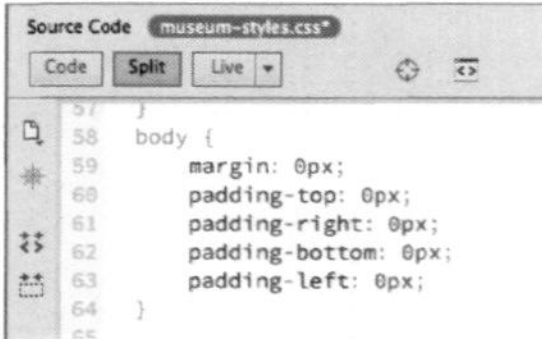

7. **With body still selected in the Selectors section of the panel, define the following Background properties for the body selector:**

background-image:	**floor.jpg**
background-size:	**cover**
background-attachment:	**fixed**

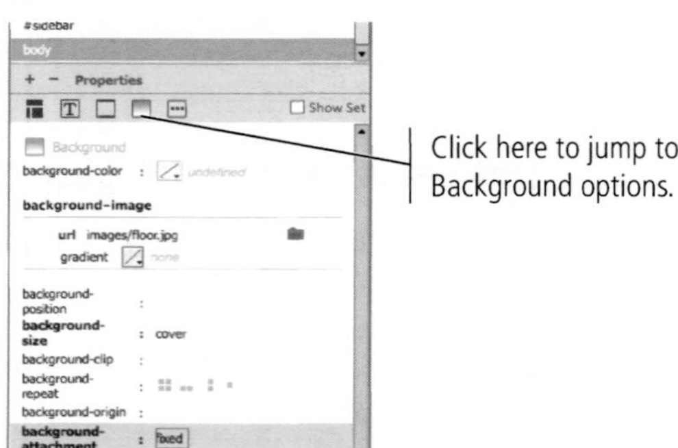

Click here to jump to Background options.

   The **background-size** property defines the size of background images.

   - If you do not define a specific background size, the image will simply display at its actual size. The same result can be achieved using the **auto** value.

     background-size: auto

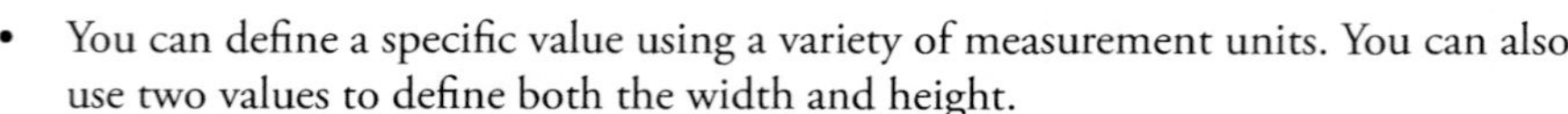

   - You can define a specific value using a variety of measurement units. You can also use two values to define both the width and height.

     background-size: 400px 600px [width height]

     Instead of specific values, you can use percentages. In this case, the background image appears as a percentage of the container.

     background-size: 80% 100% [width height]

   - The **cover** value scales the background image as large as necessary completely fill the container. If the image has a different aspect ratio than the container, some parts of the background image will be cut off.

     background-size: cover

   - The **contain** value scales the image to the largest possible size so that the entire image fits inside the container. If the image has a different aspect ratio than the container, some areas of the container will not be filled by the background image unless you tile it.

     background-size: contain

   The **background-attachment** property determines whether a background image moves when the page scrolls. By default, background images scroll with the page. When you define the **fixed** value, the background image remains in place even when the rest of the page scrolls in front of it.

8. **In the Text options, define the following properties for the body selector:**

font-family:	**Gotham, Helvetica Neue, Helvetica, Arial, sans-serif**
font-size:	**14px**
font-weight:	**300**
line-height:	**22px**

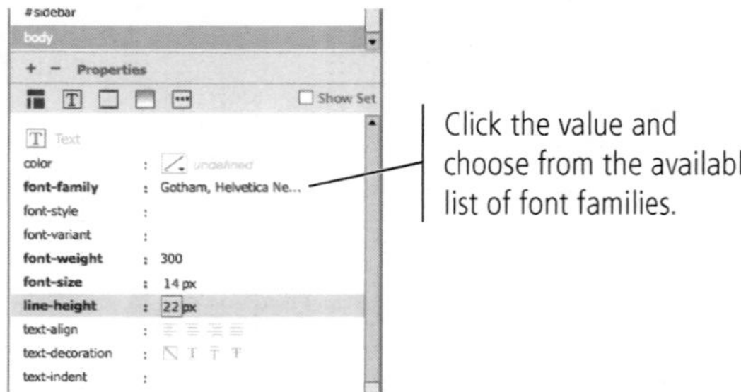

Click the value and choose from the available list of font families.

The **font-family** list defines fonts that will be used to display the text, in order of availability.

The **font-weight** property defines how thick characters should be displayed. Numeric values from 100 to 900 (in hundreds) define this option from thin to thick; 400 is approximately normal.

The **line-height** property defines the distance from one line of text to the next in a paragraph.

9. **Review the results in the Design pane.**

Web browsers have default values (which can differ) for many elements, including the body element. By specifying padding and margins of 0, you are standardizing these settings or negating any default values (called "normalizing"), so all browsers will render the body element the same way.

By this point you should begin to understand the concept of nested tags. The **<body>** tag is the parent of the tags it contains. Properties of the parent tag are automatically inherited by the child (nested) tags.

In this case, the font family, size, weight, and line height you defined for the **<body>** tag are automatically applied to content in the nested elements.

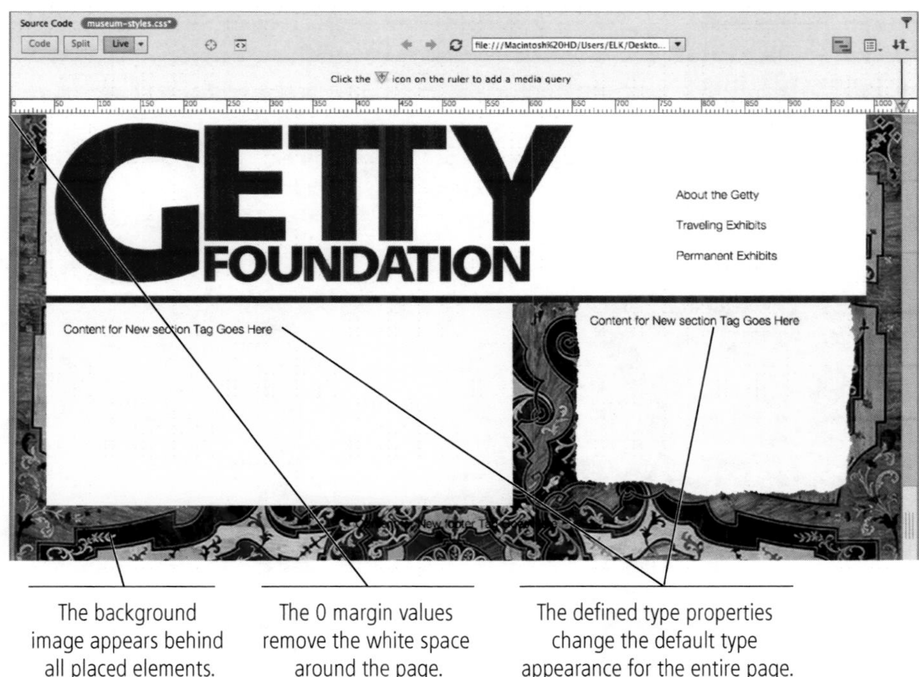

The 0 margin values remove the white space around the page.
The defined type properties change the default type appearance for the entire page.

10. **Save all files, then continue to the next stage of the project.**

Stage 2 Working with a Template

Using a template file (with the ".dwt" extension), you can create common page elements only once, rather than recreating them every time you add a new page to a site. If you modify a template, pages based on the template are updated to reflect the same changes.

When you create a Dreamweaver template, you indicate which elements of a page should remain constant (non-editable; locked) in pages based on that template, and which elements can be changed.

Create a Template

When all pages in a site will have the same basic layout, you can save the common elements as a template, and then apply the template to all pages. This workflow makes it much faster and easier to maintain consistency and complete the project.

Following the same logic, keep in mind that the museum-styles.css file in this site is attached to the design.html file — which will become the template. Any pages created from the template file will also be attached to the museum-styles.css file, so changes made in the museum-styles.css file will affect pages created from the template.

1. **With design.html from the Museum site open, turn off the Live view.**

   You can't create a template while the Live view is active.

2. **Select and delete the placeholder text in the main-copy and sidebar section elements.**

   Because you defined a minimum height for the #main-copy and #sidebar selectors, the elements do not entirely collapse in the page layout.

3. **Replace the placeholder text in the footer div with the following:**

   Site design by Against The Clock, Inc.

4. **Using the CSS Designer panel, make sure the footer selector is active and change the text color property to white.**

   It's important to realize that layout development is an ongoing evolutionary process; as you continue to work, new issues will pop up. You can always add properties to or remove properties from specific selectors, edit the values of specific properties, and add new selectors as necessary to meet a project's needs.

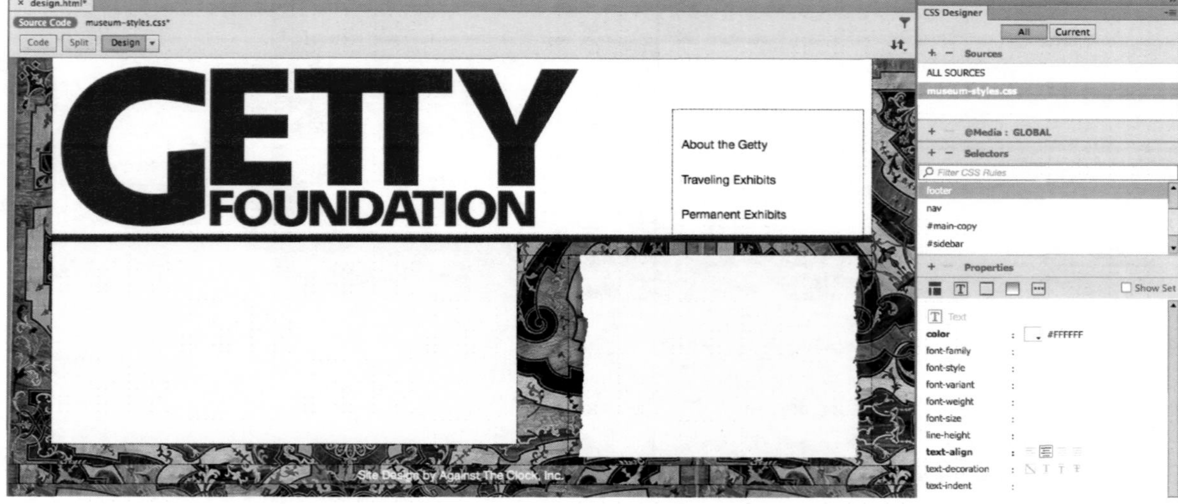

5. **Choose File>Save As Template.**

6. **In the Save As Template dialog box, make sure Museum is selected in the Site menu.**

7. **In the Description field, type `Museum Site Template`.**

   The description is only relevant in Dreamweaver; it will not appear in any page based on the template. (You can modify the template description by choosing Modify>Templates>Description.)

8. **Click Save to save the active file as a template.**

   The extension ".dwt" is automatically added on both Macintosh and Windows.

9. **Click Yes in the resulting dialog box.**

   The template is saved in a Templates folder, which Dreamweaver automatically creates for you in the local root folder of the Museum site. To ensure that all images and links function properly, you should allow Dreamweaver to update the link information as necessary.

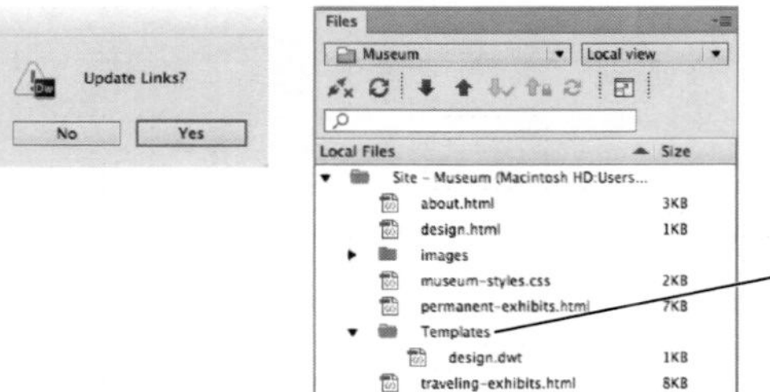

The template is automatically added to the site in a new Templates folder.

   Your template contains the layout structure you created in the first stage of this project. However, after converting the document into a template, all parts of the page become non-editable. Until you define an editable region, you won't be able to add page-specific content to any pages based on this template.

10. **Show the page source code in the Code pane.**

11. **Change the Document Title to `The Getty Foundation`.**

    When you define a title in a template file, that title is automatically applied to any page attached to the template. You are adding the basic information in the template, so you can then simply add page-specific information in each attached file.

    As you can see in the Code pane, the <title> tag is contained in special tags that define it as an editable region. This means that the title can be edited independently on any page that is attached to the template file.

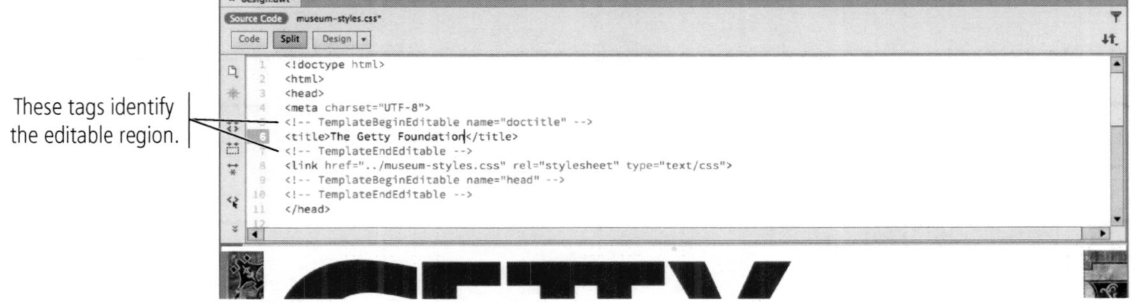

Note:

You can also create a template from the active page by choosing Insert>Template Objects>Make Template.

Note:

Do not move your templates out of the Templates folder or save any non-template files in the Templates folder. Also, do not move the Templates folder out of your local root folder. Doing so causes errors in paths in the templates.

12. **In the Design pane, click to place the insertion point in the main-copy section, then click section#main-copy in the Tag Selector to select the entire element.**

13. **Click the Editable Region button in the Templates Insert panel.**

    You can also choose Insert>Template Objects>Editable Region.

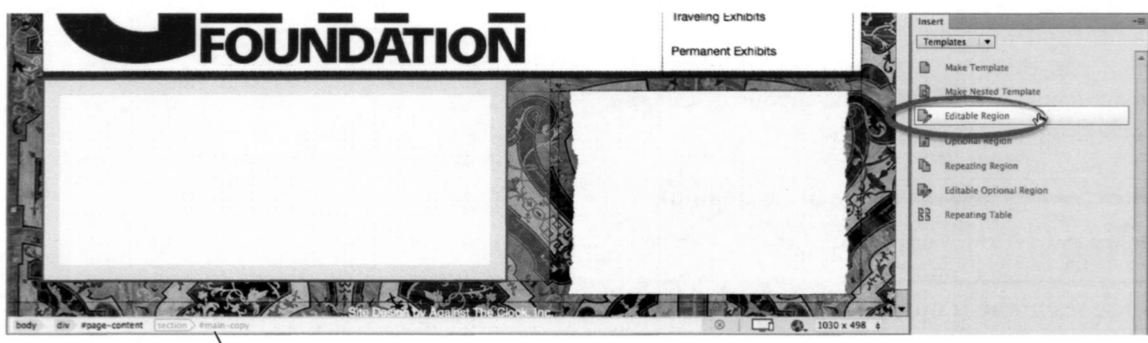

Click the section#main-copy tag to select the entire element.

14. **Type `Page Content` in the resulting dialog box and then click OK.**

    When pages are created from this template, the editable regions will be the only areas that can be modified.

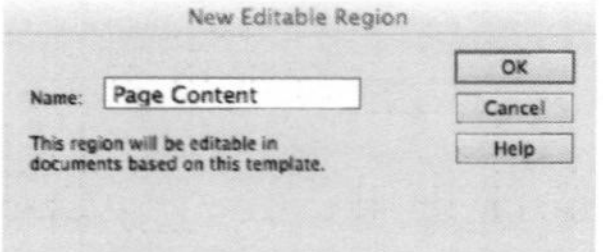

15. **In the Design pane, click the blue Page Content tag above the editable region.**

    In the Design view, editable areas are identified with a blue tag and border; these are for design purposes, and will not be visible in the resulting HTML pages. If you don't see a blue tag with the Page Content region name, open the View>Visual Aids menu and choose Invisible Elements to toggle on that option.

    Clicking this tab selects the entire object; this makes it easier for you to see the related code in the Code pane.

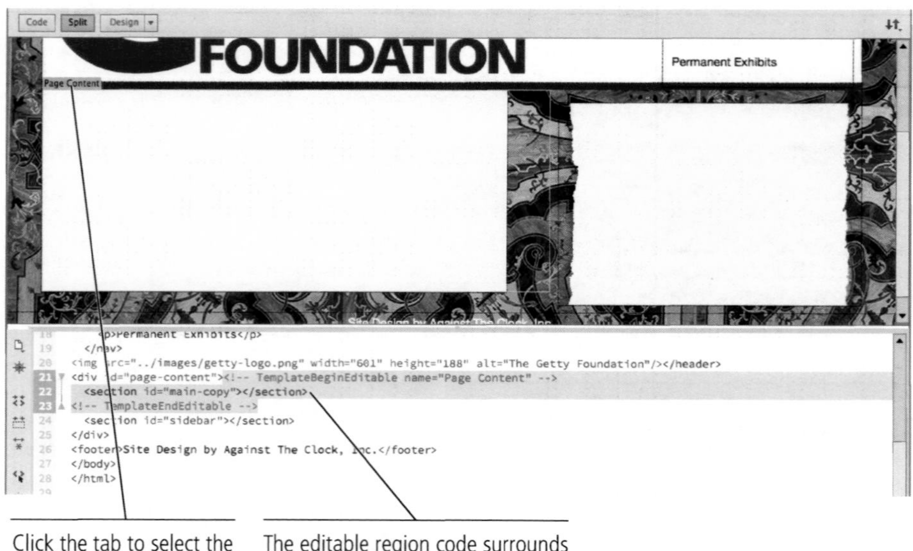

Click the tab to select the entire editable region.

The editable region code surrounds only the main-copy section.

The new editable area was added around the selected section element. Because you want the main-copy *and* sidebar sections inside the editable area, you have to edit the page code.

16. **In the page code, move the closing code of the editable region (<!-- TemplateEndEditable -->) to be after the closing tag of the section#sidebar element. Refresh the Design view and review the results.**

When something is selected in the Code pane, you can click the selected code and drag to move that code to a new position. Alternatively, you can cut (Command/Control-X) the relevant code from its original location, move the insertion point to another position, and then paste (Command/Control-V) the cut code into place.

The editable area now contains the two nested sections, but not the surrounding div#page-content element.

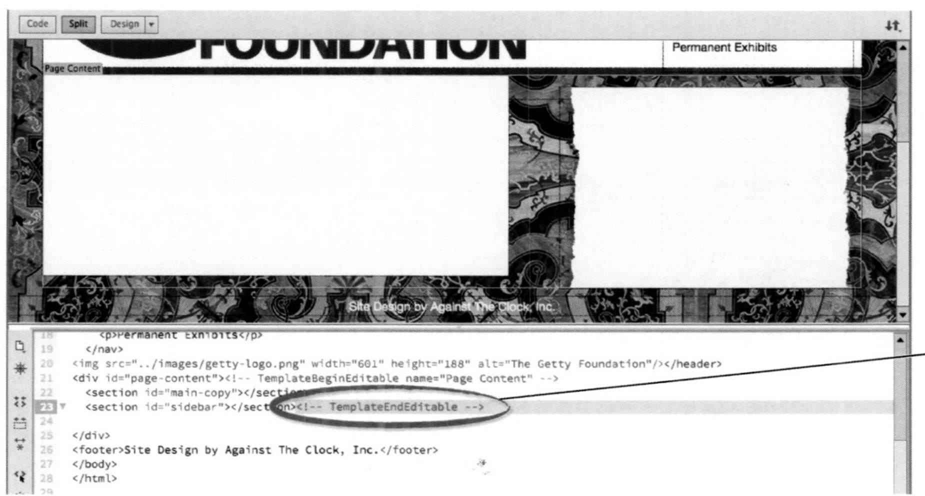

Move the ending code of the editable area after the closing tag of the section#sidebar element.

17. **Choose File>Save All, close the template file, and then continue to the next exercise.**

Unlike other applications, you do not have to use the Save As command to rewrite a Dreamweaver template. You can simply choose File>Save or press Command/Control-S.

Understanding Template Objects

Template objects consist primarily of different types of regions. These options are available in the Templates Insert panel or the Insert>Template submenu:

- **Make Template** converts an HTML file into a template, automatically prompting you to save the HTML file as a template.
- **Make Nested Template** inserts a template in a page created from an existing template.
- **Editable Region** creates areas of a template that you can modify in pages using the template. You don't add content in the regions in the template itself, but in the pages created from the template. By default, editable regions are highlighted in blue and locked regions are highlighted in yellow. (You can change these colors in the Highlighting pane of the Preferences dialog box.)
- **Optional Region** defines a section of the page that will be shown or hidden depending on the content being presented.
- **Repeating Region** creates a section of template content that you can easily duplicate (primarily used in tables and lists).
- **Editable Optional Region** combines the Optional Region functionality with the Editable Region functionality. If the Editable Optional Region is shown, the content within the region can be modified.
- **Repeating Table** creates both a table and repeating regions simultaneously. Selecting a repeating table object opens the standard table dialog box for defining rows within a repeating region.

Apply the Template to Existing Pages

Templates can be applied to existing HTML pages, basically wrapping the template around the existing content. You simply map existing page content to editable regions in the template. After the template is applied, you can begin to make whatever changes are necessary based on the actual content in the files.

1. **In the Files panel, open the Site Setup dialog box for the active site:**

   On Macintosh, open the Directory menu and click the Museum site in the list.

   On Windows, simply double-click the site name in the Directory menu without opening the menu.

   Remember, this technique opens the Site Setup dialog box for the selected site and allows you to skip the Manage Sites dialog box.

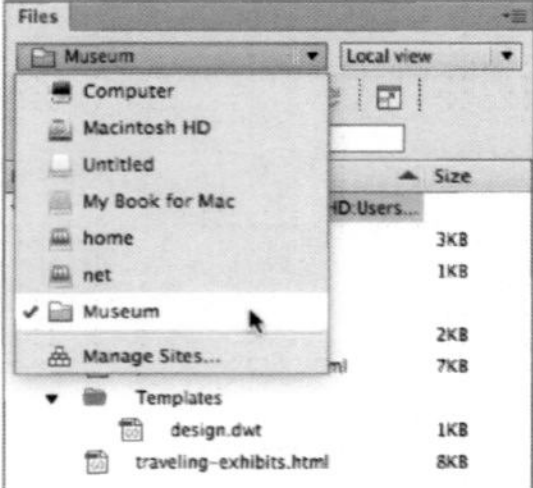

2. **Expand the Advanced Settings options and click Templates in the category list to show the related options.**

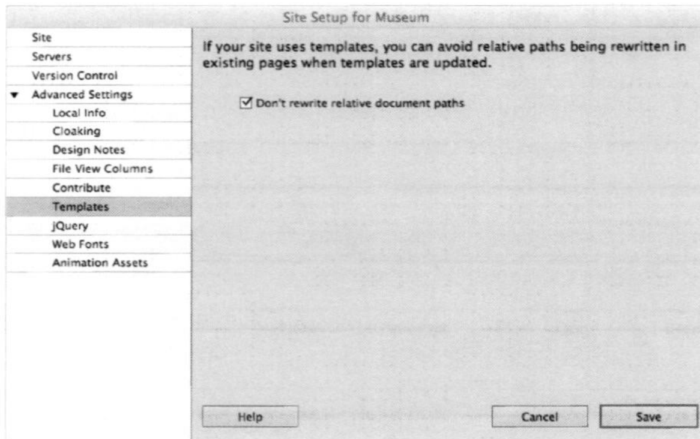

3. **Make sure the Don't Rewrite option is checked.**

   When you saved the template file, it was placed in a folder named Templates. Links from this template file to images or other pages must first go up from the Templates folder to the root folder (e.g., **../images/getty-logo.png**).

   When this template is attached to a page in the root level of the site, the same link would not be accurate. For example, the path from about.html in the root folder to the same image would simply be **images/getty-logo.png**. If this check box is not active, the links on pages where the template is attached would not work properly.

4. **Click Save to close the Site Setup dialog box.**

5. **Using the Files panel, open about.html from the root folder of the Museum site.**

Each file in the site contains two areas of content — the primary page copy, and a list of links to help users navigate through the long blocks of text. The two sections are already tagged with ids (#main-copy and #sidebar) that match the ones you used in the template file. This will direct the appropriate elements of the provided pages to appear in the defined areas of the template.

6. **Choose Modify>Templates>Apply Template to Page.**

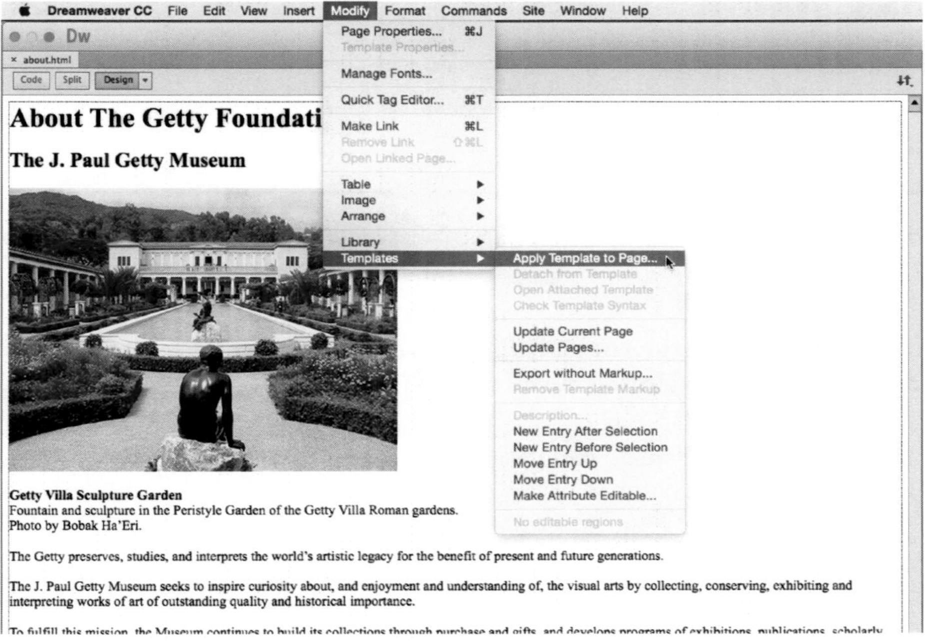

The Modify>Templates Menu in Depth

DREAMWEAVER FOUNDATIONS

Commands in the Modify>Templates menu are useful when you want to make changes to pages based on a template.

- **Apply Template to Page** applies a template to the current HTML page.
- If you don't want a page to be based on a template, **Detach from Template** separates the page from the template. Non-editable regions become editable, but changes in the template do not reflect in the page.
- **Open Attached Template** opens the template attached to a page.
- If code is written directly in the code area, there is a chance that the code might contain some errors. The **Check Template Syntax** option enables Dreamweaver to automatically check the code syntax in the template.
- **Update Current Page** updates a page if the template on which it is based is modified. Before closing the file, Dreamweaver prompts you to update the page.
- If you update only the template and not pages based on the template, you can use the **Update Pages** option to update all pages based on the template.
- **Export without Markup** exports an entire site to a different location by detaching all pages from templates on which they are based. You can also save the template information in XML by selecting Keep Template Data Files after you choose this command.
- Use **Remove Template Markup** to convert an editable region to a non-editable region.
- The **Description** is simply a textual explanation of the selected file, which does not appear in the page body.
- **New Entry After** or **Before Selection.** Repeating regions include more than one editable region, which enables you to add repeated elements such as rows of a table. (Clicking the "+" button of the repeating region's blue tab adds a new entry in the region.)
- Use **Move Entry Up** or **Down** to move a repeating element up or down.
- You can use **Make Attribute Editable** to make a specific attribute of an HTML tag editable in template-based pages.

7. **In the Select Template dialog box, make sure Museum is selected in the Site menu.**

Since this is the active site, the menu should default to the correct choice.

8. **Click design in the Templates list to select it, and make sure the Update Page... option is checked at the bottom of the dialog box.**

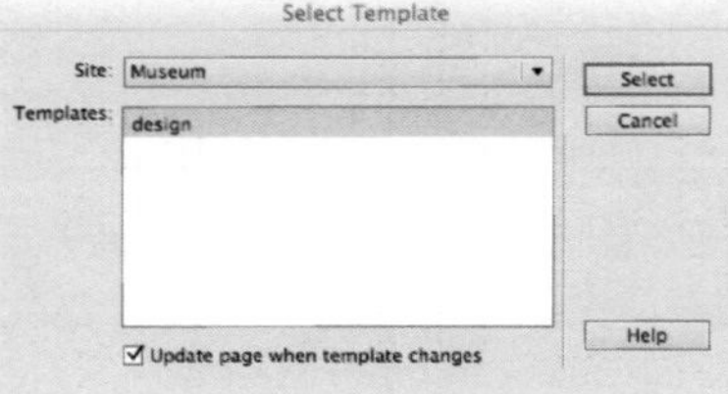

9. **Click Select to apply the template to the open page.**

In the Inconsistent Region Names dialog box that appears, you have to determine where to place the named regions of the open file relative to the editable regions in the template you selected.

10. **In the resulting dialog box, click the Document body (in the Name column) to select it. In the Move Content to New Region menu, choose Page Content.**

Remember, "Page Content" is the name you assigned to the template's editable region. The page body (named "Document body" by default) will be placed into the "Page Content" editable region when the template is applied to the page.

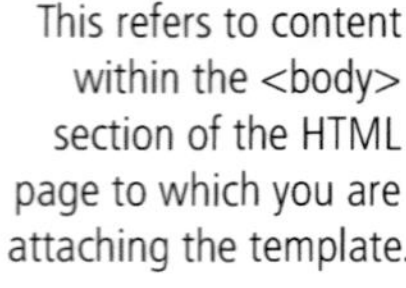

This refers to content within the <body> section of the HTML page to which you are attaching the template.

Use this menu to map file content to an editable region in the template file.

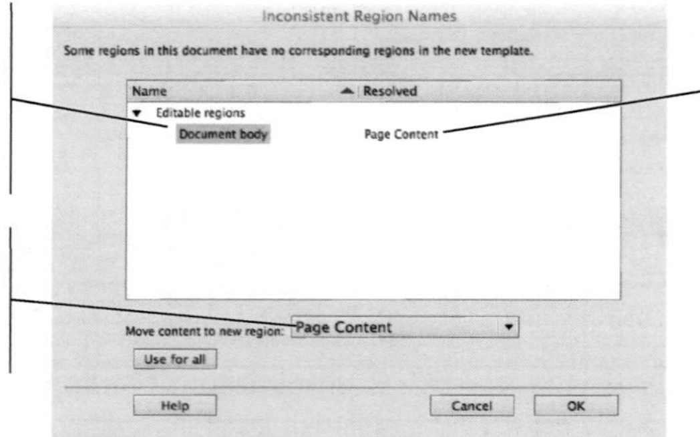

This is the name assigned to the editable region in the template file.

> ***Note:***
>
> *You can choose Nowhere in the Move Content... menu to exclude specific content in the newly "templated" page.*

Creating a New Page from a Template

DREAMWEAVER FOUNDATIONS

In addition to attaching a template to an existing page, you can also create a new HTML page from an existing template.

You can use the Assets panel (Window>Assets) to show all templates that are available in the current site. Control/right-clicking a specific template file opens a contextual menu, where you can choose New from Template.

This results in a new untitled HTML file containing all the content that is defined in the template, with the template already attached to the HTML page. Any changes in the template file will apply to files created from the template.

Pages can also be created from a template using the New Document dialog box (File>New). Choose Site Templates in the left column of the New Document dialog box, select your site in the middle column, and then choose the template you want to apply in the right column.

11. **Click OK to finalize the process.**

Because the museum-styles.css file is attached to the template, it is also attached to this page.

This tag identifies the template that is applied to the HTML file.

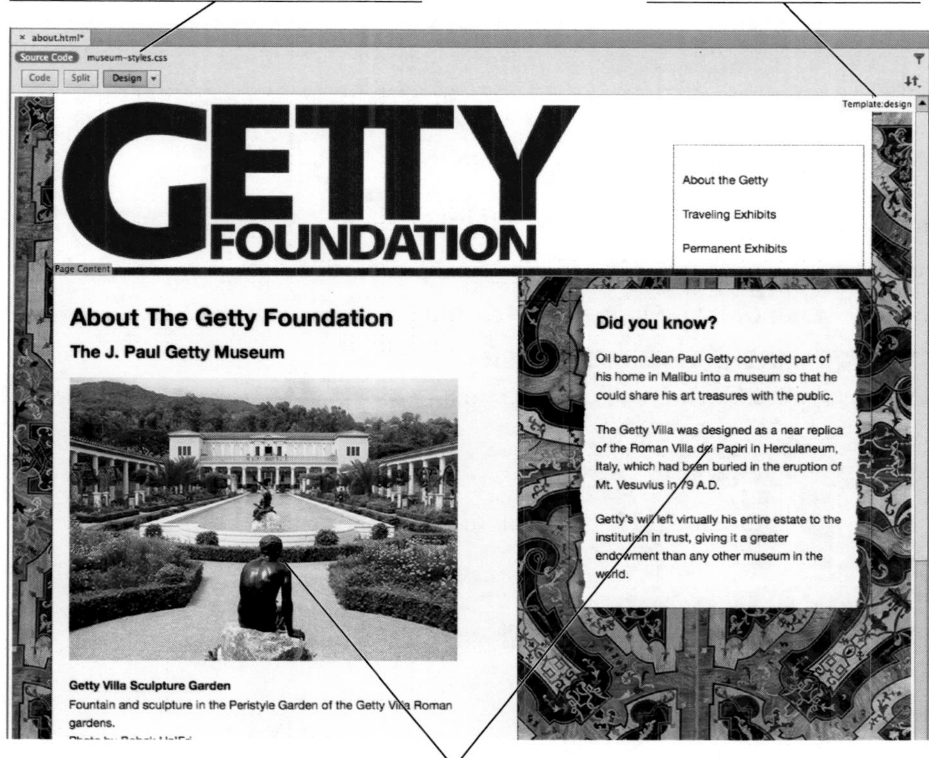

Content defined with ID attributes in the original HTML file is moved into the appropriate location in the template.

> ***Note:***
>
> *If you move the cursor over areas other than an editable region, an icon indicates that you can't select or modify that area. You can modify only the editable region.*

12. **Save the file and close it.**

13. **Repeat this process to attach the design.dwt template to the two remaining pages in the site.**

14. **Save and close any open files, and continue to the next exercise.**

Edit the Design Template

The links in the nav element for this site are common to every page in the site. Because that area is not editable in pages attached to the template, you have to define those links in the template. When you make changes to the template, those changes automatically apply to any page attached to the template — another advantage of using Dreamweaver template files.

1. **Open `design.dwt` from the Templates folder.**

2. **Create links for each paragraph in the nav element as follows:**

About The Getty	**Link to `about.html`**
Traveling Exhibits	**Link to `traveling-exhibits.html`**
Permanent Exhibits	**Link to `permanent-exhibits.html`**

3. **Choose File>Save to save the template file.**

4. **Read the resulting message, then click Update.**

   When you save changes to a template file, Dreamweaver recognizes the link from the template to pages where that template is attached. You are automatically asked if you want to update those pages to reflect the new template content.

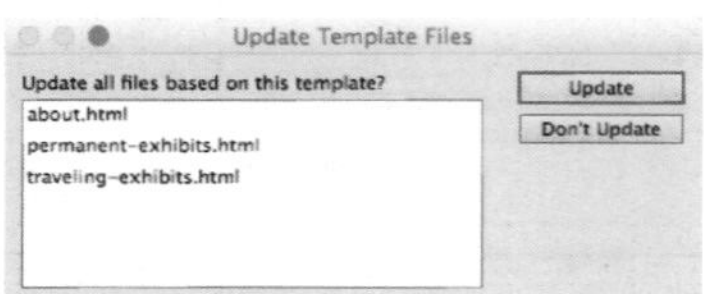

5. **When the resulting Update Pages dialog box shows "Done," click Close.**

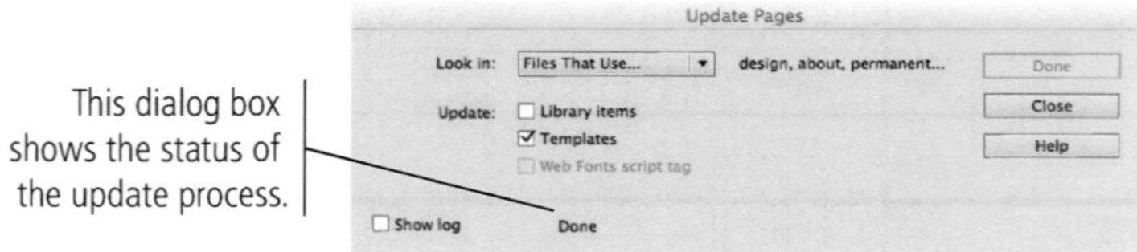

This dialog box shows the status of the update process.

6. **Close the template file, then open `about.html` from the Files panel.**

   As you can see, the links you defined in the template file are automatically added to the page that is attached to the template. This type of workflow makes it much easier to maintain consistency across an entire site — make changes to common content once in the template file, and those changes are automatically applied in any page where the template is attached.

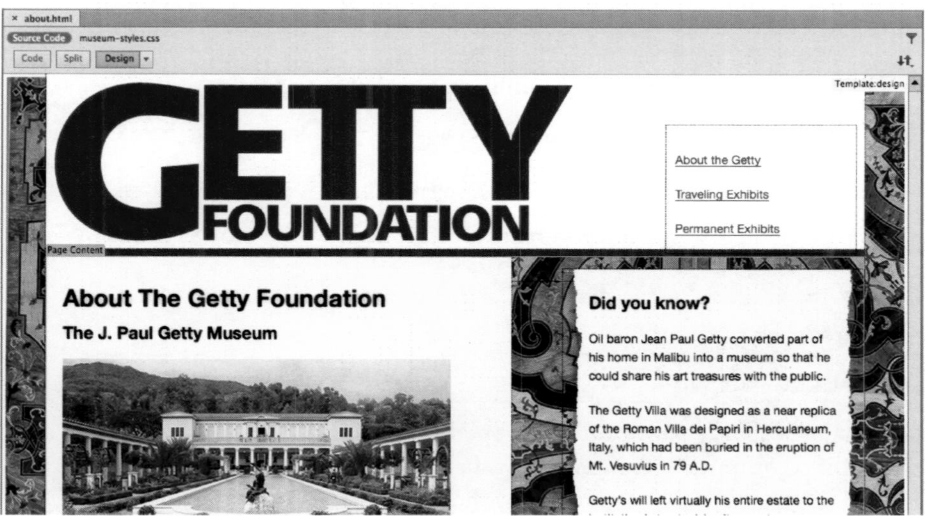

7. **Using the Properties panel, add the text `| About The Getty` (including a preceding space) to the end of the existing document title.**

8. **Click the Split button to show the page code, and scroll to the top of the code.**

   Although you did not specifically define it as an editable area, the <title> tag of each page is always editable, even when attached to a template file.

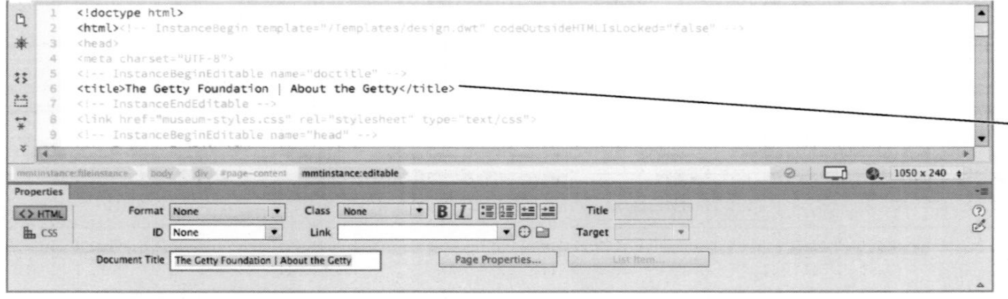

The title element in the page head is automatically an editable region.

9. **Save the file and close it.**

10. **Open `permanent-exhibits.html` and `traveling-exhibits.html`, and add appropriate text to each page title.**

11. **Save and close any open files, then continue to the next stage of the project.**

Stage 3 Using CSS to Control Content

The first stage of this project focused on building a layout with properly structured HTML; in the second stage, you created a template file to more easily apply the defined layout to multiple pages. Although defining structure is a significant part of designing pages, it is only half the story — professional Web design also requires controlling the content in pages.

In this stage of the project, you will complete a number of tasks required to present the client's information in the best possible way.

- Define CSS to format HTML elements, including headings, paragraphs, and links.
- Create a list of links for users to jump to different parts of a page.
- Define CSS to format the rollover behavior of links throughout the site.
- Define CSS to format specific elements only in certain areas of the page.
- Create and format figures and captions within the copy of each page.

Define HTML Tag Selectors

In addition to the **<body>** tag that encloses the page content, properly structured pages use HTML tags to identify different types of content. As you already know, CSS uses tag selectors to format HTML tags such as paragraphs (**<p>**), headings (**<h1>**, **<h2>**, etc.), links (**<a>**), and so on.

1. **Open `permanent-exhibits.html` from the Museum site root folder, and turn on the Live view.**

   When you are editing CSS to define the appearance of page content, it's a good idea to work in the Live view so you can see an accurate representation of the CSS rendering.

2. **In the CSS Designer panel, select museum-styles.css in the Sources list and then click the Add Selector button in the Selectors section.**

3. **Type `h1` as the selector name, then press Return/Enter twice to finalize the new selector name.**

   This tag selector defines properties for any h1 element — in other words, content surrounded by the <h1> </h1> tags. Tag selectors do not require a # character at the beginning of the name; only the actual element name is required.

4. **In the Properties section of the panel, define the following properties for the h1 tag selector:**

margin:	**0px (all four sides)**
color:	**sample the color of the client's logo**
font-size:	**30px**
text-transform:	**uppercase**

   Content block elements such as headings and paragraphs have default top and bottom margins equivalent to the current text size. It is common to modify some or all of these margins with CSS. By defining margins of 0 for <h1> tags, any subsequent paragraph or heading's top margin will determine the spacing between the elements.

The first paragraph in the text — which is formatted with the <h1> tag — is affected by the new selector definition.

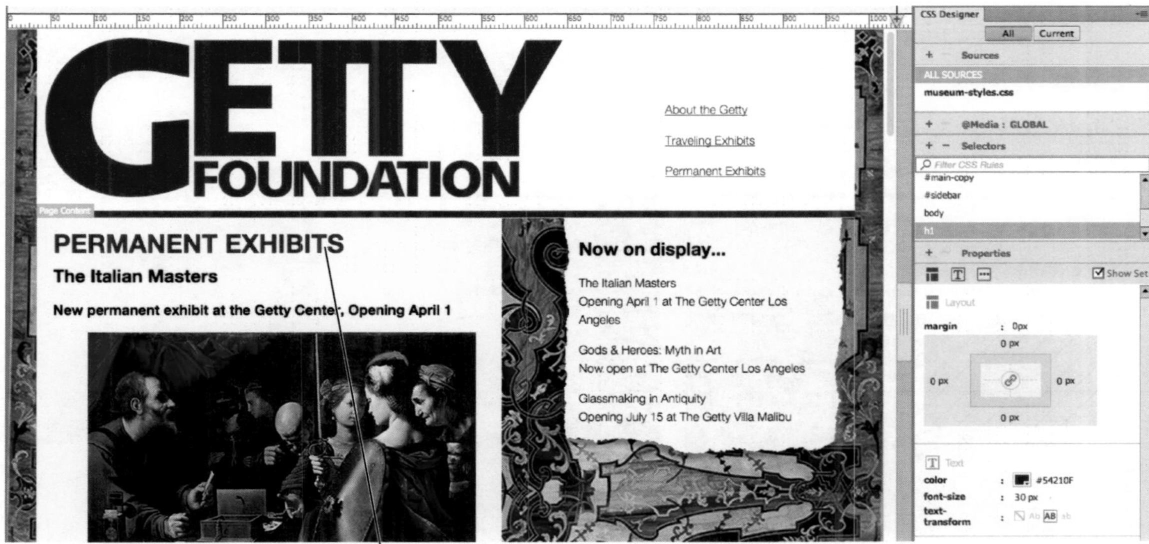

This is the h1 element.

5. **Create another tag selector for the <h2> tag, using the following settings:**

margin-top:	**30px**
margin-bottom:	**5px**
color:	**sample the color of the client's logo**
font-size:	**24px**

Note:

We have the Show Set option turned on in our screen shots to reinforce the properties you should define in each step.

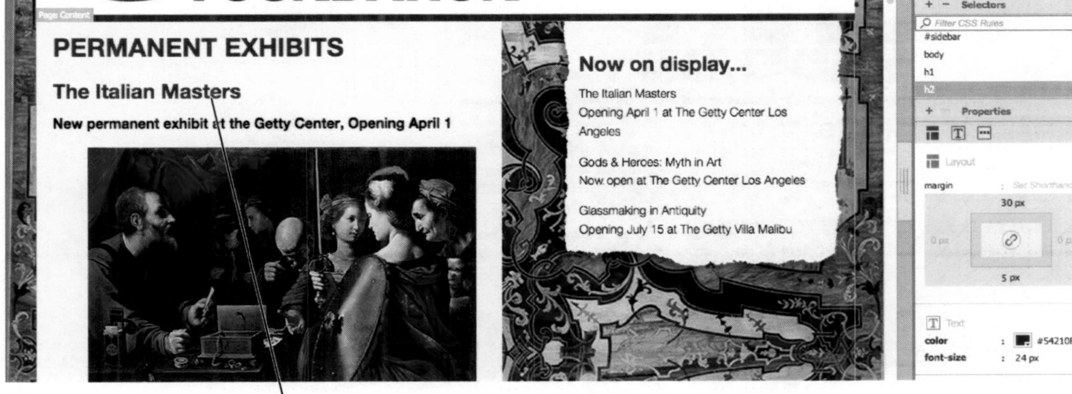

The margin settings for h2 elements are not yet apparent because the <h3> margins are still ambiguous.

5. **Create another tag selector for the <h3> tag, using the following settings:**

margin-top:	**0px**
margin-bottom:	**15px**
font-style:	**italic**
font-weight:	**400**

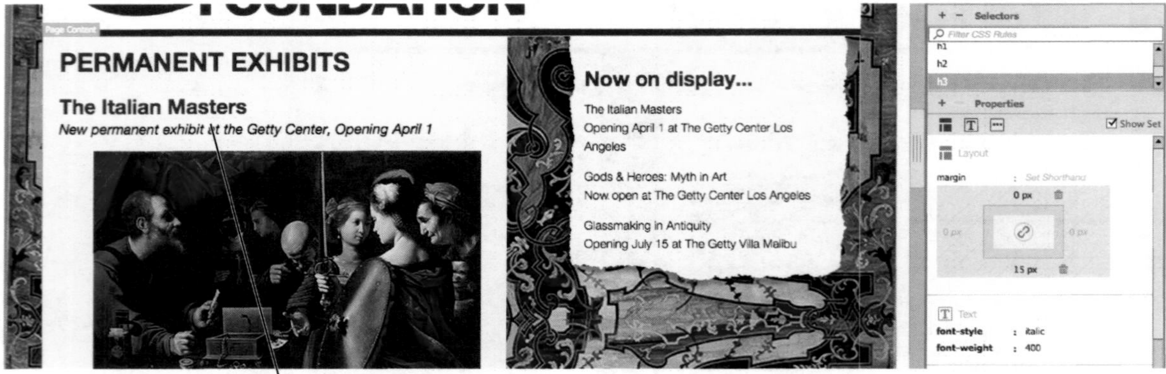

Margin settings for h2 elements are now apparent because the <h3> margins have been clearly defined.

6. **Create another tag selector for the <p> tag, using the following settings:**

margin-top:	**0px**
margin-bottom:	**10px**

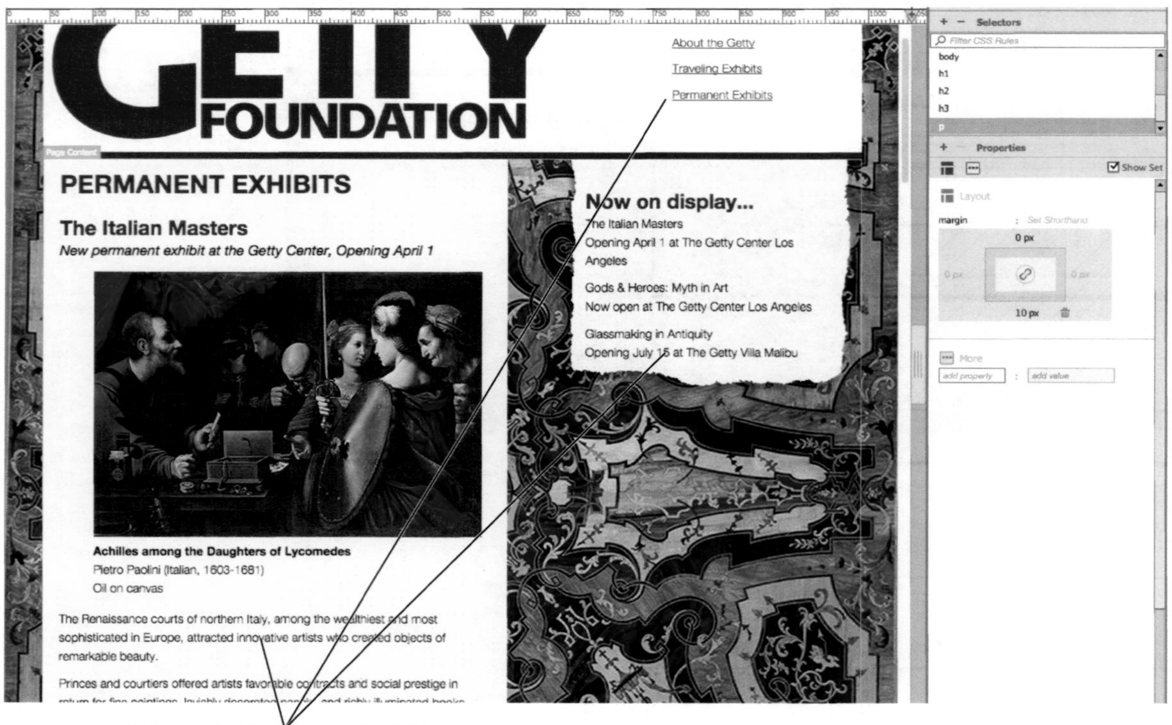

Paragraphs in all areas of the page are affected by the p selector.

8. **Add another tag selector for the <a> tag, using the following settings:**

color:	**sample the color of the client's logo**
font-weight:	**bold**
text-decoration:	**none**

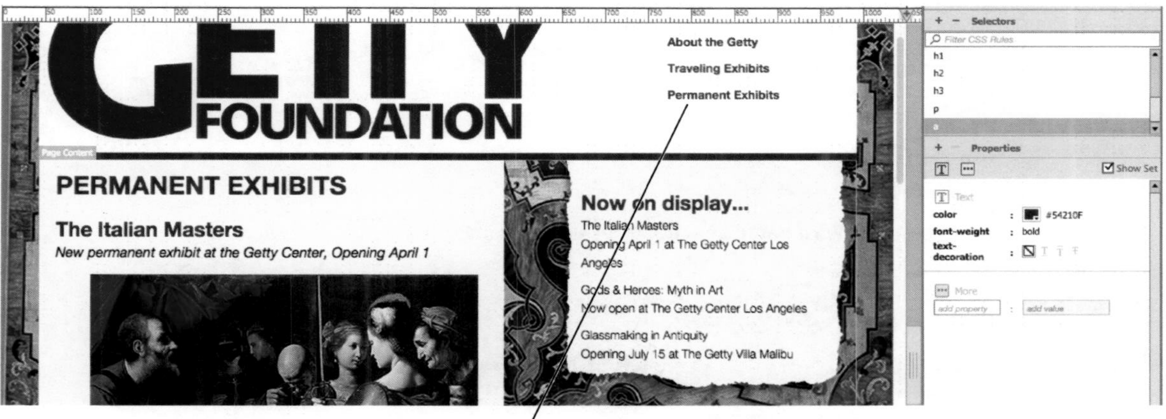

Links no longer have the default blue underline appearance.

9. **Choose File>Save All, then continue to the next exercise.**

Create Named Anchors

Documents with large blocks of copy — like the ones in this site — often benefit from named anchors, which mark specific locations on a page that can be linked from other locations within the same page or from other pages. Instead of forcing the reader to search for the information by scrolling or other means, you can create a hyperlink that points to the exact location of the information. Clicking the anchor link moves that anchor to the top of the browser window.

1. **With permanent-exhibits.html open, turn off the Live view and show the page source in the Code pane.**

   Selecting text and creating links can be a bit easier in the regular Design view.

2. **In the Code pane, click to place the insertion point immediately after the opening <h2> tag for the first h2 element.**

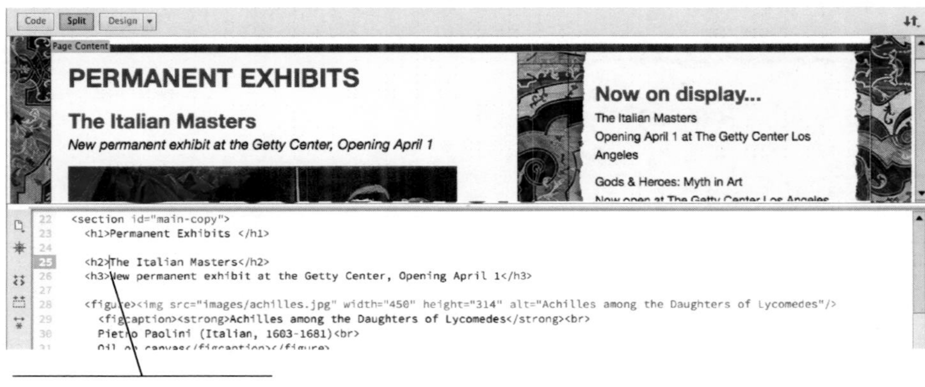

Place the insertion point after the opening <h2> tag.

3. **Type the following code:**

```
<a name="masters"></
```

As soon as you type the "/" character, Dreamweaver automatically closes the last unclosed container tag — in this case, the <a> tag.

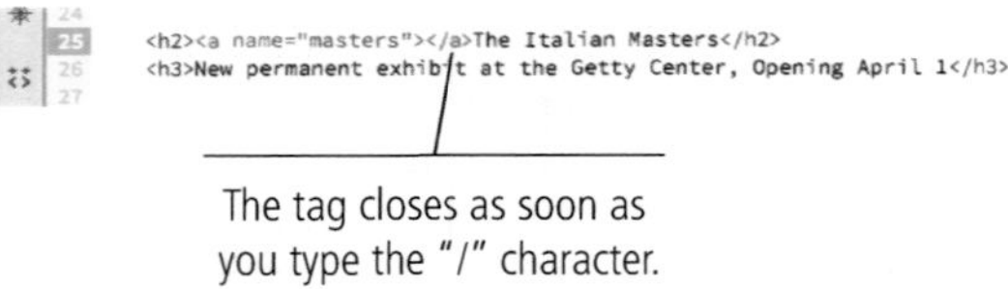

The tag closes as soon as you type the "/" character.

4. **Refresh the Design pane.**

When the Live view is not active, a named anchor appears in the page as a small anchor icon. These icons are not visible in the Live view or in the browser.

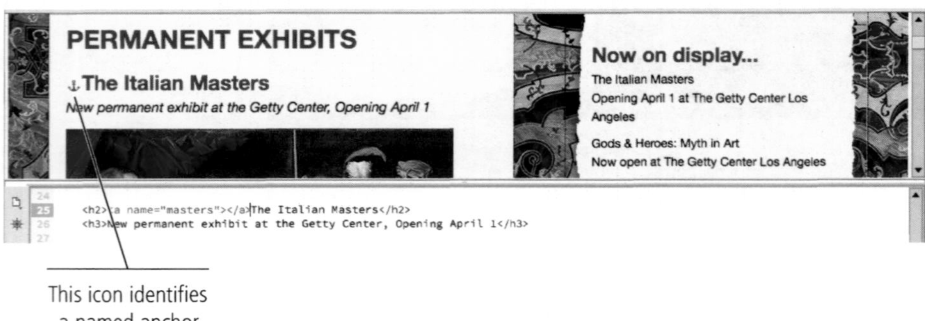

This icon identifies a named anchor.

5. **Repeat this process to add named anchors to the other h2 elements on the page. Use `gods` and `glassmaking` as the names of the related anchors.**

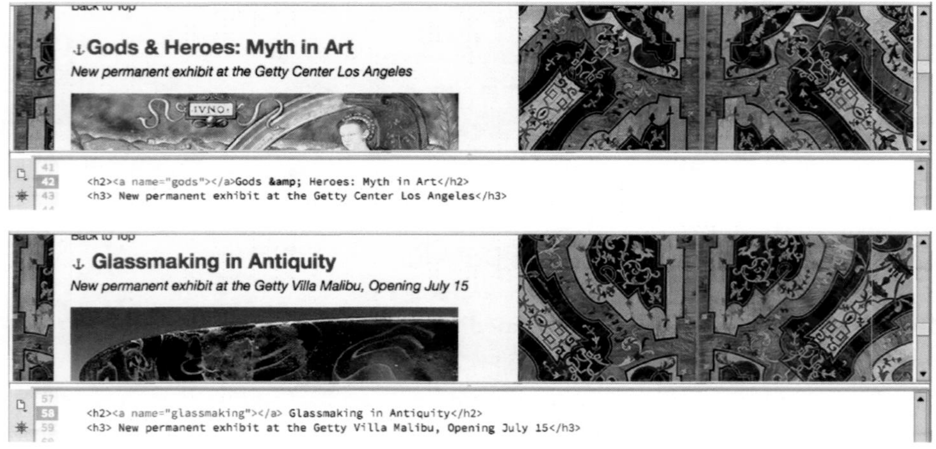

6. **In the Design pane, highlight the words "The Italian Masters" in the section#sidebar element.**

7. **Click the Hyperlink button in the HTML Insert panel.**

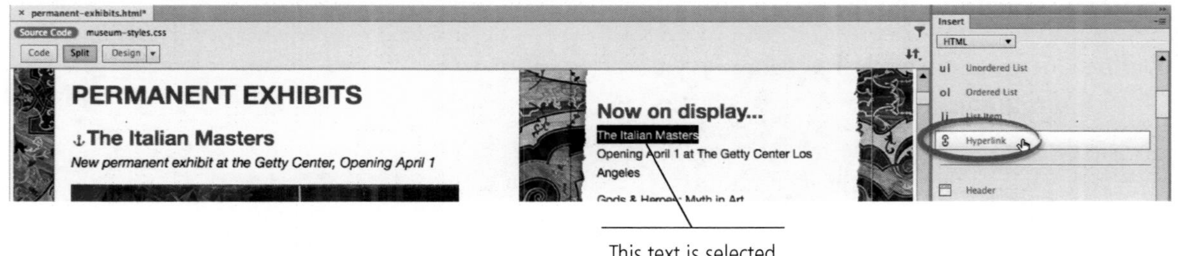

8. **In the Hyperlink dialog box, open the Link menu and choose #masters.**

This menu includes all named anchors; each anchor name is preceded by the # character.

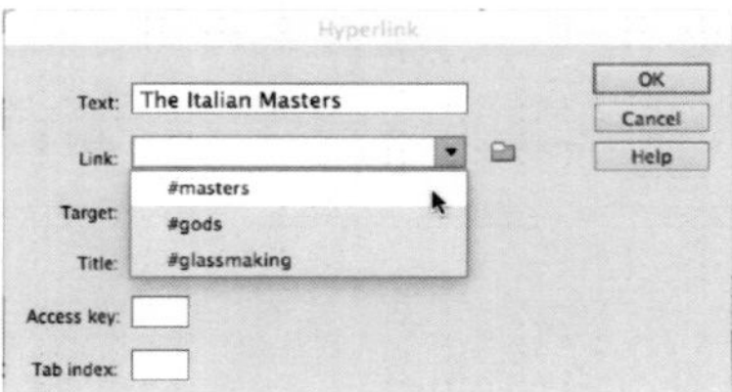

9. **Click OK to close the dialog box and create the new anchor link.**

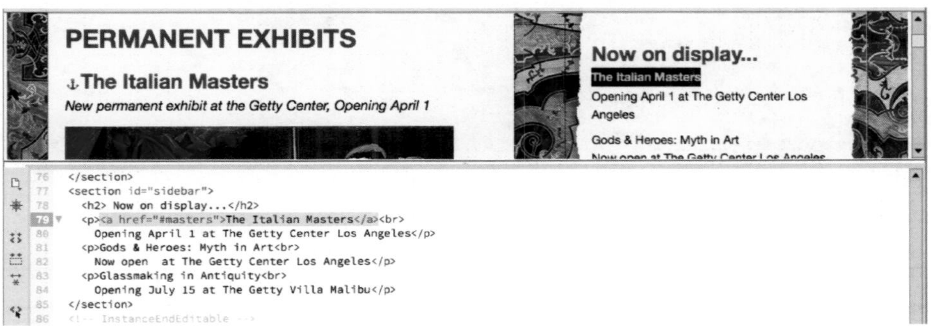

10. **Repeat Steps 6–9 to create links for the other two items in the section#sidebar element:**

Link Text	Link Target
Gods & Heroes: Myth in Art	gods
Glassmaking in Antiquity	glassmaking

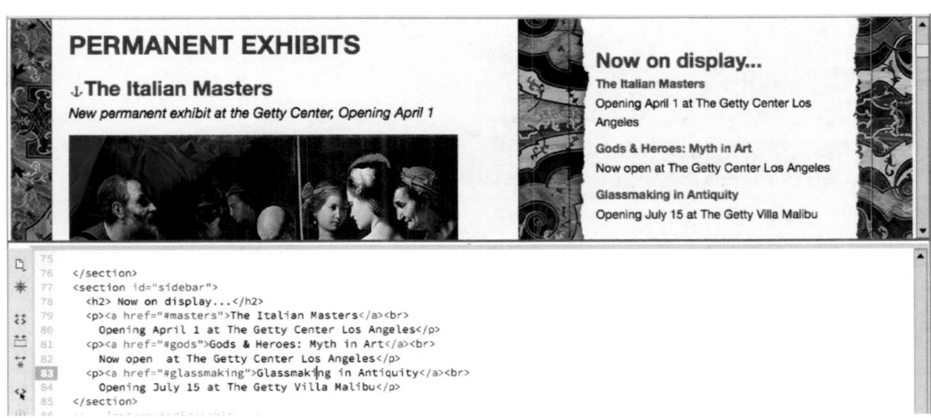

11. **In the Code pane, place the insertion point immediately after the opening <h1> tag near the top of the page.**

12. **Define a new named anchor as follows:**

```
<a name="top"></a>
```

To help the reader return to the link list from any section of the page, it is good practice to include a link to the top of the page at the end of each section.

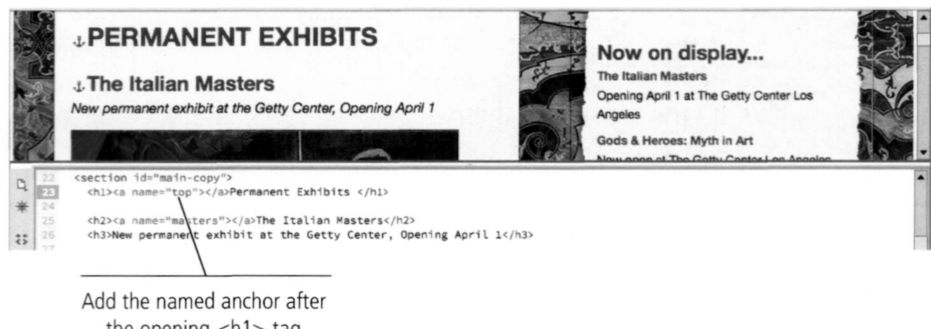

Add the named anchor after the opening <h1> tag.

13. **Select the words "Back to Top" above the second <h2> element. Create a link to the #top named anchor.**

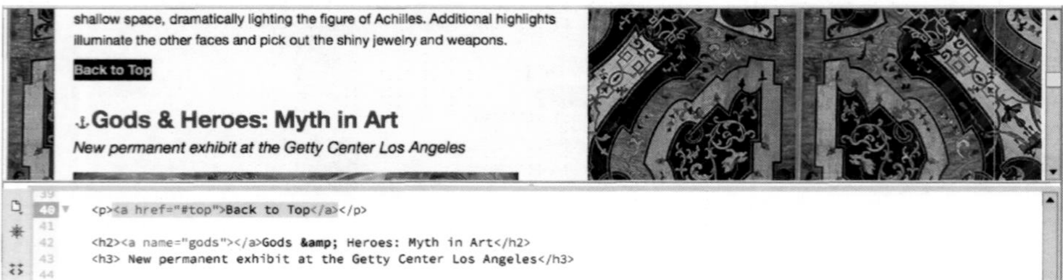

14. **Repeat Step 13 to link the remaining two "Back to Top" paragraphs to the #top anchor.**

Note:

To reduce the amount of repetitive work required to complete this project, we have already created the named anchors and links in the provided traveling-exhibits.html file.

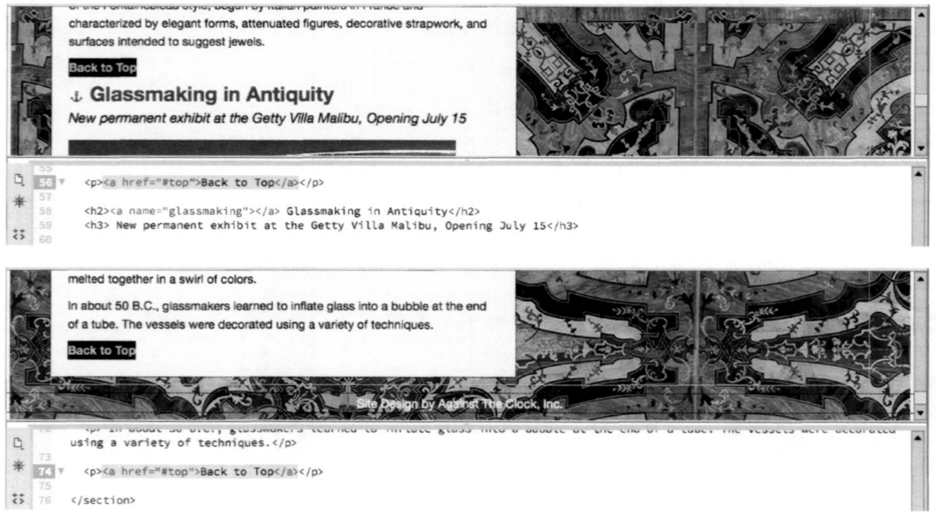

15. **Save the file and continue to the next exercise.**

Create a Pseudo-Class Selectors

A **class selector** is used when the same style needs to be applied to more than one element in a page. Unlike an ID attribute, which is used only once per page, a class attribute can be used to repeat the same style throughout the page.

As you should remember from the previous exercise, controlling the default appearance of link text is accomplished with the <a> tag selector. To affect the rollover behavior, you have to define **pseudo-classes** (or variants) of the <a> selector. Four common pseudo-classes important to the appearance of links are:

- **a:link** refers to a hyperlink that has not yet been visited.
- **a:visited** refers to a hyperlink that has been visited.
- **a:hover** refers to a hyperlink when the mouse pointer is hovering over the link.
- **a:active** refers to an active hyperlink (in other words: when the link is clicked before the mouse button is released).

Note:

For them to work correctly in all Web browsers, these pseudo-class selectors should appear in the following order in the CSS file:

a:link

a:visited

a:hover

a:active

1. **With permanent-exhibits.html open, turn on the Live view and hide the code pane.**

2. **Select museum-styles.css in the Sources section of the CSS Designer panel, then click the Add Selector button.**

3. **With the new selector name highlighted, type a:.**

   As soon as you type the colon character, a menu appears with the available pseudo-classes for the defined tag.

4. **Press the Down Arrow key until :hover is selected.**

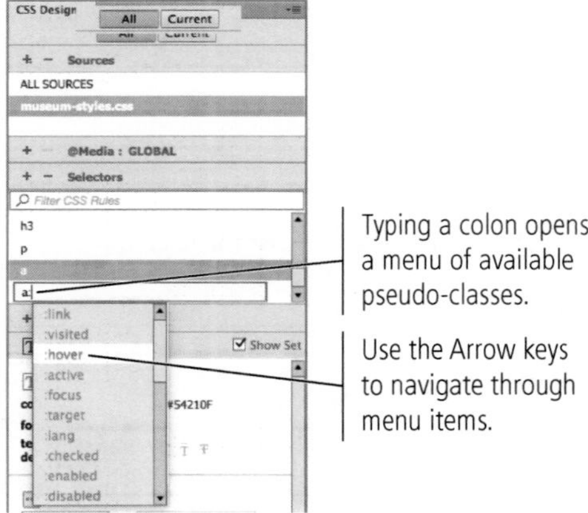

4. **Press Return/Enter to choose the :hover option, then press Return/Enter again to finalize the new selector name.**

   The full name of the new selector should be a:hover.

5. **Define the following property for the new selector:**

   color: **sample a light brown color from the background image**

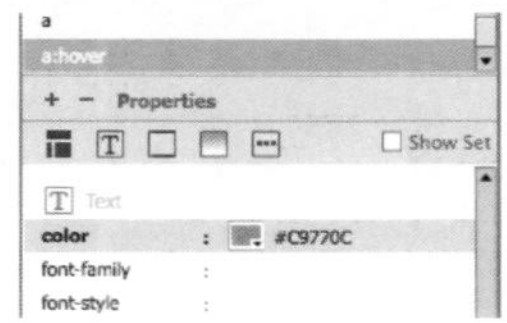

7. **With the Live view active, test the rollover property of the links in various sections of the page.**

The a:hover selector changes the color of the links in all areas of the page.

8. **Choose File>Save All, close the HTML file, then continue to the next exercise.**

Create a Figure and Figure Caption

The figure element is used to define content such as illustrations or photos that are related to the copy. The figure element is a container that can include a nested figcaption element describing the figure, which means the image and caption can be treated together as a single unit.

Note:

To minimize repetitive work, we created the figure and figcaption tags for you in the traveling-exhibits.html and permanent-exhibits.html files.

1. **Open about.html and make sure the Live view is active.**

2. **Click to select the image near the top of the section#main-copy element.**

3. **Click the Figure button in the HTML Insert panel.**

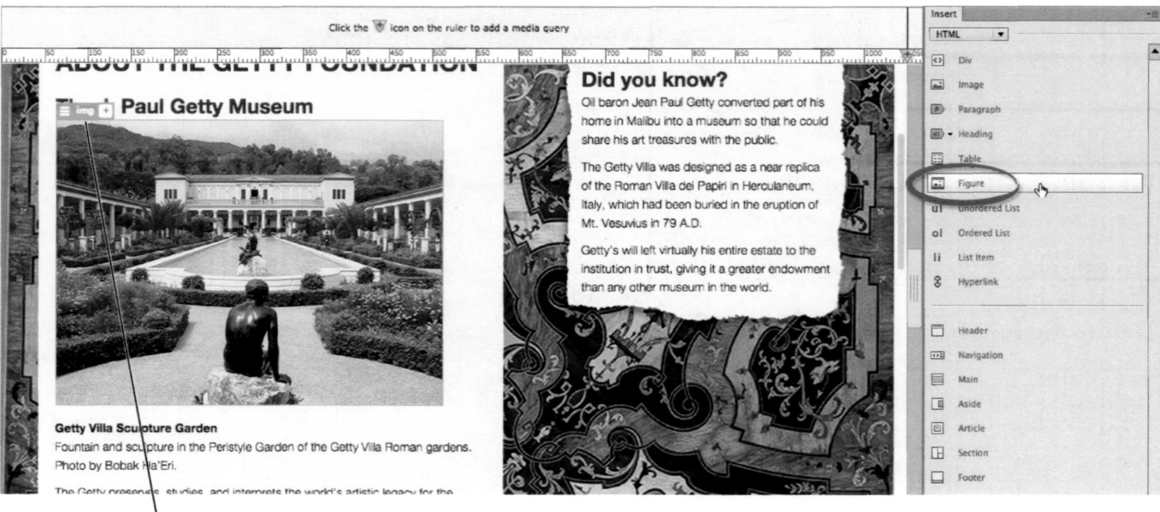

The img element is selected.

4. **Choose Before in the Position Assistant.**

   For some reason, the Wrap option is not available in this case. You have to use a workaround to move the image into the proper position inside the figure tags.

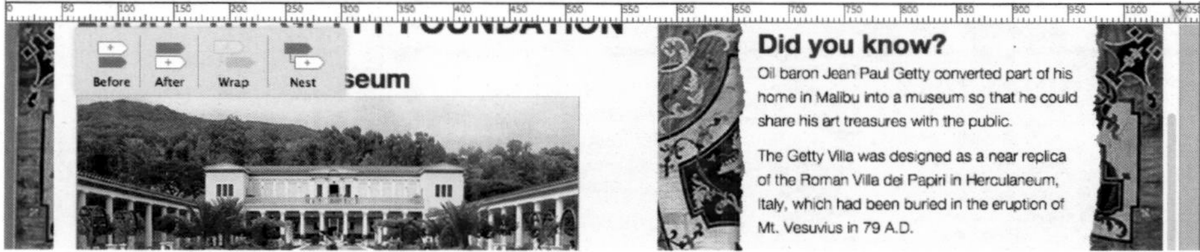

5. **Click to select the image again, then open the DOM panel.**

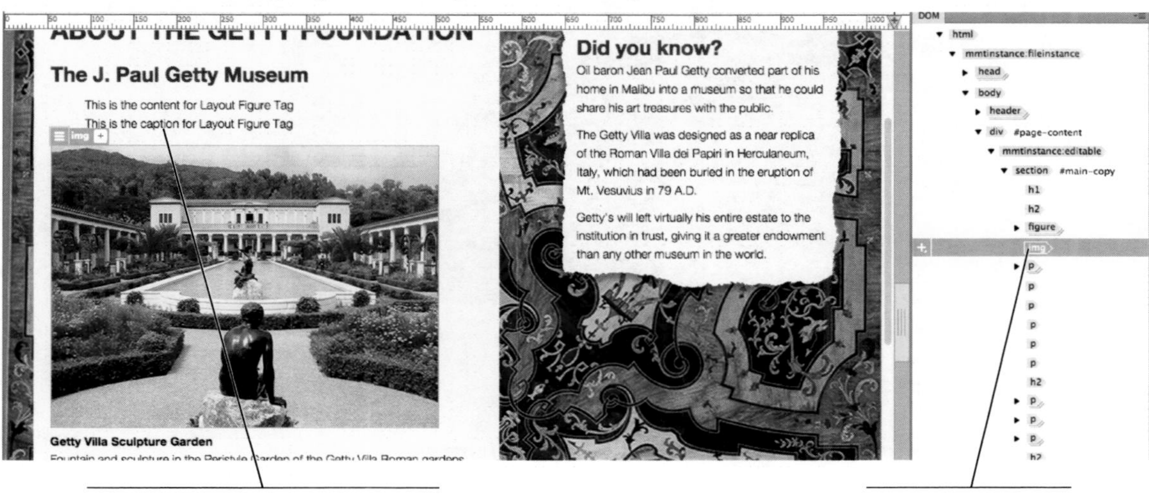

The figure element includes placeholder text for the content and the caption.

The DOM panel lists all elements in the page.

6. **In the DOM panel, click the arrow to expand the figure element.**

7. **In the panel, click the img tag and drag onto the figure element. When you don't see a green line, release the mouse button.**

   This moves the img element into the figure element; in other words, the img element becomes nested inside the figure element.

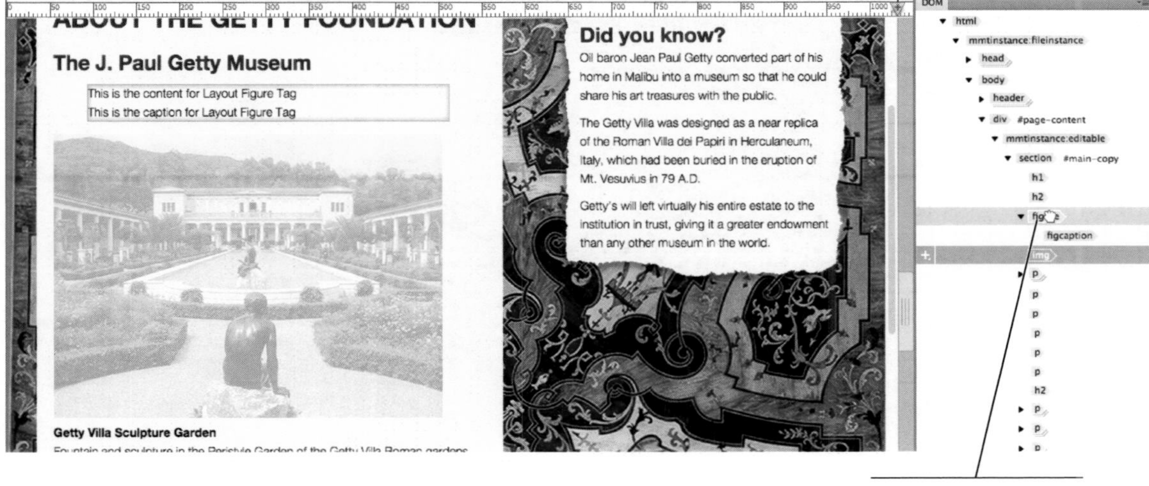

Drag the img element onto the figure element.

8. **In the Design pane, click to select the paragraph immediately below the image (beginning with Getty Villa...").**

9. **In the DOM panel, drag the selected paragraph onto the figcaption element.**

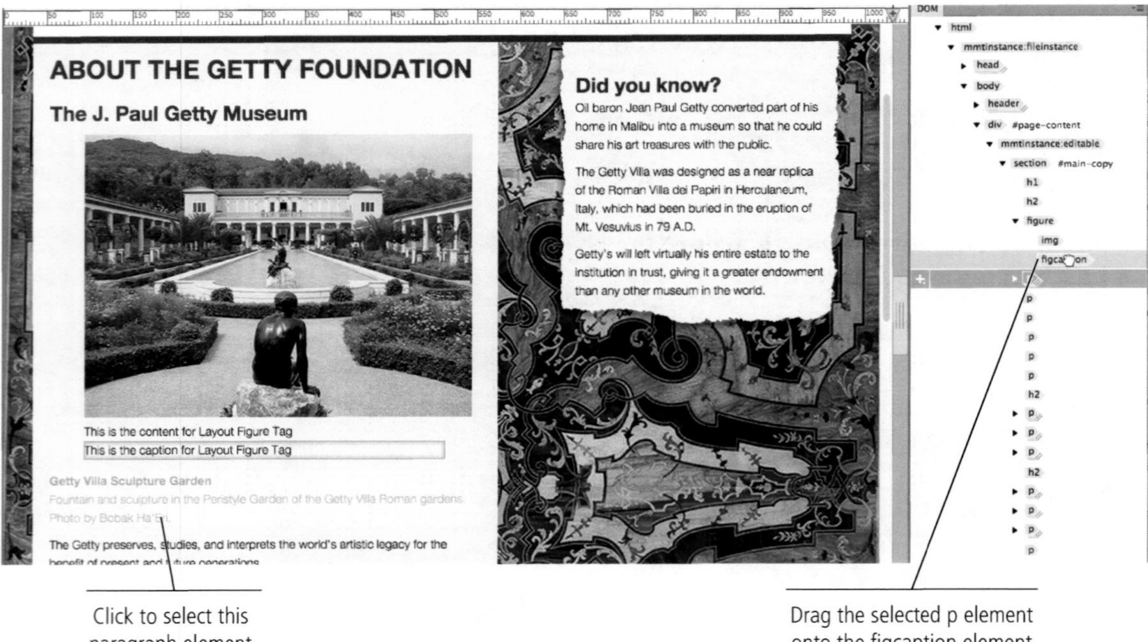

10. **In the Code pane, review the code related to the figure element.**

As you can see in the code, the img element is nested inside the figure element. The figcaption is also nested inside the figure element, which allows you to treat the image and caption as one unit by editing the figure element.

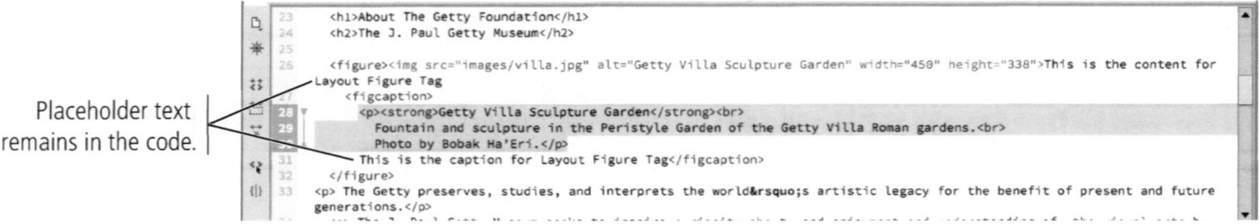

11. **Using the Code pane, delete the placeholder text that was included in the figure and figcaption elements.**

```
<figure><img src="images/villa.jpg" alt="Getty Villa Sculpture Garden" width="450" height="338">
  <figcaption>
    <p><strong>Getty Villa Sculpture Garden</strong><br>
      Fountain and sculpture in the Peristyle Garden of the Getty Villa Roman gardens.<br>
      Photo by Bobak Ha'Eri.</p></figcaption>
</figure>
<p> The Getty preserves, studies, and interprets the world&rsquo;s artistic legacy for the benefit of present and future
generations.</p>
  <p> The J. Paul Getty Museum seeks to inspire curiosity about, and enjoyment and understanding of, the visual arts by
collecting, conserving, exhibiting and interpreting works of art of outstanding quality and historical importance. </p>
  <p> To fulfill this mission, the Museum continues to build its collections through purchase and gifts, and develops
programs of exhibitions, publications, scholarly research, public education, and the performing arts that engage our diverse
```

12. **Using the CSS Designer panel, define a new tag selector named `figure` with the following settings:**

width:	**300px**
margin-top:	**0px**
margin-right:	**0px**
margin-bottom:	**10px**
margin-left:	**10px**
float:	**right**

Because the figcaption is nested inside the figure element, it is also affected by the width and float values you defined here.

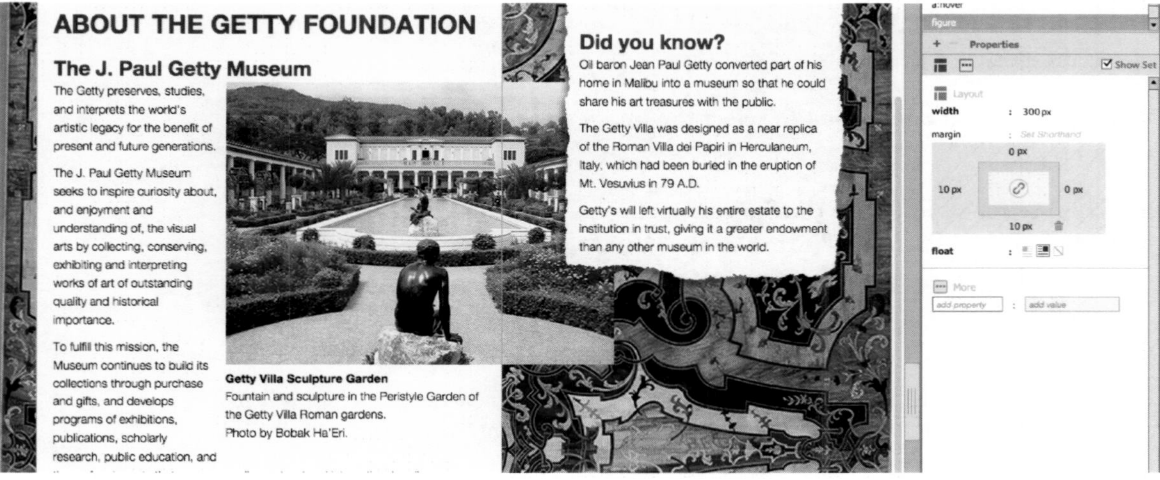

13. **Using the CSS Designer panel, define a new tag selector named `figcaption` with the following settings:**

font-style:	**italic**
font-size:	**12px**
line-height:	**15px**
text-align:	**right**

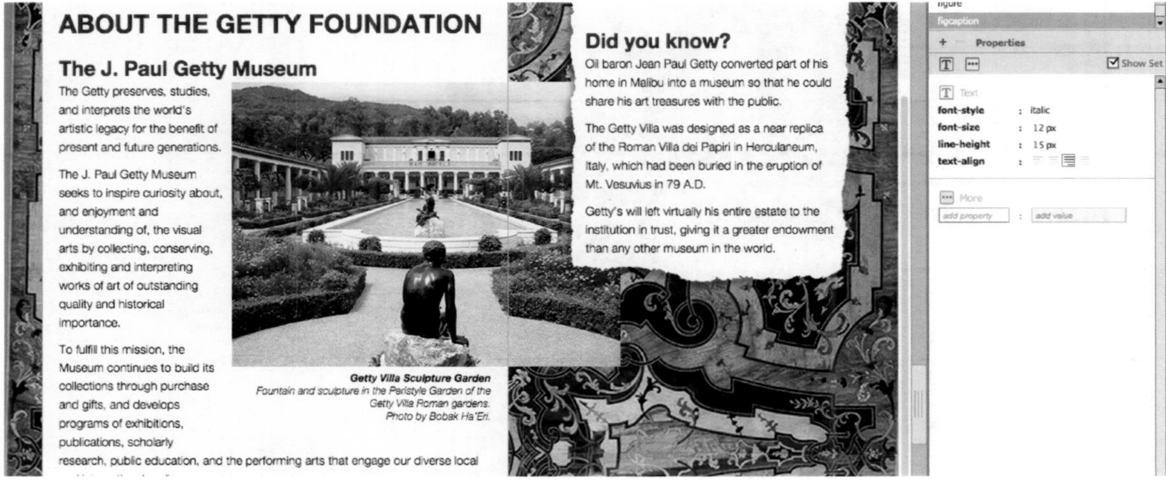

14. **Choose File>Save All, then continue to the next exercise.**

Create Descendant Selectors

Three items remain in the list of known formatting requirements:

- Images in the main-copy section should not extend past the edge of the containing section element.
- The sidebar text should be centered, and a border should appear below the h2 element in that section.
- Navigation links in the header area should be larger, and should align to the right edge of the nav container.

Each of these items refers to content in a specific area of the page. To meet these requirements without affecting similar tags in other areas, you need to define **descendant selectors** (also called compound selectors) to format certain elements only within a specific area.

1. **With about.html open, click to select the image in the section#main-copy element.**

2. **Select museum-styles.css in the Sources section of the CSS Designer panel, then click the Add Selector button to the left of the Selectors heading.**

   When an element is selected in the page layout, the new selector automatically adopts the name of the active insertion point, including all tags in the path to the active insertion point.

   This is compound or descendant selector specifically identifies where the properties will be applied: in this case, all img elements that exist in a figure element, which is in an element with the #main-copy ID attribute.

3. **Define the following properties for the new #main-copy figure img selector:**

width:	**300px**
height:	**auto**

   If you defined settings for the basic img element, you would affect all images on the page — including the logo at the top of the page. You are using a descendant selector here because you only want to affect images in the main-copy section.

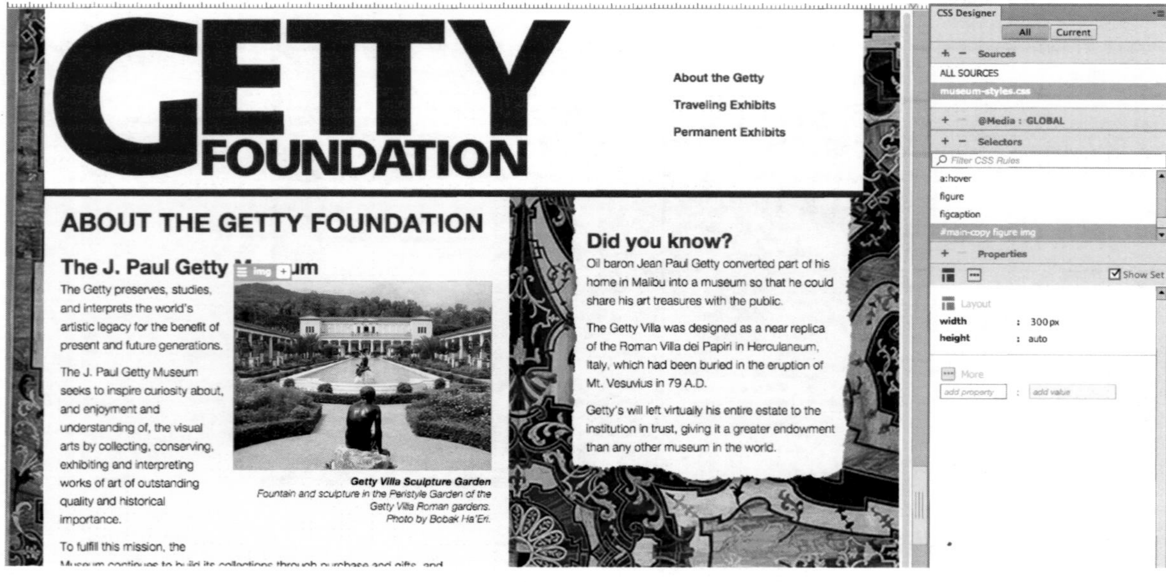

4. **Click the Add Selector button again. With the new name highlighted, type `#sidebar p`, then press Return/Enter two times to finalize the new name.**

   It is not necessary to first place the insertion point or select an object to create a descendant selector. You can simply type the appropriate selector name.

5. **Define the following settings for the #sidebar p selector:**

   text-align: **center**

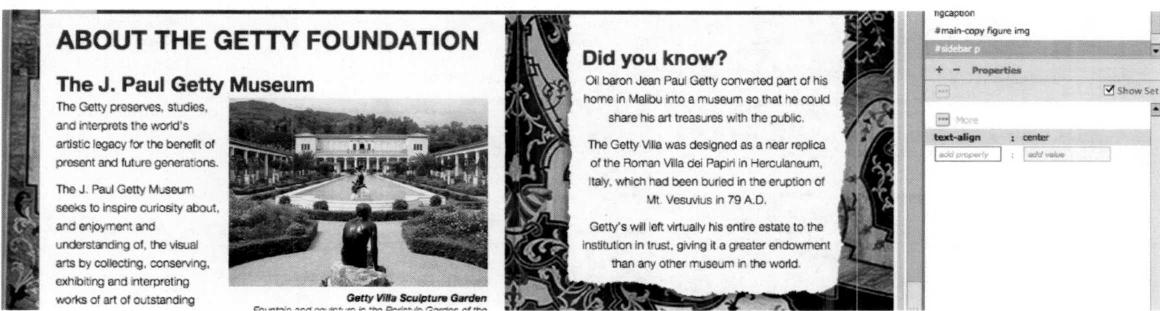

6. **Create another descendant selector named `#sidebar h2` using the following settings:**

   padding-bottom: **10px**
   text-align: **center**
   border-bottom-width: **thin**
   border-bottom-style: **solid**
   border-botom-color: **sample the brown color in the client's logo**

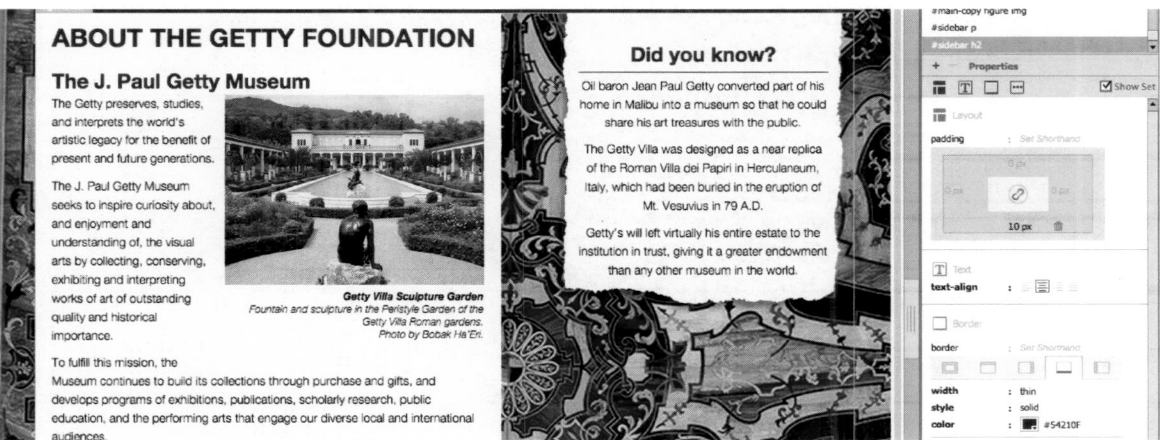

6. **Create another descendant selector named `nav p` using the following settings:**

margin-top:	**20px**
font-size:	**20px**
text-align:	**right**

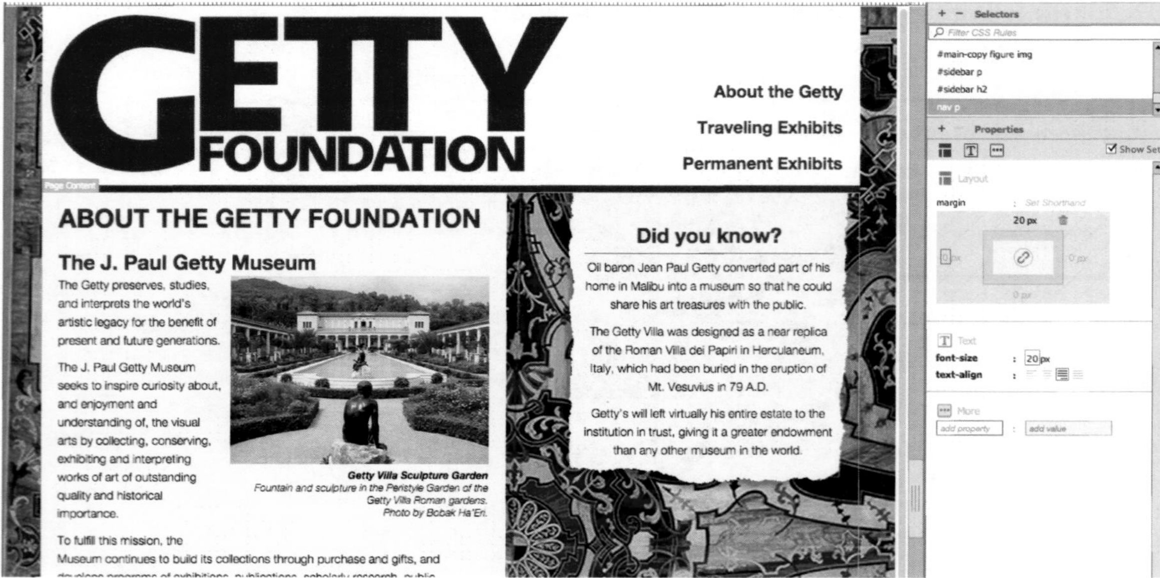

7. **Save all files (File>Save All) and close them.**

8. **Export a site definition named `Museum.ste` into your WIP>Museum folder, and then remove the Museum site from Dreamweaver.**

   If necessary, refer back to Project 6: Bistro Site Organization for complete instructions on exporting a site definition or removing a site from Dreamweaver.

Project Review

fill in the blank

1. A(n) _______________ is a flat image placed in the background of a page, used as a guide for reassembling the component pieces of the page.

2. A(n) _______________ is the formal name of a CSS rule.

3. A(n) _______________ style sheet stores CSS rules in a separate file, which can be linked to multiple HTML pages.

4. Click the _______________ button in the CSS Designer panel to create a new CSS files or define an existing external CSS file that should be used for the active page.

5. A(n) _______________ selector type is used to control unique div elements.

6. A(n) _______________ selector type is used to format specific HTML tags.

7. A(n) _______________ selector type can be used to format specific tags only within a certain div.

8. The _______________ property can be used to attach an object to the right or left side of the containing object.

9. The _______________ property exists inside the container; background properties of the container extend into this area.

10. The _______________ exists around the container; background properties of the container do not extend into this area.

short answer

1. Briefly explain two reasons why CSS is the preferred method for creating a Web page layout.

2. Briefly explain the difference between external, embedded, and inline styles.

3. Briefly explain how padding, margin, and border properties relate to the CSS box model.

Portfolio Builder Project

Use what you learned in this project to complete the following freeform exercise.
Carefully read the art director and client comments, then create your own design to meet the needs of the project.
Use the space below to sketch ideas; when finished, write a brief explanation of your reasoning behind your final design.

art director comments

You have been hired by the local chapter of the Girls & Boys Club of America to design a Web page featuring the programs that are available to local community. The club director wants the site to be easily navigable, and attractive to both children and their parents.

- ❑ Download the client-supplied resources in the **Club_Web16_PB.zip** archive on the Student Files Web page.
- ❑ Create a cohesive site design for all pages in the site.
- ❑ Create individual pages for each category that is defined by the client.
- ❑ Find one main image that supports the message of each page on the site. Look for public-domain images to minimize costs (try www.publicdomainpictures.net).

client comments

Our group serves thousands of children in the local community, especially during the summer when school is not in session. We serve children from all demographics, and we encourage kids to build relationships regardless of social or economic status.

We don't want to present too much information on any one screen, so we'd like each program to be featured on its own page. In addition to the Home page, we want individual pages for:

- Personal Development program
- Summer Tutoring program
- Overnight Adventure program
- VolunTeen Enrichment program
- Career Mentoring program

project justification

Project Summary

Cascading style sheets offer tremendous flexibility when you are designing the look and feel of a Web site. By linking multiple HTML files to a single external CSS file — with or without an HTML page template — you can experiment with options by altering the CSS selectors and immediately seeing the effect on all linked pages. In addition to this flexibility, CSS is also compliant with current Web design standards, which means pages designed with CSS are both search-engine and accessibility-software friendly.

By completing this project, you have worked with different types of selectors to control both the layout of an HTML page and the formatting attributes of different elements on different pages in the site. The site structure is entirely controlled by the selectors in the linked CSS file, so you could change the appearance of the entire site without ever touching the individual HTML pages. And the inverse is also true — you can change the content of individual pages without affecting the site structure.

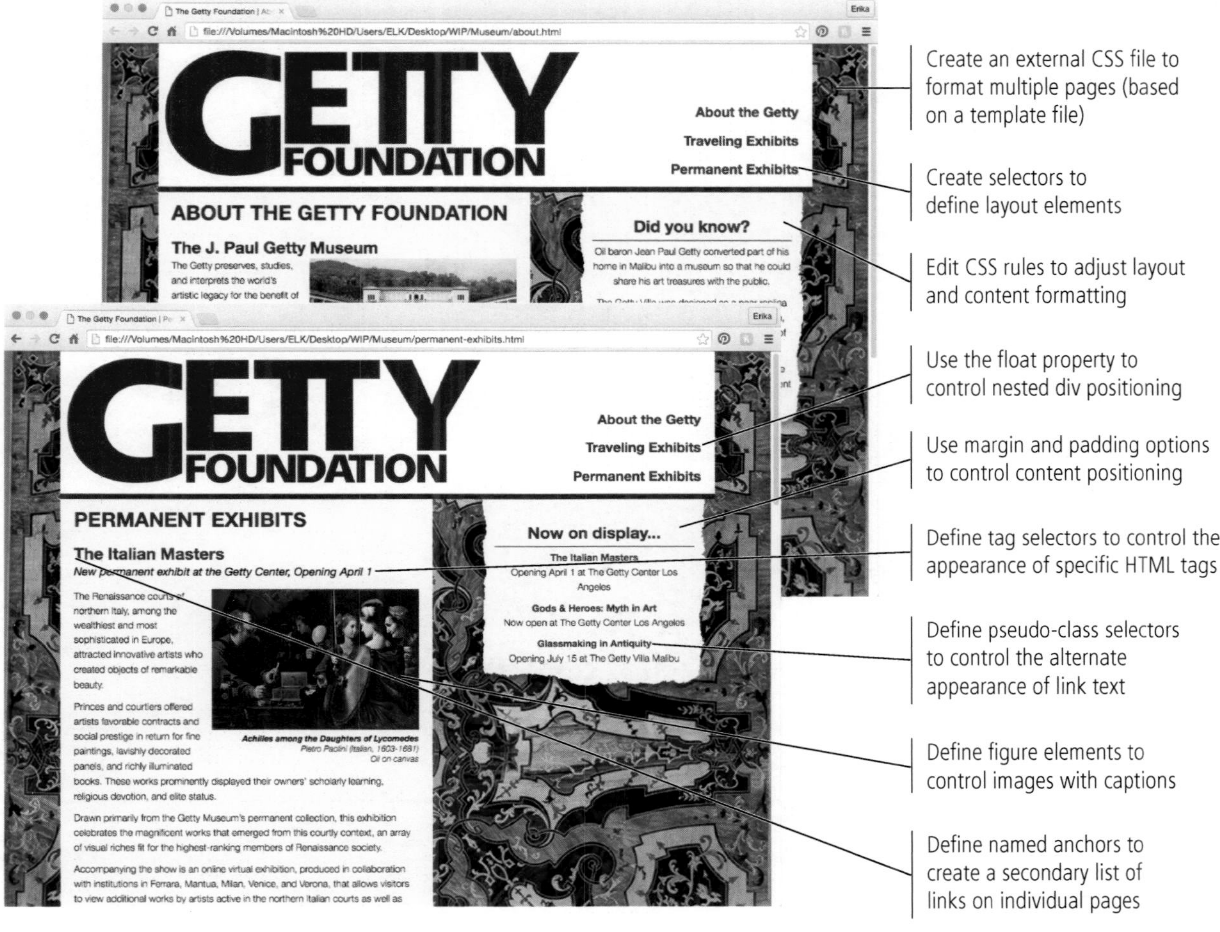

Create an external CSS file to format multiple pages (based on a template file)

Create selectors to define layout elements

Edit CSS rules to adjust layout and content formatting

Use the float property to control nested div positioning

Use margin and padding options to control content positioning

Define tag selectors to control the appearance of specific HTML tags

Define pseudo-class selectors to control the alternate appearance of link text

Define figure elements to control images with captions

Define named anchors to create a secondary list of links on individual pages

Index

Symbols

A

B

C

G

H

I

J

K

L

Q

R

S